DEPRESSIVE DISORDERS

Depressive Disorders
Facts, Theories, and Treatment Methods

Benjamin B. Wolman, Editor
George Stricker, Co-Editor

A WILEY-INTERSCIENCE PUBLICATION

JOHN WILEY & SONS, INC.

New York • Chichester • Brisbane • Toronto • Singapore

Recognizing the importance of preserving what has been written, it is a policy of John Wiley & Sons, Inc. to have books of enduring value published in the United States printed on acid-free paper, and we exert our best efforts to that end.

Library of Congress Cataloging-in-Publication Data

Depressive disorders : facts, theories, and treatment methods /
    Benjamin B. Wolman, editor : George Stricker, co-editor.
        p.   cm. — (Wiley series on personality processes)
    Includes bibliographical references.
    ISBN 0-471-61819-5
    1. Depression, Mental.   I. Wolman, Benjamin B.   II. Stricker,
George,   III. Series.
    [DNLM: 1. Depression.   WM 171 D4235]
    RC537.D4475   1990
    616.85′27—dc20   90-12101
                                                         CIP

Printed in the United States of America

90 91 10 9 8 7 6 5 4 3 2 1

Contributors

Aaron T. Beck, MD
Director
Center for Cognitive Therapy
University of Pennsylvania

Jules R. Bemporad, MD
Professor of Clinical Psychiatry
Cornell University Medical
　College
Director of Education
New York Hospital-Westchester
　Division

David J. Berndt, PhD
Associate Professor
Department of Psychiatry
The University of Chicago

Pamela C. Cantor, PhD
President, National Committee
　for Youth Suicide Prevention
Faculty, Harvard Medical School

Catherine A. Colby, PhD
Adjunct Assistant Professor
Department of Psychology
University of Western Ontario

Rebecca Curtis, PhD
Professor of Psychology
Department of Psychology
Adelphi University

Philip Erdberg, PhD
Diplomate in Clinical Psychology
American Board of Professional
　Psychology

Jerold R. Gold, PhD
Assistant Professor, Ferkauf
　Graduate School of Psychology
Yeshiva University

Robert N. Golden, MD
Associate Professor, Department
　of Psychiatry
University of North Carolina
　School of Medicine
Chief, Clinical
　Psychopharmacology Section
UNC Mental Health Clinical
　Research Center

Ian H. Gotlib, PhD
Associate Professor and
　Co-Director of Clinical
　Training
Faculty of Social Science
Department of Psychology
The University of Western
　Ontario

Harry M. Hoberman, PhD
Assistant Professor
Psychiatry and Pediatrics
Adolescent Health Program
University of Minnesota
　Hospital and Clinic

David S. Janowsky, MD
Professor and Chairman
Department of Psychiatry
University of North Carolina
　School of Medicine
Director, UNC Center for
　Alcohol Studies

Gerald L. Klerman, MD
Professor and Associate
  Chairman for Research
Department of Psychiatry
Cornell University Medical
  Center
Payne Whitney Psychiatric Clinic

Beatrice Joy Krauss, PhD
Memorial Sloan-Kettering
  Cancer Center

Herbert H. Krauss, PhD
Professor of Psychology
Hunter College, City University
  of New York
Director of Rehabilitation
  Research
The International Center for the
  Disabled

Karen L. Lombardi, PhD
Assistant Professor
Gordon F. Derner Institute of
  Advanced Psychological
  Studies
Adelphi University

Myer Mendelson, MD
Professor of Clinical Psychiatry
University of Pennsylvania
  School of Medicine
Senior Attending Psychiatrist
Institute of Pennsylvania
  Hospital

Cory F. Newman, PhD
Assistant Director of Education
Center for Cognitive Therapy
University of Pennsylvania

Lynn P. Rehm, PhD
Professor of Psychology
University of Houston

Diane E. Sholomskas, PhD
Associate Research Scientist
Department of Psychiatry
Yale University School of
  Medicine

Pamela M. Wallace, PhD
Assistant Professor
Department of Pediatrics
University of South Florida

Myrna M. Weissman, PhD
Professor of Epidemiology in
  Psychiatry
College of Physicians and
  Surgeons of Columbia
  University
Chief, Department of Clinical
  and Genetic Epidemiology
New York State Psychiatric
  Institute

Robert B. Wesner, MD
Assistant Professor of Psychiatry
University of Iowa College of
  Medicine

George Winokur, MD
The Paul W. Penningroth
  Professor and Head
Department of Psychiatry
University of Iowa College of
  Medicine

Benjamin B. Wolman, PhD
Editor-in-Chief
*International Encyclopedia of
  Psychiatry, Psychology,
  Psychoanalysis, and Neurology*

Steven Zavodnick, MD
Clinical Assistant Professor
Department of Psychiatry
Medical School of the University
  of Pennsylvania

Series Preface

This series of books is addressed to behavioral scientists interested in the nature of human personality. Its scope should prove pertinent to personality theorists and researchers as well as to clinicians concerned with applying an understanding of personality processes to the amelioration of emotional difficulties in living. To this end, the series provides a scholarly integration of theoretical formulations, empirical data, and practical recommendations.

Six major aspects of studying and learning about human personality can be designated: personality theory, personality structure and dynamics, personality development, personality assessment, personality change, and personality adjustment. In exploring these aspects of personality, the books in the series discuss a number of distinct but related subject areas: the nature and implications of various theories of personality; personality characteristics that account for consistencies and variations in human behavior; the emergence of personality processes in children and adolescents; the use of interviewing and testing procedures to evaluate individual differences in personality; efforts to modify personality styles through psychotherapy, counseling, behavior therapy, and other methods of influence; and patterns of abnormal personality functioning that impair individual competence.

IRVING B. WEINER

University of South Florida
Tampa, Florida

Preface

Depressive disorders are, at the present time, the highest ranking mental problem. Every year, more than 100 million people the world over are diagnosed as suffering from depression, and depressive disorders are ten times as frequent as schizophrenia.

Despite a great deal of thorough research there is no agreement concerning the etiology, symptomatology, and treatment methods. "Depressive disorders" covers a variety of distinct approaches and probably several distinct clinical entities. The numerous monographs and collective volumes based on impressive studies bear witness to the diversity of opinions. Every one of the *Diagnostic and Statistical Manuals of Mental Disorders* published by the American Psychiatric Association (1952, 1968, 1980, 1987) introduced new facts, new concepts, and new approaches.

The purpose of this collective volume is to put together the wealth of factual information and conceptual systems. The presentation is comprised of three parts. The first part deals with theories, the second with symptomatology, and the third with diagnostic and treatment methods. My goal was to provide an encyclopedic presentation of the entire body of empirical data, theories, and treatment methods. The 20 chapters written by 27 highly competent experts represent a brilliant galaxy of approaches based on years of thorough experimental, theoretical, and clinical work.

In working on this major project I was fortunate to obtain the highly capable cooperation of George Stricker, my Co-Editor, who did the lion's share in planning this volume and choosing our contributors. In addition, I have received most cordial and efficient guidance from Herb Reich, Senior Editor at John Wiley & Sons. I must also express my gratitude to my research assistant, Maggie McClellan, and all other people who took part in this work.

BENJAMIN B. WOLMAN

New York, New York
September 1990

Contents

PART 1

Theories of Depression

CHAPTER 1

Biological Theories of Depression

ROBERT N. GOLDEN, MD and DAVID S. JANOWSKY, MD

Biological theories regarding the etiology of depression date back to antiquity. Hippocrates is credited with advancing one of the first biological hypotheses. He felt that the accumulation of "black bile" and phlegm affected brain functioning, "darkening the spirit and making it melancholic" (Lewis, 1967). Over the centuries, theories have continued to be proposed, often reflecting the general scientific interests and advancements of the times.

During the past quarter century, hypotheses as to the biological pathogenesis of depressive illness have rapidly evolved. Some general patterns can be discerned from this evolution. Early modern proposals emphasized a deficiency model of depressive illness in which an inadequate amount of a particular substance, such as the neurotransmitter norepinephrine, was identified as the causative factor. This deficiency model of depression probably had its roots in two types of clinical data. The first of these consisted of observations of mood states of medical patients suffering from diseases involving the deficiency of a particular neurotransmitter, vitamin, or hormone, such as occurs in patients with hypothyroidism. The second consisted of observations of depressive reactions caused by pharmacological therapies which were thought to deplete particular substances, such as the depletion of norepinephrine stores by the antihypertensive agent reserpine (Golden & Potter, 1986).

As it became clear that the deficiency of a single substance was unlikely to account for all of the observed phenomena of depressive illnesses, and as scientists began to recognize the multitude of interactions that take place among neurotransmitter systems, the deficiency model began to yield to imbalance theories. In this revised model, the interactions and relative balance between two systems were addressed. Most recently, with the growing appreciation for the complexity of dynamic systems in the brain, and perhaps in reflection of general systems theory, hypotheses based on relatively subtle forms of systems dysregulation have come into prominence (Siever & Davis, 1985).

3

It is particularly challenging to develop and test biological theories of the etiology of depression. Depressive syndromes, as described elsewhere in this volume, include a constellation of symptoms that are quite "human" in character. Thus, it is much more difficult to develop an animal model or "test tube" equivalent for depression than it is for infectious or neoplastic diseases. While there are animal models for depression, they seem to be limited in capturing and quantifying some of the core, essential features of depression, including sadness, low self-esteem, and anhedonia. Also, it is difficult, although becoming less so with newer imaging techniques, to study brain function directly in people. Practical and ethical considerations eliminate some of the usual approaches to the examination of organ systems, such as the use of biopsy. Because of the incredible complexity of the brain, isolated study of small components of the system is fraught with potential problems in "missing the forest for the trees."

The emergence of new developments in technology has influenced the types of questions that can be asked, and has shaped the development of biological theories. For example, in the mid-1960s, new techniques in chromatography permitted the measurement of very small concentrations of biochemical compounds. Not coincidentally, theories regarding the role of catecholamine neurotransmitters, whose metabolites could by then be measured in body fluids, began to emerge. In the 1970s and 1980s, increasingly sophisticated techniques, including radioimmunoassays, pushed back the limit of quantification of biological compounds to incredibly minute concentrations. This development permitted the accurate measurement of various hormones whose extremely low concentrations could not be measured previously. This in turn allowed researchers to advance and test theories regarding the possible roles that various neurohormones and other trace compounds might play in the pathophysiology of depression. Currently, the technologies of molecular biology and brain imaging are developing and becoming widely available at an explosive pace. We predict that theories of depression in the 1990s will be shaped, in part, by the perspectives and insights that are offered by these techniques.

In this chapter, we present a review of selected biological theories of depression. Rather than presenting every theory, we have chosen for elaboration three biochemical hypotheses which have undergone repeated testing, modification, and retesting over many years and which continue to have heuristic value.

NOREPINEPHRINE

For more than half a century, the catecholamine norepinephrine has been recognized as a stress-related hormone. Cannon (1929) identified norepinephrine (also referred to as "noradrenaline"), along with epine-phrine, as playing a key function in mobilizing the "fight–flight" re-sponse to threatening stimuli. Hans Selye later documented the role of norepinephrine in the physiological response to stress (Selye, 1950). After it was established that norepinephrine fulfilled the requirements for being a central neurotransmitter, this biogenic amine became a cor-nerstone in biological theories of depression.

The catecholamine hypothesis of affective illness was first articu-lated more than 25 years ago (Bunney & Davis, 1965; Prange, 1964; Schildkraut, 1965). In its original formulation, it proposed that "some, if not all, depressions are associated with an absolute or relative defi-ciency of catecholamines, particularly noradrenaline, at functionally important receptor sites in the brain. Elation, conversely, may be asso-ciated with an excess of such amines" (Schildkraut, 1965). Much of the impetus for this hypothesis was originally based on the application of the "pharmacological bridge" paradigm in which clinically effective antidepressants, including the monoamine oxidase inhibitors and the tricyclic compounds, were noted to increase the availability of nore-pinephrine at brain synapses. From this observation, the pathogenesis of depression was assumed to be caused by a deficiency in available central norepinephrine prior to treatment. The catecholamine hypoth-esis also derived support from the observations of the mood-altering effects of the antihypertensive medication reserpine. This compound, which was reported to cause depressive reactions in a number of pa-tients receiving treatment for high blood pressure, was found to deplete norepinephrine from synaptic storage vesicles.

As the original catecholamine hypothesis came under close exami-nation, some questions and problems emerged. First, compounds that were expected, according to the hypothesis, to function as antidepres-sants were not found to be clinically effective. For example, cocaine and amphetamines were noted to increase central noradrenergic neu-rotransmission, yet were not effective medications in treating depres-sion. Second, the validity of the original observation that reserpine caused depression came into question. A critical review of the litera-ture by Goodwin, Ebert, and Bunney (1972) suggested that reserpine was associated with "pseudo-depression"—lethargy and sedation—rather than true clinical depression, in most of the reported cases. The 5 to 9 percent of patients who developed the full depressive syndrome while receiving this medication frequently had prior histories of de-pression, suggesting that the biological effects might be "unmasking" an underlying depressive illness, rather than causing its development de novo. More recently, the controversy regarding the putative depres-sogenic effects of decreased central noradrenergic neurotransmission has centered on propranolol and other antihypertensive agents which block beta-adrenergic receptors. Some reports support the claim that these compounds cause depression (Avorn, Everitt, & Weiss, 1986; Mattiasson & Henningsen, 1978; Petrie, Maffucci, & Woolsey, 1982; Waal, 1967), others do not (Adler & New York VAMC Study Group, 1988). Our own studies of healthy subjects without prior personal or family histories of depression suggest that propranolol can induce some, but not all, of the clinical stigmata of depression in normal subjects (Golden, Brown, et al., 1989).

Another problem with the original catecholamine hypothesis relates to the observed "lag time" in antidepressant response. Antidepressant pharmacotherapies require two to six weeks before a significant clinical response is achieved, yet the biochemical effects, including increased availability of norepinephrine, occur almost immediately upon initiation of treatment. Also, several of the "second generation" antidepressants, such as fluoxetine, do not affect norepinephrine to any appreciable degree, but are still clinically effective (Golden, Brown, Miller, & Evans, 1988).

Despite these challenges, the original catecholamine hypothesis has retained its heuristic value and has continued to undergo modification. Several new approaches have been applied to the study and testing of refined versions. The major metabolite of norepinephrine, MHPG, has been studied in the urine. Maas, Fawcett, and Dekirmenjian were the first to report decreased urinary excretion of MHPG (1968), and some, but not all, subsequent investigations have confirmed this finding. Bipolar patients demonstrate this finding most consistently, perhaps in reflection of the relative homogeneity of this group. Studies of unipolar patients have produced less consistent findings, and Schatzberg's group has demonstrated both low and high MHPG-excreting subpopulations of unipolar depressives (Schatzberg et al., 1982). It is difficult to interpret the meaning of these observations, since the estimates of the actual proportion of MHPG that originates in the brain, rather than in the peripheral sympathetic nervous system, range from 80 percent (Ebert & Kopin, 1975) down to 20 percent (Blombery, Kopin, Gordon, Marley, & Ebert, 1980).

Norepinephrine itself has been measured in plasma. Early studies found norepinephrine plasma levels were elevated not only in depressed patients (Esler et al., 1982; Lake et al., 1982; Wyatt, Portnoy, Kupfer, Snyder, & Engelmann, 1971), but in manic patients as well (Lake et al., 1982). More recently, investigators have measured the plasma norepinephrine response to a physiological "orthostatic challenge test" paradigm, in order to examine the efficiency of the noradrenergic system. In rising from a supine to an upright position, depressed patients are able to maintain cardiovascular output, but require a greater increase in plasma norepinephrine concentrations compared to healthy subjects (Rudorfer, Ross, Linnoila, Sherer, & Potter, 1985). This "inefficiency" in regulating the cardiovascular system might also be present in the noradrenergic regulation of mood in these patients, with "normal" amounts of norepinephrine being inadequate to maintain euthymic mood.

Several studies have suggested that antidepressant treatments increase the efficiency of norepinephrine systems in depressed patients. For example, such diverse treatments as electroconvulsive therapy, lithium, the monoamine oxidase inhibitor clorgyline, the tricyclic antidepressant desipramine, the unicyclic aminoketone bupropion, and the serotonin reuptake inhibitor zimelidine all decrease "whole body norepinephrine turnover," that is, the 24-hour production and elimination of norepinephrine and its metabolites (Golden, Rudorfer, Sherer, Linnoila, & Potter, 1988; Linnoila, Karoum, Calil, Kopin, & Potter, 1982; Linnoila, Karoum, & Potter, 1982; Linnoila, Karoum, Rosenthal, & Potter, 1983; Rudorfer et al., 1984). Furthermore, we have shown that desipramine, monoamine oxidase inhibitors, and the unicyclic aminoketone bupropion increase the output of the hydroxylated metabolite of melatonin, a neurohormone whose release is regulated by norepinephrine, while at the same time decreasing whole body norepinephrine output (Golden, Markey, Risby, Cowdry, & Potter, 1988). Again, as with the orthostatic challenge test, these data suggest that the physiological efficiency of norepinephrine systems in depressed patients is enhanced following treatment (Golden & Potter, 1986).

Both norepinephrine and MHPG have been studied in the cerebrospinal fluid (CSF) of depressed patients, as well as in urine and blood. These CSF studies have been inconclusive, as have direct measures of norepinephrine in autopsied brain tissue (see Willner, 1985, for review).

Studies of noradrenergic receptors and their responsivity to pharmacological "challenge" have provided yet another means for testing hypotheses regarding norepinephrine and depression. Beta-adrenergic receptors on lymphocytes provide a model for studying one type of norepinephrine receptor that is far more readily accessible than receptors in the brain. A number of studies have reported decreased responsivity to noradrenergic agonist stimulation in lymphocyte beta-adrenergic receptors in depressed patients (Extein, Tallman, Smith, & Goodwin, 1979; Mann et al., 1985; Pandey, Sudershan, & Davis, 1985). Pharmacological "challenge" paradigms have utilized the pituitary neuropeptide, growth hormone, since its release is mediated via postsynaptic alpha-2 noradrenergic receptors. Several studies have demonstrated blunted growth-hormone response to the alpha-2 agonist, or stimulating agent, clonidine in depressed patients compared to healthy control subjects (Charney et al., 1982; Checkley, Slade, & Shur, 1981; Matussek et al., 1980; Siever et al., 1982). Further, the growth-hormone response to desipramine, the tricyclic norepinephrine reuptake inhibitor, appears to be blunted in unipolar and bipolar depressed patients compared to healthy subjects (Sawa, Odo, & Nakazawa, 1980) and in acutely depressed patients compared to patients with affective illness in remission (Calil et al., 1984).

Another approach to testing the catecholamine hypothesis of depression involves the observation of the effects of pharmacological manipulation of central noradrenergic systems in depressed patients. For example, tyrosine, the amino acid precursor for catecholamine formation, has been reported to have some antidepressant activity (Gelenberg, Gibson, & Wojcik, 1982). Also, the beta-2 agonist salbutamol has shown clinical efficacy in at least one study (Belmaker, Lerer, & Zohar, 1982).

In summary, although the original formulations of the catecholamine hypothesis of depression have required modification, the role of norepinephrine in the pathogenesis of affective illness continues to merit attention and further study.

THE CHOLINERGIC–ADRENERGIC BALANCE HYPOTHESIS

In 1972, Janowsky, El-Yousef, Davis, and Sererke proposed a cholinergic–adrenergic balance hypothesis of affective illness. This hypothesis was based, in part, on the recognition that there is extensive cholinergic innervation of brain centers in the limbic system that appear to be functionally important in the regulation of mood states. The balance hypothesis postulated that affective states may represent the relative balance between cholinergic and adrenergic activity in relevant brain areas. Specifically, a relative increase in cholinergic versus noradrenergic activity could lead to clinical depression, while a relative hyperactivity of norepinephrine versus acetylcholine could lead to mania (Janowsky et al., 1972).

A substantial body of data, including clinical observations, animal studies, and controlled clinical research, supports the role for adrenergic–cholinergic balance in the regulation of mood. Outside of the central nervous system, norepinephrine–acetylcholine interactions modulate the functioning of several other important autonomic physiological systems, including the cardiovascular, gastrointestinal, and pupillary nervous systems. As described in the previous section, many anticatecholaminergic medications, such as reserpine and propranolol, have been linked with depressive symptoms, and interestingly, these medications have central and peripheral cholinomimetic properties in addition to their antiadrenergic activity. In animals, reserpine causes parasympathetic somatic effects, including salivation, lacrimation, miosis, diarrhea, akinesia, and tremor, as well as behavioral effects such as decreased locomotor activity, sedation, and decreased self-stimulation. In some people, reserpine is associated with a psychological profile that resembles some aspects of a depressive episode, including dysphoria, lethargy, anergy, sleepiness, and nightmares.

Perhaps the most striking evidence in support of the cholinergic-adrenergic balance hypothesis stems from observations of the psychological effects of cholinesterase inhibitors, which enhance cholinergic activity by retarding the degradation of acetylcholine. In the 1950s and 1960s, several research groups studied depressed and manic patients, and normal subjects who had been accidentally or experimentally exposed to insecticides containing cholinesterase inhibitors. In each instance, these cholinomimetic compounds seemed to induce anergic-inhibitory effects as well as to intensify and induce depressive symptoms (Bowers, Goodman, & Sim, 1964; Gershon & Shaw, 1961; Rowntree, Neven, & Wilson, 1950). The centrally active cholinesterase inhibitor physostigmine was found to induce a dramatic, albeit brief reduction in manic symptoms in bipolar patients, while placebo and neostigmine, a cholinesterase inhibitor that acts peripherally but does not cross the blood brain barrier, caused no such effect. Physostigmine also can switch manic patients, as well as depressed patients, into a more psychomotorically retarded depressed state (Janowsky, El-Yousef, Davis, & Sererke, 1973b; Janowsky, David, El-Yousef, & Davis, 1974). This finding has been replicated by others (Davis, Berger, Hollister, & DeFraites, 1978) and extended to include schizoaffective patients and euthymic bipolar patients maintained on lithium. More recently, Risch and colleagues described depressive reactions to physostigmine in normal volunteers (Risch, Cohen, Janowsky, Kalin, & Murphy, 1981).

Acetylcholine precursors (choline, lecithin, and deanol) have been shown to induce depressed mood. Two independent groups of researchers reported an increase in depressive symptoms in schizophrenic patients who were receiving choline for treatment of tardive dyskinesia (Davis, Hollister, & Berger, 1979; Tamminga, Smith, Chang, Haraszti, & Davis, 1976). Casey (1979) has described depressed mood, and in some cases hypomania, in a minority of patients with tardive dyskinesia treated with deanol, the presumed acetylcholine precursor. Others have described depressive reactions to choline and to lecithin in a small number of patients receiving experimental treatment with these compounds for Alzheimer's disease. Furthermore, Cohen, Miller, Lipinski, and Pope (1980) observed antimanic responses to choline in a group of bipolar patients.

The depressogenic effects of various cholinomimetic drugs may be somewhat specific to patients with affective disorders. Janowsky et al. (1974) observed that while nearly all psychiatric patients developed an inhibitory or anergic syndrome in response to physostigmine challenge, patients with depression, mania, or schizoaffective diagnoses became significantly more sad and depressed, compared to schizophrenic patients. More recently, in a study of a group of carefully diagnosed psychiatric inpatients, the dysphoric and behavior-inhibiting response to intravenous physostigmine was considerably more pronounced in patients with affective disorders than in psychiatric patients with other diagnoses (Risch, Kalin, & Janowsky, 1981). Also, in the study of the effects of deanol on patients with tardive dyskinesia, referred to above, Casey (1979) noted that the subgroup of patients with a strong history of affective disorders selectively accounted for most of the depressive response to this cholinomimetic.

One of the most widely studied and established biological markers of depression is decreased rapid eye movement (REM) sleep latency (Gillin et al., 1984). REM latency is the period of time from the onset of sleep to the initiation of the first REM period. Interestingly, REM latency can be decreased by acetylcholine and increased by norepinephrine. Depressed patients have a greater sensitivity to the effects of a cholinergic agonist on this sleep parameter. Following infusion of the acetylcholine agonist arecholine, the REM latency of depressed patients decreased to a greater degree than that of healthy subjects (Sitaram, Nurnberger, Gershon, & Gillin, 1980). This increased sensitivity to cholinergic effects was also seen in the first-degree relatives of depressed patients and in patients with anorexia nervosa who had past histories of depression (Sitaram et al., 1980). Using another agonist challenge paradigm, Sitaram, Gillin, and Bunney (1984) demonstrated another example of cholinergic hypersensitivity in depressed patients, that of exaggerated pupillary constriction following the instillation of the cholinergic agonist pilocarpine into the eyes of depressed patients, compared to healthy control subjects.

A pharmacological–behavioral approach has also been utilized in testing the cholinergic–adrenergic balance hypothesis. Stereotypic behaviors can be induced in rats by the psychostimulant methylphenidate, presumably via increased catecholaminergic activity. These methylphenidate-induced stereotypes can be antagonized by the cholinomimetic physostigmine. Similarly, methylphenidate can induce psychomotor stimulation in manic patients, including increased talkativeness, euphoric mood, and increased interpersonal interaction, and these methylphenidate-induced symptoms can be rapidly antagonized by physostigmine administration. Conversely, physostigmine can precipitate inhibitory-depressant effects, which can be reversed by methylphenidate (Janowsky, El-Yousef, Davis, & Sererke, 1973a).

While cholinomimetic drugs can produce mood-lowering and antimanic effects, centrally acting anticholinergic drugs can stimulate mood elevation. Anticholinergic antiparkinsonian medications, used to treat neuroleptic-induced parkinsonian side effects, can cause euphoria, a sense of well being, increased sociability, and a reversal of depressed mood. Furthermore, case reports describe antidepressant responses to high doses of atropine and to other anticholinergic compounds such as biperiden and trihexylphenidyl; a recent report, a tricyclic antidepressant-induced anticholinergic syndrome led to alleviation of depressive symptoms. Finally, a number of tricyclic antidepressants have substantial anticholinergic properties, although some of the second-generation antidepressants, such as trazodone and fluoxetine, do not (Janowsky et al., 1983).

Neuroendocrine studies have also been applied to the cholinergic-adrenergic balance hypothesis. Physostigmine increases serum ACTH and beta-endorphin concentrations, and these responses are exaggerated in depressed patients (Janowsky et al., 1983; Risch, Kalin, & Janowsky, 1981).

Finally, genetic studies have also examined the cholinergic-adrenergic balance hypothesis. Nadi, Nurnberger, and Gershon (1984) reported that the cultured fibroblasts of bipolar affective disorder patients and their relatives with affective disorders showed increases in muscarinic binding, compared to their nonaffectively ill relatives and to healthy controls. Such "up-regulation" of cholinergic receptors could account for increased sensitivity to acetylcholine. However, other groups have been unable to replicate these results (Kelsoe et al., 1985, 1986).

Thus, considerable evidence from a variety of approaches supports the cholinergic–adrenergic balance hypothesis of affective illness. Ongoing studies should permit the development of an even greater understanding of the role of these mechanisms in affective disease processes.

SEROTONIN

While American psychiatrists were focusing their attention on the catecholamine hypotheses of depression in the early 1960s, their British colleagues were pursuing the link between affective illness and the indoleamine neurotransmitter serotonin. The indoleamine hypothesis held that a deficiency or functional deficit in central serotonin could lead to the emergence of depressive illness (Coppen, Shaw, Malleson, Eccleston, & Gundy, 1965). Some of the original observations that supported the catecholamine hypothesis were also consistent with an indoleamine hypothesis of depression. For example, the first clinically effective antidepressants—the monoamine oxidase inhibitors and the tricyclic reuptake inhibitor imipramine—increased the availability of serotonin, as well as norepinephrine, in the brain. Coppen, Shaw, and Farrell (1963) reported that the addition of tryptophan, the amino acid precursor for serotonin formation, to pharmacotherapy with a monoamine oxidase inhibitor increased clinical effectiveness in treating depression. Other psychiatrists reported some clinical utility in administering tryptophan alone as an antidepressant. When Prange and his coworkers observed that tryptophan was effective in treating mania, they revised the indoleamine hypothesis and postulated a "permissive hypothesis" of affective illness. This theory suggested that a deficit in central serotonergic neurotransmission permits the emergence of affective illness. When coupled with decreased noradrenergic activity, depression will develop; and mania will emerge from increased noradrenergic activity in the context of decreased serotonin (Prange, Wilson, Lynn, Alltop, & Stikeleather, 1974).

Several lines of evidence support the role of a functional deficit in serotonin in depressive illness. Postmortem studies of depressed patients and suicide victims have found reduced levels of serotonin or its metabolites (Beskow, Gottfries, Roos, & Winblad, 1976; Bourne, Bunney, & Colburn, 1968; Cochran, Robins, & Grote, 1976; Lloyd, Farley, Deck, & Horneykieweiz, 1974; Shure, Campes, & Eccleston, 1967), increased serotonin-2 (5-HT2) receptor binding (Mann, Stanley, McBride, & McEwen, 1986), and decreased tritiated imipramine binding (Stanley & Mann, 1983) in brain tissue, all suggestive of decreased functional serotonergic activity. Depressed patients have decreased CSF concentrations of the serotonin metabolite 5-HIAA (Asberg & Bertilsson, 1979; Asberg, Thoren, & Traskman, 1976; Ashcroft et al., 1966; Cowdry & Goodwin, 1978), although some investigators have been unable to replicate this finding (Murphy, Campbell, & Costa, 1978). Platelets, which share several biochemical and pharmacological properties with serotonergic nerve endings, have abnormal tritiated imipramine binding (Briley, Langer, Raisman, Sechter, & Zarifian, 1980; Paul, Rehavi, Skolnik, Ballenger, & Goodwin, 1981), reduced serotonin uptake (Meltzer, Arora, Baber, & Tricou, 1981; Tuomisto & Tukiainen, 1976), aberrant seasonal variations in serotonin uptake (Malmgren, Aberg-Wistedt, & Martensson, 1989), and supersensitivity to serotonin (Brusov et al., 1989) in depressed patients, compared to control subjects.

Treatment studies also support the role of serotonin in the pathogenesis of depression. Coppen's finding of tryptophan potentiation of monoamine oxidase inhibitor antidepressant activity has been extended to include potentiation of other monoamine oxidase inhibitors and the tricyclic antidepressant clomipramine (Glassman & Platman, 1969; Walinder, Skott, Carlson, Nagy, & Roos, 1976). Another serotonin precursor, 5-hydroxytryptophan (5-HTP), has been shown to enhance the efficacy of antidepressants and on occasion to be effective as an antidepressant itself (Carroll, 1971; Kaneko, Kumashiro, Takahashi, & Hoshino, 1979; Van Praag & Van Korf, 1974). The drug p-chlorophenylalanine, which decreases serotonin synthesis, has been shown to induce a recurrence of depressive symptoms in recovered patients receiving antidepressant treatment (Shopsin, Friedman, & Gershon, 1976).

Pharmacological "challenge" tests have also been applied to the serotonin hypothesis of depression. Analogous to the challenge paradigms for norepinephrine described above, these involve the administration of drugs with selective serotonergic activity and the measurement of accompanying changes in plasma concentrations of hormones whose release is regulated by serotonin. For example, the prolactin response to IV administration of tryptophan is blunted in depressed patients (Heninger, Charney, & Sternberg, 1984), and normalizes following treatment with tricyclic antidepressants, monoamine oxidase inhibitors, and lithium (Charney, Heninger, & Sternberg, 1984; Price, Charney, Delgado, & Heninger, 1989; Price, Charney, & Heninger, 1985). Fenfluramine, a serotonin-releasing agent and uptake inhibitor, yields a blunted prolactin response in depressed patients as well (Siever, Murphy, Slater, De La Vega, & Lipper, 1984). We have recently found a blunted prolactin—as well as an ACTH—response to IV administration of clomipramine, the relatively specific serotonin uptake inhibitor, in depressed patients, compared to healthy control subjects (Golden, Hsiao, & Potter, 1989). In contrast, Meltzer's group has described an exaggerated cortisol response to the serotonin precursor 5-hydroxytryptophan (Meltzer, Umberkoman-Wiita et al., 1984); the magnitude of the cortisol response was significantly correlated with severity of depression and with suicidal activity (Meltzer, Perline, Tricou, Lowy, & Robertson, 1984). Interestingly, the exaggerated cortisol response to 5-hydroxytryptophan was seen in manic patients as well, consistent with the permissive hypothesis of affective illness described above.

Despite the wealth of supportive evidence for an indoleamine hypothesis of depression, there are limits to the conclusions that can be drawn. Not all of the findings have been consistently replicated (e.g., low CSF 5-HIAA in depressed patients). Each of the challenge paradigms described above is less than perfect in regard to specificity for serotonergic systems (Van Praag, Lemus, & Kahn, 1987). Still, the serotonin hypothesis continues to be the stimulus for increasingly sophisticated research into the biological bases of depression.

OTHER HYPOTHESES

We have reviewed selected biological theories of depression which have significant historic value as well as continued importance in the present. Many other theories regarding the biology of depressive illness are also stimulating ongoing studies. As new neurotransmitters are discovered, their possible role in affective illness and other psychiatric syndromes comes under investigation, and there are a number of peptides, as well as additional biochemical compounds, which have been recently implicated in the pathophysiology of depression (Janowsky, Golden, Rapaport, Cain, & Gillin, 1988). For example, the dopamine hypothesis of affective illness proposes that mania is associated with increased dopaminergic neuronal activity, while depression, particularly depression with psychomotor retardation, is associated with a decrease in dopaminergic activity (Willner, 1985). Phenylethylamine, an endogenous amphetamine-like monoamine, has been postulated to be involved in depression (Sabelli & Moswaim, 1974), as has the inhibitory amino acid neurotransmitter gamma-aminobutyric acid (Berrettini & Post, 1984). Recent investigations have begun to explore the possible relationship between endorphin function and affective disorders (Emrich, Vogt, & Herz, 1983). Furthermore, theories involving biological rhythms, including sleep and seasonal cycles, have now emerged (Sack & Wehr, 1988).

SUMMARY

Several lines of evidence suggest that the classic neurotransmitters, norepinephrine, acetylcholine, and serotonin, play important roles in the pathogenesis of depressive illness. Other biochemical compounds and peptides may also be involved in the etiology of some forms of mood disorders.

With so many biological theories of depression to choose from, one might wonder which theory will ultimately turn out to be the correct one. We believe the answer is that no one theory will completely explain the biological bases for depression because depression is really a syndrome, rather than a specific unitary disease state. Although we have made some progress in identifying certain subtypes (e.g., bipolar depression), we probably still are left with many overlapping entities that currently cannot be distinguished clinically from one another. Further, because it is so difficult in clinical practice to delineate depression from related disorders, let alone isolate the possible subtypes of depression, it should not be surprising that a consistent biological correlate or marker has not yet been identified. Furthermore, it is highly likely that many biological hypotheses overlap each other, and that different neurotransmitter systems interact with each other. Still, our understanding of the biology of affective illness continues to grow at a rapid pace, and we hope that this increased understanding will continue to be translated into more effective treatment for patients who are suffering from depression.

REFERENCES

Adler, L., and New York VAMC Study Group (1988). CNS effects of beta blockade: A comparative study. *Psychopharmacology Bulletin, 24,* 232–237.

Asberg, M., & Bertilsson, L. (1979). Serotonin in depressive illness: Studies of CSF 5-HIAA. In B. Saleto, P. Berner, & L. E. Hollister (Eds.), *Neuropsychopharmacology* (pp. 105–115). New York: Pergamon Press.

Asberg, M., Thoren, P., & Traskman, L. (1976). "Serotonin depression": A biochemical subgroup within the affective disorders. *Science, 191,* 478–480.

Ashcroft, G. W., Crawford, T. B. B., Eccleston, D., Charman, D. F., MacDougall, E. J., Stanton, J. B., & Binns, J. K. (1966). 5-hydroxyindole compounds in the cerebral spinal fluid of patients with psychiatric or neurological diseases. *Lancet, 2,* 1049–1052.

Avorn, J., Everitt, D. E., & Weiss, S. (1986). Increased antidepressant use in patients prescribed B-blockers. *Journal American Medical Association, 255,* 357–360.

Belmaker, R. H., Lerer, B., & Zohar, J. (1982). Salbutamol treatment of depression. In E. Costa & G. Racagini (Eds.), *Typical and atypical antidepressants: Clinical practice* (pp. 181–193). New York: Raven Press.

Berrettini, W. H., & Post, R. M. (1984). GABA in affective illness. In R. M. Post & J. C. Ballenger (Eds.), *Neurobiology of mood disorders.* Baltimore/London: Williams & Wilkins.

Beskow, J., Gottfries, C. G., Roos, B. E., & Winblad, D. B. (1976). Determination of monoamine and monamine metabolites in the human brain: Post-mortem studies in a group of suicides and in a control group. *Acta Psychiatrica Scandinavia, 53,* 7–20.

Blombery, P. A., Kopin, I. J., Gordon, E. K., Marley, S. P., & Ebert, M. (1980). Conversion of MHPG to vanillylmandelic acid: Implications for the importance of urinary MHPG. *Archives of General Psychiatry, 37,* 1095–1098.

Bourne, H. R., Bunney, W. E., & Colburn, R. W. (1968). 5-Hydroxytryptamine and 5-hydroxyindoleacetic acid in the hind brains of suicidal patients. *Lancet, 2,* 805–808.

Bowers, M. B., Goodman, E., & Sim, V. M. (1964). Some behavioral changes in man following anticholinesterase administration. *Journal of Nervous and Mental Disease, 138,* 383.

Briley, M. S., Langer, S. Z., Raisman, R., Sechter, D., & Zarifian, E. (1980). Tritiated imipramine binding sites are decreased in platelets of untreated depressed patients. *Science, 209,* 303–305.

Brusov, I. S., Beliaev, B. S., Katasonov, A. B., Zlobina, G. P., Factor, M. I., & Lideman, R. R. (1989). Does platelet serotonin receptor supersensitivity accompany endogenous depression? *Biological Psychiatry, 25,* 375–381.

Bunney, W. E., Jr., & Davis, J. B. (1965). Norepinephrine in depressive reactions: A review. *Archives of General Psychiatry, 13,* 483–494.

Calil, H. M., Lesieur, P., Gold, P. W., Brown, G. M., Zavadil, A. P., & Potter, W. Z. (1984). Hormonal responses to zimelidine and desipramine in depressed patients. *Psychiatry Research, 13,* 231–242.

Cannon, W. B. (1929). *Bodily changes in pain, hunger, fear, and rage.* New York: Appleton.

Carroll, B. J. (1971). Monoamine precursors in the treatment of depression. *Clinical Pharmacology Therapy, 12,* 743–761.

Casey, D. E. (1979). Mood alterations during deanol therapy. *Psychopharmacology, 62,* 187–191.

Charney, D. S., Heninger, G. R., & Sternberg, D. E. (1984). Serotonin function and the mechanism of action of antidepressant treatment: Effects of amitriptyline and desipramine. *Archives of General Psychiatry, 41,* 359–365.

Charney, D. S., Heninger, G. R., Sternberg, D. E., Hafstad, K. M., Giddings, S., & Landis, D. H. (1982). Adrenergic receptor sensitivity in depression: Effects of clonidine in depressed patients and healthy subjects. *Archives of General Psychiatry, 39,* 290–294.

Checkley, S. A., Slade, A. P., & Shur, E. (1981). Growth hormone and other responses to clonidine in patients with endogenous depression. *British Journal of Psychiatry, 138,* 290–294.

Cochran, E., Robins, E., & Grote, S. (1976). Regional serotonin levels in brain: A comparison of depressive suicides and alcoholic suicides with controls. *Biological Psychiatry, 11,* 283–294.

Cohen, B. M., Miller, A. L., Lipinski, J. F., & Pope, H. G. (1980). Lecithin in mania: A preliminary report. *American Journal of Psychiatry, 137,* 242–243.

Coppen, A., Shaw, D., & Farrell, J. P. (1963). Potentiation of the antidepressive effect of a monoamine-oxidase inhibitor by tryptophan. *Lancet, 1,* 79–81.

Coppen, A., Shaw, D. M., Malleson, A., Eccleston, E., & Gundy, G. (1965). Tryptamine metabolism in depression. *British Journal of Psychiatry, 111,* 993–998.

Cowdry, R. W., & Goodwin, F. K. (1978). Amine neurotransmitter studies and psychiatric illness: Toward more meaningful diagnostic concepts. In R. L. Spitzer & D. F. Klein (Eds.), *Critical issues in psychiatric diagnosis* (pp. 281–304). New York: Raven Press.

Davis, K. L., Berger, P. A., Hollister, L. E., & DeFraites, E. (1978). Physostigmine in mania. *Archives of General Psychiatry, 35,* 119–122.

Davis, K. L., Hollister, L. E., & Berger, P. A. (1979). Choline chloridine and schizophrenia. *American Journal of Psychiatry, 136,* 119–122.

Ebert, M. H., & Kopin, I. (1975). Differential labelling of origins of urinary catecholamine metabolites by dopamine-C 14. *Transactions of the American Physicians, 13,* 256–262.

Emrich, H. M., Vogt, P., & Herz, A. (1983). Possible antidepressant effects of opioids: Action of buprenorphine. *Annals of the New York Academy of Science, 398,* 108–112.

Esler, M., Turbott, J., Schwartz, R., Leonard, P., Bobik, A., Skews, H., & Jackman, J. (1982). The peripheral kinetics of norepinephrine in depressed illness. *Archives of General Psychiatry, 39,* 295–300.

Extein, I., Tallman, J., Smith, C. C., & Goodwin, F. K. (1979). Changes in lymphocyte beta-adrenergic receptors in depression and mania. *Psychiatry Research, 1,* 191–197.

Gelenberg, A., Gibson, C., & Wojcik, J. D. (1982). Neurotransmitter precursors for the treatment of depression. *Psychopharmacology Bulletin, 18,* 7–18.

Gershon, S., & Shaw, F. H. (1961). Psychiatric sequelae of chronic exposure to organophosphorous insecticides. *Lancet, 1,* 1371–1374.

Gillin, J. C., Sitaram, N., Wehr, T., Duncan, W., Post, R. M., Murphy, D. L., Mendelson, W. B., Wyatt, R. J., & Bunney, W. E., Jr. (1984). Sleep and affective illness. In R. M. Post and J. C. Ballenger (Eds.), *Neurobiology of mood disorders* (pp. 157–189). Baltimore: Williams & Wilkins.

Glassman, A., & Platman, S. R. (1969). Potentiation of monoamine oxidase inhibitor by tryptophan. *Journal of Psychiatry Research, 7,* 83–88.

Golden, R. N., Brown, T. M., Miller, H., & Evans, D. L. (1988). The new antidepressants. *North Carolina Medical Journal, 49,* 549–554.

Golden, R. N., Brown, T., Tancer, M., Mason, G., Burnett, L., & Evans, D. L. (1989). *Psychobiologic effects of beta-adrenergic blockade.* Paper presented at the 142nd Annual Meeting of the American Psychiatric Association, May 1989.

Golden, R. N., Hsiao, J., & Potter, W. Z. (1989). *Serotonergic dysregulation in mood disorders.* Paper presented at the 142nd Annual Meeting of the American Psychiatric Association, May 1989.

Golden, R. N., Markey, S. P., Risby, E. D., Cowdry, R. W., & Potter, W. Z. (1988). Antidepressants reduce whole-body norepinephrine turnover while enhancing 6-hydroxymelatonin output. *Archives of General Psychiatry, 45,* 150–154.

Golden, R. N., & Potter, W. Z. (1986). Neurochemical and neuroendocrine dysregulation in affective disorders. *Psychiatric Clinics of North America, 9,* 313–327.

Golden, R. N., Rudorfer, M. V., Sherer, M., Linnoila, M., & Potter, W. Z. (1988). Bupropion in depression: I. Biochemical effects and clinical response. *Archives of General Psychiatry, 45,* 139–143.

Goodwin, F. K., Ebert, M. H., & Bunney, W. E., Jr. (1972). Mental effects of reserpine in man: A review. In R. I. Shader (Ed.), *Psychiatric complications of medical drugs* (pp. 73–101). New York: Raven Press.

Heninger, G. R., Charney, D. S., & Sternberg, D. E. (1984). Serotonergic function in depression: Prolactin response to intravenous tryptophan in depressed patients and healthy subjects. *Archives of General Psychiatry, 41,* 398–402.

Janowsky, D. S., David, J. M., El-Yousef, M. K., & Davis, J. M. (1974). Acetylcholine and depression. *Psychosomatic Medicine, 36,* 248–257.

Janowsky, D. S., El-Yousef, M. K., Davis, J. M., & Sererke, H. J. (1972). A cholinergic–adrenergic hypothesis of mania and depression. *Lancet, 2,* 6732–6735.

Janowsky, D. S., El-Yousef, M. K., Davis, J. M., & Sererke, H. J. (1973a). Antagonistic effects of physostigmine and methylphenidate in man. *American Journal of Psychiatry, 130,* 1370–1376.

Janowsky, D. S., El-Yousef, M. K., Davis, J. M., & Sererke, H. J. (1973b). Parasympathetic suppression of manic symptoms by physostigmine. *Archives of General Psychiatry, 28,* 542–547.

Janowsky, D. S., Golden, R. N., Rapaport, M., Cain, J. J., & Gillin, J. C. (1988). Neurochemistry of depression and mania. In A. Georgotas & R. Cancro (Eds.), *Depression and mania* (pp. 244–264). New York: Elsevier.

Janowsky, D. S., Risch, S. C., Judd, L. L., Parker, D. C., Kalin, N. H., & Huey, L. Y. (1983). Behavioral and neuroendocrine effects of physostigmine in affect disorder patients. In P. J. Clayton & J. E. Barrett (Eds.), *Treatment of depression: Old controversies and new approaches* (pp. 61–74). New York: Raven Press.

Kaneko, M., Kumashiro, H., Takahashi, Y., & Hoshino, Y. (1979). L-5-HTP treatment and serum 5-HT level after L-5-HTP loading in depressed patients. *Neuropsychobiology, 5,* 232–240.

Kelsoe, J., Jr., Gillin, J., Janowsky, D. S., Brown, J., Risch, S. C., & Lumkin, B. (1985). Failure to confirm muscarine receptors on skin fibroblasts. *New England Journal of Medicine, 312,* 861–862.

Kelsoe, J., Jr., Gillin, J., Janowsky, D. S., Brown, J., Risch, S. C., & Lumkin, B. (1986). Specific ^{3}H-N-methyl scopolamine binding without cholinergic function in cultured adult skin fibroblasts. *Life Sciences, 38,* 1399.

Lake, C. R., Pickar, D., Ziegler, M. G., Lipper, S., Slater, S., & Murphy, D. L. (1982). High plasma norepinephrine levels in patients with major affective disorders. *American Journal of Psychiatry, 139,* 1315–1318.

Lewis, A. (1967). Melancholia: historical review. In A. Lewis (Ed.), *The state of psychiatry: Essays and addresses.* New York: Science House.

Linnoila, M., Karoum, F., Calil, H., Kopin, I., & Potter, W. Z. (1982). Alteration of norepinephrine metabolism with desipramine and zimelidine in depressed patients. *Archives of General Psychiatry, 39,* 1025–1028.

Linnoila, M., Karoum, F., & Potter, W. Z. (1982). Effect of low dose clorgyline on 24-hour urinary monoamine excretion in patients with rapidly cycling bipolar affective disorder. *Archives of General Psychiatry, 39,* 513–516.

Linnoila, M., Karoum, F., Rosenthal, N., & Potter, W. Z. (1983). Electroconvulsive treatment and lithium carbonate: Their effects on norepinephrine metabolism in patients with primary major depressions. *Archives of General Psychiatry, 40,* 677–680.

Lloyd, K. G., Farley, I. J., Deck, J. H. N., & Horneykieweiz, O. (1974). Serotonin and 5-hydroxy-indoleacetic acid in discrete areas of the brain stem of suicide victims and control patients. *Advances in Biochemical Psychopharmacology, 11,* 387–398.

Maas, J. W., Fawcett, J., & Dekirmenjian, J. (1968). 3-Methoxy-4-hydroxphenylglycol (MHGH) excretion in depressed states: A pilot study. *Archives of General Psychiatry, 19,* 129–134.

Malmgren, R., Aberg-Wistedt, A., & Martensson, B. (1989). Aberrant seasonal variations of platelet serotonin uptake in endogenous depression. *Biological Psychiatry, 25,* 393–402.

Mann, J. J., Brown, R. P., Halper, J. P., Sweeney, J. A., Kocsis, J. H., Stokes, P. E., & Bilezikian, J. P. (1985). Reduced sensitivity of lymphocyte beta-adrenergic receptors in patients with endogenous depression and psychomotor agitation. *New England Journal of Medicine, 313,* 715–720.

Mann, J. J., Stanley, M., McBride, A., & McEwen, B. S. (1986). Increased serotonin-2 and β-adrenergic receptor binding in the frontal cortices of suicide victims. *Archives of General Psychiatry, 43,* 954–959.

Mattiasson, I., & Henningsen, N. C. (1978, September). *Side effects during treatment with lipid-soluble beta-adrenergic blocking substances.* Paper presented at the 8th World Congress of Cardiology, Tokyo, Japan.

Matussek, N., Ackenheil, M., Hippius, H., Müller, F., Schröder, H. T., Schultes, H., & Wasilewski, B. (1980). Effect of clonidine on growth hormone release in psychiatric patients and controls. *Journal of Psychiatric Research, 2,* 25–36.

Meltzer, H. Y., Arora, R. C., Baber, R., & Tricou, B. J. (1981). Serotonin uptake in blood platelets of psychiatric patients. *Archives of General Psychiatry, 38,* 1322–1326.

Meltzer, H. Y., Perline, R., Tricou, B. J., Lowy, M., & Robertson, A. (1984). Effective of hydroxytryptophan on serum levels in major affective disorders: Relation to suicide, psychosis and depressive symptoms. *Archives of General Psychiatry, 41,* 379–387.

Meltzer, H. Y., Umberkoman-Wiita, B., Robertson, A., Tricou, B. J., Lowy, M., & Perline, R. (1984). Effective of hydroxytryptophan on serum cortisol levels in major affective disorders: Enhanced response in depression and mania. *Archives of General Psychiatry, 41,* 379–387.

Murphy, D. L., Campbell, I., & Costa, J. L. (1978). Current studies in the indoleamine hypothesis of the affective disorders. In M. A. Lipton, A. Dimascio, & K. F. Killam (Eds.), *Psychopharmacology: A generation of progress* (pp. 1235–1248). New York: Raven Press.

Nadi, N., Nurnberger, J., & Gershon, E. (1984). Muscarinic cholinergic receptors on skin fibroblasts in familial effective disorder. *New England Journal of Medicine, 311,* 225.

Pandey, G. N., Sudershan, P., & Davis, J. M. (1985). Beta adrenergic receptor function in depression and the effect of antidepressant drugs. *Acta Pharmacology and Toxicology, 56* (Supp. 1), 66–79.

Paul, S. M., Rehavi, M., Skolnik, P., Ballenger, J. C., & Goodwin, F. K. (1981). Depressed patients have decreased binding of tritiated imipramine to platelet serotonin "transporter." *Archives of General Psychiatry, 38,* 1315–1317.

Petrie, W. M., Maffucci, R. J., & Woolsey, R. L. (1982). Propranolol and depression. *American Journal of Psychiatry, 139,* 92–94.

Prange, A. J., Jr. (1964). The pharmacology and biochemistry of depression. *Diseases of the Nervous System, 25,* 217–222.

Prange, A. J., Jr. Wilson, I. C., Lynn, C. W., Alltop, L. B., & Stikeleather, R. A. (1974). L-tryptophan in mania: Contribution to a permissive hypothesis of affective disorders. *Archives of General Psychiatry, 30,* 56–62.

Price, L. H., Charney, D. S., Delgado, P. L., & Heninger, G. R. (1989). Lithium treatment and serotonergic function: Neuroendocrine and behavioral responses to intravenous tryptophan in affective disorder. *Archives of General Psychiatry, 46,* 13–19.

Price, L. H., Charney, D. S., & Heninger, G. R. (1985). Effects of tranyl-cypromine treatment on neuroendocrine, behavioral, and autonomic responses to tryptophan in depressed patients. *Life Sciences, 37,* 809–818.

Risch, S. C., Cohen, R. M., Janowsky, D. S., Kalin, N. H., & Murphy, D. L. (1981). Plasma B-endorphin and cortisol elevations accompany the mood and behavioral effects of physostigmine in man. *Science, 209,* 1545–1546.

Risch, S. C., Kalin, N. H., & Janowsky, D. S. (1981). Cholinergic challenges in affective illness: Behavioral and neuroendocrine correlates. *Journal of Clinical Psychopharmacology, 1,* 186–192.

Rowntree, D. W., Neven, S., & Wilson, A. (1950). The effects of diisopropylfluorophosphonate in schizophrenia and manic depressive psychosis. *Journal of Neurology, Neurosurgery and Psychiatry, 13,* 47–62.

Rudorfer, M., Ross, R., Linnoila, M., Sherer, M., & Potter, W. Z. (1985). Exaggerated orthostatic responsivity of plasma norepinephrine in depression. *Archives of General Psychiatry, 42,* 1186–1192.

Rudorfer, M., Scheinin, M., Karoum, F., Ross, R. J., Potter, W. Z., & Linnoila, M. (1984). Reduction of norepinephrine by serotonergic drug in man. *Biological Psychiatry, 19,* 179–193.

Sabelli, H. C., & Moswaim, A. D. (1974). Phenylethylamine hypothesis of affective behavior. *American Journal of Psychiatry, 131,* 695.

Sack, D. A., & Wehr, T. (1988). Circadian rhythms in affective disorders. In A. Georgotas & R. Cancro (Eds.), *Depression and mania* (pp. 312–332). New York: Elsevier.

Sawa, Y., Odo, S., & Nakazawa, T. (1980). Growth hormone secretion by tricyclic and nontricyclic antidepressants in healthy volunteers and depressives. In S. Z. Langer, R. Takahashi, & M. Briley (Eds.), *New vistas in depression* (pp. 309–315). New York: Pergamon.

Schatzberg, A., Orsulak, P., Rosenbaum, A., Maruta, T., Kruger, E., Cole, J., & Schildkraut, J. (1982). Toward a biochemical classification of depressive disorders. V. Heterogeneity of unipolar depressions. *American Journal of Psychiatry, 139,* 471–475.

Schildkraut, J. (1965). The catecholamine hypothesis of affective disorders: A review of supporting evidence. *American Journal of Psychiatry, 122,* 509–522.

Selye, H. (1950). *Stress.* Montreal: Acta, Inc.

Shopsin, B., Friedman, E., & Gershon, S. (1976). Parachlorophenylalanine reversal of tranylcypromine effect in depressed patients. *Archives of General Psychiatry, 33,* 811–822.

Shure, D. M., Campes, F. E., & Eccleston, E. G. (1967). 5-Hydroxytryptamine in the hind brain of depressive suicides. *British Journal of Psychiatry, 113,* 1407–1411.

Siever, L. J., & Davis, K. L. (1985). Overview: Toward a dysregulation hypothesis of depression. *American Journal of Psychiatry, 142,* 1017–1031.

Siever, L. J., Murphy, D., Slater, S., De La Vega, E., & Lipper, S. (1984). Plasma prolactin changes following fenfluramine in depressed patients compared to the controls: An evaluation of central sertonergic responsivity in depression. *Life Sciences, 34,* 1029–1039.

Siever, L. J., Uhde, T. W., Silberman, E. K., Jimerson, D. C., Aloi, J. A., Post, R. M., & Murphy, D. L. (1982). The growth hormone response to clonidine as a probe of noradrenergic receptor responsiveness in affective disorder patients and controls. *Psychiatry Research, 6,* 171–183.

Sitaram, N., Gillin, J. C., & Bunney, W. E., Jr. (1984). Cholinergic and catecholamine receptor sensitivity in affective illness: Strategy and theory. In R. M. Post and J. C. Ballenger (Eds.), *Neurobiology of mood disorders* (pp. 629–651). Baltimore: Williams & Wilkins.

Sitaram, N., Nurnberger, J., Gershon, E., & Gillin, J. C. (1980). Faster cholinergic REM sleep induction in euthymic patients with primary affective illness. *Science, 208,* 200–202.

Stanley, M., & Mann, J. (1983). Increased serotonin-2 binding sites in frontal cortex of suicide victims. *Lancet, 1,* 214–216.

Tamminga, C., Smith, R. C., Chang, S., Haraszti, J. S., & Davis, J. M. (1976). Depression associated with oral choline. *Lancet, 2,* 905.

Tuomisto, J., & Tukiainen, B. (1976). Decreased uptake of 5-hydroxytryptamine in blood platelets of depressed patients. *Nature, 262,* 596–598.

Van Praag, H. M. (1977). *Depression and schizophrenia: A contribution on their chemical pathologies* (pp. 65–92). New York: Spectrum Publications.

Van Praag, H. M., Lemus, C., & Kahn, R. (1987). Hormonal probes of central serotonergic activity: Do they really exist? *Biological Psychiatry, 22,* 86–98.

Van Praag, H. M., & Van Korf, J. (1974). 5-hydroxytryptophan as an antidepressant: The predictive value of the probenecid test. *Journal of Nervous and Mental Disease, 158,* 331–337.

Waal, H. J. (1967). Propranolol-induced depression. *British Medical Journal, 2,* 50.

Walinder, J., Skott, A., Carlson, A., Nagy, A., & Roos, B. E. (1976). Potentiation of antidepressant action of clomipramine by tryptophan. *Archives of General Psychiatry, 33,* 1384–1389.

Willner, P. (1985). Dopamine and depression: A review of recent evidence. I. Empirical studies. *Brain Research Review, 6,* 211.

Wyatt, R. J., Portnoy, B., Kupfer, D. J., Snyder, F., & Engelmann, K. (1971). Resting plasma catecholamine concentrations in patients with depression and anxiety. *Archives of General Psychiatry, 24,* 65–70.

CHAPTER 2

Psychoanalytic Views on Depression

MYER MENDELSON, MD

FREUD'S THEORY

The evolution of psychoanalytic concepts of depression has kept in step with the development of the general theory of psychoanalysis. The psychosexual phases of development, the structural theory, the broadening of the concepts of orality and anality, the increased understanding of self-esteem, and the deepening insight into the determinants of self-esteem are among the developments of the general psychoanalytic theory which became reflected in the gradually evolving understanding of depressive illness.

In 1905, Freud sketched out his theory of psychosexual development, according to which infants and children make their way through the oral, anal, and phallic phases. If this development is blocked or meets traumatic hurdles at any stage, fixation points may develop at the oral, anal, or phallic phase and ominous consequences may become integrated into the personality structure of the individual.

With the insight provided by this theory of psychosexual development, Abraham (1911, 1916, 1924) was able to observe a number of clinical examples of oral fixations in both children and adults, who obtained sensual gratification of their oral mucosa by drinking milk or eating sweets. Abraham understood these behaviors as defensive acts to prevent a threatened depression or to relieve a depression that had already occurred. He also saw the loss of appetite or the refusal to take food which may occur in depressions as acts designed to defend patients against their hostile wish to incorporate their love object by eating or incorporating it and so devouring and destroying it. As Abraham made clear, he was attempting to explain the wish contents of the depressives' unconscious fantasies and not the actual causes of melancholia in general.

In 1917 Freud was able to point to and suggest explanations for other depressive symptoms. He tried to understand the processes of self-accusation and self-vilification in delusional melancholics. He finally explained these as follows:

> If one listens patiently to the many and varied self-accusations of the melancholic, one cannot in the end avoid the impression that often the most violent of these are hardly at all applicable to the patient himself but that with insignificant modifications they do fit someone else, some person whom the patient loves, has loved or ought to love . . . so we get the key to the clinical picture.

In other words, instead of complaining, the patient is actually accusing—not himself or herself, but the person who was loved and who is now unconsciously identified with the self.

This act of identification with the lost object is accompanied by a regression to the earliest psychosexual phase of development, the oral phase. Infants' mode of relating to people is alleged to consist essentially of placing objects into the mouth and thus into themselves, as it were. This process—"oral incorporation" or "oral introjection"—allows infants to experience a sense of identity with the object world around them. Like Abraham, Freud saw the relation to the object in melancholia as colored by ambivalence, which he viewed as one of the preconditions of melancholia.

This operation is more simplistically described or conceptualized, by many unsophisticated therapists and ancillary hospital personnel, as turning the anger away from the disappointing or rejecting love object back to the self, but it is still understood by many today as the major and sometimes the only psychoanalytic paradigm for depression. Any experienced therapist will have heard from patients, or directly from colleagues, or from social workers or nurses that the patient needs to "get the anger out," to relieve depression. But psychoanalytic concepts of depression have ranged very far and wide from this brilliant but narrow clinical insight of 1917.

ABRAHAM

Abraham in 1924 corroborated and expanded Freud's observations. He very discerningly noted a relationship between obsessional neurosis and manic-depressive psychosis in two patients he had analyzed and in other patients he had treated more briefly. He reported the presence, in the manic-depressive's free periods, of ambivalence and other similarities to the typical obsessional patient, such as emphasis on cleanliness, obstinacy, and rigid attitudes about money and possessions.

Abraham theorized that, in the anal stage of psychosexual development, the patient "regards the person who is the object of his desire as something over which he exercises ownership, and that he consequently treats that person in the same way as he does his earliest piece of private property, i.e. the contents of his body, his fæces." Abraham noted the anal way in which the obsessional reacts to loss—with diarrhea or constipation, depending on certain unconscious dynamics. He believed that the depressive may regress even beyond the anal level to the oral phase, in his or her fantasies. And when recovery takes place, Abraham postulated, the patient progresses to the controlling, retentive, constipatory phase in which he or she functions fairly well—not unlike the obsessional neurotic.

Abraham believed that the melancholic has an inherited overaccentuation of oral eroticism, an increased ability or tendency to experience pleasure in the oral zone, but that this leads to excessive needs and consequently to excessive frustrations connected with the acts of sucking, drinking, eating, and kissing.

When the melancholic experiences early and repeated disappointments in love, before his oedipal wishes for his mother are resolved, Abraham postulated, a permanent linking of libidinal feelings with hostile destructive wishes overwhelms him. When he experiences disappointments in later life, "a 'frustration,' a disappointment from the side of the love object may at any time let loose a mighty wave of hatred which will sweep away his all too weakly-rooted feelings of love." Melancholia will then occur.

There have been criticisms (e.g., Blanco, 1941) of Abraham's preoccupation with unconscious libidinal and aggressive activities of the gastrointestinal tract, "as though [Abraham] had the idea that melancholia was a kind of mental indigestion." He seems to have thought of the depressive's love object chiefly as something to gratify the inordinate need for pleasurable satisfaction of the oral mucosa, that is, as something to provide continuous and unprotesting oral satisfaction and then to be held and controlled in an anal way—until the love object disappoints the patient. He then conceived of it as being angrily battered and assaulted until, at last, it is contemptuously excreted and cast aside.

In the meantime Freud, in *The Ego and the Id* (1923), had evolved his structural theory in which, by an anthropomorphic conceit, the superego became the repository of ego ideals, the representative of parental standards, and the embodiment of one's internalized objects, one's parents. It was in the context of this structural theory that Rado (1928) brought the concept of depression a little further along its evolutionary path.

As we have seen, Abraham focused on the melancholic's constitutional accentuation of oral eroticism, which made the patient vulnerable to frustrations, disappointments, and depression.

RADO

Rado, although using some of the same language, distanced himself somewhat from the gastrointestinal tract and focused instead on the psychological aspects of orality: the depressives' "intensely strong craving for narcissistic gratification" and their extreme "narcissistic intolerance." Rado saw depressives as overwhelmingly dependent for their self-esteem on the love, attention, approval, and recognition of others rather than on their own activity and achievements. He perceived depressives as unhealthily dependent on "external narcissistic supplies" and as having a correspondingly high intolerance for narcissistic deprivation—the trivial disappointments and offenses that the secure individual can shrug off.

A patient may react to disappointment with hostility and with bitterness but when this reaction fails to win back love, the patient becomes depressed. Rado understood melancholia to be "a great despairing cry for love" that takes place not in the real world but on the psychic plane. The patient has then moved from reality to psychosis.

In the years that followed, other writers confirmed the presence in melancholics of intense narcissistic cravings and of ambivalence, and they found evidence of unconscious oral and anal symbolism in their patients' dreams and fantasies. But questions were raised about the universality of some of these features.

GERO

When Gero outlined the analysis of two depressed patients in 1936, he brought understanding of the melancholic condition down from the heights of intriguing theorization to the relatively solid ground of therapeutic work. He was able to demonstrate clearly the narcissistic hunger, the intolerance of frustration, and the introjection of the love object. From analysis of one of these patients he felt able to disagree with his predecessors about the universality of the obsessional character structure in depression.

Of great significance was Gero's ability to demonstrate that the importance of "oral" experiences in infancy had less to do with the sensual gratification of the oral and gastrointestinal mucosa than with the broader and more comprehensive aspects of the mother–child relationship. "The essentially oral pleasure is only one factor in the experience satisfying the infant's need for warmth, touch, love and care." The emphasis was shifting away from the vicissitudes of psychosexual development to object-relationships.

MELANIE KLEIN

At this point mention should be made of Melanie Klein (1934, 1940) who, in England, making use of an unfamiliar dialect of the psychoanalytic tongue, had much to do with shifting the emphasis to object-relationships. Disregarding the many objectionable aspects of her *pun.* formulations and despite her tendency to discern phases of incredible savagery and hatred which she presumed to be taking place during early infancy, we must remember that it was Melanie Klein who first elaborated the theory that the predisposition to depression depended not so much on one trauma or even a series of traumatic incidents or disappointments, but rather on the quality of the mother–child relationship in the first year of life. If this relationship does not promote in the child the feeling that he or she is secure and good and beloved, the child is, according to Klein, never able to overcome a pronounced ambivalence toward love objects and is forever prone to depressive breakdowns.

The predisposition to depression, then, is not particularly characterized by specific traumatic events or overwhelming disappointments but is simply the result of the child's lack of success in overcoming early depressive fears and anxieties and the child's failure to establish an optimal level of self-esteem.

Thus, Melanie Klein's basic contribution to the theory of depression was the concept of a developmental phase during which the child has to learn how to modify ambivalence and retain self-esteem despite periodic losses of the "good mother."

The study of the determinants of self-esteem became the focus of the next two major contributors to the development of psychoanalytic concepts of depression, Bibring and Jacobson.

BIBRING

Of the two, Bibring (1953) appears easier to read but his views departed more radically from classical theory. Bibring agreed with Rado and others that the predisposition to depression results from traumatic experiences in early childhood, which bring about a fixation to a state of helplessness and powerlessness.

Previous writers had emphasized the oral fixation of the depressive, at the point where the needs "to get affection, to be loved, to be taken care of" are so prominent. Bibring acknowledged the great frequency of oral fixations in the predisposition to depression but he appealed to clinical experience to confirm his thesis that self-esteem may be diminished in ways other than by the frustration of the need for love and affection.

He had observed that self-esteem can be lowered by the frustration of other narcissistic aspirations, for example, of "the wish to be good, not to be resentful, hostile, defiant but to be loving, not to be dirty, but to be clean, etc.," which he associated with frustrations at the anal level and which would be colored by feelings of guilt and loss of control.

He also observed that self-esteem can be reduced by frustrations associated with the phallic phase such as "the wish to be strong, superior, great, secure, not to be weak and insecure." Frustrations associated with these wishes would be characterized by feelings of inadequacy and inferiority.

Bibring also deviated from the mainstream in conceiving of depression as an ego phenomenon. He did not agree with the view that depression was a product of intersystemic conflict—between the ego and the superego, for example. He thought of depression as stemming from tensions or conflicts within the ego. Here he followed Freud's view that the ego was the site of anxiety. He considered depression to be an affective state, a "state of the ego," like anxiety. Unlike Rado and others (e.g., Fenichel, 1945), he did not see depression as an attempt at reparation. Instead, he saw reparative attempts as reactions to the loss of self-esteem, reactions to the depression. He also disagreed with the view that all depressive reactions consisted of aggression redirected from the object to the self.

JACOBSON

Edith Jacobson (1953, 1954, 1964, 1971) saw self-esteem as central in depression also, and, like Bibring, considered self-esteem to be influenced by a number of variables. Jacobson sketched out a most elaborate and comprehensive model for the determinants of self-esteem and its relevance to depression. Her theoretical model is a tightly knit, complex construction based on careful exposition of the development of self- and object-representatives, the self, ego identifications, the ego ideal, and the superego.

There is not enough space in one chapter to trace the development of her model in any detail, but one can say that she made use of Hartman's (1950) careful distinction between the ego (an abstraction referring to one's psychic system, in contradistinction to the other personality substructures, the superego and the id) and the self (one's own person in contrast to other persons or things). She used Hartman's terms: "self-representations," "the endopsychic representation of one's bodily and mental self in the system ego," and, by analogy, the term "object-representations."

She visualized the self- and object-representations as cathected with libidinal and aggressive energy. When the self-representation is cathected with libidinal energy, self-esteem is said to be high; when it is cathected with aggressive energy it is more, or less, depressed, depending on the quantitative level of the aggressive cathexis.

Jacobson reviewed the developmental tasks of the establishment of self- and object-representations, the vicissitudes that led to their endowment with libidinal or aggressive psychic energy, and the factors that lead to their integration and unification and to the establishment of firm intrapsychic boundaries between them; in other words, she visualized the goals of development as including the firm establishment of one's own identity, the sharp differentiation of one's own self from others, the acquisition and maintenance of an optimal level of self-esteem, and the capacity to form satisfying object-relationships.

Among the determinants of self-esteem Jacobson considered the following. She pointed out that many developmental vicissitudes—illness, a distorted body image, domestic friction during childhood, for example—all may have an important impact on self-representation. Furthermore, the actual talents, abilities, intelligence, and other functions of the individual may obviously make it more or less easy to live up to his or her ego ideal and consequently to affect the desired level of self-esteem. The more realistic the ego ideal is, in the sense that it is within the reach of the individual's unique abilities, talents, and opportunities, the more likely it will affect the self-representation positively. The more the maturing individual becomes capable of distinguishing between the reasonable and the unreasonable, the better the control he or she will have over the ego ideal and self-representation. In other words, the more mature the self-critical ego functions, the more tempered and realistic will be the ideals and expectations. The more attainable one's ideal, the less vulnerable one's self-esteem.

Finally, since parental values and standards constitute the core of the self-critical superego functions, any discrepancy between them and one's behavior—and sometimes, one's thoughts and fantasies—may lead to guilt, which can be conceptualized as aggressive tension between the superego and the self-representation.

Thus, Jacobson agreed with Bibring that lowered self-esteem was central to depression but disputed his view of depression as an ego phenomenon and certainly disagreed with him about the role of aggression in depressive illness. Depression, by its very nature, according to Jacobson, consisted of an aggressive cathexis of the self-representation.

By "aggression," Jacobson did not of course mean aggressive behavior, acts of aggression, or even aggressive feelings, though these may be byproducts of the aggression she referred to, which was aggressive psychic energy, one of the two basic instinctual drives that Freud had postulated. Jacobson saw aggressive instinctual energy as an integral feature of any depression, in the same way that an aggressive cathexis of the self-representation is the metapsychological counterpart of the lowered self-esteem that is characteristic of depression.

THE CONCEPT OF PSYCHIC ENERGY

However, the concept of psychic energy had been exposed to an increasing drumbeat of criticism since at least the 1940s. The cadence mounted and became more emphatic throughout the 1960s and 1970s. Most analysts found it hard to accept Freud's Death Instinct, from which aggressive energy was said to derive. Many others thought of aggressive energy as secondary to stimuli rather than as a primary instinctual drive. Still others, however, became skeptical of the very concept of psychic energy. As far back as 1947, Kubie declared,

> When in doubt one can always say that some component of human psychology is bigger or smaller, stronger or weaker, more intense or less intense, more or less highly charged with "energy" or with degraded energy and by these words delude ourselves into believing that we have explained a phenomenon which we have merely described in metaphors.

In a report on a 1962 panel on psychic energy (Modell, 1963) Holt was quoted as asserting that "a basic objection to concepts such as psychic energy is that they are tautological and thus ultimately useless." In 1967 he dismissed psychic energy as "a concept [that] has steadily ramified into a conceptual thicket that baffles some, impresses many, and greatly complicates the task of anyone who tries to form a clear idea of what the basic theory of psychoanalysis is." Along the same vein Beres (1965) expressed his concern about the use of psychic energy, basically a metaphor, as an explanatory device. Bowlby (1969) even more emphatically argued that the psychic energy model can be discarded without affecting the concepts that are truly central to psychoanalysis. Waelder (1966), Grossman and Simon (1969), Rosenblatt and Thickstun (1970), Peterfreund (1971), Applegarth (1971, 1977), and others echoed the argument that psychic energy, a misleading metaphor, was being used as a tautological, inquiry-stopping explanation that should be discarded.

We return then to Jacobson's view of aggression as central to the understanding of depression. The picture of self-representation as cathected with aggressive energy does not represent an explanation of low self-esteem; it is only an alternative metaphorical way of saying that self-esteem is low. It is not explanatory, it is tautological. It expresses the same thing in different, pseudotechnical language. However, it is a mischievous formulation because it causes its readers to assume that they understand the cause of depression and thus produces premature closure.

SELF-ESTEEM

The causes of low self-esteem and depression have to do not with the vicissitudes of aggressive energy but, as Jacobson so clearly described, with a variety of other variables. These include early deprivation; the individual's appearance, talents, standards, and ideals; and his or her self-expectations. Jacobson went beyond her predecessors' focus to include the patient's object-world among the determinants of self-esteem. The patient's relationship to earliest as well as latest love objects was considered by Jacobson to be among the elements that help define his or her level of self-esteem.

Sandler and Joffe (1965) went a little further than identifying self-esteem, in their examination of the affective core of depression. From the concept of self-esteem they extracted what they labeled as "an ideal state of well-being," in the attainment of which they saw the role of the love object as that of a vehicle. According to them, when an object is lost, what is really lost is not only the object itself but the affective state of well-being for which the object was the vehicle. This produces psychic pain, which they conceived as occurring when a discrepancy exists between an actual state of a person and an ideal state of well-being. This psychic pain may mobilize the patient's typical defenses but if these fail, a feeling of helplessness results and the depressive reaction ensues.

The concept of the ego which Bibring conceptualized as the site of depression has also been strenuously criticized. Beres (1956, 1962) warned against the danger of personifying the ego and of referring to it and to the other psychic structures as if they had spatial location. He was critical of expressions that appeared to locate fantasies or affects "in" the ego or id which, he insisted, were merely theoretical constructs "which do not have existence in space." Holt (1967), Grossman and Simon (1969), and Schafer (1970) also persuasively criticized the anthropomorphism inherent in the personification of the ego.

Bibring's location of depression in the ego was his device to emphasize that not all depressions were characterized by guilt, that is, by intersystemic tensions. He bolstered his argument by citing Freud's reference to the ego as "the seat of anxiety." Bibring argued that since depression is also an affective state, the ego is therefore the "seat" of depression too, an obvious instance of reification of the ego. After all, it is the human being, the individual, who is depressed—not the ego. The ego is a theoretical abstract, not a site or a seat, as numerous authors have pointed out.

What Bibring actually accomplished was to direct attention to the clinical observation that low self-esteem and depression have other determinants than guilt. One does not need Bibring's metapsychological argument to substantiate his valuable clinical contribution.

CRITICAL EVALUATION OF THEORIES OF DEPRESSION

In this chapter I have reviewed the major voices in the gradually expanding chorus of evolving concepts of depression. I passed over others because of lack of space or because their melodies were eccentric, or repetitive, or out of key. Looking back on these contributors—the entire chorus—I am struck by the absence of the statistics that one ordinarily finds in scientific reports, and by their being replaced by clinical cases or clinical anecdotes or by no concrete clinical material at all.

A striking feature of the impressionistic pictures of depression painted by many writers is that they have the flavor of art rather than of science and may well represent profound personal intuitions as much as they depict the raw clinical data.

Abraham, for example, saw the depressed state as a complicated process of psychic digestion shot through with primitive desires, impulses, and fantasies. For Freud, melancholia was a loud, lamenting, self-tormenting period of mourning in which each and every hostile tie with the introjected love object was painfully loosened and abandoned. Melanie Klein and her disciples viewed depression as a mixture of sorrow over the loss of the love object and guilt over the hostility and rage that brought about this loss. Others, by way of contrast, thought of depression as essentially a state of starved, unhappy lovelessness not necessarily reactive to previous sadistic fantasies.

Rado pictured depression as a great, despairing cry for love and forgiveness, a drama of expiation acted out on the psychic plane following upon a loss of self-esteem.

Bibring and Jacobson both felt that there was a mechanism common to all cases of depression but differed from Rado in their conception of it. Bibring saw the fall in self-esteem as the essential element in depression and all else, including aggressiveness, as secondary phenomena. Jacobson, on the other hand, ascribed the central role in the pathology of depression to aggression and to the resulting fall in self-esteem.

The tendency of Sandler and Joffe to conceptualize the "depressive reaction" as a state of helplessness and resignation derived, of course, from Bibring's view of depression as an affective state characterized by a state of helplessness and powerlessness of the ego.

Some writers believe that the loss of love is fundamental to depression. Beres (1966) denied that either loss of love or helplessness was primary in depression but argued for the centrality of guilt. Bibring and Jacobson encompassed these partial conceptualizations in their much broader formulations.

From each personal vision of depression stem derivative explanations of one or another depressive symptom. The guilt of which the depressive complains, for example, was viewed by Abraham in conformity with his particular picture of this condition as related to the patient's cannibalistic impulses. Rado, with his conception of depression as a prolonged attempt to win back the love object, understood the patient to be guilty because of the aggressive attitude that led to the loss of the object.

SOME RECENT VIEWS

Having reviewed the major contributions to the theory of depression, I think it would be rewarding to glance at some recent (Stone, 1986) retrospective reflections of the analysis or analytic treatment of some 23 adults on the part of a senior, very experienced analyst who referred to himself correctly as conservative and even "old fashioned." He commented on both the formulations with which he agreed and those which he thought were off the mark in some measure.

After a respectful nod in the direction of "that currently vast and interesting sphere, the biology and pharmacology of depression," he very properly pointed out that his own interest lay in the dynamic understanding and treatment of depressive illness. He carefully distinguished depressive illness from those depressive affects that occur in a wide variety of pathological settings but insisted that, contrary to some other authors, depressive illness is the proper focus of theories about depression. He believed that "mourning and melancholia" remain the basic paradigm for understanding depressive illness "even though much has been added since that time." He understood "narcissistic object choice" as having more to do with the original failure of fundamental separation of self- and object-representations than Freud was able to see with the more primitive metapsychology available to him. He believed that oral symbolism and fantasies may be found in most depressions but he was inclined to agree with Gero's broader interpretation of orality and the narcissistic vulnerability to which it exposes the patient.

He disagreed with the universality of Rado's depressive manipulativeness as the intrinsic meaning of depression and with Bibring's view of helplessness as the essential factor in depression. He also disagreed with Bibring's view of the intrasystemic nature of depression and with his conception of aggression as secondary in depressive illness, but went along with him in acknowledging that the frustrations of aspirations other than oral ones can be found in depression. He could not agree with Beres's (1966) view that guilt is a pathognomonic element in depression or that it is more important than other elements.

He regarded Jacobson's "complicated metapsychology" as neither complete nor as "displacing all others" but he found it a useful formulation for the understanding of a significant number of cases.

It is interesting, in view of the many debates about aggression in depressive illness, that Stone did not "regard aggression as the manifestation of an inborn destructive drive, but rather as a forceful, painful, or destructive mode of coercing an object to the subjects' will." Stone believed that it is this aggression, deriving "from the hostile urge towards the bad parent" which, inhibited, "lends the especially tormenting quality and the extended duration to the latent efforts toward decathexis of the object."

This is a brief, unsatisfying synopsis of a profoundly interesting paper. After reviewing the various elements that are found in depressive illness, Stone very properly warned that "these elements should [not] be read into our patients but that one should be aware of their probable presence and fundamental dynamic importance."

The psychoanalytic understanding of depression is made up of certain recurring themes that weave in and out of the theoretical tapestry. These themes are the basic human themes of love, loss, hate, vulnerability, and happiness. They are elemental aspects of human life. Expressed clinically they take on designations, simultaneously both aseptic and value-laden, such as dependency, aggression, and narcissism. They lead to joy and despair, to elation and depression. In this chapter I have, of course, been primarily unconcerned with those enduring or long-lasting states of depression that we call depressive illness of one kind or another.

NEUROPHYSIOLOGIC ASPECTS

It is clear, however, that depressive illness involves much more than depressive affects, however defined or understood. The most discerning of the psychoanalytic pioneers of depression left themselves escape clauses when they wrote about depression. Freud referred to various clinical forms of melancholia, "some of them suggesting somatic rather than psychogenic affections." He wondered "whether an impoverishment of ego-libido directly due to toxins would not result in certain forms of disease." Abraham postulated a constitutional and inherited overaccentuation of oral eroticism in depression. And Jacobson agreed with Freud that psychotic depressions have psychotic components that cannot be explained on a psychological basis alone.

In the 1950s the serendipitous discovery of antidepressive medications attracted attention to the neurophysiological substructure of depression, and subsequent genetic and pharmacological contributions to the literature generated interesting hypotheses. Jacobson considered it discreet to refer to psychosomatic determinants of depression. But, generally speaking, the psychoanalytic literature focused on what went on in the consulting room and gave the extensive empirical literature hardly a glance. An example of this was shown at a psychoanalytic meeting in Jerusalem (Prego-Silva, reporter, 1978). Pollock, one of the discussants, made a reference to one of his patients who was simultaneously being treated with lithium carbonate. As far as I can gather from the report on this conference, no one took him up on what appeared to be a gross sullying of the pure stream of the analytic process.

However, there have been a few heretics. Basch (1975) flatly declared that "the depressive syndrome is a mental illness, but not necessarily a psychological illness." Wolpert, in the same year (1975), referring back to Freud's old concept of anxiety, expressed his belief that bipolar illness is an "actual neurosis," the symptoms of which have no psychological meaning.

But it was in 1985 that Arnold Cooper, a past president of the American Psychoanalytic Association, announced that investigation has shown that some symptoms or conditions, especially chronic anxiety, panic, and depressive and manic illness, have biological thresholds so low "that it is no longer useful to view the psychological event as etiologically significant." As Cooper put it, "The trigger for anxiety is a biological event as in 'actual neurosis,' but now the trigger is separation, not dammed up libido." These patients, he believed, are actually "physiologically maladapted for maintenance of homeostasis in average expectable environments."

Cooper went on to give a clinical vignette of a depressed patient whom he analyzed with only moderate success. He had to see her again two years later and at that time he arranged for her to be given a trial of imipramine to which she responded well. She was able to go on to much more effective analysis which was not this time interfered with by "anxiety and mood dysregulation."

Cooper made two important points. One was that, contrary to expectations, symptom removal may facilitate analysis, enhance self-esteem, and open up new possibilities of growth, insight, and new experiences. The second was that "there are patients with depressive, anxious and dysphoric states . . . who should not be held accountable for their difficulty in accepting separation from dependency objects, or at least they should not be held fully accountable."

He stated candidly that "as psychoanalysts we should welcome any scientific knowledge that removes from our primary care illnesses which we cannot successfully treat by the methods of our profession because the etiology lies elsewhere or that facilitates our analytic treatment by assisting us with intractable symptoms . . . . Psychoanalysis is a powerful instrument for research and treatment, but not if it is applied to the wrong patient population."

SUMMARY

I have reviewed the evolution of psychoanalytic concepts of depression from the first observations on orality and aggression through the broadening of the concept of orality and the widening of the spectrum of the determinants of self-esteem which came to be viewed more and more as central to depression. I touched upon the metapsychological battles that made many of the psychoanalytic positions look as dated as the debates of the Medieval Schoolmen, but I indicated how the clinical observations outlasted the metapsychological explanations.

Finally, I concluded at the point where psychoanalysts were just beginning to grasp that their psychoanalytic tools were inadequate for the treatment of depressive illness, but were not inadequate for many of the patients who were ill with depression after the biological aspects of their anxiety, panic, and dysphoria were relieved pharmacologically.

REFERENCES

Abraham, K. (1911). Notes on the psychoanalytic investigation and treatment of manic-depressive insanity and allied conditions. In *Selected papers on psycho-analysis* (pp. 137–156). London: Hogarth Press, 1927.

Abraham, K. (1916). The first pregenital stage of the libido. In *Selected papers on psycho-analysis* (pp. 248–279). London: Hogarth Press, 1927.

Abraham, K. (1924). A short study of the development of the libido, viewed in the light of mental disorders. In *Selected papers on psycho-analysis*. London: Hogarth Press, 1927.

Applegarth, A. (1971). Comments on aspects of the theory of psychic energy. *Journal of the American Psychoanalytic Association, 19,* 379–416.

Applegarth, A. (1977). Psychic energy reconsidered—discussion. *Journal of the American Psychoanalytic Association, 25,* 599–633.

Basch, M. F. (1975). Toward a theory that encompasses depression: A revision of existing causal hypotheses in psychoanalysis. In E. J. Anthony & T. Benedek (Eds.), *Depression and human emotions* (pp. 485–534). Boston: Little, Brown.

Beres, D. (1956). Ego deviation and the concept of schizophrenia. *Psychoanalytic Study of the Child, 11,* pp. 164–235.

Beres, D. (1962). The unconscious fantasy. *Psychoanalytic Quarterly, 31,* 309–328.

Beres, D. (1965). Structure and function in psycho-analysis. *International Journal of Psycho-analysis, 46,* 53–63.

Beres, D. (1966). Superego and depression. N. R. M. Loewenstein, L. M. Newman, M. Schur, & A. J. Solnit (Eds.), *Psychoanalysis—A General Psychology.* (pp. 479–498). New York: International Universities Press.

Bibring, E. (1953). The mechanism of depression. In P. Greenacre (Ed.), *Affective disorders* (pp. 14–47). New York: International Universities Press.

Blanco, I. M. (1941). On introjection and the process of psychic metabolism. *International Journal of Psycho-analysis, 22,* 17–36.

Bowlby, J. (1969). *Attachment and loss. I. Attachment.* New York: Basic Books.

Cooper, A. M. (1985). Will neurobiology influence psychoanalysis? *American Journal of Psychiatry, 142,* 1395–1402.

Fenichel, O. (1945). *The psychoanalytic theory of neurosis.* New York: International Universities Press.

Freud, S. (1905/1953). Three essays on the theory of sexuality. In J. Strachey (Ed. and Trans.) *The standard edition of the complete psychological works of Sigmund Freud* (Vol 7, pp. 130–243). London: Hogarth Press.

Freud, S. (1917/1957). Mourning and melancholia. *Standard edition* (Vol. 14, pp. 243–258). London: Hogarth Press.

Freud, S. (1923/1961). The ego and the id. *Standard edition* (Vol. 19, pp. 12–66). London: Hogarth Press.

Gero, G. (1936). The construction of depression. *International Journal of Psycho-analysis, 17,* 423–461.

Grossman, W. M., & Simon, B. (1969). Anthropomorphism: Motive, meaning and causality in psychoanalytic theory. *Psychoanalytic Study of the Child, 24,* 79–111.

Hartman, H. (1950). Comments on the psychoanalytic theory of the ego. *Psychoanalytic Study of the Child, 5,* 74–96.

Holt, R. R. (1967). Beyond vitalism and mechanism: Freud's concept of psychic energy. In J. H. Masserman (Ed.), *Science and Psychoanalysis* (pp. 1–41). New York: Grune & Stratton.

Jacobson, E. (1953). Contribution to the metapsychology of cyclothymic depression. In P. Greenacre (Ed.), *Affective disorders* (pp. 49–83). New York: International Universities Press.

Jacobson, E. (1954). The self and the object world: Vicissitudes of their infantile cathexes and their influence on ideational and affective development. *Psychoanalytic Study of the Child, 9,* 75–127.

Jacobson, E. (1964). *The self and the object world.* New York: International Universities Press.

Jacobson, E. (1971). *Depression.* New York: International Universities Press.

Klein, M. (1934/1948). A contribution to the psychogenesis of manic-depressive states. In *Contributions to psycho-analysis, 1921–1945* (pp. 282–310). London: Hogarth Press.

Klein, M. (1940/1948). Mourning and its relation to manic-depressive states. In *Contributions to psycho-analysis, 1921–1945* (pp. 311–338). London: Hogarth Press.

Kubie, L. S. (1947). The fallacious use of quantitative concepts in dynamic psychology. *Psychoanalytic Quarterly, 16,* 507–518.

Modell, A. H. (1963). Report, panel discussion on the concept of psychic energy. *Journal of the American Psychoanalytic Association, 11,* 605–618.

Peterfreund, E. (1971). *Information, systems and psychoanalysis. Psychological issues* (Nos. 25, 26). New York: International Universities Press.

Prego-Silva, L. E. (reporter). (1978). Dialogue on depression and other painful affects. *International Journal of Psycho-analysis, 59,* 517–532.

Rado, S. (1928). The problem of melancholia. *International Journal of Psycho-analysis, 9,* 420–438.

Rosenblatt, A. D., & Thickstun, J. T. (1970). A study of the concept of psychic energy. *International Journal of Psycho-analysis, 51,* 265–278.

Sandler, J., & Joffe, W. G. (1965). Notes on childhood depression. *International Journal of Psycho-analysis, 46,* 88–96.

Schafer, R. (1970). An overview of Heinz Hartmann's contributions to psychoanalysis. *International Journal of Psycho-analysis, 51,* 425–446.

Stone, L. (1986). Psychoanalytic observations on the pathology of depressive illness: Selected spheres of ambiguity and disagreement. *Journal of the American Psychoanalytic Association, 34,* 329–362.

Waelder, R. (1966). Adaptational view ignores "drive." *International Journal of Psychiatry, 2,* 569–575.

Wolpert, E. A. (1975). Manic-depressive illness as an active neurosis. In E. J. Anthony & T. Benedek (Eds.), *Depression and human existence* (pp. 199–221). Boston: Little, Brown.

CHAPTER 3

Existential Approaches to Depression

HERBERT H. KRAUSS, PhD and BEATRICE JOY KRAUSS, PhD

If you wish to understand a philosopher, do not ask what he says, but find out what he wants.
NIETZSCHE

Named in the aftermath of the First World War, modern existentialism became influential after the Second. In its responses to questions about the significance of human life and our responsibility to ourselves, each other, and nature, it has informed our understanding of psychopathology in general and depression in particular.

This chapter on existential approaches to depression develops along the following line. First an introduction to existential thought is presented, emphasizing thematic material. Next, a section on depression briefly overviews issues of diagnosis and etiology. Finally, contributions made by the existential orientation to the primary, secondary, and tertiary prevention of depressions are described. Throughout the chapter, content not directly related to existentialism or its approach to depression, yet deemed relevant to its argument, is touched upon.

In 1929 Fritz Heinemann's book *Geist/Leben/Existenz: Eine Einfuhrung in die Philosophie der Gegenwart* (*New Paths in Philosophy: Spirit/Life/Existence: An Introduction in Contemporary Philosophy*) (Kaufmann, 1972) gave the word *existentialism* its current sense and piqued academic and public interest in the work of those philosophers he labeled "existential." However, it was not until the publication of Sartre's essay "*L'être et le Ne'ant: Essai d'Ontologie Phenomenologique*" ("Being and Nothingness") in 1943 that existentialism became *le dernier cri* (Kaufmann, 1972). Overnight, existentialism became a topic of daily conversation and disputation in Paris (Reinhardt, 1960).

Undoubtedly the dynamics contributing to existentialism's ascension at that time were complex. This much is quite clear: the world was in crisis. France, along with most of Europe and large parts of Asia, was under the boot. The state, the capital city, the church, the university, and the family—the fundamental instrumentalities of western civilization—were either subverted by or in collaboration with

Fascist savagery. A regrounding, especially a new moral foundation, was necessary. Camus, Sartre, and others set out to provide just that foundation.

Even though existentialism flourished in the twentieth century, its aggregate of intuitions, notions, and affirmations traced roots to pre-Socratic (e.g., Heraclitus) and Aristotelian thought. After lying dormant for centuries, existential concepts burst into consciousness as a result of Kierkegaard's soul-wrenching struggles in the early nineteenth century. They grew in strength, largely through the efforts of Nietzsche, as that century progressed; they attained maturity in the twentieth century with the writings of Heidegger and Sartre (Kaufmann, 1972; Reinhardt, 1960).

BASIC TENETS

The belief that "Philosophy should begin neither with axioms nor with sense impressions, but with experiences which involve the whole individual" (Kaufmann, 1972, p. 76) is common to those considered existentialists. All existentialists accept the phenomenological method as basic and valid (Misiak & Sexton, 1973). When applied to human consciousness, this method has as its goal the simple, unprejudiced observation and description of the phenomenon experienced. Husserl, considered the founder of modern phenomenology, was Heidegger's teacher and Husserl's studies informed the work of Sartre and Merleau-Ponty. Husserl envisioned phenomenology as the methodology through which a clear comprehension of the essential (universal, absolute, unchanging) nature of reality could be discovered.

> For Husserl, reality is comprised of a rich variety of forms of being, including the essences of mathematical being, logical being, animal being, and so on, alongside with natural being.
>
> *(Jennings, 1986, p. 1234)*

Of these forms of being, human consciousness, Husserl argued, had "ontological priority."

> On the one hand, human beings are part of nature by virtue of their physical bodies. On the other hand, the world "exists" owing to human consciousness, which can behold and study that world.
>
> *(Jennings, 1986, p. 1234)*

His investigations convinced him that the quintessential property of consciousness is intentionality. The development of existential thought, from Husserl through Sartre, then followed the active tradition of Leibnitz and rejected the reactivity of Locke.

> The Lockean tradition, in brief, holds that man's mind by nature is *tabula rasa* (environmentalist learning); mind does what it is made to do (a leaning toward reactivity and behavioristics); its components are basically discrete (simple ideas), and its organization therefore a matter of cementing bonds (associationism). While not all of these doctrines are fully developed by Locke himself, his particular brand of empiricism paved the way directly for Hume, Hamilton, Mill, and later for objectivism. Darwin gave the tradition a functional turn, and borrowing from Freud gave it depth. . . . To Leibnitz, as to Kant, the intellect was perpetually self-active (not merely reactive). When Locke said *nihil est in intellectu quod non fuerit in sensu,* Leibnitz gave his famous retort . . . *excipe: nisi ipse intellectus.* To him, the inner and spontaneous workings of the mind were at least as important as its contents or productions. His concept of the self-active monad easily became the "person" who with his entelechtive strivings pursued a unique destiny.
>
> *(Allport, 1957, p. 7)*

For Husserl,

> The crucial point is that when consciousness is "seen" as it immediately presents itself, we find a bodily felt aura of implicitly meaningful felt experiencing—not explicit words, concepts, or experiences. . . . Within a given moment, this inwardly sensed experiential datum might encompass, say, a sense of inferiority, a history of paternal domination, a revengeful fantasy, a wish for autonomy, and many other meanings. However, it is the bodily sensed experiential aura that is *immediately* experienced in awareness rather than any one of these potentially conceptualized experiences. . . . [It] is the quality of implicitly meaningful "felt experiencing" that is essential: This characteristic of consciousness, like intentionality, is an essence that is eternally the same for persons in all cultures and historical ages.
>
> *(Jennings, 1986, p. 1239)*

Consequences follow from the decision to adopt the phenomenological method and the acceptance of the individual as an active, intentional being. Unlike a tree, which exists in itself (*en-soi*), Sartre asserted, man exists for himself (*pour-soi*). Central to existence *pour-soi* is decision, including the possibility of denying the potential of a human being by transforming it into an existence *en-soi*.

> The thinker who can in all his thinking forget also to think that he is an existing individual will never explain life. He merely will attempt to

cease to be a human being in order to become a book or an objective
something which is possible only for "a Munchhausen."

(Kierkegaard, 1941, p. 317)

"Man is nothing else but what he makes of himself. That is the first
principle of existentialism" (Sartre, 1945, p. 29). It is through choice
that individuals realize their unique existence: *Eligo, ergo sum*; I
choose, therefore I am. Marcel described man as a *homo viator*—never
at a goal, always on the way (Reinhardt, 1960). Magee (1982) chose a
quotation from Matthew Arnold to reflect the same perspective: "We
are between two worlds, one dead, the other powerless to be."

Choice inheres in *pour-soi*. However, what may be chosen at any
moment is constrained by an individual's situation. By no means does
existentialism intend to deny the laws of genetics or suggest we can do
absolutely that of which we dream except in dreams.

When Sartre argued that man's essence is his existence, Buytendijk
(1957, pp. 208–209) elaborated:

> Existential psychology emphasizes the analysis of the meaning of situa-
> tions in which the individual constantly finds himself involved. Situations
> of this sort are formed not only by natural and social relationships, but
> also the body and its biological constitution. . . . We may be guided by
> Merleau-Ponty's observations: *"Le corps n'est pas une chose, il est une
> situation"* (The body is not a fact, it is a situation), but we will have to add
> that the body itself is a fact, a structure of facts. . . . The study of facts is
> "natural science"; the study of the meaning of facts in the context of
> human existence is psychology.

Not only must the physical and social world be considered, but the
individual's past carries a substantial, though not decisive weight, in
regard to the possibilities of the future and decisions of the present.
Even the contributions of behavioral psychology must be considered.

> The existentialist emphasis in psychology does not, therefore, deny the
> validity of conditioning, the formulation of drives, the study of discrete
> mechanisms, and so on. It only holds that we can never explain or under-
> stand any *living* human being on that basis.

(May, 1969, p. 14)

The manner in which the simultaneous interactions of the individual's biological, social, and self-worlds will be represented eventually
is not yet clear.

Three promising alternative constructions of the representation
of the outer world in the mind have been posited. The first, Popper's
(Popper & Eccles, 1977), conceived mind to be an emergent of brain

function interacting with language and culture (both material and not), fed back through the senses to influence brain function. Eccles (Popper & Eccles, 1977) differed from Popper in that he conceptualized mind as operating directly on "liaison" formations within the cerebral cortex itself. In either case, each individual is unique. Individuals experience an emerging existence conditioned by their nervous system, the world around them (including others and the material and nonmaterial aspects of culture), and an active self.

Pribram (1986) took a different track. He argued that the basic components of the universe are neither material nor mental but separate "realizations" of informational "structure."

> The enduring "neutral" component of the universe is informational structure, the negentropic organization of energy. In a sense, this structure can be characterized as linguistic—or mathematical, musical, cultural, and so on. Dual aspects become dual realizations—which in fact may be multiple—of the fundamental informational structure. . . .
>
> Mind and brain stand for two such classes of realizations each achieved . . . by proceeding in a different direction in the hierarchy of conceptual and realized systems. Both mental phenomena and material objects are realizations and therefore realities. . . .
>
> *(p. 512)*

Information is encoded in the neuromicrostructure of the brain. Sensory transduction of energy from either the internal or external environment results in patterns of neuronal activation in the spectral domain. Pribram pointed out that such processing, if done with lens systems, is called *optical information processing*; if performed with computers, *image processing*; or if storage on photographic film is employed, *holography*.

> This mechanism has direct relevance for the mind/brain problem. Note that storage takes place in the spectral domain. Images and other contents as such are not stored, nor are they "localized" in the brain. Rather, by virtue of the operation of the local brain circuitry, usually with the aid of sensory input from the environment, images and mental events emerge and are constructed. The images *are* Gilbert Ryle's ghosts resulting from the operations of the "machine" (brain). But, when implemented (i.e. realized, materialized) through action (i.e. in the organism's environment), these ghosts *can* causally influence, through the senses, the subsequent operations of the brain.
>
> . . . A similar mechanism involving the motor mechanisms of the brain can account for intentional, planned behavior.
>
> *(p. 514)*

Whether the paradigms posited by Popper, Eccles, Pribram, or yet another, will prove convincing is unclear. However, their discussions of the relationship of matter, mind, and mentation do flesh-out phenomenological–existential notions of active processing and choice.

Although they insist individuals must choose in order to create their being, existentialists differ considerably on how that choice should be made. In fact, it is fair to say that existentialists have more concrete things to say about the grounds on which decisions should *not* be made.

Whatever the rationale, no existentialist is likely to suggest conventional wisdom as a basis for meaningful choice. Each major contributor to existentialism has stood against his times. Kierkegaard rebelled against the desiccated doctrine of "good old uncle" religion, Nietzsche against decadence, and Jaspers against cultural disarray.

Using theology to ground decision also fails for most but by no means all of those considered existentialists.

Nietzsche, Sartre, Heidegger, and Buber all speak of the "death of God," but to each it means something essentially different—to Nietzsche, the loss of a base for values that makes way for the will to power which creates new values and leads to the Superman; to Sartre, the necessity of inventing one's own values and choosing oneself as an image of man for all men; to Heidegger, a void that cannot be filled by any superman but the occasion, nonetheless, for a new succession of divine images arising out of man's clarifying thought about Being; to Buber, the "eclipse of God" which comes when God answers man's turning away by seeming to be absent Himself.

An essential difference between the so called religious existentialists, which makes them quite as varied as the nonreligious, is that some of them understand the "answers" in as thoroughly existentialist terms as the questions, while others follow an existentialist analysis of the human condition or the situation of modern man with an appeal to traditional theology as the only valid response to that situation. Although one cannot draw any clear lines here, we may distinguish between *religious existentialists,* such as Martin Buber, Franz Rosenzweig, and Gabriel Marcel, and *existentialistic theologians,* such as Soren Kierkegaard, Paul Tillich, and Jacques Maritain.

(Friedman, 1967, pp. 262–263)

Perhaps the most that can be said is that to all existentialists,

. . . human life is an adventure. For some existentialists this has implied the venture to live in constant awareness of the mystery of human existence; for others it has been the call to create meaning in an otherwise meaningless world. In both cases existentialists have asked for a life in which man continuously questions his purpose and accepts responsibility for his actions, one which truly reflects man's special position in this world. To such a life, existentialists refer when they speak of authentic existence, even though they differ widely in their interpretation of it.

(Breisach, 1962, pp. 4–5)

According to the existentialists, this then is the human condition. Each of us enters a world not made by us. We are not the master of our biology, or of our cultural heritage, or of our concrete circumstance at that time. If there is rhyme or reason, or black humor involved in our particular circumstance, it surely is not patent. Instead, when we perceive clearly our situation we experience a sense of *Geworfenheit* (throwness, like a cast of dice) (Magee, 1982). Yet, unplanned as it and our entry into it may be, "[t]he reality of the world cannot be evaded. Experience of the harshness of the real is the only way by which a man can come to his own self" (Jaspers, 1959, p. 178).

Even before we are out of the womb we are in a relationship with the woman who carries us and the world in which she lives, "In the beginning is the relationship" (Buber, 1970, p. 69). What will characterize it? Will we enter into a dialogue in which mutuality is the goal, or will the prototype for monologues disguised as dialogues be impressed upon experience? Chances are we will be seen as more object than self, both in the womb and "out" in the world.

Very early in life we perceive a lack of "everness"; it is a frightening fact (Patterson & Moran, 1988; Yalom, 1980). Later, as we grow older and cognitively more complex, we self-consciously apprehend that we are terminal (Yalom, 1980). An old German proverb reminds us, "As soon as we are born, we are old enough to die." This understanding mobilizes us, more so than any other break in the fabric of everyday life for which we are unprepared, for it is irremedial; it is the nonpareil experience of boundary. Death is the one possibility that cancels all others.

The temper of existentialism is passion. Far from shrinking from emotion, the existentialist affirms that dread, *angst, sorge* (care), fear and trembling, guilt, and anxiety are intrinsic to the situation of the individual. This ardor galvanizes the individual to action. To affirm life requires "tragic heroism" (Frankl, 1985).

Yalom (1980) schematized the failure of nerve (inauthenticity) that opposed this passion: Awareness of ultimate concern leads to anxiety which in turn leads to defense. Inauthenticity has many forms and a heavy price. Common to all forms of "bad faith" is the strangulation of being. This may manifest itself as a symptom, the distortion of time (Krauss, 1967), for example; or as the intuition of alienation attendant upon living a "second hand life" (Breisach, 1962), or in psychopathology.

DEPRESSION

As Mendelson (1974, pp. 30–31) indicated, "scientific" thinking about "depression" has nearly come full circle.

It began in the last quarter of the nineteenth century with some preliminary mutterings about heredity and morbid traits and with a search for the pathological lesions of the numerous entities of the pre-Kraepelinian era. It went on to describe the synthesis that Kraepelin accomplished so brilliantly and that brief moment in time when the psychiatric stage was swept bare of its many players to leave only those two grand protagonists, manic-depressive psychosis and dementia praecox.

The moment could not last . . . was or was not involutional melancholia included within its [manic-depression] scope? Were not neurotic depressions different from manic-depressive psychosis?

. . . Using techniques involving life histories, family studies, genetics, and considerations of age and sex, they [investigators] began to carve up the body of depressive illnesses into different shaped components. . . .

Are subgroups we now read about real or artifacts? . . . [I]t is too early to tell. But the Kraepelinian simplicity is gone. The psychiatric stage now converted into a research laboratory is once again populated by numerous players. Yet there is still a Kraepelinian flavor to it. His confident assumption of pathological lesions has been replaced by a sophisticated search for biochemical lesions. Since the Klinik has been replaced by the laboratory, we hear discussions about neurophysiology, biochemistry and endocrinology, about catecholamines and indoleamines.

Diagnostic Issues

Ample evidence has accumulated that the term *depression* denotes a variety of affective states differing among themselves biologically and phenomenologically (Mendelson, 1974). Depression, according to Kaplan and Sadock (1981, p. 358), refers to a "normal human emotion, to a clinical symptom, and to a group of syndromes or disorders." These differ among themselves both biologically and phenomenologically; the boundary dividing the normal from the pathological is sometimes as far from clear now as it was to William James. In his 1896 Lowell Lectures (James, 1984, p. 15), he said:

We make a common distinction between healthy and morbid but the fact is that we cannot make it sharp. No one symptom by itself is a morbid one—it depends rather on the part it plays. We speak of melancholy and moral tendencies, but he would be a bold man who should say that melancholy was not a part of every character. Saint Paul, Lombroso,

Kant, each is in some way an example of how melancholy in a life gives a truer sense of values.

Because it has been used so frequently to describe even minor dysphoria, some question the distinctiveness of depression as a psychopathological concept (Loehlin, Willerman, & Horn, 1988). Matters are not helped by the mounting evidence that no cross-culturally acceptable conception of depression exists (Marsella, 1980), and that depression's symptomatology varies somewhat as a function of ethnicity. Binitie (1975), for example, found that both African and European patients diagnosed as having a major depression lost interest in work and in their social environment. The Africans reported a greater number of bodily complaints than the Europeans, who experienced guilt and suicidal ideation more often than the Africans. Marsella (1980), in addition to suggesting depression is more common in western societies, found that those diagnosed as depressed in nonwestern societies were less likely to express guilt and self-abasement. Though the differential diagnosis of depression is acknowledged to be difficult, an argument may be made for its utility. Even if those so categorized are etiologically heterogeneous, the very process of classification, if done reliably and with a modicum of validity will insure at least surface similarity among those so denominated. Among the symptoms that are consistently observed in "depression" (American Psychiatric Association, 1987) are the following:

1. Diminished interest or pleasure in all or almost all activities
2. Fatigue or loss of energy
3. Feelings of worthlessness or "inappropriate" guilt
4. Diminished ability to think or concentrate, or indecisiveness
5. Feelings of hopelessness.

In part because of the variety of operations used to define it and in part because of its protean nature, estimates of the prevalence of depression vary widely. Kaplan and Sadock (1981) indicated that between 15 and 30 percent of adults in the United States experience clinically significant depressions. Of these only 25 percent will seek professional help. Recently Regier et al. (1988), using data from the NIMH Epidemiological Catchment Area Program Study, reported a lifetime prevalence for Major Depressive Disorder to be 5 to 8 percent, that for Bipolar Disorder to be 0.8 percent, and dysthymia to be 3.3 percent. Of patients with a severe primary depressive disorder of at least one month's duration, they found almost 15 percent end their lives. For the United States, they estimated the total, yearly social cost (e.g., in health care cost, sick days, wages lost, lost productivity) of major depressions to be over $16 billion.

Etiology

Many putative causes have been offered to explain the etiology of the various forms of depression. These include the genetic anomalies that have been linked to Bipolar Disorder: those found by Egeland et al. (1987) on the short arm of chromosome 11 in the Old Order Amish, and those associated with color blindness on the X-chromosome found in four Israeli families of non-European heritage (Baron et al., 1987). The possibility that antidepressant medication in some instances may contribute to inducing an unusual form of the Bipolar Disorder—rapidly cycling, alternating mania and depression—was demonstrated by Wehr, Sack, Rosenthal, and Cowdry (1988). Sundry biogenic amine hypotheses (Rosenbaum, Maruta, & Shatzberg, 1983; Schildkraut, 1977; Van Praag, 1977) have also been proposed. So too have numerous psychosocial and psychoanalytical models of variable comprehensiveness. Many of these focus upon the role that experience of helplessness plays in these disorders.

Depression's symptom configuration has been found in conjunction with a number of empirically researched circumstances. Davids (1955) and Seeman (1959) argued it is characteristic of "anomia" or alienation. Individuals experience anomia when social disruption or disorganization makes it difficult for them to view themselves as valued by society and empowered to achieve socially meaningful goals through their own actions in common effort with others. A similar theme can be perceived in Naroll's (1983) description of the consequences of weak "moral nets" in a society.

Seligman (Garber & Seligman, 1980; Seligman, 1975), in summarizing the results of an extensive laboratory research program, posited that the less the individual feels in control of his or her environment and the potential for reward and punishment it offers, the more likely he or she will be to develop a sequence of cognitive, self-esteem, emotional, and motivational deficits that constitute or at least ape the depressive syndromes. He posited that individuals first develop an inability to determine the extent to which they are capable of coping effectively with their environment; then, after becoming convinced that there is no hope for them, they become passive in the face of adversity. Eventually an affective defect—depression—ensues.

Beck (1967a, 1967b, 1976) found in depression specific idiosyncratic cognitive schemes: (a) the individual is inadequate to the challenges faced, (b) the external world is impossibly hard and unforgiving, and (c) the future holds no hope. In a similar vein, Bandura (1986) contended:

> [i]nability to influence events and social conditions that significantly affect one's life can give rise to feelings of futility and despondency, as well as anxiety. Self-efficacy theory distinguishes between two judgmental

sources of futility. People can give up trying because they seriously doubt they can do what is required. Or they may be assured of their capabilities but give up trying because they expect their efforts will not produce any results due to an unresponsive, negatively biased, or punitive social environment.

(pp. 445–446)

A sense of causal agency, Bandura believed, arises through the successes an individual achieves in producing effects through intentional action. With considerable acumen, he also suggested that the interactional characteristics of a "depressed" person are often off-putting. This leads others to avoid the person, further reducing the ability to achieve desired results.

Unlike the laboratory-based theories of depression just reviewed, the psychoanalytic depiction of depression derives its force and its "data" from clinical interactions between therapist and client.

The psychoanalytic understanding of depression is made up of certain recurring themes which weave in and out of the theoretical tapestry. These themes are the basic human themes of love and loss and hate and vulnerability and happiness. These themes are elemental aspects of human life. Expressed clinically they take on designations, simultaneously both aseptic and value-laden, such as dependency and aggression and narcissism. They lead to joy and despair, to elation and depression.

(Mendelson, 1974, p. 295)

There are many psychoanalytic descriptions of the etiology of depression. Each differs somewhat in slant and nuance. Freud himself did not articulate one definitive conceptualization of depression's origin. His most influential statements on depression derive largely from "Mourning and Melancholia" (Freud, 1917/1956) and "On Narcissism" (Freud, 1914/1962).

In "Mourning and Melancholia," Freud argued that in an important sense pathological melancholia is similar to "normal" mourning. In both conditions, something is lost. The two differ in that in mourning the loss of a loved one or a cherished ideal (as liberty), the grieving individual experiences the world as poor and empty; in melancholia the ego itself is felt to be barren.

The mourner, to use Freudian argot, has lost an object cathexis; the melancholic has experienced a narcissistic wound.

Because of various circumstances—for example, a genetic predisposition or a rejecting mother—instead of a balanced parallel development of both object and narcissistic cathexes, the ego in some instances adopts predominantly the narcissistic mode of relating to reality in general and to others in particular. These narcissistic attachments are tenuous; they are made on the basis of a "thing's" resemblance to the narcissist or the attachments' ability to satisfy the narcissist. They are disrupted when they prove unsatisfying. Obviously, as a general rule, narcissists cannot control the behavior of their apparent likenesses in the external world. They are, therefore, threatened continually with frustration, which necessarily leads to ambivalence. They love the likenesses but fear rejection, the frustration of their aims, and the subsequent loss of self-esteem. When frustrated,

> [t]he melancholic's erotic cathexis of his object thus undergoes a twofold fate: a part of it regresses to identification, but the other part, under the influence of the conflict of ambivalence, is reduced to the stage of sadism. . . .
>
> *(Freud, 1917/1956, p. 162)*

Depression is, therefore, to be considered violence against the self. To paraphrase the more prosaic language of Dollard, Doob, Miller, Mowrer, and Sears (1939), the natural consequence of the frustration of an individual's goal-directed behavior is aggression. When the source of frustration is perceived to be the individual, the self, that aggression will be self-directed.

Schafer's (1976) translation of Freud's portrayal of the genesis and dynamics of depression into "action" language provided a depiction of the "depression" that is much more in consonance with existentialism's tenor.

> . . . [w]e may say that the valuable part of Freud's account is his unsystematized presentation of depression as action. Here, the central figure is not the pathological emotional state of depression; it is the depressive agent; the one who is continuously and desperately acting egocentrically, guiltily, reproachfully, etc.; the one who is deviously, fantastically, and unconsciously attacking others while ostensibly being only self-attacking; the one who is in fact protecting loved ones from directly destructive actions; and the one who is attempting in these and other ways to regulate both self esteem and relationships with others.

> [I]n acting depressively one is unconsciously engaged in affirming or enacting the following propositions: I hate those I love (ambivalence); I interact with them lovingly insofar as they support my precarious self-esteem by being loving, admiring, attentive, and steadily available to me (narcissism), and I interact with them hatefully, even to the extent of wishing them dead, insofar as they do not relate to me in the ways I desire (ruthless destructiveness); because I cannot altogether control how they actually behave (hopelessness), and because I think of being loved as being fed (oral fixation and regression), I imagine that I eat them in order to get them inside of me where, fantastically, I can control them, punish them, protect them, and feed off them endlessly (oral aggression or cannibalism). . . .

> *(pp. 349–350)*

In addition to these independent part-theories (e.g., Bandura, Freud, Beck), attempts have been made to integrate these sometimes disparate visualizations into a comprehensive statement of depression's origin. A paper by Akiska and McKinney (1975) was typical. In it, they postulated that melancholia is a biological phase of many depressions and that the depressive syndrome is the final common pathway of various processes. Predisposing one to depression may be any and all of the following: genetic vulnerability, developmental events (early loss), psychosocial events (loss of a job), personality traits (pessimism), and physiological stressors (sleep loss). For any particular person, a somewhat different, powerful combination of these elements may be required to produce the potentially reversible, functional derangement of diencephalic mechanisms of reinforcement that Akiska and McKinney considered central to melancholia.

An appeal of these integrative conceptualizations is their recognition that the interrelationships among events, cognitions, emotions, and physiology are intricate. Unfortunately, no integrative model has yet considered fully how complicated they may indeed be. Both emotions and meaning structures may be activated from the "bottom up." Certain organic depressions seem to exemplify that process. When one allows the likelihood that both emotions and meaning structures can be activated and driven from lower-level mind structures as well as through higher-order interactions with the "external" environment, the probability of finding a final common pathway in "depression" diminishes considerably.

In summary, it is fair to suggest that the proliferation of schemata designed to describe depression reflects the heterogeneity of its phenomenology and causation and our own ignorance of these elements and their interplay. Hubris also plays a part. Mendelson's (1974, p. 289) comments with respect to the boosterism displayed by many adherents of the various psychoanalytic approaches to depression could be generalized without much strain to the advocates of the many competing and alternating models:

> To one familiar with the open confessions of ignorance in other scientific disciplines it is a little disconcerting to read so many confidently offered global conclusions in the literature on depression. This tendency to make definite pronouncements makes it appear as if legitimate uncertainty has acquired the bar sinister.

APPLICATION OF EXISTENTIAL APPROACHES TO DEPRESSION

The application of the existential outlook to depression, May advised (1969), does not obviate the need for accurate diagnosis, nor does it deny the usefulness of therapeutic interventions of demonstrated efficacy, nor does it belittle psychodynamic or behavioral insights. Rather, the existentially oriented clinician is likely to co-opt them. If nothing else, at the core of the existential perspective is the belief that it and we shall be forever unfinished. It is an exemplary open system. What the existentialist position does insist upon is that the accumulation of knowledge be considered an unending, ever enlarging quest, evolving, hopefully as Heidegger would have had it, toward "truth." The existential position further insists that, as useful as this information must prove, individuals or their circumstances can never be defined solely in its terms.

Regardless of etiology, even in primarily "organic" depressions, existentialists remind us that it is an individual, a person, who is experiencing and attempting to cope with a situation.

To cite one example, Boss (1983), explained:

We maintain that the role of physicality in organic psychoses can be described at best through the following propositions. The most we can say is, first, that there is a regular simultaneity between pathological behavior in paralytics and a certain condition of the brain. Second, what natural science interprets as frontal lobe damage caused by lues spirochetes is actually primary and direct injury to the being-in-the-world of an existing human being which destroys the bodily capacity for carrying out most of the normal, appropriate ways of responding to what a person encounters. It follows, third, that a person so affected has at his disposal only an extremely self-centered, restricted mode of human Da-sein. Strictly speaking, the substration of organic illness is only that sphere of the reduced spatiality and temporality of paralytically ill human beings which may also be interpreted, though inadequately, as defects in biophysical brain matter at a specific location in space.

(p. 215)

Yet, it might be added: it is just that paralytically ill human being who must live life. Likewise:

When patients with occipital lobectomies say that they are blind even though they are able to respond correctly to the location and configuration of visual cues . . . , how are we to deal with "blind-sight" except to distinguish their instrumental responses from their verbal reports of introspection? . . . We accept the inference that the subject has a "mental life," that his or her psychological processes are accessible by way of his or her verbal report and instrumental behaviors, and furthermore, that these different forms of behavior may reflect different processes.

(Pribram, 1986, pp. 508–509)

This individual, too, must make his or her way.

The same outlook is maintained when the constraints imposed are poverty or enslavement, wealth or position.

It is reasonable to conclude that the existentially oriented clinician may not, on the surface, offer different treatment than a clinician of another persuasion, but that the attitude of the existentially oriented clinician will differ decisively from that of a clinician of the biological or behavioral schools regardless of the growing rapprochement between existentialism and the "human sciences." Nonetheless, in the treatment of "psychopathology," attitude may prove pivotal.

Treating Depression

The existential standpoint has important contributions to make to the primary, secondary, and tertiary prevention of pathological depressions. In primary prevention (Macht, 1978), efforts are made to counteract the influence of forces that contribute to the development of a disorder, and thereby reduce its incidence. Those interventions attempt either to provide sufficient supplies necessary to maintain health, for example, vaccinations or prenatal nutritional programs, or to reduce exposure to and contamination by noxious agents. Secondary prevention activities are those which are designed to shorten the duration of severe impairment associated with already established disorders. Examples of such actions include early case finding and effective treatment. Steps taken that effectively reduce the residual deficits or sequelae of a disorder are considered tertiary prevention. Cognitive rehabilitation programs prescribed to ameliorate the functional impairments that accompany brain injury fall into that category. Of course, as with any constructed typology, the lines of demarcation that separate activities into these prevention categories are not sharply drawn at all times.

Primary Prevention

In common with most critics who "view with alarm," existentially oriented commentators on "the contemporary scene" are more adept at diagnosis than remediation. While there are stirrings in the area of existential political theory and political science (Jung, 1972) they are just stirrings. When system interventions addressing primary prevention are proposed, however, the existentially oriented critics tend to be realistic—even conservative—about the effectiveness of the course of action suggested, if not the suggestions themselves. They believe no "cure" is possible and hold that even in the best of societies authentic existence must always be a matter of individual choice and individual action. Yet, it is also clear to them that certain social configurations are more likely to facilitate good-faith action than others.

Fromm (1941, 1955, 1964, 1968), more than any other existentially oriented social psychological theorist, developed the notion of the "good" society. He constructed it on humanistic, communitarian, socialistic lines. He envisioned it as a society in which "man relates to man lovingly, in which he is rooted in bonds of brotherliness and solidarity . . . ; a society which gives him the possibility of transcending nature by creating rather than by destroying, in which everyone gains a sense of self by experiencing himself as the subject of his powers rather than by conformity, in which a system of orientation and devotion exists without man's needing to distort reality and to worship idols" (1955, p. 362).

If the ethos of the "good" society seen through Fromm's eyes bears little resemblance to the *zeitgeist* of our own, the discrepancy is not accidental. On the whole, existentially oriented clinicians see our society as pathological in itself and as generating pathology in individuals. According to Frankl (1985), we increasingly live in an "existential vacuum"; meaninglessness is spreading to the extent that it may be considered a mass neurosis. Its symptoms are depression, aggression, and addiction.

Not only is western society at large viewed as increasingly hostile to human life, but many of its institutional components, even those designed to secure the quality of life, are seen as contributing to its dissolution. The "healing arts" are but one example, as Jaspers declaimed presciently in 1931 (Jaspers, 1959, pp. 65–66).

In large measure, patients are now being dealt with in the mass according to the principles of rationalization, being sent to institutes for technical treatment, the sick being classified in groups and referred to this or that specialized department. But in this way the patient is deprived of his doctor. The supposition is that like everything else, medical treatment has now become a sort of manufactured article. . . .

A gigantic "enterprise" of medical practice is arising. . . . "Enterprise" has taken the place of individualized care. . . . Joy in the exercise of a profession on humanist lines is replaced by the joy in work that results from technical achievement. . . .

Above all, however, those who are really sick find it less and less possible to have faith in being treated thoroughly, scientifically, and intelligently by a doctor whose whole services are for the time being put at [their] service. The human being as a sick man forfeits his rights when there no longer exists any true physicians because the apparatus designed to place them at the disposal of the masses has, by its very working, make the existence of true physicians impossible.

The family provides another example:

> The family has shifted from a relatively unspecialized, task-oriented organization, bound together largely by ties derived from the performance of the widest possible range of work chores, to a highly specialized organization that is bound by emotional or expressive ties.
>
> *(Zwerling, 1968, p. 23)*

Therein lies the family's vulnerability.

> it is virtually the only social institution organized around love as a binding force. A necessary corollary of this is that the family is the only locus in which emotional budgets may be reliably balanced.
>
> *(Zwerling, 1968, p. 25)*

The image of Humanity being made Machine by the mechanisms of "civilization" is compelling. Whether the next generation, born into an age of information, will suppose us bytes is yet to be determined.

Much of the existentialist brief against western culture resembles that made by Durkheim in analyzing the consequences of the industrial revolution. He too focused upon "pathology"; his monograph "Suicide" was a brilliant example of the linkage of social structure and individual fate (Durkheim, 1951). Further, he aimed, like the existentialists, at developing remedies for the current situation short of those suggested by Luddites.

Durkheim believed western society was becoming increasingly anomic and egoistic. Anomie results from disruptions in social regularity; egoism, when the meaning structures of a society are weakened. Both lead to increases in the rate of suicide.

Durkheim's description of egoistic suicide was instructive. Egoists, according to Durkheim, suffer from "the sickness of infinity." They experience a fantastical sense of unlimited possibilities with no basis to select one over another and no assurance that they will; and they have every indication that they will not be able to motivate others to any sustained effort. Since joint effort is undoubtedly required to realize even the most primitive of goals, let alone construct self-meaning through effective action, egoists die of thirst while swimming in a sea of water.

Naroll, 1962, 1983; Krauss, 1976; and Krauss and Krauss, 1968 have provided the clearest, most ambitious, cross-cultural, empirical demonstration since Durkheim that societal characteristics can increase or dampen the rate of "mental illness." Building upon both Durkheim's and Freud's conceptualization of suicide, Naroll first undertook to discover in societies the presence of what he later termed "thwarting disorientation traits." These are recurrent and regular patterns of interaction within a culture that lead predictably to the threatened or actual disruption of interpersonal cohesion. These traits increase the difficulties individuals have in achieving biological and personal security. Frequent Warfare, Drunken Brawling, Divorce Freedom, Witchcraft Accusation (Naroll was a cross-cultural methodologist), and Defiant Homicide are five of many such traits. Naroll found that higher rates of mental illness and suicide are likely in societies with more of these traits. Conversely, reducing the frequency and intensity of these traits lowers a culture's rate of depression and its equivalents.

Naroll (1983) also focused upon those societal institutions which, if strong, have a salutary influence on mental health and, when weakened, enhance the probability of mental disorders. These he called moral nets. Moral nets make available to individuals the possibility of strong social ties, emotional warmth, punishment for transgression, myth and meaning creation, and economic and political support. The family is an exemplary moral net.

In an extensive, methodologically sophisticated investigation, Naroll demonstrated, as he predicted, that the stronger a society's moral nets, the lower was its rate of psychopathology; conversely, the weaker the moral nets, the greater was its rate of psychopathology. These findings argued cogently that to prevent depressions, exertions to strengthen the moral nets of the community and of the individual particularly at risk are required.

Even if Durkheim, Naroll, and others like them were not correct in detail, their intuitions are compelling. How but depressed can one feel if nothing and no one can be counted upon, if a common language creates no shared understanding, if no reliable mirror of one's actions is available, if no sustained action in time is possible, if one is thrown back on oneself without a structure?

Secondary Prevention

The importance of early case identification and treatment of depressive disorders has been repeatedly acknowledged (Kaplan & Sadock, 1981; Regier et al., 1988). Yet, case finding has largely been neglected by clinicians of every orientation except those working for Employee Assistance Programs (Dickman, Challenger, Emener, & Hutchinson, 1988). Only 15 to 30 percent of those experiencing depressions of "clinical" severity seek professional assistance. Existentially oriented clinicians, however, have made major contributions to the psychotherapeutic encounter in general, and to the "treatment" of "depression" in particular.

Toulmin (1988, p. 345) differentiated between the "clinical" and "scientific" attitude toward individuals requesting help for their problems.

A patient may be studied by either a clinician or by a scientist who is researching his or her current disease. The scientist's interest is in any general features the patient may share with others suffering from the same disease. The clinician's interest is in whatever can throw light on his patient, in that bed, here and now. The clinician's knowledge will be "informed by" biomedical science; but it is not, in its details, "entailed by" any biomedical theory and typically goes beyond everything that scientists can yet account for. The patient is not merely an "individual" who happens to "instantiate" a "universal law." His clinical state is local, timely, and particular, and universal theories at best throw only partial light on it.

By Toulmin's criteria, existentially oriented clinicians fall at the "clinical" end of his dichotomy.

The existentially oriented therapist encounters a client as an existential partner and has as therapeutic targets:

1. An ever deepening understanding of the life story of the individual as he or she is in the world.
2. Helping the client experience as radically as possible when and how he or she has neglected the fullness of his or her humanity.
3. Enabling the client to reactivate the full scope of his or her inner possibilities.
4. Assisting the client to achieve the restoration of his or her existential wholeness and integrity.
5. Facilitating the client's adoption of a decisive, active orientation to life, recognizing that decision often precedes knowledge (drawn from Binswanger, 1962; May, 1958; Reinhardt, 1960).

Clearly these goals have influenced greatly the practice of "humanistic" psychotherapy (Rogers, 1951, 1974). Further, the importance of relationship, meaning, active experiencing, and action in effecting therapeutic change has received substantial support from research. For those formulating an integration of psychotherapies (Beitman, Goldfried, & Norcross, 1989; Greenberg & Safran, 1989), these activities form the core of practice considerations.

To the therapist whose attitude is existential, clinical depressions, whatever else they may be—neurological dysfunction, for example—are the predictable consequences of "bad-faith" reactions of clients to their situations. "The goal of bad faith," to Sartre (1953, p. 197), "is to put oneself out of reach, it is an escape." It is designed, he wrote, to "cause me to be what I am, in the mode of 'not being what one is,' or not to be what I am in the mode of 'being what one is'" (p. 198). In a sense, bad faith resembles lying:

The ideal description of the liar would be cynical consciousness, affirming the truth within himself, denying it in his words, and denying that negative as such [p. 155]. . . . Of course we have described the ideal lie; doubtless it happens often enough that the liar is more or less the victim of his lie, that he half persuades himself of it. But the common, popular forms of the lie are also degenerate aspects of it; they represent intermediaries between falsehood and bad faith [pp. 156–157]. . . . Bad faith then has in appearance the structure of falsehood. Only what changes everything is the fact that in bad faith it is from myself that I am hiding the truth. . . . The true problem of bad faith stems evidently from the fact bad faith is *faith* [p. 202]. . . . [B]ad faith is belief; and the essential problem of bad faith is a problem of belief.

(Sartre, 1953, p. 203)

One belief, for instance, is that one's existence ought to be subordinated to that of another.

It is the whole existence of the melancholic patient which has failed to take over openly and responsibly all those possibilities of relating to the world which actually would constitute his own genuine self. Consequently, such an existence has no independent standing of its own but continuously falls prey to the demands, wishes, and expectations of others. Such patients try to live up to those foreign expectations as best they can, in order not to lose the protection and love of their surroundings. But the longer these patients allow others to govern their ways of feeling, acting, and perceiving, the more deeply indebted they become in regard to their fundamental task in life, which is to appropriate and carry out, independently and responsibly, all their authentic possibilities of relating to that which they encounter. Hence the terrible guilt feelings of the melancholic. His incessant self-accusations derive from existential guilt. The severity of his symptoms varies according to the degree in which he fails to exist as the world-openness in whose light everything encountered can unfold and shine forth in its full meaning and content.

(Boss, 1963, pp. 209–210)

Another form of bad faith may induce the "life of suicide" (Farber, 1976). According to Farber,

. . . "the life of suicide" . . . must be seen not as that situation or state of mind which *leads to* the act, but that situation in which the act-as-possibility, quite apart from whether it eventually occurs or not, has a life of its own. . . . For the man who is caught up in what I have called "the life of suicide," however, the possibility of being the author of his own death exercises a demonic and seductive fascination over him. This fascination takes different forms. There is a certain kind of person for whom the idea of suicide is a secret and cherished solution to any difficulty life may throw across his path. [p. 66] . . . —potentially despair at least—is both destroying and renewing. . . . While despair means literally the loss of hope, the movements of despair are frantically directed

toward hope; but the hope born of despair may turn to the prescriptions
of the isolated will.

(Farber, 1976)

Still other motifs of inauthenticity lead to what Maddi (1967) called
"existential neurosis." Persons who consider themselves nothing more
than actors—players of social roles—must feel powerless in the face of
social pressure. Those who believe themselves just embodiments of biological needs cannot but be impotent when injury or illness threatens
that identity. Yet as pained as such individuals may be, the stress that
precipitates existential neurosis is most likely to be that which radically
confutes their identity by forcing them to recognize its untruths: its
concrete, fragmentary, essential nature. This stressor may be the threat
of imminent death, the loss of a loved object, a significant disruption in
social order, or the accumulated impact of repeated confrontations with
the hollowness of inauthentic identity.

The equations describing depression's many sides have a fundamental sameness: fear of life and fear of extinction provoke defense. Defense
hardens into psychopathology, "a graceless, inefficient mode of coping
with anxiety" (Yalom, 1980, p. 110). "Even defensive maneuvers that
successfully ward off severe anxiety, prevent growth and result in a
constricted and unsatisfying life," Yalom indicated (p. 111). Every attempt to avert one's face from the boiling, chaotic abyss that is life is
definitive, as is the denial of the liberating force produced by the experience of dread and despair as they creatively inform our existence. So too
is the distorted experience of temporality that attends the tension between decisions already made and those needing to be made as the
individual's inevitable march to nothingness continues. Depression represents the failure of human transcendence; existential therapy's purpose is its resurrection.

Tertiary Prevention

Although there are indications that tertiary prevention efforts potentially pay large financial and moral dividends to client and society alike,
relatively little or no attention has been paid directly to such issues as:
Does existentially informed treatment ameliorate the scope and severity of residual deficits associated with some forms of depression? Does
it reduce the likelihood of secondary impairments developing? Alcohol
and drug abuse and cancer (Backman, 1989) have been implicated as
the sequelae of depression. Does it reduce the possibility of economic
invalidism by facilitating return to work? If these questions are answered affirmatively, another remains: How do existentially oriented
interventions accomplish these ends?

With its focus upon individuals and their phenomenology; its insistence upon a realistic appraisal of the life situation, and its emphasis upon decisive, responsible action with respect to it; and its stress upon transcendence, the existential attitude likely has an important contribution to make in the tertiary prevention of depression. This impression is strengthened by the mounting evidence that, for example, feelings of personal control are related to successful adaptation to chronic illness (Williams & Stout, 1985). Research also supports the existential insights that the therapist's recognition of a client's need to assume responsibility for self-regulation increases treatment compliance (Brownlee-Duffeck et al., 1987) as do reciprocally respectful client–therapist interactions (Haynes, Taylor, & Sackett, 1979). Nonetheless, considerable additional evidence must be sought and accumulated before the case for efficacy of the existential orientation in tertiary prevention is made. Topics for these investigations might be the degree to which existentially designed interventions reduce self-stigmatization and increase return to meaningful social interactions and gainful employment. Other researchers may attempt to gauge the impact of existentially oriented therapy upon the likelihood of self-destructive acts; yet others, whether individuals treated existentially are less at risk for additional "depressive episodes."

SUMMARY

The existential viewpoint brings scope, depth of field, and clarity to the appreciation of the human situation. It informs our understanding and treatment of psychopathology in general and depressions in particular.

Among the strengths of the existentialist stance, and they are many and formidable, are the following: a concern for individuals and their view of their particular circumstances; the realization that the individual is embarked upon a lifelong quest in which transcendence over local circumstances is natural; an acceptance of dread and despair as emotions which attend, motivate, and inform the actions that determine direction; and the intuition that although each individual's path is unique, others, even though they are engaged in their own voyages of discovery, may contribute necessary coordinates.

While rejecting as necessarily incomplete the premises of systems claiming truth, existentialism has been quick to borrow and apply pragmatically the techniques these alien orientations have generated, be they psychopharmacological or behavioral.

The existential attitude does have its weaknesses. One is its inability to inspire in its clinical adherents a desire to depict and elucidate the tactics of therapeutic intervention in the same detail with which they have described its strategic considerations. Another failing of existentially oriented clinicians has been their general disinterest in personally participating in the development of transpersonal methodologies and data bases. These tasks they leave to others, thereby depriving themselves of the enhancement of reality that engaging in such a process provides. That such work can be conducted profitably within a humanistic framework has been amply demonstrated by the extraordinary research program of Rogers (1951, 1974) and those influenced by him.

REFERENCES

Akiska, H. P., & McKinney, W. T., Jr. (1975). Overview of some research in depression: Integration of ten conceptual models into a comprehensive clinical frame. *Archives of General Psychiatry, 32*, 285–305.

Allport, G. W. (1957). European and American theories of personality. In H. P. David & H. V. Bracken (Eds.), *Perspectives in personality theory* (pp. 3–24). New York: Basic Books.

American Psychiatric Association. (1987). *Diagnostic and statistical manual of mental disorders* (3rd ed. rev.). Washington, DC: American Psychiatric Association.

Backman, M. E. (1989). *The psychology of the physically ill patient: A clinician's guide.* New York: Plenum.

Bandura, A. (1986). *Social foundations of thought and action: A social-cognitive theory.* Englewood Cliffs, NJ: Prentice-Hall.

Baron, M., Risch, N., Hamburger, R., Kushner, S., Newman, M., Drumer, D., & Belmaker, R. H. (1987). Genetic linkage between X-chromosome markers and bipolar affective illness. *Nature, 326*, 289–292.

Beck, A. (1967a). *Depression: Causes and treatment.* Philadelphia: University of Pennsylvania Press.

Beck, A. (1967b). *Depression: Clinical, experimental, and theoretical aspects.* New York: Harper.

Beck, A. (1976). *Cognitive therapy and the emotional disorders.* New York: International Universities Press.

Beitman, B. D., Goldfried, M. R., & Norcross, J. C. (1989). The movement toward integrating the psychotherapies: An overview. *American Journal of Psychiatry, 146*, 138–147.

Binitie, A. (1975). A factor-analytic study of depression across cultures (African and European). *British Journal of Psychiatry, 127*, 559–563.

Binswanger, L. (1962). Existential analysis and psychotherapy. In H. M. Ruitenbeek (Ed.), *Psychoanalysis and existential philosophy* (pp. 17–23). New York: Dutton.

Boss, M. (1963). *Psychoanalysis and Daseinanalysis.* New York: Basic Books.

Boss, M. (1983). *Existential foundations of medicine and psychology.* New York: Aronson.

Breisach, E. (1962). *Introduction to modern existentialism*. New York: Grove.

Brownlee-Duffeck, M., Peterson, M., Simonds, J. F., Goldstein, D., Kilo, C., & Hoette, S. (1987). The role of health beliefs in the regimen adherence and metabolic control of adolescents and adults with diabetes mellitus. *Journal of Consulting and Clinical Psychology, 55,* 139–144.

Buber, M. (1970). *I and thou*. New York: Scribner.

Buytendijk, F. J. J. (1957). Femininity and existential psychology. In H. P. David & H. V. Bracken (Eds.), *Perspectives in personality theory* (pp. 197–211). New York: Basic Books.

Davids, A. (1955). Alienation, social apperception and ego structure. *Journal of Consulting Psychology, 19,* 21–27.

Dickman, F., Challenger, R. B., Emener, W. G., & Hutchinson, W. S., Jr. (1988). *Employee Assistance Programs: A basic text*. Springfield, IL: Thomas.

Dollard, J., Doob, L. W., Miller, N. E., Mowrer, O. H., & Sears, R. R. (1939). *Frustration and aggression*. New Haven, CT: Yale University Press.

Durkheim, E. (1951). *Suicide*. J. A. Spaulding & G. Simpson (Eds.). Glencoe, IL: Free Press.

Egeland, J. A., Gerhard, D. S., Pauls, D. L., Sussex, J. N., Kidd, K. K., Allen, C. R., Hostetter, A. M., & Housman, D. E. (1987). Bipolar affective disorders linked to DNA markers on chromosome 11. *Nature, 325,* 783–787.

Farber, L. H. (1976). *Lying, despair, jealousy, envy, sex, suicide, drugs, and the good life*. New York: Harper.

Frankl, V. (1985). *The unheard cry for meaning*. New York: Washington Square.

Freud, S. (1917/1956). Mourning and melancholia. In J. Strachey (Ed. and Trans.), *Collected Papers of Sigmund Freud* (Vol. 4, pp. 152–170). London: Hogarth Press.

Freud, S. (1914/1962). On narcissism: An introduction. In J. Strachey (Ed. and Trans.), *The standard edition of the complete psychological works of Sigmund Freud* (Vol. 14, pp. 73–102). London: Hogarth Press.

Fromm, E. (1941). *Escape from freedom*. New York: Rinehart.

Fromm, E. (1955). *The sane society*. New York: Rinehart.

Fromm, E. (1964). *The heart of man*. New York: Harper.

Fromm, E. (1968). *The revolution of hope*. New York: Harper.

Friedman, M. (1967). *To deny our nothingness*. New York: Dell.

Garber, J., & Seligman, M. E. P. (Eds.). (1980). *Human helplessness: Theory and applications*. New York: Academic Press.

Greenberg, L. S., & Safran, J. D. (1989). Emotion in psychotherapy. *American Psychologist, 44,* 19–29.

Haynes, R. B., Taylor, D. W., & Sackett, D. L. (Eds.). (1979). *Compliance in health care*. Baltimore: Johns Hopkins Press.

James, W. (1984). *William James on exceptional mental states: The 1896 Lowell Lectures*. E. Taylor (Ed.). Amherst, MA: University of Massachusetts Press.

Jaspers, K. (1959). *Man in the modern age*. London: Routledge & Kegan Paul.

Jennings, J. L. (1986). Husserl revisited. *American Psychologist, 41,* 1231–1240.

Jung, H. Y. (Ed.). (1972). *Existential phenomenology and political theory: A reader.* Chicago: Regnery.

Kaplan, H. I., & Sadock, B. J. (1981). *Modern synopsis of comprehensive textbook of psychiatry III.* Baltimore: Williams & Wilkins.

Kaufmann, W. (1972). The reception of existentialism in the United States. In R. Boyers (Ed.), *The legacy of the German refugee intellectuals* (pp. 69–96). New York: Schocken.

Kierkegaard, S. (1941). *Concluding unscientific postscript.* Princeton, NJ: Princeton University Press.

Krauss, H. H. (1967). Anxiety: The dread of a future event. *Journal of Individual Psychology, 23,* 88–93.

Krauss, H. H. (1976). A psychological theory of suicide. In B. B. Wolman & H. H. Krauss (Eds.), *Between survival and suicide* (pp. 25–54). New York: Gardner.

Krauss, H. H., & Krauss, B. (1968). A cross-cultural study of the thwarting disorientation theory of suicide. *Journal of Abnormal Psychology, 73,* 353–357.

Loehlin, J. C., Willerman, L., & Horn, J. M. (1988). Human behavior genetics. *Annual Review of Psychology, 39,* 101–133.

Macht, L. B. (1978). Community psychiatry. In J. A. M. Nicholi (Ed.), *The Harvard guide to modern psychiatry* (pp. 627–649). Cambridge, MA: Harvard University Press.

Maddi, S. R. (1967). The existential neurosis. *Journal of Abnormal Psychology, 72,* 311–325.

Magee, B. (1982). *Men of ideas.* New York: Oxford.

Marsella, A. J. (1980). Depressive experience and disorder across cultures. In H. C. Triandis & J. G. Draguns (Eds.), *Handbook of cross cultural psychology: Vol. 6 Psychopathology.* Boston: Allyn & Bacon.

May, R. (1958). The origins and significance of the existential movement in psychology. In R. May, E. Angel, & H. F. Ellenberger (Eds.), *Existence* (pp. 3–36). New York: Simon & Schuster.

May, R. (1969). *Existential psychology* (2nd ed.). New York: Random House.

Mendelson, M. (1974). *Psychoanalytic concepts of depression.* New York: Spectrum.

Misiak, H., & Sexton, V. S. (1973). *Phenomenological, existential, and humanistic psychologies: A historical survey.* New York: Grune & Stratton.

Naroll, R. (1962). *Data quality control—A new research technique.* Glencoe, IL: Free Press.

Naroll, R. (1983). *The moral order: An introduction to the human situation.* Beverly Hills, CA: Sage.

Patterson, R. J., & Moran, G. (1988). Attachment theory, personality development, and psychotherapy. *Clinical Psychology Review, 8,* 611–636.

Popper, K. R., & Eccles, J. C. (1977). *The self and its brain.* Berlin: Springer-Verlag.

Pribram, K. H. (1986). The cognitive revolution and mind/brain issues. *American Psychologist, 41,* 507–520.

Regier, D. A., Hirschfeld, R. M. A., Goodwin, F. K., Burke, J. D., Jr., Lazar, J. B., & Judd, L. L. (1988). The NIMH depression awareness, recognition, and treatment program: Structure, aims, and scientific base. *American Journal of Psychiatry, 145,* 1351–1357.

Reinhardt, K. F. (1960). *The existentialist revolt: The main themes and phases of existentialism.* New York: Unger.

Rogers, C. R. (1951). *Client-centered therapy: Its current practice, implication, and theory.* Boston: Houghton Mifflin.

Rogers, C. R. (1974). In retrospect: Forty-six years. *American Psychologist, 29,* 115–123.

Rosenbaum, A. H., Maruta, T., & Shatzberg, A. F. (1983). Toward a biochemical classification of depressive disorders: VII urinary free cortisol and urinary MHPG in depression. *American Journal of Psychiatry, 140,* 314–318.

Sartre, J. P. (1945). *L'Existentialisme est un humanisme.* Paris: Nagel.

Sartre, J. P. (1953). *Existential psychoanalysis.* Chicago: Regnery.

Schafer, R. (1976). *A new language for psychoanalysis.* New Haven, CT: Yale University Press.

Schildkraut, J. J. (1977). Biochemical research in affective disorders. In G. Usdin (Ed.), *Depression: Clinical, biological, and psychological perspectives.* New York: Brunner-Mazel.

Seeman, M. (1959). On the meaning of alienation. *American Sociological Review, 24,* 783.

Seligman, M. E. P. (1975). *Helplessness: On depression, development, & death.* San Francisco: Freeman.

Toulmin, S. (1988). The recovery of practical philosophy. *American Scholar, 57,* 337–352.

Van Praag, H. M. (1977). *Depression and schizophrenia: A contribution to their clinical pathologies.* New York: Spectrum.

Wehr, T. A., Sack, D. A., Rosenthal, N. E., & Cowdry, R. W. (1988). Rapid cycling affective disorder: Contributing factors and treatment responses in 51 patients. *American Journal of Psychiatry, 145,* 179–184.

Williams, J. M., & Stout, J. K. (1985). The effect of high and low assertiveness on locus of control and health problems. *Journal of Psychology, 119,* 169–173.

Yalom, I. (1980). *Existential psychotherapy.* New York: Basic Books.

Zwerling, I. (1968). *Alienation and the mental health professions.* Richmond, VA: Virginia Commonwealth University.

CHAPTER 4

Cognitive and Behavioral Theories

LYNN P. REHM, PhD

THEORETICAL MODELS

In 1928 Ivanov-Smolensky, a physician working in Pavlov's labs, reported on his observations of a dog that appeared depressed consequent to its inability to make extremely fine discriminations in a classical conditioning task. The paper had little impact on the field of depression psychopathology and only in the past 20 years has there been a concerted effort to apply learning models to the phenomena of depression. During this recent period a number of new theories have developed. They have led to the generation of a great deal of research data on the psychopathology of depression and to the development of many new therapeutic approaches to treatment. The theories themselves have been influenced by these developments and revised theories have evolved from earlier forms.

Behavioral models were the first learning approaches to be applied to depression. The behavior modification approach to depression brought the tradition of borrowing models from the psychological laboratory and adapting them to the explanation of complex human problems such as depression. As theories have developed, the learning models of the animal laboratory have not been the only influences on the process. The psychology of learning has gone through a cognitive revolution in recent years, and current work stresses models of human learning and memory. These new cognitive models have been brought into the domain of clinical psychology generally and the psychopathology of depression in particular. Earlier theories have evolved in a cognitive direction and new theories have developed from a cognitive perspective. Social psychology has also had an influence on theory in clinical psychology, and constructs from the social psychological laboratories have been adapted to models of depression.

This chapter will describe four major theoretical models of depression that have been developed from the cognitive-behavioral perspective in clinical psychology. In each case a description of the basic elements of the initial theory will be followed by a sampling of the main lines of research generated from the theory. Specific forms of therapy derived from each theory will be described briefly with a sampling of the associated therapy research. Each theory has been revised over time, as research has introduced new problems which the theories need to account for. The chapter will trace the important developments in each theory and attempt to sum up its current status.

Depression presents a difficult problem to the cognitive-behavioral approach to theory in psychopathology because depression is quite complex in its symptomatology and etiology. The contrast with anxiety is instructive. Behavioral approaches to anxiety made great strides in theory and practice with the simplifying assumption of anxiety as a conditioned response. The analogy of the simple phobia as composed of related behavioral, cognitive, and physiological responses to a specifiable stimulus has great explanatory power. Testable models of etiology and effective forms of treatment follow from the basic metaphor. Depression is more complex in its manifestations. It includes overt behavior (e.g., sad demeanor, slowed activity, lack of responsiveness), cognition (e.g., low self-esteem, hopelessness, helplessness, negative view of the world), and somatic symptoms (e.g., loss of weight, disturbed sleep, physical complaints) that extend to almost all domains of functioning. While a precipitating event or theme can usually be identified, depression is not stimulus-bound in the way anxiety is. Depression is more constant and pervasive. From the cognitive-behavioral perspective this can be seen as a problem in response and stimulus overgeneralization. Why should the stimulus of loss of a job generalize to loss of responsivity to other, formerly enjoyable stimulus situations (e.g., going to a movie)? Why should its effects generalize to affect so much of the person's behavior (e.g., loss of interest in sex, reduced eating, and low self-esteem)? Each theoretical model had to account for these diverse phenomena, and each theory took a different approach to handling the problem. For the most part, a single symptom was selected as the core or center of depression and it was assumed that other symptoms followed as secondary effects. The chapter will attempt to highlight and contrast these different approaches to the problem of overgeneralization in depression.

REINFORCEMENT THEORY

One of the first to apply a behavioral analysis to the problem of depression was Charles Ferster (1973), who viewed depression as a generalized reduction of rates of response to external stimuli. Behavior was then no longer under the control of reinforcers that once were effective. Ferster's basic analogy in learning terms was to the process of extinction. Major losses in life could be seen as losses of important sources of reinforcement. Generalization of the effects of the loss occurred because other behavior was chained to or organized by the central source of reinforcement. The concept of chaining referred to the situation where one response was dependent on a later response, because the first functioned to gain access to the second. For example, for a man who becomes depressed after the break-up of a romance, the woman in the relationship could be thought of as having been an important and central source of reinforcement. His relationship with her may have organized much of the man's behavior, chaining it to this source of reinforcement. If in his depression he no longer goes to movies, a previously enjoyable activity (reinforcing), it is because he formerly went with her and now that source of reinforcement is not available. He might also stop reading the newspaper section that contains movie advertisements and reviews. His depression can be seen in the many behaviors that are reduced in rate.

In later elaborations of his theoretical ideas, Ferster (1977, April; 1981) stressed the analysis of verbal behavior as an important avenue for studying depression. As a verbal phenomenon, depression consists largely of complaints that are negatively reinforced by those around the depressed person.

Peter M. Lewinsohn developed similar ideas into a coherent theory and explored the ramifications of the theory in a clinical research program (Lewinsohn, 1974; Lewinsohn, Biglan, & Zeiss, 1976). In Lewinsohn's terms, depression is a response to a loss or lack of response-contingent positive reinforcement. Insufficient reinforcement in major domains of one's life leads to dysphoria and a reduction in behavior, which are the primary phenomena of depression. Other symptoms of depression such as low self-esteem and hopelessness follow from the reduced level of functioning.

According to the theory, there are three ways in which insufficient reinforcement may arise. First, the environment may be inadequate in providing sufficient reinforcement to maintain adequate functioning. For example, the loss of a job or of a loved one would represent a significant loss of a source of reinforcement. Inability to find a job, or a distressed marriage, might cause a continuing lack of reinforcement. Second, the person may lack the requisite skills to obtain reinforcement in an environment where it is potentially available. Poor interpersonal skills might prevent a person from developing satisfactory social relationships; poor communication skills might maintain a distressed marital relationship. Third, the reinforcers might be available to the person but he or she is unable to enjoy or receive satisfaction from them. The reason for this condition would ordinarily be interfering anxiety. The socially anxious person does not functionally receive the reinforcers, even if they are emitted by an amiable social environment.

Another feature of the theory is its suggestion that, once depression occurs, depressive behavior functions to elicit reinforcement from others in the form of concern and succor. The person who is experiencing insufficient reinforcement obtains reinforcement for acting in a depressed manner, which functions to maintain the depression. Furthermore, although depressive behavior elicits positive responses from others in the short run, continued depression is aversive to these others and they begin to avoid the depressed person, whose reinforcement is again reduced. The ultimate results are that the depressed behavior is maintained on a thin schedule of reinforcement, and reinforcement is still insufficient to overcome the depression in a self-perpetuating cycle.

Research

Several areas of research support elements of Lewinsohn's theory. One area concerns the relationship between mood and daily events. On the assumption that positive and negative daily events can be thought of as reinforcements and punishments, this research looks at daily mood as it is influenced by events. Positive events (rewards) should elevate mood and negative events (punishments) should depress mood. Contingency between the events and the person's behavior is assumed and not demonstrated.

Lewinsohn and his coworkers have developed instruments for assessing daily events. The Pleasant Events Schedule (MacPhillamy & Lewinsohn, 1982), a lengthy list (320 items) of potentially pleasant events, is used in two ways. In the retrospective format the subject identifies items that have occurred in a specified period of time, usually the past 30 days, and indicates the potential pleasure of each event. The first (identifying) responses are summed for an activity level score, the second (evaluating) responses yield a reinforcement potential score, and the sum of the cross-products of the two ratings is used as an index of obtained reinforcement. In its second use, the Pleasant Events Schedule, or a selected subset of its items, is employed as a daily checklist for monitoring the occurrence of positive events. Lewinsohn and Talkington (1979) developed a parallel Unpleasant Events Schedule.

Findings are generally consistent with the theory. Depressed persons have lower activity levels, report less pleasure from positive events (are unable to experience reinforcement), and obtain less total pleasure (experience a relative lack of reinforcement) compared to normals or psychiatric controls (MacPhillamy & Lewinsohn, 1974). The opposite effects occur with the Unpleasant Events Schedule scores, though with somewhat less consistency (Lewinsohn & Talkington, 1979). With treatment, scores improve on both event scales in appropriate directions (Lewinsohn, Youngren, & Grosscup, 1979).

Daily mood is positively correlated with pleasant events and negatively correlated with unpleasant events; the two types of events are uncorrelated with each other (Grosscup & Lewinsohn, 1980; Lewinsohn & Graf, 1973; Lewinsohn & Libet, 1972, Rehm, 1978). These findings are presumed to be consistent with the basic theoretical mechanism that loss or lack of reinforcement produces depression as an extension of normal sad mood. The findings also support the rationale behind attempting to increase pleasant events as a means of therapeutic intervention.

Social skill deficits in depression have been demonstrated in several studies. Lewinsohn, Mischel, Chaplin, and Barton (1980) found that depressed individuals in a group interaction were rated by themselves and by other group members as less socially skilled than either normal or psychiatric control group members. Interestingly, depressed subjects rated their own skills accurately while normals and psychiatric controls rated their own skills higher than they were rated by others. Both self-ratings and the ratings of social skill by others improved with therapy. Most studies of social skill in depression do not address the question of whether depressed persons have a true skill deficit or whether, when depressed, they merely perform in a less skilled fashion. The fact that social skills improve following treatments for depression that do not specifically target social skill (Rude, 1986) argues for the deficit being only in performance.

There is little direct research on the question of whether anxiety inhibits pleasure in depression but it is a well-recognized clinical reality that anxiety is often a feature of depression (Kendall & Watson, 1989; Maser & Cloninger, in press). Anxiety disorders often precede depressive disorders in the same individual but it is not clear that a causal relationship exists as specified in Lewinsohn's theory, that is, that anxiety interferes with reinforcement.

Therapy

Lewinsohn's work on the psychopathology of depression has been consistently paralleled by a sequence of studies developing a behavioral approach to therapy for depression. His early approach to therapy for depression (Lewinsohn, Biglan, & Zeiss, 1976) was to develop a series of depression therapy "modules." The idea of the modular approach was to match the module to the primary deficit of a particular depressed person. Thus, the person with insufficient reinforcement in his or her environment would be matched to an activity-increase therapy module in which the goals of treatment would be to identify potentially reinforcing activities and to encourage the patient, through scheduling, incentives, and the like, to engage increasingly in these activities. An interpersonal skill training module was developed to intervene in cases where social skill deficiencies were evident, and a desensitization module was developed for patients who demonstrated interfering anxiety.

Research has shown, however, that matching of patient and therapy does not seem to be important. For example, Zeiss, Lewinsohn, and Muñoz (1979) found that interpersonal, cognitive, and activity-increase modules were helpful in ameliorating depression regardless of the pattern of deficits shown by the patients at pretest, and that regardless of the therapy module that patients received, they improved in all three areas. This finding of nonspecificity is something of a problem to the theory and has led to a rethinking of the approach to therapy.

In recent years, Lewinsohn and his colleagues have taken a psycho-educational approach to therapy for depression. The rationale is that a variety of skills relevant to ameliorating depression can be taught to patients in a therapy program and their cumulative effect is likely to be more helpful than the effect of any single module. The product of this work is a structured therapy course, "The Coping with Depression Course" (Lewinsohn, Antonuccio, Breckenridge, & Teri, 1987). The 12-session course consists of sections on the overall rationale for the course, relaxation training, an activity-increase unit, a cognitive unit on constructive thinking, a social skills training unit, and a unit on developing a self-change program. The cognitive unit is related to the basic theory by the assumption that distortions of thinking can interfere with the accurate perception of reinforcement and contingencies. Brown and Lewinsohn (1984) evaluated the course in group, individual, and minimum contact (i.e., self-change) formats and found them to be equally effective.

A number of other, separately developed therapy programs share aspects of the reinforcement theory orientation. Most focus on teaching some form of interpersonal skills. A general social skill training approach was adopted by Hersen, Bellack, Himmelhoch, and Thase (1984) in a study that found social skill training to compare favorably to treatment with a tricyclic antidepressant. Marital communication skills were successfully employed in the treatment of depression in several studies (Beach & O'Leary, 1986; Jacobson, Holtzworth-Munroe, & Schmaling, 1989; McLean & Hakstian, 1979). Nezu (1986; Nezu, Nezu, & Perri, 1989) recently described a therapy program focusing on problem-solving skills training.

Comment and Recent Developments

The most problematic point in reinforcement approaches to depression is demonstration of a contingency between specific responses and reinforcement. Some group or marital interaction studies seem to point to a functional relationship between some specific verbal response classes and reactions of others. For example, depressive complaints and nagging may be negatively reinforced by spouses who give in to the complainant (Hautzinger, Linden, & Hoffman, 1982). This is the reinforcement of depressive behavior, which may have a maintaining function, but it is unlikely to explain the origin of a depressive episode. The reduction of behavior as a consequence of a loss or lack of response-contingent reinforcement is harder to demonstrate.

Overgeneralization seems to be based on an implicit assumption that a basic minimum ratio of reinforcement to behavior is required to maintain an adequate level of functioning in very broad and interrelated life domains (e.g., work; domestic or social life). The nature of these relationships is not well articulated and is only roughly translated into empirical demonstration.

In a theoretical article, Lewinsohn, Hoberman, Teri, and Hautzinger (1985) reviewed developments in research and theory of depression and pointed to needed expansions and integration of the behavioral reinforcement theory. They suggested that cognitive factors involving increased self-awareness may mediate between reduced reinforcement and dysphoria/depression. Such mediation may explain the overgeneralization of the effects of reduced reinforcement. Other suggested modifications of the theoretical approach involve consideration of feedback loops whereby the consequences of depressed behavior may affect depression-evoking events, reinforcement, and self-awareness in ways that amplify depression. It remains to be seen what kind of influence this next step in reinforcement theory will have on the field of research and practice.

LEARNED HELPLESSNESS THEORY

The Animal Model

Martin E. P. Seligman's (1974, 1975) learned helplessness theory of depression began with an animal model for the disorder. Seligman observed a phenomenon wherein animals exposed to unavoidable shock were subsequently deficient in learning an escape or avoidance response in a shuttle box apparatus (Seligman & Maier, 1967). Seligman assumed that the animals had acquired a generalized helplessness—a perception of lack of contingency between responses and outcomes. Contingency was seen as the critical factor since animals with equivalent but response-contingent shock learned later to escape and avoid like animals with no precondition.

Seligman saw in the behavior of these animals may analogies to human depression. Induction by inescapable shock was seen as parallel to the traumatic loss that often precipitates depression. The animals' behavior showed passivity, which Seligman felt paralleled the reduction in instrumental behavior typical of depressed people. Other symptom parallels included weight loss and lack of appetite. The learned helplessness effect dissipated with time, as does normal depression.

When experimental analogs of the helplessness induction experiment were conducted with humans, findings were similar. College students who were exposed to inescapable noise or unsolvable anagrams were deficient in later escape or anagram pattern recognition tasks (Miller & Seligman, 1975). Mildly depressed students behaved like those who had been through the helplessness induction procedure. Deficits in perception of contingency connected to depression were further examined in studies of expectancy shift (Abramson, Garber, Edwards, & Seligman, 1978). In these studies, subjects were given feedback of consistent success or failure on tasks described as involving skill or chance. Depressed subjects were slower to change their expectancies for success based on positive feedback, suggesting a deficiency in perception of contingency.

The Attribution Revision

As research accumulated, conceptual and empirical problems became apparent in the animal learned helplessness model of depression. One of the central conceptual issues involved the paradox of guilt in depression. If depression is based on helplessness and the perception of non-contingency between the person's behavior and outcomes, then it is difficult to explain why people should perceive themselves responsible and blame themselves for bad outcomes (Abramson & Sackheim, 1977).

In 1978 an attributional revision of the learned helplessness theory was published (Abramson, Seligman, & Teasdale, 1978). The revision adapted the social psychological ideas about attribution of responsibility. When people make inferences about the causes of events in their lives, these attributions can be categorized according to a simple dimensional structure (Weiner et al., 1971). Causes are either internal or external; that is, the event is caused either by some aspect of the person (skill, personality, or effort) or by some aspect of the outside world (the task, another person, or chance). Secondly, causal factors are either stable or unstable. That is, either they continue to function consistently over time (skills; types of easy or difficult tasks) or they are relative to the particular time of the event (how much effort was expended; luck). The two dimensions cross to make a two-by-two classification of causes.

Abramson, Seligman, and Teasdale (1978) added another dimension for their purposes. Attributed causes can also be thought of as global or specific. Global causes are general to many situations whereas specific causes apply only to limited domains. For example, a person might attribute success on an examination to general intelligence or to a skill with multiple-choice math questions.

Using these concepts, the revised model hypothesized that people develop consistent attributional styles and that a particular attributional style is typical of people at risk for depression. Such people habitually attribute negative outcomes to internal, stable, global causes and they credit positive events to external, unstable, specific causes. In other words, following a failure the depressive person accepts blame and assumes the cause is general and persisting. Following a success the same person takes no credit and assumes the success has no implication for other behavior or for the future.

A person with this depressive style is likely to make a depressive attribution when a major aversive event occurs. To make such an interpretation is to perceive oneself as helpless: I am unable to avoid failure and unable to produce success. A depressive attributional style is a vulnerability or risk factor for making a depressive attribution following an aversive event. The nature of that attribution will determine the nature of the depression. An internal attribution determines whether the person's self-esteem is affected, a stable attribution determines the chronicity of the depression, and a global attribution determines the generality of the feelings of depression. The intensity of the depression is determined not only by the aversiveness of the event but by the person's consequent attributions. The revision reconceptualizes what was a behavioral animal model into a cognitive social psychological model.

Research

An immense literature has developed from the attributional revision. A number of interrelated issues have been studied. Assessment of attributional style as a stable personality trait has been facilitated by the development of an instrument, the Attributional Style Questionnaire (ASQ) (Peterson et al., 1982). Subjects are asked to identify the most likely cause of some hypothetical positive and negative events and then to rate the cause on the three attribution dimensions (internal, stable, and global). Quite a few studies have assessed attributions by various methods and have defined depressed samples in various ways (Raps, Peterson, Reinhard, Abramson, & Seligman, 1982; Zuroff, 1980, 1981). Attributional style assessed on the hypothetical items of the ASQ is not always consistent with attributions of real events. Studies of the consistency of attributional style both during and after recovery from depression (Eaves & Rush, 1984) addressed the question of whether depressive attributions are merely a symptom of depression or a more enduring trait. Only a few prospective studies looked at the question of attributional style as a risk or vulnerability factor for depression (Metalsky, Abramson, Seligman, Semmel, & Peterson, 1982; O'Hara, Rehm, & Campbell, 1982).

Therapy

No therapy program has been developed directly from the learned helplessness perspective. Seligman (1981), however, suggested that four basic therapy strategies are consistent with the tenets of the theory. The first is environmental manipulation, which would involve putting the person in an environment that would promote the recovery of a sense of control. Psychiatric hospitalization might be one environment in which an individual might experience a sense of control over daily events. The second is skill training, to give the person actual increased ability to control the environment. Interpersonal skill training would be only one example. Third, Seligman suggested the possibility of resignation training, to help a person give up an unrealistic goal that he or she is helpless to achieve and to replace it with a more realistic and controllable goal. Fourth, attribution retraining would be directed at the depressive attributional style itself, as a means of avoiding the initiation of new depressive episodes.

Comment and Recent Developments

The learned helplessness theory has been the topic of a great deal of research, yet several issues remain problematic and are not well resolved empirically. A major issue centers on attributional inference as a stable individual difference. Attributional style is a trait-like concept and many of the problems of trait models apply. Do individuals actually develop attributional styles that are stable and consistent? The social psychological literature would suggest that this is not likely (Weiner et al., 1971). Most individuals ought to develop differentiated attributional tendencies. The child with athletic talent comes to attribute athletic success internally, but if he or she consistently does poorly in math, a successful exam score might be attributed to chance. Attributional assumptions accumulate from experience and allow people to make causal inferences as a basis for accurate predictions in the world. A depressive attribution is distorted and overgeneralized almost by definition, but in many instances there may be an element of reality. The complexity of the process does not seem to be well modeled in the theory.

Recent papers concerning the theory have suggested some additional revisions. Alloy, Clements, and Kolden (1985) and Abramson, Alloy, and Metalsky (1988) emphasized the idea that attributional style is neither a necessary nor a sufficient cause of depression but only a contributory cause or a risk factor along with many other possible risk factors. A depressive attribution about a particular adverse event is only partly predictable from attributional style. These researchers also acknowledged that many other paths to depression may exist and the model therefore applied to only a subset of depressions. Another step in the causal sequence was added by the assertion that helplessness leads to depression when it leads the person to be hopeless about the future. Hopelessness is seen as the proximal antecedent cause of only hopelessness depressions. The authors referred to this as a revised "hopelessness model of depression."

The model becomes harder to test when an unknown proportion of depressions is excluded and when multiple unspecified factors may determine whether a depressive attribution is made. It is also difficult to test the idea of a causal sequence of cognitive mediating constructs, such as helplessness to hopelessness to depression, and to separate a mediating cognition from the complex cognitive symptomatology of depression. Helplessness and hopelessness are also components of the general negative bias that depressed subjects show about themselves in all areas of inference, including self-evaluation, expectancies, and so on.

SELF-CONTROL THEORY

The relevance of models of self-control to depression was commented on early in the history of social learning approaches to psychopathology (Bandura, 1971; Marston, 1964; Mathews, 1977). Models of self-control are concerned with the ways in which people manage their behavior in order to obtain long-term goals (e.g., quit smoking, or start exercising for long-term health). In depression, people are hopeless about long-term goals and feel helpless to manage their own behavior. When a person becomes depressed, behavior organized by long-term goals deteriorates first. The depressed person may continue to meet the immediate demands of daily existence but behavior without immediate consequences is not performed.

Rehm (1977) presented a self-control model of depression which was an attempt to integrate aspects of the theories of Lewinsohn, Beck, and Seligman under a self-control framework. The framework was an adaptation of Kanfer's (1970) model of self-control. Kanfer described people's efforts at controlling their behavior to obtain long-term goals in terms of a three-stage feedback–loop process. When people see the need to change behavior to achieve a delayed goal, they begin to pay conscious attention to the relevant behavior (e.g., number of cigarettes smoked). This is the first or self-monitoring stage of the loop.

The information monitored is compared to some internal standard and a judgment is made of the valence of the behavior in a process of self-evaluation. Here the model was modified by the addition of an attributional component to self-evaluation. Self-evaluation of behavior as positive or negative is premised on having made an internal attribution for the act. Behavior perceived as externally caused is not a basis for evaluation of oneself. As such, attributional judgments act to moderate self-evaluation.

The final phase of Kanfer's model is self-reinforcement. Kanfer assumed that people are able to control and influence their own behavior using the same reinforcement principles that would apply to the control of someone else's behavior. Positive behavior toward a goal is rewarded and negative behavior is punished. Self-reward and self-punishment act as supplements to the external rewards and punishments of the environment and function to maintain behavior when external reinforcement is not immediate.

The self-control model of depression (Rehm, 1977) postulated that the behavior of depressed people could be characterized by one or more of six deficits in self-control behavior. First, depressed persons selectively attend to negative events in their lives, to the relative exclusion of positive events. This self-monitoring deficit describes the phenomenon discussed by Beck (1972) as selective attention in depression. Ferster (1973) described this as the depressed person's vigilance in anticipating aversive experiences. Second, depressed people selectively attend to the immediate as opposed to the delayed consequences of their behavior. This might be considered an overall effect of depressive self-control. Depressed persons have difficulty in looking beyond the demands of the present when making behavioral choices.

Third, depressed people set stringent self-evaluative standards for themselves. Depressed people are often perfectionistic. Standards for themselves are more stringent than those applied to others. Fourth, depressed persons make depressive attributions about their behavior. Depressed persons make internal attributions for failure and make external attributions for success. A global-specific dimension was discussed in terms of breadth of standards applied. With the advent of the attributional revision of the learned helplessness theory (Abramson, Seligman, & Teasdale, 1978), later versions of the model have simply incorporated the three-dimensional analysis of helplessness theory.

Fifth, depressed people administer to themselves insufficient contingent reward to maintain important domains of behavior, and sixth, they administer excessive self-punishment, which suppresses constructive behavior in many areas. These deficits in the self-reinforcement phase of self-control are partly the consequence of deficits in the earlier phases of self-control behavior. For example, to monitor negative events and set high standards minimizes reward and maximizes punishment.

Self-reinforcement is seen as supplementing external reinforcement. The nondepressed person is able to maintain behavior toward goals even when the external environment is not reinforcing that behavior. The depressed person is dependent on external sources of reinforcement and becomes depressed when they are insufficient, as suggested by Lewinsohn. When environmental contingencies change, the individual is faced with organizing efforts to readjust and reorient toward distant goals. The self-control model is a vulnerability model in the sense that poor self-control skills, as described above, place people at risk for depression under adverse conditions of external reinforcement.

The overgeneralization represented by depression is dealt with by the fact that self-control skills are assumed to act like a control program employed to manage all domains of behavior aimed at long-term goals. When self-control skills are called on to aid in readaptation in a major life area, poor skills will lead to maladaptation with implications for poor functioning in many areas.

Research

Research relevant to the self-control model of depression is diverse and has been reviewed elsewhere (Rehm, 1982, 1988). A few examples will be given here. Roth and Rehm (1980) examined the self-monitoring behavior of depressed and nondepressed psychiatric patients who viewed themselves interacting on videotape and counted specified positive and negative behaviors. Although there were no objective differences between groups, the depressed patients counted fewer positive and more negative behaviors than the nondepressed patients did. While the study did not distinguish between selective attention and different standards for calling an event positive or negative, it pointed to a depressive tendency to self-monitor in a biased fashion.

Rehm and Plakosh (1975), using a paper-and-pencil questionnaire, found that mildly depressed college students were more likely to express a preference for a small immediate reward in contrast to a larger delayed reward. Faced with a real, as opposed to a hypothetical choice, subjects in another study (O'Hara & Rehm, 1982) did not respond in a way related to depression scores.

Studies showing negative self-evaluation in depressed persons are plentiful (Lewinsohn et al., 1980). Performance standards of depressed persons appear to be higher because depressed persons often evaluate the same actual performance as less positive than do nondepressed persons. Shrauger and Terbovic (1976) demonstrated that low self-esteem (depressed) college students gave themselves a lower rating on a task than they gave a confederate who was duplicating the subject's performance.

Self-reinforcement studies have compared the rate at which depressed and nondepressed subjects administer token rewards and punishments to themselves based on their evaluations of their own performance. For example, Rozensky, Rehm, Pry, and Roth (1977) found that on a recognition memory task, depressed psychiatric patients self-rewarded less and self-punished more than nondepressed patients, even though their actual performance was equivalent. These studies have not usually differentiated self-reinforcement from self-evaluation.

Several scales have been developed to assess self-control behavior for research purposes. The Self-Control Questionnaire was developed explicitly to assess the deficits outlined in the self-control model of depression and it was used as a therapy outcome measure in several studies (Fuchs & Rehm, 1977; Rehm, Fuchs, Roth, Kornblith, & Romano, 1979). A Self-Control Schedule (Rosenbaum, 1980) measures a broader range of self-control behavior and has been used as an outcome or predictor variable in psychotherapy outcome studies. Heiby (1982) developed a Frequency of Self-Reinforcement Scale and has used the scale to identify depressed subjects with deficits suited to self-control therapy. Lewinsohn, Larson, and Muñoz (1982) developed a Cognitive Events Schedule with the similar purpose of assessing self-reinforcing cognitions.

Therapy

One of the research developments from this perspective has been the creation and evaluation of a therapy program based on the self-control model. Self-Control or Self-Management Therapy is a highly structured, manual-based, group-format program that presents the depression concepts of the model to participants and sends them out with weekly homework assignments to modify their self-management behavior. The program has been evaluated in six outcome studies by Rehm and his colleagues and in a number of independent replications (Rehm, 1984).

The first two studies were essentially validation studies that found the Self-Management program to be superior to nonspecific and waiting list controls (Fuchs & Rehm, 1977) and to an assertion skills comparison group (Rehm et al., 1979). The second two studies were attempts to evaluate the contribution of major components of the program, using a dismantling strategy (Kornblith, Rehm, O'Hara, & Lamparski, 1983; Rehm et al., 1981). Results indicated that outcomes did not seem to be affected by the omission of components such as the self-evaluation or self-reinforcement portions of the program. Two more studies looked at versions of the program written to focus on cognitive versus behavioral targets and their combination (Rehm, Kaslow, & Rabin, 1987; Rehm, Lamparski, Romano, & O'Hara, 1985). Results indicated equivalent effects on cognitive and behavioral outcome measures which were also independent of initial status on cognitive or behavioral measures of deficits. This nonspecificity of effects has become a common finding in the depression outcome literature.

Comment and Recent Developments

Kanfer and Hagerman (1981) presented a revised model of self-control and discussed its applicability to depression. The revision elaborated on the sequences of decisions that are made in the self-control process. For example, attributional processes are incorporated at both the self-monitoring and self-evaluation stages of regulation. In order to set the self-regulatory processes in motion, the person must have made an internal attribution about the cause of a problematic behavior. When monitored behavior is compared to a standard, an internal attribution is a necessary prerequisite for making a positive or negative judgment that will lead to self-reinforcement. The revised model also elaborated on the interaction of short- and long-term goals and standards which may be applied to specific behaviors. To date, the revised model has not led to extensive research relevant to depression.

As the depression model has been applied empirically, a number of issues have been raised. The specificity of some of the deficits to depression has been questioned (Gotlib, 1981) and the model has not been applied to the question of differentiating other forms of psychopathology. The results of the therapy outcome research have been puzzling. The self-control model appears to have utility as a heuristic for helping people understand and modify their own depressive behavior, yet it has not been demonstrated that specific deficits are remediated or that specific therapy procedures are effective. These are problems for the field of therapy for depression generally.

It has also become evident in self-control research that the original stages may not serve well for describing the separate processes involved in self-control (Rehm, 1988). For example, some of the studies often cited as evidence for negative self-monitoring in depression (Wener & Rehm, 1975; Nelson & Craighead, 1977) are actually studies of incidental memory rather than of self-observation. It would be conceptually clearer to separate self-monitoring into selective allocation of attention and a variety of inference or judgment processes. Depressed persons may choose to focus on negative events that they perceive with accuracy. Negative bias occurs in situations of ambiguity in which interpretation, inference, or judgment is involved. Estimation of numbers of negative events, self-evaluation, and attributions are all interpretive inferences that may evidence negative biases in depression when they pertain to self.

The concept of self-reinforcement has frequently been criticized (Catania, 1975), in part because of the difficulty of demonstrating in the laboratory a functional effect of a self-administered reinforcer. Alternative models of self-regulation may be desirable in order to account for the ways in which inference get translated into action. It may be more appropriate for a model applicable to depressive psychopathology

to consider how people problem-solve and plan, based on biased inferences, negative bias in recall, unrealistic standards, and negative expectancies. Rehm and Naus (in press), in a paper discussed in the next
section, presented one example of an approach to developing such a
model.

COGNITIVE THEORY

Beck's Cognitive Theory

Aaron T. Beck developed a cognitive theory that initially focused on
depression and has been expanded to other areas of psychopathology
and psychotherapy. Beck became dissatisfied with his psychodynamic
training because he felt it did not adequately account for clinical and
research phenomena he was seeing. He read George Kelly's *The Psychology of Personal Constructs* (1955) and was attracted to the cognitive conception of unique construct systems through which each
individual construes the world. From modern cognitive psychology he
adopted the theoretical construct of "schema." Schemata are structural units of stored information that also function to interpret new
experience. They act as templates against which new information is
compared and incorporated. Schemata vary from representations
of simple concepts (e.g., a chair schema operates in the simple act of
identifying an object as a chair) to complex interpretive rules (e.g.,
applying a schema about hotels allows a person to see that the bellhop
is hesitating because he expects a tip).

Beck's (1972) theory defined depression in cognitive terms. He saw
the essential elements of the disorder as the "cognitive triad": (a) a
negative view of self, (b) a negative view of the world, and (c) a negative
view of the future. The depressed person views the world through an
organized set of depressive schemata that distort experience about self,
the world, and the future in a negative direction.

A number of typical forms of cognitive distortion were identified
early in the development of the theory (Beck, 1963). Arbitrary inference
involves the arbitrary assumption that some negative event was caused
by oneself. For example, a friend appears preoccupied and the depressed person thinks, "What did I do to make him angry with me?"
Selective abstraction occurs when the person focuses on the negative
element in an otherwise positive set of information. An employer, while
congratulating the employee on a promotion, says, "Don't underestimate your future with this company." The depressive employee thinks,
"She thinks I have no self-confidence." Magnification and minimization involve overemphasizing negatives and underemphasizing positives. Inexact labeling involves giving a distorted label to an event and

then reacting to the label rather than to the event. The conversation with the boss is labeled a "criticism session," and the person anticipates being fired.

It is a basic tenet of the cognitive approach that a schematic interpretation always mediates between an experience and the emotional response to that experience. The negative, distorted cognitions that a person has in a particular situation are termed "automatic thoughts." They are automatic in the sense that the person is not aware of the interpretive process and may not be aware even of the thoughts themselves but only of the emotional consequences of the thoughts. These specific thoughts can be distinguished from underlying assumptions, which are more basic interpretive rules that form the automatic thoughts. In depression, the theme of the automatic thoughts is the perception of loss. Loss is the cognition that relates to depression. In contrast, perceptions of gain produce euphoria, perceptions of danger produce anxiety, and perceptions of offense produce anger.

Depressive schemata are activated when a major loss is perceived. An organized set of negative schemata, formed earlier in life when major losses were experienced, replaces nondistorted schemata when the person becomes depressed, and represents organized and elaborated views of self, the world, and the future. The negative schemata may be replaced in use by more realistic schemata under usual life circumstances, but they remain intact as "latent" schemata with the potential of reactivation under circumstances of loss. With time and the improvement of circumstances, these schemata may again become latent unless they are modified by some form of intervention. The overgeneralization that occurs in depression is due to the replacement of one broad network of schemata with another.

Research

A great deal of research can be considered relevant to Beck's cognitive theory of depression. A few studies will be cited that illustrate the major issues involved. The idea that depressed persons have a negative cognitive bias is widely demonstrated. When looked at in terms of the cognitive triad, it is clear that bias about self is negative, relative to interpretations of the behavior of others (Shrauger & Terbovic, 1976). A frequent and interesting finding is that these judgments of self seem more accurate than those of nondepressed persons (Alloy & Abramson, 1979; Lewinsohn et al., 1980; Roth & Rehm, 1980; Roth, Rehm, & Rozensky, 1980). People may have a positive set of expectations about their behavior that is offset during periods of depression.

Negative interpretations of the world have received less research attention, but it is clear that depressed persons perceive a higher frequency of negative events in the world and see problems as more severe and more difficult to cope with (Kuiper & MacDonald, 1983). Negative interpretations of the future have been assessed in a number of studies, in terms of expectancies for personal success and slower adjustment of these expectancies following positive feedback (Abramson et al., 1978). It is notable that negative interpretations of self are usually referenced to current and past functioning and depressed persons are negatively biased in memory about the past. "Negative view of the future" in Beck's cognitive triad is therefore not exclusive of past and present.

A basic premise of Beck's approach is that cognition intervenes between an event and the affective response to that event. One line of research relevant to this idea has been studies of mood induction by cognitive methods, for example, where subjects read a series of negative statements to induce a sad mood (Velten, 1968). Debate centers around the mechanisms of mood induction and how well they validate the premise. Zajonc (1980) argued that affect is the primary response in some cases but the issue may revolve around definition of cognition (Rachman, 1981, 1984).

The question of cognitive vulnerability to depression has been addressed in several ways. The Automatic Thoughts Scale (Hollon & Kendall, 1980) was devised to assess cognitive symptoms of a current depression. The Dysfunctional Attitudes Scale (Weissman & Beck, 1978, November), on the other hand, was devised to assess underlying assumptions that should represent an enduring trait of vulnerability to depression. Studies using these and other scales assessed patients during and after episodes of depression. Results were not consistent as to whether the trait measures remain deviant while the symptom measures improve (Eaves & Rush, 1984; Lewinsohn, Steinmetz, Larson, & Franklin, 1981). Prospective studies from this perspective have been infrequent and current evidence does not support the predictive value of measures of cognitive assumptions (O'Hara, Rehm, & Campbell, 1982).

It has been argued that "latent" depressive schemata may only be detected when the person is actually faced with a perceived loss and, therefore, a kind of challenge test will be necessary to demonstrate cognitive vulnerability. For example, negative schemata may not be manifest unless an adverse event sufficient to arouse sad affect activates them. A challenge test might assess reactions to failure and predict that the more extreme reactors in terms of altered perceptions of self, the world, and the future would be most susceptible to reactive depression. Evidence on this point to date is mixed (Blackburn & Smyth, 1985).

Therapy

Much of Beck's thinking developed in the context of clinical work with patients. Cognitive therapy developed along with the relevant theory of depression (Beck, 1976; Beck, Rush, Shaw, & Emery, 1979). Cognitive therapy is a complex collection of techniques that share the goal of making interpretations of events rational and realistic. Typically, therapy consists of a sequence of techniques focusing on behavior, then on automatic thoughts, and then on underlying assumptions. Behavioral techniques are sometimes used to get patients functioning to a level where they may better test out cognitive distortions. Patients are taught methods for identifying and recording automatic thoughts in their daily lives and are aided in refuting them. As automatic thoughts are reviewed, the underlying assumptions they represent become more clear and the therapist can use a variety of techniques to get patients to examine the rationality of their assumptions and to replace them.

The therapy relationship is seen as one of collaborative empiricism, whereby the therapist collaborates with the patient in identifying hypotheses and assumptions and in devising empirical tests of their validity in real life. As part of the therapy, the therapist closely structures sessions and frequently confirms with the patient the goals set and the progress made within sessions.

Cognitive therapy is the most thoroughly researched of the cognitive-behavioral approaches to intervention in depression. Several reviews are available (e.g., deRubeis & Beck, 1988; Dobson, 1989; Rehm & Kaslow, 1984; Williams, 1984). Most notable of the findings is that cognitive therapy has been demonstrated to produce effects equal to or superior to tricyclic antidepressants in ameliorating depression (Beck, Hollon, Young, Bedrosian, & Budenz, 1985; Blackburn, Bishop, Glenn, Whalley, & Christie, 1981; Murphy, Simons, Wetzel, & Lustman, 1984; Rush, Beck, Kovacs, & Hollon, 1977). It is also notable that the effects tend to be better maintained in terms of reducing future episodes of depression. Cognitive therapy also does as well as, or better than, other cognitive-behavioral approaches. Research on the mechanisms of therapy from the cognitive perspective is only beginning to be done.

Comment and Recent Developments

Beck's theory has been very influential in clinical psychology. It developed rapidly as a school of psychotherapy with research and application far beyond depression. As a theory it borrowed terms and constructs from cognitive psychology, without necessarily bringing with these terms some of the more specific theoretical distinctions and debates of cognitive science. Nonetheless, it facilitated the connection between clinical and cognitive psychology. Clinical psychology has often borrowed models and metaphors from more basic areas of psychology, and today cognition and memory are the mainstream of experimental psychological research.

New areas of research are developing which establish further connections between the psychopathology of depression and cognitive research. Self-referent encoding is the phenomenon wherein information about oneself is encoded and stored with existing self-schemata acting as an organizing structure. In depression, negative information is remembered better, presumably because it has been organized by predominantly negative schemata (Derry & Kuiper, 1981).

The topic of emotion and memory is rapidly expanding in both psychopathology and cognition (Blaney, 1986). Mood-congruent recall is the phenomenon whereby current mood state (episode of depression, natural mood, induced mood, and so on) influences retrieval such that memories with a similar emotional tone are more likely to be recalled (more frequently, more accurately, and with a shorter latency). When depressed, people are more likely to recall sad events and less likely to recall happy events. The related phenomenon, emotional state related learning, involves the laboratory demonstration that material learned while in one mood state is better recalled in the same mood state and that an alternate mood state interferes with recall. For example, neutral word lists learned in a sad mood are best recalled in a sad mood when other potentially interfering material has been learned in a distinctly different mood (Bower, 1981).

The effect of these new areas of research is that models are beginning to be developed that employ these concepts to explain elements of depression. Depression theory is being brought closer to cognitive psychology. Ingram (1984) discussed information processing in depression and the ways in which loss activates affective networks in memory, which in turn bias successive information processing. Teasdale (1983) developed a model in which individual differences in prior accumulated experiences of depression determine the nature and course of subsequent depression because stronger and more elaborate depressive structures are activated. Rehm and Naus (in press) attempted to describe the way in which depressive schemata about oneself may develop and how they might influence experience through the development, maintenance, recovery from, or treatment of an episode of depression. They discussed how mood can influence problem solving and planning by influencing standards and prior experiences accessed in that mood. These various papers brought the field closer to a new generation of cognitive theory in depression.

SUMMARY—AND FUTURE DIRECTIONS

For the past two decades, four theories have been prominent in accounting for the phenomena of depression from the learning or cognitive-behavioral perspective. Each approached the problem of the overgeneralized response of the depressed person to adverse circumstances. Lewinsohn explained the reduction in interrelated behaviors as the response to a loss or lack of response-contingent positive reinforcement from an important and generalized reinforcer. Seligman described the dimensions of overgeneralization in terms of a depressive attributional style leading to internal, stable, and global perceptions of helplessness following aversive events. Rehm postulated broad self-management skills that are inadequate to overcome the environment's failure to reinforce efforts toward long-term goals. Beck's cognitive theory hypothesized an extensive negative view of the world and self that is reactivated when loss is perceived.

Each of these theories was influential in shaping and developing research topics in the psychopathology of depression. The data generated influenced the theories, and revisions to the theories were presented. Each theory faced the question of whether the hypothesized deficits are actually vulnerability factors existing prior to and causally related to depression or whether they are merely concomitants or effects of depression.

Therapy conceptualizations and techniques have been developed from the theories. These therapies have been the focus of a growing body of therapy outcome research in depression. Evidence for the efficacy of these approaches now seems well established. Therapy research seems to suggest that each therapy program is effective but does not differentiate among them. Also, research has repeatedly failed to find effects specific to hypothesized deficits or to targeted outcome measures. These findings raise questions relevant to theory. New developments in theory need to take into account the fact that so many therapy strategies seem to be helpful in ameliorating so many components of the disorder.

The current theories seem to need major revision and expansion. What might be considered first drafts of new theories have appeared in the literature. Lewinsohn, Hoberman, Teri, and Hautzinger (1985), Abramson, Alloy, and Metalsky (1988), Abramson, Metalsky, and Alloy (in press), Ingram (1984), Teasdale (1983), and Rehm and Naus (in press) presented new models that attempted to expand the purview of the earlier theories. All of the current approaches are developing in a more cognitive direction and are coming closer to recent advances in cognitive psychology. Models that formerly addressed depression alone are beginning to be expanded to consider how the constructs of the theory might differentiate other emotions and disorders.

The theories also need to encompass new knowledge about depression, coming from other fields. Epidemiological data suggest that cultural changes may be producing a greater risk for depression among young people than in prior generations. Theory should be able to address these mechanisms in society (Seligman, 1989). Studies of coping and stress expand our knowledge about the ways in which ongoing stressors may have an impact on mental health and vice versa. Biological correlates of depression are being identified and need to be taken into account in psychological theories. Biological, environmental, and psychological factors seem to be related like loosely interconnected gears. The slowing down or speeding up of any one gear has an effect on the total machine. We need integrative models that suggest how biology, environment, and psychological predispositions interact in the etiology, maintenance, and resolution of depression. Significant advances have been made but new advances in cognitive-behavioral theory can also be expected.

REFERENCES

Abramson, L. Y., Alloy, L. B., & Metalsky, G. I. (1988). The cognitive diathesis-stress theories of depression: Toward an adequate evaluation of the theories' validities. In L. B. Alloy (Ed.), *Cognitive processes in depression* (pp. 3–30). New York: Guilford.

Abramson, L. Y., Garber, J., Edwards, N. B., & Seligman, M. E. P. (1978). Expectancy changes in depression and schizophrenia. *Journal of Abnormal Psychology, 87,* 102–109.

Abramson, L. Y., Metalsky, G. I., & Alloy, L. B. (in press). The hopelessness theory of depression: A metatheoretical analysis with implications for psychopathology research. *Psychological Review.*

Abramson, L. Y., & Sackheim, H. A. (1977). A paradox in depression: Uncontrollability and self-blame. *Psychological Bulletin, 84,* 838–851.

Abramson, L. Y., Seligman, M. E. P., & Teasdale, J. D. (1978). Learned helplessness in humans: Critique and reformulation. *Journal of Abnormal Psychology, 87,* 32–48.

Alloy, L. B., & Abramson, L. Y. (1979). Judgment of contingency in depressed and nondepressed students: Sadder but wiser. *Journal of Experimental Psychology, 108,* 447–485.

Alloy, L. B., Clements, C., & Kolden, G. (1985). The cognitive diathesis-stress theories of depression: Therapeutic implications. In S. Reiss & R. R. Bootzin (Eds.), *Theoretical issues in behavior therapy* (pp. 379–410). Orlando, FL: Academic Press.

Bandura, A. (1971). Vicarious and self-reinforcement processes. In R. Glaser (Ed.), *The nature of reinforcement* (pp. 228–278). New York: Academic Press.

Beach, S. R. H., & O'Leary, K. D. (1986). The treatment of depression occurring in the context of marital discord. *Behavior Therapy, 17,* 43–49.

Beck, A. T. (1963). Thinking and depression: I. Idiosyncratic content and cognitive distortions. *Archives of General Psychiatry, 9,* 324–333.

Beck, A. T. (1972). *Depression: Causes and treatment.* Philadelphia: University of Pennsylvania Press.

Beck, A. T. (1976). *Cognitive therapy and the emotional disorders.* New York: International Universities Press.

Beck, A. T., Hollon, S. D., Young, J. E., Bedrosian, R. C., & Budenz, D. (1985). Treatment of depression with cognitive therapy and amitriptyline. *Archives of General Psychiatry, 42,* 14–152.

Beck, A. T., Rush, A. J., Shaw, B. F., & Emery, G. (1979). *Cognitive therapy for depression.* New York: Guilford.

Blackburn, I. M., Bishop, S., Glenn, A. I. M., Whalley, L. J., & Christie, J. E. (1981). The efficacy of cognitive therapy in depression: A treatment trial using cognitive therapy and pharmacotherapy, each alone and in combination. *British Journal of Psychiatry, 139,* 181–189.

Blackburn, I. M., & Smyth, P. (1985). A test of cognitive vulnerability in individuals prone to depression. *British Journal of Clinical Psychology, 24,* 61–62.

Blaney, P. H. (1986). Affect and memory: A review. *Psychological Bulletin, 49,* 229–246.

Bower, G. H. (1981). Mood and memory. *American Psychologist, 36,* 129–147.

Brown, R. A., & Lewinsohn, P. M. (1984). A psychoeducational approach to the treatment of depression: Comparison of group, individual, and minimal contact procedures. *Journal of Consulting and Clinical Psychology, 52,* 774–783.

Catania, A. C. (1975). The myth of self-reinforcement. *Behaviorism, 3,* 192–199.

Derry, P. A., & Kuiper, N. A. (1981). Schematic processing and self-reference in clinical depression. *Journal of Abnormal Psychology, 90,* 286–297.

deRubeis, R., & Beck, A. T. (1988). Cognitive therapy. In L. S. Dobson (Ed.), *Handbook of cognitive-behavioral therapies* (pp. 273–306). New York: Guilford.

Dobson, K. S. (1989). A meta-analysis of the efficacy of cognitive therapy for depression. *Journal of Consulting and Clinical Psychology, 57,* 414–419.

Eaves, G., & Rush, A. J. (1984). Cognitive patterns in symptomatic and remitted unipolar major depression. *Journal of Abnormal Psychology, 93,* 31–40.

Ferster, C. B. (1973). A functional analysis of depression. *American Psychologist, 28,* 857–870.

Ferster, C. B. (1977, April). *Functional analysis of the verbal aspects of depression.* Paper presented at The Loyola University Symposium, Chicago.

Ferster, C. B. (1981). A functional analysis of behavior therapy. In L. P. Rehm (Ed.), *Behavior therapy for depression: Present status and future directions* (pp. 181–196). New York: Academic Press.

Fuchs, C. Z., & Rehm, L. P. (1977). A self-control behavior therapy program for depression. *Journal of Consulting and Clinical Psychology, 45,* 206–215.

Gotlib, I. H. (1981). Self-reinforcement and recall: Differential deficits in depressed and nondepressed psychiatric inpatients. *Journal of Abnormal Psychology, 90,* 521–530.

Grosscup, S. J., & Lewinsohn, P. M. (1980). Unpleasant and pleasant events, and mood. *Journal of Clinical Psychology, 36,* 252–259.

Hautzinger, M., Linden, M., & Hoffman, N. (1982). Distressed couples with and without a depressed partner: An analysis of their verbal interaction. *Journal of Behavior Therapy and Experimental Psychiatry, 13,* 307–314.

Heiby, E. M. (1982). A self-reinforcement questionnaire. *Behavior Research and Therapy, 20,* 397–401.

Hersen, M., Bellack, A. S., Himmelhoch, J. M., & Thase, M. E. (1984). Effects of social skill training, amitriptyline, and psychotherapy in unipolar depressed women. *Behavior Therapy, 15,* 21–40.

Hollon, S. D., & Kendall, P. C. (1980). Cognitive self-statements in depression: Development of an Automatic Thoughts Questionnaire. *Cognitive Therapy and Research, 4,* 383–395.

Ingram, R. E. (1984). Toward an information-processing analysis of depression. *Cognitive Therapy and Research, 8,* 443–478.

Ivanov-Smolensky, A. G. (1928). The pathology of conditioned reflexes and the so-called psychogenic depression. *Journal of Nervous and Mental Disease, 67,* 346–350.

Jacobson, N. S., Holtzworth-Munroe, A., & Schmaling, K. B. (1989). Marital therapy and spouse involvement in the treatment of depression agoraphobia, and alcoholism. *Journal of Consulting and Clinical Psychology, 57,* 5–10.

Kanfer, F. H. (1970). Self-regulation: Research, issues and speculations. In C. Neuringer and J. L. Michael (Eds.), *Behavior modification in clinical psychology* (pp. 178–220). New York: Appleton-Century-Crofts.

Kanfer, F. H., & Hagerman, S. (1981). The role of self-regulation. In L. P. Rehm (Ed.), *Behavior therapy for depression: Present status and future directions* (pp. 143–179). New York: Academic Press.

Kelly, G. A. (1955). *The psychology of personal constructs.* New York: Norton.

Kendall, P. C., & Watson, D. (1989). *Anxiety and depression: Distinctive and overlapping features.* San Diego: Academic Press.

Kornblith, S. J., Rehm, L. P., O'Hara, M. W., & Lamparski, D. M. (1983). The contribution of self-reinforcement training and behavioral assignments to the efficacy of self-control therapy for depression. *Cognitive Therapy and Research, 7,* 499–527.

Kuiper, S. D., & MacDonald, M. R. (1983). Schematic processing in depression: The self-based consensus bias. *Cognitive Therapy and Research, 7,* 469–484.

Lewinsohn, P. M. (1974). A behavioral approach to depression. In R. J. Friedman & M. M. Katz (Eds.), *The psychology of depression: Contemporary theory and research* (pp. 157–185). New York: Wiley.

Lewinsohn, P. M., Antonuccio, D. O., Breckenridge, J., & Teri, L. (1987). *The coping with depression course: A psychoeducational intervention for unipolar depression.* Eugene, OR: Castalia Press.

Lewinsohn, P. M., Biglan, A., & Zeiss, A. M. (1976). Behavioral treatment of depression. In P. O. Davidson (Ed.), *The behavioral management of anxiety, depression and pain* (pp. 91–146). New York: Brunner/Mazel.

Lewinsohn, P. M., & Graf, M. (1973). Pleasant activities and depression. *Journal of Consulting and Clinical Psychology, 41,* 261–268.

Lewinsohn, P. M., Hoberman, H., Teri, L., & Hautzinger, M. (1985). An integrative theory of depression. In S. Reiss & R. R. Bootzin (Eds.), *Theoretical issues in behavior therapy.* New York: Academic Press.

Lewinsohn, P. M., Larson, D. W., & Muñoz, R. F. (1982). The measurement of expectancies and other cognitions in depressed individuals. *Cognitive Theory and Research, 6,* 437–446.

Lewinsohn, P. M., & Libet, J. (1972). Pleasant events, activity schedules, and depression. *Journal of Abnormal Psychology, 79,* 291–295.

Lewinsohn, P., Mischel, W., Chaplin, W., & Barton, R. (1980). Social competence and depression: The role of illusory self-perceptions. *Journal of Abnormal Psychology, 89,* 203–213.

Lewinsohn, P. M., Steinmetz, J. L., Larson, D. W., & Franklin, J. (1981). Depression-related cognitions: Antecedent or consequence? *Journal of Abnormal Psychology, 90,* 213–219.

Lewinsohn, P. M., & Talkington, J. (1979). Studies on the measurement of unpleasant events and relations with depression. *Applied Psychological Measurement, 3,* 83–101.

Lewinsohn, P. M., Youngren, M. A., & Grosscup, S. J. (1979). Reinforcement and depression. In R. A. Depue (Ed.), *The psychobiology of the depressive disorders: Implications for the effects of stress* (pp. 291–315). New York: Academic Press.

MacPhillamy, D. J., & Lewinsohn, P. M. (1974). Depression as a function of levels of desired and obtained pleasure. *Journal of Abnormal Psychology, 83,* 651–657.

MacPhillamy, D. J., & Lewinsohn, P. M. (1982). The Pleasant Events Schedule: Studies on reliability, validity, and scale intercorrelation. *Journal of Consulting and Clinical Psychology, 50,* 363–380.

Marston, A. R. (1964). Personality variables related to self-reinforcement. *Journal of Psychology, 58,* 169–175.

Maser, J. D., & Cloninger, C. R. (in press). *Comorbidity in anxiety and mood disorders.* Washington, DC: American Psychiatric Press.

Mathews, C. O. (1977). A review of behavioral theories of depression and a self-regulation model for depression. *Psychotherapy: Theory, Research and Practice, 14,* 79–86.

McLean, P. D., & Hakstian, A. R. (1979). Clinical depression: Comparative efficacy of outpatient treatments. *Journal of Consulting and Clinical Psychology, 47,* 818–836.

Metalsky, G. J., Abramson, L. Y., Seligman, M. E. P., Semmel, A., & Peterson, C. (1982). Attributional styles and life events in the classroom: Vulnerability and invulnerability to depressive mood reactions. *Journal of Personality and Social Psychology, 43,* 612–617.

Miller, W. R., & Seligman, M. E. P. (1975). Depression and learned helplessness in man. *Journal of Abnormal Psychology, 84,* 228–238.

Murphy, G. E., Simons, A. D., Wetzel, R. D., & Lustman, P. J. (1984). Cognitive therapy and pharmacotherapy, singly and together, in the treatment of depression. *Archives of General Psychiatry, 41,* 33–41.

Nelson, R. E., & Craighead, W. E. (1977). Selective recall of positive and negative feedback, self-control behaviors, and depression. *Journal of Abnormal Psychology, 86,* 379–388.

Nezu, A. M. (1986). Efficacy of a social problem-solving therapy approach for unipolar depression. *Journal of Consulting and Clinical Psychology, 54,* 196–202.

Nezu, A. M., Nezu, C. M., & Perri, M. G. (1989). *Problem-solving therapy for depression: Theory, research, and clinical guidelines.* New York: Wiley.

O'Hara, M. W., & Rehm, L. P. (1982). Choice of immediate versus delayed reinforcement and depression. *Psychological Reports, 50,* 925–926.

O'Hara, M. W., Rehm, L. P., & Campbell, S. B. (1982). Predicting depressive symptomatology: Cognitive-behavioral models and postpartum depression. *Journal of Abnormal Psychology, 91,* 457–461.

Peterson, C., Semmel, A., Von Baeyer, C., Abramson, L. Y., Metalsky, G. I., & Seligman, E. P. (1982). The attributional style questionnaire. *Cognitive Therapy and Research, 6,* 287–299.

Rachman, S. (1981). The primacy of affect: Some theoretical implications. *Behaviour Research and Therapy, 19,* 279–290.

Rachman, S. (1984). A reassessment of the "Primacy of Affect." *Cognitive Therapy and Research, 8,* 579–584.

Raps, C. S., Peterson, C., Reinhard, K. E., Abramson, L. Y., & Seligman, M. E. P. (1982). Attributional style among depressed patients. *Journal of Abnormal Psychology, 91,* 102–108.

Rehm, L. P. (1977). A self-control model of depression. *Behavior Therapy, 8,* 787–804.

Rehm, L. P. (1978). Mood, pleasant events and unpleasant events: Two pilot studies. *Journal of Consulting and Clinical Psychology, 46,* 849–853.

Rehm, L. P. (1982). Self-management and depression. In P. Karoly & F. H. Kanfer (Eds.), *The psychology of self-management: From theory to practice* (pp. 522–570). New York: Pergamon.

Rehm, L. P. (1984). Self-management therapy for depression. *Advances in Behaviour Therapy and Research, 6,* 83–98.

Rehm, L. P. (1988). Self-management and cognitive processes in depression. In L. B. Alloy (Ed.), *Cognitive processes in depression* (pp. 143–176). New York: Guilford.

Rehm, L. P., Fuchs, C. Z., Roth, D. M., Kornblith, S. J., & Romano, J. M. (1979). A comparison of self-control and assertion skills treatments of depression. *Behavior Therapy, 10,* 429–442.

Rehm, L. P., & Kaslow, N. J. (1984). Behavioral approaches to depression: Research results and clinical recommendations. In C. M. Franks (Ed.), *New developments in behavior therapy: From research to clinical application* (pp. 155–230). New York: Haworth Press.

Rehm, L. P., Kaslow, N. J., & Rabin, A. S. (1987). Cognitive and behavioral targets in a self-control therapy program for depression. *Journal of Consulting and Clinical Psychology, 55,* 60–67.

Rehm, L. P., Kornblith, S. J., O'Hara, M. W., Lamparski, D. M., Romano, J. M., & Volkin, J. (1981). An evaluation of major components in a self-control behavior therapy program for depression. *Behavior Modification, 5,* 459–490.

Rehm, L. P., Lamparski, D., Romano, J. M., & O'Hara, M. W. (1985). *A comparison of behavioral, cognitive and combined target version of a self-control therapy program for depression.* Unpublished manuscript, University of Pittsburgh.

Rehm, L. P., & Naus, M. J. (in press). A memory model of emotion. In R. E. Ingram (Ed.), *Contemporary approaches to depression: Treatment, research and therapy.* New York: Plenum.

Rehm, L. P., & Plakosh, P. (1975). Preference for immediate reinforcement in depression. *Journal of Behavioral Therapy and Experimental Psychiatry, 6,* 101–103.

Rosenbaum, M. (1980). A schedule for assessing self-control behaviors: Preliminary findings. *Behavior Therapy, 11,* 109–121.

Roth, D., & Rehm, L. P. (1980). Relationships among self-monitoring processes, memory, and depression. *Cognitive Therapy and Research, 4,* 149–159.

Roth, D., Rehm, L. P., & Rozensky, R. A. (1980). Self-reward, self-punishment and depression. *Psychological Reports, 47,* 3–7.

Rozensky, R. A., Rehm, L. P., Pry, G., & Roth, D. (1977). Depression and self-reinforcement behavior in hospital patients. *Journal of Behavior Therapy and Experimental Psychiatry, 8,* 35–38.

Rude, S. S. (1986). Relative benefits of assertion or cognitive self-control treatment for depression as a function of proficiency in each domain. *Journal of Consulting and Clinical Psychology, 54,* 390–394.

Rush, A. J., Beck, A. T., Kovacs, M., & Hollon, S. (1977). Comparative efficacy of cognitive therapy and pharmacotherapy in the treatment of depressed outpatients. *Cognitive Therapy and Research, 1,* 17–38.

Seligman, M. E. P. (1974). Depression and learned helplessness. In R. J. Friedman & M. M. Katz (Eds.), *The psychology of depression: Contemporary theory and research* (pp. 83–113). New York: Winston/Wiley.

Seligman, M. E. P. (1975). *Helplessness: On depression, development and death.* San Francisco: Freeman.

Seligman, M. E. P. (1981). A learned helplessness point of view. In L. P. Rehm (Ed.), *Behavior therapy for depression: Present status and future directions.* New York: Academic Press.

Seligman, M. E. P. (1989). Research in clinical psychology: Why is there so much depression today? In I. S. Cohen (Ed.), *The G. Stanley Halt Lecture Series: Vol. 9.* Washington, DC: American Psychological Association.

Seligman, M. E. P., & Maier, S. F. (1967). Failure to escape traumatic shock. *Journal of Experimental Psychology, 74,* 1–9.

Shrauger, J. S., & Terbovic, M. L. (1976). Self-evaluations and assessments of performance by self and others. *Journal of Consulting and Clinical Psychology, 44,* 564–572.

Teasdale, J. D. (1983). Negative thinking in depression: Cause, effect, or reciprocal relationship? *Advances in Behaviour Research and Therapy, 5,* 27–49.

Velten, E., Jr. (1968). A laboratory task for induction of mood states. *Behaviour Research and Therapy, 6,* 473–482.

Weiner, B., Frieze, I., Kukla, A., Reed, L., Rest, S., & Rosenbaum, R. M. (1971). *Perceiving the causes of success and failure.* Morristown, NJ: General Learning Press.

Weissman, A. N., & Beck, A. T. (1978, November). *Development and validation of the Dysfunctional Attitude Scale.* Paper presented at the annual convention of the Association for the Advancement of Behavior Therapy, Chicago.

Wener, A. E., & Rehm, L. P. (1975). Depressive affect: A test of behavioral hypotheses. *Journal of Abnormal Psychology, 84,* 221–227.

Williams, J. M. G. (1984). Cognitive-behavioral therapy for depression: Problems and perspectives. *British Journal of Psychiatry, 145,* 254–262.

Zajonc, R. B. (1980). Feeling and thinking: Preferences need no inferences. *American Psychologist, 35,* 151–175.

Zeiss, A. M., Lewinsohn, P. M., & Muñoz, R. (1979). Nonspecific improvement effects in depression using interpersonal, cognitive and pleasant events focused treatments. *Journal of Consulting and Clinical Psychology, 47,* 427–439.

Zuroff, D. C. (1980). Distortions of memory and attribution in depressed, formerly depressed, and never depressed. *Psychological Reports, 46,* 415–425.

Zuroff, D. C. (1981). Depression and attribution: Some new data and a review of old data. *Cognitive Therapy and Research, 5,* 273–282.

CHAPTER 5

Depression: The Psychosocial Theory

BENJAMIN B. WOLMAN, PhD

CONCEPTUAL FRAMEWORK

DEFINING DEPRESSION

The word *depression* has been used in several different ways, to describe somewhat different issues. Since it usually relates to affects, it belongs to the class of *Affective Disorders* in DSM-III (American Psychiatric Association, 1980). Depressed individuals undergo mood changes, thus depression is included in DSM-III-R (American Psychiatric Association, 1987) in the class of *Mood Disorders*. In daily use, depression connotes a variety of negative feelings, such as disappointment, frustration, defeat, sadness, despair, weakness, helplessness, hopelessness, and so on. Apparently no scientific research could put all these feelings into one nosological class, and scientists have tried to offer a more precise and concise definition.

Abraham (1927) and Freud (1917/1956) stressed self-criticism and self-hatred. Bibring (1953), Seligman (1975), and others pointed to the feelings of defeat and helplessness. Beck (1967) and his followers emphasized a pessimistic outlook on life and a feeling of one's own hopelessness. Nemiah (1985) pointed to feelings of loneliness and sadness.

The *Random House Dictionary* has several definitions of depression. Depression in psychiatry and psychology is defined as "emotional dejection greater and more prolonged than that warranted by any objective reason." Other definitions are: "a low state of vital powers or functional activity," or "dejection, sadness, gloom."

Wolman's *Dictionary of Behavioral Science* (1989) gives the following definition: "**Depression**, as opposed to other negative feelings, such as sadness, unhappiness, frustration, sorrow or grief, is a *feeling of helplessness and blaming oneself for being helpless*. Depression is self-directed hatred usually associated with hatred directed toward others. Depression is *endogenous* when it comes from within; it is *exogenous* when it is a reaction to misfortunes."

This definition limits depression to the combination of a feeling of helplessness and self-directed accusation; it excludes other negative feelings.

Exogenous Depression

Every human being is exposed to stressful events; some events are exceedingly stressful and cause *exogenous* depression (Dohrenwend & Dohrenwend, 1974).

Exogenous depression is normal provided it is, like all other normal human emotions, appropriate, proportionate, controllable, and adjustive. Achievement and victory produce elation; frustration and defeat cause depression. When depression corresponds to what has really taken place, it does not indicate poor mental health, but feeling unhappy in victory and enjoying defeat are morbid emotional reactions. Usually joy and sorrow correspond to the magnitude of fortunate and unfortunate events. When one is ecstatically happy at irrelevant achievements and reacts with feelings of despair to mild frustrations, the reactions are pathological.

Endogenous Depression

Quite often my patients say, "I feel miserable. I have no reason to feel unhappy. I have nothing to complain about, but why do I feel so miserable?" Apparently, the depression comes from within; it is *endogenous*. A decrease in self-esteem and a low estimate of one's power form the common denominator of depressive states. The less realistic one's estimate is of one's ability to cope with hardships, the more severe is the depression. No human being can always be successful in dealing with his or her problems, and every human life represents a chain of successes and failures. Endogenous depression reflects one's disbelief in oneself and in one's ability to cope with difficulties. It is a feeling of being weak and unable to withstand hardship, of helplessness and resentment for being helpless.

THE CONCEPT OF POWER AND THE "LUST FOR LIFE"

The behavior of all living organisms has an immanent and universal goal, *survival.* All living organisms fight for survival; all of them eat to live and defend themselves against being eaten or destroyed.

The process of life is a process of oxidation, digestion, metabolism, and so on. The higher the species stands on the evolutionary ladder, the more complex are its life processes. The behavior of all organisms is an aggressive–defensive process, for each organism either devours others or protects itself, by fight or flight, against being devoured.

The entire biological process can be presented as a continuous struggle aimed at the destruction of the prey by the predator or of the predator by the prey. An organism can be forceful, full of energy, capable of providing food for itself, and well prepared for self-defense. Or it may be sick, declining, and dwindling to nothing. When the vital energies become exhausted and vitality reaches the zero point, the organism dies.

I define the *drive for survival* as follows:

> All living matter is endowed with biochemical energy derived from the universal energy. At a certain evolutionary level this biochemical energy is transformed into mental energy. Mental energy serves survival. The apparatus of discharge, the instinctual force, reflects the universal urge to fight for survival. It is the "Lust for Life," the craving of all living matter to *stay alive*.

Pavlov (1928) introduced the term "instinct of life." According to Pavlov, "All life is nothing other than the realization of one purpose, viz., the preservation of life itself, the tireless labor which may be called the general instinct of life."

Survival depends on the amount of power that enables the organism to cope with hardships and dangers. I have defined power as "the ability to satisfy needs," and survival is the arch-need and the prerequisite of all other needs. Further on, "The amount of power the individual possesses indicates how well he or she can protect life and satisfy [his or her] own and others' needs. Omnipotence is the summit of power, death is the zero point" (Wolman, 1989, p. 258).

The awareness of one's ability to defend oneself is tantamount to the feeling of power. When people believe in their own power they feel strong, elated, and happy. When people perceive themselves as being weak, they feel unhappy and are depressed. Depression is, primarily, a feeling of weakness, inferiority, helplessness, and inability to cope with adverse situations, plus self-directed resentment for being weak. Whatever the origins of the feelings of weakness and helplessness, most often they are associated with blaming oneself (Abramson & Sackeim, 1977; Beck, 1967; Peterson & Seligman, 1983).

Some human beings give up the fight. In such cases of "learned helplessness," the lack of self-confidence reduces the ability of the immune system to fight diseases. The decline in "lust for life" can make the organism defenseless (Ader & Cohen, 1984; Seligman, 1975; Simonton & Simonton, 1978).

EROS AND ARES

Vital energies can be used in two directions, to fight or to help. These two directions can be symbolically represented by two gods of ancient Greek mythology.

Ares, the ancient Greek god of war, is the symbol of aggression and destructiveness. *Eros,* the ancient Greek god of love is the symbol of caring, protecting, and loving. *Libido* is the name of the emotional energy of *Eros, destrudo* is the name of the emotional energy for *Ares.*

People can protect themselves by fight and/or by associating with others. In the philogenetic history of organic life, Ares, or hostile behavior, is definitely older than Eros, which is cooperative, loving behavior. Only after a long evolutionary process have animals become capable of helping and caring for each other. Even procreation was initially void of sex, and certainly void of love (Wolman, in press).

To love means to give, to do everything for whomever one loves. Weaklings have nothing to give, but strong individuals can give, and one needs much more power to create than to destroy. Scores of skilled workers build a house, but one half-wit can destroy it by setting it on fire. Parents, educators, and doctors help an infant to grow up, but one stray bullet can kill the human being they have nurtured.

Power is the main determinant of survival; thus, being strong makes one elated, being weak makes one depressed. Victory over obstacles makes one feel happy; defeat makes one feel miserable.

NOSOLOGY

One can develop several classificatory systems of any group of people on the basis of gender, age, race, religion, income, or any other characteristic. Every classificatory system is rational, as long as no one belongs to two categories and no case is left out.

DSM-III-R (American Psychiatric Association, 1987) introduced the following nosological system for affective disorders, changing their name to Mood Disorders. This classificatory system divides mood disorders into four groups: (a) manic disorders, (b) bipolar disorders, (c) major depressive episodes, and (d) depressive disorders. Symptomatological consideration seems to be the rationale of the system developed by the American Psychiatric Association in both DSM-III and DSM-III-R.

My nosological system (Krauss & Krauss, 1977; Wolman, 1973) is based on etiologic considerations of cause and effect. All mental disorders, including depression, are either inherited or acquired. Mental disorders caused by genetic factors are *Genosomatogenic.* Mental disorders caused by interaction with the physical or chemical environment are *Ecosomatogenic* (*Ecos* means environment). Mental disorders caused by psychological environment are *Psychosociogenic*. Interaction among the three types of factors is a frequent phenomenon; thus, clinical diagnosis is a difficult and highly responsible task (Wolman, 1978a).

PSYCHOSOCIOGENIC DETERMINANTS

Since Freud, human relations have been perceived in a broad context of growth and development, fixation, and regression. All human beings are born both lovers and haters, and the interaction in early childhood greatly influences the balance of intraindividual and interindividual cathexes of libido and destrudo.

I have introduced a division of human relationships into three types: instrumental (I), mutual (M), and vectorial (V). The instrumental, taking attitude implies concern with satisfying one's own needs; infants are takers and their psychosocial attitudes are *instrumental*. Through growth and learning they may acquire the *mutual* attitude of giving and taking; in mature sexual relations and good marriages the participants are mutual. When one becomes more mature, one may become capable of giving without taking; mature parents display a giving, *vectorial* attitude to their children (Wolman, 1973).

Observing mental patients in hospitals and in private offices, one can't help noticing three distinct patterns of behavior. Some patients are sociopathic–*hyperinstrumental* types; they care only for themselves and tend to exploit others. On the other extreme, there are the *hypervectorial* schizo-type patients, who care for others even at their own expense. The third category are the depressive *dysmutuals,* who swing from one extreme to another. The hyperinstrumental sociopaths are extremely selfish and overinvolved with themselves, the hypervectorial schizophrenics tend to be underinvolved with themselves, and the dysmutual depressives go from one extreme to the other. The hypervectorial schizo-type patients care too much for others and very little love is left for themselves. Sometimes they hate themselves for not loving enough. The depressive dysmutuals swing from being very friendly to being very hostile to themselves and to others.

The depressive dysmutuals tend to exaggerate and to advertise their feelings. They may take signs of friendliness as evidence of great love. They often imagine that other people are in love with them or hate them. A repeated pattern of these feelings often assumes the dimensions of paranoia (Kraepelin, 1921; Schwartz, 1964; Waelder, 1951; Wolman, 1973).

In 1911 Karl Abraham was the first psychoanalyst to interpret the manic-depressive disorder. Abraham proposed a most valuable hypothesis that unfortunately failed to attract much attention. At that time, Freud maintained that repressed sexuality leads to anxiety; Abraham hypothesized that repressed hostility leads to depression. Abraham's essay, with its emphasis on hostility, has influenced my thoughts (Abraham, 1927).

CATHEXIS

In psychoanalysis, cathexis means charging or investing an object or an idea with emotional energy. I have introduced the concepts of *interindividual cathexis,* which is the balance of emotional energy of libido or destrudo cathected, that is invested, in an interaction between two or more individuals; and *intraindividual cathexis,* which is the balance of destrudo or libido individuals invest in themselves, and/or in various parts of their own body. Thus, when A loves B, A invests (cathects) some of his or her libido into B, the love object. B is the receiver of these *interindividual* cathexes. Because B, as the receiver of cathexes, may feel loved and cared for, his or her *intraindividual* balance of libido cathexes is increased.

I know of no clear-cut neurophysiological interpretation of the increase of the inner emotional balance, but one can easily observe improved self-esteem, courage, and activity in people, especially children, who receive the interindividual cathexes. Most probably, the issue of cathexis is related to the neuropsychological reactions of the immune system (Ader, 1981; Ader & Cohen, 1984). The resilience in fighting diseases is determined by the immune system, its genetic predisposition, and psychosomatic reactions. Being a recipient of interindividual cathexes of libido improves the intraindividual cathexes and strengthens the immune system.

A child who does not receive adequate loads of interindividual libido cathexes feels deprived and rejected. The child's intraindividual balance of cathexes becomes inadequate, and, emotionally undernourished, the child craves love. Such children have "hungry libidos" and, as Fenichel (1945) pointed out, they become depressed "love addicts." Quite often, their need to receive love leads to a regressive behavior and to a compensatory intake of enormous quantities of food. Depression is frequently associated with obesity (Wolman, 1982a).

GENETIC PREDISPOSITION

The above described three types of psychosocial mental disorders do not include disorders caused by genetic factors such as, for instance, Down's syndrome, nor disorders caused by physical, chemical, prenatal, natal, and postnatal factors. It must be mentioned that even the three types of psychosociogenic mental disorders could be related to genetic *predisposition,* but they are not genetically transmitted (Beckham & Leber, 1985; Howells, 1980; Wolman, 1987). More about genetics in the following section.

THE LEVELS OF DISORDERS

There are distinct degrees of severity in mental disorders, but the traditional distinction between neurosis and psychosis is today a controversial issue. Pinsker and Spitzer (1977) reported that, in DSM-III, *psychoses* and *neuroses* are not used as principles of classification.

According to Pinsker and Spitzer, the term *psychotic* is used as an adjective to describe certain aspects of severity of illness. Neurosis is referred to as a speculative etiologic concept. Probably, the concept of psychoses as a group of conditions was rooted in mental hospitals at a time when no one was identified as a mentally ill person unless psychotic. But if the term psychotic describes a certain degree of impairment of reality testing, disruption of thinking process, disorganization of behavior, or inability to function, the disorder (or disorders) which causes the psychotic impairment must have been present in mild form before the psychotic level of impairment was reached.

Thus, I am using the terms neurosis and psychosis as *levels* of mental disorders, and as a link between the various degrees of endogenous depression, viewed as a nosological entity, on a continuum of neurotic symptoms (hysterias, etc.) through hysteroid character neuroses, latent psychosis, and full-blown psychotic depression. The moods of elation and depression are reflections of shifts in the balance of libidinal cathexes from self-love to object love, from self-hate to object hate, from love to hate, and vice versa.

In my nosological system, hysteria and conversions belong to the class of neuroses. They are clusters of symptoms of the basic dysmutual-depressive pathology, to be described later on. When these symptoms become fortified by rigid defense mechanisms, such as rationalization and denial, the neurosis turns into character neurosis. When the defenses prove to be inadequate, and the individual faces psychotic breakdown, but somehow desperately holds on to whatever was left from the defenses, it is latent depressive psychosis. When the defenses fail, a manifest depressive psychosis develops.

I avoid the terms *unipolar* and *bipolar,* because every manifest psychotic depression can develop depressive and manic symptoms. I also avoid the term *manic-depressive psychosis,* for there are five possible clusters of symptoms in manifest psychotic depression, to be described later on.

ETIOLOGY

Quite often, similar symptoms are caused by different causes. For instance, high body temperature is definitely a sign of disease, but it may be a sign of various diseases. Many symptoms or clusters of symptoms, such as indigestion, chest pains, headaches, and so on are not necessarily indicative of a particular disease.

Years ago, in a study of infantile autism, I arrived at the conclusion that the two theories of its organic or psychologic origin deal with two different disorders. Infantile autism type A is a neurological disorder, whereas infantile autism type B is a subtype of childhood schizophrenia, a psychosocial disorder caused by an extreme case of maternal rejection (Wolman, 1970).

One should draw a distinction between the ecosomatogenic depression caused by physical and chemical factors and the psychosociogenic depression caused by social and psychological factors. It seems in both types of depression there is a certain degree of genetic predisposition (Bertelsen, 1985; Depue & Iacomo, 1989; Gershon, 1987). It is possible that depressive disorders are a product of interaction between the genetic predisposition and environmental, psychosocial factors (Cadoret, O'Gorman, Heywood, & Troughton, 1985; Cole, Schatzberg, & Frazier, 1978). Despite a good deal of research, there is no conclusive evidence that depression is carried by genes, however. On the other side, recent immunological studies support the role of genetic predisposition.

ECOSOMATOGENIC DEPRESSION

The subject of this chapter is psychosociogenic depression, but here are a few words about ecosomatogenic depression. This depression can be caused by a variety of neurochemical factors, such as dopamine, actylcholine, norepinephrine, serotonin, and other neurobiological processes (Thase, Frank, & Kupfer, 1985). Several research works reported by Depue (1988), Post and Ballinger (1984), and others pointed to the role of dopamine. Janowsky, Risch, and Gillin (1983) and several others studied the role of acetylcholine in depression, and more research is currently going on.

GENETIC FACTORS IN PSYCHOSOCIOGENIC DEPRESSION

Despite significant research, there is no conclusive evidence that the ecosomatogenic and psychosociogenic depressions are carried by genes. However, according to Winokur and Crowe (1983), in the population identified as having bipolar depression there was an equal number of males and females, whereas among those having unipolar depression, the number of females was much higher than males. Mendlewicz (1977) suggested the hypothesis of genetic heterogeneity, and according to Farber (1982), children of bipolar depressive individuals tend to be depressed and display hyperactive, impatient, and explosive personality traits. Research by Radke-Yarrow, Cummings, Kuczynski, and Chapman (1985), of interaction between mothers who had a history of depression and their young children, showed that the children were initially anxious and, after a four-year follow-up study, exhibited a low level of social competence. Apparently, the children were somewhat affected by their depressed mothers, but it is not sure that there were genetic causal relations.

As mentioned above, the issue of genetic origin of depression is still a controversial one. Bertelsen (1985), in a research of monozygotic and dizygotic twins, supported the genetic hypothesis, whereas Tsuang, Bucher, Fleming, and Faraone (1985) did not. Apparently, although there is no final evidence concerning the genetic origin of depression, genetic predisposition to depression is a strong possibility, supported by immunological research (Loehlin, Willerman, & Horn, 1988).

THE IMMUNE SYSTEM

The immune system is involved in biochemical, endocrinological, neurological, and psychological processes. It resembles a set of interconnected bridges that link several areas of living organisms and coordinate several vital functions. When a dysfunction of the immune system causes depression, the depression is ecosomatogenic, and when the dysfunction of the immune system is caused by psychosociogenic depression, the dysfunction of the immune system is psychosomatic (Wolman, 1988).

The immune system plays a significant role in the etiology of mental disorders (Ader, 1981; Ader & Cohen, 1984; Solomon & Amkraut, 1981), possibly somewhat similar to its role in bodily diseases. The immune system may or may not react to antigens, that is, it can be immunocompetent or immunotolerant. It is my hypothesis that cancer is an autoimmune disease, whereas AIDS is an antiautoimmune disease. Both cancer and AIDS are caused by antigens, but the reaction of the immune system determines whether the organism will or will not succumb to the disease (Wolman, 1988). The responsiveness of the immune system, its strength or deficiency, cannot be unrelated to genetic factors.

Researchers are facing even more complex issues in regard to psychological aspects of the functions of the immune system. Depression, stress, mourning, severe frustration, and despair can reduce the responsiveness of the immune system and adversely affect the organism's resilience to diseases (Lipowski, 1985). According to Lipowski, psychosomatic research should take into consideration both genetic and environmental factors. The basic resilience of the immune system is, most probably, genetically determined, but overstimulation and stress may cause "excessive autonomic and cortical arousal leading to cognitive and/or motor performance. . . . Such repeated and sustained arousal may lead to physiological changes as well as behavior, enhancing the subject's general *susceptibility* to illness" (Lipowski, 1985, pp. 38–39).

FEAR OF DEATH

There are universal human emotions that are contributing factors to feeling helpless and hopeless and resenting these depressive feelings. The *fear of death,* common to all human beings, is the arch-source of depression. The fear of death inspires people to accumulate possessions, to erect monuments, and to believe in a "life after death." Religions offer a highly important consolation by promising an immortal Hereafter.

All religions link the hope for a happy life after death to what one does when one is alive. The moral principles are linked to a reward and punishment system. Ancient Greeks believed that the souls of deceased people were ferried by Charon, the gods' oarsman, and brought to the goddess of justice. The goddess of justice held a sword in one hand to make sure that justice had power, and a scale in the other hand to weigh people's sins and virtues. The sinners were sent to Hades for eternal punishment, and the virtuous individuals were sent to the peaceful Fields of Elysium. Every human being is exposed to the feeling of being weak and judged by divine powers (Schwab, 1946).

The Judeo-Christian tradition promises punishment and forgiveness for past sins. The ancient Jews were expelled from their land and "cried on the rivers of Babylonia."

The Catholic religion elaborates on hell and heaven and demands confession of—and penance for—sins. All Christian denominations have developed intricate systems describing the dependence of human beings on the promise of mercy from an all-powerful, omnipotent source.

SOCIOECONOMIC FACTORS

Freud's patients complained mainly about sexual problems; today the main problems facing patients are insecurity and depression. At the present time, economic and political insecurity greatly contribute to widespread depressive feelings. Living in the aftermath of the Great Depression, World War II, and the Holocaust, and now coping with the current proliferation of nuclear weapons and with the rampant and chaotic violence that permeates every level of humanity can hardly be expected to foster a society of secure, well-adjusted adults. Depression is a feeling of weakness, helplessness, and hopelessness associated with resenting and blaming oneself for being weak. Small wonder that depressed individuals tend to turn to alcohol and drugs, and many of them join various cults that relieve depression and give the illusion of power and control (Akiskal, Hirschfeld, & Yerevanian, 1983; Fox, 1967; Rounsaville, Weissman, Crits-Christoph, Wilber, & Kleber, 1982).

Present-day fluctuations in economic life, with the inevitable phenomena of inflation, depression, and recession, do not provide much security to the vast majority of people. Many people have no job security, and many face unemployment and poverty. But even middle- and upper-class individuals cannot be very secure because changes in the economic climate of this society may seriously affect their income and possessions. A loss of income can cause exogenous depression, but quite a few people will also blame themselves for their real or imagined inabilities in coping with their financial problems, and will develop endogenous depression as well.

PARENT–CHILD RELATIONSHIP

The feeling of security depends on one's estimate of one's own power and of the power and loyalty of one's allies. Since no human being can be omnipotent, every human being needs allies. Isolation and loneliness cause exogenous depression. When an individual believes in being lonely, it causes endogenous depression, whether or not the belief is realistic. Children cannot survive unless taken care of by adults, and children's most severe fear is the fear of abandonment (Bowlby, 1980; Joffe & Vaughn, 1982; Wolman, 1978b). An early separation from parents may cause severe depression with a host of psychosomatic symptoms such as enuresis, school phobia, asthma, and many others (Kimball, 1978). The earlier the separation, the more severe the depression (Hamburg, Hamburg, & Barchas, 1975; Levinger & Moles, 1979; Spitz, 1946a, 1946b; 1960).

The lack of maternal love causes "affect hunger." The rejected child may try to win love by intentional suffering and may escape into illness. "The discouraged child who finds that he can tyrannize best by tears will be a cry-baby, and a direct line of development leads from the cry-baby to the adult depressed patient," wrote Kurt Adler (1967, p. 332).

Many severely depressive patients come from families where no one was genuinely interested in the child's welfare. As a result of the lack of a true and meaningful relationship in childhood, the depressive individuals suffer from feelings of insecurity and rejection (Cartwell & Carlson, 1983).

Most depressive patients are exposed in childhood to a sort of emotional seesaw of acceptance and rejection. The mothers of severely depressed patients did not like their children; however, when the children were in serious trouble or gravely ill, the mothers turned around and showered them with affection. These emotional swings were conducive to a self-defeating attitude in the offspring; getting sick became the only way to win love (Kashami & Carlson, 1985; Schaffer, 1977).

In most cases, adequate maternal care is given to the infant in the first few months of life; the rejection comes somewhat later. Thus, depressed patients have a tendency to regress to infancy. Regression goes back not to the point of frustration or rejection, but before that point, to the true or imaginary era of the "lost paradise" of safety and love. In milder, neurotic cases of hysteria and depressive neurosis, the regression is usually to the oral stage in an intentional, albeit unconscious hope to win love.

Parental rejection need not be associated with pathological hostility; infants may feel rejected when the mother is sick and unable to take care of them, or when she is pregnant with another child, or when she is too busy working or is overburdened with a large family (Earle & Earle, 1961; Goldstein, 1988).

In some instances, the future depressed patient had to compete unsuccessfully against a more privileged sibling. Many depressive patients were a kind of Cinderella in their family, which was usually composed of a hostile mother, an uninterested or hostile father, and favored siblings. Some mothers preferred another child; the child who became severely depressed was the forgotten child, the "ugly duckling." In some instances the mother, father, and siblings joined in rejecting the child, telling the child how ugly and stupid he or she was.

The child who has become a depressed patient was usually the unwanted, unloved, and forgotten member of the family, treated like a burden and handicap (Hodges & Siegel, 1985; Kashami & Carlson, 1985).

As previously mentioned, the regressive process in depression goes back *not* to the *point* of frustration or rejection but *before* that point, to the true or imaginary era of the lost paradise of safety and love.

PERSONALITY DYNAMICS

Several authors have tried to relate depression to personality types, using various frames of reference; among them are Akiskal, Hirschfeld, and Yerevanian (1983), Arieti and Bemporad (1980), Becker (1977),

Millon (1981), Paykel, Klerman, & Prusoff (1976), Winokur (1983), and others.

In the following description of personality dynamics I am applying a modified psychoanalytic model (Abraham, 1927; Freud, 1933, 1949; Wolman, 1984a). As described earlier, I rejected Freud's concept of Thanatos, and I introduced the dual concept of Eros (love), associated with libido, and Ares (hate), associated with destrudo. I also added the concept of interindividual cathexis, revised Freud's structural theory, and added the concepts of *we-ego* and *vector-ego*. I modified the psychoanalytic topographic conscious, preconscious, and unconscious theory: I rejected Freud's preconscious concept and introduced the concept of *protoconscious* (Wolman & Ullman, 1986).

THE DYSMUTUAL-DEPRESSIVE DISORDER

One of the outstanding features of depression is an imbalance of libido and destrudo cathexes. Maternal gratification of the infant's needs helps in the development of a proper balance of cathexes. However, when milk is withheld from a hungry child or when it is given in an unfriendly manner, the infant is unable to develop the proper balance between inter- and intracathexes of libido and destrudo. Total rejection leads to an increased intracathexis of libido and increased intercathexes of destrudo, that is, more self-love and more hatred of others—which leads to a sociopathic personality (Wolman, 1987). When a child is expected to give more love than it receives, and the parents are overdemanding and expect the child to compensate them for their true or imaginary misfortunes, the child's libido becomes hypercathected in the parents and inadequately intracathected in itself. The child, forced to over-control his or her resentment, follows the hypervectorial path to schizophrenia. In hypervectorial, schizophrenic patients, the repressed destrudo breaks through and leads to outbursts directed against oneself and others (Wolman, 1966a, 1966b, 1970).

Well-adjusted individuals have a reasonable balance between love and hate; they love themselves and their allies and hate their enemies. Their libido is *intrapersonally* cathected in themselves and *interpersonally* cathected in other people. Their destrudo is cathected *interpersonally* in others who represent a threat to them.

The libido of depressed individuals is inadequately self-cathected; they love themselves only when others love them. They are "love hungry," as Fenichel (1945) put it.

In depressive disorders the destrudo is abundantly intra- and intercathected. Most of the time, depressive patients hate themselves. A depressed patient told me, "No one cares for me because I am a worthless person, and I hate myself for being a worthless person. I hate myself because no one loves me, but how can anyone care for me if I myself don't care for myself, and how can I care for myself if no one cares for me?"

And so the vicious cycle of depression goes on. Depression is self-perpetuating, but it can be interrupted by a true or imaginary sign of affection or admiration coming from without. Some depressed persons may indulge in an elated mood, whereas some others may reject the friendly person, thinking that there must be something wrong with that person if she or he cares for them.

Depressed individuals are exceedingly sensitive to the slightest sign of rejection or disrespect. Their self-love (self-cathected libido) is inconsistent. They tend to believe that they are good-looking and smart only when they are told so by another person, or when they are in a state of manic bliss.

Being overly dependent on the opinions of others, depressed people cannot be consistent in their self-conception. As one patient put it, "My mother, my father, my brother, my teachers, everyone hated me. So I realized that I am an ugly, stupid little boy."

Dr. Jekyll and Mr. Hyde

The feeling of being rejected is a constant feeling in depressive neurotics and psychotics. Friends and relatives of depressive patients often compare the rapidly changing attitudes to the turning off and on of hot and cold water faucets. The soft-spoken, kind, affectionate Dr. Jekyll turns into a Mr. Hyde whenever his loving attitude is not fully appreciated and repaid with high interest.

When in a loving mood, the volatile depressed individuals make exaggerated promises about great love and unlimited desire to be of help, but at the slightest disappointment, they forget what they said a short while before. Depressed patients are not calculated liars; they exaggerate in mutuality (hence the name "dysmutual"), wanting too much and giving too much. They are easily carried away by momentary feelings; they say things that bear witness to their poor sense of reality, making promises they cannot possibly fulfill.

THE SUPEREGO

The superego of depressed individuals incorporates the parental rejecting figures. The superego of the depressive dysmutuals is highly inconsistent, full of hate yet ready to embrace the ego when it is in great trouble; at such moments, depression turns into elation.

A depressed individual can be an idealist and a swindler, cruel and sentimental, religious and atheistic at the same time. Depressed individuals easily shift their moral or political identifications; they have no steady conviction, no persistent philosophy. One day they are determined to adhere strictly to the rules of religion; the next day may find them preaching the opposite.

In psychosociogenic depressions, the superego is almost continuously attacking one's ego. Guilt feeling is an outstanding feature of depression, but the content of the self-accusations has little to do with reality. In their depressed moods, patients recall events that happened a long time ago and magnify their importance.

ANTIDEPRESSIVE REACTIONS

There are several possible reactions to depression. In the peculiar imbalance of cathexes a small supply of libidinal cathexis (affection) from without may terminate the depression. Depression may be interrupted by an intake of food or fluid, by rest or play, by praise or achievement. Depressive moods come and go, and their inconsistency is one of the chief characteristics of depressive disorders.

DEFENSE MECHANISMS

The neurotic defenses against depression are the ego-protective symptoms, which include denial, dissociation, fatigue, reaction formation, and a galaxy of psychosomatic symptoms, such as headaches, gastrointestinal troubles, and so on. The ego-deficiency or psychotic symptoms include the manic state, paranoid projections, aggressive–defensive moods, and severe regression.

The term *manic-depressive disorder* is misleading: the manic mood is one of a number of possible reactions to depression. The so-called manic-depressive patients are *depressed,* that is, torn by the attacks of the superego. The manic state is an effort to deny depression and to ward it off. In a manic state, the patients display a flood of words and actions in a desperate effort to escape the feelings of guilt and depression; but even at the peak of elation the depressed feelings never completely disappear.

Manic episodes may come as a blissful reaction to profound, bottom feelings of loss and defeat; they can also be triggered by achievement or by a sign of affection from without. Mania is not a happy mood; it is a state of tension accompanied by a feeling of *power.* A patient in a manic mood acts indiscriminately, making friends with whomever he or she meets. However, the slightest opposition to these overtures may trigger depression and hostile feelings.

THE ID

The id is a carrier of impulses. In well-adjusted individuals the ego holds on to reality and restrains both the id and the superego.

In depressive states the ego is weak and subservient to the whims of the superego. Depressed patients are inattentive and lack self-discipline. Quite often, unable to withstand superego pressure, their ego merges with the id. Their contact with reality is tenuous, even on a neurotic level. Depressed patients show little perseverance, and even when endowed with excellent intellectual abilities, they are often underachievers.

The degree of their reality testing corresponds to the level of disorder. A neurotic's ego tries to ward off superego pressures by developing defense mechanisms such as rationalizations, reaction-formation, and denial. Unlike schizophrenics, depressive patients rarely lose all contact with reality. Even on the psychotic level, the depressive patients still preserve some contact with reality. However, inattention, forgetting, oblivion, distortion of truth to please people or to impress them, exaggeration, omission of detail, and lack of understanding for the feelings of others are typical of depressive patients.

One of the outstanding features of depressives is the shifting self-image. At one moment they perceive themselves as being helpless, and a while later they may feel powerful.

WE-EGO AND VECTOR-EGO

The development of we-ego and vector-ego undergoes substantial changes in depressive disorders. Normally, the we-ego develops in adolescence as a function of group identification (Wolman, 1982b). Depressed children and adolescents tend to overdo or underdo in interpersonal relations; they are either overinvolved with their peers up to the point of denying their own identity or, feeling rejected, they withdraw from social relations, or shift from one extreme to the other (Pearce, 1977). The development of the vector-ego is associated with attainment of intellectual and moral development. The depressed individuals are overdependent on approval by others, and they rarely attain the level of vector-ego (Wolman, 1982b).

PROTOCONSCIOUS

I believe that Freud's (1938/1949) topographic theory that divides the mental strata into conscious, preconscious, and unconscious layers should be revised, for there is hardly any significant distinction between the conscious and preconscious layers. The term *conscious* indicates what one is aware of at the present moment; preconscious implies what is in one's mind, but not *on* one's mind at the present moment. Obviously, preconscious is the storage room of the conscious.

One may revise the psychoanalytic topographic theory by analyzing phenomena that were almost unheard of in Freud's era. Sensory deprivation, biofeedback, and autogenic therapy were rather unknown at that time, and transcendental meditation, certain imagery processes, and parapsychological phenomena of telepathy and psychokinesis were not yet scrutinized by rigorous scientific research.

The above mentioned phenomena are neither entirely conscious nor entirely unconscious. They are not conscious because there is no reality testing, yet the individual who experiences transcendental meditation or telepathy is aware that he or she does experience these phenomena. Psychomotor epileptics who attack innocent bystanders are both aware and unaware of what they are doing; they are neither unconscious nor conscious. Their state of mind is somewhere between—it is *protoconscious*. The dichotomy between sleep and wakefulness has been undermined by the so-called *lucid dreams theory.* Lucid dreamers are asleep; thus they cannot be conscious. They are, however, aware that they are dreaming and therefore, they are not unconscious. In a lucid dream the dreamers are able to reason, remember, and act volitionally while being sound asleep and dreaming (LaBerge & Gackenbach, 1986). They are neither conscious nor unconscious; they are *protoconscious* (Wolman, 1986; Wetzel, 1984).

The dreams of depressed individuals are sometimes more rational than their waking cognitive processes. Quite often, even when they are quite depressed they have lucid dreams, and in these dreams their repressed ego presents a realistic solution to their problems and calls for rational actions.

The lucid dream enables them to experience protoconscious phenomena. Some depressive patients also have parapsychological experiences, and report extrasensory and premonition phenomena. Possibly, the lack of emotional balance contributes to the ability to regress to protoconscious and unconscious levels (Wolman, 1986).

Elated moods of depressed patients are usually protoconscious. The patients are somewhat aware of their excited mood, but they are unable to test reality or to control themselves. In a manic mood they tend to do immediately whatever they feel like doing; there is no delay, no reconsideration, no self-discipline.

SYMPTOMATOLOGY

INCONSISTENCY

One of the outstanding features of depressive disorders is *inconsistency* in practically all aspects of behavior. Depressed individuals can easily turn love into hate and vice versa; they tend to be happy and unhappy, sociable and seclusive, full of energy and passive, sleepy and unable to sleep, and so on.

Depressed individuals are highly inconsistent in their plans and actions. They may enthusiastically choose an occupation and, after a while, be thoroughly disappointed. The proverbial "other pastures are always greener" applies to depressive disorders. Depressed individuals are in a never ending search to compensate for their feelings of inadequacy. They rarely check the availability of things they wish to possess or the accessibility of things they want to accomplish. They often start a great many projects at the same time and abandon all of them in no time. They are often hypomanic to cover up their frustrations, and are critical of themselves for not having accomplished the impossible tasks. They are often irritable and angry at themselves and others.

Their decision-making processes and analysis of what they have to face, as well as other cognitive functions, vary greatly, depending on their moods (Bower, 1981; Davis & Unruh, 1981; Teasdale, 1983; Wetzel, 1984).

"LOVE ADDICTS"

Depressive patients either exude overflowing love and kindness or are irritable and hateful. They are at their best behavior when loved and admired. It is easy for them to be kind and friendly to strangers whom they expect to win over, but the same person who is a kind Dr. Jekyll for strangers may be the rude Mr. Hyde for his or her family members. Their libido and destrudo are frequently shifting. Deeply depressed psychotics are in a state of almost continual hatred toward those who reject them and toward themselves for failing to win love. Their destrudo is very active and resists sublimation, neutralization, and aim-inhibition (Abraham, 1927; Arieti, 1974; Bibring, 1953; Mendelson, 1960; Wolman, 1973, 1984b).

LEARNED HELPLESSNESS

When depressed individuals feel they cannot win love by being strong, they try to win it by being weak. Many of them can work hard toward a goal, but when they come close to a victory, they defeat themselves. They seem to recapitulate their childhood; they tried to win parental love by being successful, but this did not work. The self-defeating and self-hurting tendency of depressed patients is deeply rooted in their unconscious belief that maternal love can be won only through misery. Many depressed patients, whether on a neurotic or psychotic level, have the masochistic wish to suffer, and hope to gain love by suffering. Depressed people often fear success, and after trying hard they somehow manage to prevent it. They practice "learned helplessness" (Leites, 1979; Seligman, 1975).

Depressive moods last long and are painful, yet the patients seem to do very little to overcome their depressive feelings. They are accident-prone and often act against their own interests. They are quite sensitive to criticism coming from without, but they blame themselves for what their discreditors blame them for, as if hoping to win sympathy by willingly accepting punishment.

SEXUALITY

Depressed individuals may not be able to resolve their Oedipal complex through identification with the parent of the same sex. In most instances, maternal rejection prevents normal resolution of the family drama, and overdependency on and incestuous attachments to the parents may continue all through their life. The defense mechanism of reaction-formation makes them feel hostile toward the parent they are attracted to the most, and they are usually attracted to the more forceful, more aggressive, and more rejecting parent.

Depressed females try to attract as many men as they can in order to satisfy their desire to be loved by everyone, but they tend to lose interest in men who love them.

The combination of an absent or weak father and an aggressive mother is conducive to a tendency toward *homosexuality* in male offspring.

Depressed male patients cannot renounce their mother as a love object, nor identify with their father. Depressed males tend to perceive all women as potential lovers. They fall in and fall out of love, always in search of the loving mother. Many depressed males are impotent; they tend to boast about their victories, while actually fearing intercourse. They often pursue women they cannot win over, but as soon as they win, they run away.

OBESITY

Depressed patients are unable to love unless loved. The less love they receive, the more they need. The feelings of being loved are usually short-lived; sooner or later, these patients experience the pangs of emotional and of physical hunger. Small wonder that they may overeat constantly, as if trying to fill the emotional void. They also overeat to make themselves less attractive, less capable of an active life, less successful, and less healthy. Overeating serves to deepen their self-defeat, to prove to themselves that they are weak and unable to control their weight and behavior; in the back of their minds looms the unconscious hope of gaining love by self-destructive behavior (Wolman, 1982a).

PSYCHOSOMATIC DISORDERS

According to Katon, Kleinman, and Rosen (1982), at least 26 percent of patients who come to physicians complaining about physical disease are depressed, and their depression has led to the development of psychosomatic symptoms. Apparently, a great many psychosomatic conversion symptoms are related to underlying depressive disorders (Beckham & Leber, 1985). Exposure to stressors alone is almost never a sufficient explanation for illness, just as genetic studies have shown that biological factors alone do not cause mental disorders. According to Kurt Adler (1967), the rejected child may try to win love by intentional suffering and escape into illness. "The discouraged child who finds that he can tyrannize best by tears will be a cry-baby, and a direct line of development leads from the cry-baby to the adult depressed patient." Quite often, psychosomatic disorders represent a willful, albeit unconscious, escape into illness.

Several psychosomatic symptoms in depressive disorders are related to the immune system. According to Zegans (1982, p. 149), "Any stressful process that alters the normal physiology of hormones will naturally have an impact on immunological behavior."

Mason (1975) found that depression and mental stress can affect endocrine glands and thus disturb the functions of the immune system and reduce the organism's resilience.

Depression also reduces the organism's overall ability to fight disease. Depressed individuals are prone to develop a variety of diseases and disabilities, and many of them suffer from angina pectoris, myocardial infarction, and other cardiac diseases (Herd, 1984; Howells, 1980; Wolman, 1988).

SUICIDAL ATTEMPTS

Depressive-psychotics usually fall asleep easily and wake up very early. There is nothing to do in the wee hours, and there is no one who cares. At such moments, depressed psychotics often act under the desire to punish themselves and those who do not love them. Some of them imagine themselves dead, listening to the sobbings of their relatives, as if believing that death would win the love they failed to receive in life. Some patients imagine themselves being alive, lying in their coffin, and smiling to themselves with a feeling of victory.

Unfortunately, their suicidal attempts are all too often successful. Any sign of rejection may motivate a depressive patient to attempt suicide. Quite often, they did not want to die, but desired to be nurtured (Brown & Sheran, 1982; Hankoff & Einsidler, 1979; Miller, 1980; Pokorny, 1983; Shneidman, 1980; Wolman & Krauss, 1976).

DEPRESSIVE NEUROSIS

As mentioned in the section on nosology, I believe that there are five levels of mental disorders: neurosis, character neurosis, latent psychosis, manifest psychosis, and the total collapse of personality structure (Krauss & Krauss, 1977). Depressive neurotics are usually absent-minded, forgetful, and careless. In elated moods they are hyperactive and full of enthusiastic plans, ignoring or underestimating difficulties. Their thinking lacks precision, and they tend to confuse wish and reality. They may sound self-assured, but the slightest disappointment can put an end to their cheerful mood and make them depressed. In depressed moods they procrastinate, and they are sluggish and apathetic. They refrain from taking the initiative or engaging in active behavior, always expecting defeat and preaching gloom.

There are three main neurotic syndromes: *depressive, dissociative,* and *conversion* (i.e., conversion-hysteria) *reaction.* The neurotic depressive syndrome is associated with anxiety states and feelings of inadequacy. Neurotic-depressive patients tend to blame themselves for noncommitted errors. They are accident-prone in an unconscious wish for self-punishment.

Amnesia and the so-called "split personality" are typical symptoms of the dissociative syndrome. Instead of facing difficulties, patients deny them. In extreme cases of dissociation, patients tend to forget their own name and past experiences. Fugue, split personality, loss of memory, and loss of identity help them to escape self-blame.

In the conversion-hysteria syndrome, the patients develop a galaxy of psychosomatic symptoms that can imitate almost every possible physical disease. Hysterical symptoms can be quite frequent, even in psychotic-depressive patients in their prepsychotic years, but as long as the hysterical psychosomatic symptoms prevail, the patients are not psychotic yet (Anthony & Benedek, 1975; Gold, Pottash, Extein, & Sweeney, 1981; Herd, 1984).

DEPRESSIVE CHARACTER NEUROSIS

Rationalization is the choice defense mechanism of depressive character neurotics. They tend to give to themselves and others shallow advice, such as "Keep smiling," "Don't worry," "Let's face it," "Everyone does it," "Never too late," and so on. Depressive character neurotics tend to be hyperactive and gregarious. Quite often, they comment on their true or imaginary hardships, blaming the world and defending themselves. They often say, "Crooks and thieves are successful, and honest people have no chance." A patient who failed in business made himself believe that he "sacrificed himself for his family, and never gave up," and that the business failure was caused by "enemies" who hated his great virtues.

DEPRESSIVE PSYCHOSIS

In most cases, the transition from neurosis to psychosis is an erosion rather than a catastrophic event. Most often, latent depressive psychotics feel that they are failures, that they have never done anything sensible, that their lives have been a waste, and that no one likes them; at the same time they will quite often try to give the impression that they are happy and successful individuals. Mild euphoric moods prevail, but depressed moods, occurring in the early morning hours, are distinct signs of deterioration. Their moods usually improve at evening, but their sleep is often quite disturbed (Luce, 1970).

Depressive latent psychotics often act as if in a frenzy, undertaking a great many activities aimed at warding off the oncoming depression. One patient of mine, a musician, decided to become a physicist, a mathematician, a philosopher, a historian of art, and an anthropologist in addition to being a composer, a conductor, and an impresario. A female patient was "collecting men," by letting herself become involved with casual acquaintances and total strangers. Another patient started half a dozen projects, contacted scores of people, made hundreds of appointments, and kept dreaming up new, grandiose, and never-to-be-concluded projects.

The term *vacationing ego* describes the mentality of latent depressive psychotics. It seems as if all functions of the ego shrink to one task: the warding off of the superego's hostility. Latent depressive psychotics tend to accept commitments they cannot meet, alternate exaggerated friendliness with isolation, undersell or oversell their services, underspend or overspend their money, and act in a thoughtless way whenever their wish to impress others is at stake.

THE FIVE SYNDROMES OF MANIFEST DEPRESSIVE PSYCHOSIS

There are five clinical syndromes in the manifest depressive psychosis. These syndromes are descriptive categories related to observable symptoms and personality structure. Occasional transitions from one clinical pattern to another have been observed (American Psychiatric Association, 1987; Grinker, Miller, Sabshin, Nunn, & Nunnally, 1961; Kaplan & Sadock, 1985; Wolman, 1973).

In the first syndrome, *major depression,* the ego has lost its control over the id and the superego. The patients are at the mercy of their irrational impulses and are unable to follow a rational path of behavior. They torture themselves with guilt feelings for true or imaginary transgressions.

The second syndrome is *mania,* a frantic and hyperoptimistic frame of mind that aims at covering up the deep and torturous depression.

The third syndrome is *paranoia.* When the ego, battered by the superego, resorts to projection and externalizes superego pressure, the patient perceives the world as a rejecting and punishing mother who some day will be forced to accept her suffering child.

The fourth syndrome is *agitated depression.* When the weak ego is unable to withstand the assaults of the superego and can't control the demanding id, the patient is continuously irritable, hates oneself and the whole world, and is in the throes of depression. Agitated depression often leads to suicidal attempts.

The last syndrome is *simple deterioration,* when both the ego and the superego are defeated and the primitive, uninhibited impulses of the id take over.

Major Depression

The first syndrome is the so-called *major depression* (American Psychiatric Association, 1980, 1987). The symptoms of the major depression include passivity and helplessness associated with irritability and anger directed toward oneself (Krauss & Krauss, 1977; Mendelson, 1960).

Major depression is a psychotic syndrome; the ego has lost whatever control it had over the id impulses and is unable to restrain the superego's hostile attitudes. Major-depression (i.e., psychotic) patients may cross streets on red lights, eat in an unrestrained manner, or refuse to eat. Their biological rhythm is disrupted, and their sleeping patterns are disorganized. Quite often, they refuse to get up in the mornings and may, unless prodded, spend their days in bed in total passivity.

Depressed psychotics lose concern for their personal hygiene and appearance. They don't mind wearing dirty and torn garments, and are unable to relate to other people although they wish to be taken care of. Their cognitive functions oscillate from total incoherence to an almost normal way of thinking (Leight & Ellis, 1981; Teasdale, 1983; Usdin, 1977; Wetzel, 1984).

Their pervading feeling of guilt may lead to suicidal attempts. Some of their self-accusations are remotely related to reality, but some are of a hallucinogenic nature (Nelson & Charney, 1981; Winokur, Clayton, & Reich, 1969; Winokur & Crowe, 1983).

The Manic Syndrome

Manic moods can start when patients experience a severe blow to their self-esteem and/or feelings of security. They may lose a close relative or friend, a job, status, prestige, property, or money. Quite often, the manic moods are precipitated by a sudden and severe failure of efforts.

Introjection of the image of the rejecting parent is typical for all depressive disorders. The introjected image is usually hostile, but only up to a certain point. The patient reactivates his or her childhood experiences as if invoking the superego to do what the mother did: "I see how unhappy you are. Now I will take care of you and reward you for your misfortunes." The superego, as it were, embraces the failing ego and acts the way the rejecting mother acted when she felt sorry for her suffering child.

There is no reality principle in a manic mood, no self-discipline, and no self-control. Manic patients do whatever they feel like doing. If they are sexually aroused, they may proposition the first person they meet. Psychotic depressed patients regress to a stage they experienced before they felt rejected and depressed. They regress to the "lost-paradise stage," to early childhood and infantile bliss (Arieti, 1974).

Psychotic delusions and hallucinations are often associated with *delusions of martyrdom,* of being lost and found, of being a Cinderella saved by a Prince Charming or a slave led by the Messiah to the lost paradise. Psychotic depressed patients often dream of a disaster that will force the mother to love them (Bibring, 1953; Hodges & Siegel, 1985). However, even in a manic mood, patients seem to be protoconsciously aware of the underlying depressed feelings. Their thoughts shift from one issue to another and from one grandiose plan to another. In manic moods they dream of a great many actions; but they refrain from the practical steps that could bring disappointment.

Paranoia

One of the psychotic reactions against depression is paranoia, a projection mechanism in which the patient is saying to himself or herself: "I do not hate myself. They hate me."

This projective-paranoid mechanism is used by the ego in many disorders. It occurs whenever the ego, attacked by the superego, has not given up, but is unable to test reality and uses projection.

The same mechanism takes place in schizophrenia, when the ego is exposed to intolerable accusations from the superego (Wolman, 1983). Patients who elicited hate by their hostile behavior deny that they were ever hostile; they believe they are innocent victims of enemies (Wolman, 1987).

In depressive disorders the projections become systematized and reproduce the Cinderella story of the persecuted child who will finally be rewarded. Paranoiacs believe themselves to be martyrs, persecuted by a bad mother or anyone else, but ultimately to be helped by the mother of their dreams.

A man ran away from the Army during World War II because he believed two men in his platoon had been ordered to kill him. All soldiers, he said, were cowards who fought only when forced to, but he was a military genius who could "smash Germany with one big blow." He went to his colonel with his inventions, but ". . . the envious colonel would not let me become famous" and turned his proposals down. The patient believed that the colonel gave orders to shoot him on the next day and to steal his plans. The patient deserted.

Paranoia represents a combination of elation and of denial of depression. It is the martyr-hero complex—a dramatization of an unfairly persecuted person who eventually will be rewarded for innocence.

Paranoia has been linked to the depressive psychosis by several authors. According to Kanzer (1952), guilt feelings lead to regression, to a magic omnipotence, and/or to submission to the imaginary prosecutor. Internalization of the rejecting parental figure is the basic psychological mechanism of paranoia. According to Salzman (1960), the paranoid megalomania is an effort to deny one's low self-esteem. Kraepelin (1921) noticed the wish for grandiosity and excessive ambition in depressives; their persecution complex offers a detour of the desire to be admired.

In all cases of paranoia I have seen, paranoia was a reaction against unbearable feelings of depression. All paranoiacs share the wish of the rejected child whose misery will eventually gain the mother's love.

The Agitated-Depressive Syndrome

Not all dysmutual-depressive psychotics are capable of the manic-denial or of the paranoia-projective maneuver. Agitated-depressive patients may, occasionally, be calm, especially when they have the chance to outshine others, but since no one can always be successful, the elated moods are short-lived (Wetzel, 1984; Wolman, 1973).

Agitated-depressive patients are full of gloom and anger. One patient described his mood in the following way: "I feel like jumping out of my skin. You'd better lock me up before I strangle my wife and my child. I cannot stand them; I hate them and hate myself. The best thing would be to put an end to everything." A female patient, tortured by her moods, was hospitalized voluntarily and felt better on the ward where she "took care of all those crazy characters." She became very active, a sort of assistant and advisor to the doctors and nurses. After she was discharged from the hospital, she found life bleak, and regressed.

Hate and self-hate are the main symptoms of the agitated-depressive syndrome. The defeated ego does not exercise reality testing; a casual approval by a nurse gave a female patient new enthusiasm for living, but her son's lack of interest provoked a violent and self-destructive reaction. In agitated-depressive patients the slightest sign of rejection unleashes uncontrollable outbursts of violent behavior directed against themselves and others.

Simple Deterioration Syndrome

In the simple deterioration syndrome in depressive psychosis the patients regress into parasitic life as if hoping that somebody will take care of them. They give up any efforts to live a normal life. One man who held a menial job in a mailroom found a dark corner where he hid and slept. When he was discovered, he was fired. His reaction was, "I knew this was going to happen. They are just unfair! Don't they understand that life is too hard for me!"

Simple deteriorated psychotics refuse to exert themselves. Their "sleepy ego" merges with the id. There isn't much reality principle left, and there is no self-discipline. The id's law of immediate gratification rules their regressive behavior.

Simple deteriorated psychotics of the dysmutual type go down the social ladder. If they have some money, they usually spend it in a senseless manner. Some of them become addicted to drugs or alcohol and some become street bums and beggars.

In the simple deterioration syndrome the patients renounce love for others and the need to be loved by anyone. They accept defeat and give up all effort. They may sleep on a bench on a street or hang around in a public place, begging. They do not care any more for anything. When life gets too difficult, they may turn on the gas and put an end to it all. Defeated, depressed, rejected, and forgotten by all, the simple deterioration depressive psychotic does not care to live any longer (Brown & Sheran, 1982; Hankoff & Einsidler, 1979; Roy, 1982).

SUMMARY

The term *depression* is used to describe a variety of negative feelings, such as frustration, disappointment, mourning, and so on. Depression as a psychopathological term means the *feeling of helplessness associated with blaming oneself for being helpless.* Helpless anger directed against oneself and others and feeling guilty for being weak are the essential elements of depression.

There are two distinct types of depression, albeit their symptoms are quite similar. The distinction is based on etiologic factors. The first type, ecosomatogenic depression, is caused by biochemical factors; the second type, psychosociogenic depression, is caused by psychological factors.

Both types of depression can be caused by inner (endogenous) or outer (exogenous) factors.

There is probably a genetic predisposition to both types of depression.

There are three basic types of interaction with others: instrumental, mutual, and vectorial. Well-adjusted adults interact in an instrumental manner in the breadwinning functions, in a mutual manner in friendship and sexual relations, and in a vectorial manner in the parenting relation. Classification of mental disorders in the nosological system follows the division of three major psychopathological types: sociopathic hyperinstrumentals, depressive dysmutuals, and schizo-type hypervectorials. Psychosocial depression is dysmutual, that is, related to imbalances and shifts in moods and social relations.

The etiology of depressive-dysmutual disorders is chiefly related to faulty parent–child interaction. The parents of depressive patients show no affection toward nor interest in their children, except when the children are gravely ill or in a desperate situation.

Children exposed to the parental emotional seesaw feel rejected and blame themselves for being rejected. They often wish to suffer, for that was the only way they gained love. In the masochistic streak of depression, depressed individuals hate themselves for not being loved and hate others for not loving them.

One may distinguish five levels of severity in depression: (a) depressive neurosis, (b) depressive character neurosis, (c) latent depressive psychosis, (d) manifest depressive psychosis, and (e) total collapse of personality structure.

There are five possible syndromes in psychotic depression: (a) major depression, (b) mania, (c) paranoia, (d) agitated depression, and (e) simple deterioration. The division into unipolar or bipolar depression seems to be superfluous, for elation is one of the defense mechanisms of escape from depression.

REFERENCES

Abraham, K. (1927). *Selected papers on psychoanalysis.* London: Hogarth Press.

Abramson, L. Y., & Sackeim, H. A. (1977). A paradox in depression: Uncontrollability and self-blame. *Psychological Bulletin, 84,* 835–852.

Ader, R. (Ed.) (1981). *Psychoneuroimmunology.* New York: Academic Press.

Ader, R., & Cohen, N. (1984). Behavior and the immune system. In W. D. Gentry (Ed.), *Handbook of behavioral medicine.* New York: Guilford.

Adler, K. (1967). Adler's individual psychology. In B. B. Wolman (Ed.), *Psychoanalytic techniques.* New York: Basic Books.

Akiskal, H. S., Hirschfeld, R., & Yerevanian, B. I. (1983). The relationship of personality to affective disorders: A critical review. *Archives of General Psychiatry, 40,* 801–810.

American Psychiatric Association (1980). *Diagnostic and statistical manual of mental disorders: DSM III.* Washington, DC: Author.

American Psychiatric Association (1987). *Diagnostic and statistical manual of mental disorders: DSM III-R.* Washington, DC: Author.

Anthony, J., & Benedek, T. (Eds.) (1975). *Depression and human existence.* Boston: Little, Brown.

Arieti, S. (1974). Manic-depressive psychosis and psychotic depression. In S. Arieti (Ed.), *American handbook of psychiatry* (Vol. 3). New York: Basic Books.

Arieti, S., & Bemporad, J. R. (1980). The psychological organization of depression. *American Journal of Psychiatry, 137,* 1360–1365.

Beck, A. T. (1967). *Depression: Clinical, experimental, and theoretical aspects.* Philadelphia: University of Pennsylvania Press.

Becker, J. (1977). *Affective disorders.* Morristown, NJ: General Learning Press.

Beckham, E. E., & Leber, W. R. (Eds.) (1985). *Handbook of depression: Treatment, assessment and research.* Homewood, IL: Dorsey Press.

Bertelsen, A. (1985). Controversies and consistencies in psychiatric genetics. *Acta Psychiatrica Scandinavia, 71,* 61–75.

Bibring, E. (1953). The mechanism of depression. In P. Greenacre (Ed.), *Affective disorders.* New York: International Universities Press.

Bower, G. (1981). Mood and memory. *American Psychologist, 36,* 129–138.

Bowlby, J. (1980). *Attachment and loss.* New York: Basic Books.

Brown, T. R., & Sheran, T. J. (1982). Suicide prediction: A review. *Life Threatening Behavior, 2,* 67–98.

Cadoret, R. J., O'Gorman, T. W., Heywood, E., & Troughton, E. (1985). Genetic and environmental factors in major depression. *Journal of Affective Disorders, 9,* 155–164.

Cartwell, D. P., & Carlson, G. A. (Eds.) (1983). *Affective disorders in childhood and adolescence.* New York: Medical Scientific Books.

Cole, J. O., Schatzberg, A. F., & Frazier, S. H. (Eds.) (1978). *Depression: Biology, psychodynamics, and treatment.* New York: Plenum.

Davis, H., & Unruh, W. (1981). The development of the self-schema in adult depression. *Journal of Abnormal Psychology, 90,* 125–133.

Depue, R. A. (1988). *Neurobehavioral systems: Personality and psychopathology.* New York: Springer.

Depue, R. A., & Iacomo, W. G. (1989). Neurobehavioral aspects of affective disorders. *Annual Review of Psychology, 40,* 457–492.

Dohrenwend, B. P., & Dohrenwend, B. S. (Eds.) (1974). *Stressful life events: Their nature and effects.* New York: Wiley.

Earle, A. M., & Earle, B. V. (1961). Early maternal deprivation and later psychiatric illness. *American Journal of Orthopsychiatry, 31,* 181–186.

Farber, S. L. (1982). Genetic diversity and differing reactions to stress. In L. Goldberger & S. Bresnitz (Eds.), *Handbook of stress.* New York: Free Press.

Fenichel, O. (1945). *The psychoanalytic theory of neurosis.* New York: Norton.

Fox, R. (1967). Alcoholism and reliance on drugs as depressive equivalents. *American Journal of Psychotherapy, 21,* 585–595.

Freud, S. (1917/1956). Mourning and melancholia. In J. Strachey (Ed. and Trans.), *The standard edition of the complete psychological works of Sigmund Freud* (Vol. 14). London: Hogarth Press.

Freud, S. (1933). *New introductory lectures on psychoanalysis.* New York: Norton.

Freud, S. (1938/1949). *An outline of psychoanalysis.* New York: Norton.

Gershon, E. S. (1987). Genetics. In F. K. Goodwin & K. R. Jamison (Eds.), *Manic-depressive illness.* Oxford: Oxford University Press.

Gold, M. S., Pottash, A. L. C., Extein, I., & Sweeney, D. R. (1981). Diagnosis of depression in the 1980's. *Journal of the American Medical Association, 245,* 1562–1565.

Goldstein, M. J. (1988). The family and psychopathology. *Annual Review of Psychology, 39,* 283–299.

Grinker, R. R., Miller, J., Sabshin, M., Nunn, R., & Nunnally, J. C. (1961). *The phenomena of depression.* New York: Hoeber.

Hamburg, D., Hamburg, B. A., & Barchas, J. D. (1975). Anger and depression in perspective of behavioral biology. In L. Levi (Ed.), *Emotions: Their parameters and measurement.* New York: Raven Press.

Hankoff, L. D., & Einsidler, B. (Eds.) (1979). *Suicide theory and clinical aspects.* Littleton, MA: PSG Publishing Co.

Herd, J. A. (1984). Cardiovascular diseases and hypertension. In W. D. Gentry (Ed.), *Handbook of behavioral medicine* (pp. 222–281). New York: Guilford.

Hodges, K. K., & Siegel, L. J. (1985). Depression in children and adolescents. In E. E. Beckham & W. R. Leber (Eds.), *Handbook of depression: Treatment, assessment and research.* Homewood, IL: Dorsey Press.

Howells, J. G. (Ed.) (1980). *Advances in family psychiatry.* New York: International Universities Press.

Janowsky, D. S., Risch, S. C., & Gillin, J. C. (1983). Adrenergic-cholinergic balance and the treatment of affective disorders. *Progress in Neuropharmacology and Biological Psychiatry, 7,* 297–307.

Joffe, L. S., & Vaughn, B. E. (1982). Infant–mother attachment. In B. B. Wolman (Ed.), *Handbook of developmental psychology.* Englewood Cliffs, NJ: Prentice-Hall.

Kanzer, M. (1952). Manic-depressive psychoses with paranoid trends. *International Journal of Psychoanalysis, 33,* 34–42.

Kaplan, H. I., & Sadock, B. J. (Eds.) (1985). *Comprehensive textbook of psychiatry.* Baltimore: Williams & Wilkins.

Kashami, J. H., & Carlson, G. A. (1985). Major depressive disorders in a preschooler. *Journal of the American Academy of Child Psychiatry, 24,* 490–494.

Katon, W., Kleinman, A., & Rosen, G. (1982). Depression and somatization: A review. *American Journal of Medicine, 72,* 127–135.

Kimball, C. P. (1978). Diagnosing psychosomatic situations. In B. B. Wolman (Ed.), *Clinical diagnosis of mental disorders: A handbook.* New York: Plenum.

Kraepelin, E. (1921). *Manic-depressive insanity and paranoia.* Edinburgh: Livingston.

Krauss, H. H., & Krauss, B. J. (Eds.) (1977). Nosology: Wolman's system. In B. B. Wolman (Ed.), *International encyclopedia of psychiatry, psychology, psychoanalysis, and neurology* (Vol. 8). New York: Aesculapius–Van Nostrand Reinhold.

LaBerge, S. P., & Gackenbach, J. (1986). Lucid dreaming. In B. B. Wolman & M. Ullman (Eds.), *States of consciousness.* New York: Van Nostrand Reinhold.

Leight, K. A., & Ellis, H. C. (1981). Emotional mood states, strategies, and state-dependency in memory. *Journal of Verbal Learning and Behavior, 20,* 251–275.

Leites, N. (1979). *Depression and masochism.* New York: Norton.

Levinger, G., & Moles, D. (Eds.) (1979). *Divorce and separation: Context, causes and consequences.* New York: Basic Books.

Lipowski, Z. J. (1985). *Psychosomatic medicine and liaison psychiatry.* New York: Plenum.

Loehlin, J. C., Willerman, L., & Horn, J. M. (1988). Human behavior genetics. *Annual Review of Psychology, 39,* 101–133.

Luce, G. G. (1970). *Biological rhythm in psychiatry and medicine.* Washington, DC: US Department of Health, Education and Welfare.

Mason, J. W. (1975). Psychologic stress and endocrine function. In F. J. Sachar (Ed.), *Topics in endocrinology.* New York: Grune & Stratton.

Mendelson, M. (1960). *Psychoanalytic concept of depression.* Springfield, IL: Thomas.

Mendlewicz, J. (1977). Affective disorders: Genetics. In B. B. Wolman (Ed.), *International encyclopedia of psychiatry, psychology, psychoanalysis, and neurology* (Vol. 1). New York: Aesculapius–Van Nostrand Reinhold.

Miller, J. (1980). Helping the suicidal client: Some aspects of assessment. *Psychotherapy: Theory, Research, and Practice, 17,* 94–100.

Millon, T. (1981). *Disorders of personality: DSM III, Axis III.* New York: Wiley.

Nelson, J. C., & Charney, D. S. (1981). Delusional and non-delusional unipolar depression. *American Journal of Psychiatry, 138,* 328–333.

Nemiah, J. (1985). Neurotic depression. In H. I. Kaplan & B. J. Sadock (Eds.), *Comprehensive textbook of psychiatry.* Baltimore: Williams & Wilkins.

Pavlov, I. P. (1928). *Lectures on conditioned reflexes.* New York: Liveright.

Paykel, E. S., Klerman, G. L., & Prusoff, B. A. (1976). Personality and symptom patterns in depression. *British Journal of Psychiatry, 129,* 327–334.

Pearce, J. (1977). Depressive disorders in childhood. *Journal of Child Psychology and Psychiatry, 18,* 79–82.

Peterson, C., & Seligman, M. E. P. (1983). Learned helplessness and victimization. *Journal of Social Issues, 39,* 103–116.

Pinsker, H., & Spitzer, R. L. (1977). Classification of mental disorders, DSM III. In B. B. Wolman (Ed.), *International encyclopedia of psychiatry, psychology, psychoanalysis, and neurology* (Vol. 3). New York: Aesculapius–Van Nostrand Reinhold.

Pokorny, A. D. (1983). Prediction of suicide in psychiatric patients. *Archives of General Psychiatry, 40,* 249–257.

Post, R. M., & Ballinger, J. C. (Eds.) (1984). *Neurobiology of mood disorders.* Baltimore: Williams & Wilkins.

Radke-Yarrow, M., Cummings, E. M., Kuczynski, L., & Chapman, M. (1985). Patterns of adjustment in two and three year olds in normal families and families with parental depression. *Child Development, 56,* 884–893.

Rounsaville, B. J., Weissman, M. M., Crits-Christoph, K., Wilber, C., & Kleber, H. (1982). Diagnosis and symptoms of depression in opiate addicts. *Archives of General Psychiatry, 39,* 151–156.

Roy, A. (1982). Risk factors for suicide in psychiatric patients. *Archives for General Psychiatry, 39,* 1089–1095.

Salzman, L. (1960). Paranoid state—theory and therapy. *A.M.A. General Archives of Psychiatry, 2,* 679–693.

Schaffer, H. R. (Ed.) (1977). *Studies in mother–infant interaction.* New York: Academic Press.

Schwab, G. (1946). *Gods and heroes: Myths and epics of ancient Greece.* New York: Pantheon.

Schwartz, D. A. (1964). The paranoid-depressive existential continuum. *Psychiatric Quarterly, 38,* 690–706.

Seligman, M. E. P. (1975). *Helplessness: On depression, development, and death.* San Francisco: Freeman.

Simonton, D. C., & Simonton, S. (1978). Belief systems and management of the emotional aspects of malignancy. *Journal of Transpersonal Psychology, 7,* 29–47.

Shneidman, E. S. (1980). Psychotherapy with suicidal patients. In T. B. Karasu & L. Bellack (Eds.), *Specialized techniques in individual psychotherapy.* New York: Brunner-Mazel.

Solomon, G. E., & Amkraut, A. A. (1981). A psychoneuroendocrinological effect of the immune response. *Annual Review of Microbiology, 35,* 155-184.

Spitz, R. (1946a). Anaclitic depression: An inquiry into the genesis of psychiatric conditions in early childhood. *Psychoanalytic study of the child* (Vol. 1). New York: International Universities Press.

Spitz, R. (1946b). Hospitalism: An inquiry into the genesis of psychiatric conditions in early childhood. *Psychoanalytic study of the child* (Vol. 2). New York: International Universities Press.

Spitz, R. (1960). Motherless infants. In N. Haimowitz & T. Haimowitz (Eds.), *Human development.* New York: Crowell.

Teasdale, J. (1983). Negative thinking in depression: Cause, effect, or reciprocal relationship? *Advances in Behavior Research and Therapy, 5,* 3-25.

Thase, M. E., Frank, E., & Kupfer, D. J. (1985). Biological processes in major depression. In E. E. Beckham & W. R. Leber (Eds.), *Handbook of depression: Treatment, assessment, and research.* Homewood, IL: Dorsey Press.

Tsuang, M. T., Bucher, K. T., Fleming, J. A., & Faraone, S. V. (1985). Transmission of affective disorders: An application of segregation analysis to blind family study data. *Journal of Psychiatric Research, 19,* 23-29.

Usdin, G. (Ed.) (1977). *Depression: Clinical, biological and psychological perspectives.* New York: Brunner-Mazel.

Waelder, R. (1951). The structure of paranoid ideas: A critical survey of various theories. *International Journal of Psychoanalysis, 32,* 167-177.

Wetzel, J. W. (1984). *Clinical handbook of depression.* New York: Gardner Press.

Winokur, G. (1983). The validity of familial subtypes in unipolar depression. *McLean Hospital Journal, 2,* 17-37.

Winokur, G., Clayton, P. J., & Reich, T. (1969). *Manic-depressive illness.* St. Louis: Mosby.

Winokur, G., & Crowe, R. R. (1983). Bipolar illness: the sex-polarity effect in affectively ill family members. *Archives of General Psychiatry, 40,* 57-58.

Wolman, B. B. (1966a). *Vectoriasis praecox or the group of schizophrenias.* Springfield, IL: Thomas.

Wolman, B. B. (1966b). *Dr. Jekyll and Mr. Hyde: A new theory of the manic-depressive disorder.* New York: New York Academy of Sciences.

Wolman, B. B. (1970). *Children without childhood: A study of childhood schizophrenia.* New York: Grune & Stratton.

Wolman, B. B. (1973). *Call no man normal.* New York: International Universities Press.

Wolman, B. B. (Ed.) (1978a). *Clinical diagnosis of mental disorders: A handbook.* New York: Plenum.

Wolman, B. B. (1978b). *Children's fears.* New York: Grosset and Dunlop.

Wolman, B. B. (Ed.) (1982a). *Psychological aspects of obesity.* New York: Van Nostrand Reinhold.

Wolman, B. B. (1982b). Interactional theory. In B. B. Wolman (Ed.), *Handbook of developmental psychology.* Englewood Cliffs, NJ: Prentice-Hall.

Wolman, B. B. (1983). Schizophrenia. In B. B. Wolman (Ed.), *The therapist's handbook* (rev. ed.). New York: Van Nostrand Reinhold.

Wolman, B. B. (1984a). *The logic of science in psychoanalysis.* New York: Columbia University Press.

Wolman, B. B. (1984b). *Interactional psychotherapy.* New York: Van Nostrand Reinhold.

Wolman, B. B. (1986). Protoconscious and psychopathology. In B. B. Wolman & M. Ullman (Eds.), *Handbook of states of consciousness.* New York: Van Nostrand Reinhold.

Wolman, B. B. (1987). *The sociopathic personality.* New York: Brunner-Mazel.

Wolman, B. B. (1988). *Psychosomatic disorders.* New York: Plenum.

Wolman, B. B. (1989). *Dictionary of behavioral science.* New York: Plenum.

Wolman, B. B. (in press). *Moral behavior.*

Wolman, B. B., & Krauss, H. H. (Eds.) (1976). *Between survival and suicide.* New York: Gardner Press.

Wolman, B. B., & Ullman, M. (Eds.) (1986). *Handbook of states of consciousness.* New York: Van Nostrand Reinhold.

Zegans, L. S. (1982). Stress and the development of somatic disorders. In L. Goldberger & S. Bresnitz (Eds.), *Handbook of stress.* New York: Free Press.

CHAPTER 6

Genetics of Affective Disorders

ROBERT B. WESNER, MD and GEORGE WINOKUR, MD

A regular finding in the study of affective disorders is that persons with these illnesses often cluster within families. All major psychiatric disorders appear to result at least partially from an inherited predisposition and in that manner are not unlike other medical disorders such as diabetes or coronary artery disease. The theory that affective disorders and other medical disorders share common genetic modes of transmission can be a difficult concept to follow, if one assumes that mental disorders are purely abnormal psychological reactions to environmental events. This is not to say that the environment plays no role in the development and course of these disorders. In fact, the environment probably plays a large role in the development and course of mental disorders and other medical disorders as well.

For example, it is quite clear that coronary artery disease runs in families (Wolinsky, 1979); having a first-degree relative with the disorder is considered to be a risk factor. It is also hypothesized that the environment may influence the course of coronary artery disease. Smoking, obesity, lack of exercise, and high dietary fat content are all environmentally controlled factors that may influence the course of the illness (Messerli, 1986). A person with a genetic predisposition to coronary artery disease will have different physiological reactions to these environmental factors that one who does not possess that predisposition. The heart and blood vessels are then the substrate for the environment to act upon. The physical and metabolic abnormalities that are the product of the genetic diathesis (congenital predisposition) will interact with the environment to produce the usual features of coronary artery disease (i.e., atheromas, reduced coronary blood flow, and angina). Removing or minimizing the environmental factors in coronary artery disease may stall the onset of the disorder, produce clinically insignificant changes, or entirely prevent the development of any manifestation of the disorder. The underlying congenital predisposition, however, remains constant.

The interaction between the environment and genetic factors may be played out similarly in the affective disorders. Certain environmental or biological events in genetically susceptible persons possibly may lead to episodes of affective illness. The combination of environmental and biological genetic factors is the liability that a given individual will develop an affective disorder.

The genetics of any mental disorder can be researched in a variety of ways. In this chapter we will discuss four major research paradigms—twin studies, adoption studies, family studies, and genetic marker studies.

TWIN STUDIES

Twin studies compare the concordance rates for monozygotic and dizygotic twin pairs. Monozygotic twins possess identical sets of genes. Dizygotic twins share only 50 percent of the genes they inherited from their parents and in that manner are exactly the same as other sibling pairs. If a disorder is genetically transmitted, then monozygotic twins should show a higher concordance rate than dizygotic twins because of their identical genetic material. A major assumption in these studies is that environmental factors are controlled, since twins raised by their biological parents share identical environments. Although environmental influences may be important, studies of psychological traits in twins indicate that monozygotic twins who have highly similar environments do not on average show any greater concordance for personality traits or IQ than monozygotic twins with less environmental similarity (Loehlin & Nicholas, 1976).

Five twin studies of affective illness are shown in Table 6.1. The hypothesis of a genetic component for affective disorders is supported by the repeated finding of a higher concordance in monozygotic than in dizygotic pairs. Pooling the data from all studies, an overall concordance rate of 63.8 percent is observed for monozygotic and 14 percent for dizygotic pairs. In a large study using the Danish twin register, Bertelsen and colleagues identified 110 same-sex twin pairs in which at least one had affective disorder (Bertelsen, 1979). Twins were personally interviewed and zygocity was established using serologic markers or, if both twins were not alive, anthropometric methods. Of 55 monozygotic twin pairs, 58.3 percent were concordant for affective disorder whereas only 17.3 percent of the 52 dizygotic pairs were concordant.

In a study of 12 monozygotic twin pairs reared apart, using data gleaned from published series, 67 percent were concordant for affective disorder, a figure strikingly similar to the pooled figure of 63.8 percent (Price, 1968).

TABLE 6.1. Concordance Rates for Affective Illness in Monozygotic and Dizygotic Twins[a]

	Monozygotic Twins		Dizygotic Twins	
Study	Concordant Pairs/ Total Pairs	Concordance (%)	Concordant Pairs/ Total Pairs	Concordance (%)
Slater (1953)	4/7	57.1	4/17	23.5
Kallman (1954)	25/27	92.6	13/55	23.6
Harvald & Hauge (1965)	10/15	66.7	2/40	5.0
Allen, Cohen, Pollin, & Greenspan (1974)	5/15	33.3	0/34	0.0
Bertelsen (1979)	32/55	58.3	9/52	17.3
Totals	*76/119*	*63.8*	*28/198*	*14.1*

[a]Data not corrected for age. Diagnoses include both bipolar and unipolar illness.

Source: Adapted from: Nurnberger, J. I., Goldin, L. R., & Gershorv, E. S. (1986). Genetics of psychiatric disorders. In G. Winokur & P. Clayton (Eds.), *The medical basis of psychiatry* (pp. 486–521). Philadelphia: Saunders.

ADOPTION STUDIES

Adoption studies attempt to separate genetic susceptibility from environmental factors. A demonstration that offspring reared away from their biological parents have higher than expected rates of illness would be a persuasive argument for inheritance.

Adoption studies can be carried out in a number of ways. The simplest method is to identify a group of adopted affected individuals and compare them to a control group of unaffected adoptees. The adoptive and biological parents of both groups would be studied for the presence of illness. If the biological parents of ill adoptees show higher rates of illness than the biological parents of control adoptees and both sets of adoptive parents, then a genetic factor can be said to be present. An adoption study can also be done by identifying ill parents who adopt away their children. These offspring can be compared to adopted-away children born to unaffected parents. A complicated adoption study, the cross-fostering study, compares children of affected biological parents reared by well adoptive parents to children of well biological parents reared by ill adoptive parents.

Adoption studies do not provide information about the mode of transmission. They have been criticized because unknown and unquantifiable factors such as demographics and selection practices among adoption agencies may place children in environments where nongenetic risk factors are prevalent.

The families of adult bipolar adoptees and three control groups were studied by Mendlewicz and Rainer (1977). In addition to the adoptive and biological parents of 29 bipolar adoptees, the study included the biological parents of 31 bipolar nonadoptees, the adoptive and biological parents of 22 unaffected adoptees, and the biological parents of 20 individuals who developed polio. The polio group was added to control for the effect of raising a disabled child. Interviews were conducted blind to the clinical status of the adoptees.

Table 6.2 shows the diagnoses of the adoptive and biological parents. The biological parents of the bipolar adoptees and nonadoptees showed similar rates of affective disorder (31 percent vs 26 percent). These same parents showed higher rates of affective illness than either the adoptive or biological parents of normal adoptees, and higher rates than the parents of polio patients. Three major points can be made from this study. First, the hypothesis of a genetic contribution to bipolar affective disorder is supported by these data. Second, the excess amount of unipolar disorder seen in the biological parents of all bipolar patients supports the notion that unipolar illness in some cases stems from the same genetic abnormality as bipolar illness. Lastly, the data show that unipolar illness is more common in the adoptive parents than bipolar disorder. In fact, only one case of bipolar disorder was found in the adoptive parents.

TABLE 6.2. Affective Illness in Parents of Bipolar Adoptees and Controls

Group	Diagnosis of Parent	Adoptive Parents	Percent Ill	Biological Parents	Percent Ill
Bipolar	Bipolar	1		4	
adoptees	Unipolar	6	12%	12	31%
N = 29	Other affective disorder	0		2	
Bipolar	Bipolar	—	—	2	
nonadoptees	Unipolar	—	—	11	26%
N = 31	Other affective disorder	—	—	3	
Normal	Bipolar	0		0	
adoptees	Unipolar	3	10%	1	2%
N = 22	Other affective disorder	1		0	
Poliomyelitis	Bipolar	—	—	0	
	Unipolar	—	—	4	10%
N = 20	Other affective disorder	—	—	0	

Data from "Adoption Studies Supporting Genetic Transmission in Manic-Depressive Illness" by J. Mendlewicz and J. Rainer, 1977. *Nature, 268,* 326–329.

This suggests that unipolar disorder is probably a heterogeneous group of illnesses, with some being related to bipolar illness and others perhaps not genetically mediated at all.

Wender, Kety, and Rosenthal (1986) studied the biological and adoptive families of 71 adoptees with affective disorders and 71 matched control adoptees with no illness. Biological relatives of ill adoptees had significantly higher rates of affective disorder (bipolar and unipolar) compared to the biological relatives of controls. Alcohol abuse and dependence was also seen in greater frequency among the biological relatives of ill adoptees, supporting earlier findings that in some cases affective disorders and alcoholism may be genetically related. The most significant finding was a striking increase in completed suicide in the biological relatives of ill adoptees, compared to those of controls.

In a study by Cadoret, 83 adoptees were selected from adoption records showing evidence that their biological parents had mental disorders (Cadoret, 1978). Forty-three matched controls were also obtained. All adoptees and at least one adoptive parent were interviewed. All data were collected blind to the diagnosis of the biological parents. Eight adoptees were found to have one biological parent with an affective disorder. Three of these adoptees were diagnosed as having an affective disorder, all of which were unipolar illnesses (38 percent). The remaining 75 adoptees in the experimental group and the 43 controls had four (5 percent) and four (9 percent) cases of unipolar depression respectively. The differences in the observed rates of affective illness in the adoptees of biological parents with affective disorder compared to those without such a disorder are significant.

In a large study of 2,966 adoptees born in Sweden and adopted out prior to age three, Von Knorring and colleagues identified 56 adoptees with affective disorders and 59 with substance abuse (Von Knorring, Cloninger, Bohman, & Sigvardsson, 1983). Each affected adoptee was matched to one of 115 control adoptees with no mental illness. Adoptees with affective disorder showed no higher rates of affective disorder in either the biological or adoptive parents when compared to parents of matched controls. There was, however, a trend for nonpsychotic depressed adoptees to have more mothers with affective disorders than normal controls. Adoptees with affective disorder did show a significant increase in biological mothers with substance abuse compared to mothers of adoptees with no illness. No general concordance of any specific psychiatric diagnosis was observed between adoptees and biological parents.

It should be pointed out that all subjects in this study were diagnosed by medical records only. Subjects identified as having no psychiatric illness could have, in fact, had episodes of illness that were treated but not recorded, misdiagnosed, or not treated at all. In support of this, not one of the eight parents of adoptees with psychotic depression was diagnosed as having affective disorder. Although this is possible and is similar to the rate found in the controls, it is much lower than the rate observed in studies where relatives are directly examined. Despite its shortcomings, the study does suggest that some cases of unipolar depression may not be genetically transmitted.

FAMILY STUDIES

Family studies are easily applied to the research of the genetics of affective disorders and have been its cornerstone. Studies such as these usually begin with an affected individual (proband) and study all available relatives. Two basic types of family research are recognized. The family history method involves obtaining all pedigree information from the proband only. Studies of this nature have been criticized because other affected family members may conceal their illnesses or may have milder forms of illness that would go unnoticed by others (Andreasen, Endicott, Spitzer, & Winokur, 1977). In general, family history studies are biased by underreporting. The second, more complete type of family study involves the direct examination of all available relatives.

Family studies are useful in delineating the range of disorders that may be associated with a single genetic vulnerability. For example, Winokur demonstrated through a series of family studies that unipolar depression, alcoholism, and sociopathy cluster in certain kindreds, suggesting that all three stem from the same genetic abnormality (Winokur, 1972). When two or more disorders appear to be genetically related, they are referred to as a spectrum.

A family study attempts to identify all affected persons. In order to show that an illness is familial, the rates of illness in the relatives of probands must be higher than the rates of the same illness in controls. The statistic used to compare families of probands to controls is called the morbid risk—the ratio of the number of ill relatives divided by the total number of relatives at risk for the disorder. The calculation of the number at risk for the disorder must take into account variable age of onset. In order to do this, the number of relatives who are in a particular decade is multiplied by the percentage of affected persons who first become ill by that decade of their lives. This product is called the Bezugziffer (BZ). For each decade, BZs are summed and the total number is used in the calculation of the morbid risk (Nurnberger, Goldin, & Gershon, 1986).

The familial concentration of affective disorders has been clearly demonstrated in numerous family studies. Table 6.3 shows the lifetime prevalence of affective disorders in first-degree relatives of patients and controls. Of the eight studies listed, eight identified bipolar

TABLE 6.3. Morbid Risk for Bipolar and Unipolar Disorders in First-Degree Relatives of Patients and Controls

	Number at Risk	Morbid Risk (%) Bipolar	Unipolar
Bipolar probands:			
Angst (1966)	161	4.3	13.0
Perris (1966)	627	10.2	0.5
Winokur & Clayton (1967b)	167	10.2	20.4
Helzer & Winokur (1974)	151	4.6	10.6
Gershon, Baron, & Leckman (1975)	341	3.8	6.8
Smeraldi, Negri, & Melica (1977)	172	5.8	7.1
Taylor, Abrams, & Hayman (1980)	601	4.8	4.2
Gershon, Goldin, Weissman, & Nurnberger (1981)	598(572)[a]	8.0	14.9
Unipolar probands:			
Angst (1966)	811	0.3	5.1
Perris (1966)	684	0.3	6.4
Gershon, Baron, & Leckman (1975)	96	2.1	11.5
Smeraldi, Negri, & Melica (1977)	185	0.6	8.0
Taylor, Abrams, & Hayman (1980)	96	4.1	8.3
Gershon, Goldin, Weissman, & Nurnberger (1981)	138(133)	2.9	16.6
Normal probands:			
Gershon, Baron, & Leckman (1975)	518(411)	0.2	0.7
Gershon, Goldin, Weissman, & Nurnberger (1981)	217(208)	0.5	5.8

[a]Total number at risk for bipolar illness appears first. The number in parentheses represents the number at risk for unipolar disorder when known.
Source: Adapted from: Gershon, E. S., Hamovit, J., Guroff, J. J., Dibble, E., Leckman, J. F., Sceery, W., Targum, S. D., Nurnberger, J. I., Goldin, L. R., & Bunney, W. E. (1982). A family study of schizo affective, bipolar I, bipolar II, unipolar and normal control probands. *Archives of General Psychiatry, 39,* 1157–1167.

probands, six identified unipolar probands, and two utilized unaffected controls. Bipolar and unipolar probands had more relatives ill with either disorder than did normal control probands. The most common affective disorder seen in the relatives of either unipolar or bipolar probands was unipolar disorder. This suggests that at least in some families bipolar and unipolar illnesses are different phenotypic expressions of the same genetic illness.

As seen from Table 6.3, morbid risk figures vary widely among studies. There are many reasons for these observed variations. Diagnostic criteria employed, method of data collection, and cultural factors all vary and may be responsible for the differences observed. Studies utilizing a family history method tend to underestimate prevalences, whereas direct examination of all available relatives tends to produce a higher figure that may be a more correct estimate of the true prevalence.

Although each study has its own flaws with respect to methodology and cannot be directly compared to the others, each shows a clear increase in affective disorder among first-degree relatives of ill probands. Taken together, family studies support the genetic hypothesis in the transmission of affective disorders.

Family, twin, and adoption studies, regardless of methodological flaws, all support the hypothesis of a genetic component for affective disorder. Just how affective disorder is transmitted is not known. Segregation analysis of family study data has failed to show the exact mode of transmission for any affective disorder (Gershon, Bunney, Leckman, Van Eerdewegh, & De Bauche, 1976). There are likely to be several reasons for this, but in order to proceed with this discussion two definitions are needed: *Genotype* is the actual inherited genetic material, and *phenotype* is the observed effect of the genotype.

Genotype and Phenotype

Since the environment may play a role in the development of the disorder, the absence of critical environmental factors may obscure the mode of transmission: Certain individuals with a genetic predisposition (affected genotype) and no environmental input may not show the disease (affected phenotype) at all. The finding that monozygotic twins fail to show 100 percent concordance for affective disorders suggests that the disease may not manifest itself in all persons who possess the gene. Reduced penetrance, the term applied to this phenomenon, may play a role in many mental disorders—schizophrenia and anxiety disorders, as well as affective disorders. Any genetic illness with low penetrance would clinically appear to be uncommon even though the actual frequency of the disease gene may be high. The possibility that many individuals could be carriers without overt illness would make it nearly impossible to determine the mode of transmission from family study data alone. Reduced penetrance implies that the disease gene does not manifest itself at any time in a carrier's lifetime, assuming that the carrier has lived through the entire age of risk for the disorder. The accepted ages of risk for bipolar and unipolar disorder are 20–50 years and 20–70 years respectively (Paykel, 1982). Since affective disorders have a variable age of onset, the penetrance of a disease gene may be age-dependent. In any family study there will be a large number of individuals who may be gene carriers but who have not yet reached the age where the illness manifests itself. The ideal family for segregation analysis would be a large kindred with the youngest generation well into the age of risk and with a clear unilateral source of illness. Since family studies examine pedigrees only at one point in time, many younger family members who may be carrier would be classified as unaffected, thereby obscuring the path of transmission.

Until now it has been assumed that a single disease gene leads to a defined single phenotype. This assumption may not be valid for clinical psychiatry; there is evidence that phenotypes may vary from person to person even though they may contain the same genetic material. Winokur described a clinical spectrum of disorders termed *depression spectrum disease,* which includes sociopathy, unipolar depression, and alcoholism (Winokur, 1972). This clustering appeared to breed true, and a closer look at the families studied showed that the cases of depression were commonly seen in women under the age of 40 who had unstable personalities; alcoholism and sociopathy were more commonly seen in males. Winokur's work suggested that the three disorders may stem from a single genetic abnormality that manifests itself differently due to sex effect and/or perhaps other undetermined environmental or biological factors. Other clinical studies have shown affective disorder to cluster with eating disorders and panic disorder in certain families (Cantwell, Sturzenberger, Burrows, Salkin, & Green, 1977; Leckman, Weissman, Merikangas, Pauls, & Prusoff, 1983). Even among affective disorders, the wide range of possible phenotypes includes bipolar I, bipolar II, unipolar, cyclothymia, dysthymia, and schizoaffective disorder. Whether all these disorders stem from the same genetic diathesis is a matter for debate, but the fact that many kindreds do show more than one type of disorder suggests that, for at least some families, single genetic abnormalities produce a variety of phenotypes.

Since affective disorders are not determined from laboratory or other biological/physical exams, the diagnosis is made purely from the description of the disorder made by the patient and sometimes by a knowledgeable informant. The absence of objective tests for diagnosis means that other disorders with a different pathophysiology may mimic an affective illness. Examples include hypothyroidism, reactive depression, Cushing's disease, and bereavement. Cases such as these, called phenocopies, may be clinically indistinguishable from primary affective disorders. Phenocopies are probably common in studies of unipolar depression (depending upon the diagnostic criteria used) and would certainly obscure efforts to find the mode of transmission in the families involved.

Heterogeneity

The last and perhaps most difficult obstacle to uncovering the mode of transmission for any affective disorder is heterogeneity. Genetic heterogeneity is a factor in many diseases. For example, diabetes in

its variety of forms may stem from several different genetic abnormalities. Early onset (insulin-dependent) and late onset (non-
insulin-dependent) have different pathophysiologies and it has been
demonstrated that non-insulin-dependent diabetes is familial but the
insulin-dependent form is not (Unger & Foster, 1985). In a study of a
heterogeneous illness, detecting the mode of transmission would be
nearly impossible. A variety of genetic mechanisms would be in play
and each would have its own mode of transmission. In an attempt to
limit the heterogeneity factor, families showing X-linked inheritance
have been singled out for analysis. In these cases there is a father-to-
son transmission because fathers can pass only a Y chromosome on
to their sons. It is assumed in these cases that the genetic abnormality
is limited to the X chromosome, thereby excluding all of the auto-
somes. In X-linked dominant transmission, females would be affected more often because they possess two X chromosomes and
therefore have twice the risk of getting a disease gene. Winokur and
colleagues observed both an excess of ill females and a lack of male-
to-male transmission in a study of 62 bipolar probands (Winokur,
Clayton, & Reich, 1969). They postulated an X-linked dominant
mode of transmission for bipolar illness in these selected kindreds.
These data and others, however, have been reanalyzed, and neither
an X-linked or an autosomal single-major-locus model of transmission could explain totally the cases of bipolar illness observed in
these families (Bucher et al., 1981; Bucher & Elston, 1982). X-linked
dominant transmission was also postulated by Mendlewicz and Fleiss
in a series of bipolar probands but a reanalysis of these data found
that the X-chromosome single-major-locus model did not fit their
data (Mendlewicz & Fleiss, 1974; Van Eerdewegh, Gershon, & Van
Eerdewegh, 1980). Data from families suggesting X linkage remain
conflicting and the results obtained vary, based on assumptions
made and statistical methods used. The hypothesis of an X-linked
form of affective disorder is likely to be viable but probably accounts
for only a minority of cases.

As mentioned earlier, variable phenotype may hinder segregation
analysis studies and thereby obscure the mode of transmission. This
issue has been taken up by a number of researchers in the analysis of
family study data. Gershon and colleagues have hypothesized that
unipolar, bipolar I, bipolar II, and schizoaffective disorders are all
part of a continuum stemming from a common genetic background
with multiple thresholds (Gershon et al., 1982). Their family study
data are in support of that model. Further support for the concept
of variable expressivity comes from work by Winokur. In one
study (Winokur, 1984), the morbid risks for affective disorder in
first-degree relatives of bipolar and unipolar probands were nearly
identical. In another study (Winokur, Kadrmas, & Crowe, 1986),

first-degree relatives of schizoaffective bipolars were found to have morbid risks for affective disorder similar to those of first-degree relatives of other bipolar probands. Smeraldi, Fiammetta, Heimbuch, and Kidd (1981) found that the probands' polarity did not predict illness in relatives.

Sex differences in the transmission of affective disorders have been demonstrated. Winokur and Clayton found that ill mothers more often transmitted their illness to daughters than to sons whereas ill fathers transmitted their illness with equal frequency to both sons and daughters (Winokur and Clayton, 1967a). Angst, Frey, Lohmeyer, and Zerbin-Rudin (1980) demonstrated that first-degree female relatives of female probands had higher morbidity risks than other relatives. At this point it is clear that the mode of transmission for affective disorders is not known and is likely to be complex, even though the familial clustering of these illnesses is easily demonstrated.

GENETIC MARKER STUDIES

Genetic markers pose a new method to uncover the inheritability of affective disorders. It is possible that genetic markers may uncover subtypes of illness that are linked to a particular marker, thereby directly addressing the problems of heterogeneity and variable expressivity.

The search for genetic markers linked to mental disorders has included studies of color blindness, blood group polymorphisms, HLA (human leukocyte antigen) types, and DNA (deoxyribonucleic acid) markers. The methodology used in these studies is called linkage analysis. This method determines the probability that a genetic marker and a disease trait are inherited together, suggesting that they are physically close to one another on the same chromosome. Marker loci must be polymorphic; that is, they must have at least two forms so that one form can be demonstrated to be linked to a particular disease. Additionally, the mode of inheritance for the marker locus must be known. If linkage can be demonstrated between marker locus and disease locus, it is convincing evidence for the presence of a genetic component, since it is unlikely that environmental influences would cause such an association.

Linkage

To demonstrate linkage, it is necessary to employ mathematical models to estimate the likelihood of linkage. The lod (log of the odds ratio) score method of Morton tests the hypothesis of linkage between two loci (marker and disease) when the mode of transmission of each locus is known (Morton, 1955). This method assumes that the gene frequency and penetrance for the disease and marker loci are known. It is also assumed that there is no population association between the marker and disease loci and that random mating occurs. The pattern of segregation seen between the marker and disease loci is compared to the probability of observing the same pattern if the two loci are not linked (random assortment). The probability of linkage is expressed in terms of the recombination fraction called theta. On a given chromosome, genes can recombine at the time of meiosis. Genes that lie far apart will recombine more frequently than genes that are close together. If a marker locus and disease locus are tightly linked, then they should recombine infrequently. Theta takes on a value between zero and one half. A recombination fraction of one half means that the loci are expected to recombine 50 percent of the time; that is, they segregate independently and are not linked. At the other extreme, a recombination fraction of zero means that the loci are expected never to recombine and always to segregate together. Using these recombination fractions a lod score is defined as:

$$\text{LOD Score} = \log_{10} \frac{\text{probability of observing a family for } \theta < \frac{1}{2}}{\text{probability of observing a family for } \theta = \frac{1}{2}}$$

A lod score of 1.0 indicates that linkage is 10 times more likely than no linkage. LOD scores are calculated for several values of theta because there is no way of directly determining its exact value. The recombination fraction that gives the highest score is considered to be the best estimate of theta. By convention, a lod score of 3.0 is required to establish linkage. A score of -2.0 excludes linkage. Intermediate scores indicate that not enough information is available to make a conclusion on linkage and more families would need to be studied in order to confirm or exclude linkage. LOD scores can be summed across families so that several families, each giving a small positive or negative lod score, can be taken together to provide evidence confirming or excluding linkage. Statistical software packages are available that will compute lod scores on personal computers.

The lod score method has certain disadvantages when applied to the genetics of mental disorders. First, the method requires that the mode of inheritance for both the marker locus and disease locus be known. In most cases the mode of inheritance for the marker locus is known but very little is known about the mode of transmission for the disease locus. As mentioned earlier, the exact mode of inheritance for *any* mental disorder is unknown at this time. Most genetic marker studies using the lod score method for psychiatric disorders assume that the trait is transmitted in an autosomal-dominant fashion, with reduced penetrance. This assumption may not be valid.

The lod score method works best with diseases that show complete penetrance. Although newer versions of statistical packages that compute lod scores include functions to account for age-dependent and incomplete penetrance, the fact that psychiatric disorders do not show complete penetrance reduces the value of the lod score method for these types of disorders. Genetic marker studies using the lod score method have had to make estimates of disease penetrance, and these estimates have varied widely. At this time there is no way of estimating the true penetrance for any mental disorder (Kennedy et al., 1988). This is unfortunate because the penetrance function is highly sensitive to minor changes and it has been demonstrated that lod scores can vary widely, depending on what value of penetrance is used for the disease gene. Another disadvantage of the lod score method is that it is most powerful for large, multigenerational families, which are difficult to come by in clinical psychiatry. The lod score method can be easily applied to small, nuclear families, but obtaining the large number required to calculate a meaningful lod score can be difficult.

The sib-pair method of Penrose was developed to study linkage of various diseases to HLA loci but can be applied to other genetic markers as well (Penrose, 1953). In this method, affected sib-pairs are compared for the presence of a specific marker. If the affected pairs share the marker together more often than can be expected to result from chance alone, then a case can be made for an association between the marker and the disease. This method requires fewer assumptions than the lod score method. It does not require complete pedigrees, or that the mode of inheritance be known, or that the gene frequency and penetrance of the disease and marker loci be known. For these reasons, the sib-pair method is useful for diseases thought to have low penetrance. A specific disadvantage of the sib-pair method is that, to be informative, it requires highly polymorphic loci. Other, less polymorphic loci can be used in a sib-pair analysis but very large sample sizes are required to obtain adequate results.

Both the lod score method and the sib-pair method calculate probabilities of linkage. Both can be applied to specific clinical situations and each has its own distinct advantages and disadvantages. A major problem for both of these methods, however, is that neither can adequately address the issue of genetic heterogeneity. Both methods assume that the disease in question is caused by the same genetic locus in each person. If genetic heterogeneity is present, then pooling families or sib-pairs would lead to erroneous results.

Color blindness, XG blood group marker, and glucose-6-phosphate dehydrogenase (G6PD) deficiency are three X chromosome markers that have been studied for linkage to bipolar illness. Interest in the possibility of a genetic locus for bipolar illness on the X chromosome started after Winokur presented a family in which X-linked color blindness segregated with manic-depressive illness in a large kindred (Winokur, Clayton, & Reich, 1969). Shortly thereafter, Mendlewicz reported evidence of linkage of bipolar illness to the red cell XG locus, which is on the opposite arm of the X chromosome as color blindness (Mendlewicz, Fleiss, & Fieve, 1975). Mendlewicz reported linkage between bipolar illness and G6PD deficiency in a single large pedigree (Mendlewicz, Linkowski, & Wilmotte, 1980). Alternatively, Gershon found no evidence of linkage to either color blindness or XG blood group in a series of families (Gershon, 1980). It is clear that research on the X chromosome has yielded conflicting results, with some pedigrees showing evidence for linkage to color blindness, XG blood group, and G6PD deficiency, and others showing no evidence of linkage. These conflicting results may be due in part to methodological uncertainties, but the presence of genetic heterogeneity may also be a factor. In a recent study of genetic linkage of bipolar illness to G6PD deficiency and color blindness, Baron reported a maximum lod score of 7.52 assuming homogeneity and 9.17 assuming heterogeneity for the disorder (Baron et al., 1987). His results provide confirmation that a major psychiatric disorder can be caused by a single genetic trait. It appears from these data that the existence of an X-linked locus is involved in the etiology of some cases of bipolar disorder.

The HLA locus on chromosome 6 has been a source of some interest. In one of the early studies of HLA and affective disorder, Shapiro reported an increased frequency of HLA BW16 in patients (Shapiro, Block, Rafaelson, Ryder, & Srejgaard, 1976). Smeraldi reported that affected sib-pairs shared HLA haplotypes more often than would be expected from chance alone (Smeraldi, Negri, Melica, & Scorza-Smeraldi, 1978). Other studies have failed to show a significant association of HLA haplotypes in affective disorder (Goldin, Clerget-Darpoux, & Gershon, 1982). Weitkamp, reporting data from a sib-pair study of HLA haplotypes, found that the frequency of haplotype sharing did not deviate from random (Weitkamp, Stancer, Persad, Flood, & Guttormsen, 1981). Other studies have also failed to demonstrate any relationships between HLA and affective disorder. In summary, studies of association between HLA haplotypes and affective disorder have yielded inconsistent results.

Several other autosomal markers have been tested for linkage to affective disorders. Depending on the method of diagnosis used and the statistical analysis employed, weak evidence of linkage to several autosomal markers has been demonstrated. An overview of selected recent studies of linkage between affective disorders and autosomal markers is presented in Table 6.4. Depression spectrum disease had shown weak linkage to haptoglobin and compliment factor 3 in two

TABLE 6.4. Linkage Studies of Affective Disorders and Protein Polymorphisms

Study	Diagnostic System	Statistical Analysis	Significant Results
Tanna, Winokur, Elston, & Go (1976)	DSD[a]	Sib-pair	Provisional linkage to C3 and HP
	FPDD[b]	Sib-pair	Provisional linkage to GC, PCM1
Tanna, Go, Winokur, & Elston (1977)	FPDD	LOD Score	Provisional linkage to GC
Tanna, Go, Winokur, & Elston (1979)	DSD	LOD Score	Provisional linkage to HP
Johnson, Hunt, Robertson, & Doran (1981)	BP + UP[c]	LOD Score	Provisional evidence for GC; excluded ABO, RH, HP
Goldin & Gershon (1983)	BP + UP	LOD Scores	Provisional evidence for MNS
Fieve, Go, Dunner, & Elston (1984)	BP + UP	Sib-pair	Provisional linkage to PEPA
Hill, Wilson, Elston, & Winokur (1988)	DSD & FPDD	Sib-pair	Provisional linkage to MNS for FPDD & ORM for DSD

[a] DSD = Depression Spectrum Disease
[b] FPDD = Familial Pure Depressive Disease
[c] BP + UP = Bipolar and Unipolar Disorders

studies (Tanna, Winokur, Elston, & Go, 1976a; Tanna, Go, Winokur, & Elston, 1979). Provisional evidence of linkage has also been reported for PGM1 and GC in two separate studies of familial pure depressive disease families (Tanna, Winokur, Elston, & Go, 1976b; Tanna, Go, Winokur, & Elston, 1977). Three studies that took bipolar and unipolar illness together as a single illness found provisional evidence of linkage to PEPA in one study, to MNS blood group marker in another, and to GC blood group marker in a third (Fieve, Go, Dunner, & Elston, 1984; Goldin, Gershon, Targum, Sparkes, & McGinniss, 1983; Johnson, Hunt, Robertson, & Doran, 1981). In a recent study by Hill, Wilson, Elston, and Winokur (1988), indications of linkage between familial pure depressive disease and MNS blood group marker and between depression spectrum disease and orosomucoid on chromosome 9 were found to support previously reported findings. All of these protein polymorphism studies share methodological flaws with other genetic studies. The differences in methods used may, in part, explain the differences observed.

DNA Marker Studies

Advancement in molecular biological techniques has allowed geneticists to study specific DNA markers and their relationships to specific disease loci. These advances have led to the chromosomal localization of genes responsible for several diseases, including Huntington's chorea, Duchenne's dystrophy, and cystic fibrosis. The discovery of polymorphic DNA probes has provided a new method to test genetic hypotheses using probes that are specific for a particular marker. Investigators can see whether a particular disease is linked to a marker detected by a DNA probe. Polymorphic DNA probes can recognize specific nucleic acid and sequences that have been cut with restriction enzymes derived from bacteria. These specific nucleic acid sequences are referred to as restriction fragments and each is a characteristic length. Each individual's DNA contains restriction sites that are inherited in a Mendelian fashion. When a specific DNA probe binds to a fragment that has been cleaved by a restriction enzyme, the combination is referred to as a restriction fragment length polymorphism (RFLP). RFLPs can be examined in families evidencing affective illness to see which RFLPs may cosegregate with the illness. RFLPs that always cosegregate with the illness can be considered tightly linked to the disease locus.

To date, five DNA marker studies of affective disorders have been carried out. The first by Egeland et al. (1987) examined a large Amish kindred for linkage of bipolar affective disorder to markers on chromosome 11. It was demonstrated in their study that bipolar illness in the Amish kindred was linked to the Harvey-ras oncogene on the short arm of chromosome 11 with a maximum lod score of 4.32 at a recombination fraction of 0. Additionally, a weaker linkage to the insulin locus was shown. The insulin locus is adjacent to the Harvey-ras locus, and a maximum lod score of 2.63 was obtained at a recombination fraction of 0. Four additional studies of the Harvey-ras oncogene and insulin gene have failed to demonstrate evidence of linkage in other families (Detera-Wadleigh et al., 1987; Gill, McKeon, & Humphries, 1988; Hodgkinson et al., 1987; Wesner, Scheftner, Palmer, Crowe, & Winokur, 1990). In a separate DNA marker study, Mendlewicz et al. (1987) presented evidence of linkage of factor 9 on the X chromosome to bipolar illness in selected kindreds. A maximum lod score of 3.10 was obtained at a recombination fraction of .11.

DNA marker studies of affective disorders are new and they await replication. The fact that no replication has been successful suggests that there are methodological flaws even within the reported DNA marker studies. DNA marker technology should provide a powerful tool to look at the genetics of all mental disorders. As the technology improves, we would hope that the ability to analyze specific areas of the genome will improve to the point that we will be able to find valid genetic markers for all major psychiatric illnesses.

SUMMARY

Affective disorders appear to have a genetic component. Twin, adoption, family, and biological marker studies all provide some evidence to support this idea. Once valid genetic causes for affective disorder are found, the interaction between the environmental and genetic factors can be better understood.

REFERENCES

Allen, M. G., Cohen, S., Pollin, W., & Greenspan, S.I. (1974). Affective illness in veteran twins: A diagnostic review. *American Journal of Psychiatry, 131,* 1234–1239.

Andreasen, N. C., Endicott, J., Spitzer, R. L., & Winokur, G. (1977). A family history method using diagnostic criteria, reliability, and validity. *Archives of General Psychiatry, 34,* 1229–1235.

Angst, J. (1966). Zur Atiologie und Nosolgie endogoner depressiver Psychosen. In *Monographien ans dem Gesamtgebrete der Neurologie und Psychiatrie* (No. 112). Berlin: Springer-Verlag.

Angst, J., Frey, R., Lohmeyer, B., & Zerbin-Rudin, E. (1980). Bipolar manic depressive psychosis: Results of a genetic investigation. *Human Genetics, 55,* 237–254.

Baron, M., Risch, N., Hamberger, R., Mandel, B., Kushner, S., Newman, M., Drumer, D., & Belmaker, R. H. (1987). Genetic linkage between X-chromosome markers and bipolar affective illness. *Nature, 236,* 289–292.

Bertelsen, A. (1979). A Danish twin study of manic depressive disorders. In M. Schou & E. Strongren (Eds.), *Origin, prevention, and treatment of affective disorders* (pp. 227–239). London: Academic Press.

Bucher, K. D., & Elston, R. C. (1982). The transmission of manic-depressive illness: I. Theory, description of the model, and summary of results. *Journal of Psychiatric Research, 16,* 53–63.

Bucher, K. D., Elston, R. C., Green, R., Whybrow, P., Helzer, J., Reich, T., Clayton, P., & Winokur, G. (1981). The transmission of manic-depressive illness: II. Segregation analysis of three sets of family data. *Journal of Psychiatric Research, 16,* 65–78.

Cadoret, R. (1978). Evidence of genetic inheritance of primary affective disorder in adoptees. *American Journal of Psychiatry, 135,* 463–466.

Cantwell, D. P., Sturzenberger, S., Burrows, J., Salkin, B., & Green, J. K. (1977). Anorexia nervosa: An affective disorder. *Archives of General Psychiatry, 34,* 1087–1093.

Detera-Wadleigh, S. D., Berrettini, W. H., Goldin, L. R., Boorman, D., Anderson, S., & Gershon, E. (1987). Close linkage of c-Harvey-ras I and the insulin gene to affective disorders is ruled out in three North American pedigrees. *Nature, 325,* 806–808.

Egeland, J. A., Gerhard, D. S., Pauls, D. L., Sussex, J. N., Kidd, K. K., Allen, C. R., Hostetter, A. M., & Hausman, D. E. (1987). Bipolar affective disorders linked to DNA markers on chromosome 11. *Nature, 325,* 783–787.

Fieve, R. R., Go, R., Dunner, D. L., Elston, R. C. (1984). Search for biological/genetic markers in a long-term epidemiological and morbid risk study of affective disorders. *Journal of Psychiatric Research, 18,* 425–445.

Gershon, E. S. (1980). Nonreplication of linkage to X-chromosome markers in bipolar illness. *Archives of General Psychiatry, 37,* 1200.

Gershon, E. S., Baron, M., & Leckman, J. F. (1975). Genetic models of the transmission of affective disorders. *Journal of Psychiatric Research, 12,* 301–317.

Gershon, E. S., Bunney, W. E., Leckman, J. F., Van Eerdewegh, M., & De Bauche, B. A. (1976). The inheritance of affective disorders: A review of data and of hypotheses. *Behavioral Genetics, 6,* 227–261.

Gershon, E. S., Goldin, L. R., Weissman, M. N., & Nurnberger, J. I. (1981). Family and genetic studies of affective disorders in the Eastern United States: A provisional summary. In C. Perris, G. Struwe, & B. Jansson (Eds.), *Biological psychiatry* (pp. 157–162). Amsterdam: Elsevier.

Gershon, E. S., Hamovit, J., Guroff, J. J., Dibble, E. D., Leckman, J., Sceery, W., Targum, S. D., Nurnberger, J. I., Goldin, L., & Bunney, W. E. (1982). A family study of schizoaffective, bipolar I, bipolar II, unipolar and normal control probands. *Archives of General Psychiatry, 39,* 1157–1167.

Gill, M., McKeon, P., & Humphries, P. (1988). Linkage analysis of manic depression in an Irish family using H-ras I and INS DNA markers. *Journal of Medical Genetics, 25,* 634–637.

Goldin, L. R., Clerget-Darpoux, F., & Gershon, E. S. (1982). Relationship of HLA to major affective disorders not supported. *Psychiatry Research, 7*, 29–45.

Goldin, L. R., Gershon, E. S., Targum, S. D., Sparkes, R. S., & McGinniss, M. (1983). Segregation and linkage analysis in families of patients with bipolar, unipolar, and schizoaffective disorders. *American Journal of Human Genetics, 35,* 274–287.

Harvald, B., & Hauge, M. (1965). Hereditary factors elucidated by twin studies. In J. V. Neal, M. W. Shull, W. J. Shaw, (Eds.), *Genetics and the epidemiology of chronic diseases* (Publication 1163, pp. 61–76). Washington, DC: Public Health Service.

Helzer, J. E., Winokur, G. (1974). A family interview study of male manic depressives. *Archives of General Psychiatry, 31,* 73–77.

Hill, E. M., Wilson, A. F., Elston, R. C., & Winokur, G. (1988). Evidence for possible linkage between genetic markers and affective disorders. *Biological Psychiatry, 24,* 903–917.

Hodgkinson, S., Sherrington, R., Gurling, H., Marchbanks, R., Reeders, S., Mallet, J., McInniss, M., Petursson, H., & Brynjolfsson, J. (1987). Molecular genetic evidence for heterogeneity in manic depression. *Nature, 325,* 805–806.

Johnson, G. F., Hunt, G. E., Robertson, S., & Doran, T. J. (1981). A linkage study of manic depressive disorders with HLA antigens, blood groups, serum proteins and red cell enzymes. *Journal of Affective Disorders, 3,* 43–58.

Kallman, F. (1954). Genetic principles in manic depressive psychosis. In P. H. Hoch & J. Zubin (Eds.), *Depression* (pp. 1–24). New York: Grune & Stratton.

Kennedy, J. L., Guiffra, L. A., Moises, H. W., Cavalli-Sforza, L. L., Pakstis, A. J., Kidd, J. R., Catiglione, C. M., Sjogren, B., Wetterberg, L., & Kidd, K. K. (1988). Evidence against linkage of schizophrenia to markers on chromosome 5 in a Northern Swedish pedigree. *Nature, 336,* 167–170.

Leckman, J. F., Weissman, M. M., Merikangas, K. R., Pauls, D. L., & Prusoff, B. A. (1983). Panic disorder and major depression: Increased risk of depression, alcoholism, panic and phobic disorders in families of depressed probands with panic disorder. *Archives of General Psychiatry, 40,* 1055–1060.

Loehlin, J. C., & Nicholas, R. C. (1976). *Heredity, environment and personality: A study of 850 sets of twins.* Austin, TX: University of Texas Press.

Mendlewicz, J., & Fleiss, J. L. (1974). Linkage studies with X-chromosome markers in bipolar and unipolar illnesses. *Biological Psychiatry, 9,* 261–294.

Mendlewicz, J., Fleiss, J. L., & Fieve, R. R. (1975). Linkage studies in affective disorders: The XG blood group in manic depressive illness. In R. R. Fieve, D. Rosenthal, & H. Brill (Eds.), *Genetic research in psychiatry* (pp. 289–304). Baltimore: Johns Hopkins University Press.

Mendlewicz, J., Linkowski, P., & Wilmotte, J. (1980). Linkage between glucose-6-phosphate dehydrogenase deficiency in manic depressive psychosis. *British Journal of Psychiatry, 137,* 337–342.

Mendlewicz, J., & Rainer, J. D. (1977). Adoption studies supporting genetic transmission in manic depressive illness. *Nature, 268,* 326–329.

Mendlewicz, J., Simon, P., Sevy, S., Charon, F., Brocas, H., Legros, S., & Vassart, G. (1987). Polymorphic DNA marker on X-chromosome in manic depression. *Lancet, 1,* 1230–1232.

Messerli, F. H. (1986). *Risk factors in cardiovascular disease* (Vol. 4, pp. 1–24). Philadelphia: Saunders.

Morton, N. E. (1955). Sequential tests for the detection of linkage. *American Journal of Human Genetics, 7,* 277–318.

Nurnberger, J. I., Goldin, L. R., & Gershon, E. S. (1986). Genetics of psychiatric disorders. In G. Winokur & P. Clayton (Eds.), *The medical basis of psychiatry* (pp. 486–521). Philadelphia: Saunders.

Paykel, E. S. (1982). *Handbook of affective disorders.* New York: Guilford.

Penrose, L. S. (1953). The general purpose sibpair linkage test. *Annals of Eugenics, 18,* 120–124.

Perris, C. (1966). A study of bipolar (manic-depressive) and unipolar recurrent depressive psychoses. *Acta psychiatrica Scandinavia (suppl.), 194,* 15–44.

Price, J. (1968). The genetics of depressive behavior. In A. Coppen & A. Walk (Eds.), *Recent developments in affective disorders* (pp. 37–54). *British Journal of Psychiatry* special publication no. 2.

Shapiro, R. W., Block, E., Rafaelson, O. J., Ryder, L. P., & Svejgaard, A. (1976). Histocompatibility antigens and manic depressive disorders. *Archives of General Psychiatry, 33,* 823–825.

Slater, E. (1953). Psychotic and neurotic illnesses in twins. *Medical Research Council of Great Britain Special Report Series.* London: Her Majesty's Stationery Office.

Smeraldi, E., Fiammetta, N., Heimbuch, R. C., & Kidd, K. K. (1981). Familial patterns and possible modes of inheritance of primary affective disorders. *Journal of Affective Disorders, 3,* 173–182.

Smeraldi, E., Negri, F., & Melica, A. M. (1977). A genetic study of affective disorder. *Acta Psychiatrica Scandinavia, 56,* 382–398.

Smeraldi, E., Negri, F., Melica, A. M., & Scorza-Smeraldi, R. (1978). HLA system and affective disorders: A sibship genetic study. *Tissue Antigens, 12,* 270–274.

Tanna, V. L., Go, R. C., Winokur, G., & Elston, R. C. (1977). Possible linkage between groups specific component and pure depressive disease. *Acta Psychiatric Scandinavia, 55,* 111–115.

Tanna, V. L., Go, R. C., Winokur, G., & Elston, R. C. (1979). Possible linkage between alpha haptoglobin and depression spectrum disease. *Neuropsychobiology, 5,* 103–113.

Tanna, V. L., Winokur, G., Elston, R. C., & Go, R. C. P. (1976a). A linkage study of depression spectrum disease. The use of the sibpair method. *Neuropsychobiology, 2,* 52–62.

Tanna, V. L., Winokur, G., Elston, R. C., & Go, R. C. P. (1976b). A linkage study of pure depression disease. The use of the sibpair method. *Biological Psychiatry, 11,* 767–771.

Taylor, M. A., Abrams, R., & Hayman, M. A. (1980). The classification of affective disorders: A reassessment of the bipolar, unipolar dichotomy. *Journal of Affective Disorders, 2,* 95–109.

Unger, R. A., & Foster, D. W. (1985). Diabetes mellitus. In J. D. Wilson & D. W. Foster (Eds.), *Williams textbook of endocrinology* (pp. 1018–1080). Philadelphia: Saunders.

Van Eerdewegh, M., Gershon, E. S., Van Eerdewegh, P. (1980). X-chromosome threshold models of bipolar manic depressive illness. *Journal of Psychiatric Research, 15,* 215–238.

Von Knorring, A., Cloninger, C. R., Bohman, M., & Sigvardsson, A. (1983). An adoption study of depressive disorders and substance abuse. *Archives of General Psychiatry, 40,* 943–950.

Weitkamp, L. R., Stancer, H. C., Persad, E., Flood, C., & Guttormsen, S. (1981). Depressive disorders and HLA: A gene on chromosome 6 that can affect behavior. *New England Journal of Medicine, 305,* 1301–1306.

Wender, P. H., Kety, S. S., & Rosenthal, D. (1986). Psychiatric disorders in the biological and adoptive families of adoptive individuals with affective disorders. *Archives of General Psychiatry, 43,* 923–929.

Wesner, R. B., Sheftner, W., Palmer, P. J., Crowe, R., & Winokur, G. (1990). The effect of comorbidity and gene penetrance on the outcome of linkage analysis in a bipolar family. *Biological Psychiatry, 27,* 241–244.

Winokur, G. (1972). Depression spectrum disease: Description in a family study. *Comprehensive Psychiatry, 13,* 3–8.

Winokur, G. (1984). Psychosis in bipolar and unipolar affective illness with special reference to schizoaffective disorder. *British Journal of Psychiatry, 145,* 236–242.

Winokur, G., & Clayton, P. (1967a). Family history studies: II. Sex differences and alcoholism in primary affective illness. *British Journal of Psychiatry, 113,* 973–979.

Winokur, G., & Clayton, P. (1967b). In J. Wortis (Ed.), *Recent advances in biological psychiatry* (Vol. 9). New York: Plenum.

Winokur, G., Clayton, P., & Reich, T. (1969). *Manic depressive illness.* St. Louis: Mosby.

Winokur, G., Kadrmas, A., & Crowe, R. R. (1986). Schizoaffective mania: Family history and clinical characteristics. In A. Marneros & M. T. Tsuang (Eds.), *Schizoaffective psychoses.* Berlin-Heidelberg: Springer-Verlag.

Wolinsky, H. (1979). Atherosclerosis. In P. B. Beeson, W. McDermott, & J. B. Wyngaarden (Eds.), *Cecil textbook of medicine* (pp. 1218–1223). Philadelphia: Saunders.

PART 2

Symptomatology

CHAPTER 7

Depressive States and Somatic Symptoms

KAREN L. LOMBARDI, PhD

DEPRESSION AND SOMATIZATION FROM AN EMPIRICAL PERSPECTIVE

Depressive states, from both phenomenological and symptomatic points of view, often include such bodily disturbances as insomnia or hypersomnia, anorexia, weight loss, loss of energy and libido, anhedonia, psychomotor agitation or retardation, and difficulty in thinking or concentrating. These vegetative signs may move into more elaborated somatic constellations, such as headaches, backaches, or chronic pain, and may involve any organ system: the central nervous system, the peripheral nervous system, or the cardiovascular, respiratory, genitourinary, gastrointestinal, or endocrine systems. Although somatization may be symptomatic of hysteria, anxiety disorders, obsessive-compulsive character pathology, borderline conditions, or grief reactions, many researchers (Katon, Kleinman, & Rosen, 1982a; Lesse, 1967; Lloyd, 1986) suggest that somatization most frequently is represented in affective disorders and particularly in major depression. Somatization is seen as serving the function of masking depression (Lesse, 1967); somatizers do not necessarily present with depressive affect and may instead find their way to primary care physicians to seek relief for their presenting somatic complaints (Katon et al., 1982a). As reported in an extensive review of the empirical literature (Katon et al., 1982a), research studies using various depression inventories indicate that when depression is not self-reported, but presents as somatic symptoms to primary care physicians, the diagnosis of depression is missed in more than 95 percent of the cases. Even more importantly, 12 to 35 percent of the patients of primary care physicians are estimated to be significantly depressed.

What accounts for the somatic presentation of affective states? It has been suggested that somatic symptoms are amplifications of

normal physiological sensations that become distorted through hyper-
awareness, hypersensitivity, and selective attention (Lloyd, 1986). Cultural factors, including cultural inhibitions against the direct
experience of depressive affect and the lack of vocabulary for emotional expression, have also been implicated (Goldberg & Bridges,
1988; Katon et al., 1982a; Lloyd, 1986). Somatization appears related
to increased age, family history, and previous physical illness; it appears to decrease as socioeconomic status gets higher. Symptoms most
commonly expressed in depressive patients are those of the autonomic
nervous system (sweaty palms, trembling, tachycardia, perspiration,
and breathlessness), sleep disturbances, dry mouth, and fatigue
(Wittenborn & Buhler, 1979), which suggest an association between
depression and anxiety. Some researchers (Burns & Nichols, 1972)
suggested a relationship among character traits, family history, and
somatization. Several differences were found in comparisons of depressives who had no localized somatic symptoms to depressives with
chest symptoms of nonexertional breathlessness, including sighing res-
piration and acute hyperventilation; heaviness in the sternum; and
depressive themes of preoccupation with death from chest and heart
disease. Depressives with chest symptoms tended to be more obsessional, to recall prolonged breathlessness in a parent, and to have lost a
first-degree relative within the past three years, suggesting that issues
of identification and of loss may be related not only to somatization
but to the particular somatic symptoms involved.

In some studies (Goldberg & Bridges, 1988; Katon, Kleinman, &
Rosen, 1982b) somatization was regarded as a coping or defense mechanism. In the medical literature, somatization of depression traditionally has been described as an unconscious defensive maneuver on the
part of the patient, with the assumption made that intrapsychically
focusing on somatic symptoms instead of on an emotion will protect
the person from psychological pain. Cross-cultural and historical perspectives reveal that depressives in non-European and non-Western
cultures tend to somatize much more frequently, which suggests that
somatization is a cultural orientation. Goldberg and Bridges (1988)
saw somatization as a basic mechanism of the human species for responding to stress. They postulated that in societies in which the individual tends to be submerged in the group, somatization is a relatively
common means of expression of stress. In individualistic societies,
which tend to the narcissistic idealization of the self, somatizing has
been replaced by psychologizing, a more recent cultural orientation.

In a study carried out in an urban area of England, Goldberg and
Bridges collected groups of psychologizers and somatizers who were
interviewed and asked to complete various personality and attitude
scales. Interestingly, although psychologizers and somatizers were
equally anxious, psychologizers were much more likely to report

depression than were somatizers. Given the relationship between depression and somatization, the finding seems contradictory on the surface. However, the authors posited that somatization functions as a defense against blame. Those who somatize tend not to report depression, nor do they see themselves as mentally ill or as responsible for their life predicaments. Inferentially, we might then posit that those who acknowledge their affect, and see themselves as agents in their own lives, somatize less. Goldberg and Bridges asserted that, in somatizers, blame is handled through projection (for example, a Yoruba who attributes his bodily symptoms to witchcraft), through introjection (for example, a hypochondriacal Britisher who attributes his bodily symptoms to undiagnosed cancer), or through a combination of both (for example, a person who believes she has some sort of disease which the doctor has been unable to diagnose, and it's the doctor's fault). Again, we might infer that those who tend more to integrative experience and to a sense of personal agency in their own lives somatize less.

CLASSIC VIEWS OF SOMATIZATION AND DEPRESSION

> The modern term "psychosomatic" disturbances has the disadvantage of suggesting a dualism that does not exist. Every disease is "psychosomatic," for no "somatic" disease is entirely free from psychic influence . . . .
>
> *(Fenichel, 1945, p. 237)*

Classic psychoanalytic theory has made some serious attempts to address the mind—body dualism common in Western thought. While continuing to value the development of intellect and the rational mind above more "primitive" expressions of emotional and somatic existence, these attempts have tried to understand the consequences for the human organism of repressing both feelings and thoughts. In classic psychoanalytic theory, somatization was regarded as an unconscious expression, through bodily discharge, of thoughts and feelings that were unacceptable to the individual. When an individual experienced affect on a visceral level, without awareness of the mental experience, the somatization served as an equivalent for the recognition of the affect. Unlike fully experienced affects, which would be connected to mental awareness, affect equivalents had diminished discharge value to the individual, and tended to become chronic expressions of anxiety. Somatization was seen as the bodily result of unconscious attitudes, a substitute outlet for the expression of warded-off conflicts or impulses. For example, the muscular tension that accompanies an unacceptable experience of anger can result in chronic back or neck pain. A woman who develops hives on her chest when wearing a low-cut dress may be expressing conflicts about being admired and sexually desired.

Somatization, though precipitated by intrapsychic events, utilizes physical channels as a means of discharge. Somatization is linked to regression of the ego, which cannot effectively contain anxiety or neutralize aggression (Schur, 1955). We might, then, see somatization as aggression turned inward or, in more modern terms, as the process of the body attacking the self. Freud (1917/1957) originally attributed somatization to repressed hostility, which emerges either as self-reproach and depression (melancholia) or as an hysterical mode of punishment through the development of bodily symptoms. In either case, at the root of the need for punishment is posited unconsciously felt responsibility for the death, or loss of love, of a loved one.

In an early treatise on the psychosomatics of health and disease, Groddeck (1923/1949) was a proponent of the fallaciousness of separating body and mind. That each continually affects and informs the other, and that the total organism is animated by a life force (the It, which Freud later reformulated as the id) which is expressed through illness as well as through health, is Groddeck's unique contribution. Disease cannot be isolated from the total personality; disease is the It expressing itself through the self.

Groddeck's continued relevance to contemporary thought on psychosomatics is twofold. First, his focus was on the relation between inner and external life and the continuing relevance of one to the other. In describing the physical treatment of patients, he inquired into the personal function of their symptoms. For example, when an orange peel appeared on a path and led to a patient's breaking his arm, Groddeck investigated what personal purpose might be served through this event. "Since everything has at least two sides, we can always consider it from two points of view, and shall find, if we take the trouble, that for every event in life there is both an external and an internal cause" (Groddeck, 1923/1949, p. 234). Second, he viewed somatization as a defense against rejection and loss. "Thus it implants near the loving mouth which is yearning for kisses a disfiguring eczema; if in spite of that I am kissed, then indeed I shall be happy, but if the kiss is not forthcoming, then it is not because I am unloved but because of the revolting eczema (p. 96)."

DEVELOPMENTAL CONSIDERATIONS OF SOMATIZATION AND DEPRESSION: ANACLITIC DEPRESSION

Throughout early explorations of the etiology of somatization were woven themes of depression and loss. Later work with children, from clinical pediatric (Winnicott, 1936/1978), empirical (Spitz, 1946, 1951; Spitz & Wolf, 1946), and longitudinal case study (Harmon, Wagonfeld, & Emde, 1982) perspectives, provided striking confirmatory evidence of such a relationship. From his pediatric experience, Winnicott suggested that various appetite disorders reached back to the child's experience in the first months of life and became involved in defenses against anxiety and depression. Winnicott was speaking of relatively "normal" or typical children seen in pediatric practice, who developed feeding difficulties as infants or who became anorectic or bulimic or suffered bouts of stomachache or intestinal spasms as young children.

Spitz's work was with children from unusual circumstances—infants in foundling homes who were separated from their mothers and their original family environment for prolonged periods of time. Spitz's original foundling home subjects showed not only severe developmental delays in language, socialization, motor skills, and intellectual functioning, but also severe somatic symptoms, including significantly lowered resistance to disease and higher morbidity rates. Those children who did recover had, on follow-up, a high incidence of eczema and other skin disturbances. Spitz referred to this syndrome as "hospitalism," which might be better called "institutionalism." The children in this original sample suffered both separation from family and institutional emotional neglect, although they were well cared for physically. In most cases, neither maternal care nor family life was restored to these children.

Further studies (Spitz & Wolf, 1946) of a more discrete syndrome developed by infants separated from their mothers during the second half of the first year of life also revealed a relationship between somatization and depression. Called anaclitic depression, the syndrome is characterized by weepiness and apprehension, withdrawal from the environment, retardation of development, psychomotor retardation, anorexia, weight loss, and insomnia. Symptoms developed four to six weeks following the separation from the mother, and continued until reunion, which was generally effected within three months of the original separation. These symptoms appeared to be somatic expressions of depressive affect, specifically related to the loss of the love object.

Why should depressive affect take the path of somatic expression? In infancy and early childhood, in particular, we might speculate that since the words to express grief over loss are not available, the body becomes the readiest vehicle of expression. Developmentally, it was thought by some theorists (A. Freud, 1970; Group for the Advancement of Psychiatry, 1966) that in infancy there is a sort of semipermeable membrane between psychic and somatic experience, so that there is easy access from mind to body, and from body to mind. Bodily excitations such as hunger, cold, or pain may easily be "discharged" through mental pathways in the form of affects such as anxiety or rage.

Conversely, mental distress may be "discharged" through bodily disturbances of digestion, elimination, the skin, and so on. Spitz (1951) succinctly stated the ego psychological view of somatization:

> . . . [T]he psychic system is not yet differentiated from the somatic system in the infant. What we might call psyche at this stage is so completely merged with the physical person that I would like to coin for it the term *somato-psyche*. Subsequently the psychic and somatic systems will be progressively delimited from each other. . . . [I]n the course of the first six months a psychological steering organization will be segregated from the somato-psyche. . . . This organized, structured, conscious steering organization is the nucleus of what we call the ego, a body ego in the beginning. It is thus delimited from the remaining conscious part of the somato-psyche, which we will designate as the id.
>
> *(p. 256)*

The idea here is that in infancy and early childhood, there is more "overflow" or permeability between mental and bodily experience. With development and maturation, experiences from each of these domains form structuralized systems which are increasingly differentiated from each other. What Spitz failed to stress is the continued linkage, especially on unconscious levels, between psyche and soma throughout life.

AN OBJECT RELATIONAL VIEW OF PSYCHOSOMATIC EXISTENCE

As Freud (1923) originally stated, the ego is first and foremost a body ego, not merely a surface but the projection of a surface. What I intend to delineate are original tendencies toward integration of mind and body, as expressed through psychosomatic existence. Dissociations of mind from bodily experience, resulting from relational experiences that mold the development of the self, predispose the individual to somatic symptomatology and to depressive states.

Object relational perspectives focus on the ability to tolerate depressive affect, which is seen as adaptive and developmentally appropriate. Depression is considered a basic ego state; the focus, then, is on various prototypes of the capacity or the failure to accept depressive affect and depressive states (Winnicott, 1962/1965; Zetzel, 1965). The depressive position is an achievement in emotional development (Klein, 1940/1975; Winnicott, 1954-5/1978), a movement from the ruthlessness and part-object orientation of the early relating which is characteristic of infancy, to the capacity to recognize both the self and the other as whole persons, capable of both loving and of hating. Along with this recognition of the fundamental separateness and integrity of self and other comes the beginning of empathy, of the capacity for concern. Stern (1985) similarly described this achievement as the discovery of intersubjectivity: with the recognition of the separateness of self comes the discovery that subjective states can be shared. This realization involves apprehending that others, distinct from oneself, can hold or entertain a mental state which is similar to the one held by the self. The term Stern gives to this realization is the acquisition of a theory of separate minds. Paradoxically, the recognition of the separateness of self allows for the realization that inner subjective experience is potentially shareable with someone else. This developmental achievement, whether called the depressive position or the discovery of intersubjectivity, is thought to occur between six months of age and a year.

Why should depressive affect be associated with such a positive and remarkable achievement? Because, as the infant, who is a whole person, is able to identify with the whole person of the mother and other primary figures, the infant begins to recognize that the one loved so dearly is also the one hated in the bad or the hard-going moments. In Kleinian (1940/1975) terms:

> . . . the introjection of the whole loved object gives rise to concern and sorrow lest that object should be destroyed [by negative affects of frustration, hatred, and rage], and that these distressed feelings and fears . . . constitute the depressive position . . . . In short, persecution (by "bad" objects) and the characteristic defenses against it, on the one hand, and pining for the loved ("good") object, on the other, constitute the depressive position.

> *(p. 348)*

The anxieties of the depressive position are twofold: those that center on concern for the other and those that center on concern for the self. Anxieties about the love object include concern that the object may be damaged or even destroyed during those moments of frustration and hatred. Anxieties about the self include fantasies about one's insides or inner life, and concerns that good internal objects will be lost due to one's own bad impulses. In mourning (and in Spitz's babies who suffered anaclitic depression), there is the actual loss of the loved person, which in its extreme may cause one to feel hopeless about relationships and external contacts in general; pathological mourning is an example of such a state. In the depressive position, there is the recognition that one's own anger and hatred may lose both the loved object and the internally felt goodness of the self.

Hypochondriacal symptoms can be seen as manifestations of either paranoid or depressive anxieties (Klein, 1935/1975). Somatic symptoms which in fantasy represent attacks of persecuting objects are typically paranoid. Those symptoms which are handled through projection—as the Yoruba, referred to earlier, who attributes his symptoms to witchcraft; or the Italian peasant who attributes her headaches to the evil eye—are examples. Somatic symptoms that derive from the fantasied attacks of bad internal objects on good ones, in which the individual is identified with the sufferings of the good objects, are typically depressive. For example, a well-behaved, phobic, eight-year-old boy who was unable to ask directly for food talked, in his therapy sessions, of a hunger monster inside him that was never satisfied. The monster would eat wood and metal and could eat up the whole room if it were let out.

The ways in which individuals work through their depressive position determine their capacities for full relationships and for healthy living. Healthy reparative tendencies, which serve to integrate aspects of love and aggression so that they can be experienced in relation to self and others without fearing sadism and destruction, would mitigate tendencies to somatization. The ability to tolerate depressive affect is linked to the recognition of one's own aggression, and to the capacity to "make good" for destruction wreaked on loved objects. The inability to tolerate depressive states is reflective of an internal state in which the individual feels not only abandoned by all good objects, but subject to attack by all bad ones. The sense of guilt that accompanies this state of affairs is often turned against the self, in the form of somatic "attacks."

SPLITTING AND DISSOCIATION

> The mind does not exist as an entity in the individual's scheme of things provided the individual psyche-soma or body scheme has come satisfactorily through the very early developmental stages; mind is then no more than a special case of the functioning of the psyche-soma.
>
> *(Winnicott, 1949/1978, p. 244)*

In this passage, Winnicott was addressing the dissociations that occur when the natural integrative processes within the individual are disrupted by a bad (as opposed to good-enough) environment. Mind and body are not dichotomous, with the mind localized in one place and the body in another. Rather, there is a process of mutual interrelation between psychic and somatic aspects of the growing individual, with each informing the experience of the other. Like Freud's (1923/1961) body ego and Stern's (1985) core sense of self, Winnicott saw the body, as it is experienced by the individual, as forming the core of the imaginative, created self.

Early psychosomatic development, along healthy lines, entails the continuity of being. The ordinary good-enough mother, who actively adapts to the baby's needs in the beginning, and then gradually fails to adapt by continuing with her own life, provides the environment which facilitates "going-on-being." During this early phase, the infant develops a self: psychosomatic existence begins to take on a personal, individual pattern, which Winnicott referred to as the psyche "indwelling" in the soma (1960/1965). This indwelling, which is constituted by the integration of motor, sensory, and functional experiences, is the basis for the construction of the self, of personal reality and personal experience. Impingements, withdrawal, and erratic relating on the part of primary caretakers constitute environmental failures to which the infant must react and adapt. These failures interfere with the integration of the self, with the infant's natural tendency to acquire a personal psychic reality and personal body scheme. In infancy, as well as in later life, symptoms such as eating and sleeping disorders, suicidal ideation, and other psychosomatic difficulties are likely to surface as reflections of early disintegrative experiences of psychosomatic existence.

In this view, psychosomatic symptoms are regarded as special instances of splitting or dissociation (Gaddini, 1978; James, 1979; Szasz, 1957; Winnicott, 1966). These failures of mind-body integration can be seen as:

1. Failures in the early mother-child relationship
2. Defenses
3. Means of forging a true identity.

Developmentally, psychosomatic splits arise from failures in the early relationship between mother (and other primary caretakers) and infant. Parental impingements, withdrawals, and failures of empathy require adaptations on the part of the infant which force precocious compliance and a consequent loss of spontaneity and self-integration. The lack of physical and psychical mutuality between parent and child in infancy interferes with the natural integration of psyche and soma; psyche, then, is narcissistically damaged and turns, at best, to false selfconstructions. In adapting a false self-compliance, the developing child builds up a set of false relationships (Winnicott, 1960/1965). These operate as if they are real, but they lead to a sense of inner disconnection and futility. One of the consequences of this inner disconnection is dissociation from bodily experience, which is then expressed psychosomatically.

When psychosomatic symptoms are taken seriously on a medical level, the search for medical relief can give purpose to life and distract attention from the inner sense of futility (James, 1979); such symptoms, then, constitute a defensive process. Hypochondriasis best fits this model of defense. A more compelling model is that proposed by Winnicott, which posited that psychosomatic symptoms serve to defend the individual against the dangers that arise out of integration of the personality. The somatic defense operates to protect the individual from the experience of depressive anxiety associated with the sense that the good object has been lost not through environmental failure, but through the individual's own destructiveness. In other words, somatization serves to mitigate the guilt, blame, and self-hatred that arise when depressive affect cannot be tolerated in the individual.

SOMATIZATION AND IDENTITY

Somatization also functions as a means of forging an identity and of regaining integration. Psychosomatic symptoms may be seen as a function of the self, rather than as the specific symbolic expression of a conflict. One of the aims of psychosomatic illness "is to draw the psyche from the mind back to the original intimate association with the soma" (Winnicott, 1949/1978, p. 254). In drawing attention to the dissociation, the symptom is an attempt by the individual to heal the split between mind and body, between idea and affect. The very fact that the symptoms are bodily symptoms demonstrates that the psychosomatic linkage is not altogether lost. Paradoxically, through the depersonalized experience of the somatization, the individual is attempting to get in touch with the possibility of psychosomatic integration and the personalized self.

In conclusion, two short clinical vignettes will be offered as illustrations. The first, reported by Szasz (1957), concerns a woman who developed somatic symptoms which took the form of hypochondriacal preoccupation with various parts of her body, including tingling in the extremities, "bubbly feelings" in the head, "shocks" through her body, and severe constipation. These symptoms developed soon after the woman suffered a miscarriage at six months, which was precipitated by a fall on the ice. Szasz viewed her symptomatology as the ego treating the body (in contrast to the self) as the lost object. This woman failed to work through the loss of her pregnancy with depression and grief; rather, she transferred the lost object to the body and expressed her unfelt grief through somatic attacks. In this case example, the somatization was specifically linked to loss and to this woman's inability to mourn for the fantasied damage done.

The second is an autobiographical account (Cardinal, 1983) of a psychoanalytic journey from illness to health, where the illness contained, among other things, life-threatening somatic symptoms of chronic uterine bleeding. Innumerable medical consultations and medical treatment failed to stem the bleeding; psychoanalysis did. In Cardinal's experience, finding the words to say it constituted the "cure." She quoted Boileau, *L'Art Poetique:* "What one truly understands clearly articulates itself, and the words to say it come easily." Healing her splits, integrating what were formerly dissociated and disintegrative bits of her experience into a whole, real sense of her personal self, allowed Cardinal to "dwell within herself" in psychosomatic health.

SUMMARY

Both research and clinical data suggest that somatic symptomatology is a frequent correlate of depressive states. Classic psychoanalytic theory has attempted to address the mind-body dualism common in Western thought by regarding somatization as an unconscious expression, through bodily discharge, of thoughts and feelings unacceptable to the individual. Developmental and object relations perspectives tend to relate somatization to problems with the ability to contain depressive affect and depressive states. The ways in which individuals work through the depressive position, including integration of good and bad self and object experiences, determine their capacities for full relationships and for healthy living. Early psychosomatic development, along healthy lines, entails a continuity of self experience which may be disrupted by impingements, withdrawal, and erratic relating on the part of primary caretakers. Such disruptions interfere with the integration of self. In childhood, as in later life, psychosomatic difficulties are likely to surface as reflections of such early disintegrative experiences. In this view, psychosomatic symptoms are regarded as special instances of splitting or dissociation. The somatic defense serves to mitigate the guilt, blame, and self-hatred that arise when depressive affect cannot be tolerated in the individual. Paradoxically, through the depersonalized experience of somatization, the individual is attempting to get in touch with the possibility of psychosomatic integration and the personalized self.

REFERENCES

Burns, B. H., & Nichols, M. A. (1972). Factors related to the localization of symptoms to the chest in depression. *American Journal of Psychiatry, 121,* 405–409.

Cardinal, M. (1983). *The words to say it.* Cambridge, MA: Van Vactor & Goodheart.

Fenichel, O. (1945). *The psychoanalytic theory of neuroses.* New York: Norton.

Freud, A. (1970). The symptomatology of childhood: A preliminary attempt at classification. *The Psychoanalytic Study of the Child, 25,* 19–41.

Freud, S. (1957). Mourning and melancholia. In J. Strachey (Ed. and Trans.), *The standard edition of the complete psychological works of Sigmund Freud* (Vol. 14, pp. 243–258). London: Hogarth Press. (Original work published 1917.)

Freud, S. (1961). The ego and the id. In J. Strachey (Ed. and Trans.), *The standard edition of the complete psychological works of Sigmund Freud* (Vol. 19, pp. 12–66). London: Hogarth Press. (Original work published 1923.)

Gaddini, R. (1978). Transitional object origins and the psychosomatic symptom. In S. A. Grolnick & L. Barkin (Eds.), *Between reality and fantasy: Transitional objects and phenomena.* New York: Jason Aronson.

Goldberg, D. P., & Bridges, K. (1988). Somatic presentations of psychiatric illness in primary care setting. *Journal of Psychosomatic Research, 32,* 137–144.

Groddeck, G. (1949). *The book of the It.* New York: Vintage Books. (Original work published 1923.)

Group for the Advancement of Psychiatry (1966). *Psychopathological disorders in childhood: Theoretical considerations and a proposed classification.* New York: Brunner/Mazel.

Harmon, R. J., Wagonfeld, S., & Emde, R. N. (1982). Anaclitic depression: A follow-up from infancy to puberty. *Psychoanalytic Study of the Child, 37,* 76–94.

James, M. (1979). The non-symbolic nature of psychosomatic disorder: A test case of both Klein and classical theory. *International Review of Psychoanalysis, 6,* 413–422.

Katon, W., Kleinman, A., & Rosen, G. (1982a). Depression and somatization: A review. Part I. *The American Journal of Medicine, 72,* 127–135.

Katon, W., Kleinman, A., & Rosen, G. (1982b). Depression and somatization: A review. Part II. *The American Journal of Medicine, 72,* 241–247.

Klein, M. (1975a). The psychogenesis of manic-depressive states. In *Love, guilt, and reparation.* (pp. 262–289) New York: Delacorte Press. (Original work published 1935.)

Klein, M. (1975b). Mourning and its relation to manic-depressive states. In *Love, guilt, and reparation.* (pp. 344–369) New York: Delacorte Press. (Original work published 1940.)

Lesse, S. (1967). Hypochondriasis and psychosomatic disorders masking depression. *American Journal of Psychotherapy, 21,* 607–620.

Lloyd, G. G. (1986). Psychiatric syndromes with a somatic presentation. *Journal of Psychosomatic Research, 30,* 113–120.

Schur, M. (1955). Comments on the metapsychology of somatization. *Psychoanalytic Study of the Child, 10,* 119–164.

Spitz, R. (1946). Hospitalism. *Psychoanalytic Study of the Child, 2,* 113–117.

Spitz, R. (1951). The psychogenic diseases of infancy. *Psychoanalytic Study of the Child, 6,* 255–275.

Spitz, R., & Wolf, K. M. (1946) Anaclitic depression. *Psychoanalytic Study of the Child, 2,* 313–342.

Stern, D. (1985). *The interpersonal world of the infant.* New York: Basic Books.

Szasz, T. S. (1957). A contribution to the psychology of bodily feelings. *Psychoanalytic Quarterly, 26,* 25–47.

Winnicott, D. W. (1978). Appetite and emotional disorder. In *Through paediatrics to psychoanalysis*. London: Hogarth Press. (Original work published 1936.)

Winnicott, D. W. (1978). Mind and its relation to the psyche-soma. In *Through paediatrics to psychoanalysis*. London: Hogarth Press. (Original work published 1949.)

Winnicott, D. W. (1965). The theory of the parent–infant relationship. In *The maturational processes and the facilitating environment*. New York: International Universities Press. (Original work published 1960.)

Winnicott, D. W. (1965). A personal view of the Kleinian contribution. In *The maturational processes and the facilitating environment*. New York: International Universities Press. Original work published 1962.)

Winnicott, D. W. (1966). Psychosomatic illness in its positive and negative aspects. *International Journal of Psychoanalysis, 47,* 510–516.

Winnicott, D. W. (1978). The depressive position in normal emotional development. In *Through paediatrics to psychoanalysis*. London: Hogarth Press. (Original work published 1954-5.)

Wittenborn, L. & Buhler, R. (1979). Somatic discomforts among depressed women. *Archives of General Psychiatry, 36,* 465–471.

Zetzel, E. R. (1965). Depression and the incapacity to bear it. In M. Schur (Ed.), *Drives, affects, and behavior* (Vol. 2). New York: International Universities Press.

CHAPTER 8

Mood Disorders and Self-Defeating Behaviors

REBECCA CURTIS, PhD

Mood disorders lead to a variety of symptomatic self-defeating behaviors, many of which contribute to perpetuation of negative affect. The present chapter will examine these behaviors, but will also attempt to delineate what is known about the self-defeating behaviors that make people more vulnerable to mood disorders. The chapter will first examine the cognitive style of depressed persons and persons vulnerable to depression and will then explore the consequences of cognitive styles for physical health and performance in academic, job, social, and general life situations. Next, experimental studies of the effects of cognitions and mood on behavior will be reviewed. Finally, consideration will be given to the possibility that a cluster or clusters of enduring behavioral patterns, which might qualify as depressogenic personality styles, make people vulnerable to depression. The chapter does not attempt to provide a comprehensive review of the extensive literature on this topic, but does try to highlight the major findings.

COGNITIVE STYLE AND SELF-DEFEATING BEHAVIORS

Considerable research and clinical data have clarified the cognitive styles of depressed persons in contrast to those of nondepressed persons. After Beck (1967) identified a depressive triad of negative feelings about the self, the world, and the future, many research investigations examined the cognitive processes of depressed individuals (Abramson, Seligman, & Teasdale, 1978; Alloy, 1982, 1988; Derry & Kuiper, 1981; Peterson & Seligman, 1984). Research on depressives' cognitive styles has focused primarily upon their negative self-schemata and their self-defeating attributional style. These aspects of depressives' cognitive styles will be discussed and the behaviors related to them will be examined subsequently.

Self-Views of the Depressed

Depressives rate themselves more poorly than nondepressed patients do on a variety of personality traits (Laxter, 1964; Lunghi, 1977). When evaluating themselves in comparison to others, they see themselves as inferior in such important areas as intelligence, attractiveness, and social status (Alloy & Ahrens, 1987). They have also been found to have low self-esteem (Beck, 1976; Nadich, Gargan, & Michael, 1975). Depressives engage in self-focusing after failure (Pyszczynski & Greenberg, 1985) and fail to exhibit the self-serving information search of nondepressed persons (Pinkley, LaPrelle, Pyszczynski, & Greenberg, 1988).

Experiments have also shown that normals show superior memory for positive rather than negative self-referential material, but depressives recall more negatively toned personal information about themselves (Lishman, 1972), or show equal recall for both types of material (Derry & Kuiper, 1981; Kuiper & Derry, 1982; Kuiper & MacDonald, 1982). Research demonstrates that normal, nondepressed people have self-schemata with positive content, which increases their efficiency in processing and recalling positive self-referent information (Alloy, Greenberg, Clements, & Kolden, 1983; Davis, 1979a, 1979b; Davis & Unruh, 1981; Derry & Kuiper, 1981; Greenberg, Vazquez, & Alloy, 1988; Hammen, Marks, Magol, & deMayo, 1985; Hammen, Miklowitz, & Dyck, 1986; Ingram, Smith, & Brehm, 1983; Kuiper & Derry, 1982; Kuiper & MacDonald, 1982; Kuiper, Olinger, MacDonald, & Shaw, 1985; Ross, Mueller, & de la Torre, 1986). In contrast, the self-schemata of depressives appear to be either negative (Derry & Kuiper, 1981) or unstable, containing both positive and negative content (Ingram et al., 1983; Kuiper et al., 1985; Kuiper & Derry, 1982; Kuiper & MacDonald, 1982). Recent work by Greenberg et al. (1988) showed that depressed persons endorse more depression-related negative adjectives as self-descriptive than do either normal or anxious subjects. Kuiper, MacDonald, and Derry (1983) and Greenberg et al. (1988) noted that whether depressed people possess strong negative self-schemata or mixed content schemata may depend on the severity of their symptoms (Kuiper & Derry, 1982) or the chronicity of their symptoms (Davis, 1979a, 1979b; Davis & Unruh, 1981). Kuiper et al. (1983) suggested that mild depressives may have an "overload" of positive and negative information, which impairs efficient processing of all self-referent material.

The research on the negative self-schemata of depressives has frequently shown that, when their depression lists, their schemata resemble those of nondepressed persons (Hamilton & Abramson, 1983; Lewinsohn, Steinmetz, Larson, & Franklin, 1981). Some research, however, has demonstrated that negative life events that are congruent with the depressogenic self-schema are associated with depression whereas schema-irrelevant events are not.

Thus, the negative self-schema of depressed persons appears to be a concomitant of depression and not a marker of it. In an attempt to predict those persons who are vulnerable to depression, Kuiper and Olinger (1986) developed a "self-worth contingency model of depression." They proposed that excessively rigid and inappropriate rules for guiding one's life constitute a cognitive predisposition to depression. A number of such rules or dysfunctional attitudes were identified by Beck (Beck, Rush, Shaw, & Emery, 1979) and can be measured by the Dysfunctional Attitudes Scale (DAS) developed by Oliver and Baumgart (1985) and used by Dobson and Shaw (1986). Examples of such dysfunctional attitudes are: "If I do not do well all of the time, people will not respect me," or "If someone disagrees with me, it probably indicates that he does not like me," or "My value as a person depends upon what others think of me" (Kuiper, Olinger, & MacDonald, 1988, p. 296). According to their model, the self-worth of depressed persons depends upon their self-worth contingencies being met. Support for this model was obtained by Olinger, Kuiper and Shaw (1987).

Kuiper et al. (1988) found that persons scoring high in vulnerability to depression as measured by the DAS, but low in depression as measured by the BDI, rated their Perceived Popularity as quite high, even higher than nonvulnerable depressed subjects rated theirs. As their depression level increased, however, vulnerable subjects showed a marked decrease in Perceived Popularity. For subjects scoring low on the DAS there was little difference in Perceived Popularity across differing levels of depression. Kuiper et al. interpreted these data as demonstrating that vulnerable individuals who are not depressed perceive themselves as currently meeting their self-worth contingencies. Vulnerable individuals who are depressed do not see themselves as meeting their criteria for self-worth and begin to focus upon negative aspects of the self.

Further support for the self-worth contingency model was obtained in a study of perception of similarity to others (Swallow & Kuiper, 1987). Vulnerable, nondepressed subjects perceived themselves as more similar to others than did nonvulnerable or depressed individuals. As the level of depression increased, vulnerable subjects displayed the largest decrease in similarity ratings. A large body of research in social psychology has demonstrated that when people perceive others as similar to themselves, they like them more (Byrne, 1971; Griffit, 1974; Kaplan, 1972) and are more cooperative (Krauss, 1966). Depressed persons' views of others will be discussed at greater length in the section that follows.

Views of Reality and of Other People

The realism and the accurate perceptions of the depressed in many situations, in contrast to the illusions and inaccurate perceptions of the nondepressed, have now been well-documented (Abramson & Alloy, 1981; Alloy & Abramson, 1979, 1982; Alloy, Abramson, & Viscusi, 1981; Benassi & Mahler, 1985; Vazquez, 1987).

These findings have challenged the original assumptions of Beck's (1967) cognitive theory of depression and Seligman's (1975) learned helplessness theory, which said that depressed persons negatively distort reality. Alloy and Abramson (1988) recently reviewed the judgments and inferences of depressed and nondepressed persons in six areas: judgment of control, attribution, expectancy/prediction, recall of feedback, self-evaluation, and social comparison. These studies indicated that depressive realism and nondepressive illusions of control are robust phenomena, but that there are some exceptions. The realism of the depressed and their attributional evenhandedness occur only for themselves and not for others. For example, Golin, Terrell, and Johnson (1977) found that depressed students had inappropriately high expectancies of success when an experimenter rolled the dice, but accurate expectancies when they rolled the dice themselves. In contrast, nondepressed students were accurate when the experimenter rolled the dice, but inappropriately high in their expectancies when they rolled the dice themselves. Golin, Terrell, Weitz, and Drost (1979) subsequently replicated these findings with psychiatric patients. The depressed also underestimated the amount of positive feedback they received (Buchwald, 1977; Wener & Rehm, 1975), whereas nondepressed students (Buchwald, 1977) and nondepressed psychiatric outpatients (DeMonbreun & Craighead, 1977) overestimated the amount of positive feedback they received.

The low self-esteem of the depressed and social comparison theories (Festinger, 1954; Morse & Gergen, 1970; Schachter, 1959) led Alloy and others to suggest that depressed people would see others in highly positive terms. Research has shown that depressed people do view "people in general" more favorably than do normal, nondepressed people (Alloy & Abramson, 1988; Martin, Abramson, & Alloy, 1984; Tabachnik, Crocker, & Alloy, 1983; Vazquez & Alloy, 1987). Nondepressed people evaluate "people in general" more negatively, but not their best friends (Vazquez & Alloy, 1987). Although research generally has indicated that depressed people evaluate others favorably, Beck's theory suggests that they expect others to treat them poorly. A recent study by Janoff-Bulman and Hecker (1988) supported this idea. These researchers found that depressed people see others as more malevolent and themselves as more vulnerable.

Depressed persons are more accurate in their perceptions of the degree to which they are liked by others than are nondepressed persons, who overestimate the extent to which they are liked (Strack & Coyne, 1983). Experimental research suggests that the illusion of the nondepressed should facilitate their actually being liked and the perception of the depressed should lead to their being liked less (Curtis & Miller, 1986; Swann & Read, 1981b). The expectancy confirmation effects of these beliefs will be discussed later in this chapter.

EXPLANATORY STYLE

Many studies have examined the attributional styles of depressed people. In a review of these studies by Sweeney, Anderson, and Bailey (1986), the authors conclude that depressed persons are more likely to attribute negative life events to their own inadequacy and, to a lesser extent, to attribute positive life events to external, unstable, and specific causes (Abramson, Alloy, & Metalsky, 1988; Abramson, Metalsky, & Alloy, 1988).

Health

Although the evidence is inconsistent, it has been suggested that depressed people are at a greater risk for illness than nondepressed people (Schleifer, Keller, Siris, Davis, & Stein, 1985). Schleifer et al. found that decreased lymphocyte function is associated specifically with depression and not related to hospital effects or, nonspecifically, to other psychiatric disorders. Peterson and Seligman (1987) obtained data showing that explanatory style predicts illness. Controlling for depression and physical illness at the onset of the study, Peterson and Seligman measured self-reports of illness after one month and after one year, and reports of visits to physicians after one year. A negative explanatory style predicted illness at both of the later times, on measures of self-report and visits to physicians. In a replication and extension of that study, using the same variables, the variables that related to explanatory style were related to illness: unhealthy habits, low self-efficacy to change the habits, and the occurrence of stressful life events. The authors noted that bad life events are likely to precede pessimism as well as to follow from it. In another correlational study of members of the Baseball Hall of Fame, Peterson and Seligman found that external, unstable, and specific explanations for good events in newspaper quotations from 1900–1950 were correlated with living a shorter life, for a sample of 24 men. Internal, stable, and global explanations of bad events were also correlated with living a shorter life, for a sample of 30 players. Peterson, Seligman, and Vaillant (1988) demonstrated that pessimistic explanatory style at age 25 predicted poor health at ages 45 through 60 for a sample of 99 university graduates, even when physical and mental health at age 25 were controlled. Scheier and Carver (1985), using the Life Orientation Test, discovered that optimistic college students reported fewer physical symptoms at two different assessment periods—the beginning of the last four weeks of the semester and the end of the semester.

Academic Achievement and Job Performance

Explanatory style has been linked with poor performance by university students. Habitual explanation of bad events as having internal, stable, and global causes predicted poor academic performance, even when Scholastic Aptitude Test scores were held constant in a study by Kamen and Seligman (cited in Peterson & Bossio, 1989). Peterson and Barrett (1987) reported that this explanatory style predicted lower grades for university freshmen, when initial ability, measured by the SAT, and initial depression, measured by the Beck Depression Inventory, were held constant. Their research also showed that students with a negative explanatory style were less likely to hold specific academic goals or to make use of academic advising. Explanatory style was also found to be correlated with depression and school achievement in elementary school children and to predict changes in depression over time. This research demonstrated that explanatory style and bad life events interacted to make children vulnerable to depression. Depression had a significant negative correlation with California Achievement Test scores and a positive correlation with helpless behaviors in the classroom. Similarly, explanatory style was correlated with achievement test scores and teachers' ratings of helpless behaviors in the classroom. In a work environment, negative explanatory style predicted poor productivity and quitting among life insurance sales agents (Seligman & Schulman, 1986).

The attribution of failure to stable, global, internal factors is associated with decreased effort and decreased persistence on tasks. Changing the explanation for an outcome to unstable, specific causes, such as lack of effort, has proved beneficial, leading to improved performance in both adults and children (Andrews & Debus, 1978; Chapin & Dyck, 1976; Foersterling, 1985; LaNoue & Curtis, 1985).

COPING WITH STRESS

Optimism has been found to be positively related to active, problem-focused strategies of coping with stress and negatively related to disengagement (Scheier, Weintraub, & Carver, 1986). Optimists reported that they were more likely to seek out social support and less likely to rely on denial or distancing. Optimism is related to positive coping outcomes (Carver & Gaines, 1987; Reker & Wong, 1985; Scheier & Carver, 1985, Study 3; Strack, Blaney, Ganellen, & Coyne, 1985; Strack, Carver, & Blaney, 1987), and to the success with which treated alcoholics move from the treatment setting into mainstream society (Strack et al., 1987). Optimists are more likely to complete aftercare programs successfully than are more pessimistic persons.

Optimism is negatively related to the development of postpartum depression. Carver and Gaines (1987) assessed depression and dispositional optimism during the third trimester of pregnancy and again three weeks after childbirth. Not surprisingly, optimism was inversely related to depression at each assessment period. When the researchers controlled for initial level of depression, however, the relationship between optimism and depression still had a significantly negative correlation. Humphries (cited in Scheier & Carver, 1988) reported similar findings with office workers undergoing major changes in their work procedures.

PERFORMANCE ON COGNITIVE AND SOCIAL TASKS

Performance on Psychomotor and Cognitive Tasks

Depressed persons perform more poorly than normals on cognitive tasks involving short-term memory (Glass, Uhlenhuth, & Weihreb, 1978; Sternberg & Jarvik, 1976; Williams, Little, Scates, & Blockman, 1987) and reaction time (Friedman, 1964; Hall & Stride, 1954; Martin & Rees, 1966). Laboratory research has indicated that low expectations about performance lead to poor performance (see Feather, 1982, for a review). Kuhl (1982) suggested that expectations are the best predictor of achievement motivation. Curtis (1989b) and Andrews (in press) argued that low expectations and the self-confirming attributions of failure to a lack of ability lead to a self-perpetuating cycle of low effort and poor performance. That the lack of effort on the part of the depressed is not totally an unmodifiable consequence of the depressed mood state was demonstrated in recent research by Frankel and Snyder (1987). In a laboratory study, they divided college students at the median of their distribution of scores on the Beck Depression Inventory (Beck, 1967). The depressed group, but not the nondepressed group, persisted significantly longer at a task when told it was highly difficult than when told it was moderately difficult. With difficulty as an excuse for poor performance, the depressed exerted greater effort. Snyder and Frankel (1989) argued that the low effort of the depressed in some situations appears to protect their already fragile sense of self-esteem.

Social Interactions

Coyne (1976a, 1976b) proposed a social interaction model of depression. According to this model, depressed persons provide little reinforcement to others and receive little in return. Although little evidence has been provided that such behaviors lead to depression, research has clearly indicated that such behaviors are characteristic of people who are already depressed. Furthermore, the lack of an intimate social relationship is a vulnerability factor in depression (Brown & Harris, 1978). Depressed people are seen by observers as performing more poorly in social interactions (Coyne, 1976a; Gotlib, 1982; Lewinsohn, Mischel, Chaplin, & Barton, 1980). They speak more slowly and softly, maintain less eye contact, are less pleasant, and show a less aroused facial expression than normals although they do not differ from control subjects who are not depressed but show some other form of psychological deviation (Youngren & Lewinsohn, 1980). Hautzinger, Linden, and Hoffman (1982), in an examination of distressed couples with and without a depressed partner, found many differences in the verbal interaction of the couples. The depressed partners were more likely to talk about their negative mood, cry, give expression of their negative somatic and psychological well-being, give a negative self-evaluation, offer help, demand help, and ask questions about the partner's well-being. The nondepressed partners in the depressed couples demonstrated a positive feeling, mood, and self-esteem, but gave more negative partner evaluations and were more demanding. The nondepressed couples communicated more positive well-being, more positive partner evaluations, and more agreement with their partner's statements. Hinchliffe and his associates (Hinchliffe, Hooper, & Roberts, 1978; Hinchliffe, Hooper, Roberts, & Vaughan, 1975) demonstrated that, after successful inpatient drug treatment, the interaction differences between depressed and nondepressed couples disappeared, but Hautzinger et al. believed this improvement to be unstable and short-lived. For example, Paykel and Weismann (1973) noted that submissive dependency improved when depression was alleviated, but that interpersonal friction and inhibited communication showed little change and appeared to reflect enduring personality disturbances. Coyne (1976b) determined that depressed persons were more likely to be rejected by others and induced negative affect in others. Subsequent studies have consistently demonstrated that depressed people are rejected, but have failed to show consistent negative mood induction in others (see Gutman, 1986, for a review). For example, Howes and Hokanson (1979) had confederates act in a depressed role, a normal role, or a physically ill role. Subjects who interacted with a depressed confederate responded with a higher rate of silence and negative comments and a lower rate of responding. They expressed a level of direct support similar to that of subjects with the "physically ill" confederate and greater than that of subjects with the normal confederate. Hokanson, Sacco, Blumberg, and Landrum (1980), in an experimental study with college students who were depressed, nondepressed with other psychological problems, or normal, found that depressed persons given a high-power role behaved in an exploitive and noncooperative manner and showed elevated communications of self-devaluation, sadness, and helplessness. These behaviors elicited noncooperativeness, extrapunitiveness, and expressions of helplessness in their normal partners. Depressives in the low-power role communicated self-devaluation and helpless messages and, additionally, blamed their partner for their situation.

According to Coates and Peterson (1982), nondepressed subjects tend to dislike others who talk about their problems. Others may react with general avoidance (Lewinsohn & Shaffer, 1971; Lewinsohn, Weinstein, & Shaw, 1969), or, if reluctant to express negative feelings verbally, may express them through nonverbal behaviors, such as fewer smiles and less eye contact (Davis, 1961; Hinchliffe et al., 1978; Kleck, Ono, & Hastorf, 1966).

Lack of Assertiveness

Several studies have shown that depressed people exhibit deficits in social skills and assertiveness (Barbaree & Davis, 1984), fail to express an opinion or do so in a whining and ineffective manner (Weissman & Paykel, 1974), and report a high level of discomfort when attempting to behave in an assertive manner (Youngren & Lewinsohn, 1980). Recently, Olinger et al. (1987; cited in Kuiper et al., 1988) found support for the co-occurrence of nonassertiveness and attitudinal vulnerability to depression. Their work was based upon Ludwig and Lazarus' (1972) hypothesis (cited in Kuiper et al., 1988, p. 302) that nonassertive persons are characterized by "(1) the desire to be liked by everyone, (2) perfectionism and self-criticism, (3) unrealistic expectations and excessive criticism of others, and (4) the labeling of assertive behavior as inappropriate."

In a study by Olinger et al. (1987), vulnerable subjects failed to use appropriate strategies for dealing with interpersonal conflicts and felt greater discomfort when behaving assertively than did the normal controls. The vulnerable subjects who were not currently depressed displayed the same assertion deficits as depressed individuals. Kuiper et al. (cited in Kuiper et al., 1988) demonstrated that subjects who score high on the DAS (Oliver & Baumgart, 1985) display heightened levels of public self-consciousness and social anxiety even when they are not depressed.

Self-Disclosure of Depressed Persons

What differences exist between the self-disclosures of depressed and nondepressed persons and what are the effects of the depressed person's disclosures? Carpenter (1987) suggested that the excessive focus on the self in depressives made it difficult for them to attend adequately to social cues and to benefit from social interaction. He suggested that fatigue, loss of pleasure, and reduced concentration interfered with effective interpersonal behavior. Finally, he suggested that the negative mood resulted in deficient disclosure.

Research on the self-disclosure of depressives has demonstrated an interaction with the degree of the person's self-monitoring. High self-monitors are more concerned, are more sensitive to cues others provide (Snyder, 1979), and make more accurate interpretations of others' nonverbal communications (Mill, 1984). At relatively high depression levels for college students, high self-monitors reported more satisfaction with the support they received from friends when disclosing their distress (Coates and Winston, 1987). A significant negative relationship between reported distress disclosure and depression was also obtained, showing that people who said they talked about their problems more were less distressed at the moment.

In another study, depressed subjects viewed negative self-disclosure topics concerning their work, financial status, personality, and so on, to be more appropriate for discussion by themselves and others than did normal subjects (Kuiper & McCabe, 1985). Vulnerable subjects who were currently not depressed displayed the same views of topic appropriateness as did depressed subjects.

Hostility and Conflict

Although no research was located indicating that depressed persons are able to express their anger in a forceful or effective manner, the self-reports of the depressed reveal that their feelings of aggression are conscious and not inaccessible or warded off as Abraham (1927) and Fenichel (1945), respectively, had suggested. Hostility may be more obvious in males than in females (Gjerde, Block, & Block, 1988), but considerable hostility is expressed by women in close relationships even though it is not always apparent in interviews (Weissman, Klerman, & Paykel, 1971).

MASKED DEPRESSION, SUBSTANCE ABUSE, AND ANTISOCIAL BEHAVIORS

Experimental research has demonstrated that alcohol relieves anxiety for some people in certain situations (Levenson, Sher, Grossman, Newman, & Newlion, 1980). Alcoholism is believed to mask depression in the general population, especially in men. Clinical observations and research have shown that depression occurs as frequently in men as in women in cultures such as the Amish, where alcohol is not used

(Egeland & Hostetter, 1983), yet depression is more common among women in the general population. Research has also shown that a gene associated with vulnerability to depression in women is associated with alcoholism in men (Robinson, Davis, Nies, Ravaris, & Sylvester, 1971; Winokur, 1972). Many researchers have noted that truancy, running away, and antisocial or delinquent behaviors, especially in adolescents, mask depressive experiences (Chwast, 1961; Glaser, 1967; Toolan, 1962, 1974; Weiner, 1975).

MANIC SELF-DEFEATING BEHAVIORS

Very little research has focused upon the behaviors of manic patients. Janowsky, El-Yousef, and Davis (1974) found that in-patient manic patients were more likely to test limits, try to make others feel responsible for plans gone awry, be sensitive to and exploit the "soft spots" of others, attempt to divide staff, flatter, and evoke anger than either schizoaffective or schizophrenic patients. This pattern of behavior had been previously identified by Janowsky, Leff, and Epstein (1970). Bipolar manic-depressives in remission, however, were found not to differ on measures of positive mental health and measures of external orientation, including the Personal Orientation Inventory, the Marlow–Crowne Social Desirability Scale, Levenson's Internal and Powerful Others Locus of Control Scale or the Embedded Figures Test (MacVane, Lange, Brown, & Zayat, 1978). Remitted bipolars' inferences about the causes of failures have been found to resemble those of depressives, however, although their scores on a traditional measure of self-esteem (the Self-Report Inventory-II) did not differ from the normals (Winters & Neale, 1985). These data suggest that bipolar patients have the negative self-schema and depressive attributional style found in depressives, although their negative feelings are not revealed on usual self-report inventories.

EXPERIMENTAL STUDIES OF THE RELATIONSHIP BETWEEN MOOD AND BEHAVIOR

Perhaps because of the ethical implications of inducing a negative affect in experimental research participants, considerably more laboratory and field studies have investigated the effects of a positive mood on behavior than the effects of a depressed mood. This research was reviewed recently by Isen (1987). The finding that positive affect produces certain effects does not necessarily imply that negative affect will give rise to its opposite. Certainly, however, depressed people should be less likely, in many cases, to exhibit the behaviors associated with positive affect. Isen reviewed research on positive affect and social behavior, memory, and problem-solving. Some of these findings will be reported here.

Isen cited twelve studies demonstrating that people induced to have happy feeling are more likely to help others than are people in control groups. This finding holds for both children and adults. Happy people are more likely to volunteer to help someone, but less likely to volunteer to annoy someone (Isen & Levin, 1972). Other limits to their willingness to help have also been reported. Isen and Simmonds (1978) found that subjects who found a dime in a telephone booth were more likely than controls to help someone by reading and evaluating statements they were told would put them in a good mood, but less likely to read statements they were told would put them in a bad mood. Furthermore, persons who felt good were more likely than persons in a control condition to help a cause they favored, but less likely to help a cause they did not like (Forest, Clark, Mills, & Isen, 1979).

People who feel good tend to reward themselves more than control subjects (Mischel, Coates, & Raskoff, 1968) and to display greater preference for positive rather than negative self-relevant information. They are more willing to initiate conversations with others (Batson, Coke, Chard, Smith, & Taliaferro, 1979; Isen, 1970) and to express liking for others (Gouaux, 1971; Griffit, 1970; Veitch & Griffit, 1976); they are less aggressive (Baron, 1984; Baron & Ball, 1974) and more cooperative (Carnevale & Isen, 1986). People in a good mood are more cautious in threatening situations, and more willing to take a risk when the threat is of little consequence (Arkes, Herren, & Isen, 1988; Isen & Geva, 1987; Isen & Patrick, 1983).

Isen reviewed several studies showing that positive affect speeds up the recall of positive memories (Teasdale & Fogarty, 1979) and increases the recall of positive material (Laird, Wagenar, Halol, & Szegda, 1982; Nasby & Yando, 1982; Teasdale & Russell, 1983). Isen also showed that people in a good mood are more likely to give a positive evaluation than others (Isen, 1987; Isen, Daubman, & Nowicki, 1987). The affect at the time of learning appears to influence the material learned more than the affect at the time of retrieval influences the type of material recalled. For example, Bower, Gilligan, and Montiero (1981) showed that people induced to feel good at the time of learning, but not induced to feel good at the time of recall, remembered more facts about persons described as happy. Isen suggested that positive affect may give rise to an enlarged cognitive context, that is, a wide range of associated thoughts. She found that people induced to feel positive affect give more unusual word associations (Isen, Johnson, Martz, & Robinson, 1985) and show improved creative problem-solving, both social and nonsocial. For example, Isen et al. (1987) found that positive affect improved performance on the Remote Associates Test, whereas negative affect and affectless arousal did not. Similarly, persons in whom happiness was induced were better able to recall words when an obscure theme was not provided, but showed no advantage when it was provided (Isen et al., 1987). In a bargaining task, persons with positive affect were more likely to reach agreement and to reach the optimal agreement possible (Carnevale & Isen, 1986). Whereas positive affect appears to broaden association and attention there is some earlier work showing that negative affect leads to a restriction of attention and categorization (Bruner, Malter, & Papanek, 1955; Easterbrook, 1959).

The implications of the work on positive affect are that such affect facilitates a broad range of behaviors enhancing social relationships and problem solving. In contrast to persons with positive affect, persons lacking it exhibit impaired helping, cooperation, and creative problem-solving.

EXPERIMENTAL STUDIES OF THE RELATIONSHIP BETWEEN NEGATIVE SELF-SCHEMATA AND SELF-DEFEATING BEHAVIORS

The low self-esteem of the depressed person was suggested by Freud (1917/1957) and other psychoanalytic writers (Arieti & Bemporad, 1978; Bibring, 1953; Fenichel, 1945; Gaylin, 1968; Jacobson, 1953; Rado, 1928) as well as Beck (1967). Research on expectancy confirmation and self-verification processes has shown that people act in ways that confirm their negative self-schemata. Andrews (in press) has drawn upon this research to propose a "self-confirmation model" of depression.

Swann and Read (1981a) found that subjects sought information that would confirm their self-conception, regardless of whether they held self-concepts that they were assertive or nonassertive. In their research the subjects chose to read answers to questions another individual had completed about them that either probed for assertiveness, such as, "What makes you think that this is the type of person who will complain in a restaurant if the service is bad?" or probed for evidence of unassertiveness, such as, "Why would this person not be likely to complain if someone cuts into line in front of him or her at a movie?" In a second experiment, subjects even paid money for each piece of feedback they wished to examine. Subjects who perceived themselves as unassertive purchased more "unassertive" than "assertive" feedback and subjects who perceived themselves as assertive purchased more "assertive" feedback. In other research (Swann & Read, 1981b), subjects rated themselves as relatively likable or dislikable to others. They were then led to believe that a person with whom they would be interacting viewed them favorably or unfavorably. When allowed to examine statements on slides that their prospective partners had ostensibly selected to summarize their initial perceptions, subjects spent more time reading the statements when the partner's appraisal was expected to confirm their self-conceptions. Self-likables spent a longer time reading the statements in the favorable conditions whereas self-dislikables spent a longer time reading the statements in the unfavorable condition. In a subsequent study (Swann & Read, 1981b, Investigation II), participants elicited reactions from their partners that confirmed their self-conceptions, especially when they suspected their interaction partners' appraisals might disconfirm their self-conceptions. Participants also were found to preferentially recall feedback consistent with their self-conceptions. When people receive feedback that is inconsistent with their self-conceptions, their intimate partners, but not strangers, act to discredit the inconsistent information even when it is positive (Swann & Predmore, 1985). Curtis and Miller (1986) found that when people believe that another person dislikes them, even when the belief is erroneous, they act in ways that make the belief come true. People led experimentally to believe that they were disliked disagreed more with their partners, expressed less similarity, and had a more negative general attitude. When the interaction was over, they were actually liked less than persons who had been led experimentally to believe that they were liked (Curtis & Miller, 1986). People choose mates who see them as they see themselves (Swann & Pelham, 1990). They also regard information consistent with their self-concepts, even when it is negative, as more accurate and as delivered by a more competent evaluator. Persons with a negative self-concept believe unfavorable feedback, even though they feel upset hearing it (Swann, Griffin, Predmore, & Gaines, 1987).

All of this research suggests that once a depressogenic self-schema is activated by loss, failure, or stress, people will act in ways to make reality confirm it. Although the experimental research has focused upon negative self-schemata and expectancies, it seems reasonable to assume that these "negative" views are similar to those held by depressed persons and, probably, by many persons with bipolar disorder.

DEPRESSION, SELF-DEFEATING BEHAVIOR, AND CHRONIC PERSONALITY DISPOSITIONS

Depressed persons may be diagnosed as suffering from a wide variety of personality disorders, each characterized by particular types of self-defeating behaviors. They are most commonly diagnosed, however, as either avoidant or dependent personality disorders (Frank, Kupfer, Jacob, & Jarren, 1987; Shea, Glass, Pilkonis, Watkins, & Doherty, 1987). Leary's (1957) account of the depressive personality stresses the self-effacing/masochistic style of this person, but Horowitz, Rosenberg, Baer, Ureno, and Villasenor (1987) and more recently Andrews (in press) consider the dependent depressive as a separate subtype. Blatt, Quinlan, Chevron, and McDonald (1982) have also differentiated the self-critical and dependent types of depressed personalities, similar to the masochistic and dependent subtypes described by Leary.

Recently, with the Self-Defeating Personality Disorder (SDPD; formerly called Masochistic Personality) given provisional status in DSM-III-R and considered for inclusion in DSM-IV, the question has arisen as to whether persons with this particular cluster of behaviors are suffering primarily from symptoms of depression. The behaviors listed as descriptive of persons with a self-defeating personality disorder are as follows:

A. A pervasive pattern of self-defeating behavior, beginning by early adulthood and present in a variety of contexts. The person may often avoid or undermine pleasurable experiences, be drawn to situations or relationships in which he or she will suffer, and prevent others from helping him or her, as indicated by at least five of the following:

   (1) chooses people and situations that lead to disappointment, failure, or mistreatment even when better options are clearly available

   (2) rejects or renders ineffective the attempts of others to help him or her

   (3) following positive personal events (e.g., new achievement), responds with depression, guilt, or a behavior that produces pain (e.g., an accident)

   (4) incites angry or rejecting responses from others and then feels hurt, defeated, or humiliated (e.g., makes fun of spouse in public, provoking an angry retort, then feels devastated)

   (5) rejects opportunities for pleasure, or is reluctant to acknowledge enjoying himself or herself (despite having adequate social skills and the capacity for pleasure)

   (6) fails to accomplish tasks crucial to his or her personal objectives despite demonstrated ability to do so, e.g., helps fellow students write papers, but is unable to write his or her own

   (7) is uninterested in or rejects people who consistently treat him or her well, e.g., is unattracted to caring sexual partners

   (8) engages in excessive self-sacrifice that is unsolicited by the intended recipients of the sacrifice

B. The behaviors in A do not occur exclusively in response to, or in anticipation of, being physically, sexually, or psychologically abused.

C. The behaviors in A do not occur only when the person is depressed.

(American Psychiatric Association, 1987, pp. 373–374.)

Certain characteristics of persons with an SDPD, such as pessimism, rejection of opportunities for pleasure, rejection of efforts to help, self-criticism, guilt, disinterest in caring partners, and failure to complete tasks may all be seen in patients suffering from depression. Akiskal (1983), Liebowitz (1987), and Vaillant and Perry (1985) criticized inclusion of the SDPD in DSM-III-R on the grounds of its conceptual overlap with other diagnostic categories, primarily depression and passive–aggressive and dependent personality disorders.

Curtis (1988) suggested, on the other hand, that although persons with SDPD may become depressed, the behaviors associated with this personality style usually allow the person to maintain a sense of control and to avoid depression. The social psychological literature on choosing to suffer in nonclinical samples demonstrates that people making such a "choice" believe they are improving future outcomes (Curtis, 1989a). Levey (1983) found that men who engaged in self-handicapping behavior in a laboratory experiment were more likely to feel depressed as measured by the Beck Depression Inventory, but also to feel a higher sense of control.

SUMMARY

Many self-defeating behaviors of the depressed seem to be concomitants of the depressed mood state. Other behaviors, related to the preexisting view of the self, of the world, and of causality appear to make some people more vulnerable to depression after stressful life events than others. Although people with dependent and self-effacing personality styles may be particularly prone to depression, further investigations into the ways in which views of self and others and means of coping with failure and loss are learned would be useful in the prevention of the development of depressogenic behavior patterns. Particularly necessary is further research examining how induced self-sacrifice and induced dependence (Langer & Benevento, 1978) lead to depressogenic self-schemata and attributional styles.

REFERENCES

Abraham, K. (1927). Notes on the psycho-analytical investigation and treatment of manic-depressive insanity and allied conditions. In D. Bryan and A. Strachey (Trans.), *Selected papers on psychoanalysis*. London: Hogarth Press.

Abramson, L. Y., & Alloy, L. B. (1981). Depression, nondepression, and cognitive illusions: A reply to Schwartz. *Journal of Experimental Psychology: General, 108*, 436–447.

Abramson, L. Y., Alloy, L. B., & Metalsky, G. I. (1988). The cognitive diathesis-stress theories of depression: Toward an adequate evaluation of the theories' validities. In L. B. Alloy (Ed.), *Cognitive processes in depression* (pp. 3–30). New York: Guilford.

Abramson, L. Y., Metalsky, G. I., & Alloy, L. B. (1988). The hopelessness theory of depression: Does the research test the theory? In L. Y. Abramson (Ed.), *Social cognition and clinical psychology: A synthesis* (pp. 33–65). New York: Guilford.

Abramson, L. Y., Seligman, M. E. P., & Teasdale, J. (1978). Learned helplessness in humans: Critique and reformulation. *Journal of Abnormal Psychology, 87,* 49–74.

Akiskal, H. (1983). Dysthmic disorder: Psychopathology of proposed chronic depressive subtypes. *American Journal of Psychiatry, 140,* 11–20.

Alloy, L. B. (1982). The role of perceptions and attributions for response-outcome noncontingency in learned helplessness: A commentary and discussion. *Journal of Personality, 50,* 443–479.

Alloy, L. B. (1988). *Cognitive processes in depression.* New York: Guilford.

Alloy, L. B., & Abramson, L. Y. (1979). Judgment of contingency in depressed and nondepressed students: Sadder but wiser? *Journal of Experimental Psychology: General, 108,* 441–485.

Alloy, L. B., & Abramson, L. Y. (1982). Learned helplessness, depression, and the illusion of control. *Journal of Personality and Social Psychology, 42,* 1114–1126.

Alloy, L. B., & Abramson, L. Y. (1988). Depressive realism: Four theoretical perspectives. In L. B. Alloy (Ed.), *Cognitive processes in depression* (pp. 223–265). New York: Guilford.

Alloy, L. B., Abramson, L. Y., & Viscusi, D. (1981). Induced mood and the illusion of control. *Journal of Personality and Social Psychology, 41,* 1129–1140.

Alloy, L. B., & Ahrens, A. H. (1987). Depression and pessimism for the future: Biased use of statistically relevant information in predictions for self versus others. *Journal of Personality and Social Psychology, 52,* 366–378.

Alloy, L. B., Greenberg, M. S., Clements, C., & Kolden, G. (1983, August). *Depression, anxiety, and self-schemata: A test of Beck's theory.* Paper presented at the meeting of the American Psychological Association, Anaheim, CA.

American Psychiatric Association (1987). *Diagnostic and statistical manual of mental disorders* (3rd ed., rev.). Washington, DC: Author.

Andrews, G. R., & Debus, R. L. (1978). Persistence and the causal perception of failure: Modifying cognitive attributions. *Journal of Educational Psychology, 70,* 154–166.

Andrews, J. D. W. (in press). Psychotherapy of depression: A self-confirmation model. *Psychological Review.*

Arieti, S., & Bemporad, J. (1978). *Severe and mild depression.* New York: Basic Books.

Arkes, H., Herren, L. T., & Isen, A. M. (1988). The role of potential loss in the influence of affect on risk-taking behavior. *Organizational Behavior and Human Decision Processes, 42,* 181–193.

Barbaree, H. E., & Davis, R. B. (1984). Assertive behavior, self-expectations, and self-evaluations in mildly depressed university women. *Cognitive Therapy and Research, 8,* 153–172.

Baron, R. A. (1984). Reducing organizational conflict: An incompatible response approach. *Journal of Applied Psychology, 69,* 272–279.

Baron, R. A., & Ball, R. L. (1974). The aggression-inhibiting influence of nonhostile humor. *Journal of Experimental Social Psychology, 10,* 23–33.

Batson, C. D., Coke, J. S., Chard, F., Smith, D., & Taliaferro, A. (1979). Generality of the "Glow of goodwill": Effects of mood on helping and information acquisition. *Social Psychology Quarterly, 42,* 176–179.

Beck, A. T. (1967). *Depression: Clinical, experimental, and theoretical aspects.* New York: Harper & Row.

Beck, A. T. (1976). *Cognitive therapy and the emotional disorders.* New York: International Universities Press.

Beck, A. T., Rush, A. J., Shaw, B. F., & Emery, G. (1979). *Cognitive therapy of depression.* New York: Guilford.

Benassi, V. A., & Mahler, H. I. M. (1985). Contingency judgments by depressed college students: Sadder but not always wiser. *Journal of Personality and Social Psychology, 49,* 1323–1329.

Bibring, E. (1953). The mechanism of depression. In P. Greenacre (Ed.), *Affective disorders.* New York: International Universities Press.

Blatt, S., Quinlan, D., Chevron, E., & McDonald, C. (1982). Dependency and self-criticism: Psychological dimensions of depression. *Journal of Consulting and Clinical Psychology, 50,* 113–124.

Bower, G. H., Gilligan, S. G., & Montiero, K. P. (1981). Selectivity of learning caused by affective states. *Journal of Experimental Psychology: General, 110,* 451–473.

Brown, B. W., & Harris, T. (1978). *Social origins of depression: A study of psychiatric disorders in women.* New York: Free Press.

Bruner, J. S., Malter, J., & Papanek, M. L. (1955). Breadth of learning as a function of drive-level and maintenance. *Psychological Review, 62,* 1–10.

Buchwald, A. M. (1977). Depressive mood and estimates of reinforcement frequency. *Journal of Abnormal Psychology, 86,* 443–446.

Byrne, D. (1971). *The attraction paradigm.* New York: Academic Press.

Carnevale, P. J., & Isen, A. M. (1986). The influence of positive affect and visual accession: The discovery of integrative solutions in bilateral negotiation. *Organizational Behavior and Human Decision Processes, 37,* 1–13.

Carpenter, B. N. (1987). The relationship between psychopathology and self-disclosure: An interference/competence model. In V. J. Derlega & J. H. Berg (Eds.), *Self-disclosure: Theory, research, and therapy* (pp. 203–227). New York: Plenum.

Carver, C. S., & Gaines, J. G. (1987). Optimism, pessimism, and postpartum depression. *Cognitive Therapy and Research, 11,* 449–462.

Chapin, M., & Dyck, D. G. (1976). Persistence in children's reading behavior as a function of N length and attribution retraining. *Journal of Abnormal Psychology, 85,* 511–515.

Chwast, J. (1961). Depressive reactions as manifested among adolescent delinquents. *American Journal of Psychotherapy, 21,* 575–584.

Coates, D., & Peterson, B. A. (1982). Depression and deviance. In G. Weary & H. L. Mirels (Eds.), *Integrations of clinical and social psychology* (pp. 154–170). New York: Oxford University Press.

Coates, D., & Winston, T. (1987). The dilemma of distress disclosure. In V. J. Derlega & J. H. Berg (Eds.), *Self-disclosure: Theory, research, and therapy* (pp. 231–255). New York: Plenum.

Coyne, J. C. (1976a). Depression and the response of others. *Journal of Abnormal Psychology, 85,* 186–193.

Coyne, J. C. (1976b). Toward an interactional description of depression. *Psychiatry, 39,* 28–40.

Curtis, R. C. (1988, August). *Self-defeating personality: Diagnosis and treatment.* Symposium presented at the annual meeting of the American Psychological Association, Atlanta, GA.

Curtis, R. C. (1989a). Choosing to suffer or to . . . ? Empirical studies and clinical theories of masochism. In R. C. Curtis (Ed.), *Self-defeating behaviors: Experimental research, clinical impressions, and practical implications* (pp. 189–214). New York: Plenum.

Curtis, R. C. (1989b). Integration: Conditions under which self-defeating and self-enhancing behaviors develop. In R. C. Curtis (Ed.), *Self-defeating behaviors: Experimental research, clinical impressions, and practical implications* (pp. 343–359). New York: Plenum.

Curtis, R. C., & Miller, K. (1986). Believing another likes or dislikes you: Behaviors making the beliefs come true. *Journal of Personality and Social Psychology, 51,* 284–290.

Davis, F. (1961). Deviance disavowal: The management of strained interaction by the visibly handicapped. *Social Problems, 9,* 120–132.

Davis, H. (1979a). Self-reference and the encoding of personal information in depression. *Cognitive Therapy and Research, 3,* 97–110.

Davis, H. (1979b). The self-schema and subjective organization of personal information in depression. *Cognitive Therapy and Research, 3,* 415–425.

Davis, H., & Unruh, W. R. (1981). The development of self-schema in adult depression. *Journal of Abnormal Psychology, 90,* 125–133.

DeMonbreun, B. G., & Craighead, W. E. (1977). Distortion of perception and recall of positive and neutral feedback in depression. *Cognitive Therapy and Research, 1,* 311–329.

Derry, P. A., & Kuiper, N. A. (1981). Schematic processing and self-reference in clinical depression. *Journal of Abnormal Psychology, 90,* 286–297.

Dobson, K. S., & Shaw, B. F. (1986). Cognitive assessment with major depressive disorders. *Cognitive Therapy and Research, 10,* 13–31.

Easterbrook, J. A. (1959). The effect of emotion on cue utilization and the organization of behavior. *Psychological Review, 66,* 183–201.

Egeland, J. A., & Hostetter, A. M. (1983). Amish Study I: Affective disorders among the Amish. *American Journal of Psychiatry, 140,* 56–61.

Feather, N. T. (1982). Actions in relation to expected consequences: An overview of a research program. In N. T. Feather (Ed.), *Expectations and actions* (pp. 53–59). Hillsdale, NJ: Erlbaum.

Fenichel, O. (1945). *The psychoanalytic theory of neurosis.* New York: Norton.

Festinger, L. (1954). A theory of social comparison processes. *Human Relations, 7,* 117–140.

Foersterling, F. (1985). Attributional retraining: A review. *Psychological Bulletin, 98,* 495–512.

Forest, D., Clark, M. S., Mills, J., & Isen, A. M. (1979). Helping as a function of feeling state and nature of the helping behavior. *Motivation and Emotion, 3,* 161–169.

Frank, E., Kupfer, D., Jacob, M., & Jarren, D. (1987). Personality features and response to acute treatment in recurrent depression. *Journal of Personality Disorders, 1,* 14–26.

Frankel, A., & Snyder, M. L. (1987, September). Egotism among the depressed: When self-protection becomes self-handicapping. In R. C. Curtis (Chair), *Self-defeating behaviors: Situational and dispositional factors.* Symposium conducted at the annual meeting of the American Psychological Association, New York.

Freud, S. (1957). Mourning and melancholia. In J. Strachey (Ed. and Trans.), *The standard edition of the complete psychological works of Sigmund Freud* (Vol. 14, pp. 239–258). London: Hogarth Press. (Original work published 1917.)

Friedman, A. S. (1964). Minimal effects of severe depression on cognitive functioning. *Journal of Abnormal and Social Psychology, 69,* 237–243.

Gaylin, W. (Ed.). (1968). The meaning of despair. In *Psychoanalytic contributions to the understanding of depression.* New York: Science House.

Gjerde, P. F., Block, J., & Block, J. H. (1988). Depressive symptoms and personality during late adolescence: Gender differences in the externalization-internalization of symptom expression. *Journal of Abnormal Psychology, 97,* 475–986.

Glaser, K. (1967). Masked depression in children and adolescents. *American Journal of Psychotherapy, 21,* 565–574.

Glass, R. M., Uhlenhuth, E. H., & Weihreb, H. (1978). Imipramine reversible cognitive deficit in outpatient depressives. *Psychopharmacology Bulletin, 14,* 10–13.

Golin, S., Terrell, F., & Johnson, B. (1977). Depression and the illusion of control. *Journal of Abnormal Psychology, 86,* 440–442.

Golin, S., Terrell, F., Weitz, J., & Drost, P. L. (1979). The illusion of control among depressed patients. *Journal of Abnormal Psychology, 88,* 454–457.

Gotlib, I. H. (1982). Self-reinforcement and depression in interpersonal interaction: The role of performance level. *Journal of Abnormal Psychology, 91,* 3–13.

Greenberg, M. S., Vazquez, C. V., & Alloy, L. B. (1988). Depression versus anxiety: Differences in self- and other-schemata. In L. B. Alloy (Ed.), *Cognitive processes in depression* (pp. 109–142). New York: Guilford.

Griffit, W. B. (1970). Environmental effects on interpersonal affective behavior: Ambient effective temperature and attraction. *Journal of Personality and Social Psychology, 15,* 240–244.

Griffit, W. B. (1974). Attitude similarity and attraction. In T. L. Huston (Ed.), *Foundations of interpersonal attraction.* New York: Academic Press.

Gutman, M. (1986). Depression and the response of others: Reevaluating the reevaluation. *Journal of Abnormal Psychology, 95,* 99–101.

Hall, K. R. L., & Stride, E. (1954). Some factors affecting reaction times to auditory stimuli in mental patients. *Journal of Mental Science, 100,* 462–477.

Hamilton, E., & Abramson, L. (1983). Cognitive patterns and major depressive disorder: A longitudinal study in a hospital setting. *Journal of Abnormal Psychology, 92,* 173–184.

Hammen, C. L., Marks, T., Magol, A., & deMayo, R. (1985). Depressive self-schemas, life stress, and vulnerability to depression. *Journal of Abnormal Psychology, 94,* 303–319.

Hammen, C., Miklowitz, D., & Dyck, D. (1986). Stability and severity parameters of depressive self-schema responding. *Journal of Social and Clinical Psychology, 4,* 23–45.

Hautzinger, M., Linden, M., & Hoffman, N. (1982). Distressed couples with and without a depressed partner: An analysis of their verbal interaction. *Journal of Behavior Therapy and Experimental Psychiatry, 13,* 307–314.

Hinchliffe, M. R., Hooper, D., & Roberts, F. J. (1978). *The melancholy marriage.* New York: Wiley.

Hinchliffe, M. R., Hooper, D., Roberts, F. J., & Vaughan, R. V. (1975). A study of interaction of depressed patients and their spouses. *British Journal of Psychiatry, 126,* 164–172.

Hokanson, J. E., Sacco, W. P., Blumberg, S. R., & Landrum, G. C. (1980). Interpersonal behavior of depressed individuals in a mixed-motive game. *Journal of Abnormal Psychology, 89,* 320–332.

Horowitz, L., Rosenberg, S., Baer, B., Ureno, G., & Villasenor, V. (1987). *The inventory of personal problems.* Unpublished manuscript, Stanford University, Palo Alto, CA.

Howes, M. J., & Hokanson, J. E. (1979). Conversational and social responses to depressive interpersonal behavior. *Journal of Abnormal Psychology, 88,* 625–634.

Ingram, R. E., Smith, T. W., & Brehm, S. S. (1983). Depression and information processing: Self-schemata and the encoding of self-referent information. *Journal of Personality and Social Psychology, 45,* 412–420.

Isen, A. M. (1970). Success, failure, attention and reaction to others: The warm glow of success. *Journal of Personality and Social Psychology, 15,* 294–301.

Isen, A. M. (1987). Positive affect, cognitive processes and social behavior. In L. Berkowitz (Ed.), *Advances in experimental social psychology* (Vol. 20, pp. 203–253). New York: Academic Press.

Isen, A. M., Daubman, K. A., & Nowicki, G. P. (1987). Positive affect facilities creative problem solving. *Journal of Personality and Social Psychology, 52,* 1122–1131.

Isen, A. M., & Geva, N. (1987). The influence of positive affect on acceptable level of risk: The person with a large canoe has large worry. *Organizational Behavior and Human Decision Processes, 39,* 145–154.

Isen, A. M., Johnson, M. M. S., Martz, E., & Robinson, G. (1985). The influence of positive affect on the unusualness of word association. *Journal of Personality and Social Psychology, 48,* 1413–1426.

Isen, A. M., & Levin, P. F. (1972). The effect of feeling good on helping: Cookies and kindness. *Journal of Personality and Social Psychology, 21,* 384–388.

Isen, A. M., & Patrick, R. (1983). The effect of positive feelings on risk-taking: When the chips are down. *Organizational Behavior and Human Performance, 31,* 194–202.

Isen, A. M., & Simmonds, S. F. (1978). The effect of feeling good on a helping task that is incompatible with good mood. *Social Psychology Quarterly, 41,* 345–349.

Jacobson, E. (1953). Contribution to the metapsychology of cyclothymic depression. In P. Greenacre (Ed.), *Affective disorders.* New York: International Universities Press.

Janoff-Bulman, R., & Hecker, B. (1988). Depression, vulnerability, and world assumptions. In L. B. Alloy (Ed.), *Cognitive processes in depression* (pp. 177–192). New York: Guilford.

Janowsky, D. S., El-Yousef, M. K., & Davis, J. M. (1974). Interpersonal maneuvers of manic patients. *American Journal of Psychiatry, 131,* 250–255.

Janowsky, D. S., Leff, M., & Epstein, R. S. (1970). Playing the manic game. *Archives of General Psychiatry, 22,* 252–261.

Kaplan, M. F. (1972). Interpersonal attraction as a function of similar and dissimilar attitudes. *Journal of Experimental Research in Personality, 6,* 17–21.

Kleck, R., Ono, H., & Hastorf, A. H. (1966). The effects of physical deviance upon face-to-face interaction. *Human Relations, 19,* 425–436.

Krauss, R. M. (1966). Structural and attitudinal factors in interpersonal bargaining. *Journal of Experimental Social Psychology, 2,* 42–55.

Kuhl, J. (1982). The expectancy-value approach within the theory of social motivation: Elaborations, extensions, critique. In N. T. Feather (Ed.), *Expectations and actions* (pp. 125–160). Hillsdale, NJ: Erlbaum.

Kuiper, N. A., & Derry, P. A. (1982). Depressed and nondepressed content self-reference in mild depressives. *Journal of Personality, 50,* 67–69.

Kuiper, N. A., & MacDonald, M. R. (1982). Self and other perception in mild depressives. *Social Cognition, 1,* 223–239.

Kuiper, N. A., MacDonald, M. R., & Derry, P. A. (1983). Parameters of a depressive self-schema. In J. Suls & A. G. Greenwald (Eds.), *Psychological perspectives on the self* (Vol. 2, pp. 191–217). Hillsdale, NJ: Erlbaum.

Kuiper, N. A., & McCabe, S. B. (1985). The appropriateness of social topics: Effects of depression and cognitive vulnerability on self and other judgments. *Cognitive Therapy and Research, 9,* 371–379.

Kuiper, N. A., & Olinger, L. J. (1986). Dysfunctional attitudes and a self-worth contingency model of depression. In P. C. Kendall (Ed.), *Advances in cognitive-behavioral research and therapy* (Vol. 5, pp. 115–142). New York: Academic Press.

Kuiper, N. A., Olinger, L. J., & MacDonald, M. R. (1988). Vulnerability and episodic cognitions in a self-worth contingency model of depression. In L. B. Alloy (Ed.), *Cognitive processes in depression* (pp. 289–309). New York: Guilford.

Kuiper, N. A., Olinger, L. J., MacDonald, M. R., & Shaw, B. F. (1985). Self-schema processing of depressed and nondepressed content: The effects of vulnerability to depression. *Social Cognition, 3,* 77–93.

Laird, J. D., Wagenar, J. J., Halol, M., & Szegda, M. (1982). Remembering what you feel: The effects of emotion on memory. *Journal of Personality and Social Psychology, 42,* 646–657.

Langer, E. J., & Benevento, A. (1978). Self-induced dependence. *Journal of Personality and Social Psychology, 36,* 886–893.

LaNoue, J. B., & Curtis, R. C. (1985). Improving women's performance in mixed-sex situations by effort attributions. *Psychology of Women Quarterly, 9,* 337–356.

Laxter, R. M. (1964). Self-concept changes of depressive patients in general hospital treatment. *Journal of Consulting Psychology, 28,* 214–219.

Leary, T. (1957). *Interpersonal diagnosis of personality.* New York: Ronald Press.

Levenson, R. W., Sher, K. J., Grossman, L. M., Newman, J., & Newlion, D. B. (1980). Alcohol and stress response dampening: Pharmacological effects, expectancy, and tension reduction. *Journal of Abnormal Psychology, 89,* 528–538.

Levey, C. A. (1983). *Self-handicapping behavior: When and why do people engage in it?* Unpublished doctoral dissertation, Adelphi University, Garden City, NY. Dissertation Abstracts International, 44/04B, p. 280. (University Microfilms, 8329708-1983.)

Lewinsohn, P. M., Mischel, W., Chaplin, W., & Barton, R. (1980). Social competence and depression: The role of illusory self-perceptions. *Journal of Abnormal Psychology, 89,* 203–212.

Lewinsohn, P. M., & Shaffer, M. (1971). The use of home observations as an integral part of the treatment of depression: Preliminary report and case studies. *Journal of Consulting and Clinical Psychology, 37,* 87–94.

Lewinsohn, P. M., Steinmetz, J., Larson, D., & Franklin, J. (1981). Depression-related cognitions: Antecedent or consequences? *Journal of Abnormal Psychology, 90,* 213–219.

Lewinsohn, P. M., Weinstein, M. S., & Shaw, D. A. (1969). Depression: A clinical research approach. In R. D. Rubin & C. D. Franks (Eds.), *Advances in behavior therapy*. New York: Academic Press.

Liebowitz, M. (1987). Commentary on the criteria for self-defeating personality disorder. *Journal of Personality Disorders, 1*, 197–199.

Lishman, W. A. (1972). Selective factors in memory, Part 2: Affective disorder. *Psychological Medicine, 2*, 248–253.

Ludwig, L. D., & Lazarus, A. A. (1972). A cognitive and behavioral approach to the treatment of social inhibition. *Psychotherapy: Theory, Research, and Practice, 9*, 204–206.

Lunghi, M. E. (1977). The stability of mood and social perception measures in a sample of depressive in-patients. *British Journal of Psychiatry, 130*, 598–604.

MacVane, J. R., Lange, J. D., Brown, W. A., & Zayat, M. (1978). Psychological functioning of bipolar manic-depressives in remission. *Archives of General Psychiatry, 35*, 1351–1354.

Martin, D. J., Abramson, L. Y., & Alloy, L. B. (1984). The illusion of control for self and others in depressed and nondepressed college students. *Journal of Personality and Social Psychology, 46*, 125–136.

Martin, I., & Rees, L. (1966). Reaction times and somatic reactivity in depressed patients. *Journal of Psychosomatic Research, 9*, 375–382.

Mill, J. (1984). High and low self-monitoring individuals: Their decoding skills and empathic self-disclosure. *Journal of Personality, 52*, 372–388.

Mischel, W., Coates, B., & Raskoff, A. (1968). Effects of success and failure on self-gratification. *Journal of Personality and Social Psychology, 10*, 381–390.

Morse, S., & Gergen, K. J. (1970). Social comparison, self-consistency, and the concept of self. *Journal of Personality and Social Psychology, 16*, 148–156.

Nadich, M., Gargan, M., & Michael, L. (1975). Denial, anxiety, and the discrepancy between aspiration and achievements as components of depression. *Journal of Abnormal Psychology, 84*, 1–9.

Nasby, W., & Yando, R. (1982). Selective encoding and retrieval of affectively salient information. *Journal of Personality and Social Psychology, 43*, 1244–1255.

Olinger, L. J., Kuiper, N. A., & Shaw, B. F. (1987). Dysfunctional attitudes and stressful life events: An interactive model of depression. *Cognitive Therapy and Research, 11*, 25–40.

Oliver, J. M., & Baumgart, E. P. (1985). The Dysfunctional Attitude Scale: Psychometric properties and relation to depression in an unselected adult population. *Cognitive Therapy and Research, 9*, 161–167.

Paykel, E. S., & Weissman, M. M. (1973). Social adjustment and depression. *Archives of General Psychiatry, 28*, 659–663.

Peterson, C., & Barrett, L. C. (1987). Explanatory style and academic performance among university freshmen. *Journal of Personality and Social Psychology, 53*, 603–607.

Peterson, C., & Bossio, L. M. (1989). Learned helplessness. In R. C. Curtis (Ed.), *Self-defeating behaviors: Experimental research, clinical impressions, and practical implications* (pp. 235–257). New York: Plenum.

Peterson, C., & Seligman, M. E. P. (1984). *Content analysis of verbatim explanations.* Unpublished manuscript, University of Pennsylvania, Philadelphia.

Peterson, C., & Seligman, M. E. P. (1987). Explanatory style and illness. *Journal of Personality, 55,* 237–265.

Peterson, C., Seligman, M. E. P., & Vaillant, G. E. (1988). Pessimistic explanatory style is a risk factor for physical illness: A thirty-five-year longitudinal study. *Journal of Personality and Social Psychology, 55,* 23–27.

Pinkley, R., LaPrelle, J., Pyszczynski, T., & Greenberg, J. (1988). Depression and the self-serving search for consensus after success and failure. *Journal of Social and Clinical Psychology, 6,* 235–244.

Pyszczynski, T., & Greenberg, J. (1985). Depression and preference for self-focusing stimuli following success and failure. *Journal of Personality and Social Psychology, 49,* 1066–1075.

Rado, S. (1928). The problem of melancholia. *International Journal of Psychoanalysis, 9,* 420–438.

Reker, G. T., & Wong, P. T. P. (1985). Personal optimism, physical and mental health: The triumph of successful aging. In J. E. Birren & J. Livingston (Eds.), *Cognition, stress, and aging* (pp. 134–173). Englewood Cliffs, NJ: Prentice-Hall.

Robinson, D. S., Davis, J., Nies, A., Ravaris, C., & Sylvester, D. (1971). Relation of sex in aging to monoamine oxidase activity in human brain, plasma, and platelets. *Archives of General Psychiatry, 24,* 536.

Ross, M. J., Mueller, J. H., & de la Torre, M. (1986). Depression and trait distinctiveness in the self-schema. *Journal of Social and Clinical Psychology, 4,* 46–59.

Schachter, S. (1959). *The psychology of affiliation.* Stanford, CA: Stanford University Press.

Scheier, M. F., & Carver, C. S. (1985). Optimism, coping, and health: Assessment and implications of generalized outcome expectancies. *Health Psychology, 4,* 219–247.

Scheier, M. F., & Carver, C. S. (1988). A model of self-regulation: Translating intention into action. In L. Berkowitz (Ed.), *Advances in experimental social psychology* (Vol. 21, pp. 303–346). New York: Academic Press.

Scheier, M. F., Weintraub, J. K., & Carver, C. S. (1986). Coping with stress: Divergent strategies of optimists and pessimists. *Journal of Personality and Social Psychology, 51,* 1257–1264.

Schleifer, S. J., Keller, S. E., Siris, S. G., Davis, K. L., & Stein, M. (1985). Depression and immunity. *Archives of General Psychiatry, 42,* 129–133.

Seligman, M. E. P. (1975). *Helplessness: On depression, development, and depth.* San Francisco: Freeman.

Seligman, M. E. P., & Schulman, P. (1985). Explanatory style as a predictor of productivity and quitting among life insurance agents. *Journal of Personality and Social Psychology, 50,* 832–838.

Shea, M., Glass, D., Pilkonis, P., Watkins, J., & Doherty, J. (1987). Frequency and implications of personality disorders in a sample of depressed outpatients. *Journal of Personality Disorders, 1,* 27–42.

Snyder, M. (1979). Self-monitoring processes. In L. Berkowitz (Ed.), *Advances in experimental social psychology* (Vol. 12, pp. 25–86). New York: Academic Press.

Snyder, M. L., & Frankel, A. (1989). Making things harder for yourself: Pride and joy. In R. C. Curtis (Ed.), *Self-defeating behaviors: Experimental research, clinical impressions, and practical implications* (pp. 131–157). New York: Plenum.

Sternberg, D. E., & Jarvik, M. E. (1976). Memory functions in depression. *Archives of General Psychiatry, 33,* 219–224.

Strack, S., Blaney, P. H., Ganellen, R. J., & Coyne, J. C. (1985). Pessimistic self-preoccupation, performance deficits, and depression. *Journal of Personality and Social Psychology, 49,* 1075–1085.

Strack, S., Carver, C. S., & Blaney, P. H. (1987). Predicting successful completion of an aftercare program following treatment for alcoholism: The role of dispositional optimism. *Journal of Personality and Social Psychology, 53,* 579–584.

Strack, S., & Coyne, J. C. (1983). Social confirmation of dysphoria: Shared and private reactions to depression. *Journal of Personality and Social Psychology, 44,* 798–806.

Swallow, S. R., & Kuiper, N. A. (1987). The effects of depression and cognitive vulnerability to depression on judgments of similarity between self and other. *Motivation and Emotion, 11,* 157–167.

Swann, W. B., Jr., Griffin, J. J., Predmore, S. C., & Gaines, B. (1987). The cognitive-affective crossfire: When self-consistency confronts self-enhancement. *Journal of Personality and Social Psychology, 52,* 881–889.

Swann, W. B., Jr., & Pelham, B. W. (1990). *Embracing the bitter truth: Positivity and authenticity in social relationships.* Manuscript submitted for publication.

Swann, W. B. Jr., & Predmore, S. C. (1985). Intimates as agents of social support: Sources of consolation or despair. *Journal of Personality and Social Psychology, 49,* 1609–1617.

Swann, W. B., Jr., & Read, S. J. (1981a). Self-verification processes: How we sustain our self-conceptions. *Journal of Experimental Social Psychology, 17,* 351–372.

Swann, W. B., Jr., & Read, S. J. (1981b). Acquiring self-knowledge: The search for feedback that fits. *Journal of Personality and Social Psychology, 41,* 1119–1128.

Sweeney, P. D., Anderson, K., & Bailey, S. (1986). Attributional style in depression: A meta-analytic review. *Journal of Personality and Social Psychology, 50,* 974–991.

Tabachnik, N., Crocker, J., & Alloy, L. B. (1983). Depression, social comparison, and the false-consensus affect. *Journal of Personality and Social Psychology, 45,* 688–699.

Teasdale, J. D., & Fogarty, S. J. (1979). Differential effects of induced mood on retrieval of pleasant and unpleasant events from episodic memory. *Journal of Abnormal Psychology, 88,* 248–257.

Teasdale, J. D., & Russell, M. L. (1983). Differential effects of induced mood on the recall of positive, negative, and neutral words. *British Journal of Clinical Psychology, 22,* 163–172.

Toolan, J. M. (1962). Depression in children and adolescents. *American Journal of Orthopsychiatry, 32,* 404–415.

Toolan, J. M. (1974). Masked depression in children and adolescents. In S. Lesse (Ed.), *Masked depression* (pp. 141–164). New York: Jason Aronson.

Vaillant, G. E., & Perry, J. C. (1985). Personality disorders. In H. I. Kaplan & B. J. Sadock (Eds.), *Comprehensive textbook of psychiatry* (4th ed., pp. 958–986). Baltimore: Williams & Wilkins.

Vazquez, C. V. (1987). Judgment of contingency: Cognitive biases in depressed and nondepressed subjects. *Journal of Personality and Social Psychology, 52,* 419–431.

Vazquez, C. V., & Alloy, L. B. (1987). *Schematic memory processes for self- and other-referent information in depression versus anxiety: A signal detection analysis.* Unpublished manuscript, Northwestern University, Evanston, IL.

Veitch, R., & Griffit, W. (1976). Good news–bad news: Affective and interpersonal effects. *Journal of Applied Social Psychology, 6,* 69–75.

Weiner, I. B. (1975). Depression in adolescence. In F. F. Flack & S. C. Draghi (Eds.), *The nature and treatment of depression* (pp. 99–117). New York: Wiley.

Weissman, M. M., Klerman, G. L., & Paykel, E. S. (1971). Clinical evaluation of hostility in depression. *American Journal of Psychiatry, 128,* 261–266.

Weissman, M. M., & Paykel, E. S. (1974). *The depressed woman: A study of social relationships.* Chicago: University of Chicago Press.

Wener, A. E., & Rehm, L. P. (1975). Depressive affect: A test of behavioral hypotheses. *Journal of Abnormal Psychology, 84,* 221–227.

Williams, J. M., Little, M. M., Scates, S., & Blockman, N. (1987). Memory complaints and abilities among depressed older adults. *Journal of Consulting and Clinical Psychology, 55,* 595–598.

Winokur, G. (1972). Family history studies VIII: Secondary depression is alive and well and . . . *Diseases of the Nervous System, 33,* 94–99.

Winters, K. C., & Neale, J. M. (1985). Mania and low self-esteem. *Journal of Abnormal Psychology, 94,* 282–290.

Youngren, M. A., & Lewinsohn, P. M. (1980). The functional relation between depression and problematic interpersonal behavior. *Journal of Abnormal Psychology, 89,* 333–341.

CHAPTER 9

Symptoms, Prevention, and Treatment of Attempted Suicide

PAMELA C. CANTOR, PhD

In 1969 and 1970 I was a National Institute of Mental Health Fellow in Psychiatry at the Johns Hopkins Medical School, Phipps Psychiatric Center, where, with a group of distinguished faculty and interested students, I studied suicide. At that time we considered eight questions essential to our understanding of self-inflicted death:

1. Are individuals who attempt suicide like those who commit suicide or are they different?
2. Are attempted suicide and completed suicide the same, or are they distinct entities?
3. Is suicide a disease or a symptom?
4. Can suicidal individuals be identified before the event?
5. What are the symptoms that put them at risk?
6. What is it that drives people to suicide?
7. Are people who attempt or commit suicide pathologically disturbed or can they be "normal"?
8. How can individuals be prevented from taking their own lives?

Twenty years later these questions are still crucial to the field—and 20 years later we have only a few of the answers. Let us look at each question.

ATTEMPTERS AND COMPLETERS

Are attempters and completers alike or are they different? There is consensus that suicide attempters and suicide completers need to be seen as separate, but overlapping, populations (Farberow, 1989). A prior suicide attempt may be a clue to future suicide, but as often it is not.

Are attempted suicides and completed suicides discrete acts? Twenty years ago I proposed, for purposes of research clarity, the continuum model of suicide, with suicide placed at the far end of the continuum and suicide attempts at the beginning. I suggested that individuals who attempted suicide should be seen, not as one homogeneous group, but rather as at least two subgroups divided according to motivation: those who attempted suicide but did not wish to end their lives, and those who attempted suicide with the intention of dying. Attempters in this latter category could be considered more like those who commit suicide, because the only difference between those who live and those who die is the lethality of their attempt (Cantor, 1972). Take, for instance, Carl, a young man who stabbed himself in the heart. He missed death by $\frac{1}{16}$ of an inch. When someone like Carl dies, we look at his personality and life events as characteristic of completers. When the person lives, we examine him as an attempter. He would be no different either way. The difference is found in the $\frac{1}{16}$ of an inch—not in the person.

Prior to 1970, the vast majority of studies on attempted and completed suicide did not make any distinction beyond whether an individual survived or died. Anyone who lived was an attempter, anyone who died was a completer. This dichotomous approach made much of our research useless.

A second major flaw in suicide research was the absence of control groups. Researchers would study a group of suicidal individuals and make claims about them, only to realize later that the same claims could be made for other behaviors as well.

Even at the present time, research on attempters and committers is still so confounded that we are certain of only one crucial difference between the population who survive an attempt and the population who die. That difference is gender. The ratio of suicides committed by males to those committed by females is almost five to one, and the ratio of males to females for attempted suicide is the reverse. Rates for males committing suicide increased by 50 percent during the past decade while the increase for females was only two percent (Kupfer, 1989).

A DISEASE OR A SYMPTOM?

To the question, is suicide a disease or a symptom, finally there is a strong consensus of reply among the experts: Suicide is a symptom and not a disease entity. This means that suicide can be the outcome of any number of psychological or physical conditions and that attempted suicide can be an intermediate point in any number of circumstances.

Certain symptoms or behaviors do appear frequently, however, in the histories of individuals who attempt or commit suicide. Depression is the symptom most frequently mentioned. Even if an individual is suffering from depression, however, it does not mean that he or she is about to kill himself or herself. Not all individuals who are depressed are suicidal and not all individuals who are suicidal are necessarily depressed (Cantor, 1987a).

While depression is the symptom most often associated with suicidality, the significant factors that put a person at risk have more to do with behavioral and cognitive changes than with the diagnosis of depression.

A person is considered at risk if he or she has:

1. Made a suicide attempt or gesture.
2. Discussed or threatened suicide.
3. Made a specific plan to take his or her own life.
4. Been preoccupied with death.
5. Known someone who has committed suicide.
6. Identified with someone who has died violently, modeled his or her actions on that person's behavior, or been traumatized by that person's death.
7. Been abusing drugs or alcohol.
8. Poor impulse control; been known to act impulsively or violently.
9. No strength to tackle any problem and is blind to any way out.
10. Cognitive rigidity and constricted vision—has rejected all suggestions and is convinced that suicide is the only solution.
11. Perfectionist standards and is convinced that life should be perfect and nothing less than perfect is acceptable.
12. Recently experienced a loss. This could be an actual loss or it could be the loss of self-esteem. Loss may be the only factor on this list directly related to depression.

The symptoms of suicide that are related to depression are sleep and eating disturbances. These symptoms, however, can also be related to anxiety.

Individuals who have eating disorders and who are depressed or anxious appear to have a defect in the opiod systems and in the metabolic functions of their brain. It is not entirely clear, however, whether the defect and neurochemical changes are the result of the anorexia or bulimia (known to affect the central nervous system through caloric deprivation), or the cause of the symptoms. Norepinephrine and serotonin levels are lower in individuals with anorexia and bulimia. Both remain low, however, in individuals who have maintained healthy eating patterns for almost two years, leading researchers to speculate that the lower levels of norepinephrine and serotonin were present prior to the eating disturbance. Thus, eating problems may have their origins in neurochemical dysfunction, and depression and anxiety may be symptoms of the underlying biological problems (Fava, Copeland, Schweiger, & Herzog, 1989).

A third symptom of depression associated with suicidal behavior is that of extreme lethargy coupled with pessimism. A fourth symptom is overt hostility. A fifth is withdrawal and isolation and the sixth recently identified risk factor, related to both depressive illness and suicide, is serotonin. Low serotonin level or difficulties in serotonin regulation predispose one to violent behavior and suicide (Asberg, et al., 1981).

ETIOLOGIC FACTORS

Twenty years ago, suicidologists did not mention biochemistry or genetic predisposition except to deny the fact that suicide could be inherited. Today suicidologists admit that suicide does run in families and cite the genetic basis for manic-depressive psychosis and schizophrenia and the inherited tendency to low serotonin level, which can put a person at risk.

What is it that actually drives people to suicide? I have stated that suicide is a symptom and not a disease, and suicide can be the result of psychiatric illness, physical illness, or biochemical imbalance. It is possible, as well, that some suicidal individuals may not be psychiatrically disturbed, but rather only temporarily stressed to the point of not wanting to live. It is also established that the symptoms of suicide potential can lead to other outcomes. If all of the foregoing statements are true, how can we ever identify the origins of suicide?

An example will further illustrate this dilemma. The break-up of a relationship might be the final straw that triggers a serious depression in a person with a history of manic-depressive illness. Is it the heartbreak, the depression, the stress, or manic-depressive tendencies that are responsible for the person's suicide attempt? And if this person also has a dysfunctional family or few friends, should we blame isolation or lack of social supports for the suicidal behavior?

The question then becomes: How do these different risk factors contribute to the outcome of suicide potential, and with what weight? Or is the number of factors the important criteria? In order to answer these questions we might better ask: What is it that keeps people from attempting or committing suicide? To date, few have taken this approach.

It is clear that psychiatric illness does predispose one to suicide, but it is also clear that it is not a necessary variable. Further, it is not clear exactly which psychiatric illnesses predispose one to suicide (Cantor, 1989b; Shaffer, 1989).

The psychopathologies most frequently documented as related to suicide are affective disorders (primarily depression), conduct disorders, and substance abuse. Personality traits such as impulsiveness and aggression, and borderline and antisocial personality disorders are often cited as well. And one recent study claims anxiety and panic symptoms are the best indicator of future suicidal potential (Weissman, Klerman, Markowitz, & Ouellette, 1989).

The literature and folklore lead us to believe that suicide occurs among depressed individuals. Current studies, however, refute this and point to other areas of risk such as anxiety, substance abuse, biochemical and neurochemical dysfunction, and the psychosocial factors of lack of support, stress, chronic illness, and chance.

Moreover, the actual vulnerability of an individual to suicide may fluctuate from day to day. This raises the question of whether suicide is more often the result of mental illness or of the vagaries and stresses of life, be they hormonal, biochemical, or situational.

For example, take a 16-year-old who breaks up with his girlfriend after he has been cut from the final tryouts for the hockey team and has been humiliated in front of his teammates. His former girl's new interest is the captain of the team and the 16-year old's pride is severely damaged. He goes to a party and gets high. He hopes to see his girl and patch things up, but he drinks too much and leaves feeling despondent. He does not have the life experience to know that tomorrow may bring a new love. He just lives for today and today was not so hot. As he drives into his family's garage, his eye catches his father's rifle hanging on the wall. He takes it down. He may be at risk for suicide. Is it the heartbreak, the humiliation, the alcohol, or the gun? Which of the factors is causing the vulnerability? Is it a temporary vulnerability or will this boy be at continual risk for suicide?

One goal of suicidologists is to identify individuals at risk so we can prevent people from killing themselves; yet we cannot seem to agree on something as basic as the significant factors for suicide potential. The most important breakthrough in research in the past 20 years has come from the identification of serotonin, and while this has great importance in the field of mental illness, it is of little practical value to most professionals or individuals on the front lines of prevention.

In sum, the factors that can lead to suicide and attempted suicide are diverse and nonspecific. The list of biochemical, behavioral, psychological, and social characteristics that are linked to suicide includes:

- Alcohol and drug abuse
- Mental illness—with much controversy as to which illnesses are most heavily represented

- Impulsive and antisocial behaviors
- Severe stress, shame, or loss

Those that are suicide-specific are now reduced to:

- A history of previous suicide behaviors or a family history of violence or suicide
- Witnessing a suicide
- Low concentrations of serotonin metabolite, 5-hydroxinodoleacetic acid (5-HIAA), and homovanillic acid (HVA) in the cerebrospinal fluid
- Access to a lethal weapon such as a gun, a car, or drugs.

We are now at a point where we can tackle the question: Is mental illness a necessary prerequisite for suicidal behavior or can "normal" individuals attempt or even commit suicide?

NORMALITY

There are four major perspectives on normality (Sabshin, 1967): normality as utopia, normality as process, normality as average, and normality as health. Normality as utopia is an ideal state of self-realization which is almost never realized. Normality as process is a longitudinal interpretation of behavior where only the successful unfolding of developmental tasks can adequately prove normality. Normality as average is a statistical perspective according to which the most common behaviors are considered normal for that group. Normality as health refers to a reasonable rather than an optimal state, and is defined by the absence of pathology, pain, or limitation of action.

Parents are concerned primarily with the last two definitions: Is my child like everyone else and is he free from pain? Kids are concerned with normality as average, especially when they want something their parents may not approve of. They invoke this definition when they say: "But Mom, all the kids are drinking; I don't want to be different." Or, "Everyone is having sex." Parents may not consider these "normal," but, they may, in fact, be average for this age group.

What is normal and average, however, may not be normal and healthy. Cavities, for instance, are average—more people have them than not—but on one would tell you that having holes in your teeth is a sign of health. Contemplating suicide is so common among teenagers that studies that span the past two decades show that teenagers who do not think about suicide are the ones who deviate from the norm

(Cantor, 1976; McCormack, 1987); but no one would tell you that contemplating suicide is a sign of health.

For clinicians, the most valuable definition of normal is that of health. Normality as utopia implies that just about everyone is disturbed and this is as clinically useless as implying that no one is disturbed. Normality as process is of concern to us, but it means that we have to wait a lifetime for the verdict. Relying on normality as average means we would not concern ourselves with adolescents who drink, as long as most of their peers drink as well, and we would not treat heroin addicts as long as they live in a community of addicts.

Yet judgments of normality cannot be free from the context in which they occur. One example is ritual suicide, a behavior that has a different meaning for the Japanese in Japan than it does for Japanese in the United States. Using the definition of normal as health, however, we can include the capacity for social interaction and harmony within an immediate society at the same time we assume the individual is free from pain, discomfort, and disability.

I see a lot of teenagers in my practice. Many are average and some are even healthy. Many of them function at a high level but have met very few of life's problems, and when they hit a snag, they do not know how to cope. It would be an error to ask: To what diagnostic category does their pathology belong? Rather, I must ask: Why is this young person suicidal at this time? How can I work to keep this person alive? How can I help this youngster to face his problems and take control of his own life? How can I teach him to be more resilient? How can I help him to believe that he has value? These are questions of coping skills and self-esteem, not questions of pathology.

To stretch this point, it is possible that attempting suicide could be considered adaptive under the "right" circumstances. Consider the youngster who comes from a family where the adults are so wrapped up in their own affairs that they do not have the time to notice their child's distress. The adolescent decides to call attention to his problems in a very dramatic fashion. He does not intend to die, he only wants people to notice that he needs help. His suicide attempt might get that help; it might be an instructive way of rallying his family. It would be my job as a clinician to teach this youngster other, more constructive, less risky ways of getting the attention he wants, but I would not necessarily claim that this young man was self-destructive.

Consider another youngster who is in love and his girlfriend tells him she wants to break it off. He goes to a bar and drowns his sorrows in too many beers. As he is driving home, he is apprehended by the police for "driving under the influence" and taken to a holding cell to sober up. It is hours before his father can be reached. The boy has been intimidated and left alone. When his father receives the phone call he screams at his son in bitter disappointment. The boy is afraid of facing his father's rage. Rather than deal with the anticipated consequences, he tries to hang himself with his belt. Is this young man pathologically disturbed, or a "normal" kid with less resiliency than we would like and a victim of circumstances at a vulnerable moment in time?

Perhaps, then, for many individuals who commit suicide, we need to consider psychopathology or biochemical deficiencies. However, many are individuals with reduced coping skills, who are without psychopathology but temporarily are without the will to live. They have passed their threshold of tolerance.

Suicidal behavior may fit the same paradigm as alcohol behavior. Thinking about suicide, like thinking about alcohol, may be both average and healthy. Attempting suicide, like drinking socially, could be average and could, under certain circumstances, be considered adaptive—if one attempts suicide to correct a situation one perceives as nearly impossible. This would be like drinking for health purposes. Attempting suicide or committing suicide with the intent of killing oneself, like abusing alcohol with the intent of never sobering up, would not be considered either statistically average or a sign of health.

Perhaps a better analogy would be to that of sex. Thinking about sex is normal—both average and healthy. Having sex is normal—both average and healthy. Doing nothing but thinking about sexual activity, to the exclusion of all else, is neither average nor good for your health.

If we think of all individuals who talk about, gesture, attempt, or commit suicide as seriously disturbed, we will stigmatize people and make them reluctant to go for help. If those whose job it is to identify individuals at risk only concern themselves with people who show serious pathology, we will miss many individuals whose lives we could save.

Shneidman (1990) made this point strongly when he wrote: To understand suicide I would eschew the dreary demographic facts of age, sex and race, and I would ignore the obfuscating psychiatric categories of schizophrenia, depression and borderline states—and assume that 100 percent of individuals who committed suicide, were, in one way or another, significantly perturbed, not psychiatrically disturbed.

Debate on this question continues. Some professionals think that in order to be suicidal one must be psychiatrically disturbed. Others think that, given the "right" set of circumstances, almost anyone could be suicidal.

Without definitive answers to this and other questions, the prevention of suicide becomes an extremely elusive goal, but one that we continue to try to reach. Whom should we be targeting for prevention and how should we be trying to reach them?

PREVENTION

Suicide prevention can be approached on two different levels: the social and the traditional. The social approach encompasses public education and environmental risk reduction. The traditional view encompasses the different forms of clinical treatment. If suicide is the result of both social and psychological problems, for effective prevention, a combined approach would be best.

In the past 20 years, the focus of national suicide prevention programs has been on youth because the suicide rate for this age group has risen dramatically and continues to remain high. Every decade we expect 50,000 of our young people to commit suicide and in the same time period, we estimate about 5 million young people will attempt suicide (Cantor, 1987c).

We have managed to decrease the mortality statistics for every age group in the United States, with the exception of young people, who now have a higher death rate than they did 20 years ago. This is primarily due to increases in suicide and homicide, the two types of death that are more heavily influenced by social factors than any other. The discussion of the broader aspects of prevention that follows focuses on youth suicide.

Youth Suicide

Thus far, in suicide prevention, the social approach has meant education. To make the point that education is a form of prevention, let me give you an example.

Ben was a high school student in Massachusetts. He came into school one morning and went directly to the nurse's office, where he called a crisis intervention center. He spoke for half an hour, hung up the phone, and walked to his classroom, gathering students along the way. "Come see me," he said. "Come see the most sensational act of the century. You don't want to miss this!" He walked into his classroom, opened his desk, pulled out a gun, and shot himself. After a few agonizing days in intensive care, Ben died, leaving a trail of devastation in his wake.

If anyone had been familiar with the risk factors, if anyone had known what to look for, it would have been noticed that Ben was in trouble. He had missed a lot of school, had bruises on his neck—probably from previous attempts at hanging himself—and gave away his favorite records saying he would not need them anymore. He had been writing about suicide, and he had been calling a crisis line. He had a gun. If anyone had knowledge about the warning signs or about how to intervene, Ben might be alive today (Cantor, 1987a).

Educational intervention is difficult to evaluate because of an absence of data. Over a period of years, however, it is estimated that public education could reduce the suicide rate among our young people by 20 percent (Cantor, 1987b).

The second aspect of the broad treatment approach to prevention is limitation of the availability of lethal agents, particularly guns. Guns account for more suicides than all other methods combined: 65 percent of all teen suicides are committed with firearms. Some 25 million households have handguns and one-half keep their handguns loaded. Many more keep rifles. Suicidal individuals are impulsive and having a loaded gun in the house is an invitation to disaster.

I recognize that eliminating guns would not resolve the underlying problems that drive people to suicide, but it would result in fewer deaths. Consider the analogy of mandatory seatbelts: Seatbelts do not make people better drivers, but seatbelts improve the chances of surviving a collision. Removing guns will not make people more content with their lives, or healthier individuals, but the absence of lethal weapons gives them a chance to survive and work on their problems.

Studies estimate that 70 percent of gun victims could not have obtained them if there had been handgun regulations. Fifty percent of these individuals might have used another method. Thus, the reduction in firearm accessibility could save the lives of approximately 20 percent of our youngsters (Cantor, 1987c).

When highly lethal methods of suicide are less available, there is evidence to show that individuals do not necessarily switch to other means. When the English converted their home heating gas from deadly coke gas to low lethality natural gas, their suicide rate dropped 33 percent. This rate remained constant despite the bleak economic picture in England, which would ordinarily have been expected to lead to an increase in suicide.

Poisoning, usually with prescription medicine, is the second most common method of suicide, accounting for 11.3 percent of all suicides. The availability of lethal drugs could be limited by restricting the number of tablets permitted with each prescription. This kind of legislative restriction on sedative and hypnotic drugs is thought to be largely responsible for the decline in the suicide rate in Australia in the 1960s and 1970s. In addition, tricyclic antidepressants could be sold with an emetic or antidote. If an individual overdosed and then had a change of mind or was found, an antidote could be given and a life could be saved. The projection is that this could save approximately 3 percent of teen suicides a year (Cantor, 1989a).

Thus, the prevention strategies that would appear to have the greatest impact on youth suicide are the limitation of the availability of firearms and medications, together with education programs in positive mental health.

DIAGNOSIS AND TREATMENT

The clinician's responsibility, in the more traditional approach to treating suicidal individuals, is to make an appropriate diagnosis and plan beneficial treatment.

The important point to remember in diagnosis is that if suicidal behavior is a symptom and not a disease entity it can appear in almost any diagnostic category and we would do better to approach suicidal individuals with a therapeutic model that looks for where they are well rather than where they are "sick."

Treatment is the final step in helping a person cope with the conflicts that generate a suicidal crisis. The most appropriate choices for treatment of suicidal individuals seem to be supportive psychotherapy, followed by insight-oriented psychotherapy or family therapy.

Supportive psychotherapy will reinforce the person's defenses and help control disturbing thoughts and feelings. Unlike psychoanalytic therapy, it focuses on present difficulties and avoids probing the past or the unconscious. It is most effectively used with a patient who is experiencing anxiety, stress, or turmoil (as in most suicidal states), or when an individual with psychotic potential becomes overtly psychotic or goes into acute decomposition with psychotic overtones.

In diagnostic terms, the therapist can use supportive psychotherapy most effectively with psychotic and borderline patients and as an initial approach with patients who have neurotic difficulties or character disorders. With fragile individuals, a supportive approach may be all that can be accomplished. It may be the best initial approach for those who have less fragile organization but reduced capacity to cope.

The therapist might order medication, to relieve anxiety or decrease depression, or hospitalization, to protect the patient and ease the strain on the patient and the family. Medication or hospitalization can allow the family a chance to regroup their emotional resources.

Once the goals of supportive psychotherapy are achieved, the therapist can move to insight-oriented therapy focusing on the patient's life situation.

Family therapy is used when the patient's difficulties reflect ongoing difficulties with the family or when there is identifiable pathology in other family members. The goal is to help the family become aware of the underlying emotional conflicts and to open up the potential for change. The focus is on the process and not on the individual.

Regardless of the model one chooses—cognitive therapy, behavior therapy, psychoanalytic psychotherapy, family therapy, or any other method of therapy—the way in which treatment is conducted is a more important factor than the treatment model.

The key in working with suicidal individuals is to be warm and responsive without being too familiar or effusive. It is rarely (if ever) beneficial to remain aloof because suicidal individuals, already sensitive to rejection, will interpret analytic anonymity as rejection and feel alienated from the therapist.

Patients want to see their therapists as a powerful source of wisdom. Many suicidal individuals want to see their therapists as more than powerful, they want to see them as omnipotent. A therapist must tell the patient that as much as the therapist may want to be there when needed, no therapist can be available 24 hours every day and night.

Individuals who are suicidal very often are self-centered (even though they may feel they have no self and no center). They expect their therapist to be waiting by the phone and do not understand if their therapist is not there at precisely the moment they need intervention. There is often a fragile balance between life and death, a balance as fragile as a response on the other end of the phone. The therapist must make his or her human limitations known.

Another issue in working with suicidal patients is that of fatigue and burnout for the therapist. Freud said that a doctor who sees 10 patients a day is exposing a concealed attempt at suicide. Imagine what Freud would have said about the therapist who sees 10 suicidal patients a day—perhaps that the attempt is no longer concealed.

SUMMARY

It is now many years after Freud, more than 50 years since the publication in 1938 of Karl Menninger's landmark book on suicide, *Man Against Himself,* and nearly the end of the 20th century. Are we any closer to resolving the questions of self-destruction and suicide?

We have taken some steps forward: We now recognize the fact that children and adolescents can and do commit suicide, we have greatly improved methods of data collection, we have increased national awareness of the loss of life by suicide, we have implemented programs of public education and programs of community response to crisis, and we have furthered our understanding of the biological origins of depression, schizophrenia, manic-depressive psychosis, and violent behaviors.

In many ways, however, we seem to have taken steps backward. We are destroying ourselves and each other at ever increasing rates and in ever increasing numbers by homicide and suicide, with guns, automobiles, drugs, and toxic pollution, and we are threatened by total global destruction with nuclear weapons of our own making.

In the past half-century since Menninger wrote *Man Against Himself,* we have continued to look to medical science, psychology, sociology, anthropology, biochemistry, epidemiology, psychiatry, and religion for the answers to our questions on the etiology, the symptoms, the prevention, and the treatment of suicide. Yet, 50 years after Menninger, 20 years after Johns Hopkins, and almost into the 21st century, the answers of individual and global self-destruction still elude us.

REFERENCES

Asberg, M., Bertilsson, L., Rydin, E., Schalling, D., Thoren, P., & Träskman-Benz, L. (1981). Monoamine metabolites in cerebrospinal fluid in relation to depressive illness, suicidal behavior and personality. In B. Angrist, G. Burrows, M. Lader, O. Ling jaerde, G. Sedvall, & D. Wheatley (Eds.), *Recent advances in neuropsycho-pharmacology* (pp. 257–271). Oxford and New York: Pergamon Press.

Cantor, P. C. (1972). *Personality and status characteristics of the female youthful suicide attempter* (Doctoral dissertation, Columbia University).

Cantor, P. (1976). Personality characteristics found among youthful female suicide attempters. *Journal of Abnormal Psychology, 85,* 324–329.

Cantor, P. C. (1987a). *Young People in Crisis: How You Can Help* [Film and teaching manual]. National Committee on Youth Suicide Prevention, American Association of Suicidology and Harvard Medical School. Available from National Committee on Youth Suicide Prevention, 22 Florida Avenue, Staten Island, NY 10305.

Cantor, P. (1987b). Recommendations for epidemiological interventions. *Report of the Presidential Task Force on Youth Suicide.* Washington, DC: National Institute of Mental Health, Department of Health and Human Services, Center for Disease Control.

Cantor, P. (1987c). *National strategies to reduce teen suicide.* Testimony before Senate Subcommittee on Juvenile Justice, U.S. Senate Committee on the Judiciary, Washington, DC.

Cantor, P. (1989a). Intervention strategies: Environmental risk reduction for youth suicide. *Report of the Secretary's Task Force on Youth Suicide, 5,* 285–294. U.S. Dept. of Health and Human Services, Public Health Services.

Cantor, P. (1989b, October). *Suicide update.* Video broadcast for Medi Vision, Washington, DC.

Farberow, N. L. (1989). Preparatory and prior suicidal behavior factors. *Report of the Secretary's Task Force on Youth Suicide, 2,* 34–55.

Fava, M., Copeland, P. M., Schweiger, U., & Herzog, D. (1989). Neurochemical abnormalities of anorexia nervosa and bulimia nervosa. *American Journal of Psychiatry, 156,* 963–971.

Kupfer, D. J. (1989). Summary of the National Conference on Risk Factors for Youth Suicide. *Report of the Secretary's Task Force on Youth Suicide, 2,* 9–16.

McCormack, P. (1987, September 12). *One out of three top students considered suicide.* UPI Press Release.

Menninger, K. (1938). *Man against himself.* New York: Harcourt.

Sabshin, M. (1967). Psychiatric perspectives on normality. *Archives of General Psychiatry, 17,* 258–264.

Shaffer, D. (1989, October). *Suicide update.* Video broadcast for Medi Vision, Washington, DC.

Shneidman, E. S. (1990). In E. C. Walker (Ed.) *A history of clinical psychology in autobiography.* New York: Brooks Cole.

Weissman, M. M., Klerman, G. L., Markowitz, J. S., & Ouellette, R. (1989). Suicidal ideation and suicide attempts in panic disorder and attacks. *New England Journal of Medicine, 321,* 1209–1214.

CHAPTER 10

Levels of Depression

JEROLD R. GOLD, PhD

Discussions of depression inevitably seem to convey concerns about the quantity and the topography of that disorder. Patients and clinicians are alike in their questions and descriptions, which include information about the "depth," the "extent," and the "severity" of the disorder. A cross-sectional study, formal or informal, of a group of depressed persons will quickly yield opinions about which patients are "more" or "less" depressed, and about "how much" those levels of depression are influencing the functioning of those individuals. Depressed persons tend to describe their past, present, and even future experiences in quantitative terms ("I'm less depressed than I was a month ago"), and topographic metaphors abound in their self-descriptions ("I've reached the depths," "I hit bottom," "I am down in the dumps").

This chapter attempts to provide an overview of the quantity and topography of depressive phenomenology. The most typical and widely referred-to levels or types of depression will be described, as will the most salient and current conceptual and empirical concerns in the areas of nosology and diagnosis. Issues of development, etiology, course, and prognosis will be referred to but will receive only passing mention because these topics are discussed more fully and adequately elsewhere in this volume.

ISSUES IN THE CLASSIFICATION OF LEVELS OF DEPRESSION

Depressive symptoms differ in intensity, severity, scope, and configuration from person to person. However, any account of the history of attempts to name and to classify depressive syndromes will mention the extensive debate between those who believe that depression is a single or unitary disorder, and those who accept the notion that there are two or more distinct, discrete syndromes which share certain signs and symptoms. This debate has been labeled the unitary/dualist debate (Beck, 1967), the monist/dualist controversy (Nemiah, 1975), and the one-factor/two-factor controversy (Levitt, Lubin, & Brooks, 1983), and it probably has other names in the literature as well.

The unitary or single-disorder position usually is linked to the work of Aubrey Lewis in England in the 1930s (Beck, 1967). Lewis is described as introducing the *spectrum* conception to the study of depression, which holds that the different presentations of depression, in terms of scope and severity, are merely varying surface manifestations of a continuous, single, underlying disorder. The binary or two-disorder position can be traced to the work of Kraepelin (1921), who identified two distinct and separate types of depression, which he named manic-depressive illness, and psychogenic depression.

Since Kraepelin's time, a plethora of dichotomies have been applied to describe and to name the specific levels or subtypes of depression. Beck (1967) listed four major dualities which have been used in the context of binary theory: agitated vs. retarded depression, endogenous vs. exogenous depression, reactive vs. autonomous depression, and neurotic vs. psychotic depression. Levitt et al., (1983) added to this list the terms manic-depressive psychosis vs. psychogenic depression, vital vs. personal depression, and physiological vs. psychological depression. Rush (1986) extended this list further with the dimensions of psychotic vs. nonpsychotic depression, primary vs. secondary depression, anergic-hypoactive vs. anxious-agitated, and the triad of familial pure depression vs. depressive spectrum disorder vs. sporadic depression. This surely is not an exhaustive list of available names and dichotomies.

The official *Diagnostic and Statistical Manuals* (DSM) of the American Psychiatric Association (1952, 1968, 1980, 1987) introduced their own terminology into the general framework of the binary, two-disorder theory. The particular diagnostic labels used in these manuals will be discussed in detail in the next section of this chapter.

A substantial research literature has developed out of the unitary–binary controversy, in an attempt to determine the "true" nature of depression. A complete answer to this question, if in fact it does exist, has eluded students of depression to this date, although some authors insist that partial solutions have been found. These research efforts have been handicapped by the lack of consensual, validated, and reliable operational definitions of depression and of the various hypothesized subtypes which are the foci of the studies (Zung, 1977). These research efforts have been hindered also by diagnostic biases across settings and examiners, and by instruments and interviews of questionable validity and reliability (Levitt et al., 1983).

Beck (1967) concluded a review of the research that was available in the mid-1960s by stating that these studies had failed to establish clear, qualitative differences between Type 1 depressions (endogenous, autonomous, psychotic) and Type 2 depressions (neurotic, reactive, exogenous), but that quantitative differences between these subtypes were robust and reliable, which Beck believed lent some credence to two-factor theory. Mendels and Cochrane (1968) focused on a group of factor-analytic studies of depressive symptomatology and found that these studies consistently yielded two orthogonal factors. These factors were judged to be consistent with the clinical stereotypes of reactive and endogenous depression, with the major differentiation being the loading of the latter on somatic symptoms. However, these studies have been critiqued and to some (Kendell, 1977), discredited, because of methodological and conceptual flaws inherent in the factor-analytic procedure.

An extensive cross-cultural study of the presentation and phenomenology of depression was conducted by the World Health Organization in the early 1980s (1983). This study included 1,209 patients drawn from psychiatric centers in Teheran, Iran; Basel, Switzerland; Montreal, Canada; Tokyo, Japan; and Nagasaki, Japan. The subjects were assessed via a series of interviews and with specially constructed questionnaires, and the data were analyzed though a variety of factor-analytic and multivariate statistical procedures. The WHO researchers identified three distinct levels or types of depression which differed reliably with respect to history, symptoms, and severity. These types were named *Endogenous Depression,* which accounted for 57 percent of the sample; *Psychogenic Depression,* applicable to 37 percent of patients; and *Other Depression* (the remaining 6 percent). Psychogenic Depressions were more frequent than Endogenous Depressions in the Montreal center, while in all of the other sites the proportions of the two disorders were reflective of the numbers reported above. A core group of symptoms most typical of depression was noted; it included affects of sadness, joylessness, anxiety, tension, and guilt; cognitive symptoms of ideas of worthlessness, inadequacy, and failure, loss of the ability to attend and to concentrate, and self-criticism; and motivational symptoms of a loss of energy and of interest in others. Endogenous Depressions were distinguished by a reliable constellation of additional symptoms which included early morning awakening, diurnal mood variation, retardation in cognitive functioning, psychomotor retardation, and suicidal ideation. Psychogenic Depression was correlated with a higher frequency of symptoms of aggression and irritability, and the absence of the endogenous constellation. A multivariate factor analysis yielded three orthogonal factors which discriminated between the two levels. Endogenous Depression was found to load significantly on a factor labeled Anergia/Retardation, while Psychogenic Depression loaded significantly on the factors of Premorbid Abnormal Personality and on Dejected Mood. An item analysis of the various questionnaires used in the study found that the presence of ongoing psychological stress and of a history of psychopathology in childhood or adolescence was typical of Psychogenic Depression, while items associated with Endogenous Depression referred to psychomotor retardation, early morning awakening, and repeated past depressive episodes. The WHO group concluded that these results were supportive of the traditional division of depression into reactive and endogenous types.

Rush (1986) reviewed and discussed the various dichotomies that have been used to differentiate depressive subtypes, and found that more questions than answers still remain. He noted—to look at one traditional duality—that we do not possess sufficient evidence to conclude that psychotic depressions differ in kind from nonpsychotic depressions, and that endogenous and reactive depression cannot be separated on the basis of an identifiable precipitant. Rush also noted that the premorbid personalities of patients with reactive and psychotic depressions have not been demonstrated to differ significantly. He indicated that the endogenous vs. reactive dichotomy does have some validity in differentiating patients on a variety of neuroendocrine, REM (rapid eye movement), and sleep variables, and in studies of clinical and blood plasma responses to antidepressant medication.

Cohen and Winokur (1988) wrote that the research which had attempted to disprove or to demonstrate the existence of distinct types of depression was flawed by a lack of operational definitions, poor instrumental reliability, and investigator biases. They concluded that empirical support for the separation of Type 1 depressions (psychotic, endogenous, autonomous) and Type 2 depressions (reactive, neurotic, psychogenic) is minimal at best. However, they reported that recent work utilizing the Research Diagnostic Criteria (Spitzer & Endicott, 1978) and the Washington University Feighner criteria (Feighner, Robins, & Guze, 1972) has yielded four reliable subtypes of depression: endogenous depression, situational depression, psychotic depression, and incapacitating depression. However, they noted that most patients display symptoms typical of two or more of these categories.

This limited review of the literature cannot offer an exhaustive presentation of specific studies. However, the authors cited will highlight for the reader the general state of affairs in past and current efforts at establishing and validating a nosology of levels or subtypes of depression. The literature offers some support for the idea that different types of depression do "exist," but this support is limited and many findings are contradictory and simply add to the debate.

As a result of this lack of an empirically validated and consensual system with which to identify specific levels of depression, the rest of this chapter will be organized around the traditional, clinically derived categories familiar to students of depression. Those levels of depression generally labeled as neurotic, psychotic, chronic, masked, and secondary depressions will be examined in terms of diagnostic criteria, symptoms, and phenomenology. Where relevant and available, current empirical data about each level will be mentioned as well.

LEVELS OF DEPRESSION

Neurotic Depression

Also known as reactive depression, mild depression, depressive neurosis, and psychogenic depression, this level of depressive psychopathology was first identified and classified as a unique disorder by Kraepelin (1921), who coined the label psychogenic depression. Kraepelin excluded a particular form of depression from the group of depressive illnesses he had studied extensively (manic-depressive disorder, involutional melancholia, and neurasthenic depression) on the basis of a presumed difference in etiology. The dysphoria, hopelessness, and associated behavioral symptoms of psychogenic depression were judged by Kraepelin to be reactions and responses to stressful, disappointing, or thwarting life experiences and/or environmental situations. Further, he observed that the course of psychogenic depression primarily was affected and channeled by subsequent experience and interaction with the interpersonal world, and that the depressive person's mood would and could vary considerably, even during the most acute, severe parts of the depressive episode, when the patient's attention was directed away from his or her disappointment or loss toward a more neutral or positive subject. The three types of depressive illnesses from which psychogenic depression was differentiated by Kraepelin shared, in his view, a biological etiology and were refractory to environmental influence and treatment.

Beck (1967) noted that until about 1950 the syndrome of reactive, exogenous, or psychogenic depression was not linked specifically to the concept of neurosis. Instead, reactive or exogenous depressions were judged by many clinicians to occur in otherwise healthy individuals whose premorbid personality structure was unremarkable for the presence of neurotic psychopathology. These depressions were construed therefore as isolated but exaggerated responses to loss or disappointment, while the separate syndrome of neurotic depression was called upon to describe a psychogenic depression in an individual with a known or hypothesized history of neurotic maladjustment or disturbance. Since reactive depressions and neurotic depressions were highly similar, if not identical in symptomatology and course and in appearing to have a psychological origin with an environmental precipitant, the two concepts gradually became fused into one with a variety of interchangeable names. Also influencing the fusion of these categories into one syndrome (Beck, 1967) was the then dominant psychodynamic perspective on psychopathology, in which all nonpsychotic disorders are conceptualized as arising out of neurotic anxiety and conflict.

The first edition of the *Diagnostic and Statistical Manual* (DSM) of the American Psychiatric Association (1952) labeled this category of depression the Psychoneurotic Depressive Reaction, and described it as a reaction that has as a precipitant or stimulus some current situation in the patient's life. Most frequently this situation is a loss and is correlated with feelings of guilty responsibility and with self-deprecation and self-hatred for past actions and failures. This diagnostic category was designated as equivalent to "reactive depression" and was differentiated from psychotic depressive reactions on the criteria of life history and absence of malignant symptoms. A depressed individual whose depression could be traced to a specific precipitant or precipitants, whose premorbid character structure was neurotic, who had a history free of reports of mood swings, and whose depression was *not* accompanied by such severe symptoms as suicidal rumination, delusions, hallucinations, severe psychomotor retardation, profound retardation of thought, stupor, intractable insomnia, or hypochondrial preoccupation, would be diagnosed as suffering from psychoneurotic depressive reaction. Patients whose clinical presentations included these symptoms, and whose history indicated repeated mood swings and a cyclothymic personality structure, would be diagnosed as suffering from the more severe type of depression, Psychotic Depressive Reaction.

DSM-II (1968) relabeled the disorder *Depressive Neurosis,* and described it as a "disorder . . . manifested by an excessive reaction of depression due to an internal conflict or to an identifiable event such as the loss of a love object or cherished possession" (p. 49). This description extends the range of possible precipitants to those occurring intrapsychically, but retains the essential point of view of DSM-I. Interestingly, both editions of DSM skimped significantly on descriptions of the signs and symptoms of this (and other) disorders, a condition which the latest revisions have been designed to rectify (see below).

DSM-III and its later revision (American Psychiatric Association, 1980, 1987) do not contain a diagnostic label which is strictly equivalent or applicable to the level of neurotic or reactive depression. The diagnosis of Adjustment Disorder with Depressed Mood may be somewhat relevant. This label refers to a a maladaptive response to a known psychosocial precipitant, which leads to either social and/or occupational impairment or excessive symptoms such as depressed mood, tearfulness, and hopelessness. Another diagnostic category mentioned by some authors as roughly equivalent to neurotic/reactive depression is Dysthymic Disorder. This diagnosis is made when the depressive periods present are marked by depressed mood or anhedonia, and by at least three of 13 common depressive symptoms (see "Chronic

Depression" below). The absence of psychotic features also is required to establish this diagnosis. However, a fourth criterion is the requirement that the depressive symptoms have been present for at least two years, which would differentiate this disorder from depressions which in the past would have been labeled neurotic or reactive.

Most clinical descriptions of the presentation of neurotic/reactive depression overlap considerably, if not completely. A few authorities on this subject will be cited here to provide a general picture of the phenomenology of this level of depression.

Nemiah (1975) reported that neurotic/reactive depression almost invariably is a response to some life situation or intrapsychic event, the meaning of which is to lower or damage the person's sense of self-worth or self-esteem. In those individuals whose self-esteem is relatively consistent or robust, a major, shattering event may be necessary to produce the requisite negative changes in self-evaluation. Persons with fragile self-esteem may lapse into depression following an experience or occurrence which seemingly is trivial in "objective" terms, but which has significant narcissistic meaning to the individual. The most frequent precipitants of neurotic/reactive depressions are separations from or losses of loved ones due to rejection, physical leave-taking, or death. However, any event, whether objective or purely "fantastic" (intrapsychic), can trigger a depression if the person construes the situation in such a way that his or her self-esteem is threatened or lowered.

Other writers (Fenichel, 1945; Kolb, 1973) also stressed the role of a precipitant in this level of depression but emphasized the role of anxiety rather than self-esteem as the critical intrapsychic issue. In this view, a loss, separation, or disappointment produces in the patient an unconscious wish and/or affect which is responded to with guilt, shame, sadness, and anxiety. The depressive symptoms thus are thought to be defenses or compromise formations which serve to mask and to unconsciously express the person's conflicting wishes toward the lost person or object.

Central to the symptoms of neurotic/reactive depression are such affective phenomena as loneliness, sadness, and despair (Nemiah, 1975); issues of self-esteem such as self-criticism, self-deprecation, and self-hatred (Freud, 1917/1950); motivational and behavioral symptoms including helplessness, impotence, and resignation (Bibring, 1953; Seligman, 1975); and cognitive sets of pessimism, hopelessness, and poor self-evaluation (Beck, 1967). These psychological symptoms are usually accompanied by physical symptoms (Beck, 1967; Nemiah, 1975). Each area just mentioned will be described in greater detail below.

Although many cognitive theorists now dispute the etiological importance of affect in depression, phenomenologically and experientially, it is these symptoms that typically dominate the neurotic/reactive depressive's daily life, and which become a primary, if not the first, target for intervention by the clinician. Neurotic/reactive depression is typified by the emotions of sadness, despair, loneliness, and melancholy. Often, these feelings are accompanied by a significant level of anger, irritation, and contempt directed toward others and toward the world in general—affects that are usually secondary responses to the dysphoria and sense of isolation (Nemiah, 1975). The neurotic/reactive depressive often describes his or her inner world as being "gray," "dead," or "empty," usually a symbolization of the affective states of emotional withdrawal, and experiences a loss of interest in and of ability to maintain affective ties to others (Freud, 1917/1950). His or her sadness, pain, and despair often are tinged with a sense of the self and the world having been altered or damaged so that something of significance is missing from life, and there often is a correlated sense of guilt and/or shame for being the locus or the cause of this emptiness and damage. These emotions can intensify greatly in a neurotic/reactive depression and may persist for long periods of time, but the presence and severity of dysphoria are dependent upon and modifiable by both environmental and intrapsychic variables. As a result, considerable shifts in the type and intensity of affect experienced in a neurotic/reactive depression often are observed. Similarly, most patients with this type of depression retain some capacity to observe and to reflect upon their emotional suffering, and find these affects to be ego dystonic (Arieti & Bemporad, 1978) or ego alien, in that the patient recognizes and is able to acknowledge that his or her emotions are not justified entirely or are inappropriate to the objective circumstances of the present situation.

Freud (1917/1950) was among the first to describe poor self-esteem as a sphere of depressive phenomenology, and his work was followed and amplified by such writers as Bibring (1953), Beck (1967), and Arieti and Bemporad (1978), to name only a select few. These writers all emphasized the neurotic/reactive depressive's extreme tendency toward self-criticism, self-loathing, and self-hatred. The patient relies upon excessively harsh, rigid, demanding, and unrealistic standards and expectations to evaluate his or her thoughts, emotions, and behavior. Each experience is inspected and poked into for signs of failure or inadequacy, and any shortcomings, errors, incomplete acts, awkwardness, or related "sins" are responded to by the patient with violently hateful and attacking judgments. Often, a particular dimension of life and experience becomes the central issue upon which the self is evaluated, and the dimensions selected will differ across patients. Attractiveness, intelligence, productivity, morality, social popularity, and success are among the issues that may be singled out or may occur in particular combinations as evaluative criteria; the negative evaluations and attacks on the self lead to a variety of negative views of the self and to a myriad of dysphoric affects, including guilt, shame, sadness, and despair (Beck, 1967). Often the neurotic/reactive depressive is able to evaluate the behavior of other people in a much more accepting and realistic way, and sometimes finds his or her severe and relentless deprecation to be alien, bizarre, and unjustified, but feels powerless to change or ameliorate these attitudes. The ability to comfort, forgive, and appreciate the self often is flawed or extremely fragile in this disorder. Self-love typically is highly conditional and based upon excessive, perfectionistic standards.

Motivational changes are a major characteristic of this level of depression. The neurotically depressed person sees no way out of his or her pain, and despite wishing for help, often becomes apathetic, lethargic, and passive. The patient often is reluctant to do things he or she knows will be ameliorative, and withdraws from social interaction, sexual and familial relationships, hobbies, sports, and domestic, occupational, or academic responsibilities. Often, grooming and appearance suffer as well. A general and pervasive sense of joylessness and anhedonia may loom large in the person's consciousness, though these and other motivational symptoms are not absolute and sometimes will respond to efforts from others. These symptoms may be reflective of what Seligman (1975) termed "learned helplessness," which is a conviction that one's behavior has been, is, and will be ineffective with regard to obtaining life's gratifications and satisfactions. Such an outlook understandably leads to a sense of impotence and futility and to a reluctance or unwillingness to act.

Cognitive therapists, largely following Beck (1967), identify ideational symptoms as the primary causal factors in neurotic/reactive depression. Regardless of the validity of these hypotheses, the "depressive triad" identified by Beck (1967) figures largely in the phenomenology of most, if not all, neurotic depressions. This triad includes negative evaluations of the self (discussed in more detail above), negative evaluations of the environment, and a negative outlook for the future. Essentially, the patient castigates and finds fault within himself or herself; construes the world as depriving, frustrating, hostile, cold, empty, frightening, overwhelming, or unmanageable; and can see or admit to no chance for improvement or change in the future. Again, many neurotic/reactive depressives are more realistic in their evaluations of the lives and prospects of others, and experience their depressive cognitions as ego dystonic and unrealistic, but unavoidable and dominant in their psychologies.

Patients with neurotic/reactive depressions usually are thought (Nemiah, 1975) to be free of the more severe somatic and biological symptoms which are typical of more severe depressions (see the next section, "Psychotic Depressions"). However, such symptoms as lethargy and a loss of physical energy are common, as are uncomfortable but mild to moderate changes in sleep patterns, appetite, and weight. Patients may complain of vague somatic distress, pain, or tension, and will present with unhappy, glum, and "weighted-down" appearance (Kolb, 1973).

The empirical status of neurotic/reactive depression is unclear. Certain studies, such as the WHO (1983) study cited earlier in this chapter, lent support for the existence of this level of depression as a separate disorder, typified by a history of neurosis or character pathology, an identifiable precipitant or precipitants, and symptoms primarily of a cognitive, affective, and motivational nature, which are less severe than in other types of depression. Cohen and Winokur (1988) cited recent studies of unipolar depressive disorders which have yielded a reliable, discrete subtype of depression that they labeled "depressive spectrum" disease:

> Neurotic-reactive depression could be defined as a depression in a person with an unstable personality who has a tendency to react with depression, anxiety, and hostility when confronted with difficult life circumstances. These cases are associated with a family history of alcoholism in a number of studies. In a sense this closed the circle. The "Type 2," or neurotic-reactive depression of characterological depression, or depression spectrum disease patient, is one who has a stormy life-style, attributes his/her illness to a life event, has lifelong personality problems and is more likely to have a family history of alcoholism. The criteria for a neurotic-reactive depression are equally as good as the criteria for an "endogenous" depression. In fact, they may be better in light of the fact that they utilize lifelong characteristics rather than evanescent symptoms.
>
> *(p. 91)*
>
> • • •
>
> In any event, it seems clear now that diagnostic criteria such as the Feighner criteria or the RDC or the DSM-III criteria in fact do define a syndrome but they do not define diseases. There do seem to be at least two separate valid entities within the unipolar depressive group, i.e., neurotic-reactive depression (depression spectrum disease) and endogenous depression (familial pure depressive disease).
>
> *(p. 92)*

However, other authors believe that the separation of this level of depression is artifactual and is based primarily on the failure to study patients with neurotic/reactive depressions longitudinally and with procedures of sufficient validity and reliability. Fulwiler and Pope (1987), in a review of the literature, concluded that a neurotic/reactive type of depression could not be differentiated from endogenous depressions. Rush (1986) reported that a series of studies indicated that almost all depressions can be linked to an identifiable precipitant, thus canceling one of the most frequently cited discriminators between neurotic/ reactive and endogenous depressions. Akiskal et al. (1979) reported that follow-up of patients with neurotic/reactive depressions indicated that at least 50 percent of these patients develop deeper, more serious depression which meets the criteria for endogenous depression. Akiskal (1983) also reported that when patients with DSM-II Depressive Neurosis diagnoses are compared to controls with DSM-II Cyclothymic Personality Disorder (the diagnosis used for patients with chronic or characterological depressions), the groups are more similar than they are different, in terms of course, history, and response to treatment.

These and other differences in findings and opinions leave us to conclude that the jury is still out with regard to the empirical status of this level of depression.

Psychotic Depressions

Depressions of this level of intensity, scope, and severity have been labeled and described variously as the depressive phase of manic-depressive illness, psychotic depressions, severe depressions, endogenous depression, and involutional melancholias. Kraepelin (1921), in his pioneering work, identified the more severe, presumably endogenously derived affective illnesses to be a single disorder with three subtypes. The overall class of pathology he identified as Manic-Depressive Illness, and he included in this class the disorder itself as well as the variants of Involutional Melancholia and Neurasthenic Depression. Kraepelin's theory became the focus of considerable and intense debate in descriptive psychiatry as various factions argued for or against a unitary grouping of the more severe depressions.

The original edition of the DSM (American Psychiatric Association, 1952) deviated from the unitary position and offered three diagnostic possibilities for severe depressions: Psychotic Manic-Depressive Reaction, Psychotic Depressive Reaction, and Involutional Reaction.

The second edition of the DSM (American Psychiatric Association, 1968) retained the first two of these diagnoses and described them in the following ways. Psychotic Depressive Reaction was differentiated from the other types of severe depression on the basis of a presumptive psychogenic etiology. The criteria included a depressive mood attributable to an identifiable experience. The patient's history contained no evidence of repeated depressions or of mood swings, which, if present would have pointed to the diagnosis of manic-depressive illness. Psychotic Depressive Reaction was differentiated diagnostically from Neurotic Depressive Reaction on the basis of whether the depression caused a noticeable impairment in the patient's reality testing or functional adequacy. If such impairments were noted, a psychotic level diagnosis was indicated.

Manic-depressive illness, depressed type, was defined as a disorder comprised of exclusively depressive episodes marked by severely depressed mood, mental and motor retardation, and the possible appearance of illusions, hallucinations, and delusions which were attributable to the mood disorder. This syndrome was understood to be a biological or endogenous disorder, with no clear precipitant in the environment or on an intrapsychic level.

The Involutional Psychotic reaction of DSM-I was renamed Involutional Melancholia in DSM-II (American Psychiatric Association, 1968) and was described as a disorder which had its onset in the involutional period and which had symptoms of worry, agitation, anxiety, and severe depression. Frequent and delusionally proportioned feelings of guilt and preoccupations around somatic issues were features. The disorder differed from manic-depressive illness in the absence of previous occurrences; it differed from psychotic depressive reaction in that there was no identifiable precipitant.

Both manic-depressive illness, depressed type, and involutional melancholia were grouped in DSM-II under the heading of major affective disorders, a group of psychoses which are:

> characterized by a single disorder of mood, either extreme depression or elation, that dominates the mental life of the patient and is responsible for whatever loss of contact he has with his environment. The onset of the mood does not seem to be related directly to a precipitating life experience and therefore is distinguishable from psychotic depressive reaction and depressive neurosis.
>
> *(American Psychiatric Association, 1968, p. 37)*

DSM-III and DSM-III-R (American Psychiatric Association, 1980, 1987) offer two possible diagnostic categories for severe depressions: Bipolar Disorder, and Major Depression. Bipolar Disorder has three subtypes, two of which, the mixed type and the depressed type, are potentially applicable to severe depressions. The essential differentiating feature between Bipolar Disorder and Major Depression is a history of at least a single manic episode. A positive history yields a diagnosis of one of the subtypes of Bipolar Disorder, while a negative history eventuates in the label of Major Depression. There are five criteria that lead to either diagnosis. The first is dysphoric mood. The second is at least seven signs such as changes in appetite leading to weight loss or gain, insomnia, or hypersomnia; psychomotor agitation or retardation; loss of libido and/or loss of interest or pleasure in usual activities; loss of energy and fatigue; feelings of worthlessness, self-reproach, and/or excessive and inappropriate guilt; diminished or impaired cognitive processes, including poor attention and concentration, slowed thinking, and indecisiveness; and recurrent suicidal ideation, wishes to be dead, suicide attempts, and thoughts of death. A third criterion is the absence of preoccupation with mood-incongruent delusions and hallucinations, and absence of bizarre behavior, when an affective syndrome is absent. The fourth criterion is that the affective symptoms are not superimposed on schizophrenia, schizophreniform disorder, or paranoid disorder; and the last criterion is that the symptoms are unrelated to any Organic Mental Disorder or to Uncomplicated Bereavement.

Major depressive episodes in either Bipolar Disorder or in Major Depression can be further classified in DSM-III as occurring with Psychotic Features when symptoms include depressive stupor (the person is mute or unresponsive), hallucinations, delusions, or gross failure of reality testing. A subdiagnosis of Melancholia can be added when there is a loss of pleasure and anhedonia, and three of the following: depressed mood, diurnal mood variation, early morning awakening, psychomotor agitation or retardation, anorexia or weight loss, or excessive or inappropriate guilt.

DSM-III does not contain a separate diagnostic category for Involutional Melancholia. Presumably, persons who would have received this diagnosis in the past will meet the current criteria for Bipolar Disorder or for Major Depression.

Despite these differentiations and etiologic considerations, a consolidation of labels has occurred with these syndromes similar to that discussed in the area of neurotic or reactive depression: many writers use the terms *endogenous depression, severe depression,* or *psychotic depression* interchangeably. With few exceptions, which will be noted below, the depressive episodes in the DSM-III diagnoses of Bipolar Disorder and Major Depression are thought to be equivalent as well, especially since the criteria for depression are shared by these two disorders.

The phenomenologies and symptoms of the three types of severe or psychotic depressions are essentially similar. Beck (1967), Gibson (1975), Arieti and Bemporad (1978), and Cohen and Winokur (1988) pointed out that these syndromes, if they are valid entities, require nonsymptomatic criteria to establish differential diagnoses. As a result, the following description of psychotic level depression will not be specific to any of the hypothesized subtypes.

Arieti and Bemporad (1978) suggested that severe or psychotic level depressions are typified by a classic and historically repetitive triad of psychological symptoms: a generalized and intense melancholic affect; disordered and disturbed cognitive and perceptual processes, in which thinking is slowed, blunted, and blocked, and is marked by idiosyncratic and distorted content; and psychomotor retardation. These authors also noted that psychotic level depressions are typified by the appearance of a variety of severe somatic disturbances and dysfunctions, and that severe or psychotic depressions usually are ego syntonic:

> The patient who is depressed to a psychotic degree has undergone predominantly a severe emotional transformation, but he believes that his way of feeling is appropriate to the circumstances in which he lives. Thus, he does not fight his disorder, as the psychoneurotic does, but lives within it. In many cases he even seems to nourish it. In this respect he resembles persons who are affected by character neuroses and do not even know the pathological nature of their difficulties. . . .

> The severely depressed person may neglect feeding himself to the point of starvation; he may be so inactive as to be unable to take care of even the most elementary needs, he may think he is justified in believing that there is nothing good in life and death is preferable. He also considers any attempt to improve his life to be worthless, and in some cases he feels guilty in the absence of reasons which would make other people feel guilty. . . . He considers his mood consonant with what appears to him the reality of the situation. Thus he seems to have characteristics which would make appropriate the designation "psychotic." Only in a minority of cases do delusions, especially of guilt, and hallucinations occur.

> *(Arieti & Bemporad, 1977, pp. 59–60)*

The melancholic mood in psychotic level depressions sometimes appears to be a gradual exacerbation of a chronic characterological pattern of sadness, withdrawal, and dejection; for other patients, this dysphoria is quite different and distinct from the norm. The onset of the symptomatic mood usually is typified by unexplained and prolonged bouts of tearfulness, despairing dejection, wistfulness and nostalgia for lost happiness and for better times in the past, and extended and severe feelings of grief, loss, and emptiness. In some of these cases (presumably those of the psychotic depressive reaction type), there may exist an initial event which provided the stimulus for these feelings; in others (most likely depression as part of a manic-depressive or involutional melancholic syndrome), a precipitant is absent or cannot be identified. Regardless of presence or absence of a precipitant, the dysphoric emotions remain at a severe and intense pitch for an extended period of time, and the person's mood is uninfluenceable by environmental or internal efforts. In fact, as time passes, the melancholia seems to become even more severe and disabling, and the patient experiences interference in his or her thought processes; loses the ability to concentrate, focus attention, or direct his or her thoughts; loses interest in and feels unable to work, sleep, or engage in sex, recreation, or familial/social activities. Often, the person is listless and agitated and becomes extremely anxious and confused when faced with minor decisions and seemingly insignificant frustrations.

The inner experience of this disorder frequently is described by patients with words such as "dead," "wasted," "diseased," and "consumed," to list just a few. The patient reports a severe anhedonia and a sense that previously valued persons, things, and objects have lost meaning. The self is experienced as empty, unresponsive, frozen, or paralyzed, and as being hateful, disgusting, evil, unlovable, and deserving of punishment, destruction, and death. These ideas are often accompanied by severe, intense feelings of guilt, shame, humiliation, and embarrassment. The patient usually cannot cite particulars with regard to justifying this view of the self, but the ideas and emotions themselves, as mentioned above, are syntonic and acceptable to the patient. Predictably, suicidal ideation is a frequent correlate of this melancholic mood, and suicide attempts occur with regularity. Arieti and Bemporad (1978) report that 75 percent of patients with severe depressions experience repetitive suicidal ideation, and at least 15 percent make serious attempts to end their own lives.

The melancholic mood in psychotic depressions is accompanied by profound and remarkable cognitive dysfunctions and symptoms. The content of the patient's cognitive activities is dominated by ideas and images of defeat, death, destruction, and an enduring outlook of futility, hopelessness, and pessimism. These ideas may be preceded or accompanied by obsessive or phobic preoccupations, or by aggressive and/or sexual ruminations. As the depression deepens, ideas of doom, gloom, and failure acquire greater permanence and importance. The patient is unable to think of anything but his or her failures, weaknesses, and flaws, and believes that great and terrible misfortunes will befall the patient, his or her family and friends, and even the world—all because of something the patient has/has not done in the past or will or will not be able to do in the future. In sum, the patient's thinking is dominated by the themes of failure, guilt, self-blame and condemnation, hopelessness, and sin, and these contents, although unexplainable on the basis of facts, are experienced as congruent or true to the self by the patient. The patient cannot admit into consciousness any contradictory, pleasant ideas or turn his or her thoughts to neutral, ego-distant issues. Thinking in severe depression appears to lose its role and function as an adaptive, information-processing function. Instead, it becomes an internally oriented process, the role of which is to register and transmit mental pain (Arieti & Bemporad, 1978).

Along with these cognitive contents, there are noticeable dysfunctions in the processes of thinking and perception. Attention and concentration are disrupted and impaired, as is the person's ability to direct, guide, and focus his or her thinking. Reading, writing, thinking, and speaking often become cumbersome, slowed, or blocked entirely, and are experienced as requiring extreme effort. A certain subgroup of psychotic depressions is accompanied by gross delusions, hallucinations, and failures in reality testing. Brown (1988) noted that different studies report a rate of delusions in 5 to 30 percent of psychotically depressed patients. These delusions usually focus on contents of guilt and sin, ideas of reference and of persecution, somatic disease, poverty, or nihilism. Brown (1988) reported the example of a patient whose anorexic symptoms were caused by the delusion that her bowels, bladder, and body had rotted to the point that food and water would fall out of her. Another patient blamed himself for the starvation of his family because he had failed them financially, though they were in fact well fed and economically secure. Hallucinations in this disorder are rare but include the types of contents just mentioned. Arieti (1974) noted that, in psychotic depressions, hallucinations usually are milder and less distinct than in schizophrenia, and are secondary and responsive to the patient's prevailing mood.

Severe/psychotic depressions are marked by changes in behavior; the most frequently observed is psychomotor retardation or retarded hypoactivity (Arieti, 1974; Arieti & Bemporad, 1978; Beck, 1967; Gibson, 1975; Nemiah, 1975). The patient simply stops behaving as frequently and as quickly as he or she did in the premorbid state. Talking and acting, even for the most basic tasks of life (eating, grooming, bathing) are slowed, postponed, or abandoned. The person is lethargic, indifferent, and disinterested in interpersonal situations; the frequency of spontaneous speech and interaction diminishes, often disappearing completely. In the most severe instances, *depressive stupor* may appear. This is thought to be (Arieti & Bemporad, 1978) the most severe form of depressive psychomotor and behavioral disturbance, and takes the form of total withdrawal from the environment, to the point that the patient becomes completely mute, unmoving, and unresponsive. Patients in this state cannot care for even their most basic needs, usually remain in bed, and require spoon feeding, or tubal or intravenous nutrition. They are prone to malnutrition and other severe physical complications.

The other correlated physical/behavioral symptoms of this disorder are changes in sleep patterns and appetite, weight loss or gain, and diurnal mood variation. Most psychotic depressions are accompanied by insomnia, early morning awakening, and loss of appetite and weight.

Certain authors believe that the differential diagnosis of the various types of psychotic level depressions can be made by comparing symptoms on the behavioral and physical dimensions. In contrast to the similarities in affective and cognitive symptoms, these subgroups seem to differ on these variables. For example, Gibson (1975) reported that the phenomenology of depression in cases of involutional melancholia is relatively equivalent to the depressions described above, with the exception that patients with involutional disorders demonstrate high levels of psychomotor agitation and experience anxiety and psychological agitation as additional parts of their melancholic process.

Stokes (1988) suggested that although patients with bipolar illness who are depressed resemble patients with unipolar depression to a considerable degree, the depressed bipolar patients tend to have weight gains, increased food intake, and symptoms of hypersomnia, while unipolar patients become anorexic, lose weight, and typically complain of insomnia. Brown (1988) reported that psychotically depressed patients who report delusions among their symptoms differ from non-delusional psychotic depressives on several behavioral indices. He stated that a number of studies have indicated that delusional depressives experience greater degrees of guilt, and are more cognitively ruminative, display more behavioral agitation, and are more severely retarded psychomotorically. Delusional depressives also demonstrate higher levels of depression on such measures as the Hamiliton Depression Scale. At this point in time, such findings are useful in directing further research but do not as yet add up to a sufficiently substantial knowledge base for a conclusive portrait of unique subtypes of psychotic level depression.

Research in this area is not as conflicted and as contradictory as the research mentioned in the discussion of neurotic/reactive depression. Few would doubt the validity and reliability of a diagnosis of a depression of severe proportions, and the debated issues that are attached to this level of depression are concerned with more finely tuned diagnostic and classificatory questions. These efforts are exemplified by attempts to establish clear, reliable, and valid demarcations between unipolar and bipolar disorders (Stokes, 1988) and psychotic vs. nonpsychotic manifestations of major depressive disorder or of endogenous depression (Brown, 1988; Cohen & Winokur, 1988). At this point in time research has not yet yielded unanimity with regard to the definitive criteria for such distinctions.

Chronic Depression

There is a subgroup of patients whose depressions do not follow the generally accepted rule that depression is a time-limited, self-correcting process. These patients may remain depressed for months, years, or decades without significant change in mood, cognition, or affect. It is not uncommon to interview such a person and to have that patient state that he or she cannot remember a time when he or she was not depressed. These patients often trace the onset of their condition back to childhood or to adolescence. Interestingly, many persons with this type of depression report that they first realized that they were "depressed" only lately. Until the condition was diagnosed professionally or became recognizable to the patient in some other way, many such persons assumed that their dysphoria was "normal," that is, that their depressed mood and thinking were universal.

This level of depression is an extremely controversial disorder, according to many authorities. The existence of a chronic form of depression has been discussed since the early part of this century, but the nature and features of the disorder have been the subject of disagreement until the present day. As Akiskal (1983) noted, chronic depression has had a very large number of names, including "depressive temperament," "depressive personality," "hysteroid dysphoria," "characterological depression," "neurotic depression," and "chronic mild depression." Chronic depression has been construed as a mild precursor to a full-blown manic-depressive disorder, as a type of personality disorder, or as a separate and unique affective disorder.

Kraepelin (1921) introduced the term depressive temperament to describe the condition of chronic depression which he understood to be a milder, somewhat stable predecessor to manic-depressive illness. He described depressive temperament as sharing most, if not all, of the symptoms of the manic-depressive syndrome in form and type, with the symptoms occurring in attenuated quantities or levels.

An alternative conceptualization of chronic depression as a type of personality disorder or character problem was put forth by such psychoanalytic writers as Fenichel (1945) and Bemporad (1976). Schneider (1959) also deviated from Kraepelin's viewpoint, identifying chronic depression as a type of psychopathy (his term for personality disorder). He separated chronic depression from the other, biologically derived affective disorders. DSM-II (American Psychiatric Association, 1968) placed chronic depressions with Cyclothymic Personality Disorder, Asthenic Personality Disorder, or Neurasthenic Neurosis.

In the past two decades many investigators have classified chronic depression as an affective disorder without identifying it as a type of neurosis or of character disorder, or as a forerunner of any other form of affective disorder (Spitzer, Endicott, & Robins, 1978). This is the approach taken by the authors of DSM-III and DSM-III-R (American Psychiatric Association, 1980, 1987). These manuals place chronic depressions under the diagnostic label of Dysthymic Disorder. There are four defining characteristics of this syndrome. The first is a depressed mood for the majority of the day, on most days, for at least two years. The second criterion is the presence while depressed of two of six possible depressive symptoms: poor appetite or overeating, insomnia or hypersomnia, low energy or fatigue, low self-esteem, poor concentration or difficulty in making decisions, or feelings of hopelessness. A third criterion for this diagnosis is that during the immediately preceding two-year period the patient does not report having been free of a depressed mood for longer than two months. The last criterion is the absence of clear evidence of a major affective disorder. These requirements have been judged by some (Elliot, 1989; Kocsis & Frances, 1988) to be overly similar to the diagnostic criteria for Major Depression, resulting in a blurring of boundaries between the two disorders. As Kocsis and Frances (1988) suggested, an empirical and theoretical consensus upon the nature and appearance of chronic depression is still elusive. There is at least one existing study (Hirschfeld, Klerman, Andreason, Clayton, & Keller, 1986) which concluded that there are two and possibly more patterns of life experience related to the development of chronic depression. In some patients, chronic depression was found to be the result of a failure to recover from an acute major depressive episode, while in others it was unrelated to an acute episode. In this latter group, chronic depression was in itself the major type of psychopathology present. These data were interpreted by Elliot (1989) as suggestive that chronic depression may not be a single disorder.

The patient who suffers from a chronic depression lives under the weight of his or her symptoms for an extended period of time. These depressive symptoms generally are rated as mild to moderate by patients and by clinicians and researchers (Arieti & Bemporad, 1978; Bemporad, 1976; Kocsis & Frances, 1988) and tend to cluster around the cognitive and affective dimensions of depression. The more severe behavioral and somatic features found in psychotic depressions are absent or attenuated (Kocsis & Frances, 1987). Chronic depression seems then to be identifiable primarily by enduring negative and dysfunctional cognitive, perceptual, and attitudinal patterns or traits, and by correlated or resulting dysphoric affects and moods. Persons with chronic depression consistently view themselves, the future, and the world through the lenses of Beck's (1967) depressive triad: negative evaluations of the self, pessimism about the future, and a corresponding sense of the world as barren, depriving, depleting, or rejecting. In neurotic and psychotic depressions these cognitions are present but they are hypothesized to be latent or absent when the person is not in the midst of an acute episode. In other words, the depressogenic cognitions are believed to be atypical of the person's premorbid approach to life. The chronic depressive appears to construe experience through these sets in a pervasive and unremitting way, unchanged from any other previous state or time. The patient does not seem to have insight into the effect these ways of thinking have on his or her life, and demonstrates little effort at changing or correcting these attitudes. Other depressogenic beliefs are omnipresent and reside in the person's mind in an ego syntonic manner, including those ideas most expressive of the motivational issue of learned helplessness. As a result, the patient's affective life is dominated by gloom, hopelessness, disappointment, guilt, self-blame, poor self-esteem, and, often, an unwillingness to harbor ambitions, take risks, or commit to goals because failure and disappointment always are anticipated. A full-blown depressive syndrome is not present and the person sometimes does not consider himself or herself to be depressed. These ideas, affects, and traits frequently are accompanied by feelings of anger, resentment, bitterness, jealousy, envy, and alienation, usually all correlated with the person's ideas about the unfairness of his or her inevitable deprivation and suffering. Chronic depressives often complain of fatigue and lack of energy. They feel overburdened and overwhelmed by familial, social, occupational, and recreational activities, which they usually partake of with diminished or absent pleasure, and at the subjective cost of considerable psychic energy.

Bemporad (1976) described chronic depression as distinguished by a stable background of dysphoric feeling on a day-to-day basis, usually activated by very minor frustrations or setbacks. The depressive symptoms are a part of the person's ongoing personality structure, so that there is a flattening of affect and a loss of optimism. Joy, excitement, and pleasure are systematically but unconsciously minimized or perverted by the depressive character structure. Akiskal (1983) identified a group of chronically depressed patients whom he labeled as having "early onset dysthymic disorders." These patients suffer from relatively permanent impairments of self-esteem and from depressogenic cognitive structures. Their ongoing functioning is marked by mild to moderate, and essentially stable, depressive affect. Elliot (1989), in an unpublished master's thesis conducted under this writer's supervision, found that patients with DSM-III Dysthymic Disorder have lower self-esteem than do patients with Major Depression, but that Major Depressives have more severe cognitive dysfunctions (retardation, poor attention and concentration), higher levels of depressive affect, and more severe vegetative symptoms. Elliot (1989) placed the depressive cognitive triad at the "center of chronic depression." but concluded that chronic depression

> . . . is a disorder that has measurable cognitive, personality, interpersonal, and familial characteristics. . . . These characteristics put serious constraints on the capacity of those who suffer from them. Dysthymics are severely limited in their capacity to cope. They appear to possess cognitive attributional styles which preclude them from engaging in adaptive, self-corrective behavior, and from reinforcing themselves for having completed any endeavor. Their dilemmas are not subjectively perceived to be of their own creation, nor do they believe that their situations will ever change.

> *(p.27)*

Chronic depression has been discussed in the context of a newly identified level or type of depression, which is currently known as Double Depression (Keller & Shapiro, 1982). This level consists of a severe and acute depressive episode which is diagnosable as DSM-III Major Depression, and occurs in an individual who previously was diagnosed as suffering from Dysthymic Disorder. At the present time, the empirical status of this syndrome is uncertain. Miller, Norman, and Dow (1986) reported few distinguishing psychological characteristics in groups of patients with double depressions or with major depressions. They found that double depressives suffered from the current episode of major depression for a longer time, and had more severe depressive symptoms, than did the control group. Klein, Taylor, Harding, and Dickstein (1988) found that double depressives had higher levels of self-criticism, negative cognitions, depressive personality traits, and stress reactivity, together with lower levels of social extraversion, than did a group of patients with major depression. There are no specific diagnostic guidelines or agreed-upon clinical portraits available at this time.

Masked Depression

The idea of the existence of a syndrome of masked depression is a debatable and philosophically difficult construct for many students of depression. This label, applied synonymously with the diagnosis of *depressive equivalent,* refers to patients who have behavioral, psychological, or somatic symptoms which "mask" and symbolically express an underlying depression. Kennedy and Weisel (1946) reported on a phenomenon of "manic-depressive equivalents" in patients whose overt symptoms consisted of somatic dysfunctions, which hid a psychotic-level affective disorder. Berner, Katschnig, and Poldinger (1973) and Geisler (1973) reported that many psychophysiological and physical symptoms in actuality reflected underlying depressive pathology. The list of symptoms thought to be depressive equivalents included symptoms that resembled angina, nervous dystonia, cardiovascular disorders, cholecystitus, colitis, diverticulitis, food allergy, neoplasm, and pernicious anemia. Braceland (1966/1978) noted that the most common symptoms of masked depression were general abdominal pain, fatigue, headache, anorexia, insomnia, and gastrointestinal distress. Stafford (1977) mentioned that a variety of psychodynamic, cognitive, behavioral, and biological studies provide some limited support for the existence of this syndrome. The evidence that Stafford reviewed is particularly applicable to addictive and alcoholic patients, whose substance abuse is thought to reflect an attempt to cover up and to ameliorate the dysphoria of depression. Clinically, this idea has gained a certain acceptance because of the observation that when addicts and alcoholics are prevented from obtaining chemical gratification, depression often results. Similarly, the recovery phase in these disorders often is marked by the emergence of depression. However, these observations are open to the opposite interpretation as well. The similarities in dynamics between substance abusers and depressives, and the presence of depression in the recovery phase, may be *caused* by the chemical dependency. If this latter explanation is more accurate, the depressions experienced by addicts and substance abusers might better be understood as *secondary depressions,* rather than as a "flowering" of a previously hidden depression.

Fulwiler and Pope (1987), in a review of the relationship of depression and personality disorder, suggested that many of the DSM-III Axis II personality disorders might better be looked at as "partial affective syndromes" or as reflecting what Akiskal (1983) labeled a "subsyndromal affective illness." Fulwiler and Pope (1987) pointed out that many of the diagnostic criteria for the various Axis II disorders overlap or are identical to the criteria for Dysthymic Disorder or for Major Depression. They believed that the abnormal behavior typical of personality disorders can and does obscure an additional and perhaps more basic affective disorder, particularly when that affective pathology is subsyndromal in extent and severity.

The validity of the construct of subsyndromal depression received some support from a group of studies wherein it was found that depressives, personality disorders, and alcoholics share similar family histories of drug abuse, alcoholism, and affective illness, and that these three groups often respond equivalently to antidepressant medication (Fulwiler & Pope, 1987). However, this concept and the older concept of masked depression are far from universally accepted. Critics suggest that the disorder is an artifact of methodological problems and of the confusion of correlative findings with causation.

Secondary Depression

Depression as an affect, mood, or syndrome can accompany or follow almost any medical or psychiatric illness. It also may be the consequence of temporary biochemical alterations, such as the effects of medications, alcohol use, fatigue, prolonged sleep deprivation, or malnutrition. The symptoms and phenomenology of secondary depressions are similar, if not identical, to one of the levels of primary depression which have been described above (Cohen & Winokur, 1988). Cognitive, affective, motivational, and vegetative changes may dominate the clinical picture singly or in combination, and the secondary depression may resemble a neurotic/reactive, psychotic, or chronic depression in severity and course. The presence of a primary medical or psychiatric illness, or of a biochemical derangement, or of the history of at least one of these precursors, therefore is necessary to establish the diagnosis of secondary depression (Cameron, 1987).

Certain secondary depressions may be related clinically and conceptually to the group of neurotic/reactive depressions, and might best be named Psychogenic Secondary Depression. These secondary depressions seem to result from the patient's reaction to, or appraisal of, his or her medical or psychiatric illness or the consequences of that illness. For example, a patient who has lost physical capabilities due to a stroke, or who has been disfigured by an accident, may respond to those changes with the cognitions typical of neurotic depression, thus eliciting depressive mood and behavior. In essence, the illness, psychopathology, or physical failing becomes the precipitant noted in the previous discussion of neurotic depression. Other secondary depressions may be more purely endogenous in that they are caused by biochemical processes associated with an initial disease process. Probably many secondary depressions are mixed, with regard to reactive and endogenous causation. A neurological or hormonal disorder that biologically produces secondary depressive symptoms will yield in the patient a psychological response to both the original disease and the resulting disorder. This response may exacerbate the depression if it falls within the parameters of depressive appraisal and cognition, effectively adding a reactive element to a secondary depression which was begun by endogenous processes.

SUMMARY

This chapter is concerned with the phenomenology and overt behavioral and psychological manifestations of the different types or "levels" of depressive psychopathology. Traditional typologies derived from clinical lore and observation and described and reviewed, as are the latest attempts to identify and delineate discrete classes of depression in DSM-III and DSM-III-R (American Psychiatric Association, 1980, 1987). The history of the unitary vs. dual disorder controversy is reviewed, as are current studies which attempt to test the utility of nosological work and to validate or disprove the commonly accepted differentiation of depression into such levels as neurotic-reactive, endogenous-psychotic, and characterological. Other traditional levels of depression, including masked depression, and secondary depression are discussed as well.

REFERENCES

Akiskal, H. (1983). Dysthymic disorder: Psychopathology of proposed depressive subtypes. *American Journal of Psychiatry, 140,* 11–20.

Akiskal, H., Rosenthal, R., Rosenthal, T., Kashgarian, M., Khani, M., & Pozantian, V. (1979). Differentiation of primary affective illness from situational, symptomatic, and secondary depression. *American Journal of Psychiatry, 136,* 635–643.

American Psychiatric Association. (1952). *Diagnostic and statistical manual of mental disorders* (DSM). Washington, DC: Author.

American Psychiatric Association. (1968). *Diagnostic and statistical manual of mental disorders* (2nd ed.; DSM-II). Washington, DC: Author.

American Psychiatric Association. (1980). *Diagnostic and statistical manual of mental disorders* (3rd ed.; DSM-III). Washington, DC: Author.

American Psychiatric Association. (1987). *Diagnostic and statistical manual of mental disorders* (3rd ed. rev.; DSM-III-R). Washington, DC: Author.

Arieti, S. (1974). Manic-depressive psychosis and psychotic depression. In S. Arieti (Ed.), *American handbook of psychiatry (Vol. III)*. New York: Basic Books.

Arieti, S., & Bemporad, J. (1978). *Severe and mild depression*. New York: Basic Books.

Beck, A. (1967). *Depression: Causes and treatment*. Philadelphia: University of Pennsylvania Press.

Bemporad, J. (1976). Psychotherapy of the depressive character. *Journal of the American Academy of Psychoanalysis, 4,* 347–372.

Berner, P., Katschnig, H., & Poldinger, W. (1973). What does the term "masked depression" mean? In P. Kielholz (Ed.), *Masked depression*. Bern: Huber.

Bibring, E. (1953). The mechanism of depression. In P. Greenacre (Ed.), *Affective disorders*. New York: International Universities Press.

Braceland, F. (1978). Depressions and their treatment. Cited in S. Arieti & J. Bemporad, *Severe and mild depression*. New York: Basic Books. (Original work published 1966.)

Brown, R. (1988). Delusional depression. In J. Mann (Ed.), *Phenomenology of depressive illness*. New York: Human Sciences Press.

Cameron, O. (Ed.) (1987). *Presentations of depression*. New York: Wiley.

Cohen, M., & Winokur, G. (1988). The clinical classification of depressive disorders. In J. Mann (Ed.), *Phenomenology of depressive illness*. New York: Human Sciences Press.

Elliot, A. (1989). Manifestation of symptom differences among chronic and major depressives as measured by the Hamilton rating scale for depression. Unpublished master's thesis, Yeshiva University, New York.

Feighner, J., Robins, E., & Guze, S. (1972). Diagnostic criteria for use in psychiatric research. *Archives of General Psychiatry, 26,* 57–63.

Fenichel, O. (1945). *The psychoanalytic theory of neurosis*. New York: Norton.

Freud, S. (1950). Mourning and melancholia. In J. Strachey (Ed. & Trans.), *The standard edition of the complete psychological works of Sigmund Freud*. London: Hogarth Press. (Original work published 1917.)

Fulwiler, C., & Pope, H. (1987). Depression in personality disorder. In O. Cameron (Ed.), *Presentations of depression*. New York: Wiley.

Geisler, L. (1973). Masked depression in patients suspected of suffering from internal disease. In P. Kielholz (Ed.), *Masked depression*. Bern: Huber.

Gibson, R. (1975). Manic-depressive illness. In A. Freedman, H. Kaplan, & B. Sadock (Eds.), *Comprehensive textbook of psychiatry.* Baltimore: Williams & Wilkins.

Hirschfeld, R., Klerman, G., Andreason, N., Clayton, P., & Keller, M. (1986). Psychosocial predictors of chronicity in depressed patients. *British Journal of Psychiatry, 148,* 648–654.

Keller, M., & Shapiro, R. (1982). Double depression: Superimposition of acute depressive episodes on chronic depressive disorders. *American Journal of Psychiatry, 143,* 24–28.

Kendell, R. (1977). The classifications of depression: A review of contemporary confusion. *British Journal of Psychiatry, 129,* 15–29.

Kennedy, F., & Weisel, B. (1946). The clinical nature of manic depressive equivalents and their treatment. *Transactions of the American Neurological Association, 71,* 96–103.

Klein, D., Taylor, E., Harding, K., & Dickstein, S. (1988). Double depression and episodic major depression: Demographic, clinical, familial, personality, and socioenvironmental characteristics and short term outcome. *American Journal of Psychiatry, 145,* 1226–1231.

Kocsis, J., & Frances, A. (1987). A critical discussion of DSM-III dysthymic disorder. *American Journal of Psychiatry, 144,* 1534–1542.

Kocsis, J., & Frances, A. (1988). Chronic depression. In J. Mann (Ed.), *Phenomenology of depressive illness.* New York: Human Sciences Press.

Kolb, L. (1973). *Modern clinical psychiatry.* Philadelphia: Saunders.

Kraepelin, E. (1921). *Manic depressive insanity and paranoia.* Edinburgh: Livingstone.

Levitt, E., Lubin, B., & Brooks, J. (1983). *Depression.* Hillsdale, NJ: Erlbaum.

Mendels, J., & Cochrane, C. (1968). The nosology of depression: The endogenous–reactive concept. *American Journal of Psychiatry, 124,* 1–11.

Miller, I., Norman, W., & Dow, N. (1986). Psychosocial characteristics of "double depression." *American Journal of Psychiatry, 143,* 1042–1044.

Nemiah, J. (1975). Neurotic depression. In A. Freedman, H. Kaplan, & B. Sadock. *Comprehensive textbook of psychiatry.* Baltimore: Williams & Wilkins.

Rush, A. (1986). The diagnosis of affective disorders. In A. Rush & K. Altschuler (Eds.), *Depression.* New York: Guilford Press.

Schneider, K. (1959). *Clinical psychopathology.* New York: Grune & Stratton.

Seligman, M. (1975). *Helplessness: On depression, development, and death.* San Francisco: Freeman.

Spitzer, R., & Endicott, J. (1978). *Schedule for affective disorders and schizophrenia.* New York: Psychiatric Institute.

Spitzer, R., Endicott, J., & Robins, E. (1978). *Research diagnostic criteria for a selected group of functional disorders.* New York: Biometrics Research.

Stafford, T. (1977). Masked depression and depressive equivalents. In W. Fann, I. Karacan, A. Pokorny, & R. Williams (Eds.), *Phenomenology and treatment of depression.* New York: SP Publications.

Stokes, P., (1988). Bipolar disorders. In J. Mann (Ed.), *Phenomenology of depressive illness.* New York: Human Sciences Press.

World Health Organization (WHO). (1983). *Depressive disorders in different cultures.* Geneva: Author.

Zung, W. (1977). Operational diagnosis and depression. In W. Fann, I. Karacan, A. Pokorny, & R. Williams (Eds.), *Phenomenology and treatment of depression.* New York: SP Publications.

PART 3

Diagnostic and Treatment Methods

CHAPTER 11

Interviewing Methods

DIANE E. SHOLOMSKAS, PhD

This chapter will focus on new developments in the use of standardized interview methods for the diagnosis of affective and other mental disorders in patient, community, and cross-cultural samples. Discussion will be limited to instruments used to derive diagnoses; instruments that quantify severity or measure symptom change, such as the Hamilton Depression Rating Scale (Hamilton, 1960), are not included.

BACKGROUND AND HISTORY

Over the past three decades, increasing emphasis has been placed on the explication and refinement of diagnostic nosology and on the development of standardized interviewing techniques for deriving differential diagnoses. Although the classification and description of affective disorders is still a controversial and continually evolving process, three diagnostic systems have dominated the clinical and research fields: the Feighner criteria (Feighner et al., 1972), the Research Diagnostic Criteria (Spitzer, Endicott, & Robins, 1978), and the American Psychiatric Association's *Diagnostic and Statistical Manual of Mental Disorders,* DSM-III(1980) and DSM-III-R(1987).

Prior to the 1950s, the primary sources of information about mental disorders were textbook descriptions, reported case histories, and clinical presentations. The clinician's interview was the method by which this information was obtained. Early attempts to develop a classification system, nomenclature, and standard descriptions of mental disorders began in 1952 with the publication of the first *Diagnostic and Statistical Manual* (DSM-I) by the American Psychiatric Association. In the early 1970s, trends toward the specification and standardization of diagnostic categories culminated in the publication of the Feighner criteria. This publication, a milestone for the development of a reliable and valid nosology, described diagnostic criteria for 14 psychiatric disorders. These included a distinction between primary affective disorders (depression and mania) and secondary affective disorders (depression or mania in the presence of another preexisting nonaffective disorder or a life-threatening physical illness). Although these criteria, derived from clinical and research experience, were not considered definitive for any category, they offered a method of uniformly communicating and describing patients' conditions.

In addition, Feighner et al. (1972) described five phases for demonstrating diagnostic validity in psychiatric disorders:

1. Clinical description—the phenomenological description of the condition.
2. Laboratory studies—the discovery or development of physiological, chemical, and anatomical findings that are consistently and reliably found in the presence of the specific disorder.
3. Delimitation from other disorders—the description of exclusion criteria for overlapping conditions so that the disorder defined describes the most homogenous group.
4. Follow-up studies—used to describe the outcome of the original clinical condition. It is postulated that in the absence of knowledge about the etiology of a condition, marked differences in outcome would suggest that the original cases did not comprise a homogenous group or were inaccurately diagnosed. Diagnostic heterogeneity, or change in the condition, has been regarded as a threat to the validity of the original diagnosis.
5. Family studies—based on the observation that many disorders run in families. The assumption that a high prevalence of illness in family members increases the likelihood of a valid diagnosis is made independently of the etiology (genetic versus environmental) of the condition.

Although these advances in the development of criteria for diagnostic categories moved the field closer to uniform sets of diagnostic criteria, standardized uniform procedures for collecting requisite information were absent.

Concerns with both the validity of psychiatric disorders and the reliability of diagnosis motivated the development of structured diagnostic interviews to be used with explicit criteria or classification schemes. It has long been recognized that diagnostic disagreement results from a lack of reliability or from inconsistencies occurring in the clinical interview. There are two fundamental sources of these disagreements: *information variance* and *criterion variance*. Information variance (Spitzer, Endicott, & Robins, 1975) refers to the different resources the clinician may use to gather information about a patient's condition. For example, one clinician may always interview family members as a source of data about a diagnosis, and another clinician may routinely question the patient about symptoms and difficulty in functioning, but neither of these clinicians may routinely use both sources. The end result is diagnostic disagreement between these two clinicians.

Criterion variance refers to the rules of inclusion or exclusion used by the clinician to establish a diagnosis. For example, in DSM-III the diagnosis of Panic Disorder is excluded if Agoraphobia is diagnosed, whereas in DSM-III-R Panic Disorder may be diagnosed as coexisting with Agoraphobia. Other sources of variability that contribute to error in the clinical interview originate in the patient's presentation (subject variance) and in changes in the disorder over time (occasion variance). Another source of unreliability, observation variance, refers to the clinician's differential focus on aspects of the patient's presentation. For example, one clinician may emphasize agitated behavior while another may emphasize suicidal ideation.

There are two methods for controlling these sources of variance. One is to reduce information variance with the use of structured clinical interviews. The other is to develop more uniform, standardized descriptions, names, and guidelines for diagnostic categories (Spitzer et al., 1975). These methods, in conjunction with instruction of clinicians in observational and interviewing techniques, will serve to greatly reduce variability in the clinical interview.

In the mid-1970s the National Institute of Mental Health (NIMH) Clinical Research Branch Collaborative Program on the Psychobiology of Depression sponsored the development of interview procedures and diagnostic criteria for the purpose of establishing reliable procedures for making diagnostic judgments. The commonly used structured diagnostic interview schedules and their companion diagnostic criteria are described here in detail.

DIAGNOSTIC INTERVIEW SCHEDULES AND COMPANION DIAGNOSTIC CRITERIA

The Schedule for Affective Disorders and Schizophrenia (SADS)/The Research Diagnostic Criteria (RDC)

The Schedule for Affective Disorders and Schizophrenia (SADS; Endicott & Spitzer, 1978) and the Research Diagnostic Criteria (RDC; Spitzer et al., 1978) are products of the NIMH Clinical Research Branch Collaborative Program. The SADS is a standardized, semistructured interview designed to gather systematically the information needed to derive a differential diagnosis for the 25 diagnostic categories of the RDC. The SADS follows the rhythm of a clinical interview and uses a three-pronged format of questioning about mood, symptoms, and impairment. The sequence of questions provides information that includes or excludes other specific diagnoses. In addition, the SADS gathers descriptive information about the course of illness, the age of onset, the number and duration of episodes, and other associated features.

There are three versions of the SADS: (a) the Regular Version (SADS), (b) the Lifetime Version (SADS-L), and (c) the Change Version (SADS-C). The Regular Version is organized into two parts. Part I focuses on the phenomenology of the current condition and documents the features of the current condition for two fixed time periods, the week prior to the interview and the time when the condition was at its worst in the recent course of the illness. Part I permits the quantification of current symptoms on a six-point severity scale for both time periods, a feature that makes the SADS an appropriate measure of change. Part I also permits for subtyping, which has facilitated the testing of hypotheses related to the course and onset of certain subtypes of affective disorders, such as endogenous depression. In contrast, Part II derives a lifetime description of the condition by focusing on both the description of past periods of illness and the current problem.

The SADS Regular Version is useful for interviewing inpatients or outpatients for both current episodes of illness and follow-up studies of treatment outcome.

The Lifetime Version of the SADS (SADS-L) is similar to Part II of the SADS Regular Version; however, the time period assessed by the SADS-L is only the past. This version of the SADS is useful for assessing individuals who have no current episode of illness and is appropriate for cases in which extensive information about the phenomenology of the disorders is not needed. SADS-L is useful for interviewing outpatients or for interviewing relatives of patients about themselves, and has been used with community populations to obtain information about the prevalence and incidence of these disorders.

The Change Version (SADS-C) contains the subset of items from Part I of the SADS which includes scales to measure the level of severity in the week prior to the evaluation and is therefore an efficient way to quantify change in the current condition. The SADS-C assesses change in the presentation of symptoms for current conditions or episodes of depression, mania, anxiety, alcohol and drug abuse, psychosis, or schizophrenia. It is most useful for documenting change in the conditions of inpatients or outpatients.

Which Affective Disorders Are Diagnosed by the SADS Interview?

Manic Disorder, Hypomanic Disorder, Bipolar with Mania (Bipolar I), Bipolar with Hypomania (Bipolar II), Major Depressive Disorder, nine subtypes of Major Depressive Disorder (i.e., Primary, Secondary, Endogenous, Situational), Minor Depressive Disorder, Intermittent Depressive Disorder, Cyclothymic Personality Disorder, and Labile

Personality are all diagnosable. "Rule-outs" are included to differenti-ate Schizoaffective Depressed or Manic from these affective disorders.

Who Administers the SADS?

Individuals knowledgeable about psychopathology and experienced in interviewing clinical populations, such as psychiatrists, clinical psy-chologists, and psychiatric social workers, are most suited for adminis-tering the SADS because the SADS requires the interviewer to make judgments about the clinical concepts and symptoms. The SADS may be administered by research personnel or other professionals working in the field who have had special training. Training of personnel in the administration of the SADS is facilitated by the use of videotaped SADS interviews, role playing, and direct interview with patients (Gib-bon, McDonald-Scott, & Endicott, 1981). The authors of the SADS have developed an interviewer manual which includes guidelines for conducting the interview as well as definitions of terms.

How Much Time Is Required to Administer the SADS?

An experienced interviewer requires about 1 ½ to 2 hours to adminis-ter a SADS interview. This time will vary with the version of the SADS used, the details of the history, and the mental condition of the inter-viewee.

Reliability

Psychometric information about the SADS Regular Version was ob-tained from four treatment facilities participating in the NIMH-sponsored Pilot Study of the Psychobiology of Depressive Disorders (Endicott & Spitzer, 1978). Joint interview and test–retest methods of testing reliability were used with 150 inpatients admitted with a diag-nosis of Mania or Major Depression. Joint interview intraclass coeffi-cients ranged from .82 to .99. Test–retest reliabilities for 60 inpatients retested over a time period of 48 hours to one week ranged from .49 to .93 (intraclass r). The SADS items were highly internally consist-ent, as demonstrated by Cronbach alphas of .97 for Mania and .83 to .88 for Major Depression. The exceptions were for items assessing Formal Thought Disorder (Cronbach alpha = .47) and Anxiety (Cron-bach alpha = .58).

Validity

Concurrent validity for SADS items was tested with scales measuring both patients' and relatives' reports of the patient's condition. The Katz Adjustment Scale for the subject (KAS-S) and for the relatives (KAS-R) and the Symptom Checklist 90 (SCL-90) were used. The correlations ranges (r) of the SADS depression-related items were: with the KAS-R, $r = .42$ to .58; with the SCL-90, $r = .47$ to .68; and with the KAS-S,

r = .37 to .46 (Endicott & Spitzer, 1978). Overall, there is some evidence for SADS concurrent validity for patient self-reported depression items. The SADS has been shown to be useful for discriminating between groups and for testing hypotheses about the classification and subtyping of affective disorders (Cornell, Milden, & Shimp, 1985; DeJonghe, Ameling, & Assies, 1988; Endicott & Spitzer, 1979). The SADS interview and RDC diagnostic manual appear to derive relatively stable lifetime diagnoses. Diagnostic agreement after a follow-up interval of 1 ½ to 2 years was Kappa = .83 for Mania and Kappa = .76 for Major Depression (Spitzer et al., 1978).

Scoring

Precoded score sheets for the various SADS interviews and RDC have been developed. The advantage of the SADS scoring in comparison to other instruments is that the SADS interviews may be scored by the interviewer using the RDC manual. Computerized scoring algorithms have also been developed by researchers to score the SADS using RDC criteria. Good agreement has been reported between computer-generated diagnoses and interviewer-generated diagnoses. However, the major constraint for computer-generated diagnoses is the limitations of the diagnostic system (Spitzer, Endicott, Cohen, & Fleiss, 1974).

Availability

The SADS interviews and RDC manuals are available from the Research Assessment and Training Unit, 722 West 168 Street, Room 341, New York, NY 10032. In addition, the Research Assessment and Training unit offers material for instruction in the use of the SADS and RDC. The SADS has been translated into some foreign languages. Versions are available in Spanish, French, and Japanese, among others (Miriam Gibbon, personal communication, May, 1989).

Diagnostic Interview Schedule (DIS)/Feighner Criteria; Research Diagnostic Criteria; DSM-III (1980) and DSM-III-R (1987)

The National Institute of Mental Health (NIMH) Diagnostic Interview Schedule (DIS) was developed by Robins and her colleagues (Robins, Helzer, Croughan, & Ratcliff, 1981) at the specific request of the division of Biometry and Epidemiology of NIMH for use in large-scale epidemiological studies. The immediate application of the DIS was for the Epidemiological Catchment Area (ECA) projects for gathering data on the prevalence of psychopathology and psychiatric disorders in the community at large (see Regier et al., 1984, for details). There was need for an instrument that could be administered by a nonclinician interviewer but would be capable of deriving differential diagnoses. The Renard Diagnostic Interview (RDI) (Helzer, Robins, Croughan, & Welner, 1981), the predecessor of the DIS, had been developed and was fully specified in terms of initial questions and subroutines for probing. The RDI contained a symptom scoring system which permitted the scoring of presence or absence of a symptom with severity ratings as well as scoring for the presence of a symptom in the context of other conditions, such as drugs or medical illness. The RDI, therefore, was chosen to be the model on which the DIS was based. In addition, the DIS was specifically designed to meet the need for an instrument which could provide diagnostic information for three diagnostic systems: the Feighner criteria (Feighner et al., 1972), the RDC (Spitzer et al., 1978), and the DSM-III (American Psychiatric Association, 1980, 1987).

The DIS interview assesses information for 32 DSM-III diagnostic categories, nine of the 25 RDC diagnoses, and 14 of the Feighner criteria disorders (see Robins et al., 1981, for a detailed description). There have been three revisions of the DIS since its development and a new version that derives DSM-III-R diagnoses is near completion (Philip Leaf, personal communication, May, 1989).

The DIS is a structured interview designed to make complex diagnostic decisions. A probe flow-chart method is utilized to carry the interviewer through the decision tree of positive or negative responses. The DIS Version Three contains approximately 263 items which inquire about respondents' symptoms or problems experienced currently or over a lifetime. Current symptoms are assessed for four time periods: the past two weeks, the past month, the past six months, and the past year. Other descriptive information, such as age at the last symptom, age at onset of the first symptom, or age at seeking medical help for the symptom, is also gathered. One of the features of the DIS is the differentiation of the diagnostic significance of symptoms, that is, the severity of the symptom and whether the symptom is attributable to physical illness. The DIS has been shown to be useful for identifying patients who are medically ill and who also have treatable psychiatric problems (Lustman, Harper, Griffith, & Clouse, 1986). The overlap between physical and psychiatric symptoms and the proper assignment of cause are difficult determinations in the process of differential diagnosis. The DIS, therefore, may be helpful in systematically studying the overlap between physical and emotional problems.

Which Affective Disorders Are Diagnosed by the DIS?

The DSM-III diagnoses are Major Depression, Dysthymic Disorder, Bipolar Disorder, and Manic Disorder; the Feighner criteria diagnoses are Depression and Mania; and the RDC criteria diagnoses are Major Depressive Disorder and Manic Disorder.

Who Administers the DIS?

The DIS was designed for administration by a nonclinician interviewer who is well trained in interview methods. Interviewers can be trained to administer the DIS in about two weeks. Clinically trained professionals may also use this instrument.

How Much Time Is Required to Administer the DIS?

An experienced interviewer can administer the DIS in 45 to 90 minutes.

Reliability

The initial psychometric properties of the DIS were tested on 216 inpatients, outpatients, and nonpatients. Reliability studies were conducted so that all subjects were interviewed twice, once by a nonclinician and once by a psychiatrist. Kappa coefficients of agreement fell around .60 for most disorders, with perfect agreement (1.00) for Anorexia Nervosa and Pathological Gambling but lower agreement (Kappa = .30) for Panic Disorder and Somatization Disorder. Recently, the DIS was administered to 220 psychiatric inpatients and compared to chart diagnoses. Agreement between DIS and chart diagnoses ranged from Kappa .39 to −.03 and was adequate for Affective Disorders but poorest for Phobias (Erdman et al., 1987).

Validity

Because the standard for validity for the DIS has been the psychiatrist's examination and diagnosis, the method for demonstrating validity has been to compare the lay interviewers' DIS to the psychiatrist's interview, conducted with or without the use of the DIS (Anthony et al., 1985; Helzer et al., 1985; Helzer, Spitznagel, & McEvoy, 1987). Helzer et al. (1985) reported that the agreement between lay interviewer and psychiatrist ranges from 79 to 96 percent for most diagnostic categories. Clinicians' diagnoses, upon reinterview, confirmed the diagnoses assigned by lay interviewers the majority of the time; for example, the lay interviewer DIS diagnosis of Major Depression was confirmed by the clinician 82 percent of the time. In contrast, Panic Disorder, Simple Phobia, and Obsessive-Compulsive Disorders showed confirmation rates at around 50 percent (Robins, Helzer, Ratcliff, & Seyfried, 1982). Lay interviewers have been reported to underdiagnose Major Depression (Anthony et al., 1985), Alcohol Dependence, Somatization Disorder, and Panic Disorder (Robins et al., 1982) and to overdiagnose Obsessive-Compulsive Disorder (Anthony et al., 1985). Diagnoses most accurately assigned by lay interviewers were for those cases with current and severe disorders. While there is some concern about the inconsistencies in lay versus clinician diagnoses, investigators have attributed the diagnostic variability to problems with the standard (the use of the psychiatrist's diagnosis as the validity criterion), the reinterview method, and the limitations of the Kappa statistic (Robins, 1985).

An alternative method of demonstrating the validity of the DIS has been to study the DIS predictive power in terms of health outcomes at follow-up. The lay interview DIS compared well to physicians' diagnoses for 370 ECA subjects at one-year follow-up for diagnostic consistency, actual health outcomes, and information about family psychiatric history in first-degree relatives (Helzer et al., 1987). The DIS validity studies have led to the improvement and revision of the DIS three times since 1981, especially for diagnoses such as Panic Disorder and Somatization Disorder.

The DIS has been translated into Spanish and has been used with patients and community samples in Puerto Rico (Canino et al., 1987). Overall, a comparison of clinician and nonclinician diagnoses with the Spanish version of the DIS shows much the same findings as with the original English version. There is good agreement in diagnoses when lay interviewers and clinicians collect data with the DIS; the poorest agreement occurs when the lay interviewer diagnosis is compared to the clinician's diagnosis obtained without the use of the DIS. For example, agreement for lay interviewers and clinicians when both used the DIS was Kappa = .55 for Major Depression, while agreement for lay interviewers' DIS diagnosis compared to clinicians' diagnosis without the use of the DIS was Kappa = .18 for Major Depression. The specificity of the Spanish DIS for identifying disorders is good but the sensitivity (the ability to detect the presence of a problem) is more variable. This is also true for the English version of the DIS.

Scoring

The DIS items are scored in a precoded closed-ended format. Computer programs derive and designate the diagnoses according to the three diagnostic systems and indicate how recently the disorder has been active. A computerized program for a personal computer, the Apple DIS, has been developed (Comings, 1984).

Availability

The DIS interviews, manuals, and information about computer scoring are available from Lee N. Robins, PhD, Washington University School of Medicine, 4940 Audubon Avenue, St. Louis, MO 63110.

Comparison of the SADS and the DIS

A systematic investigation of the SADS and DIS was conducted with 42 patients hospitalized for the treatment of alcohol problems (Hesselbrock, Stabenau, Hesselbrock, Mirkin, & Meyer, 1982). The two interviews were conducted within three to four days of each other by different interviewers. The diagnoses were assigned with the RDC criteria. Interrater reliability was excellent, with Kappas of .83 for the SADS and .94 for the DIS. Diagnoses derived from these two interviews showed good concordance. For example, Kappas of .74 were obtained for a current diagnosis of Major Depression without subtyping and Kappas of .72 for past episodes of Major Depression. Poorer concordance between the SADS and the DIS was demonstrated for Antisocial Personality disorder and for Drug Use.

The DIS took longer to administer (about 75–90 minutes) than the SADS (about 60–70 minutes). Overall, the SADS requires a greater investment in training time because the interviewer will be making diagnostic decisions, but the advantage of this is greater specificity in diagnoses. One of the advantages of the DIS is that it gathers more complete information in each category because there are no screening questions, diagnostic hierarchy, or interviewer judgment skip-outs. Both instruments are useful for deriving Axis I diagnoses. The DIS provides for separate coding of a medical condition or physical injury, while the SADS provides for the interviewers to rule out these factors as part of their differential diagnoses. The DIS more systematically documents overlapping medical conditions, therefore enabling an Axis III diagnosis. The SADS permits the clinician to rule out any coexisting physical condition but depends on the clinician to make the final judgment. The DIS has a component for Organic Mental Disorders while the SADS requires the clinician to judge the presence of these problems prior to administering the SADS interview. In addition, nonclinician-administered structured interviews are being used more frequently in clinical and treatment settings, expanding the application of the DIS from its original use in epidemiological surveys (Klerman, 1985).

The Structured Clinical Interview for DSM-III-R (SCID)/DSM-III-R (1987)

Modifications in the diagnostic systems over the past decade and the increased use of the DSM-III system have made the utility of the SADS interview more limited to research settings. A structured interview which was designed for the clinically trained interviewer but which derived DSM-III and DSM-III-R (American Psychiatric Association, 1980, 1987) diagnoses was needed. The Structured Clinical Interview for DSM-III-R (SCID) was developed for this purpose by Spitzer, Williams, Gibbon, and First (1988a, 1988b). The SCID is in the process of being refined and several field trials have been initiated to assess its reliability and validity. The SCID is a semistructured interview comprised of diagnostic modules for each major Axis I diagnostic category. These diagnostic modules provide the clinician or researcher with the flexibility to customize the interview and therefore to add or delete diagnostic modules that may not be relevant. The SCID assesses problems occurring within two time periods: the past month (current) and lifetime (illness occurring at any time, "ever"). The SCID is comprised of open-ended questions as well as specific probes. The interview follows the rhythm of the clinician's differential diagnostic interview. Interviewees' responses are coded in one of four ways: ? = inadequate information; 1 = absent or false; 2 = subthreshold (threshold for criterion is almost but not completely met); and 3 = threshold (criterion is met). Information about the onset, course of illness, partial or full remission, impairment or Global Assessment Functioning (GAF), and differentiation of symptoms from organic causes is documented in the SCID.

There are three versions of the SCID: (a) the Patient Version (SCID-P), (b) the Outpatient Version (SCID-OP) and (c) the Nonpatient Version (SCID-NP). The Patient Version of the SCID was designed for use with psychiatric inpatients. This version has a diagnostic module tailored for making differential diagnoses of psychotic disorders because psychotic states are more likely to be found in inpatient populations. There are nine modules in the SCID-P: mood syndromes, psychotic and associated symptoms, psychotic disorders (differential), mood disorders, psychoactive substance use disorders, anxiety disorders, somatoform disorders, eating disorders, and adjustment disorders. The SCID-P also has an overview section, which focuses on the presenting problem, and a score sheet for current and lifetime diagnoses.

In contrast to the Patient Version, the Outpatient Version (SCID-OP) is tailored for the screening of psychotic symptoms since outpatients are less likely to present in active psychotic states. There are eight modules in the SCID-OP.

The Nonpatient Version (SCID-NP) was designed for use with individuals not identified as psychiatric patients. Therefore, the SCID-NP is appropriate for use in community surveys, family studies, medical clinics, or other research settings. The SCID-NP, like the SCID-OP, includes only the psychotic screening module. However, the three versions of the SCID are easily converted from one to another by adding or removing the appropriate score sheet, overview, and psychotic modules.

Which Affective Disorders Are Diagnosed by the SCID?

The DSM-III-R diagnoses are Bipolar Disorder (Mania and Hypomania), Cyclothymia, Major Depression, Dysthymia, and Mood Disorders Not Otherwise Specified.

Who Administers the SCID?

A clinician who is familiar with psychopathology and experienced in differential diagnosis should administer the interview because clinician judgments for thresholds of criteria are required.

How Much Time Is Required to Administer the SCID?

A SCID may be administered in about one hour, but the time to administer will vary with the clinical condition of the respondent.

Reliability

Recently, the reliability of the SCID interview and its ability to differentiate between Major Depression and Generalized Anxiety Disorders was tested in 75 outpatients (Riskind, Beck, Berchick, Brown, & Steer, 1987). Interrater agreement for the clinician's initial diagnosis derived with the SCID interview and a second clinician's rating of the videotaped interview yielded high overall diagnostic agreement with 83 percent agreement and a Kappa coefficient of .74. Agreement for the SCID diagnosis of Major Depression was Kappa = .72, showing good agreement between raters for this diagnostic category. The SCID has been translated into Chinese and was used to diagnose 42 psychiatric inpatients hospitalized in China (Wilson & Young, 1988). An American psychiatrist conducted a SCID interview with patients, using a translator, and assigned DSM-III diagnoses. Within seven days a Chinese psychiatrist reinterviewed these patients without the SCID and assigned diagnoses using the Chinese system. Seventy-nine percent of the patients received the same diagnosis. The nine cases of disagreement were largely in the diagnostic category of Schizophrenia and Schizoaffective Disorders.

Validity

A comparison of the SCID and the DIS and their ability to derive similar diagnoses was tested on 41 inpatients hospitalized for the treatment of substance use, who were interviewed seven to 21 days after admission (Rounsaville, Kosten, Williams, & Spitzer, 1987). Diagnostic agreement between DSM-III (DIS interviews) and DSM-III-R (SCID interviews) was satisfactory for Alcohol, Barbiturates, and Cannabis use with Kappas of .78, .74, .77, respectively. The DSM-III-R system of diagnosis was shown to increase the likelihood of diagnosing individuals as meeting criteria for alcohol use because one of the DSM-III criteria, alcohol behavior leading to social consequences, has been removed. The SCID may also be sensitive for differentiating syndromes in which there is symptom similarity, such as Anxiety Disorders (Riskind et al., 1987). More information about the reliability and validity of the SCID will be forthcoming as the field trials are completed.

Scoring

The SCID interview contains a detailed summary score sheet which the clinician completes with use of the DSM-III-R manual for the diagnostic criteria. The SCID instruments are precoded for data entry. A computer scoring system is not currently available.

Availability

The SCID has been translated into several foreign languages and is being used in Japan, Puerto Rico, and China.

The SCID interviews come with a detailed instruction manual (Spitzer et al., 1988a). Instructional videotapes as well as SCID workshops are available for training in the use of the SCID.

Information about the SCID interviews and training may be obtained by writing to Robert Spitzer, MD, Janet B. Williams, PhD, or Miriam Gibbon, MSW, at Biometrics Research Department, New York State Psychiatric Institute, 722 West 168th Street, New York, NY 10032.

NEW INSTRUMENTS

The overwhelming popularity of structured diagnostic instruments for use both in research and in clinical settings has lead to continued work in the development of new instruments or the updating of more well established instruments. Information about these newer instruments may assist the interested reader in following further developments in the literature.

The Composite International Diagnostic Interview (CIDI)/International Statistical Classification of Diseases, Injuries, and Causes of Death, Ninth Revised Edition (ICD-9); DSM-III (1980) and DSM-III-R (1987)

In 1979 the World Health Organization (WHO) and the United States Alcohol, Drug Abuse, and Mental Health Administration (ADAMHA) began a collaboration to work toward establishing more uniform diagnostic definitions and criteria for the investigation of mental, alcohol, and drug disorders worldwide. A task force on diagnostic instruments had been mandated to create two diagnostic interviews, one to be used with clinical populations and the other with the general population. The Composite International Diagnostic Interview (CIDI; Robins et al., 1988) was created for the purpose of diagnostic assessment in the general population. To date, most European investigators have relied on the clinician-administered Present State Examination (PSE; Wing, Cooper, & Sartorius, 1974) and the International Statistical Classification of Diseases . . . (ICD-9; WHO, 1977). In the 1980s, use of the DIS with large segments of the United States population and with international populations convinced investigators of the feasibility of using this instrument for deriving diagnoses with the three diagnostic systems. Therefore, the development of the CIDI was based on combining 63 PSE items with the components and overall format of the DIS. The CIDI is similar in structure and format to the DIS. It is a structured interview that may be administered by a nonclinician. The questions are fully spelled out and the responses are codes in a closed-ended format. Clinical judgment is not a part of the decision-making process in the coding of responses. The CIDI is scored and the 40 DSM-III diagnostic categories (American Psychiatric Association, 1980) are derived with the use of a computer. Initial field trials of the CIDI began in 1988, and the CIDI is being tested worldwide at 19 sites (see Robins et al., 1988, pp. 1074–1075 for details). The CIDI will not only be updated to derive ICD-10 and DSM-III-R diagnoses but also will provide comparability to previous work in the field by retaining both DSM-III and PSE diagnoses.

In contrast to the CIDI, which will be used for the general population, the proposed international diagnostic instrument for use with clinical populations is the Schedule for Clinical Assessment in Neuropsychiatry (SCAN) (Robins et al., 1988). Information about this instrument will be forthcoming.

The creation of these diagnostic instruments and the development of more uniform criteria for diagnoses move investigators closer to the realization of the goals of more reliable cross-cultural comparisons, more uniform methods of communication about diagnoses, and more precise information about mental health worldwide.

SUMMARY

This chapter discussed the most reliable and frequently used interviewing methods available for the diagnosis of Affective Disorders. Interviews described are (a) the Schedule for Affective Disorders and Schizophrenia, (b) the Diagnostic Interview Schedule, (c) the Structured Clinical Interview for DSM-III-R, (d) the Composite International Diagnostic Interview, and (e) the Schedule for Clinical Assessment in Neuropsychiatry. Each interview method has been designed for use with a companion diagnostic system, (a) the Feighner Criteria, (b) the Research Diagnostic Criteria, (c) the Diagnostic and Statistical Manual of Mental Disorders, and (d) the International Statistical Classification of Diseases, Injuries, and Causes of Death. Descriptions were given about personnel qualified to administer the interviews, the time required, the scoring procedures and sources for obtaining the interview schedules. Finally, the diagnostic reliabilities, sensitivities, specificities, and documentation of the validity of diagnoses obtained with these interviewing methods were presented. This chapter will assist the clinician or researcher in choosing appropriate interviewing methods for the diagnosis and assessment of Affective Disorders.

REFERENCES

American Psychiatric Association. (1980). *Diagnostic and statistical manual of mental disorders* (3rd ed; DSM-III). Washington, DC: Author.

American Psychiatric Association. (1987). *Diagnostic and statistical manual of mental disorders* (3rd ed. rev. DSM-III-R). Washington, DC: Author.

Anthony, J. C., Folstein, M., Romanoski, A. J., VonKorff, M. R., Nestadt, G. R., Chahal, R., Merchant, A., Brown, C. H., Shapiro, S., Kramer, M., & Gruenberg, E. M. (1985). Comparison of the lay Diagnostic Interview Schedule and a standardized psychiatric diagnosis: Experience in eastern Baltimore. *Archives of General Psychiatry, 42,* 667–675.

Canino, G. J., Bird, H. R., Shrout, P. E., Rubio-Stipec, M., Bravo, M., Martinez, R., Sesman, M., Guzman, A., Guevara, L. M., & Costas, H. (1987). The Spanish Diagnostic Interview Schedule: Reliability and concordance with clinical diagnoses in Puerto Rico. *Archives of General Psychiatry, 44,* 720–726.

Comings, D. E. (1984). A computerized Diagnostic Interview Schedule (DIS) for psychiatric disorder. In M. D. Schwartz (Ed.), *Using Computers in Clinical Practice: Psychotherapy and Mental Health Applications.* (pp. 195–203). New York: Haworth Press.

Cornell, D. G., Milden, R. S., & Shimp, S. (1985). Stressful life events associated with endogenous depression. *Journal of Nervous and Mental Disease, 173,* 470–476.

DeJoghe, F., Ameling, E., & Assies, J. (1988). An elaborate description of the symptomatology of patients with Research Diagnostic Criteria endogenous depression. *Journal of Nervous and Mental Disease, 176,* 475–479.

Endicott, J., & Spitzer, R. L. (1978). A diagnostic interview: The Schedule for Affective Disorders and Schizophrenia. *Archives of General Psychiatry, 35,* 837–844.

Endicott, J., & Spitzer, R. L. (1979). Use of Research Diagnostic Criteria and the Schedule for Affective Disorders and Schizophrenia to study affective disorder. *American Journal of Psychiatry, 136,* 52–56.

Erdman, H. P., Klein, M. H., Greist, J. H., Bass, S. M., Bires, J. K., & Machtinger, P. E. (1987). A comparison of the Diagnostic Interview Schedule and clinical diagnosis. *American Journal of Psychiatry, 144,* 1477–1480.

Feighner, J. P., Robins, E., Guze, S. B., Woodruff, R. A., Winokur, G., & Muñoz, R. (1972). Diagnostic criteria for use in psychiatric research. *Archives of General Psychiatry, 26,* 57–63.

Gibbon, M., McDonald-Scott, P., & Endicott, J. (1981). Mastering the art of research interviewing. *Archives of General Psychiatry, 38,* 1259–1262.

Hamilton, M. (1960). A rating scale for depression. *Journal of Neurology, Neurosurgery and Psychiatry, 23,* 56–62.

Helzer, J. E., Robins, L. N., Croughan, J. L., & Welner, A. (1981). Renard Diagnostic Interview. *Archives of General Psychiatry, 38,* 393–398.

Helzer, J. E., Robins, L. N., McEvoy, L. T., Spitznagel, E. L., Stoltzman, R. K., Farmer, A., & Brockington, I. F. (1985). A comparison of clinical and Diagnostic Interview Schedule diagnoses: Physician reexamination of lay-interviewed cases in the general population. *Archives of General Psychiatry, 42,* 657–666.

Helzer, J. E., Spitznagel, E. L., & McEvoy, L. (1987). The predictive validity of lay Diagnostic Interview Schedule diagnoses in the general population: A comparison with physician examiners. *Archives of General Psychiatry, 44,* 1069–1077.

Hesselbrock, V., Stabenau, J., Hesselbrock, M., Mirkin, P., & Meyer, R. (1982). A comparison of two interview schedules: The Schedule for Affective Disorders and Schizophrenia—lifetime and the National Institute of Mental Health Diagnostic Interview Schedule. *Archives of General Psychiatry, 39,* 674–677.

Klerman, G. L. (1985). Diagnosis of psychiatric disorders in epidemiologic field studies. *Archives of General Psychiatry, 42,* 723–724.

Lustman, P. J., Harper, G. W., Griffith, L. S., & Clouse, R. E. (1986). Use of the Diagnostic Interview Schedule in patients with diabetes mellitus. *Journal of Nervous and Mental Disease, 174.* 743–746.

Regier, D. A., Myers, J. K., Kramer, M., Robins, L. N., Blazer, D. G., Hough, R. L., Eaton, W. W., & Locke, B. Z. (1984). The NIMH Epidemiologic Catchment Area Program: Historical context, major objectives, and study population characteristics. *Archives of General Psychiatry, 41,* 934–941.

Riskind, J. H., Beck, A. T., Berchick, R. J., Brown, G., & Steer, R. A. (1987). Reliability of DSM-III diagnoses for Major Depresssion and Generalized Anxiety Disorder using the Structured Clinical Interview for DSM-III. *Archives of General Psychiatry, 44,* 817–820.

Robins, L. N. (1985). Epidemiology: Reflections on testing the validity of psychiatric interviews. *Archives of General Psychiatry, 42,* 918–924.

Robins, L. N., Helzer, J. E., Croughan, J., & Ratcliff, K. S. (1981). National Institute of Mental Health Diagnostic Interview Schedule: Its history, characteristics, and validity. *Archives of General Psychiatry, 38,* 381–389.

Robins, L. N., Helzer, J. E., Ratcliff, K. S., & Seyfried, W. (1982). Validity of the Diagnostic Interview Schedule, version II: DSM-III diagnoses. *Psychological Medicine, 12,* 855–870.

Robins, L. N., Wing, J., Wittchen, H. U., Helzer, J. E., Babor, T. F., Burke, J., Farmer, A., Jablenski, A., Pickens, R., Regier, D. A., Sartorius, N., & Towle, L. H. (1988). The Composite International Diagnostic Interview: An epidemiologic instrument suitable for use in conjunction with different diagnostic systems and in different cultures. *Archives of General Psychiatry, 45,* 1069–1077.

Rounsaville, B. J., Kosten, T. R., Williams, J. B., & Spitzer, R. L. (1987). A field trial of DSM-III-R psychoactive substance dependence disorders. *American Journal of Psychiatry, 144,* 351–355.

Spitzer, R. L., Endicott, J., Cohen, J., & Fleiss, J. L. (1974). Constraints on the validity of computer diagnosis. *Archives of General Psychiatry, 31,* 197–203.

Spitzer, R. L., Endicott, J., & Robins, E. (1975). Clinical criteria for psychiatric diagnoses and DSM-III. *American Journal of Psychiatry, 132,* 1187–1192.

Spitzer, R. L., Endicott, J., & Robins, E. (1978). Research Diagnostic Criteria: Rationale and reliability. *Archives of General Psychiatry, 35,* 773–782.

Spitzer, R. L., Williams, J. B., Gibbon, M., & First, M. B. (1988a). *Instructional manual for the Structured Clinical Interview for DSM-III-R* (SCID, 6/1/88 Revision). Biometrics Research Department, New York State Psychiatric Institute.

Spitzer, R. L., Williams, J. B., Gibbon, M., & First, M. B. (1988b). *Structured Clinical Interview for DSM-III-R—Outpatient and Patient Versions* (SCID-OP 6/1/88, SCID-P 6/1/88). Biometrics Research Department, New York State Psychiatric Institute.

Wilson, L. G., & Young, D. (1988). Diagnosis of severely ill inpatients in China: A collaborative project using the Structured Clinical Interview for DSM-III (SCID). *Journal of Nervous and Mental Disease, 176,* 585–592.

Wing, J. K., Cooper, J. E., & Sartorius, N. (1974). *The description and classification of psychiatric symptoms: An instruction manual for the PSE and CATEGO system.* London: Cambridge University Press.

World Health Organization. (1977). *Manual of the International Statistical Classification of Diseases, Injuries, and Causes of Death* (Vol. 1, 9th rev.). Geneva: Author.

CHAPTER 12

The Projective Assessment
of Affective Disorders

PHILIP ERDBERG, PhD

*The gloomy person is one to whom everything looks black, while the cheerful person is
said to see everything through rose-colored glasses.*

[RORSCHACH, 1921/1942, p. 99.]

It is now well past half a century since Hermann Rorschach introduced his technique for the assessment of psychological structure and
function. From the very beginning, it was clear that projective methods, as they came to be known (Frank, 1939), had special utility in the
description of affective operations. Rorschach devoted considerable
attention in his 1921 *Psychodiagnostics* to theorizing and case discussion about disorders of affect. And essentially all of those who have
built on the foundation of Rorschach's work have underscored the
important role that projective techniques can play in the assessment of
affective operations (Beck, 1944; Bellack, 1986; Exner, 1986; Klopfer
& Kelley, 1942; Piotrowski, 1957; Rapaport, Gill, & Schafer, 1945).
Over the years, researchers and clinicians have identified a group of
projective variables that seem to have particular utility in the assessment of emotion. Within the past decade, workers have utilized discriminant techniques to analyze these variables and generate clusters
that are of value in the diagnosis of endogenous depression and suicide
potential. This chapter provides a discussion of these variables and the
clusters that can be generated from them.

CHROMATIC COLOR

There has been an ongoing sense that the use of chromatic color on the
Rorschach can be associated with affective operations. Rorschach
(1921) focused on the responsiveness to emotionally charged situations
signaled by the use of chromatic color in the production of responses.

Other workers have been more interested in utilizing chromatic color responses to describe the individual's modulation of emotional exchanges with the environment. The combination of these approaches allows the Rorschach to provide a two-stage model of affective operations: how open the individual is to processing emotionally complex material and how well controlled his or her affective responses to these situations will be.

The Rorschach's ability to provide data about how responsive an individual is to processing emotionally charged material depends on the proportion of chromatic color responses to other kinds of answers. As chromatic color increases, individuals are more easily hypnotized (Brennen & Richard, 1943), are more likely to alter their judgments on the basis of interaction with others (Linton, 1954), and are more likely to score high on a sensation-seeking measure (Exner, 1986). Exner followed Beck's approach in generating a variable called the affective ratio, to provide a single number indication of the individual's responsiveness to the Rorschach's three fully chromatic cards. Exner suggested that the ratio is associated with a "psychological receptiveness to emotionally provoking stimuli" (1986, p. 381), and presented data to show that it is normatively higher in younger children and decreases gradually through the developmental years to adulthood.

A second index that comes from an analysis of chromatic color operations on the Rorschach provides some data about the person's ability to modulate his or her emotional behavior when he or she does respond affectively. This variable is developed by calculating the balance of form-dominated (FC) color responses ("a pink flower that has that perfect bowl shape like a tulip") as opposed to more color-dominated (CF or C) percepts ("it just looks all red like blood"). This balance, which is called the FC:CF + C ratio, provides data about how well the individual is able to insert an objective component into responses in affectively charged situations. Younger children tend to load on the CF + C side of the ratio, while older teenagers and adults typically have about twice as much FC in their records as they do CF and C. Interestingly, only 47 percent of an adult outpatient character disorder sample had even one FC in their records as opposed to 98 percent of an adult nonpatient group. On the other hand, psychosomatic outpatients had records in which FC was typically around four times CF and C, suggesting emotional overcontrol in comparison with the 2:1 ratio that is expected with nonpatients (Exner, 1986, 1990a).

If we view the affective ratio as a measure of emotional responsivity and the FC:CF + C ratio as suggestive of ability to modulate affective behavior, the Rorschach can be helpful in providing a rather thorough description of affective responsivity and control. As noted, the changes in these variables over the developmental years are consistent with the increasing ability to limit responsivity and to structure emotional exchanges that characterize these years. In adulthood, high retest correlations (Exner, 1986) suggest that these variables tap an enduring aspect of affective operation.

ACHROMATIC COLOR

As Rorschach noted, the use of the achromatic color features of his inkblots may be associated with a dysphoric stance that involves the internalization of affect. Depressed patients are significantly more likely to articulate achromatic color when they describe how they produce their Rorschach responses, and these kinds of responses are also more frequent in individuals diagnosed as obsessive, psychosomatic, or schizoid. As depressed inpatients move toward discharge, they tend to give significantly fewer achromatic color responses than they did at the beginning of treatment. Achromatic color responses are also less frequent in individuals classified as passive-aggressive or sociopathic (Exner, 1986).

All of these findings tend to suggest that achromatic color signals the disequilibrium that occurs when affect is held in, regardless of the level of awareness that accompanies this defense. Data on a variety of depressive groups suggest that this internalization frequently may be relatively unconscious. But an interesting study (Exner, 1986) of delinquent adolescents currently undergoing dispositional evaluation indicated that they had more achromatic color in their records than a group of nondelinquent teenagers. These data suggest that the relatively conscious decision to limit affective interchanges which likely characterized the delinquents during evaluation was accompanied by a Rorschach elevation in achromatic color during that period. Interestingly, the use of achromatic color decreased significantly on retest after the dispositional decisions had been made.

VISTA

The use of the lighter–darker aspects of the Rorschach inkblots to create a sense of depth or dimensionality (vista) appears to be associated with a quite negative introspective process. These vista responses occur in 56 percent of inpatient depressives, a striking contrast to the 20 percent finding for adult nonpatients (Exner, 1990a). Vista appears associated with painful, unrealistic self-focus that is characterized by a significant tendency to maximize and distort problems. The individual is unable to put positive and negative aspects in perspective during this intensely negative self-evaluation, severely compromising self-esteem.

COLOR-SHADING BLENDS

The presence in a single Rorschach response of both a chromatic color and an achromatic color or lighter–darker shading variable (such as vista) is suggestive of a sort of approach–avoidance conflict in relation to the expression of affect. As noted above, chromatic color is associated with affective interaction with the environment, while achromatic color and shading signal the presence of much more internalized and painful emotional experiences. Applebaum and Colson (1968) speculated that these blends are associated with a conflict about the appropriateness of affective discharge that results in constriction of emotionally complex behavior.

EGOCENTRICITY INDEX

The egocentricity index (Exner, 1986) is a Rorschach-derived variable that has significant ability to describe the individual's assignment of importance to himself or herself in relation to others. If the egocentricity index is high, as it is in younger children, it is likely that the individual attaches more importance to self than to others. If this index is low, as it is for depressed individuals, it would appear that the person devalues himself or herself in comparison with others. As an example, Thomas, Exner, and Baker (1982) found that as the egocentrictiy index went lower, the difference between "real" and "ideal" self-descriptions on an adjective checklist became significantly greater. Exner (1986, p. 396) concluded that a low egocentricity index ". . . appears to signal negative self-esteem, that is, placing a low value on personal worth, probably because of a sense of failure to meet desires and/or expectations for oneself. It seems reasonably clear that a low Index is a precursor to an increase in the frequency and/or intensity of depressive experiences."

MORBID CONTENT

The presence of content that is described as dead, dying, spoiled, broken, or dysphoric is noteworthy in both inkblot and thematic apperception measures (Exner, 1986; Bellak, 1986). There is a significant negative relationship between morbid content on the Rorschach and the egocentricity index, suggesting the likelihood of damaged self-concept. Exner (1986) has also suggested the likelihood of a quite pessimistic stance for individuals whose Rorschach productions contain elevated amounts of morbid content.

To this point we have described a group of variables that would appear to be of value in the assessment of affective operations. Over the past several years, researchers have utilized discriminant function techniques to generate groups of Rorschach variables that could reliably separate individuals with affective disorders from the rest of the psychiatric population. It would appear that, at least to some extent, this is possible, and it is not surprising that some of the variables we have discussed turn out to play significant roles in these empirical findings. The next part of this chapter will discuss three such clusters, the suicide constellation, the depression index, and the coping deficit index.

SUICIDE CONSTELLATION

The Rorschach's ability to generate a cluster of variables that can identify suicide-prone individuals has been one focus of Exner's research for well over a decade. In 1977, a study by Exner and Wylie generated a constellation of variables that demonstrated 75 percent accuracy in identifying the Rorschachs of individuals who had effected suicide within sixty days of taking the test. A study reported later by Exner (1986) with a new sample of 101 effected suicides showed the test's ability to identify 83 percent of these individuals. If the group was subdivided in terms of the lethality of the act which had caused death, the constellation of Rorschach variables was able to identify 92 percent of these suicidal individuals while including only 12 percent false positives from a depressed but nonsuicidal group and no individuals from a nonpatient group. Although the suicide constellation is the most powerful psychometric measure currently available for the evaluation of suicide potential, it should be noted that Exner's study reported a false negative rate of 17 percent and the above-mentioned false positive rate of 12 percent with depressive controls. As Exner noted (1986, p. 411), there are ". . . clear relationships between demographic and/or behavioral variables and effected suicide, and it is unlikely that any test data, taken alone, will provide a greater discrimination of suicidal risk."

DEPRESSION AND COPING DEFICIT INDICES

Individuals eligible for diagnoses involving dysthymia or major affect disorder are quite varied. Because of this heterogeneity, initial attempts to generate a Rorschach cluster to discriminate individuals so diagnosed from the rest of the psychiatric population were largely unsuccessful (Exner, 1986). More recently, however, Exner (1990b) has reported some results which suggest substantial promise in the test's ability to help diagnosticians working within current nosologies.

In an attempt to understand the heterogeneity that characterizes patients who receive depressive diagnoses, Exner (1990b) reviewed the recent diagnostic and theoretical literature. It suggested that affective diagnoses are often given to patients who present with three relatively discrete clinical pictures: 1) emotional depression (tearful, distraught individuals), 2) cognitive depression (pessimistic, self-defeating individuals), and 3) helplessness (inadequate individuals with poor coping skills). He then studied 684 patients who could be placed in one of these three groups on the basis of clinical and diagnostic description. The emotionally depressed and cognitively depressed groups showed substantial overlap, but these two groups differed notably from the group whose clinical presentation was one of helplessness.

Exner then utilized a discriminant function methodology to develop an index, the Depression Index, that combines 15 Rorschach variables into seven tests. If the individual is positive for five of these tests, it is likely that he or she has significant depressive features of an emotional or cognitive nature. Findings of six or seven are highly suggestive that a primary diagnosis of some sort of depressive disorder will be given. Initial work with the Depression Index suggested that it was able to identify approximately 85% of the 471 patients whose diagnosis for affective disorders involved clinical presentations of either emotional or cognitive depression. In another group of impatient depressives 75% had findings of at least five on the Depression Index. False positive rates for this index were extremely low, with a 4% figure in a recent sample of 700 nonpatients (Exner, 1990a).

A second index followed in an attempt to identify that subset of individuals receiving depressive diagnoses whose clinical presentation was one of helplessness and inadequacy. This index, the Coping Deficit Index, combines ten Rorschach variables to make up five tests. Exner (1990b) reported that 81% of the 177 individuals not positive for the Depression Index and with a clinical presentation of helplessness were positive for the Coping Deficit Index if a cutoff score of at least four of the five tests was used. Again, false positives on the index were very low, approximately 3% for nonpatient adults.

The development of these two indices is promising in suggesting that the Rorschach may be specifically helpful for clinicians working within current diagnostic guidelines.

SUMMARY

A review of the topics we have discussed will suggest that projective techniques cover a substantial part of the spectrum of affective operations. Responsivity to emotion and the ability to modulate affective behavior, internalization of affect, and self-concept are the most important components for which projective assessment can provide information. The combination of these techniques with a variety of other approaches can provide the sort of comprehensive picture of an individual that ultimately results in effective intervention.

REFERENCES

Applebaum, S. A., & Colson, D. B. (1968). A reexamination of the color-shading Rorschach Test response. *Journal of Projective Techniques and Personality Assessment, 32,* 164.

Beck, S. J. (1944). *Rorschach's test. I. Basic processes.* New York: Grune & Stratton.

Bellak, L. (1986). *The TAT, CAT, and SAT in clinical use.* Larchmont, NY: Grune & Stratton.

Brennen, M., & Richard, S. (1943). Use of the Rorschach Test in predicting hypnotizability. *Bulletin of the Menninger Clinic, 7,* 183–187.

Exner, J. E. (1990a). *A Rorschach Workbook for the Comprehensive System* (3rd ed.). Asheville, NC: Rorschach Workshops.

Exner, J. E. (1990b). *Alumni Newsletter.* Asheville, NC: Rorschach Workshops.

Exner, J. E. (1986). *The Rorschach: A comprehensive system. Vol. 1* (2nd ed.). *Basic foundations.* New York: Wiley.

Exner, J. E., & Wylie, J. R. (1977). Some Rorschach data concerning suicide. *Journal of Personality Assessment, 41,* 339–348.

Frank, L. K. (1939). Projective methods for the study of personality. *Journal of Psychology, 8,* 343–389.

Klopfer, B., & Kelley, D. (1942). *The Rorschach technique.* Yonkers, NY: World Book.

Linton, H. B. (1954). Rorschach correlates of response to suggestion. *Journal of Abnormal and Social Psychology, 49,* 75–83.

Piotrowski, Z. (1957). *Perceptanalysis.* New York: Macmillan.

Rapaport, D., Gill, M., & Schafer, R. (1945). *Diagnostic psychological testing.* Chicago: Yearbook Publishers.

Rorschach, H. (1921). *Psychodiagnostik.* Bern: Bircher. (English translation, Bern: Hans Huber, 1942).

Thomas, E. E., Exner, J. E., & Baker, W. (1982). Ratings of real versus ideal self among 225 college students. Rorschach Workshops study no. 287 (unpublished).

CHAPTER 13

Inventories and Scales

DAVID J. BERNDT, PhD

The assessment of depression necessarily involves many levels of focus. An appropriate diagnosis, for example, may draw upon psychopharmacological evaluation, social and family history, structured diagnostic interviews, psychiatric and/or behavioral ratings, and self-report inventories and questionnaires. Since no one has yet isolated an effective phenotypical marker for depression, a combination of several of the above approaches is most appropriate, if diagnosis of major depressive disorder is the goal. However, when lack of resources and time forces clinicians and researchers alike to use only one of the above, inventories and scales, either self-reported or rated by others, may be relied upon with too little caution. These instruments, however, are useful when appropriately evaluated. This chapter discusses several of these instruments, with a focus on their reliability and validity.

Depression inventories and scales are most appropriately used for the assessment of severity and frequency of depressive symptoms and features. The analysis of symptom patterns is another frequent use. Because depressed individuals are relatively more accurate at self-reporting their states than are those with other psychiatric diagnoses (e.g., schizophrenia, behavior disorders), the usefulness of these measures is apparent.

The emergence of structured diagnostic interviews and more reliable diagnoses from objective standards such as Spitzer, Endicott, and Robins' (1978) Research Diagnostic Criteria (RDC) and DSM-III and DSM-IV (American Psychiatric Association, 1980, 1988) has had an immense impact on American psychiatry and psychology. No longer constrained by low agreement (reliability) between clinicians on diagnosis, researchers and clinicians alike are less hesitant to believe the accuracy of their diagnosis. A consequence of this new confidence is for a similar optimism to lead some researchers to use self-report or observer ratings of depression to actually identify cases. Research on case identification is minimal, and skepticism is necessary until researchers demonstrate that the diagnoses are accurate and valid. Until such research develops sufficient data, scales should be supplemented whenever possible by (minimally) a structured diagnostic interview.

This chapter will briefly discuss the history of self-report and observer rating scales. The four most widely used measures will be evaluated in considerable depth. Several newer instruments will then be more briefly discussed, many of which are still evolving and have yet to be comprehensively tested by the research community, despite their frequent use.

A BRIEF HISTORY OF INVENTORIES AND SCALES

A casual reader of today's literature might well conclude that only a few instruments, such as the Beck (Beck, Ward, Mendelson, Mock, & Erbaugh, 1961) Depression Inventory (BDI), are used in the assessment of depression. Four instruments, including the BDI, are currently the most widely used inventories and scales for the assessment of depression; they will be discussed in depth in the next section. However, these instruments emerged as the profession's standards within a historical context. This section briefly reviews the evolution of inventories and scales for the measurement of depression.

Jasper (1930) was the first to propose an instrument, the Depression–Elation Scale (D–E), that attempted to measure depression in a self-report format. Jasper envisioned his scale as tapping a general depression factor (Spearman, 1904). He assumed that not only depression–elation, but optimism–pessimism, and enthusiasm-apathy were all subsumed under a general single dimension. His 40-item trait measure of depression included 20 nonpersonal items focused on such topics as pessimism or apathy for sociopolitical institutions. The other 20 items resembled more closely today's subjective self-report items. All items were rated on a five-point scale and took into account how difficult it was to answer the question.

Chant and Myers (1936) were the first to employ Thurstone-type scaling to the assessment of depression. This instrument contained 22 items with values ranging from .3 for "I wish I had never been born" to 10.7 for "Life could not be better for me" (Chant & Myers, 1936, p. 35). The score was the average score of all items checked "yes."

Guilford and Guilford (1939) developed the third published scale that attempted to isolate depression from other constructs. The Guilfords developed their 17-item factor-D as part of an early study of introversion–extroversion, and were more concerned with personality than with psychopathology. The scale is remarkable in that it was the first instrument that benefited from the emerging reliance upon factor analysis to evaluate scales.

World War II brought psychology out of its academic confines and thrust it prominently into a clinical partnership with psychiatry, especially in the area of assessment. In depression studies, the self-report literature was dominated for two decades by Hathaway and McKinley's (1942) MMPI-D scale. The 60-item scale remains one of the most widely used measures, and will be evaluated in the next section.

Between the 1942 publication of the MMPI-D scale and 1967, the four most widely used measures gained their foothold. In 1961 a scale was published by a psychoanalytic psychiatrist (Beck et al., 1961), which went on to become the most widely used self-report measure of depression. In addition to its early arrival on the scene, low-cost distribution with no formal publisher, and psychometric improvement over the MMPI-D, the BDI's popularity was clearly tied to the fame of its author, who became a leading cognitive-behavioral theorist.

In 1965 the Zung Self-rating Depression Scale (SDS; Zung, 1965) gained a strong foothold, especially among physicians, who received free copies of the SDS from a manufacturer of antidepressant medication. The primary alternatives to these three measures have been observer-rating scales, the most widely used of which is Hamilton's (1967).

In the following decades, other inventories and scales evolved. Lubin (1965) developed an adjective checklist that permitted a quick state measure with several parallel forms. Wessman and Ricks (1966) developed an instrument specifically for assessment of repeated measures. Their scale was the first to provide the advantage of measuring 16 different affects. The measures, however, were theoretically derived and have not been properly evaluated psychometrically.

Costello and Comrey (1967) were the first researchers to develop a depression scale that specifically reduces the role of anxiety. A very thorough research process resulted in two orthogonal measures of trait anxiety and depression. Other scales developed in the late 1960s included a psychodynamically oriented scale by Leckie and Withers (1967), and another attempt at multiple symptom assessment by Hunt, Singer, and Cobb (1967). Internal consistency for the measure by Hunt et al. was unacceptably poor for the individual symptoms. Popoff's (1969) brief test was aimed at measuring depression in medical populations, with several "covert" items derived to detect somatization of depression.

Two of the more innovative measures of depression were developed in the late 1960s and 1970s. The Visual Analogue Scale (Aitken, 1969) is a simple and useful state measure of depression. In its modified form it is simply a 100-mm line. Respondents are asked to indicate their current mood by placing a mark on the line between the anchors "worst" and "best." Another measure, developed by Cohen and Rau (1972), requires respondents to select faces that represent how they feel. Both measures share the advantages of requiring minimal literacy and possibly offering less cultural bias than most other instruments.

Surprisingly few inventories have emerged in the 1970s and 1980s. The 40-item Institute for Personality and Ability Testing (IPAT) Depression Scale was developed by Krug and Laughlin (1976). The most recently developed observer-rating scale, by Montgomery and Asberg (1979), has received little attention outside of Britain. The Wakefield Scale (Snaith, Ahmed, Mehta, & Hamilton, 1971) evolved into the Leeds Scale (Snaith, Bridge, & Hamilton, 1976), which is, again, used primarily by the Europeans.

Several instruments that emerged from this period have, however, begun to receive wider attention. Perhaps the best known is Radloff's (1977) Center for Epidemiological Studies Depression Scale (CES-D). Its 20 items were a composite of items from other scales. In part because of its use in a national epidemiological study, Radloff's instrument rapidly captured the interest of researchers.

The Carroll Rating Scale for Depression (Carroll, Fielding, & Blashki, 1973) is a self-report measure that translates the Hamilton (1967) Rating Scale for Depression (HRSD) to self-report format. It is widely used in drug studies, and by those who share Hamilton's concern that the Beck and other self-report instruments focus too closely on mood and ignore somatic components.

The Multiscore Depression Inventory (Berndt, Petzel, & Berndt, 1980) was the first depression inventory to develop reliable subscales for 10 features of depression. It is also available in a brief 47-item format that measures nine of the 10 symptoms and features. A comparable children's form is also available (Berndt & Kaiser, in press).

The Depressive Experiences Questionnaire (Blatt, D'Afflitti, & Quinlan, 1976) is derived from psychodynamic literature, and is popular among researchers who are interested in Blatt's et al. (1976) concepts of anaclitic and introjective depression.

EVALUATION OF FOUR WIDELY USED SCALES

Four inventories and scales are clearly the most widely used by most researchers and clinicians. As noted earlier, the Beck Depression Inventory (BDI) (Beck et al., 1961) is used by psychology researchers almost to the exclusion of even the other three major instruments (Berndt et al., 1980). Because these four instruments are so widely used, they will be discussed and evaluated in depth. In the next section, four promising instruments that are emerging as important contributions to assessment of depression will be more briefly evaluated.

The Beck Depression Inventory (BDI)

The most widely used self-report measure of depression is the Beck Depression Inventory. Although initially designed to be administered by trained interviewers, the 21-item scale with a four-alternative multiple-choice format quickly circulated in self-report format throughout academic and clinical settings. Despite its widespread use, the BDI was revised in 1971 and copyrighted in 1978 (Beck, Rush, Shaw, & Emery, 1979). It may be purchased from test publishers and is available for computerized administration and scoring.

The BDI reflects nearly 30 years of research and well over 1,000 studies. Few comprehensive reviews of its psychometric properties have been published outside of Beck's own group. The most thorough review to date is a paper by Beck, Steer, and Garbin (1988).

Description

Most authors fail to distinguish between the 1961 (Beck et al., 1961) and 1978 (Beck et al., 1979) copyrighted versions of the BDI. Beck et al. (1988) point out that only 6 of the 21 items remain unchanged. Beck and Steer (1984) analyzed internal consistency and item properties of the original and revised versions, and concluded that they were similar, and Lightfoot and Oliver (1985) found high correlation between the two instruments in college students ($r = .94$), although the 1961 version had slightly lower mean scores than the 1978 version. Future users of the BDI should clearly indicate which of the two versions they use.

A short (13-item) version of the BDI (Beck & Beck, 1972) has also been used. Although the forms correlate well, little research has been done on the short form, and the factor structure appears significantly different (Berndt, 1979; Gould, 1982). Reliability appears adequate from the studies cited, but the short form must be used with caution at this stage, until it has received more comprehensive study.

Reliability

One reason the BDI gained its foothold across the country is that it was the first self-report measure with good reliability. Internal consistency ranges from a low of .73 (Gallagher, Nies, & Thompson, 1982) in a nonclinical population to .95 in two studies (Coleman & Miller, 1975; Steer, McElroy, & Beck, 1982). Internal consistency appears adequate for both clinical and nonclinical samples, with the psychiatric samples generally midway between .80 and .90 and the nonpsychiatric samples at a comparable reading.

Test–retest reliability is complicated to evaluate because the 1961 form's instructions were phrased more as a state measure and the 1978 version's instructions implied desire for a traitlike response. Because few researchers differentiate the versions, it is not a simple task to evaluate. Two of the lowest test–retest reliabilities were published with the state instructions. Bailey and Coppen (1976) reported $r = .65$ over one week, and May, Urquhart, and Tarran (1969) reported a three-week reliability of .48. Both of these studies used psychiatric samples, which may have contributed more variability.

In nonpsychiatric samples, the highest test–retest reliability reported was by Lightfoot and Oliver (1985) over two weeks (.90). More typical coefficients were in the .60s and .70s, still appropriate for periods from one week to four months.

Validity

Because so much research has been done with the BDI, a tremendous amount of validity data exist. Concurrent validity correlation coefficients have been, on average, in the .70s for the HRSD (Davies, Burrows, & Poyton, 1975), although the range is from a low of .41 (Carroll et al., 1973) to a high of .86 (Steer, Beck, & Garrison, 1986). Among self-report measures, the worst concurrent validity is with the MMPI-D scale (at least nine studies below .65), although these results may reflect more upon psychometric properties with the MMPI-D scale than the BDI. Correlations with the Zung have tended to be adequate (Blatt, Quinlan, Chevron, McDonald, & Zuroff, 1982), with the exception of some studies with nonclinical samples. Lubin's (1965) Depressive Adjective Checklist (DACL) is most frequently used in nonclinical samples, where correlations are routinely below .70; however, in a clinical sample (Byerly & Carlson, 1982) the correlation was .73. Correlation with the Multiscore Depression Inventory (Berndt, Berndt, & Byars, 1983) was .76 in a medical sample.

Construct validity is extensive for the BDI, and relevant variables from REM sleep difficulty (Akiskal, Lemmi, Yerevanian, King, & Belluomini, 1982) to suicidal behaviors (Emery, Steer, & Beck, 1981) have demonstrated its usefulness. Factorial structure has been studied in at least 20 studies (see review in Beck et al., 1988).

Final Comments

Several problems with the BDI must be kept in mind. First, in nonclinical populations there is tremendous skew, making sensitivity to subtle changes in mood hard to measure. The Carroll et al. (1973) concerns, that self-report measures like the BDI do not go beyond mood, are still noteworthy, and it is best to combine the BDI with either a structured diagnostic interview or an observer rating. The BDI warrants use for research and clinical purposes as a measure of severity of depressed mood, or as a screening measure to detect possible cases of depression.

MMPI-D

The MMPI-D (depression) scale (Hathaway & McKinley, 1942) is the "grandaddy" of all depression self-report measures, and still is used frequently, either as part of the entire inventory or as a 60-item true–false scale. Hindsight permits easy criticism of the MMPI-D scale for its psychometric failures, but readers should remember that at the time it was developed it was far superior to any similar measure, and most of today's psychometric concerns evolved out of research that attempted to improve the MMPI and its scales. The publishers are revising the MMPI; the long-awaited revision is imminent. Perhaps some of the criticisms raised here will be remedied in the version for the 1990s.

Reliability and Cohesiveness

One troublesome problem for researchers is the lack of homogeneity of the scale. Internal consistency reliabilities are below acceptable standards. Test–retest reliability is comparably low. The problem arises from the lack of a cohesive construct. Factor-analytic studies (Comrey, 1957; O'Conner, Stefic, & Gresock, 1957) have demonstrated that the scale is factorially complex. For example, among 60 items, Comrey found nine factors, and the one appearing to measure depression consisted of only five items that loaded higher than .30. More recently, construct validity of the original scale was disputed on the grounds that it measures personality rather than illness (Snaith et al., 1971).

Several authors attempted to improve on the original scale by refinement. McCall (1958) found 26 items from the original 60 which he determined to be face valid: The 26 items did discriminate better than the other items between a depressed and nondepressed clinical sample. Similarly, Dempsey (1964) developed a short version of the MMPI-D and isolated a single dimension. The item scale had better internal consistency, but it shared many items with Comrey's (1957) largest factor, described as measuring neuroticism.

Cantor's (1960) attempt to develop a short form appears to have been more widely accepted because of adequate internal consistency and some evidence of concurrent validity. Stein (1968) used the entire MMPI item pool and derived clusters, one of which was labeled depression and apathy (versus positive and optimistic outlook), although the cluster shared only 10 items with the original scale. Rosen's (1962) Depression Reaction Scale was also developed empirically, by choosing items that discriminated a group of neurotic depressives from other psychiatric patients. The 42 items shared only four items with the MMPI-D. The most true to the original scale was the revision by Harris and Lingoes (1955), and the depression measure computed by them is now used frequently.

Not one of these scales, however, was developed with the benefit of the increased reliability and validity of diagnosis gained from structured diagnostic interviews and objective criteria such as DSM-III and DSM-IV (American Psychiatric Association, 1980, 1988). The next revision, it is hoped, will use modern methods to isolate items that are psychometrically sound.

Validity

Lacking construct validity, the complex MMPI-D scale has been difficult to validate, although among hundreds of publications many studies do support its usefulness. Typical of the critical studies, however, is one by McNair (1974), which demonstrated that the MMPI-D is less sensitive to drug intervention than other scales are. Correlations with concurrent measures demonstrate that the 60-item version is clearly below today's psychometric standards (Beck et al., 1988; Blatt et al., 1982).

Most of the credible evidence for validity comes from the use of the scale in combination with other scales on the MMPI. Profile analyses are widely accepted among users of the MMPI. Dahlstrom, Welsh, and Dahlstrom (1972) concluded that none of the revisions was superior to the original scale, and most researchers who use it rely primarily on profile analyses.

Summary and Evaluation

The MMPI-D scale is still widely used, despite its need for modernization. The forthcoming MMPI-II (Hathaway & McKinley, 1989) will probably remedy some of the problems. Clinicians and researchers continue to use it because of its ease of administration (especially computerized versions) and the continued popularity of the original MMPI in its entirety. There is little support for the use of the 60-item scale, although it may still be useful in profile analyses.

One very major concern is the poor normative basis for computation of scores. While some publishers provide up-to-date normative data, the Minnesota group awaits the revision and continues to rely on old norms not appropriately general or stratified by age or geography.*

---

* The MMPI-II manual was received just prior to this volume's press date. Few changes have been made to the MMPI-D scale. Three items were affected. The major problems discussed above appear to have been carried into the revised version. The most obvious deficiency is the continued lack of adolescent norms. The publisher had reassured this author that the standard and computerized versions of the revised version would have adequate adolescent norms, unlike the current version. The manual (Hathaway & McKinley, 1989) instead refers readers back to the original norms, which were inappropriate at best. Other publishers do have well-developed adolescent norms, including some computerized versions, but the user must be alert to this major omission in the version distributed by the owners of the copyrighted version.

This is most problematic with the use of the MMPI for adolescents, who, when compared with the 1940s normal adults, appear depressed. This problem disappears for published versions that use good adolescent norms.

Computer users especially should be careful to see that clients are evaluated with the appropriate age norms; the failure to do so may well violate ethics of psychology and other responsible professions. Computer versions of the MMPI are useful if supported by sound clinical interpretation by a qualified psychologist. A good discussion of several computerized versions of the MMPI is in a book by Lachar (1974).

Zung Self-Rating Depression Scale

Zung's (1965) Self-Rating Depression Scale (SDS) has been one of the most widely used measuring instruments, especially in psychiatric and medical settings. Its ease of use and of scoring is its most attractive feature. Twenty items require respondents to rate themselves on four-point, Likert-type scales, anchored by the extremes of "none or little of the time" and "most or all of the time." The scale is balanced: half the items are symptomatically negative, the other half are positive. It is particularly easy to score with a plastic overlay, and it is available also in interviewer rating scale form (Zung, 1972).

The SDS, like all well-known instruments, is not without its detractors. Because the items were taken verbatim from interviews of psychiatric patients, the wording is considered objectionable by some nonpsychiatric patients (Froese, Vasquez, Cassem, & Hackett, 1974). Hamilton (1972) criticized the scale for not including items on hypochondriasis, guilt, and retardation; Hamilton also believed the suicide question was poorly written. Another problem is that the anchor points, representing frequency of occurrence, result in mild, persistent symptoms counting more than severe, infrequent symptoms (Carroll et al., 1973). For chronic patients, the requirement to compare their present state with previous conditions presents difficulties.

Reliability

Surprisingly little research on reliability has been reported for the Zung. Knight, Waal-Manning, and Spears (1983) report an alpha coefficient of .79, which is modest but adequate. Evaluation of test–retest reliability remains a question for future researchers.

Validity

While there is a paucity of information on reliability, its widespread use provides considerable information on its validity. McNair (1974) pointed out that it is one of the more sensitive instruments in studies evaluating drug interventions. Adequate-to-good validity coefficients are obtained with the HRSD, the BDI, and the Multiscore Depression Inventory (Berndt, 1986; Brown & Zung, 1972; Turner & Romano, 1984; Zung, 1965).

The SDS appears to discriminate depressed patients from nondepressed patients and normal respondents (Zung, 1965). With outpatients or less severely depressed patients, its ability to discriminate severity of depression seems less clear. Although Biggs, Wylie, and Ziegler (1978) reported different scores by level of rated depression in outpatients, Carroll et al. (1973) found the SDS inadequate for severity ratings.

Summary and Evaluation

Zung's SDS, with its ease of use and established validity with inpatients, will continue to be used, especially in inpatient studies on effectiveness of interventions. More reliability data, especially test–retest, are needed, and, because of its extreme wording and still unproven validity in less severely depressed settings, the SDS must be used with caution in non-inpatient or nonpsychiatric settings. As a screening instrument it may have some value, but recommended cutoff scores should not be substituted for diagnosis.

The Hamilton Rating Scale for Depression (HRSD)

Although other rating scales of depression are preferred, the first (Hamilton, 1960) remains the most widely used today. The HRSD can be administered independently, or extracted from the structured SADS (Schedule for Affective Disorders and Schizophrenia) interview (Endicott & Spitzer, 1978).

The original scale involved 21 items, only 17 of which were to be counted in a total score, following a brief interview (Hamilton, 1960). The current instrument has evolved from two modifications of the original HRSD. Anchor points for each of the items were added. Of the original 17 items, nine are five-point scales (0–4) and eight are three-point scales (0–2). In addition, three items assessing helplessness, hopelessness, and worthlessness were added for the NIMH Treatment of Depression Collaborative Research Project (Elkin, Parloff, Hadley, & Autry, 1985).

Rating scales such as the HRSD have certain advantages over self-report measures. Foremost is the ability to rate noncognitive measures such as retardation. Another significant asset is that lack of literacy or severe disorganization of the patient does not disrupt the assessment.

Reliability

The most thorough evaluation of the psychometric properties of the HRSD may be found in a review by Hedlund and Vieweg (1979). Sparse information on internal consistency exists, and with the authors' intent to assess a heterogeneous set of symptoms, low internal consistency is not surprising. Schwab, Bialow, and Holzer (1967) reported item-total correlations ranging from .45 to .78; however, Bech, Bolwig, Kramp, and Refaelsen (1979) reported item correlation with a median of .47 and a range from − .02 to .81. Some of the items may detract from the usefulness of the HRSD as a global measure of severity, and this warrants further research.

More important, however, is interrater reliability. Published materials by the author leave considerable ambiguity for rater training, and it is surprising that interrater reliability has been remarkably good. Hedlund and Vieweg's (1979) review found nine studies with interrater reliability of .84 or above, and only one with a reliability inadequately low. O'Hara and Rehm (1983) found that acceptable reliability ($r = .76$) could be achieved with undergraduates who had been trained for only five hours. Most researchers employing the SADS have both skill and training, so the version extracted from the structured interview is likely to be reliable. Evidence from Endicott, Cohen, Nee, Fleiss, & Sarantakos, (1981) indicated such interrater reliability may be in the low .90s.

Validity

The review by Hedlund and Vieweg (1979) provided the best discussion. The scale demonstrated adequate concurrent validity, whether with clinicians' ratings, the BDI, the SDS, or the Multiscore Depression Inventory (Berndt, 1986; Hedlund & Vieweg, 1979).

The HRSD has been widely used to assess the impact of therapeutic interventions, whether psychopharmacological or psychotherapeutic, as in the NIMH Collaborative Research Project. One problematic tendency is to use a specified criterion for defining a case, most typically a cutoff score of 17 for inpatients (see Endicott et al., 1981) or 14 for outpatients (Sotsky & Glass, 1983). When such a criterion is combined with a structured diagnostic interview and preferably other criteria as well, then such a cutoff may be useful. Even in these circumstances, further research must clarify the optimum level for specificity and sensitivity.

Summary and Evaluation

The Hamilton (1960, 1967) Rating Scale for Depression is the most widely used rating scale for depression. It has impressive interrater reliability and considerable evidence of validity, but further research on reliability (internal consistency and test–retest) may improve the scale. With further psychometric study, this long-time standard might be improved by enhancement of internal consistency, if validity is not sacrificed.

Used with self-report and/or interviews like the SADS, the HRSD makes an excellent addition to an assessment battery when identifying "cases." As a measure of severity of depression it also seems an excellent choice as a complement to a more mood-oriented self-report measure.

OTHER INVENTORIES AND SCALES

While the BDI, SDS, HRSD, and MMPI-D are the best known instruments, several others have received increasing attention in recent years and fill needs not met directly by these four instruments. This section focuses on instruments that have made important contributions to the literature and show promise of having greater impact in ensuing years.

CES-D

Radloff's (1977) Center for Epidemiological Studies Depression Scale may be the best-normed trait measure of self-reported depression. It was used in a large national epidemiological study and while the results are not available to the public, the eventual publication of complete norms, stratified by a variety of demographic variables, will increase the usefulness of the scale. A 20-item composite of several other scales, the CES-D is brief to administer; individuals are asked to respond to a scale (0–3) on the basis of frequency of occurrence during the prior week, with 0 for no days, and 3 for five to seven days.

Internal consistency reliability of the CES-D is good. For patient groups, coefficient alpha and Spearman-Brown coefficients were .90 and .92; for normal respondents, they were in the mid .80s. Test–retest reliability after six months was an adequate .54 (Radloff, 1977). Correlations with concurrent measures are favorable, ranging from .70 with Lubin's DACL (1965) to .81 with the BDI and .90 with the Zung SDS (1965) in recovered depressed patients (Weissman, Prusoff, & Newberry, 1975).

The biggest problem with self-report measures is reliance on cutoff scores from one instrument. The author recommends a cutoff of 16, and while this has sufficed for some research with adults, it has been problematic, especially with false negatives, for adolescents (Boyd, Weissman, Thompson, & Myers, 1982; Lewinsohn & Teri, 1982). Lack of specificity and sensitivity may be problematic for researchers, but clinicians tempted to use cutoff scores with this or other self-report measures should consider the consequences of missing 34–36 percent of depressed patients, or overdiagnosing the disorder by a 2:1 ratio.

In fairness, this problem exists throughout assessment, where a simple cutoff score facilitates research design or provides easy "rules of thumb" for students. Even in the "hard" sciences, sensitivity and specificity are not better with the dexamethasone suppression test. As mentioned at the beginning of the chapter, a combination of two or three levels of assessment is preferable.

The Multiscore Depression Inventory

Only one of the current depression scales in wide use provides reliable scores for a variety of subscales assessing "symptoms and features" of depression. The Multiscore Depression Inventory (MDI; Berndt, 1986; Berndt et al., 1980) is too recently published to have been held to the close scrutiny of many of the instruments reviewed, but the initial evidence is encouraging. Lanyon (1984) described the MDI as being developed with "extensive care," and with potential for good validity.

The MDI measures a global "severity" of depression in a trait format and provides 10 nonoverlapping subscales that measure guilt, lack of energy, irritability, learned and instrumental helplessness, sad mood, pessimism, low self-esteem, social introversion, and cognitive difficulty. A brief (47-item) version (Berndt, Petzel, & Kaiser, 1983) takes only 10 minutes and provides reliable scores on nine of the ten subscales. The full-scale MDI consists of 118 items with a yes/no forced-choice format. It is easily scored using a plastic overlay, and a computerized testing report is also available from the publisher.

Internal consistency of the global scale is an impressive .97 with a medical outpatient sample (Berndt, Berndt, & Byars, 1983). The same study reported subscale reliabilities in the high .80s and low .90s for most of the 12-item subscales. The briefer scale (Berndt, Berndt, & Byars, 1983) sacrifices very little internal consistency. Test–retest reliability for this instrument is the highest of all measures surveyed (Berndt & Kaiser, 1980) and most of the subscales also remain stable over a 3–4-week period, with the exception of instrumental helplessness.

Concurrent validity with the BDI, SDS, DACL, Popoff, and Zung are all above .70 (Berndt, 1986; Berndt, Petzel, & Kaiser, 1983). Some initial validity evidence supports the MDI's usefulness with clinical subgroups, but much of the research using profile analyses, such as the study comparing inpatient depressed and conduct-disordered patients (Berndt & Zinn, 1982), awaits replication by independent researchers.

The MDI demonstrates a consistent factor structure, and both factor and cluster analyses support the validity of the separate subscales (Berndt, 1981). The short form's factor structure is consistent with results from the long form, which led the authors to eliminate one subscale that did not hold up under analysis (Berndt, Berndt, & Kaiser, 1984).

Normative and validity data for adolescents are available for the MDI (Berndt, 1986), but the children's version (Berndt & Kaiser, in press) may prove more useful with younger patients. A unique aspect of the children's adaptation is the use by Berndt and Kaiser of children to generate the items, which were subsequently refined empirically. Normative data are available for ages eight through eighteen. Computerized reports can be obtained from the test publisher, but as always should be interpreted by a trained psychologist.

Depression Adjective Checklist

Lubin's (1965) Depression Adjective Checklist (DACL), the first state measure of depression, is useful in research projects looking for transient mood changes. The checklist format takes only 2–3 minutes for 32–34 adjectives, and the adjectives have high face validity. The multiple forms permit repeated assessments without the contamination of using the same instrument more than once.

Internal consistency is quite good, from .80 to .93 (Lubin, 1965); test–retest reliability over short intervals is similarly good. While concurrent validity evidence is not high, the instrument is different from most other measures in its focus on mood and its purely state format. It is also the least confounded with social desirability, of all the depression scales discussed (Christenfeld, Lubin, & Satin, 1978).

Carroll Rating Scale for Depression

Another measure (Carroll, Feinberg, Smouse, Rawson, & Greden, 1981) that gained quick recognition is the Carroll Rating Scale for Depression (CRS). The CRS follows the more heterogeneous item content of the HRSD. As such, the CRS attempts to go beyond depressive mood items, and more somatic items are included.

The 52-item scale has a yes/no forced-choice format. While the correspondence between the two measures is not one for one, 13 of the 17 CRS items correlated more strongly with their item counterpart on the HRSD than with other items. Also in common with the HRSD is some problem with heterogeneity. Although initial reliability (split-half) was .87, the individual item-total correlations ranged from .05 to .78. Again, the new scale will inevitably be refined and either removing or revising some items will improve the scale.

Concurrent validity data indicate that the CRS and HRSD correlate .71 to .80, and .76 with the BDI (Carroll et al., 1981; Feinberg, Carroll, Smouse, & Rawson, 1981). There is some question whether the CRS is comparable with the HRSD for assessment of severity with moderate to high severity depression (Feinberg et al., 1981).

Factor-analytic and construct validation of the CRS await further research. Nevertheless, because of Carroll's deserved reputation in the psychiatric research community, the scale will see continued use in the future.

SUMMARY

Inventories and scales for the assessment of depression are useful tools for researchers and clinicians who use them with appropriate awareness of their strengths and weaknesses.

Although the Beck Depression Inventory is the most popular, several other instruments have usefulness for different purposes, and no one instrument is particularly useful in isolation. In combination with the structured diagnostic interviews developed in the past two decades and objective diagnostic criteria, these instruments can be useful as measures of severity, as screening devices, or for assessment of the course and symptomatology of depression.

REFERENCES

Aitken, R. C. B. (1969). Measurement of feelings using visual analogue scales. *Proceedings of the Royal Society of Medicine, 62,* 989–993.

Akiskal, H. S., Lemmi, H., Yerevanian, B., King, D., & Belluomini, J. (1982). The utility of the REM latency in psychiatric diagnosis: A study of 81 depressed outpatients. *Psychiatry Research, 7,* 101–110.

American Psychiatric Association. (1980). *Diagnostic and statistical manual of mental disorders* (3rd ed.). Washington, DC: Author.

American Psychiatric Association. (1988). *Diagnostic and statistical manual of mental disorders* (4th ed.). Washington, DC: Author.

Bailey, J., & Coppen, A. (1976). A comparison between the Hamilton Rating Scale and the Beck Inventory in the measurement of depression. *British Journal of Psychiatry, 128,* 486–489.

Bech, P., Bolwig, T., Kramp, P., & Refaelsen, O. (1979). The Beck–Refaelsen Mania Scale and the Hamilton Depression Scale. *Acta Psychiatrica Scandinavia, 59,* 420–430.

Beck, A. T., & Beck, R. W. (1972). Screening depressed patients in family practice. A rapid technique. *Postgraduate Medicine, 52,* 81–85.

Beck, A. T., Rush, A. J., Shaw, B. F., & Emery, G. (1979). *Cognitive therapy of depression.* New York: Guilford Press.

Beck, A. T., & Steer, R. A. (1984). Internal consistencies of the original and revised Beck Depression Inventories. *Journal of Clinical Psychology, 40,* 1365–1367.

Beck, A. T., Steer, R. A., & Garbin, M. G. (1988). Psychometric properties of the Beck Depression Inventory: 25 years of evaluation. *Clinical Psychology Review, 8,* 77–100.

Beck, A. T., Ward, C. H., Mendelson, M., Mock, J., & Erbaugh, J. (1961). An inventory for measuring depression. *Archives of General Psychiatry, 4,* 561–571.

Berndt, D. J. (1979). Taking items out of context: Dimensional shifts with the short form of the Beck Depression Inventory. *Psychological Reports, 45,* 569–570.

Berndt, D. J. (1981). How valid are the subscales of the Multiscore Depression Inventory? *Journal of Clinical Psychology, 37,* 564–570.

Berndt, D. J. (1986) *Multiscore Depression Inventory Manual.* Los Angeles: Western Psychological Services.

Berndt, S. M., Berndt, D. J., & Byars, W. D. (1983). A multiinstitutional study of depression in family practice. *Journal of Family Practice, 16,* 83–87.

Berndt, D. J., Berndt, S. M., & Kaiser, C. F. (1984). Multidimensional assessment of depression. *Journal of Personality Assessment, 48,* 489–494.

Berndt, D. J., & Kaiser, C. F. (1980). An exploration of some reliability results for the Multiscore Depression Inventory. *Psychological Reports, 47,* 823–826.

Berndt, D. J., & Kaiser, C. F. (in press). *Manual for children's version of the Multiscore Depression Inventory.* Los Angeles: Western Psychological Services.

Berndt, D. J., Petzel, T., & Berndt, S. M. (1980). Development and initial evaluation of a Multiscore Depression Inventory. *Journal of Personality Assessment, 44,* 396–403.

Berndt, D. J., Petzel, T. P., & Kaiser, C. F. (1983). Evaluation of a short form of the Multiscore Depression Inventory. *Journal of Consulting and Clinical Psychology, 51,* 790–791.

Berndt, D. J., & Zinn, D. (1982). Prominent features of depression in affective and conduct-disordered inpatients. In D. Offer, K. Howard, & E. Ostrov (Eds.), *Patterns of adolescent self-image* (pp. 45–56). San Francisco: Jossey-Bass.

Biggs, J. T., Wylie, L. T., & Ziegler, V. E. (1978). Validity of the Zung Self-Rating Depression Scale. *British Journal of Psychiatry, 132,* 381–385.

Blatt, S. J., D'Afflitti, J., & Quinlan, D. M. (1976). Experiences of depression in normal young adults. *Journal of Abnormal Psychology, 85,* 383–389.

Blatt, S. J., Quinlan, D. M., Chevron, E. S., McDonald, C., & Zuroff, D. (1982). Dependency and self-criticism: Psychological dimensions of depression. *Journal of Consulting and Clinical Psychology, 50,* 113–115.

Boyd, J. H., Weissman, M. M., Thompson, W. D., & Myers, J. K. (1982). Screening for depression in a community sample. Understanding the discrepancies between depression symptom and diagnostic scales. *Archives of General Psychiatry, 39,* 1195.

Brown, G. L., & Zung, W. W. K. (1972). Depression scales: Self-physician-rating? A validation of certain clinincally observable phenomena. *Comprehensive Psychiatry, 13,* 361–367.

Byerly, F. C., & Carlson, W. A. (1982). Comparison among inpatients, outpatients, and normals on three self-report depression inventories. *Journal of Clinical Psychology, 38,* 797–804.

Cantor, A. (1960). The efficacy of a short form of the MMPI to evaluate depression and morale loss. *Journal of Consulting Psychology, 24,* 14.

Carroll, B. J., Feinberg, M., Smouse, P. E., Rawson, S. G., & Greden, J. F. (1981). The Carroll Rating Scale for Depression I. Development, reliability and validation. *British Journal of Psychiatry, 138,* 194–200.

Carroll B. J., Fielding, J. M., & Blashki, T. G. (1973). Depression rating scales: A critical review. *Archives of General Psychiatry, 28,* 361–366.

Chant, S. N. F., & Myers, C. R. (1936). An approach to the measurement of mental health. *American Journal of Orthopsychiatry, 6,* 134–140.

Christenfeld, R., Lubin, B., & Satin, M. (1978). Concurrent validity of the depression adjective checklist in a normal population. *American Journal of Psychiatry, 135,* 582–584.

Cohen, B. D., & Rau, J. H. (1972). Nonverbal technique for measuring affect using facial expression photographs as stimuli. *Journal of Consulting and Clinical Psychology, 38,* 449–451.

Coleman, R. E., & Miller, A. J. (1975). The relationship between depression and marital maladjustment in a clinic population: A multitrait–multimethod study. *Journal of Consulting and Clinical Psychology, 43,* 647–651.

Comrey, A. L. (1957). A factor analysis of items on the MMPI depression scale. *Educational and Psychological Measurement, 17,* 578–585.

Costello, C. G., & Comrey, A. L. (1967). Scales for measuring depression and anxiety. *Journal of Psychology, 66,* 303–313.

Dahlstrom, W. G., Welsh, G. S., & Dahlstrom, L. E. (1972). *An MMPI handbook, vol. 1: Clinical interpretation.* Minneapolis: University of Minnesota Press.

Davies, B., Burrows, G., & Poyton, C. (1975). A comparative study of four depression rating scales. *Australian and New Zealand Journal of Psychiatry, 9,* 21–24.

Dempsey, P. (1964). A unidimensional depression scale for the MMPI. *Journal of Consulting Psychology, 28,* 364–370.

Elkin, I., Parloff, M., Hadley, S., & Autry, I. (1985). The NIMH Treatment of Depression Collaborative Research Program. *Archives of General Psychiatry, 42,* 305–316.

Emery, G. D., Steer, R. A., & Beck, A. T. (1981). Depression, hopelessness, and suicidal intent among heroin addicts. *International Journal of the Addictions, 16,* 425–429.

Endicott, J., Cohen, J., Nee, J., Fleiss, J., & Sarantakos, S. (1981). Hamilton Depression Rating Scale, extracted from regular and change versions of the Schedule for Affective Disorders and Schizophrenia. *Archives of General Psychiatry, 38,* 98–103.

Endicott, J., & Spitzer, R. L. (1978). A diagnostic interview: The Schedule for Affective Disorders and Schizophrenia. *Archives of General Psychiatry, 35,* 837–844.

Feinberg, M., Carroll, B. J., Smouse, P. E., & Rawson, S. G. (1981). The Carroll Rating Scale for Depression III. Comparison with other rating instruments. *British Journal of Psychiatry, 138,* 205–209.

Froese, A., Vasquez, E., Cassem, N. H., & Hackett, T. P. (1974). Validation of anxiety, depression, and denial scales in a coronary care unit. *Journal of Psychosomatic Research, 18,* 137–141.

Gallagher, D., Nies, G., and Thompson, L. W. (1982). Reliability of the Beck Depression Inventory with older adults. *Journal of Consulting and Clinical Psychology, 50,* 152–153.

Gould, J. (1982). A psychometric investigation of the standard and short form Beck Depression Inventory. *Psychological Reports, 51,* 1167–1170.

Guilford, J. P., & Guilford, R. B. (1939). Personality factors D, R, T, and A. *Journal of Abnormal and Social Psychology, 34,* 23–36.

Hamilton, M. (1960). A rating scale for depression. *Journal of Neurology, Neurosurgery, and Psychiatry, 23,* 56–62.

Hamilton, M. (1967). Development of a rating scale for primary depressive illness. *British Journal of Social and Clinical Psychology, 6,* 278–296.

Hamilton, M. (1972). Rating scales and depression. In P. Kielholz (Ed.), *Depressive illness: Diagnosis, assessment, treatment.* Baltimore: Williams & Wilkins.

Harris, R. E., & Lingoes, J. C. (1955). Subscales for the MMPI: An aid to profile interpretation. Mimeographed materials, Dept. of Psychiatry, University of California at San Francisco.

Hathaway, S. R., & McKinley, J. C. (1942). A multiphasic personality schedule. *Journal of Psychology, 14,* 73–84.

Hathaway, S. R., & McKinley, J. C. (1989). *Minnesota Multiphasic Personality Inventory—2.* Minneapolis: University of Minnesota Press.

Hedlund, J., & Vieweg, B. (1979). The Hamilton Rating Scale for Depression: A comprehensive review. *Journal of Operational Psychiatry, 10,* 149–162.

Hunt, S. M., Jr., Singer, K., & Cobb, S. (1967). Components of depression. *Archives of General Psychiatry, 16,* 441–448.

Jasper, H. H. (1930). The measurement of depression–elation and its relation to a measure of extroversion–introversion. *Journal of Abnormal and Social Psychology, 25,* 307–318.

Knight, R. G., Waal-Manning, H. J., & Spears, G. F. (1983). Some norms and reliability data for the State Trait Anxiety Inventory and the Zung SRDS. *British Journal of Clinical Psychology, 22,* 245–249.

Krug, S. E., & Laughlin, J. E. (1976). *Handbook for the IPAT depression scale.* Champaign, Il: Institute for Personality and Ability Testing.

Lachar, D. (1974). *The MMPI: Clinical assessment and automated interpretation.* Los Angeles: Western Psychological Services.

Lanyon, R. I. (1984). Personality assessment. *Annual Review of Psychology, 35,* 667–701. p. 684

Leckie, E. V., & Withers, R. F. J. (1967). A test of liability to depressive illness. *British Journal of Medical Psychology, 40,* 273–282.

Lewinsohn, P., & Teri, L. (1982). Selection of depressed and nondepressed subjects on the basis of self-report data. *Journal of Consulting and Clinical Psychology, 50,* 590–591.

Lightfoot, S. L., & Oliver, J. M. (1985). The Beck inventory: Psychometric properties in university students. *Journal of Personality Assessment, 49,* 434–436.

Lubin, B. (1965). Adjective checklists for measurement of depression. *Archives of General Psychiatry, 12,* 57–62.

May, A. E., Urquhart, A., & Tarran, J. (1969). Self-evaluation of depression in various diagnostic and therapeutic groups. *Archives of General Psychiatry, 21,* 191–194.

McCall, R. J. (1958). Face validity of the D scale of the MMPI. *Journal of Clinical Psychology, 14*, 77–80.

McNair, D. M. (1974). Self-evaluations of antidepressants. *Psychopharmacologia, 37*, 77–80.

Montgomery, S. A., & Asberg, M. C. (1979). A new depression scale designed to be sensitive to change. *British Journal of Psychiatry, 134*, 382–389.

O'Connor, J., Stefic, E., & Gresock, C. (1957). Some patterns of depression. *Journal of Clinical Psychology, 13*, 122–125.

O'Hara, M., & Rehm, L. (1983). Hamilton rating scale for depression: Reliability and validity of judgements of novice rates. *Journal of Consulting & Clinical Psychology, 51*, 318.

Popoff, L. M. (1969). A simple method for diagnosis of depression by the family physician. *Clinical Medicine, 76*, 24–30.

Radloff, L. S. (1977). The CED-D scale: A self-report depression scale for research in the general population. *Applied Psychological Measurement, 1*, 358–401.

Rosen, A. (1962). Development of MMPI scale based on a reference group of psychiatric patients. *Psychological Monographs, 76*, 527 (Whole No.), 1-25.

Schwab, J., Bialow, M., & Holzer, C. (1967). A comparison of two rating scales for depression. *Journal of Clinical Psychology, 23*, 94–96.

Snaith, R. P., Ahmed, S. N., Mehta, S., & Hamilton, M. (1971). Assessment of the severity of primary depressive illness: Wakefield Self-Assessment Depression Inventory. *Psychological Medicine, 1*, 143–149.

Snaith, R. P., Bridge, G. W. K., & Hamilton, M. (1976). The Leeds scales for the self-assessment of anxiety and depression. *British Journal of Psychiatry, 128*, 156–165.

Sotsky, S., & Glass, D. (1983). *The Hamilton Rating Scale. A critical appraisal and modification for psychotherapy research.* Paper presented at the annual convention of the Society for Psychotherapy Research, Sheffield, England.

Spearman, C. (1904). "General Intelligence" objectively determined and measured. *American Journal of Psychology, 15*, 201–293.

Spitzer, R. L., Endicott, J., & Robins, E. (1978). Research diagnostic criteria. *Archives of General Psychiatry, 35*, 773–782.

Steer, R. A., Beck, A. T., & Garrison, B. (1986). Applications of the Beck Depression Inventory. In N. Sartorius & T. A. Ban (Eds.), *Assessment of depression* (pp. 121–142). Geneva, Switzerland: World Health Organization.

Steer, R. A., McElroy, M. G., & Beck, A. T. (1982). Structure of depression in alcoholic men: A partial replication. *Psychological Reports, 50*, 723–728.

Stein, K. B. (1968). The TSC scales: The outcome of a cluster analysis of 550 MMPI items. In P. McReynold (Ed.), *Advances in Psychological Assessment, vol. 1*. Palo Alto, CA: Science and Behavior Books.

Turner, J. A., & Romano, J. M. (1984). Self-report screening measures for depression in chronic pain patients. *Journal of Clinical Psychology, 40*, 909–913.

Weissman, M. M., Prusoff, B., & Newberry, P. B. (1975). *Comparison of CES-D, Zung, Beck self-report depression scales* (Technical Report ADM 42-47-83).

Rockville, MD: Center for Epidemiologic Studies, National Institute of Mental Health.

Wessman, A. E., & Ricks, D. F. (1966). *Mood and personality.* New York: Holt.

Zung, W. W. K. (1965). a self-rating depression scale. *Archives of General Psychiatry, 12,* 63–70.

Zung, W. W. K. (1972). The depression status inventory: An adjunct to the self-rating depression scale. *Journal of Clinical Psychology, 28,* 539–543.

CHAPTER 14

Somatic Therapies of Depression

STEVEN ZAVODNICK, MD

For several decades, consensus has been building toward the idea that some physiologic disruption of brain function underlies the syndromes of severe unipolar and bipolar depression. While psychotherapy and somatic therapies may have additive effects in the treatment of depressive states (Weissman, 1979), most experienced clinicians agree on the value of somatically based therapies in the treatment of such symptoms as disordered sleep, appetite, energy, interest, and concentration, in moderate and severe depressions. This chapter is intended to provide an overview of the use of tricyclic antidepressants (TCAs), monoamine oxidase inhibitors (MAOIs), second-generation antidepressants, lithium, and electroconvulsive therapy (ECT). The perspective will be practical, even impressionistic, rather than critical and quantitative. In an attempt to extract clues that might be useful in the treatment of patients prior to the complete resolution of controversial or theoretical issues, the benefit of clarity may be attended by the risk of oversimplification. Because the focus is on depression, no attempt to deal with possibly related conditions such as eating, panic, and obsessive-compulsive disorders will be made.

TRICYCLIC ANTIDEPRESSANTS

There is a rough specificity in the action of the various somatic treatments for depression. The most severe depressions, including psychotic or delusional depressions, respond best to electroconvulsive treatment or to a combination of tricyclic antidepressant and neuroleptic. Nonpsychotic, nonbipolar depressed patients are the group in which the response to tricyclic antidepressants is clearest. Bipolar patients may show antidepressant responses to lithium. Atypical depression marked by symptoms such as anxiety, phobia, reactive mood, and reversed vegetative symptoms is thought to be one syndrome that responds best to monoamine oxidase inhibitors. Dysthymic patients are viewed by a number of clinicians as exhibiting a preferential response to monoamine oxidase inhibitors or, perhaps, to a second-generation agent such as fluoxetine. This response specificity is only approximate. Tricyclic antidepressants may be helpful in some patients exhibiting atypical depression or dysthymia, monoamine oxidase inhibitors may be effective in some patients with severe depressions, and lithium may be useful as an adjunct to other drugs and in some unipolar patients. Nevertheless, in the absence of more rigorously defined predictors, fragmentary findings must serve as a guide to clinical intuition.

The efficacy of tricyclic antidepressants (TCAs) in the treatment of acute depression and the prevention of relapse has been well demonstrated (Davis, 1976; Klein & Davis, 1969). Patients with acute unipolar depression of at least moderate intensity constitute the core group responding to these agents with reported rates of improvement ranging from 65 to 90 percent. This patient group may be considered a subset of the DSM diagnostic category Major Depression. Disagreements concerning both diagnosis and treatment increase as the focus moves away from this core group. Joyce and Paykel (1989) suggested that response to TCAs is less clear at both extremes of the spectrum of severity, with bipolar depression and with chronic depressions. Severe depressions with psychotic symptoms probably do not respond optimally to TCAs alone (Glassman, Kantor, Shostak, 1975), although TCA–neuroleptic combination treatment (Nelson & Bowers, 1978) and electroconvulsive therapy have been reported to be effective. Problems evaluating the specific efficacy of TCAs in mild depressions include identification of cases, a sizable placebo response rate, and weighing the benefits of alleviating mild distress against significant drug side effects. In bipolar depression the risks of TCA treatment include the induction of mania and the less common occurrence of rapid cycling. Although there is some disagreement about the frequency with which a switch into mania occurs (Lewis & Winokur, 1982), clinical experience suggests that this happens often enough and presents enough of a management problem to warrant considerable caution with this patient group. The drug treatment of chronic depressions has been little studied in any systematic fashion, although anecdotes suggest some responsiveness of patients in this group to both TCAs and monoamine oxidase inhibitors.

Tricyclic antidepressants and their usual dose range in physically healthy adult patients are listed in Table 14.1. These drugs are a group of rather similar chemical structures; they include compounds related to imipramine, amitriptyline, and doxepin. The dose range of these drugs is 150–300 mg daily with the exception of nortriptyline and protriptyline, which are given in one-half and one-fifth of the usual dose respectively. Higher plasma levels of nortriptyline are associated with reduced response to the drug. Protriptyline is metabolized more slowly than the other agents in this series.

TABLE 14.1. Tricyclic Antidepressants

	Range of Daily Dosage (mg)
amitriptyline	150–300
nortriptyline	75–150
protriptyline	30– 60
imipramine	150–300
desipramine	150–300
chloripramine	150–300
trimipramine	150–300
doxepin	150–300

In the past, putative differences between TCAs have been emphasized, based upon differing potencies in blocking the reuptake of norepinephrine and serotonin in the laboratory. Differential response of patient groups to hypothetically serotonergic and noradrenergic antidepressants has not been clinically demonstrated with sufficient consistency. Current thinking is that similarities among the various TCAs are probably more important than differences (Montgomery, 1987). The members of this TCA group with more pronounced in vitro effects on serotonin are typically biotransformed in vivo into metabolites—for example, nortriptyline and desmethylchlorimipramine—with pronounced noradrenergic effects. The entire class of TCAs is probably most accurately thought of as a group of agents predominately affecting norepinephrine. Rather than the common practice of sequential drug trials involving a series of similar agents, careful attention to dose and duration of a course with a single TCA seems a more effective treatment strategy.

Drug dosage is a critical variable in the clinical use of TCAs. Underdosing is the most common error, perhaps because of the difficulty many patients encounter in tolerating the side effects of the more sedating, hypotensive, and anticholinergic drugs of this group when given in adequate dose. A figure of 3.5 mg/kg has been suggested (Glassman, Perel, Shostak, Kantor, & Fleiss, 1979) for drugs with a 150–300 mg range yielding an average daily dose well over 200 mg/d. Plasma drug levels may be helpful in allowing for variability in patients' ability to metabolize TCAs (Gold, Lydiard, Pottash, & Martin, 1987). With nortriptyline, a better drug response has been associated with plasma levels between 70 and 140 ng/ml; responsiveness is reduced both below and above this therapeutic window. Improvement with imipramine has been associated with blood levels of imipramine plus desipramine over 225 ng/ml. Possibly, improvement with desipramine requires blood levels over 125 ng/ml (Nelson, Jatlow, Quinlan, & Bowers, 1982). The usual current methods of measuring TCA plasma levels do not yield information on other active, quantitatively important metabolites (e.g., 10-hydroxynortriptyline) or variations in drug–protein binding which may increase or decrease the active, free drug fraction. The author agrees with the suggestion of Gold et al. (1987) favoring the use of nortriptyline in most TCA trials, in view of the clearer dose response relationship with this drug as well as the significant reduction in side effects when the secondary amine metabolites (nortriptyline, desipramine) are used in preference to the tertiary amine parents (amitriptyline, imipramine).

One technique for prescribing TCAs consists of starting treatment with a dose of 75 mg h.s. and titrating upward, as tolerated, to the range of 200–300 mg nightly. Given the long elimination half-lives of TCAs, there is no need for multiple daily doses. Despite its higher milligram potency, nortriptyline is usually well tolerated by healthy patients at a 75 mg starting dose. For many patients, upward titration is unnecessary because the effective dose is usually half that of most TCAs. Plasma levels may be obtained in the second or third week of treatment, ideally five to 10 days after reaching a stable dose level, and the drug dose can be adjusted with respect to the indicated range. Drug dose should be reduced with the occurrence of significant side effects, in the hope that tolerance will develop and permit the attainment of an adequate treating dose. For elderly patients and those with significant cardiovascular disease, starting doses should be lower and increases more gradual. The author's method is to start cardiac patients on 25 mg of nortriptyline daily and increase by 25 mg/week, with careful clinical assessment for the emergence of new cardiovascular symptoms, EKG, and nortriptyline plasma level determination prior to each new dose increase. There is some evidence suggesting that maintaining patients toward the lower end of the nortriptyline therapeutic window can minimize the likelihood of cardiac toxicity while preserving the possibility for the desired clinical response (Glassman & Bigger, 1981; Roose, 1987).

Response to antidepressant drugs of all types is usually not seen until three or four weeks after the therapeutic dose is reached. One group of patients has been described with a good response in week five or week six of a drug trial (Quitkin et al., 1987). There is little reason to continue TCA alone beyond six weeks if response has not been forthcoming. At this point the addition of an adjunctive agent such as lithium or tri-iodothyronine or an alternative antidepressant treatment should be considered.

Drug side effects frequently present a limiting factor in the successful use of TCAs. Patients' inability to tolerate sedative, hypotensive, or other autonomic effects may interfere with the goal of achieving a satisfactory dose/plasma level and the desired clinical response. Secondary amine tricyclics, nortriptyline and desipramine, were initially explored in the hope that, by using the metabolite compounds rather than the parent drugs, response lag might be shortened. This hope was not realized. However, the secondary amines do have the advantage of markedly less severe side effects than the original agents in the TCA series. While there is no evidence for any difference in efficacy among any of the TCAs, the reduced propensity for side effects and the better understanding of the relationship between plasma level and patient response, in the author's opinion, render nortriptyline and desipramine the agents of choice within this group of drugs.

Central nervous system side effects include sedation, induction of psychosis, confusional states, and tremor. Sedation may be marked with tertiary amine TCAs, prolonging the time to reach the effective dose range. Tolerance to this side effect usually occurs with a more gradual increase in drug dose over a period of weeks. Sedation is typically mild or absent with nortriptyline or desipramine. Patients with a prior history of psychosis, either schizophrenia or mania, are at risk for the reactivation of psychotic symptoms with TCA treatment. The magnitude of the risk for schizophrenic patients has not been assessed but is probably considerable. Some clinicians feel that adjunctive neuroleptics serve a protective function in this regard, although this has not been carefully studied. It has been estimated that 15 percent of the bipolar population may have an episode of mania in association with TCA treatment (Bunney, 1978). The induction of rapid cycling from mania to depression is another well-know risk with these agents (Wehr & Goodwin, 1979). Occasionally patients who were not previously known to be manic may exhibit mania or hypomania only while taking TCAs, leading some investigators to classify this group as part of the bipolar spectrum. Confusional states are commonly encountered with TCA overdose, especially in elderly patients, for whom doses used in younger patients prove to be excessive. These phenomena are related to the central anticholinergic effects of TCAs and to milder degrees of memory impairment that may be dose-related with the more strongly anticholinergic antidepressant drugs. Some patients given TCAs may exhibit a fine resting tremor. When necessary, low dose propranolol (e.g., 20–40 mg/d) may be prescribed to alleviate this.

Autonomic nervous system side effects include both antiadrenergic and anticholinergic actions. Orthostatic hypotension is the most serious of the antiadrenergic side effects; patients may be symptomatic with the ever present dangers of syncope, falls, and fractured bones. Nortriptyline has been reported as the TCA with the lowest incidence of orthostasis (Roose, 1981). The degree of orthostatic drop seen during treatment may be correlated with measured orthostatic changes prior to the initiation of therapy. Curiously, there have been observations (Jarvik, Read, Minty, & Neshkes, 1983; Schneider, Sloan, Staples, & Bender, 1986) of a positive correlation between the magnitude of orthostatic hypotension noted prior to antidepressant treatment and a positive response to this treatment in geriatric patients. The theoretical implications of this are intriguing, suggesting some relationship between the responsiveness of the sympathetic nervous system to postural changes and the responsiveness of the brain to drug treatment. A recent report (Price & Heninger, 1988) described the use of yohimbine, a centrally active sympathetic agonist pressor agent, in the management of hypotension with TCAs. Impotence and ejaculatory difficulties are additional sympatholytic TCA side effects that may be encountered. While the autonomic mechanism is unclear, orgasmic dysfunction in women is not uncommon (Harrison et al., 1986). Dosage reduction may be helpful in some of these situations.

Peripheral anticholinergic effects include blurred vision, dry mouth, constipation, and urinary difficulties. These effects are less severe with the secondary amines. Tolerance may develop over a period of weeks with some patients; others may be aided with symptomatic measures (e.g., hard candies, citrus fruit slices for xerostomia, bulk laxatives for constipation). Frank urinary retention is not especially common, but many patients experience urinary hesitancy, dribbling, or a sensation of bladder fullness after voiding. Patients being treated for chronic glaucoma may be prescribed TCAs with ophthalmologic consultation. Rarely, an attack of acute narrow-angle closure may be precipitated, typically in a patient not previously known to have ophthalmologic problems. Symptoms of an acute attack of narrow-angle glaucoma are a sharp pain in the eye and halos surrounding point sources of light. Immediate consultation is mandatory as delay may result in loss of vision. The treatment is surgical.

Cardiovascular side effects are a source of concern since the majority of depressed patients belong to an age group where concurrent cardiac disease is common. With proper attention, caution, and consultation when necessary, this need not be a bar to effective treatment, even in patients with known cardiac disease. Hypotension related to adrenergic blockade, heart rate increases with anticholinergic (antivagal) effects, and a quinidine-like effect consisting of antiarrhythmic actions at low to moderate plasma levels with increasing degrees of conduction blockade at higher dose levels have been described (Ziegler, Co, & Biggs, 1977). Once again, the secondary amine TCAs seem to be considerably safer with regard to the cardiovascular system because hypotensive and anticholinergic effects are less with these agents. Plasma level monitoring may help in determining the lowest effective doses to use with these patients. In addition to baseline and follow-up EKG, patients should be monitored for anginal symptoms, symptoms suggesting cardiac arrhythmia, and blood pressure measurements both sitting and standing prior to and during the course of treatment. If necessary, beta blocking agents may be used to protect against increases in heart rate and myocardial demand. Glassman's group (Giardina, Bigger, Glassman,

Perel, & Kantor, 1979) described decreases in premature atrial and ventricular contractions over a month-long imipramine trial in depressed patients. With TCA overdose, second- and third-degree heart block may be seen. TCAs are contraindicated in the acute phase following myocardial infarction. How long this contraindication must be observed is unclear. Six months would seem a reasonable and conservative, though entirely arbitrary figure.

TCA overdosage should be treated with considerable caution. Attention to possible suicidal ideation and intent is important in prescribing, since a 10-day supply of medication at usual doses may be lethal. Smaller medication supplies, more frequent physician visits, enlisting a family member or friend to control medication, or inpatient treatment are alternatives to manage this risk. Symptoms of overdose include delirium, mydriasis, flushing, dry mucosae, decreased bowel and bladder activity, cardiac arrhythmia, seizure, and coma. Patients should be treated in an intensive setting with cardiac monitoring for a 24–48-hour period because reduced gastrointestinal motility may lead to delayed absorption and late worsening of symptoms. Physostigmine 1–2 mg intravenously can produce dramatic, rapid reversal of central and peripheral anticholinergic toxicity. The duration of action of physostigmine is about two hours—rather brief relative to the half-life of the TCAs, which approximate 20 hours and may be prolonged with large overdoses. Physostigmine doses must be repeated frequently when patients exhibit clinical worsening a few hours after the last dose. Many emergency room and intensive care unit physicians prefer conservative management of TCA overdoses, avoiding any concomitant and potentially complicating medications. The use of physostigmine is roughly analogous to the use of naloxone in opiate overdose—a maneuver that is both diagnostic and therapeutic and should be employed whenever the severity of overdose symptoms warrants.

MONOAMINE OXIDASE INHIBITORS

The antidepressant action of the monoamine oxidase inhibitors (MAOIs) was discovered as a result of the chance observation of euphoria in tuberculosis patients under treatment with isoniazid, an antituberculosis agent with MAOI activity. There has been a decided upsurge of interest in drugs of this class in the United States over the past 10 years (Quitkin, Rifkin, & Klein, 1979), although they have been available since the late 1950s. The new attention may be because of an improved understanding of the spectrum of activity of these agents, the dose–response relationship, and the management of dietary restrictions and other drug side effects. While there is clearly some overlap in the efficacy of MAOIs and TCAs, it is important to realize that there are subpopulations of patients who seem to respond preferentially to MAOIs. Some patients with the diagnosis of major depression may respond only to MAOIs; others, only to TCAs, or to both, or to neither drug group. Impressionistic observations such as these rest mainly on anecdotal reports rather than on controlled comparison studies so it is difficult to assign even rough quantitative estimates as to the size of these groups. Two other diagnoses for which specific MAOI responsiveness has been suggested are atypical depressions—mixed syndromes of anxiety and depression in patients with preserved mood reactivity and pronounced anxious, phobic, and hypochondriacal symptoms—and chronic or characterologic depression, that is, dysthymia. The responsiveness of atypical depression to MAOIs has been well studied and reviewed. The use of this group of drugs in chronic depressions is only hinted at by suggestion of effectiveness in patients bearing the older diagnostic label *neurotic depression* (Nies, 1983). Another use of MAOIs has been in patients with bipolar depression in the hope, as yet unsubstantiated, that the tendency of TCAs to induce mania or rapid cycling in this patient group might be avoided.

In addition to a sharpened focus on groups of depressed patients who may preferentially respond to MAOIs, greater awareness of the effective dose range of these compounds (see Table 14.2) has contributed to their resurgence in clinical practice. It has been reported (Robinson Nies, Ravaris, Ives, & Bartlett, 1978) that 80 percent or greater inhibition of platelet monoamine oxidase is associated with a higher rate of response to MAOIs. As the measurement of platelet MAO inhibition is not generally available in routine clinical laboratories, the practical application has been an upward movement in the doses prescribed. The dose range of phenelzine is thought to be 60–90 mg daily and of tranylcypromine 40–60 mg daily, in order to attain this level of MAOI inhibition. Anecdotally, occasional patients are described tolerating and responding to doses two or three times higher! There has been interest in more specific MAOIs, with preferential affinity for one of several enzymatic subtypes. To date, the hopes for either reduced toxicity or enhanced clinical response have not been realized. Questions remain about efficacy and whether in vitro specificity is retained at the clinical doses required.

As with TCAs, the basic clinical technique in using MAOIs is to start patients at a low dose, usually one or two tablets daily, increasing

TABLE 14.2.   Monoamine Oxidase Inhibitors

Drug	Dose (mg/d)
isocarboxazid	40–60
phenelzine	45–90
tranylcypromine	30–60

over a two- to four-week period to the presumed effective dose range, as tolerated. There is a three- to six-week lag between the time that the effective dose range is reached and clinical response is seen. Patients should be advised verbally and in writing about the specific dietary and medication incompatibilities, in order to reduce the risk of hypertensive crisis.

Although many physicians are duly concerned about the risks of using MAOIs, excessive caution is not warranted. Experience has shown that given proper instruction (Davidson, Zung, & Walker, 1984) most patients are able to observe adequate precautions regarding diet and medication and that, given this precondition, the risk of serious hypertensive crisis is low. Other side effects with MAOIs are frequently neither severe nor problematic and patients often tolerate these agents better than TCAs (Nies & Robinson, 1982).

Central nervous system side effects of MAOIs include insomnia, sedation, nervousness, and psychotoxicity. Overstimulation may appear early in treatment with MAOIs. Susceptible patients complain that the medication makes them feel "hyper." This symptom is more frequently seen with tranylcypromine. Psychotoxicity refers to the ability of MAOIs to exacerbate the symptoms of schizophrenia and to induce mania or hypomania in bipolar patients. Whether these phenomena are seen less often with MAOIs than TCAs is uncertain; however, clinically it is not uncommon to encounter MAOI-induced elations, the absence of good statistical data notwithstanding. Some degree of insomnia or lesser sleep disturbance is quite common with MAOI treatment.

Hypotension is the most frequent side effect encountered in routine MAOI use. This is of the orthostatic type and may be a limiting factor in treatment. The risk of syncope, falls, and related injuries is a serious consideration. The use of sodium chloride tablets (3–6 Gm daily) has been described anecdotally as a means of increasing intravascular fluid volume to reduce drug-induced orthostasis (Munjak, 1984). This measure is practical only in younger patients with good cardiovascular tone. Hypotension is more frequent with phenelzine.

Dry mouth, blurred vision, and constipation are seen with MAOIs. The mechanism of this is obscure as these drugs are devoid of anticholinergic activity. Anorgasmia, ejaculatory inhibition, paresthesia, and myoclonus are occasional side effects seen. These may be dose-related and may reflect autonomic and peripheral nervous system toxicities.

Monoamine oxidase in the intestinal lining normally serves to protect against pressor effects of dietary amines derived from degradation of protein foodstuffs into component amino acids. MAOIs currently in use inhibit monoamine oxidase in a variety of tissues, including the gastrointestinal tract, permitting absorption of pharmacologically active quantities of dietary pressor agents. Prior to an understanding of

TABLE 14.3. Foods and Medications to Avoid with MAOIs

Foods:

Cheese (except cream cheese, cottage cheese; includes cheese sauces)
Pepperoni, salami, bologna, summer sausage
Canned and smoked meats
Chicken liver, beef liver
Smoked salmon, anchovies, caviar, pickled herring, sardines
Fava beans (broad beans, horse beans, Italian green beans)
Yeast beverages (baked goods are safe)
Red wine
Beer (especially dark beers)

Medications:

Decongestants
Cold, cough, allergy remedies
Appetite suppressants
Stimulants
Epinephrine (in dental, other local anesthetics)
Antidepressants
Meperidine, morphine

this, the risk of hypertensive crisis and even rare cerebrovascular hemorrhage was a chief reason for the reluctance of many psychiatrists to employ MAOIs. With proper education, most patients are able to observe a MAOI diet reducing the risk of severe hypertensive crisis to acceptable levels. Foods to be avoided are listed in Table 14.3. These include most forms of cheese, preserved meats and fish, liver, fava beans, brewer's yeast products (not baked goods), red wines, and dark beers. Important interactions with medications include all sympathominetic amines (decongestants, appetite suppressants, stimulants, epinephrine in local anesthetics) and opiate analgesics. Antihistamines that are not combined with sympathominetic decongestants, acetylsalicylic acid, and acetaminophen may be permitted. TCAs should be avoided in combination with MAOIs except with special experience and close monitoring of patients. The combination of fluoxetine and MAOIs may be hazardous. Symptoms of hypertensive crisis include a pounding headache, sweating, pallor, and palpitations. Patients should be directed to the nearest medical setting for blood pressure monitoring and possible intervention. Some psychiatrists advise patients to carry alpha adrenergic blocking agents (e.g., phentolamine 50 mg or chlorpromazine 50 mg) to be used in the case of inadvertent dietary indiscretion. Dietary and medication precautions should be continued for two weeks after MAOIs are discontinued as these are irreversible enzymatic inhibitors and the additional time is required for new enzyme synthesis.

SECOND-GENERATION ANTIDEPRESSANTS

During the 1980s a series of unrelated, nontricyclic, non-MAOI antidepressants were introduced to American psychiatry (Table 14.4). These
have been referred to as heterocyclic or second-generation antidepressants, although neither term is particularly informative in either a
chemical or clinical sense. In this section these agents will be compared
to TCAs from the standpoint of target patient population, efficacy, and
side effects.

Amoxapine is a demethylated derivative of the neuroleptic drug
loxapine. It is not a TCA although there are rough structural similarities (a three-ring central moeity with a nitrogen-containing albeit
cyclical side chain attached to the central ring). The pharmacology of
amoxapine is similar to that of the TCAs: it affects norepinephrine
reuptake and receptors as well as the ability to block dopamine receptors, which it shares with the neuroleptic agents. Efficacy was similar
to that of TCAs in a patient population that included inpatients and
outpatients with the diagnosis of major depression (Feighner, 1983).
The side effect profile is very similar to that of the TCAs, with the
addition of the entire spectrum of acute extrapyramidal effects occasionally reported with this drug. It appears to be no safer than TCAs in
the overdose situation.

Maprotiline is described as a tetracyclic antidepressant. The structure of this drug is quite reminiscent of desipramine: an extra ring is
found attached to the center ring of the tricyclic structure perpendicu-
lar to the plane of the molecule. The pharmacology is also rather like
that of desipramine, with specific effects on norepinephrine reuptake
and postsynaptic receptors. The population in which maprotiline has
been used, its efficacy, side effects, and overdose lethality are quite
similar to those of the TCAs. Because this drug has an elimination
half-life more than twice as long as that of the TCAs, there is a tendency for this agent to accumulate to rather high blood levels if given in
the usual TCA dose range. After several years on the United States
market, the drug's dose recommendations were changed by the

TABLE 14.4.   Second-Generation
Antidepressants

Drug	Dose (mg)
amoxapine	150–300
maprotiline	75–225
trazodone	150–300
fluoxetine	20– 80
bupropion	200–450

manufacturer to suggest slower dose increases and a maximum dose about two-thirds that of the TCAs.

Trazodone is both structurally and pharmacologically distinct. A triazolopyridine, it is thought to exert effects mainly by blocking the reuptake of and receptors for serotonin and may be viewed as a mixed serotonin agonist–antagonist. The drug also exhibits effects upon postsynaptic beta adrenergic receptors. In patients with major depression, trazodone is described as having similar efficacy to the TCAs (Schatzberg, Dessain, O'Neil, Katy, & Cole, 1987). It has enjoyed fairly extensive use in geriatric depressed patient groups. Two major areas of advantage for this drug are side effects and overdoses. Main side effects for trazodone are limited to sedation and occasional gastrointestinal discomfort. Priaprism is an infrequent side effect, noted as a curiosity and because there have been cases with permanent loss of erectile function. Immediate drug discontinuation and urological consultation are recommended. Although there are sporadic reports of cardiac arrhythmia, trazodone is generally well-tolerated from the cardiovascular standpoint and should be considered one of the drugs of choice for the medically fragile depressed patient. Overdose lethality is low.

Fluoxetine has been described (Fuller & Wong, 1987) as the most specifically serotonergic antidepressant currently available in the United States. It is a potent inhibitor of serotonin reuptake with little effect on other neurotransmitter systems. Fluoxetine has a long elimination half-life (in the range of one to three days) with an active metabolite, norfluoxetine, whose half-life is on the order of one to two weeks. Two practical consequences of this are that the drug need not be given every day (e.g., if lower doses are desired) and that fluoxetine is recommended to be discontinued five weeks prior to an MAOI trial. This drug has been used in a patient population that is different from the patients usually treated with TCAs. Patients who responded to fluoxetine were mainly outpatients with symptoms of moderately severe, chronic depression as opposed to the more severe, acute depressions that tend to respond to TCA treatment. This patient group probably includes a mixture of patients with a diagnosis of major depression in the mild to moderate range of severity as well as patients with dysthymia. Fluoxetine is generally quite well tolerated. A minority of patients may experience nervousness or insomnia and for this reason the drug is generally given in the morning. Headache and nausea, the other common side effects, usually abate with dose reduction. Although experience is limited, the drug is thought to be safe after overdoses. Overall, fluoxetine is a drug with major advantages over TCAs from the standpoint of patient tolerance and safety and a different spectrum of activity that is skewed toward the less severe, less acute depressed patient.

Bupropion is another novel antidepressant drug which has structural similarities to the psychomotor stimulants. The mechanism of action is thought to involve the neurotransmitter dopamine, setting it apart from the TCAs, MAOIs, and other second-generation antidepressants. This drug has been as effective as TCAs in research trials involving inpatient and outpatient groups with major depression (Zung, 1983). Clinical experience suggests that there are patients who respond to this agent after failing to improve with MAOIs, TCAs, and other second-generation antidepressants. Side effects are usually not problematic and are quite similar to those seen with fluoxetine—occasional nervousness, insomnia, headache, or nausea—although the drugs are dissimilar. Because of the modest risk of seizure with doses higher than 450 mg daily, these doses are not recommended and the manufacturer suggests that this drug be reserved for patients who fail to respond to other antidepressants.

LITHIUM

Lithium salts are generally considered to be either second-line or adjunctive agents in the treatment of depression in unipolar patients. Evidence for lithium's ability to prevent the recurrence of depression in the maintenance treatment of bipolar patients is clear (Davis, 1976). There is some support for the use of lithium as an acute antidepressant in bipolar patients, in maintenance treatment of recurrent unipolar depressions, and, occasionally, in the acute treatment of unipolar depression (Jefferson, Greist, Ackerman & Carroll, 1987; Ramsey & Mendels, 1980). There is little published work on the use of lithium in atypical depression or dysthymic disorder. An area that has excited considerable interest in recent years is the use of lithium as an adjunct to TCAs, MAOIs, and second-generation antidepressants in the acute treatment of unipolar depression. Dramatic responses have been described within 2 to 14 days after the addition of lithium to standard antidepressant treatment in patients who initially appeared to be treatment-refractory (de Montigny & Cournoyer, 1987). Patients responding included a small number with psychotic symptoms, a group who may not respond well to TCA alone. Lithium doses were in the 900–1,200 mg daily range with few additional side effects seen and no clear correlation between serum lithium levels and clinical response. It is not clear how long to continue combined treatment after a positive response; some patients maintained their improvement after the early discontinuation of lithium. The number of patients studied in a controlled fashion has not been large and, in some cases, lithium was added to another agent after trials lasting only three weeks so that it is difficult to be accurate about the likelihood of response with this treatment. It may be on the order of 50–75 percent. In view of the low risk and the usual need for a four- to six-week trial when switching from a failed antidepressant treatment to another, an intervening two-week period of adjunctive lithium therapy seems a reasonable second step prior to initiating a new antidepressant in any patient not responding to the first drug selected.

Maintenance treatment for the prevention of recurrent depression has been described with lithium levels toward the lower range of those used in the treatment of bipolar disorders, 0.5–0.8 mEq/1 (Hullin, 1980). Side effects should be mild in this range and can include tremor, thirst, polyuria, and possibly some of the subtler central nervous system complaints such as decreased concentration and memory. The typical patient will experience no side effects at this dose. Suppression of thyroid function indices and occasional hypothyroidism are to be expected with chronic treatment. Lithium intoxication is the most severe problem to be encountered with the use of this agent. This may occur with intentional or accidental ingestion of excess lithium, acute renal disease impairment of lithium excretion, or conditions causing sodium depletion with compensatory renal retention of both sodium and lithium (e.g., thiazide diuretic use, febrile illness, sodium loss through perspiration with heavy exercise). Symptoms are a combination of gastrointestinal and central nervous system toxicities: nausea, vomiting, or diarrhea combined with tremor, incoordination, dysarthria, or drowsiness. The serum lithium level is usually, but not always, above the range of 1.0–1.5 mEq/1. The diagnosis of lithium intoxication should be made clinically. Early recognition and discontinuation of lithium treatment while underlying causes are explored and corrected usually leads to resolution of symptoms in a few days without sequellae.

Medical conditions complicating lithium therapy include hypothyroidism, decreased renal function, congestive heart failure, and pregnancy. Hypothyroid patients may be treated with lithium so long as thyroid function is monitored closely and additional thyroid hormone supplementation is provided as necessary. Patients with decreased renal function will exhibit proportionately decreased ability to excrete lithium ion. Prescribed lithium doses must be lowered accordingly. In patients with congestive heart failure, it must be recalled that lithium behaves much like sodium physiologically. The lithium dose may act like a salt load, exacerbating the degree of failure if this is not taken into account. Additionally, thiazide diuretics may raise serum lithium levels via a mechanism involving increased proximal renal tubular resorption. Lithium treatment, when indicated, must proceed cautiously with closer than usual attention to both fluid balance and serum lithium levels. Lithium is probably teratogenic (Sitland-Marken, Rickman, Wells, & Mabie, 1989) and should be avoided during pregnancy, particularly during the first trimester. Lithium is excreted in therapeutic concentrations in breast milk. Breast feeding is contraindicated while lithium treatment is in progress.

Evaluation of the patient prior to lithium therapy should include a medical history and physical exam, including urinalysis, CBC, creatinine, BUN, thyroid function studies, and chest X-ray. Women of childbearing age should have a pregnancy test as it is lithium exposure during early, often undiagnosed pregnancy that carries the greatest risk. Patients may be started on 600–900 mg lithium salt daily with plasma lithium levels obtained every four or five days. As noted above, a target level of 0.6 mEq/1 is probably adequate for the treatment of depression. Once stable lithium levels are attained, monitoring every one to three months is sufficient. For long-term maintenance, thyroid stimulating hormone, serum creatinine, and urine specific gravity should be monitored semiannually. At the present the optimal time period for continuing lithium used to potentiate another antidepressant is not certain. It might be reasonable to discontinue either the lithium or the antidepressant after a month or two.

THYROID POTENTIATION

Thyroid potentiation with triiodothyronine has been found useful for the past 20 years in converting TCA nonresponders to responders and in shortening the lag period for TCA response (Prange, 1987; Prange, Wilson, Rabon, & Lipton, 1969). Triiodothyronine is used rather than thyroxine as the shorter half-life (one day vs. seven days) allows for more rapid clearance should discontinuation become necessary. This treatment is not dependent upon a diagnosis of frank or subclinical hypothyroidism. Indeed, in hypothyroid patients, often correction of the endocrine abnormality is the only treatment needed to modify associated psychiatric symptoms. In euthyroid depressed patients the dose range for antidepressant potentiation is usually 25 to 50 mcg triiodothyronine daily in the morning. Response may be seen within two weeks and supplemental thyroid medication is usually discontinued after a month. Side effects may include sympathetic nervous system overactivity and cardiac arrhythmia. Despite impressive results in controlled trials with as many as 75 percent of nonresponders improving with T_3 addition (Goodwin, Prange, Post, Muscattola, & Lipton, 1982), this treatment has not been as enthusiastically utilized as might be expected. The reasons for this are unclear. Whether there is overlap, nonoverlap, or some other relationship between patients responding to lithium or thyroid potentiation has not been investigated.

ELECTROCONVULSIVE THERAPY

Electroconvulsive therapy (ECT), first used by Ugo Cerletti in 1938, continues to be among the most demonstrably effective treatments for severe depressive states (Klein & Davis, 1969). Severe depressions—including those in patients with psychotic symptoms, catatonia, acutely suicidal depressed patients, and patients failing to respond to drug treatments—constitute the main indication for ECT. ECT is generally not used for mild, atypical, or chronic depression. In severe depression, the response rate to ECT often exceeds 80 percent (Fink, 1987). The main drawbacks to the use of this treatment are availability and relapse. Surveys have demonstrated (Asnis, Fink, & Saferstein, 1978) a pattern that suggests underutilization of ECT in public hospital settings when compared to university and private hospitals. While diagnostic differences between the populations served may account for some of these findings, it is suspected that ECT, with its modestly increased demands for equipment, staff, and training is less often available to patients in public mental hospitals. Relapse is a major issue in treating all patients with affective disorders. In a review (Davis, 1976) of maintenance treatment in depression it was shown that over 50 percent of treated patients suffer relapse within a few months without continuation of treatment. A similar number of patients experience relapse after a successful course of ECT (Kiloh, 1982). The clinician is left with the choice of attempting maintenance treatment with a drug whose efficacy is uncertain or maintenance ECT. Anecdotal reports suggest that maintenance ECT at intervals ranging from once weekly to once every four to six weeks is often effective.

The addition of barbiturate anesthesia and muscle relaxation agents 20 years ago reduced the subjective distress and physical trauma associated with older convulsive techniques. Recent modifications include unilateral ECT treatments, reduction in the electrical stimulus used, close physiologic monitoring, and electroencephalographic monitoring. While there are still unresolved controversies regarding the efficacy of unilateral versus bilateral treatment and brief-pulse, square-wave stimuli versus sine-wave stimuli, the overall result is a tendency toward less associated memory disruption, lower exposure of the brain to electricity, better control of oxygenation and hypertension during treatments, and more attention to the adequacy of the cerebral seizure for effective treatment.

There is general agreement (Fink, 1979; Snaith, 1981) that a majority of patients will respond to six to eight ECT treatments, although individualization of the number of treatments based upon clinical response is the basic principle. Two factors contributing to longer courses of ECT may be the not uncommon occurrence of missed or abbreviated seizures and the poorly substantiated practice of prescribing several treatments beyond the point of clinical response in the hope that they will solidify patient recovery. Fink (1979) observed that the induction of adequate generalized seizures may be more difficult with unilateral electrode placement and brief-pulse stimulation, which led some physicians to resist these modifications. The practice of some experienced clinicians is to begin a series of treatments with unilateral, brief-pulse ECT and then switch to bilateral ECT if there is no response by a certain point in the treatment course or to sine wave stimuli if difficulty in producing a generalized convulsion is encountered.

The main side effect of ECT is the acute confusional state which is related to the number of treatments, patient age, and whether the stimulus is administered to the dominant cerebral hemisphere. Memory dysfunction is minimal with unilateral, nondominant hemisphere ECT. With bilateral treatments, the severity of anterograde amnesia usually increases with increasing number of ECT treatments. Memory function is typically recovered one to two months after the cessation of ECT, although recall of events occurring during the acute amnestic period is usually lost. Delirium during the immediate post-ECT, postanesthesia recovery period may be encountered. This typically resolves spontaneously in under an hour. Benzodiazepines or neuroleptics have been used to manage this when necessary. Transient elevation in blood pressure and cardiac arrhythmias are usually managed quite easily by anesthesia personnel. Fatalities with ECT are rare. Kalinowsky (1975) cited a series greater than 100,000 treatments with a death rate of 0.003 percent despite the fact that many treated patients were elderly with concomitant cardiovascular and other medical problems. Caution is in order in the acute period following myocardial infarction, although most psychiatrists would consider ECT to be safer than TCAs here. Uncontrolled elevation in intracranial pressure is the strongest contraindication to ECT.

SUMMARY

The somatic treatment of depression is far from ideal. Tricyclic antidepressants have a fairly wide spectrum of action, being effective in major depressions of varying degrees of severity, some atypical depressions, and some dysthymias. The addition of neuroleptics may extend the range of these agents to psychotic depression. Potentiation with lithium or thyroid hormone may improve efficacy; however, it remains considerably less than complete. Side effects with TCAs are significant. Monoamine oxidase inhibitors are particularly efficacious in the treatment of atypical depression. Some patients with major depression and some with dysthymia may respond, although the statistics for this are quite uncertain. Side effects with these drugs may be bothersome and the adverse interaction with foods and medications render this a not uncomplicated treatment. Lithium has a special place in the treatment of bipolar patients, as a potentiator of other antidepressants, and, perhaps, in continuation therapy. Side effects are usually mild, but effectiveness is clearly less than complete. The second generation of antidepressants has yielded a number of chemically distinct agents, typically with fewer and less severe side effects than the TCAs and MAOIs. The clinical range of these agents is not clear at the present time. There are no suggestions that effectiveness is greater than that of TCAs when patients are considered as a group. Electroconvulsive therapy is quite effective for a narrow range of severe depressions. It is not indicated in dysthymia or atypical depression. Underutilization, management of relapses, and emotional resistance to electrical stimulation of the brain are the major problems with this treatment. The biological treatment of depression is just beginning. Psychiatrists are called upon for diagnostic acumen and clinical perspicacity in the selection and management of problems in treatment. Many of the conditional statements in this section need to be addressed by clinical research. There is much to do while awaiting the millenium.

REFERENCES

Asnis, G., Fink, M., & Saferstein, S. (1978). ECT in metropolitan New York hospitals: A survey of practice, 1975–1976. *American Journal of Psychiatry, 135,* 479–482.

Bunney, W. E. (1978). Psychopharmacology of the switch process in affective illness. In K. Killam, A. DiMascio, & M. Lipton (Eds.), *Psychopharmacology: A generation of progress.* New York: Raven Press.

Davidson, J., Zung, W. W. K., & Walker, J. I. (1984). Practical aspects of MAO inhibitor therapy. *Journal of Clinical Psychiatry, 45* (sec. 2), 81–84.

Davis, J. M. (1976). Overview: maintenance therapy in psychiatry: II. Affective disorders. *American Journal of Psychiatry, 133,* 1–13.

de Montigny, C., & Cournoyer, G. (1987). Lithium addition in treatment of resistant depression. In J. Zohar & R. H. Belmaker (Eds.), *Treating resistant depression.* New York: PMA Publishing.

Feighner, J. P. (1983). The new generation of antidepressants. *Journal of Clinical Psychiatry, 44* (sec. 2), 49–55.

Fink, M. (1979). *Convulsive therapy: Theory and practice.* New York: Raven Press.

Fink, M. (1987). ECT: A last resort treatment for resistant depression? In J. Zohar & R. H. Belmaker (Eds.), *Treating resistant depression.* New York: PMA Publishing.

Fuller, R. W., & Wong, D. T. (1987). Serotonin reuptake blockers in vitro and in vivo. *Journal of Clinical Psychopharmacology, 7* (supp.), 365–435.

Giardina, E. G., Bigger, J. T., Glassman, A. H., Perel, J. M., & Kantor, S. J. (1979). The electrocardiographic and antiarrhythmic effects of imipramine hydrochloride at therapeutic plasma concentrations. *Circulation, 60,* 1045–1052.

Glassman, A. H., & Bigger, J. T. (1981). Cardiovascular effects of therapeutic doses of tricyclic antidepressants. *Archives of General Psychiatry, 38,* 815–820.

Glassman, A. H., Kantor, S. J., & Shostak, M. (1975). Depression, delusions, and drug response. *American Journal of Psychiatry, 132,* 716–719.

Glassman, A. H., Perel, J. M., Shostak, M., Kantor, S. J., & Fleiss, J. L. (1979). Clinical implications of imipramine plasma levels for depressive illness. *Archives of General Psychiatry, 34,* 197–204.

Gold, M. S., Lydiard, R. B., Pottash, A. L. C., & Martin, D. M. (1987). The contribution of blood levels to the treatment of resistant depression. In J. Zohar & R. H. Belmaker (Eds.), *Treating resistant depression.* New York: PMA Publishing.

Goodwin, F. K., Prange, A. J., Jr., Post, R. M., Muscattola, G., & Lipton, M. A. (1982). L-triiodothyronine converts tricyclic antidepressant non-responders to responders. *American Journal of Psychiatry, 139,* 334–338.

Harrison, W. M., Rabkin, J. G., Ehrhard, A. A., Stewart, J. W., McGrath, P. J., Ross, D., Quitkin, F. M. (1986). Effects of antidepressant medication on sexual function: A controlled study. *Journal of Clinical Psychopharmacology, 6,* 144–149.

Hullin, R. P. (1980). Minimum serum lithium levels for effective prophylaxis. In F. N. Johnson (Ed.), *Handbook of lithium therapy.* Baltimore: University Park Press.

Jarvik, L. F., Read, S. L., Minty, J., & Neshkes, R. E. (1983). Pretreatment orthostatic hypotension in geriatric depression: Predictor of response to imipramine and doxepin. *Journal of Clinical Psychopharmacology, 3,* 368–372.

Jefferson, J. W., Greist, J. S., Ackerman, D. L., & Carroll, J. A. (1987). *Lithium encyclopedia for clinical practice.* Washington: American Psychiatric Press.

Joyce, P. R., & Paykel, E. S. (1989). Predictors of drug response in depression. *Archives of General Psychiatry, 46,* 89–99.

Kalinowsky, L. B. (1975). Electric and other convulsive treatments. In S. Arieti (Ed.), *American handbook of psychiatry, V. Treatment* (2nd ed.). New York: Basic Books.

Kiloh, L. G. (1982). Electroconvulsive therapy. In E. S. Paykel (Ed.), *Handbook of affective disorders.* New York: Guilford.

Klein, D. F., & Davis, J. M. (1969). *Diagnosis and drug treatment of psychiatric disorders.* Baltimore: Williams & Wilkins.

Lewis, J. L., & Winokur, G. (1982). The induction of mania: A natural history study with controls. *Archives of General Psychiatry, 39,* 303–306.

Montgomery, S. A. (1987). Does it make sense to change tricyclic antidepressants in resistant depression? In J. Zohar & R. H. Belmaker (Eds.), *Treating resistant depression.* New York: PMA Publishing.

Munjak, D. J. (1984). The treatment of phenelzine-induced hypotension with salt tablets: Case report. *Journal of Clinical Psychiatry, 45*, 89–90.

Nelson, J. C., & Bowers, J. B. (1978). Delusional unipolar depression: Description and drug treatment. *Archives of General Psychiatry, 35*, 1321–1328.

Nelson, J. C., Jatlow, P., Quinlan, D. M., & Bowers, M. B. (1982). Desipramine plasma concentration and antidepressant response. *Archives of General Psychiatry, 39*, 1419–1422.

Nies, A. (1983). Clinical application of MAOI's. In G. D. Burrows, T. R. Norman, & B. Davies (Eds.), *Antidepressants*. Amsterdam: Elsevier.

Nies, A. & Robinson, D. S. (1982). Monoamine oxidase inhibitors. In E. S. Paykel (Ed.), *Handbook of affective disorders*. New York: Guilford.

Prange, A. J., Jr. (1987). L-triiodothyronine (T_3): Its place in the treatment of TCA-resistant depressed patients. In J. Zohar & R. H. Belmaker (Eds.), *Treating resistant depression*. New York: PMA Publishing.

Prange, A. J., Jr., Wilson, T. C., Rabon, A. M., & Lipton, M. A. (1969). Enhancement of imipramine antidepressant activity by thyroid hormone. *American Journal of Psychiatry, 126*, 457–469.

Price, L. H., Heninger, G. R. (1988). Can yohimbine be used to treat orthostatic hypotension associated with the use of desipramine and other antidepressants? What general and/or specific strategy do you recommend for treating orthostatic hypotension? *Journal of Clinical Psychopharmacology, 8*, 384.

Quitkin, F., Raskin, J. D., Markowitz, J. M., Stewart, J. W., McGrath, P. J., & Harrison, W. (1987). Use of pattern analysis to identify true drug response. *Archives of General Psychiatry, 44*, 259–264.

Quitkin, F., Rifkin, A., & Klein, D. F. (1979). Monoamine oxidase inhibitors: A review of antidepressant effectiveness. *Archives of General Psychiatry, 36*, 749–760.

Ramsey, T. A., & Mendels, J. (1980). Lithium in the acute treatment of depression. In F. N. Johnson (Ed.), *Handbook of lithium therapy*. Baltimore: University Park Press.

Robinson, D. S., Nies, A., Ravaris, C. L., Ives, J. O., & Bartlett, D. (1978). Clinical pharmacology of phenelzine. *Archives of General Psychiatry, 35*, 629–635.

Roose, S. P., Glassman, A. H., Giardina, E. G. V., Walsh, B. T., Woodring, S., & Bigger, J. T. (1987). TCAs in depressed patients with cardiac conduction disease. *Archives of General Psychiatry, 44*, 273–275.

Roose, S. P., Glassman, A. H., Siris, S. G., Walsh, B. T., Bruno, R. L., & Wright, L. B. (1981). Comparison of imipramine- and nortriptyline-induced orthostatic hypotension: A meaningful difference. *Journal of Clinical Psychopharmacology, 1*, 316–319.

Schatzberg, A. F., Dessain, E., O'Neil, P., Katy, D. L., & Cole, J. O. (1987). Recent studies on selective serotonergic antidepressants: Trazodone, fluoxetine, and fluvoxamine. *Journal of Clinical Psychopharmacology, 7* (supp.), 445–495.

Schneider, L. S., Sloan, R. B., Staples, F. R., & Bender, H. (1986). Pretreatment orthostatic hypotension as a predictor of response to nortriptyline in geriatric depression. *Journal of Clinical Psychopharmacology, 6,* 172–176.

Sitland-Marken, P. A., Rickman, L. A., Wells, B. G., & Mabie, W. C. (1989). Pharmacologic management of acute mania in pregnancy. *Journal of Clinical Psychopharmacology, 9,* 78-87.

Snaith, R. P. (1981). How much ECT does the depressed patient need? In R. L. Palmer (Ed.), *Electroconvulsive therapy: An appraisal.* Oxford: Oxford University Press.

Wehr, T. A., & Goodwin, F. K. (1979). Rapid cycling in manic-depressives induced by tricyclic antidepressants. *Archives of General Psychiatry, 36,* 555–559.

Weissman, M. M. (1979). The psychological treatment of depression. *Archives of General Psychiatry, 36,* 1261–1269.

Ziegler, J. E., Co, B. T., & Biggs, J. T. (1977). Plasma nortriptyline levels and EKG findings. *American Journal of Psychiatry, 134,* 441–443.

Zung, W. W. K. (1983). Review of placebo, controlled trials with bupropion. *Journal of Clinical Psychiatry, 44* (sec. 2), 104–114.

CHAPTER 15

Psychoanalytic Therapy of Depression

JULES R. BEMPORAD, MD

BASIC PRINCIPLES

The proven effectiveness of antidepressant medication and other somatic treatments in rapidly ameliorating episodes of depression has led some therapists to question what role, if any, psychoanalysis, or long-term individual psychotherapy, retains in the optimal care of depressed individuals. These questions could be answered by pointing out that not all depressives respond to somatic treatments or that these therapeutic measures appear to affect different aspects of the depressive clinical spectrum than does psychotherapy. However, these counterarguments against skepticism regarding the efficacy of psychotherapy, while valid, would miss the inherent contribution that this form of treatment provides to depressive illness. Psychoanalytic psychotherapy is not a specific treatment for the symptoms of depression present during a clinical episode. The vegetative signs (such as anergia, insomnia, or anorexia) appear to respond best to somatic intervention. The paralyzing dysphoric mood may, at times, be relieved by psychotherapy initially, if the patient gains a sense of optimism upon embarking on a new treatment or if the patient has finally found a therapist who understands his or her plight. However, this early improvement can be found in most forms of interpersonal verbal therapies and cannot be credited to the particular mode of psychoanalytic therapy.

Psychoanalytic therapy does not attack depressive symptoms but hopes to reduce the magnitude and recurrence of clinical depression by improving the individual's ability to cope with his or her environment and by increasing emotional resiliency to formerly depressogenic events. As Strupp, Sandell, Waterhouse, O'Malley, and Anderson (1982) have observed, this form of therapy attempts to strengthen the patient's fundamental adaptive capacities. Therefore, the aim is to change personality structure rather than to ameliorate symptoms. These symptoms are treated indirectly, as it is hoped that when the individual better withstands those experiences which had previously resulted in decompensation, he or she will be subject to fewer and less severe instances of depression. The alteration in personality is achieved through the analysis of the two major facets of psychoanalytic therapy: resistance and transference, which are the essential concepts defining this form of treatment. In *The History of the Psychoanalytic Movement* (1914), Freud clearly emphasized these two features as essential to psychoanalytic therapy:

It may be thus said that the theory of psychoanalysis is an attempt to account for two striking and unexpected facts of observation which emerge whenever an attempt is made to trace the symptoms of a neurotic back to their sources in his past life: the facts of transference and of resistance. Any line of investigation which recognizes the two facts and takes them as the starting point of its work may call itself psychoanalysis, though it arrives at results other than my own.

(p. 16)

In the many decades since these words were written, transference and resistance have remained the essential concepts defining psychoanalytic psychotherapy (Greenson, 1967). Resistance is the individual's largely unconscious method of impeding the conscious awareness of his intrapsychic world. Transference represents the unconscious misrepresentation of people in current life to conform to characteristics of individuals who were significant in the past. The patient is unaware of this inappropriate distortion but is affected greatly by the vicissitudes of his relationships with individuals who have become the objects of his transference reactions. While some practitioners would analyze transference reactions only when they themselves have become their object, others would include distortions of individuals other than the therapist as suitable for investigation and interpretation. On a broader basis, overcoming resistance means coming to grips with those distortions about oneself and others that were developed in the formative years in the interactions with family or other significant individuals, and the examination of transference indicates an appreciation of how these atavistic beliefs continue to influence individuals in their adult life. As Offenkrantz and Tobin (1974) pointed out, the psychoanalytic task may be divided into two major phases: the first is to make the here-and-now experience with the therapist allow for the discovery of how the past is still alive in the patient's perceptions and behavior, and the second is to show the patient how the present situation is markedly different from the past.

In the context of a close and trusting relationship, the patient gradually understands those hidden pathogenic aspects of the self which in turn the therapist identifies, interprets according to a meaningful system, and, hopefully, transforms into more appropriate appraisals of reality. Since much of what is hidden is linked to painful memories and realizations, there is a constant effort to resist this awareness and change.

In summary, psychoanalytic therapy is the attempt to prevent future recurrences of depressive illness or to relieve a less episodic chronic depression, by restructuring the personality so that the patient no longer succumbs to the defeats, losses, or frustrations that in the past had precipitated an intensification of dysphoric mood to clinical proportions.

This form of therapy is lengthy, expensive, and, for the patient, at times rather unpleasant because unwelcomed discoveries about the self are crystallized or a painful past is remembered and, partially, relived. Psychoanalytic therapy is thus not applicable to everyone who has experienced depression. It may be contraindicated in the very severely ill who have suffered a psychotic episode or who may have a biological basis for their disorder, such as manic-depressives. These individuals may not be able to withstand the rigors of analytic work and may become worse as they experience intense emotions or the evocation of a transference distortion. At the other end of the spectrum, some individuals may be too healthy to undergo the financial or emotional costs inherent in this form of therapy. Even psychologically sound individuals experience depression following a severe loss or disappointment. In fact, the ability to bear depression and learn from it may be a sign of maturity and strength (Gut, 1989). An individual who manifests an "adjustment disorder" may wish to be analyzed as a process of self-discovery but this therapy is not specifically indicated therapeutically for this form of depression. These two groups, the very sick and the very healthy, can still benefit from modified psychotherapy, which is primarily confrontative, supportive, and concerned mainly with one's current situation. This is particularly true of healthy individuals who are temporarily devastated by a profound life event. Because of their psychological stamina and their history of optimal functioning, the emotional needs for sharing and support of such individuals often are overlooked and they are treated only by somatic treatments. All too often, these depressed individuals go through a period of painful isolation and while in this state may decide on choices that are later regretted from the hindsight of regained health. Short-term psychotherapy can do much in allowing these individuals a close, open relationship in a time of urgent need; by putting the depressive episode in proper perspective, psychotherapy prevents their grasping at ultimately poor solutions.

In contrast to these forms of depression, psychoanalytic therapy appears best indicated for two forms of mood disorder. One is the so-called "characterological depression" in which the mood disturbance is perpetuated by the individual's everyday way of living. His or her values, relationships, and modes of self-assessment reinforce a chronic state of depression whose intensity may fluctuate with the vicissitudes of external events. The other form is episodic, with periods of relatively depression-free functioning between clinical decompensations. These individuals are able to fend off depressive mood for variable periods of time by psychologically aberrant life-styles, only to fall ill once more when their mode of defense is no longer possible. Some protect themselves from depression by entering into masochistic, dependent relationships with others who they believe will offer them the love and security that are so desperately desired. Others strive toward the achievement of an all-encompassing and lofty goal which they hope will prove their worth to others. However, the unrealistic and excessive degree to which these defenses are utilized for maintenance of self-esteem produces a constant vulnerability to depression (Arieti & Bemporad, 1978). Individuals with both characterological and episodic forms of depression present with histories of long-standing maladaptive personality patterns, with distorted beliefs about themselves and others, and with gross difficulties in establishing a sense of self-worth. It is toward these underlying pathogenic processes, rather than toward manifest symptomatology, that psychoanalytic therapy is directed.

PROCESS OF THERAPY

The following sections attempt to describe the framework for the course of therapy with depressed patients. Generalization is difficult because each individual presents with idiosyncratic vulnerabilities, defenses, and distortions as well as a specific past history and current situation. Therefore, the characteristics discussed here are, at best, those that many depressives share to some degree. Similarly, for expository purposes, the course of therapy is divided into three major stages, although such a conceptualization is artificial and does not represent accurately the frequent need to deal with each of the three proposed stages simultaneously. Perhaps, rather than considering each stage as emerging in a temporal context, these should be understood as the major therapeutic tasks to be achieved with depressives, during any part of the therapy.

Most depressed individuals present for treatment in the midst of a clinical episode, when their psychic life is filled with despair and anxiety. They present themselves as anguished or empty, feeling that their environment offers little satisfaction and that they are less than adequate as human beings. Their helplessness in altering their internal state and their lack of hope of ever feeling better lead them to desire relief from their pain over any other therapeutic goal. In the past, for severely depressed patients, this time had often been allotted to the therapist's forming an alliance with the patient while waiting for the acute episode to pass of its own accord. The availability of antidepressant medication has helped to shorten this period somewhat for some patients. However, even with the benefits of pharmacological intervention, the patient still maintains a negative outlook on life and, justifiably, sees the self as having undergone a considerable ordeal. The depressed patient may sense himself or herself as helpless, isolated, and debilitated, relying unrealistically on the therapist for nurturance and support. Not infrequently there is an early idealization of the therapist which can only lead to later disappointment and resentment when the therapist cannot live up to the expectation of the patient.

Jacobson (1971, 1975) wrote specifically about problems in transference during the early sessions with depressives. She described how these patients become overinvolved with their therapists and experience an initial improvement because they have formed illusory expectations of nurturance. They express devotion to the therapist but eventually will demand equal devotion in return and, when this is not received, will leave treatment, become angry, or experience an intensification of their depressive symptoms. Kolb (1956) also noted that the beginning of treatment with depressives is stressful to the therapist because of the guilt-provoking dependency of the patient. He wrote:

> The depressed patient demands to be gratified. He attempts to extract or force the gratification from the therapist by his pleas for help, by his exposure of his misery, and by suggesting that the therapist is responsible for leaving him in his unfortunate condition.

The therapist should be warm and encouraging but consistently make clear that the burden of therapy and cure rests on the patient's shoulders. Idealization should be detected early and transference distortions corrected as these arise. In this regard, the therapist must be honest about his or her own shortcomings and the limitations of psychotherapy to produce miraculous and rapid cures. This openness, which was recommended by Kolb (1956), is very important since the depressive has all too often been raised in an atmosphere of deceit, manipulation, and secret obligations and must be shown that it is possible to be honest and forthright without being criticized or abandoned.

INSIGHT

Once the symptoms of the acute episode have begun to abate, the patient should be encouraged to look inward toward the causes of the dysphoria. This search involves the patient's relating the precipitating factor for the clinical episode to a particular personality organization. The environmental loss, frustration, or rejection that provokes a severe depression has a deeper meaning for the individual; it threatens a needed sense of self and his or her sources of narcissism. Therefore, what appears to the casual observer as a trivial event may reverberate with a deep-seated fear and shame in the vulnerable individual. This inward search not only initiates a long process of self-understanding but also helps the individual to become "psychologically minded" by paying attention to dreams, feelings, and passing thoughts which in the past may have been dismissed from consciousness. The search for the meaning of a precipitant also dispels some of the patient's sense of helplessness, demonstrating that depression does not arise out of the blue but is related to factors within the patient and, thus, is potentially under his or her control.

An illustration of this initial process is the therapy of an executive who, after performing very successfully in his work, was offered the opportunity to start his own business, a prospect that would have allowed him the autonomy and increased wealth which he strongly desired. He was very excited about this change in career and fantasized himself as becoming rich and important. However, as the time approached for this career move to occur, he began doubting himself and experiencing anxiety and fear over his ability to direct his own business. He ascribed his former success to luck and believed that the move would expose him as inadequate and a failure. His estimation of himself as a worthless businessman generalized to his assessment of himself as a husband, father, and, eventually, total human being. He was certain that he did not have the strength or knowledge to accept any responsibility and that he needed to hide his numerous inadequacies. As this alteration in attitude transpired, he lost all motivation for work (which had been his major preoccupation), felt exhausted, could not sleep, not eat, and refused to see friends or family. He withdrew to his bed where he obsessed over his alleged failures, berated himself for having left his secure job, and contemplated suicide as a means of escaping his shameful predicament. In this condition, he was hospitalized and treated with anxiolytics and antidepressants which moderated his intensive dysphoria but left him still pessimistic and confused.

When seen in therapy, he could not understand why he had become depressed. He knew that his decompensation had started when he seriously contemplated going into business for himself but why this prospect, which promised so much, had resulted in his decompensation remained a mystery to him. As he discussed the possible meaning that this event might have for him, he realized that he had never been his own boss but always relied on senior executives to direct his activities, even when such direction was unnecessary. He discovered that he excessively used older men as sources of security that would ensure, in some magical manner, the success of his ventures. This unrealistic dependency was traced to his relationship with his deceased, autocratic father who repeatedly judged the patient as incapable of functioning on his own and constantly requiring his guidance. The patient noted feelings for his immediate superior similar to those he had felt toward his father. He also confessed that he truly believed that his boss, like his father had in the past, would become angry with him for daring to be independent and would seek revenge in some terrible manner.

The patient also became aware of the great sense of loss that he would experience in leaving his mother since the new business would be situated in another city. He had not recognized his dependency on his mother, with whom he spoke every day and whom he visited a few times a week. She was the one person in his world who could make him feel loved and worthy, but only if he followed her implicit instructions of obedience and loyalty. She had always encouraged him to be successful but had punished any attempt at autonomy. In reviewing this relationship, he noted that his mother never got along with any of his girlfriends and always managed to create scenes when she and his wife got together. He also recalled a previous, milder depressive episode (which was suppressed via alcohol abuse) when his mother became emotionally distant after he married.

Finally, the patient remembered that, as a child, he had been sent abruptly to boarding school, allegedly because of a severe illness in a sibling. He had felt terribly lonely, ineffectual, and unliked in that setting, which seemed to confirm his parental estimation of him. He failed in his schoolwork and was sent home in shame and disgrace. These revelations vividly presented to this patient the reasons why so benign an event as an excellent career opportunity could result in a disastrous decompensation. Past events took on new meanings as he allowed himself to integrate bits of history into overall themes. Similarly, his current functioning was appreciated more deeply as he discovered how these basic themes continued to affect his sense of self and all that this implied.

The establishing of a therapeutic relationship characterized by openness and realistic expectations, the realization that the clinical episode is the resultant of premorbid personality organization, and the connecting of the precipitating events with particular maladaptive modes of gaining and maintaining a sense of worth comprise the major objectives of the first stage of therapy.

The patient's realization that his or her basic beliefs are irrational or that everyday reactions are self-defeating does not automatically ensure that self-conceptions or previous activities will change automatically. Characterological psychopathology is not easily relinquished, for these older, ingrained patterns have offered security, predictability, structure, and occasional gratification. The patient would gladly relinquish the symptoms but resists changes in the personality that forms the basis of these very dreaded symptoms. The overcoming of these resistances and the gradual process of change comprise the middle stage of therapy. This is the time of "working through," the real battleground of therapy, which has frequent advances, regressions, and stalemates. The fundamental struggle involves the depressive's giving up excessive reliance on external props for self-esteem and risking to venture into new modes of deriving pleasure and meaning. The resistances that are usually encountered are a fear that one's life will be totally empty without the familiar, if stifling, structure that the former beliefs and adaptations had provided and a crippling anxiety that one will be abandoned or ridiculed if he or she dares to break the childhood taboos.

A chronically depressed woman, whose illness was perpetuated by what she perceived to be an unhappy marriage, began to understand that her experiences with her father had been so humiliating and painful that she would not allow herself to care about any man. She feared that if she let herself become vulnerable by truly loving a man, he would use this opportunity to exploit her and would reject her in a sadistic manner. These modes of defense against narcissistic injury had been developed in reaction to actual mistreatment of her as a child, continued to direct her involvement with others as an adult when they were no longer appropriate, and served only to rob her of a sense of commitment and mutuality with others. As a result she continuously needed to find fault with her husband, so that she could not love him and thus be open to his inevitable rejection. She pretended to love him but secretly found him effeminate and ineffectual, and thus unworthy of her true devotion. These defensive operations were explored in therapy whereupon the patient recognized her distorted view of her husband and began to make an effort to allow herself to see him more realistically. As she succeeded in letting herself be more open to him, she began to enjoy intercourse with him and to look forward to their making love. In this context, she dreamed that she was married to a famous movie star who actually resembled her husband in appearance. In the dream, she was thrilled at having such a desirable husband and was eagerly awaiting going to bed with him. When they were having sex, the husband did not perform and weighed heavily on her body, as if uninterested in her. Suddenly, an older woman discovered them and began to loudly berate and criticize the patient. The scene in the dream switched to her being in the kitchen with the movie-star husband and her noticing that he really was not very manly or desirable, and, in so reasoning, felt more comfortable with him and with herself.

RESISTANCE

This dream dramatically illustrates the depressive's desire to give up older, established distortions and an opposing desire to maintain these for fear of greater injury. In spite of the patient's acknowledging that these older beliefs are erroneous and that characterological defenses only serve to perpetuate a lack of enjoyment or involvement in life, the risk of relinquishing these archaic convictions continue to surface and to obstruct change. Therapy, at this stage, involves a repeated identification and interpretation as these depressogenic thoughts and evaluations recur in the patient's life.

TRANSFERENCE

These underlying themes regularly permeate the therapeutic setting with the patient transferentially distorting the therapist to conform to significant figures of the past, despite a simultaneous awareness of the inappropriateness of these projections. One depressed woman became increasingly anxious and unable to speak freely in sessions. She confessed that she believed that the therapist's warm and empathic manner was but a disguise underneath which his true sadistic and critical nature was ready to humiliate the patient. She experienced dreams at this time in which the therapist was transformed during her sessions into her father who then embarrassed her for being weak and lazy, ultimately refusing to treat anyone so unworthy and dismissing her from therapy.

This woman's transferential distortion illustrates the depressives' basic feeling of worthlessness and unlovability. She, like other depressives, could not conceive of being liked for herself alone but believed that others would tolerate her only if she enhanced their lives. For the depressive, love is never given freely; it has to be earned through spectacular achievements, model conduct, slavish devotion, or masochistic behavior. Furthermore, there is the conviction that the love of significant others is available but somehow the individual has not strived sufficiently to merit being loved. In patients who are prone to severe depression, this sense of unworthiness may be quite pervasive and its conscious realization evokes profound dysphoria. Part of this sadness is due to the simultaneous conclusion that their parents, in fact, did not love them as children. Despite verbal expressions of the promise of love, their parents actually used them in order to fulfill their own needs or may have harbored aggressive feelings toward them as children. Painful as this realization may be, it may be utilized to demonstrate to these patients that a perceived and actual lack of being loved was not due to some deficiency on their part but to an inability of the parents to offer security and benevolence. Therefore, there should be the expectation that others may love the patients for themselves, even if the parents were incapable of so doing. These others, who are encountered in adult life, do not necessitate the stifling and inhibiting manipulations that were learned in order to obtain some assurances of affection or regard from the parents. The patient mentioned above became ill when her superior at work, for whom she had expended all of her energies in order to obtain favor, hired another female assistant who was perceived as being preferred by the all-important superior. This core sense of unworthiness is more blatantly exemplified by another woman who became severely depressed when her husband unexpectedly amassed a large amount of money in his business. This patient believed that her now wealthy husband would no longer need her and would abandon her for more desirable women.

The pervasive low self-regard of the depressive and the compensatory need for external reassurance of worth from the therapist characterize the typical transference reaction of the analytic process. Fears of rejection, abandonment, and brutal criticism at the hands of the therapist regularly intrude into the analytic relationship even after a secure therapeutic alliance has been consolidated. These negative expectations echo the ever present possibility of narcissistic injury that was experienced repeatedly and capriciously as a child.

One depressed patient who had made considerable gains in achieving a more satisfactory image of herself and of others, including the therapist, had discussed her improvement with a close friend, demonstrating a greater sense of trust in others and the ability to reveal herself more openly. To her surprise and satisfaction, the friend confirmed her improvement. She also expressed the desire to go into treatment and asked the patient to convey to her therapist that she would be calling him for a recommendation. After relating this information to her therapist, the patient, in the following sessions, caustically criticized the therapist's office decor, his demeanor, and other aspects of the treatment situation. When this abrupt change in what had been a positive view of therapy was pointed out, the patient revealed that since her conversation with her friend she had felt sure that the therapist would take on the friend in treatment and would prefer the friend to herself, since she believed her friend to be prettier and smarter. When asked by the therapist if she had not considered that his treating her friend simultaneously would complicate her treatment and put an additional burden on her therapy, the patient replied that she had thought of this possibility but dismissed it because therapists needed to make money and would not turn down an additional patient. The gist of her response was that she was not sufficiently important or interesting as an individual to merit appropriate care and that others would put their own needs or desires before her own. When the patient learned that her friend had indeed called her therapist but that, rather than treating her himself, he had referred her to a colleague, she reacted with complete surprise. She could not conceive of her being worthy of consideration in her own right. Her transferential distortion of the therapist as a re-embodiment of her exploitative father was corrected by the actual sequence of events. She saw her therapist differently and she saw herself as being entitled to consideration and care. She also realized that her initial referral of her friend was an attempt to ingratiate the therapist by finding patients for him and ensuring his gratitude (an action she later regretted when she thought it would relinquish her to a less favored status). This sequence of events helped to disconfirm her childhood sense of self in a concrete, lived-out fashion and to form a new and more realistic self-regard.

ANXIETY

The other major theme that regularly emerges in the therapy of depressed individuals is a horrifying fear that the gratifying of desire and impulses will result in abandonment, criticism, or some other eventuality that will negatively affect the individual. This pleasure anxiety is evident in almost all of depressives' activities except for some rare and secret gratifications that are hidden from others. From the histories related, future depressives were not permitted to express the natural exuberance of childhood and the normal hedonism of that stage of development was met with stern disapproval from parents. The pursuit of personal satisfaction is viewed as evidence of a severe disloyalty to the family and a wanton betrayal of the welfare of others. Even achievements such as excellent grades or athletic awards are understood to be one's repayment to the family for their support rather than a source of pleasure or esteem. Doing things "just for the fun of it" is perceived as a terrible self-indulgence that will incur the wrath or the loss of needed others. One depressed patient who had to travel frequently on business had no difficulty in leaving home for extended periods of time. However, when she was awarded a free vacation because of her exemplary work, she was convinced that in her absence her parents would become ill or die, or her house would be burglarized, or she would lose her job. She could not tolerate the "shame" of publicly having fun and anticipated punishment for her holiday. Another depressed patient who had made a great deal of money despaired that he did not enjoy his wealth but saw it only as insurance against certain disaster. His childhood was spent in a gloomy household with portents of ever present doom and an undercurrent of despair. His one memory of warmth and enjoyment came from his frequent visits to a neighborhood gas station where the mechanics "adopted" him and taught him how to repair cars. As an adult, he longed to buy antique cars and renovate them as a source of pleasure but could not bring himself to waste his time on such unproductive pursuits. Whenever he dared to realize this dream, he was overcome with the fear that he would lose all of his money or that other people would no longer respect him because of this frivolous behavior.

In therapy, patients will attempt to win praise by hard work and the shunning of pleasurable activities, much as they had done in childhood with their parents. This self-imposed anhedonia may be identified, as it is acted out and revealed, as an outmoded manner of obtaining security at the expense of independent satisfaction. Over time, the patient may confess "secret" desires that had been suppressed for fear of jeopardizing the needed parental relationship. These are usually quite healthy, although unproductive, aspirations that give existence a sense of joy and pleasure.

PROGRESS IN THERAPY

As patients improve, they may take up hobbies or allow themselves to spend money on entertainment. One depressed patient finally allowed himself to take flying lessons, another allowed himself to buy fashionable, expensive clothes, while another started writing short stories for his own amusement. The endeavors are regularly met initially with anxiety and shame since these are believed to result in abandonment or criticism. As patients realize that their attainment of autonomous gratification does not result in catastrophe and as the therapist applauds rather than condemns these activities, a sense of freedom and inner contentment slowly materializes. With each progressive step in therapy, the childhood roots of the former sanctions to independence are explored and discussed in the light of adult experience. Once the patients understand that with maturity comes a degree of autonomy and freedom from the control of significant others, they are well along the path toward change.

The last stage of treatment concerns environmental barriers to change more than intrapsychic ones. As patients change their behaviors and values as a result of therapy, significant others in their immediate environment may resist these changes. Colleagues, employers, but most specifically spouses may react negatively to the new and, for them, alarming or irritating sense of self that emerges in the therapeutic process. Individuals who interact with the patients in everyday life truly want them to be cured and certainly do not wish them to once again succumb to episodes of clinical depression. However, they also do not want to give up the former type of relationship, which fostered recurrent episodes of melancholia.

Another task of the final stage of therapy is a coming to terms with the ghosts of the past. Too often there is a rapid transition from an idealization of past authorities to a bitter resentment of these same people. Patients should understand that the pathogenic actions of parents (or other childhood influences) were a result of their own pathology and that these childhood idols were just ordinary people with the usual limitations along with their positive attributes. It is most important that patients appreciate their own willful participation in recreating their childhood situation in adult life, regardless of how they were treated as children.

The overriding goal of this stage, however, is the consolidation of the changes that have been achieved. Certain superficial characteristics that are indicative of deeper change may help the therapist gauge the patients' improvement. Almost all of these manifestations revolve around the patients' new independence and ability to derive meaning and pleasure directly from everyday activities. For example, creativity bespeaks the confidence to try new things. Spontaneity also reflects an ability to act with assurance, without constantly having to appraise how others will view one's behavior. The ability to take one's failures (and the failures of others) philosophically and with a sense of humor indicates an end to the hypermoral coloring of all events as "good" or "bad." Being able to take failure in stride indicates that patients do not feel themselves evil or worthless if they do not achieve their every objective and, in turn, that their self-esteem is realistically independent of life's vicissitudes. A most important indicator of change is that patients no longer work only to obtain praise or to master some remote goal, but instead gain satisfaction from everyday life.

Another manifestation of change is a growing interest in others, not for what they can supply to one's self-esteem but because they are important and interesting in themselves. In losing their manipulativeness, patients may experience true empathy for the first time, seeing others as similar to but separate from themselves. Therapy is then seen as an endeavor that involves sharing and learning rather than as a constant struggle to obtain needed feedback from a transferentially distorted other. Therapy should remain *the* place where patients can express themselves without fear or shame until they are able to form other such relationships in their everyday life.

REFERENCES

Arieti, S., & Bemporad, J. (1978). *Severe and mild depression: The psychotherapeutic approach.* New York: Basic Books.

Freud, S. (1914). The history of the psychoanalytic movement. In J. Strachey (Ed. and Trans.). The *standard edition of the complete psychological works of Sigmund Freud* (Vol. 14). London: Hogarth Press.

Greeson, R. (1967). *The technique and practice of psychoanalysis.* New York: International Universities Press.

Gut, E. (1989). *Productive and unproductive depression.* New York: Basic Books.

Jacobson, E. (1971). *Depression.* New York: International Universities Press.

Jacobson, E. (1975). The psychoanalytic treatment of depressed patients. In E. J. Anthony & T. Benedek (Eds.), *Depression and human existence.* Boston: Little, Brown.

Kolb, L. C. (1956). Psychotherapeutic evolution and its implications. *Psychiatric Quarterly, 30;* 1–19.

Offenkrantz, W. & Tobin, A. (1974). Psychoanalytic psychotherapy. *Archives of General Psychiatry, 30,* 593–606.

Strupp, M. M., Sandell, J. A., Waterhouse, G. J., O'Malley, S. S., & Anderson, J. L. Psychodynamic therapy: Theory and research. (1982). In J. Rush (Ed.), *Short-term psychotherapies for depression* (pp. 215–250). New York: Guilford.

CHAPTER 16

Behavioral Treatments for Unipolar Depression

HARRY M. HOBERMAN, PhD

The rich theoretical and empirical literature that has developed attests to the value and efficacy of behavioral treatments for unipolar depression. In a number of ways, behavioral approaches to the treatment of depression have led the way in the development of a scientific study of the psychotherapy of episodes of psychopathology. Within a relatively short period of time, both the quantity and sophistication of behavioral treatments for depression have increased dramatically. A variety of behaviorally oriented treatment packages for depressive disorders have developed and considerable evidence exists for the efficacy of each of these programs. A number of thoughtful and comprehensive reviews of this extensive literature have appeared (Blaney, 1981; Craighead, 1981; DeRubeis & Hollon, 1981; Hersen & Bellack, 1982; Lewinsohn & Hoberman, 1982). Beyond the cumulative support for their efficacy, behavioral approaches are worth considering for a number of reasons. Behavioral therapies offer the patient new or enhanced behavioral and cognitive skills as well as new ways of thinking about himself or herself. By focusing on the interaction of patients with their environment, such therapies allow for the modification of predisposing or etiologically significant interactions by helping the patient to change those interactions. Additionally, as Rush and Beck (1978) noted, behavioral interventions can be utilized to increase compliance with pharmacotherapy and to decrease premature termination from biological treatments. Finally, depressed persons who either refuse or cannot take antidepressant medication, or who do not respond to adequate trails of pharmacological agents, may respond to behavioral therapies. As clinicians increasingly accept the value and power of behavioral approaches in the treatment of psychiatric disorders, practitioners have the opportunity to select from a range of therapeutic formulations and, thus, to match potential interventions with the particular needs of their patients and the parameters of their treatment settings.

CONCEPTUAL PERSPECTIVES

Current behavioral approaches to the treatment of depression can best be understood and appreciated against the background of the conceptual foundations of behavior therapy in general, as well as early attempts by behaviorists to generate and test theory-based treatments for depression.

Conceptual Foundations of Behavior Therapy

The development of behavioral approaches to the treatment of psychological disorders had its basis in two initially distinct but sequential movements within psychology. First, beginning in the early part of this century, investigators increasingly attempted to explain human behavior on the basis of experimental studies of learning. Thus, psychologists such as Thorndike (1931) and Skinner (1953) argued for the importance of the "law of effect" and the role of behavioral consequences in learning, with Skinner also emphasizing the role of the environment rather than undocumented mental entities in determining behavior. A second and somewhat later force in the genesis of behavior therapy was rooted in an increasing dissatisfaction with the predominant intrapsychic conceptions of abnormal behavior and related treatment approaches. More particularly, certain theorists and practitioners were motivated to explore alternative models of treatment primarily because: (a) there was difficulty in testing critical assumptions of psychodynamic approaches, and empirical support was lacking when those assumptions could be tested; (b) the current diagnostic schemes had few implications for understanding the etiology, prognosis, or treatment of the disorders they defined; and (c) there was a general belief that, as Eysenck's (1952) study had suggested, the efficacy of traditional psychotherapy had yet to be established. As a result of the dissatisfaction with available psychotherapeutic orientations, a variety of theorists and therapists endeavored to develop therapeutic approaches based on the clinical utility of learning concepts. These initial theories and practices based on experimental studies of behavior constituted the basis for the field of behavior therapy.

Currently, behavior therapy can best be understood more as a general scientific approach to the understanding of behavior and its treatment rather than as having a specific theoretical basis or consisting of any specific set of techniques. Kazdin (1982) has suggested that behavior therapy can best be characterized by a number of assumptions:

1. A reliance on findings or techniques derived from general psychology, especially the psychology of learning
2. A view of the continuity of normal and abnormal behavior

3. A direct focus on the maladaptive behavior for which an individual seeks treatment
4. An emphasis on the assessment of behavior across domains and situations, for the delineation of both an individual's behavior and the influences that may contribute to, and thus may be used to change, that behavior
5. A belief that the process of treatment should be closely tied to the continual assessment of problematic target behaviors so that the outcome of therapy can be measured by monitoring changes in target behaviors

Additionally, behavior therapy is marked by its focus on current rather than historical determinants of behavior and on the specification of treatment in objective and operational terms so that procedures can be replicated.

Behavioral Theories of Depression

The predominant behavioral theories of depression fall in the domain of what is known as social learning theory. Social learning theory assumes that psychological functioning can best be understood in terms of continuous reciprocal interactions among personal factors (e.g., cognitive processes, expectancies), behavioral factors, and environmental factors, all operating as interdependent determinants of one another. From the perspective of social learning theory, people are seen as capable of exercising considerable control over their own behavior, and not simply as reactors to external influences; rather, they are viewed as selecting, organizing, and transforming the stimuli that impinge upon them. People and their environments are seen as reciprocal determinants of one another (Bandura, 1977).

Lewinsohn and his colleagues articulated the seminal behavioral theory of depression which has guided much of the empirical study of behavioral treatments of unipolar depression. According to Lewinsohn, Biglan, and Zeiss (1976), low rates of positive reinforcement (e.g., rewarding experiences) and/or high rates of aversive experiences are the central mediating factors in the onset of depression. Thus, the critical assumption of behavioral theories of depression is that a low rate of behavior (e.g., social withdrawal), dysphoric feelings, and negative cognitions are the product of low rates of rewarding experiences and/or high rates of negative experiences. These conditions were theorized to occur as a result of several factors: (a) The person's immediate environment may have few available positive experiences or may have many punishing aspects; (b) the capacity to enjoy positive experiences may be reduced and/or the sensitivity to aversive events may be heightened;

and (c) the person may lack the skills necessary to obtain available positive experiences and/or to cope effectively with aversive events. Evidence for each of these possibilities was shown by several studies (e.g., Lewinsohn, Youngren, & Grosscup, 1979) and was reviewed by Lewinsohn and Hoberman (1982).

Recently, Lewinsohn, Hoberman, Teri, and Hautzinger (1985) proposed a new theoretical model of the etiology and maintenance of depression. This integrative model of depression, presented schematically in Figure 16.1, represents an attempt to collate the findings of our epidemiological (Lewinsohn, Hoberman, & Rosenbaum, 1988) and treatment outcome studies (Zeiss, Lewinsohn, & Muñoz, 1979) with an increasing body of work in social psychology on the phenomenon of self-awareness (Carver & Scheier, 1982; Duval & Wicklund, 1973). The proposed etiological model, while tentative, represents the phenomena and conditions which are most often involved in the development and maintenance of depression. One of the strengths of this model is its incorporation of a number of different characteristics and processes that can influence the occurrence of depression. In so doing, the theory accounts for the great heterogeneity that characterizes both depression and depressives. According to the integrative theory of depression, the depressogenic process consists of the following components:

1. Antecedents are empirically defined as all events that increase the probability for the future occurrence of depression. In the literature to date, all of these "evoking events" fall under the general rubric of stressors, including life events, microstressors, and chronic difficulties. In particular, stressors related to marital distress, social exits, and work problems exhibit an especially strong relationship to the later development of depression.

2. The occurrence of *antecedents* is assumed to initiate the depressogenic process to the extent that they disrupt substantial, important, and relatively automatic behavior patterns of individuals. Much of everyday behavior appears to be "scripted" and, consequently, automatic and requiring very little mental effort. Yet, these scripted patterns constitute aspects of an individuals' behavior repertoire that are typical and crucial to a person's everyday interactions with the environment. Consequently, if antecedent or depression-evoking events do disrupt expected, automatic patterns of behavior, they are likely to elicit an immediate negative emotional response (e.g., dysphoria).

3. Such disruptions and emotional upset are assumed to be related to depression to the extent that they lead to a reduction of positive experiences and/or to an elevated rate of aversive experience; that is, they shift the balance of the quality of a person's interactions with the environment in a negative direction.

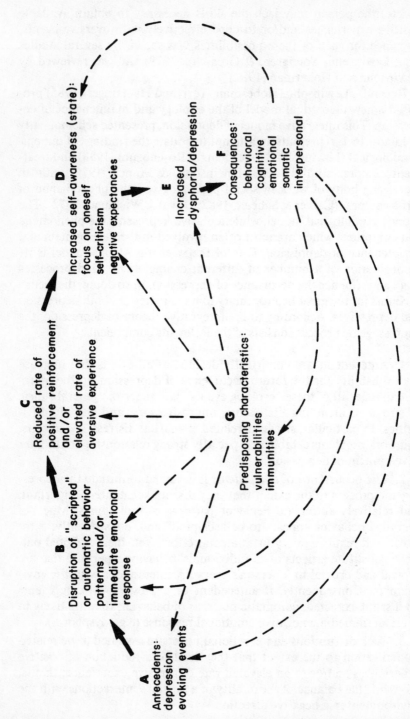

Figure 16.1. Schematic representation of variables involved in the occurrence of unipolar depression.

A
Antecedents:
depression
evoking events

B
Disruption of "scripted"
or automatic behavior
patterns and/or
immediate emotional
response

C
Reduced rate of
positive reinforcement
and/or
elevated rate of
aversive experience

D
Increased self-awareness (state):
focus on oneself
self-criticism
negative expectancies

E
Increased
dysphoria/depression

F
Consequences:
behavioral
cognitive
emotional
somatic
interpersonal

G
Predisposing characteristics:
vulnerabilities
immunities

4. A continued inability to reverse the depressogenic process to this point (e.g., to cope with behavioral disruption through decreasing negative experiences or increasing positive ones and, thus, producing a resumption of scripted behavior and/or neutral or positive affect) is hypothesized to lead to a heightened state of self-awareness. Such a state of increased self-awareness has been shown to have a number of relevant ramifications to depressive onset. First, given a situation that involves a behavioral standard (e.g., successful coping with evoking events and their subsequent emotional and behavioral disruption), self-awareness has been shown to increase self-evaluation and self-criticism when such a standard is not matched. Second, as negative outcome expectancies about future efforts to reverse the depressive cycle increase and individuals continue to be self-focused, their response is likely to be one of behavioral withdrawal and further self-criticism. In addition, heightened self-awareness has been shown to result in greater self-attribution for outcomes. In short, the elicitation of a state of heightened self-awareness breaks through an individual's self-protective, self-enhancing cognitive schema (e.g., Lewinsohn, Mischel, Chaplin, & Barton, 1980) and increases the individual's consciousness of having failed to live up to his or her expected standards of coping and, consequently, engenders a state of self-denigration and behavioral withdrawal.

5. Another important consequence of a heightened state of self-awareness is an intensification or magnification of affective reactions. The occurrence of disrupting antecedent events typically evokes some initial negative affect (e.g., sadness). Given an ongoing situation where an individual feels responsible for the occurrence of a stressor and/or attributes an inability to reverse the depressive cycle to himself or herself, dysphoria is likely to be the predominant emotional response. Thus, self-awareness will serve to magnify both the initial and continuing dysphoria.

6. Feeling increasingly dysphoric, in turn, is assumed to lead to many of the biological, behavioral, cognitive, emotional, and interpersonal changes that have previously been shown to be correlated with depression (e.g., appetite loss, slowed behavior, or social withdrawal). These changes are presumed to "lock in" the increased state of self-awareness and heightened dysphoria, creating a "vicious cycle" that serves to maintain the depressive state indefinitely.

7. The proposed model allows for a great variety of individual and environmental differences to both increase and decrease the risk of a depressive episode at a number of points during the depressogenic process. It is assumed that there are both predisposing vulnerabilities (e.g., being female, between ages 20 and 40, previous history of depression, and so on) and protective immunities (e.g., high self-perceived

social competence, competence in social interaction, generalized coping skills, high frequency of pleasant events, and so on).

The integrative model, in addition to taking into account much of what is empirically known about depression, provides potential explanations for a number of important aspects of depression. The explanatory value of this integrative theory of depression, a more detailed description of the model, and a more elaborated empirical documentation of the processes implicated in the model is presented in Lewinsohn et al. (1985). The utility of the integrative model of depression for the clinician is twofold: First, it takes into account much of what has been learned through treatment outcome studies of depression, and, second, it provides direction to the practitioner for the development and application of efficacious treatment programs.

In particular, the integrative model of depression highlights the probability that depressive episodes are the outcome of multiple events and processes. Of equal importance, it suggests that unipolar depression is a product of the transformation of behavior, affect, and cognition in the face of changing interactions between individuals and their environment. Therapeutically, it implicates a number of environmental, behavioral, affective, and cognitive phenomena as the targets of treatment. These include: stabilizing or reversing environmental changes (e.g., eliciting events); providing or enhancing means of coping with antecedent events that cannot be reversed and with the disruption of scripted behavior; decreasing the state of self-focus and the intensity of dysphoric affect; reducing critical self-evaluation and self-attribution for the failure to reverse the depressogenic process; reversing behavioral withdrawal and other correlates of the depressive episode; and remediating any predisposing vulnerabilities that facilitated the depressogenic process and that may, in turn, be maintaining the depressive episode. By selecting among these potential intervention strategies, behavioral treatments for depression aim to decrease the rate of negative experiences and increase the rate of positive experiences.

BEHAVIORAL STRATEGIES FOR TREATING DEPRESSION

A theory, however, is only a set of abstract statements suggesting general treatment goals for depressed persons (or at least certain kinds of depressives). A comprehensive treatment approach must also have a strategy. A treatment strategy translates the theory into a set of general operations and procedures that can be used to formulate treatment goals for the depressed person and to direct the elements of the treatment process. The guiding assumption in the treatment of depressed patients is that alterations in the frequency, quality, and range of the patients' activities and social interactions are the most common foci for achieving changes in the quality and frequency of positive experiences.

Diagnostic and Functional Assessment

First, an assessment for differential diagnosis must occur to determine whether depression is *the,* or at least *a,* problem for the individual. Individuals who are experiencing an episode of depression may manifest a heterogeneity of symptoms; additionally, symptoms of depression, and depression itself, occur in a large number of patients suffering from medical and other psychiatric disorders. Consequently, if depression is a presenting problem, an adequate medical and psychiatric history must be obtained to determine whether the depression is secondary to physical illness or a medical regime, or subsequent to a manic or hypomanic episode. In all these cases, it would be important to recommend an individual for specific assessment and treatment for the primary condition before proceeding with behavioral treatment for the depression. Existing assessment instruments (the Beck Depression Inventory (BDI): Beck, Ward, Mendelson, Mock, & Erbaugh, 1961; the Center for Epidemiologic Studies Depression Scale (CES-D): Radloff, 1977) allow a clinician to describe a patient in regard to depression severity and to delineate the specific constellation of symptoms shown by that patient as well as the absence or presence of other psychiatric conditions (the Schedule for Affective Disorders and Schizophrenia (SADS): Endicott & Spitzer, 1978; the Research Diagnostic Criteria (RDC): Spitzer, Endicott, & Robins, 1978).

While differential diagnosis may be common to behavioral as well as other treatment approaches, the second stage of assessment is relatively specific to behavioral interventions. A functional diagnosis or analysis of depressive behavior involves pinpointing specific person–environment interactions and events related to a particular patient's depression. This part of the diagnostic process is needed to guide the formulation of a specific, individualized treatment plan designed to change the events contributing to a particular patient's depression.

The prototypical means of identifying behavioral events and activities functionally related to depression involves the use of the Pleasant Events Schedule (PES; MacPhillamy & Lewinsohn, 1971) and the Unpleasant Events Schedule (UES; Lewinsohn, 1975a). Both of these tests have been described in greater detail elsewhere and test manuals providing normative data are available (Lewinsohn, 1975a, 1975b; MacPhillamy & Lewinsohn, 1982). Briefly, each schedule consists of 320 items assumed to represent an exhaustive sample of interactions with the environment that many people find pleasant or unpleasant. The client first rates the frequency of each event's occurrence during the past month, and then rates the subjective impact of the events. The frequency ratings are assumed to reflect the rate of occurrence of the events during the past month. The subjective impact ratings are assumed to indicate the individual's potential for positive experiences (e.g., enjoyability) and for negative experiences (e.g., aversiveness). Cross-product scores of the frequency and impact ratings are assumed to reflect the total amount of positive and negative experiences during the past month. Normative data on both schedules allow evaluation of the client's scores relative to others of the same sex.

Conceptualization of Presenting Problems

Another important strategy essential to behavior therapy for depression involves the development of a shared conceptualization of a patient's presenting problems between the therapist and the patient. Patients usually enter therapy with their own conceptualizations or definitions of their problems. As McLean (1981) wrote, depressed patients often see themselves as victims of their moods or environmental forces. Rarely do patients see their behaviors and/or their interpretations of their behaviors and/or the behaviors of others as causes for the depression. To complicate things further, increasing numbers of the lay and professional community are convinced that there is always a predominantly biogenic cause of unipolar depression. This is often meant to imply the insignificance of psychological and environmental variables as causal factors. Thus, depressed patients often initially assume a passive stance; that is, they believe that something analogous to a physical disease has happened to them. Although they may emphasize specific behavioral problems (e.g., sleeplessness, lack of social involvement, obsessive thoughts), typically the focus is on "depression." Thus, it usually takes a considerable amount of work to move patients from a construct usage of the term *depression* to a recognition of the importance of specific problematic behavioral events that may be related to their dysphoria.

One goal of the initial phase of treatment is for therapist and patient to redefine the patient's problems in terms that will give the patient both a sense of control and a feeling of hope and in terms that will lead to specific behavioral interventions. Thus, the therapist tries to understand the patient's description and definition of the problem but may not uncritically accept the patient's view of the problem. Instead, therapist and patient attempt to redefine the problem in terms that are acceptable to both of them. Information obtained through the functional assessment of depressive behavior may be especially useful in developing a shared understanding of the genesis and maintenance of the patient's depression. It is the reformulation or conceptualization phase, then, that sets the stage for behavioral change; it is essential for successful treatment that the patient and the therapist evolve a common conceptualization with common expectations. This conceptualization should be such as to lead naturally to specific behavioral changes that will benefit the patient in real-life situations.

There are numerous ways in which the patient and therapist can evolve a common conceptualization. The manner in which the therapist discusses the presenting problem, the kinds of questions asked, the type of assessment procedure employed, the content of the therapy rationale, and the kinds of initial homework assignments given are all used to evolve a common patient–therapist conceptualization. It is important to do a great deal of "structuring" in the initial phase of treatment of depressed patients so that there will be a clear and mutual understanding of expectations, goals, time commitments, and other conditions.

Monitoring of Mood and Activities

Continual feedback between ongoing assessment and treatment interventions especially characterizes behavioral treatments for depression. From the first day of therapy, the depressed patient is typically asked to monitor and rate his or her mood on a daily basis for the duration of treatment. These ratings can be made on a simple nine-point visual analog scale (where a one indicates very happy and a nine, very depressed). In rating their moods on a daily basis, depressed individuals are provided the opportunity to note variations in their mood. Daily mood variations also permit the therapist to note particular days when a patient is more or less depressed and to explore the specific circumstances and/or repeated patterns influencing fluctuations in an individual's mood.

Similarly, patients are often asked to monitor the occurrences of pleasant and aversive events on a daily basis. Therapists typically prefer to generate an individualized list of events and activities for the individual to track. The main purpose of daily monitoring of activities and mood is to enable the patient and the therapist to become aware of the covariance that typically exists between mood and the rates of occurrences of pleasant and unpleasant activities. Inspection of a graph of the daily mood and event scores provides an easy means of estimating concomitant changes in the levels of these variables. Lewinsohn and his associates (Lewinsohn, 1976; Lewinsohn, Sullivan, & Grosscup, 1980) have pioneered the use of computerized analysis of PES and UES ratings to provide the basis for constructing a personalized activity schedule. This computer analysis provides the means of pinpointing precisely the specific events most highly correlated with mood fluctuations.

Patients are taught to graph and to interpret their daily monitoring data. They seem to understand intuitively the relationship between unpleasant events and mood. However, the covariation between pleasant events and mood is typically a relevation to patients. *Seeing* these relationships on a day-to-day basis impresses on patients, in a powerful way, how the quantity and the quality of their daily interactions have an important impact on their depression. Now, the depression is no longer a mysterious force, but an understandable experience. Patients, in a very real sense, learn to diagnose the determinants of their own depression.

Progressive Goal Attainment and Behavioral Productivity

An increase in goal-defined behavior is essential to all behavioral treatments for depression. McLean (1981) has described a number of issues concerning goals common to depressed patients. He notes that many depressives are often problem- or crisis-focused and are unable to identify goals they wish to pursue. Typically, when depressed persons are able to formulate personal goals, their goals are unrealistically high and their criteria for achievement are expressed in a stringent, all-or-none manner. Depressed individuals, thus, are frequently characterized by frustration in attempting goals that have a low probability of attainment or, in those cases where goals are absent or undefined, by an aimless reactivity to the environment. In both cases, the general result of these deficiencies in goal setting is likely to be a decrease in purposeful behavior, particularly behavior that might have antidepressive consequences.

Given these deficits in goal setting and goal-related behavior, a major behavioral treatment strategy involves educating depressed individuals with regard to goals and goal-directed behavior. Depressives are taught to routinely set, plan, and review their goals. Each goal that is defined must be clearly relevant to the patient's needs. As Biglan and Dow (1981) note, patients are encouraged to decide on their own priorities among goals and are encouraged to take global goals (e.g., happiness, success) and break them down into more specific, delimited, and attainable goals. After defining realistic objectives (e.g., aspects of the person or environment that can be changed), performance tasks are graduated "into as small units as are necessary in order to reduce the task demands to the point that successful performance is relatively guaranteed" (McLean, 1976, p. 80). Throughout treatment, an ongoing effort is made to keep intermediate treatment goals mutually meaningful and specific.

The emphasis in behavior therapy for depression is that thoughts and feelings can be most effectively influenced by behavior change. Consequently, a graduated, goal-oriented, behavioral focus is established early in treatment and the utility of this position is identified throughout the course of therapy. The focus on behavioral productivity is accomplished through the employment of regular homework assignments that emphasize gradual behavioral change designed to ensure a high probability of successful performance on the part of the depressive.

Contracting and Self-Reinforcement

Another central element of behavioral treatments for depression involves the "activation" of the depressed individuals' motivation by way of increasing their behavioral output. Both the assessment and the treatment of a depressed patient require effort on the patient's part. The patient may be asked to take steps that involve substantial changes in daily activities. We advise patients to make specific agreements with themselves to give themselves rewards, but only if they perform the specific tasks agreed upon. Reinforcers may take many forms, such as material rewards or time to do things patients enjoy but don't do. The patients' responses on the PES, or activity schedules, also suggest potential rewards. Contracting is recommended because experience has shown that it facilitates the accomplishment of goals for many patients.

Another important means of cultivating motivation in depressed patients involves developing their ability and inclination to self-reinforce. The criteria for acknowledging its achievement are determined at the time the goal is set. If and when the goal is accomplished, the behavior therapist provides appropriate praise for this success. More importantly, the patient is encouraged (and reinforced) for employing any of a number of self-reinforcing practices. Other motivational tactics used include making the next appointment contingent on the completion of certain tasks and reducing patient fees for keeping appointments and for completing assignments.

Specific Skills—Remediation and Therapeutic Decision Making

Behavioral theories of depression place considerable weight, etiologically speaking, on an increase in competence-enhancing and pleasurable activities, particularly where there are specific performance and skill deficits. Depressed individuals, as a group, show marked deficiencies in such areas as social skills, coping with stressors, and cognitive self-regulation (Lewinsohn & Hoberman, 1982). Hence, a significant aspect of all behavioral treatment programs for depression involves the systematic remediation of the performance and skill deficits presented by depressed patients. Treatment approaches thus focus on teaching depressed patients skills they can use to change detrimental patterns of interaction with their environment, as well as the skills needed to maintain these changes after the termination of therapy. Specific skills training interventions will vary from case to case; they will range from highly structured standardized programs to individually designed ad hoc procedures.

Training typically involves the following processes: didactic introduction to the skills involved; modeling and coaching by the therapist; role playing and rehearsal; practice by the patient during and after treatment sessions; and application of the skills in the real world. Among the variety of specific skills a therapist may employ in treating depressed individuals in behavioral treatment programs for depression are: self-change skills; contingency management skills; social skills such as assertiveness and communication skills; relaxation and stress management skills; identification and increase of rewarding activities; and a number of cognitive and self-control skills. Consequently, this is the aspect of therapy on which behavioral treatment programs differ the most from each other: different programs (and different therapists) often emphasize the application of different skills to reach similar strategic goals.

It must be remembered that, as individuals, depressed persons are remarkably heterogeneous with regard to symptoms, presenting problems, and functional difficulties. This fact points to the importance of therapeutic decision making in the behavior therapy of depressed individuals. Treatment decision making must necessarily be a dynamic process involving the nature of a patient's performance deficits, the nature of a patient's personal and social environmental resources, and ongoing treatment response (McLean, 1976).

Structural Parameters of Therapy

Behavioral treatment approaches are typically designed to be applied within a prespecified number of sessions. The time limit should be determined for each patient on the basis of the period of time that likely will be required to achieve the treatment goals. The existence of a time limit makes it essential for both the therapist and the patient to define and accept treatment goals they can reasonably expect to be accomplished during the allotted time. Of course, when deemed necessary by the patient or the therapist, treatment goals and time limits can be, and are, renegotiated.

Outcome Evaluation

A paramount concern of behavior therapy is the accountability of the therapist to the patient. This means that the selection and continuation of specific treatment techniques must be justified on the basis of the ongoing evaluation of the patient's progress. Evaluation involves periodic assessment not only of changes in depression level but also of the concomitant changes in the events presumed to be related to the patient's depression. This two-pronged approach to assessment allows the therapist to evaluate the effectiveness of treatment, change the targeted behavior patterns, and then determine whether these steps are accompanied by changes in depression level.

Practical Concerns in Implementing Behavioral Treatments

Patient compliance with the procedures suggested by behavioral strategies for treating depression is the critical element in the actualization of behavior change. The behavioral approach requires considerable effort on the part of the patient and is dependent on the patient's keeping accurate records, being willing to learn how to chart the daily monitoring data, and agreeing to carry out other assignments from time to time. The crucial factor in eliciting a patient's cooperation is the therapist's ability to present a convincing rationale for the procedures. The therapist must be able to convince the patient that the self-monitoring and other assignments are an integral part of helpful treatment.

SPECIFIC BEHAVIORAL TREATMENT PROGRAMS

A variety of treatment programs, grounded in behavioral theories and sharing the general strategies described, have been developed and their efficacy examined. Despite commonalities, each of these programs differs in the employment of different tactics to accomplish goals pinpointed during the assessment process. Across treatment programs, behavioral treatment tactics are aimed at increasing positive experiences and decreasing unpleasant ones. These tactics, or specific interventions, typically fall into three general categories: (a) those that focus on implementing changes in the actual environment of a patient; (b) those that focus on teaching depressed individuals skills they can use to change problematic patterns of interaction with their environment; and (c) those that focus on decreasing the aversiveness and enhancing the pleasantness of person–environment interactions. Various combinations of these different tactics constitute the specific behavioral treatment programs for depression.

Decreasing Unpleasant Events and Increasing Pleasant Events

Lewinsohn, Sullivan, and Grosscup (1980) have described a behavioral program that aims to change the quality and the quantity of the depressed patient's interactions with the environment in the direction of increasing positive and decreasing negative interactions. The treatment is time-limited (12 sessions) and highly structured; a therapy manual is available to assist in the implementation of specific tactics. An activity schedule (Lewinsohn, 1976) is constructed, consisting of 80 items rated by the patient as most pleasant and frequent and 80 items rated by the patient as most unpleasant and frequent. Patients begin daily monitoring both of the occurrence of pleasant and unpleasant activities and of their mood. They continue this daily monitoring for the duration of treatment. Subsequently, the treatment proceeds in two phases. In the first phase, treatment provides assistance to the patient in decreasing the frequency and subjective aversiveness of unpleasant events in his or her life and then, in the second phase, concentrates on increasing pleasant ones.

Reducing the Intensity of Aversive Events

The therapy begins by teaching patients to manage aversive events. Patients often overreact to unpleasant events and allow themselves to interfere with their engagement in, and enjoyment of, pleasant activities. Relaxation training is, therefore, introduced early in treatment, with the goal of teaching patients to be more relaxed generally but especially in specific situations in which they feel tense. Relaxation training is provided because feelings of anxiety and tension tend to make unpleasant events more aversive and to reduce patients' enjoyment of pleasant activities. Anxiety and tension also tend to impair the clear thinking required for making decisions, planning, and learning new skills. Relaxation training has become a multipurpose tactic. It is a procedure that is easy to master, and patients tend to become particularly involved with it. Relaxation training (in particular, the practice sessions with the therapist) also seems to enhance certain nonspecific, but positive, components in the therapeutic process. The relaxation methods represent a modified version of the technique developed by Jacobson (1929) for inducing deep muscular relaxation. The patient is also assigned to read a book (Benson, 1975; Rosen, 1977) that presents all the practices one needs to know and follow in inducing progressive muscular relaxation.

Cognitive skills are intended to facilitate changes in the way patients think about reality. The locus of control over thoughts can clearly be identified as being in the patient since only the patient can observe his or her thoughts. Patients may monitor their thoughts, their connection to environmental events, and their mood every day. They are taught to discriminate between positive and negative thoughts, necessary and unnecessary thoughts, and constructive and destructive thoughts.

A number of cognitive self-management techniques have been utilized, including thought stopping and "premacking" positive thoughts (Mahoney & Thoresen, 1974) and Meichenbaum and Turk's "self talk" procedure (1976). Patients may be asked to schedule a "worrying time" or to engage in a "blowup" technique whereby potentially negative consequences are progressively exaggerated. Rational-emotive concepts may be covered and a procedure for disputing irrational thoughts may be presented (Ellis & Harper, 1961; Kranzler, 1974). All techniques are presented as skills that, to become maximally useful must be learned and practiced.

Reducing the Frequency of Aversive Events

The "decreasing unpleasant events" aspect of therapy then proceeds with pinpointing a small number of negative interactions or situations that trigger the patient's dysphoria. In order to reduce the aversiveness of these situations, the therapist has available a wide range of tactics. Typically, they fall into three categories: stress management skills, reducing aversive social interactions, and facilitating time management.

The stress management skills employed are based on techniques and procedures described by Meichenbaum and Turk (1976) and by Novaco (1975). Stress management training involves teaching patients to recognize objective signs of dysphoria early in the provocative sequence. The patients become aware of pending aversive situations and the effect that they are having on them. Components of "cognitive preparation" involve teaching patients specific skills needed for dealing with aversive situations and preparing for aversive encounters: self-instruction, in vivo relaxation, problem-solving skills, and other task-oriented skills.

Tactics aimed at allowing the patient to change the quantity and the quality of his or her interpersonal relationships typically cover two aspects of interpersonal behavior: assertion and interpersonal style of expressive behavior. For assertion, a covert modeling procedure based on Kazdin's works (1976) has been utilized in a sequence involving instruction, modeling, rehearsal, and feedback. After the concept of assertion is presented, patients read *Your Perfect Right* (Alberti & Emmons, 1974) and a personalized list of problematic situations is developed by the patient and the therapist. The therapist may model some assertive possibilities for the patient; after that, the patient is encouraged to take over and to rehearse assertiveness using the covert modeling procedure. Transfer to in vivo practices is planned and monitored during later sessions.

Work on the interpersonal style of the patient involves the same format of instruction, modeling, rehearsal, and feedback. Patients and therapists together set goals (usually small and easily attained) based on preassessment problems and the patient's preferences. Typical goals may include responding with more positive interest to others, reducing complaints or "whining," increasing activity level and discussion, or changing other verbal aspects of behavior.

Daily planning and time management training is another general tactic included in the program. At this stage, patients read and make considerable use of selected chapters from Lakein's *How to Get Control of Your Time and Your Life* (1974). Depressed individuals typically make poor use of their time, do not plan ahead and, therefore, have not made the preparations (e.g., getting a baby sitter) needed in order to take advantage of opportunities for pleasant events. The training aims also to assist patients to achieve a better balance between activities they want to do and activities they feel they are obligated to do. Using a time schedule, patients are asked to preplan each day and each week.

Increasing Pleasant Activities

The weekly and daily planning also lays the groundwork for patients to schedule specific pleasant events which become the focus of the second phase of treatment. In helping patients to increase their rate of engagement in pleasant activities, the emphasis is on setting concrete goals for this increase and on developing specific plans for things patients will do. Patients make use of their activity schedule to identify events that they enjoy. Specific goals for increasing the actual amount of enjoyment are established and monitored. Patients are taught to distinguish events, behaviors, and feelings that interfere with the enjoyment of activities and to use relaxation, cognitive techniques, social skills, and so on to increase their enjoyment of these activities. Small but systematic increases in the number of pleasant activities are implemented by each patient over a period of several weeks and the effects on their mood are self-monitored. Beyond increasing simply the number of pleasant events, patients are assisted in distinguishing and enacting pleasant events that have a particularly strong relationship to a more positive mood. Patients are especially encouraged to increase their pleasant social activities. Patients and therapists set goals for such increases based on the patients' current frequency of social activity. Goals are gradually increased over several sessions. A more detailed description of this individualized treatment procedure and case illustrations are presented in papers by Lewinsohn, Sullivan, and Grosscup (1980).

With regard to the efficacy of this behavioral intervention, Lewinsohn, Youngren, and Grosscup (1979) examined the relationship between reinforcement and depression across four samples of depressives. Over the course of treatment, they found that the rate of positive reinforcement increased as a function of improvement in clinical depression level. Similarly, the rate of experienced aversiveness, or the reaction to unpleasant events, diminished as clinical depression decreased.

Social Interaction Therapy

The social interaction theory of depression postulated by McLean (1976, 1981) considers the depressed person's interaction with his or her social environment to be crucial for both the development and the reversal of depression. As McLean views it, depression results when individuals lose the ability to control their interpersonal environment. When ineffective coping techniques are utilized to remedy situational life problems, the consequence may be a decrease in positive events and, thus, depression. Social interaction therapy aims to maximize the patient's competence in specific coping skills.

Social interaction therapy incorporates behavioral and cognitive techniques. Consequently, social interaction therapy places a marked emphasis on therapeutic decision making that involves appropriate intervention components. It is also distinguished by its incorporation of procedures for including relevant social network members (e.g., spouses) as integral components of treatment.

The therapist's evaluation includes the patient's living arrangements, marital status and satisfaction, and employment status and satisfaction. McLean stresses the importance of obtaining the patient's own criteria for improvement and maintaining a treatment that focuses on data management; explicit performance criteria are monitored by the patient throughout therapy.

Six specific therapeutic components are suggested by McLean: communication training, behavioral productivity, social interaction training, assertiveness training, decision-making and problem-solving training, and cognitive self-control. While the first three components are utilized in the treatment of all depressed patients, the latter three are employed based upon assessment of a patient's particular deficiencies in the problem areas. Perhaps the most distinctive component of social interaction therapy involves communication training between the patient and his or her spouse or significant other. Therapy includes a structured form of communication training to counteract aversive marital interactions and a constricted quantity in range of interactions. Communication exercises aim to provide opportunities for positive feedback, to enhance self-esteem, and to facilitate other forms of social interactions. Additionally, the inclusion of a relevant social network member is important in the promotion of social interaction and in maintaining treatment effects. At the end of treatment, patients are assisted to prepare for future episodes of depression, and contingency plans are established and rehearsed.

McLean, Ogston, and Grauer (1973) developed a therapeutic program based on the aforementioned components and found it to produce significant changes in problematic behaviors and in verbal communication styles. In a large-scale treatment outcome study conducted by McLean and Hakstian (1979), 178 moderately clinically depressed patients were selected by interview screening and psychometric criteria. Subjects were randomly assigned to one of four treatment conditions: behavior therapy as described by McLean (1976), short-term traditional psychotherapy, relaxation training, and medication (amitriptyline). Experienced therapists were selected on the basis of their preferred treatment modality. Patients encouraged their spouses or significant others to participate in treatment sessions, which took place weekly over 10 weeks. The results obtained demonstrated the unequivocal superiority of the behavioral intervention. Behavioral therapy was best on nine out of 10 outcome measures immediately after treatment, and marginally superior at a three-month follow-up (best on seven of 10 outcome measures). Additionally, behavior therapy conditions showed a significantly lower attrition rate (5 percent) than the other conditions, which had dropout rates of 26 to 36 percent. The medication condition was found to have the highest attrition rate. The traditional psychotherapy treatment proved to be the least effective at both the posttreatment and follow-up evaluation periods; generally, it fared worse than the control condition (relaxation training).

Social Skills Training for Depression

Based on Lewinsohn's (1975a) earlier writing on depression, a behavioral program for treating depression was developed by combining social skill techniques utilized in Lewinsohn's (1975b) early research with social skill procedures developed with other types of psychiatric patients (Hersen, Bellack, & Himmelhoch, 1982). This approach, Social Skills Training (SST) (Bellack, Hersen, & Himmelhoch, 1981a), assumes that the depressed patient has either lost socially skillful responses as the result of anxiety, the course of psychiatric illness, or hospitalization, or that the patient never possessed social skills in his or her behavioral repertoire. Consequently, treatment is conceived of as a reeducation or education for depressed patients and employs instruction, feedback, social reinforcement, modeling, coaching, behavioral rehearsal, and graded homework assignments. The actual implementation of therapeutic interventions is based on a careful behavioral analysis of social skill deficits. Typically, treatment takes place over 12 weekly therapy sessions followed by six to eight booster sessions spread over a six-month period. SST can best be understood as focusing on a matrix that has types of social situations on one axis and types of social skills on the other. Since social skills tend to be situation-specific, training is provided in each of four social contexts: (a) with strangers; (b) with friends; (c) with family members or in heterosocial interactions; (d) at work or school. The importance of each of these four contexts is prioritized by each individual. Within each area, specific social problems are delineated and dealt with hierarchically in order of increasing difficulty. Treatment across the different social contexts is seen as ensuring generalization of social skills across a variety of situations. Three types of social skills, which are viewed as being especially relevant to depression, are the primary focus of social skills training. *Positive assertion* refers to the expression of positive feelings toward others. Instruction in positive assertion concentrates on giving compliments, expressing affection, offering approval and praise, and making apologies; particular emphasis is placed on responding at appropriate times with the appropriate nonverbal components. *Negative assertion* refers to the expression of displeasure and to standing up for one's own rights. Training in this skill concerns refusing unrealistic requests, requesting new behavior from others, compromising and negotiating, and expressing disapproval or annoyance. Here, treatment aims to demonstrate that the reactions of others will be less negative than expected and less painful than continuing passivity and submissiveness. The third target of this treatment is *conversational skills,* including the ability to initiate, maintain, and end conversation. Patients are coached to avoid "sick talk" and to be more positively reinforcing to others.

For each social context–social skill deficit, the training program emphasizes four individual components. The skills training component involves learning specific response skills. Assessment is conducted through a role-playing task. Intervention targets are identified and the patient is provided with a rationale for his or her responding. Specific succinct instructions are provided for what the patient should do in a given situation. Following this, a number of serial trials occur in which the patient observes the therapist model a response. The patient then performs the response. Discrete response behaviors are taught singly and sequentially, with regular feedback and positive reinforcement. Since behaviors that are not overlearned have been shown to drop out in stressful situations, the second component of social skills training involves practice both within therapy sessions and outside therapy. Appropriate homework assignments designed to lead to reinforcement are made and monitored by the patient and therapist. Social perception training is an additional treatment component and includes instruction in the social meaning of various response cues, familiarity with social mores, attention to the relevant aspects of interaction context, and ability to accurately predict interpersonal consequences. Finally, in the self-evaluation and reinforcement component, depressives are trained to evaluate their responding more objectively and to employ self-reinforcements; the therapist provides objective and appropriate criteria for judgment if the patient is too negative in self-evaluation.

Two pilot studies of SST (Hersen, Bellack, & Himmelhoch, 1980; Wells, Hersen, Bellack, & Himmelhoch, 1979) demonstrated that this intervention resulted in improvement both in specific social skills and in scores on self-report and psychiatric rating scales. Two larger studies of SST were reported by Bellack, Hersen, and Himmelhoch (1981b, 1983) and four different treatments (amitriptyline, SST plus amitriptyline, SST plus placebo, and psychotherapy plus placebo) were employed across 72 female outpatients. All treatments produced statistically significant and clinically meaningful changes in symptoms and social functioning. Thus, SST plus placebo was as effective as amitriptyline alone or psychotherapy plus placebo. However, a greater proportion of patients were significantly improved in the SST plus placebo condition. In addition, Bellack, Hersen, and Himmelhoch (1983) found that patients treated with SST plus placebo showed the greatest improvement on measures of social skills and were most similar to normal women after treatment. Further, there was a significant difference in dropout rate across the treatment conditions—from a low of 15 percent in the SST plus placebo to as high as 56 percent in the amitriptyline alone condition (Bellack, et al., 1981b).

An Operant Reinforcement Approach

An operant reinforcement method of treating depression was described by Azrin and Besalel (1981). Like other behavioral programs, this one stresses an increase of reinforcement. However, Azrin and Besalel also report on a number of distinctive tactics designed to facilitate the amelioration of depression.

Depressed individuals are asked to identify at least four changes they desire. Each objective is to be stated in behavioral terms, if possible, and in terms of specific frequencies or duration. Patients are asked to rate their degree of happiness in each of eight areas: household responsibilities, sex, communication, social activities, finances, care of children, independence, and personal habits. On the basis of these assessment procedures, treatment tactics are discussed initially with the patient and a behavioral contract is signed by both the therapist and patient outlining their responsibilities to one another.

More specifically, a number of instruments are presented to the patient which emphasize positive rather than problematic aspects of his or her life; these forms serve as the basis for the management of positive reinforcements during the course of treatment. Patients indicate which of 15 attitudinal statements, reflecting quasi-universal positive attributes, apply to them. On the basis of this desirable attitude list, patients write down as many "nice qualities about themselves" as they can think of. Next, a "happiness reminder" list of 18 items, reflecting generally positive types of events or situations, is utilized as a basis for generating a personalized list of activities and events that have been pleasant, meaningful, or previously interesting to the patient. Additionally, patients are asked to indicate which events on a possible pleasant activities list of 50 recreational activities apply to them. A list of probable pleasant activities is constructed for each patient and each item is rated on a one-to-four scale as to degree of enjoyment obtained for each activity. Another list, this one of all persons liked by the patient, is also constructed. Employing these various lists of potentially reinforcing events, activities, and persons, the therapist helps the patient to arrange a daily and weekly schedule for engagement in reinforcing activities.

Azrin and Besalel (1981) also reported on techniques to directly combat the negative mood of depression. Employing an overcorrection rationale, the therapist teaches the depressed individual to engage in compensatory, positive statements whenever a depressive state or response occurs. Each positive statement is derived from the "nice qualities" list described earlier and serves the purpose of self-praise. Patients are also asked to review a list of 42 severe traumatic events (e.g., "My house burned down"), few, if any, of which apply to a given person; this tactic is designed to induce behavioral contrasts with the patient's own life situation. Similarly, the depressed person is asked to respond to a form emphasizing positive aspects of stress-related severe depression, including possibly negative aspects of their life situation if their problem had not occurred and any benefits that occurred because of the problem. Each of these procedures is intended to refocus the patient's affective experience.

Reinforcer-facilitating social skills are taught to depressed persons whose depression is influenced by unsatisfactory social relationships. Individuals are taught to give compliments and show appreciation, to request reinforcers (e.g., compliments or appreciation) from others, to react to annoyance caused by others, to make agreements with others, and to identify probable reinforcers of friends. In addition, patients are encouraged to engage in "happy talk" with friends, focusing on pleasant (not problem-solving) topics of mutual interest.

Finally, common sources of depression are addressed directly through skill remediation. Individuals with marital, vocational, employment, and other specific problems are assisted in translating amorphous complaints into specific behavioral objectives. Patients are then helped to implement those objectives through condensed interventions for marital, vocational, employment, and academic concerns.

Treatment utilizing these tactics takes place over four to 10 sessions. Particular procedures are discussed and practiced throughout treatment as necessary. Patients utilize self-reminder forms on which they record activities assigned to be carried out for each day between treatment sessions. These activities include each of the individualized goals, the activities scheduled by the therapist, and various positive interactional activities relevant to the specific individual. During treatment meetings, this form serves as the starting point of discussion and emphasizes what the depressed individual has done to help himself or herself. The therapist reviews the form and accomplishments of the previous week and then assigns and helps the patient to practice further intervention tactics. In contrast to other behavioral interventions, there is no attempt to have the patient master one procedure before proceeding to the next one. Rather, as noted earlier, all potentially relevant techniques are introduced initially and then applied as appropriate.

The Coping with Depression Course

The Coping with Depression (CWD) course is a multimodal, psycho-educational group treatment for unipolar depression. The major vehicle for treatment is an explicit educational experience designed to teach people techniques and strategies for coping with the problems that are assumed to be related to their depression. Thus, the course emphasizes the attainment of knowledge and skills over an intensive relationship with a therapist. The CWD course consists of 12 two-hour sessions conducted over eight weeks. Sessions are held twice a week during the first four weeks of treatment, and once a week for the final four weeks. One-month and six-month follow-up sessions, called "class reunions," are held to encourage maintenance of treatment gains.

The first two sessions of the CWD course are devoted to the definition of course ground rules, the presentation of the social learning view of depression, and instruction in basic self-help skills. The next eight sessions are devoted to the acquisition of skills in four specific areas: (a) learning how to relax; (b) increasing pleasant activities; (c) changing aspects of one's thinking; and (d) improving both the quality and quantity of one's social interactions. Each of the sessions in these four specific areas makes use of similar skills and techniques described earlier as part of the individualized treatment program for depression. Two sessions are devoted to each skill. The final two sessions focus on maintenance and prevention issues.

The course is a highly structured, time-limited, skill-training program that makes use of a text, *Control Your Depression* (Lewinsohn, Muñoz, Youngren, & Zeiss, 1978), from which reading assignments are made; a participant workbook (Brown & Lewinsohn, 1979) that was developed to supplement the text; and an Instructor's Manual (Steinmetz et al., 1979), to ensure comparability of treatment across instructors. A more detailed description of the course is provided in Lewinsohn, Antonuccio, Steinmetz, and Teri (1984).

The participant workbook contains goal statements, assignments for each session, and monitoring forms for recording specific behaviors, thoughts, and feelings relevant to the class assignments. Group time is divided among lecture, review of the assignments, discussion, role playing, and structured exercises. The instructor's main goals are to deliver the course information accurately, to promote the effective application of the information, to help participants solve problems related to the material, and to facilitate a supportive group interaction.

An important feature of the CWD course is that participants are able to meet effectively in groups, to assist each other in overcoming their depression. With relatively few exceptions (Barrera, 1979; Lewinsohn, Weinstein, & Alper, 1970), previous cognitive behavioral treatments have been offered exclusively in an individual therapy mode. This is not surprising since most authorities in the area of group therapy (Yalom, 1975) advise against homogeneous groups of depressed patients. The CWD results indicate that, within the structure presented by the course, depressives work together very effectively. Another feature of the course is that it presents a cost-effective, community-oriented outreach approach to impact on the great majority of depressives who never avail themselves of the services of clinics and mental health professionals. The educational focus reduces the stigma involved in seeking "psychiatric" or "psychological" treatment, which is especially important to the elderly depressed.

Several outcome studies have been conducted with the Coping with Depression course. Brown and Lewinsohn (1984) compared the CWD course to individual tutoring based upon the CWD course, a minimal phone contact intervention, and a wait-list control group. Teri and Lewinsohn (1981) compared the CWD course to individual behavior therapy for depression (Lewinsohn, Sullivan, & Grosscup, 1980). In both of these studies, the improvement shown by depressed individuals participating in the CWD course was substantial at post-treatment and was maintained at both one-month and six-month follow-up. The results indicated that the differences among all active treatment conditions were small and not statistically significant. In two other studies (Steinmetz, Lewinsohn, & Antonuccio, 1983; Hoberman, Lewinsohn, & Tilson, 1988), similar rates of improvement were demonstrated.

Both course leader and participant variables have been studied in relation to positive outcomes in the CWD courses. Antonuccio, Lewinsohn, and Steinmetz (1982) found that even though leaders differed significantly on many therapist variables (e.g., therapist warmth, enthusiasm, and so on), there was no significant effect for therapist differences; that is, the instructors did not differ in how much improvement their respective participants displayed at the end of the course. Both Steinmetz et al. (1983) and Hoberman et al. (1988) examined individual predictors of outcome for CWD participants. Summarizing the results of these studies, the most robust predictors of recovery from depression following treatment were: (a) lower pretreatment levels of depression, (b) higher social functioning, (c) perceived mastery over events, (d) optimism regarding treatment outcome, and (e) early positive perceptions of group cohesiveness.

In recent years, investigators have modified the CWD course and studied its effectiveness with populations other than middle-aged adult depressives. To treat depressed adolescents, Clarke and Lewinsohn (1986) added interventions incorporating basic communication, negotiation, and conflict resolution skills into the basic CWD course program. Both Clarke (1985) and Lewinsohn, Clarke, Hops, Andrews, and Osteen (1988) demonstrated significant improvements for clinically depressed adolescents as a result of treatment with the CWD course for adolescents. A modification of the CWD course, the Life Satisfaction Course (Steinmetz, Zeiss, & Thompson, 1984), was developed for use with depressed elderly persons and was found to be efficacious (Thompson, Gallagher, Nies, & Epstein, 1983; Breckenridge, Zeiss, Breckenridge, & Thompson, 1985). Finally, a pilot study has shown that inpatients with "drug refractory" depression responded favorably to a modified version of the CWD program (Antonuccio et al., 1983).

The CWD course has also been studied as a means of preventing episodes of depression among individuals presumed to be at elevated risk of developing such episodes. Muñoz, Ying, Armas, Chan, and Gurza (1987) modified the CWD course and employed it with low-income, minority medical outpatients, a group known to be at high risk for future depressive episodes. Results indicated that participants receiving the CWD course showed a significantly greater decrease in the level of depressive symptoms and lower rates of depressive disorder (Muñoz et al., 1988). Similarly, Manson and colleagues (Manson, 1988; Manson, Moseley, & Brenneman, 1988) are conducting a study of a modified version of the CWD course for use as a preventive intervention with Native Americans aged 45 and older.

COMMON OUTCOMES OF BEHAVIORAL TREATMENT FOR DEPRESSION AND THE MECHANISM OF CHANGE

Clearly, a number of well-defined behavioral treatment programs for unipolar depression presently exist. All of these treatment programs share a basic conceptualization of the etiology of depression which emphasizes changes in the quality of an individual's interactions with the environment. Behavioral theories assume that the depressed patient has acquired maladaptive reaction patterns that can be unlearned. Symptoms are seen as important in their own right rather than simply as manifestations of underlying conflicts, and treatments are aimed at the modification of relatively specific behaviors and cognitions rather than a general reorganization of the patient's personality. All behavioral treatments, to date, are structured and time-limited. For each specific behavioral treatment program, empirical support for its therapeutic efficacy has been demonstrated. Each program appears to produce significant decreases in depression level and depressive symptomatology, although relatively little difference in outcome measures has been observed between treatment programs or modalities. It seems clear that at least certain behavioral treatment programs ameliorate depression in the same degree or better than antidepressive medications and that a significantly lower number of patients drop out of behavioral treatments. In fact, a recent study by Steinbrueck, Maxwell, and Howard (1983) presented a meta-analysis of 56 outcome studies of drug therapy and psychotherapy (most of which were cognitive and/or behavioral in nature) in the treatment of unipolar depression in adults. Their results suggest that psychotherapy had an average effectiveness almost twice that of chemotherapy.

Two significant questions arise. First, by what mechanism(s) are behavioral treatments effective? Second, how is it that all the different behavioral treatment programs appear to be similarly effective? With regard to the first question, the contention of cognitive-behavioral approaches has been that changes in symptoms are effected by modifying behaviors or thoughts that are presumed to cause those symptoms. Thus, changes in cognitive and behavioral skills and, consequently, different outcomes are theorized to be the critical mechanism of change. A meta-analysis of placebo-controlled behavior therapy studies indicated that the specific effects of behavior therapies are twice as great as the nonspecific effects (Bowers & Clum, 1988). These findings suggest that some dimensions of such interventions do contribute to outcomes beyond a placebo effect of treatment.

However, relatively little attention has been focused on determining whether the specific cognitive or behavioral changes do, in fact, occur as a result of behavioral treatments for depression. Available studies suggest a somewhat contradictory set of affairs. To date, few studies have attempted to investigate the mechanism of change in behavioral treatments for depression. Williams (1988) examined adolescents who received the adolescent version of the CWD course. She found that, despite significant improvements in depression, treated patients did not appear to improve in the actual skills presumed to produce the change in depression. These results suggest that actual skills or behavior change may not play the significant role in the CWD course and by extension in other behavioral treatments.

Even when specific interventions are employed in the treatment of depression, there appears to be no selective impact on target behaviors. Zeiss, Lewinsohn, and Muñoz (1979) compared brief behavioral interventions based upon increasing pleasant activities, improving social skills, or reducing negative conditions. They found that participants receiving different treatments all improved equally in their activities, social skills, and cognitions. Similar results were reported by Rehm, Rabin, Kaslow, and Willard (1982). In studies comparing cognitive therapy and pharmacotherapy (Rush, Beck, Kovacs, Weissenberger, & Hollon, 1982; Simons, Garfield, & Murphy, 1984), both depressed persons who received cognitive therapy and those who received antidepressant medication evidenced similar changes in cognitions over the course of treatment.

Yet, there is evidence that matching specific treatment techniques to patients with particular target problems can produce particular benefits. McKnight, Nelson, Hayes, and Jarrett (1983) found that patients with social skills difficulties and irrational cognitions improved more after receiving specific interventions for those deficits than after interventions not related to their presenting problem areas. Simons, Lustman, Wetzel, and Murphy (1985) similarly showed that patients who scored high on a measure of learned resourcefulness (Rosenbaum, 1980) did better in cognitive therapy than in pharmacotherapy. The results of these studies suggest that it may be clinically efficacious to match particular treatment components to types of target problem areas that patients present.

With regard to the mechanism of change for behavioral interventions for depression, several possibilities exist. While perhaps not all patients demonstrate changes in the particular skills targeted by behavioral intervention, it may be the case that allocating one or two sessions per skill or problem area is insufficient to produce actual behavior change. In addition, given the results of the studies by McKnight et al. (1983) and Simons et al. (1985), it may be that only certain patients with particular target problem areas will demonstrate specific changes in behavior or cognition. Such changes may be obscured by analyses of total samples of patients. The lack of differential treatment response for unique interventions suggests two potential, but related, mechanisms of change. First, while actual behavioral or cognitive change may not be the means of change for all patients, clearly some aspect of cognitive-behavioral interventions is efficacious above and beyond a simple placebo or nonspecific event. Given the results of Zeiss et al. (1979), Rehm et al. (1982), and others, it may be argued that behavioral treatment programs are effective to the degree they employ some common "core" of strategies as opposed to any specific intervention. Specific techniques may be less important in these treatments than structural characteristics of the treatments. With these conditions present, a second component of change may operate: an increased sense of self-efficacy based upon self-perceived mastery. Such a notion harkens back to Frank (1961), who theorized that treatment is effective to the extent that it succeeds in restoring "morale" to a demoralized client.

Thus, the authors of two treatment outcome studies for behavioral treatments of depression have offered their hypotheses as to the critical components for successful short-term behavioral treatments for depression. Zeiss et al. (1979) concluded that efficacious behavioral treatments should include the following characteristics:

1. Therapy should begin with an elaborated, well-planned rationale.
2. Therapy should provide training in skills that the patient can utilize to feel more effective in handling his or her daily life.

3. Therapy should emphasize independent use of these skills by the patient outside of the therapy context, and thus provide enough structure so that the attainment of independent skills is possible for the patient.

4. Therapy should encourage the patient's attribution that improvement in mood is caused by the patient's increased skillfulness and not by the therapist's skillfulness.

Similarly, McLean and Hakstian (1979) noted that high structure, a social learning rationale, goal attainment focus, and increasing social interaction were significant elements in the behavioral treatment of depression.

SUMMARY

Behavioral treatments for depression are among the most popular and effective of available interventions. Initially grounded in the principles of learning and in the need for demonstrated effectiveness of psychotherapy, current behavioral theories of depression have become systemic and multidimensional. A core set of strategies informs the different models of behavioral treatments for depressive disorder. At the same time, each behavioral program includes unique tactics for improving the quality of the depressed person's interactions with his or her world. It is clear to date, that, while simple and practical, behavioral interventions are quite powerful in the acute treatment of depression. Further research efforts should be directed at strengthening the content and structure of the behavioral programs both to increase their effectiveness with patients who present with multiple problems and psychiatric disorders and to reduce the likelihood of recurrent depressions. In addition, by elucidating the mechanism of therapeutic action of behavioral tactics, both the understanding of etiological factors in depression and the effectiveness of interventions should be enhanced.

REFERENCES

Alberti, R. E., & Emmons, M. I. (1974). *Your perfect right*. San Luis Obispo, CA: Impact.

Antonuccio, D. O., Akins, W. T., Chatham, P. M., Monagan, J. A., Tearnan, B. H., & Zeigler, B. L. (1983). An exploratory study: The psychosocial group treatment of drug-refractory unipolar depression. *Journal of Behavior Therapy and Experimental Psychiatry, 15,* 309–313.

Antonuccio, D. O., Lewinsohn, P. M., & Steinmetz, J. I. (1982). Identification of therapist differences in a group treatment for depression. *Journal of Consulting Clinical Psychology, 50,* 433–435.

Azrin, N. H., & Besalel, V. A. (1981). An operant reinforcement method of treating depression. *Journal of Behavior Therapy and Experimental Psychiatry, 12,* 145–151.

Bandura, A. (1977). *Social learning theory.* Englewood Cliffs, NJ: Prentice-Hall.

Barerra, M. (1979). An evaluation of a brief group therapy for depression. *Journal of Consulting and Clinical Psychology, 47,* 413–415.

Beck, A. T., Ward, G. H., Mendelson, M., Mock, J., & Erbaugh, J. (1961). An inventory for measuring depression. *Archives of General Psychiatry, 4,* 561–571.

Bellack, A. S., Hersen, M., & Himmelhoch, J. (1981a). Social skills training for depression: A treatment manual. *Journal Supplement Abstract Service Catalog of Selected Documents, 11,* 36.

Bellack, A. S., Hersen, M., & Himmelhoch, J. (1981b). Social skills training, pharmacotherapy, and psychotherapy for unipolar depression. *American Journal of Psychiatry, 138,* 1562–1567.

Bellack, A. S., Hersen, N., & Himmelhoch, J. M. (1983). A comparison of social skills training, pharmacotherapy, and psychotherapy for depression. *Behavior Research and Therapy, 21,* 101–107.

Benson, H. (1975). *The relaxation response.* New York: Morrow.

Biglan, A., & Dow, M. G. (1981). Toward a "second generation" model of depression treatment: A problem-specific approach. In L. P. Rehm (Ed.), *Behavior therapy for depression: Present status and future directions.* New York: Academic Press.

Blaney, P. H. (1981). The effectiveness of cognitive and behavior therapies. In L. P. Rehm (Ed.), *Behavior therapy for depression: Present status and future directions.* New York: Academic Press.

Bowers, T. G., & Clum, G. A. (1988). Relative contribution of specific and non-specific effects: Meta-analysis of placebo-controlled behavior therapy research. *Psychological Bulletin, 103,* 315–323.

Breckenridge, J. S., Zeiss, A. M., Breckenridge, J., & Thompson, L. (1985). Behavioral group with the elderly: A psychoeducational model. In D. Upper & S. Ross (Eds.), *Handbook of behavioral group therapy.* New York: Plenum Press.

Brown, R., & Lewinsohn, P. M. (1979). *A psychoeducational approach to the treatment of depression: Comparison of group, individual and minimal contact procedures.* Unpublished memo, University of Oregon, Eugene.

Brown, R., & Lewinsohn, P. M. (1984). A psychoeducational approach to the treatment of depression: Comparison of group, individual, and minimal contact procedures. *Journal of Consulting and Clinical Psychology, 52,* 774–783.

Carver, C. S., & Scheier, M. F. (1982). Control theory: A useful conceptual framework for personality, social, clinical, and health psychology. *Psychological Bulletin, 92,* 111–135.

Clarke, G. N. (1985). *A psychoeducational approach to the treatment of depressed adolescents.* Unpublished doctoral dissertation, University of Oregon, Eugene.

Clarke, G. N., & Lewinsohn, P. M. (1986). *Leader manual for the Adolescent Coping With Depression Course.* Unpublished manuscript, Oregon Research Institute.

Craighead, W. E. (1981). Behavior therapy for depression: Issues resulting from treatment studies. In L. P. Rehm (Ed.), *Behavior therapy for depression: Present status and future directions.* New York: Academic Press.

DeRubeis, R. J., & Hollon, S. D. (1981). Behavioral treatment of affective disorders. In L. Michelson, M. Hersen, & S. Turner (Eds.), *Future perspectives in behavior therapy* (pp. 103–129). New York: Plenum.

Duval, S., & Wicklund, R. (1973). Effects of objective self-awareness on attribution of casualty. *Journal of Experimental and Social Psychology, 9,* 17–31.

Ellis, A., & Harper, R. A. (1961). *A guide to rational living.* Hollywood, CA: Wilshire Book.

Endicott, J., & Spitzer, R. I. (1978). A diagnostic interview: The Schedule for Affective Disorders and Schizophrenia. *Archives of General Psychiatry, 35,* 837–844.

Eysenck, H. J. (1952). The effects of psychotherapy: An evaluation. *Journal of Consulting Psychology, 16,* 319–324.

Frank, J. D. (1961). *Persuasion and healing.* Baltimore: Johns Hopkins Press.

Hersen, M., & Bellack, A. S. (1982). Perspectives in the behavioral treatment of depression. *Behavior Modification, 6,* 95–106.

Hersen, M., Bellack, A. S., & Himmelhoch, J. M. (1980). Treatment of unipolar depression with social skills training. *Behavior Modification, 4,* 547–556.

Hersen, M., Bellack, A. S., & Himmelhoch, J. M. (1982). Skills training with unipolar depressed women. In J. P. Curran & P. M. Monti (Eds.), *Social competence and psychiatric disorders: Theory and practice.* New York: Guilford Press.

Hoberman, H. H., Lewinsohn, P. M., & Tilson, M. (1988). Group treatment of depression: Individual predictors of outcome. *Journal of Consulting and Clinical Psychology, 56,* 393–398.

Jacobson, E. (1929). *Progressive relaxation.* Chicago: University of Chicago Press.

Kazdin, A. E. (1976). Effects of covert modeling, multiple models, and model reinforcement on assertive behavior. *Behavior Therapy, 7,* 211–222.

Kazdin, A. E. (1982). History of behavior modification. In A. S. Bellack, M. Hersen, & A. E. Kazdin (Eds.), *International handbook of behavior modification and therapy* (pp. 3–32). New York: Plenum.

Kranzler, G. (1974). *You can change how you feel.* Eugene, OR: Author.

Lakein, A. (1974). *How to get control of your time and your life.* New York: New American Library.

Lewinsohn, P. M. (1975a). The behavioral study and treatment of depression. In M. Hersen, R. M. Eisler, & P. M. Miller (Eds.), *Progress in behavior modification* (Vol. 1). New York: Academic Press.

Lewinsohn, P. M. (1975b). *The unpleasant events schedule.* Unpublished manuscript, University of Oregon, Eugene.

Lewinsohn, P. M. (1976). Activity schedules in the treatment of depression. In C. E. Thoreson & J. D. Kromholtz (Eds.), *Counseling methods.* New York: Holt.

Lewinsohn, P. M., Antonuccio, D. O., Steinmetz, J. L., & Teri, L. (1984). *The Coping with Depression course: A psychoeducational intervention for unipolar depression.* Eugene, OR: Castalia Publishing.

Lewinsohn, P. M., Biglan, T., & Zeiss, A. (1976). Behavioral treatment of depression. In P. Davidson (Ed.), *Behavioral management of anxiety, depression, and pain* (pp. 91–146). New York: Brunner/Mazel.

Lewinsohn, P. M., Clarke, G. N., Hops, H., Andrews, J., & Osteen, V. (1988). *Cognitive-behavioral group treatment of depression in adolescents.* Unpublished manuscript, Oregon Research Institute.

Lewinsohn, P. M., & Hoberman, H. M. (1982). Depression. In A. S. Bellack, M. Hersen, & A. E. Kazdin (Eds.), *International handbook of behavior modification and therapy* (pp. 397–429). New York: Plenum.

Lewinsohn, P. M., Hoberman, H. H., & Rosenbaum, M. (1988). A perspective study of risk factors for unipolar depression. *Journal of Abnormal Psychology, 97,* 251–264.

Lewinsohn, P. M., Hoberman, H. M., Teri, L., & Hautzinger, M. (1985). An integrative theory of depression. In S. Reiss & R. Bootzin (Eds.), *Theoretical issues in behavior therapy.* New York: Academic Press.

Lewinsohn, P. M., Mischel, W., Chaplin, W., & Barton, R. (1980). Social competence and depression: The role of illusory self-perceptions. *Journal of Abnormal Psychology, 89,* 203–212.

Lewinsohn, P. M., Muñoz, R. F., Youngren, M. A., & Zeiss, A. M. (1978). *Control your depression.* Englewood Cliffs, NJ: Prentice-Hall.

Lewinsohn, P. M., Sullivan, J. M., & Grosscup, S. J. (1980). Changing reinforcing events: An approach to the treatment of depression. *Psychotherapy: Theory, research, and practice, 47,* 322–334.

Lewinsohn, P. M., Weinstein, M., & Alper, T. (1970). A behavioral approach to the group treatment of depressed persons: A methodological contribution. *Journal of Clinical Psychology, 26,* 525–532.

Lewinsohn, P. M., Youngren, M. A., & Grosscup, S. J. (1979). Reinforcement and depression. In R. A. Dupue (Ed.), *The psychobiology of depressive disorders: Implications for the effects of stress.* New York: Academic Press.

MacPhillamy, D. J., & Lewinsohn, P. M. (1971). *The pleasant events schedule.* Unpublished manuscript, University of Oregon, Eugene.

MacPhillamy, D. J., & Lewinsohn, P. M. (1982). The pleasant events schedule: Studies on reliability, validity, and scale intercorrelation. *Journal of Consulting and Clinical Psychology, 50,* 363–380.

Mahoney, M. J., & Thoresen, C. E. (1974). *Self-control: Power to the person.* Monterey, CA: Brooks/Cole Publishing.

Manson, S. M. (1988). *Overview: A preventive intervention trial for older American Indians.* Unpublished manuscript, University of Denver.

Manson, S. M., Moseley, R. M., & Brenneman, D. L. (1988). *Physical illness, depression, and older American Indians: A preventive intervention trial.* Unpublished manuscript, Oregon Health Sciences University.

McKnight, D. I., Nelson, R. O., Hayes, S. C., & Jarrett, R. B. (1983). *Importance of treating individually assessed response classes in the amelioration of depression.* Unpublished mimeograph, University of North Carolina, Greensboro.

McLean, P. (1976). Therapeutic decision-making in the behavioral treatment of depression. In P. Davidson (Ed.), *Behavioral management of anxiety, depression, and pain* (pp. 54–89). New York: Brunner/Mazel.

McLean, P. (1981). Remediation of skills and performance deficits in depression: Clinical steps and research findings. In J. Clarkin & H. Glazer (Eds.), *Behavioral and directive strategies* (pp. 172–204). New York: Garland.

McLean, P., & Hakstian, A. R. (1979). Clinical depression: Comparative efficacy of outpatient treatments. *Journal of Consulting and Clinical Psychology, 47,* 818–836.

McLean, P., Ogston, K., & Grauer, L. (1973). A behavioral approach to the treatment of depression. *Journal of Behavior Therapy and Experimental Psychology, 4,* 323–330.

Meichenbaum, D., & Turk, D. (1976). *The cognitive-behavioral management of anxiety, depression, and pain.* New York: Brunner/Mazel.

Muñoz, R. F., Ying, Y. W., Armas, R., Chan, F., & Gurza, R. (1978). The San Francisco Depression Prevention Research Project: A randomized trial with medical outpatients. In R. F. Muñoz (Ed.), *Depression prevention: Research directions* (pp. 199–215). Washington, DC: Hemisphere Press.

Muñoz, R. F., Ying, Y. W., Bernal, G., Perez-Stable, E. J., Sorensen, J. L., & Hargreaves, W. A. (1988). *The prevention of clinical depression: A randomized controlled trial.* Unpublished manuscript, University of California, San Francisco.

Novaco, R. W. (1975). *Anger control.* Lexington, MA: Heath.

Radloff, L. S. (1977). The CES-D scale: A self-report depression scale for research in the general population. *Applied Psychological Measurement, 1,* 358–401.

Rehm, L. P., Rabin, A. S., Kaslow, N. J., & Willard, R. (1982). *Cognitive and behavioral targets in a self-controlled therapy program for depression.* Paper presented at the annual meeting of the Association for the Advancement of Behavior Therapy, Los Angeles.

Rosen, G. M. (1977). *The relaxation book.* Englewood Cliffs, NJ: Prentice-Hall.

Rosenbaum, M. (1980). A schedule for assessing self-controlled behaviors: Preliminary findings. *Behavior Therapy, 11,* 109–121.

Rush, A. J., & Beck, A. T. (1978). Behavior therapy in adults with affective disorders. In M. Hersen & A. S. Bellack (Eds.), *Behavior therapy in the psychiatric setting.* Baltimore: Williams & Wilkins.

Rush, A. J., Beck, A. T., Kovacs, M., Weissenberger, J. A., & Hollon, S. D. (1982). Affects of cognitive therapy and pharmacy therapy on hopelessness and self-concept. *American Journal of Psychiatry, 139,* 862–866.

Simons, A. D., Garfield, S. L., & Murphy, G. E. (1984). The process of change in cognitive therapy and pharmacotherapy: Changes in mood and cognitions. *Archives of General Psychiatry, 41,* 45–51.

Simons, A. D., Lustman, P. J., Wetzel, R. D., & Murphy, G. E. (1985). Predicting response to cognitive therapy of depression: The role of learned resourcefulness. *Cognitive Therapy and Research, 9,* 79–89.

Skinner, B. F. (1953). *Science and human behavior.* New York: Free Press.

Spitzer, R. L., Endicott, J., & Robins, E. (1978). Research diagnostic criteria: Rationale and reliability. *Archives of General Psychiatry, 35,* 773–782.

Steinbrueck, S. M., Maxwell, S. E., & Howard, G. S. (1983). A meta-analysis of psychotherapy and drug therapy in the treatment of unipolar depression with adults. *Journal of Consulting and Clinical Psychology, 51,* 856–863.

Steinmetz, J. L., Antonuccio, D. O., Bond, M., McKay, G., Brown, R., & Lewinsohn, P. M. (1979). *Instructor's manual for Coping with Depression course.* Unpublished mimeograph, University of Oregon, Eugene.

Steinmetz, J. L., Lewinsohn, P. M., & Antonuccio, D. O. (1983). Prediction of individual outcome in a group intervention for depression. *Journal of Consulting and Clinical Psychology, 51,* 331–337.

Steinmetz, J. L., Zeiss, A. N., & Thompson, L. W. (1984). The life satisfaction course: An intervention for the elderly. In D. Upper & S. M. Ross (Eds.), *Handbook of behavioral group therapy.* New York: Plenum.

Teri, L., & Lewinsohn, P. M. (1981). *Comparative efficacy of group vs. individual treatment of unipolar depression.* Paper presented at meeting of the Association for the Advancement of Behavior Therapy, San Francisco, CA.

Thompson, L. W., Gallagher, D., Nies, G., & Epstein, D. (1983). Evaluation of the effectiveness of professionals and nonprofessionals as instructors of Coping with Depression classes for elders. *The Gerontologist, 23,* 390–396.

Thorndike, E. L. (1931). *Human learning.* New York: Appleton.

Wells, K. C., Hersen, M., Bellack, A. S., & Himmelhoch, J. (1979). *Social skills training for unipolar depressive females.* Paper presented at meeting of the Association for the Advancement of Behavior Therapy, Atlanta, GA.

Williams, J. A. (1988). *The role of coping skills in the treatment of depressed adolescents.* Unpublished doctoral dissertation, University of Oregon, Eugene.

Yalom, I. D. (1975). *The theory and practice of group psychotherapy.* New York: Basic Books.

Zeiss, A. N., Lewinsohn, P. M., & Muñoz, R. S. (1979). Nonspecific improvement effects in depression using interpersonal, cognitive and pleasant events focused treatments. *Journal of Consulting and Clinical Psychology, 47,* 427–439.

CHAPTER 17

Cognitive Therapy of Affective Disorders

CORY F. NEWMAN, PhD and AARON T. BECK, MD

Of all the psychological ailments that plague modern humans, perhaps the most pervasive are the affective disorders. These mood syndromes, including major depression, dysthymia, and bipolar disorder, exact a great toll—diminished quality of life, disturbances of physical well-being, disrupted relationships, interference with academic and vocational performance, and threats to life itself. Traditionally, pharmacotherapy has been the treatment of choice; however, in the past 20 years we have witnessed the rise of short-term psychotherapies for the affective disorders, with special emphasis on unipolar depression.

The cognitive theory of depression (Beck, 1967, 1976; Beck, Rush, Shaw, & Emery, 1979) is at the forefront of such psychotherapeutic approaches, with substantial outcome data supporting its efficacy in both relieving symptomatology (Beck, Hollon, Young, Bedrosian, & Budenz, 1985; Blackburn, Bishop, Glen, Whalley, & Christie, 1981; Dobson, in press; Gallagher & Thompson, 1982; Hollon et al., 1986; Murphy, Simons, Wetzel, & Lustman, 1984; Rush, Beck, Kovacs, & Hollon, 1977; Shaw, 1977; Taylor & Marshall, 1977), and preventing subsequent relapse (Blackburn, Eunson, & Bishop, 1986; Evans et al., 1986; Kovacs, Rush, Beck, & Hollon, 1981; Simons, Murphy, Levine, & Wetzel, 1986). Furthermore, Dobson's (in press) meta-analysis of 21 outcome studies provided compelling evidence for the efficacy of cognitive therapy relative to other therapeutic modalities in the treatment of depression. Specifically, Dobson found that cognitive therapy produced a significantly greater magnitude of positive change than did wait-list conditions, no-treatment controls, pharmacotherapy, behavior therapy, and other psychotherapies.

In this chapter we will outline the standard course of cognitive therapy for the affective disorders, highlighting the theoretical and empirical rationales for each component and providing illustrative examples. Our attention will focus primarily on unipolar depression, because the cognitive theory and therapy data are most plentiful in this domain; however, we will endeavor to demonstrate the application of cognitive therapy to dysthymic (the so-called "depressive personality") and bipolar disorders as well, by noting special issues that arise in treating these populations.

MAJOR PREMISES AND HISTORICAL FOUNDATIONS

Cognitive therapy posits that an individual's affective state is highly influenced by the manner in which the individual perceives and structures his or her experiences (Beck, 1963, 1967, 1976). Depressed persons tend to bias negatively the information that they process, and they do so across three domains—the self, the personal world, and the future, the *cognitive triad*. Depressed individuals therefore are prone to conclude incorrectly or prematurely that they are failures or bad persons, or deserve some other unshakable pejorative label (bias against the self); that their life situation is intolerably harsh, joyless, unfair, and painful (bias toward the personal world); and that these conditions will never find remediation (bias toward the future). This bleak expectation of unremitting suffering puts depressed individuals at risk for suicidal ideation, intention, or action.

Clinical and empirical evidence has shown that depressed patients consistently and systematically distort their interpretations of events so as to conform to their negative, hopeless beliefs (Beck, 1974; Hamilton & Abramson, 1983; Karoly & Ruehlman, 1983; Krantz & Hammen, 1979; Lewinsohn, Larson, & Muñoz, 1982; Rogers & Forehand, 1983; Roth & Rehm, 1980; Teasdale & Fennell, 1982; Weissman & Beck, 1978). This depressive mindset locks the patients into a closed system of perceptual processing, so that more positive, disconfirming information is minimized or ignored. As a result, their misery is perpetuated, even when there may be little objective reason to continue to feel negative and hopeless.

As a clinical response to these phenomena, cognitive therapy is a collaborative process of investigation, reality testing, and problem solving between therapist and patient (Weishaar & Beck, 1986). The patient's negative views of the self, life, and the future are treated not as established facts but as hypotheses to be tested. The patient is taught how to evaluate objectively the evidence for and against depressive cognitions via a number of structured techniques, both verbal and behavioral in format. These may include behavioral experiments, logical discourse, imagery restructuring, problem solving, role playing, and so on. As the patient learns to generate alternative interpretations for experiences and to actively solve problems, his or her fundamental depressive beliefs are relinquished and therapeutic change is effected.

Furthermore, the active role that the patient takes in his or her treatment provides the necessary tools to continue to cope with difficulties and setbacks after therapy has ended.

There are a number of notable theoretical precursors to Beck's cognitive therapy, dating back as far as the Greek Stoic philosophers, whose phenomenological approach posited that an individual's views of self and world determined his or her feelings and actions. In the twentieth century, emphasis on the importance of conscious subjective experience can be found in the works of ego-oriented theorists such as Adler (1936), Horney (1950), and Sullivan (1953). Kelly (1955) went a conceptual step further by writing that a person's *construal* of his or her environment is the primary determinant of his or her emotional and behavioral reactions. Additionally, Ellis (1962) advanced the notion of the causal relation between thoughts and emotions by emphasizing the role of "irrational beliefs" in dysphoria.

Beck's formulation of cognitive theory and therapy resulted from his clinical and experimental findings that depressed individuals were prone to idiosyncratic cognitive distortions centering around themes of loss and deprivation (Beck, 1961, 1963; Beck & Hurvich, 1959; Beck & Ward, 1961). These consistent results forced Beck to reformulate his view of depression, which originally had been more in line with his psychoanalytic training, to incorporate the negative bias in cognitive processing as being fundamental to the disorder (Weishaar & Beck, 1986). This theory, while primarily attending to the patient's cognitions, does not by fiat downplay the significance of the patient's feelings, behaviors, or biochemistry. Each of these components is seen as a legitimate point of intervention. However, ". . . experience suggests that when we change depressive cognitions, we simultaneously change the characteristic mood, behavior, and (we presume) biochemistry of depression" (Beck & Young, 1985, p. 207).

The influence of behavior therapy is quite apparent in cognitive therapy as well. In addition to heavily emphasizing an empirical approach, the structure and process of cognitive therapy include such elements as agenda setting, goal setting, concretizing and solving problems, formulating and testing hypotheses, and assigning self-help homework for the patient to complete between therapy sessions.

While sharing some aspects with other orientations, cognitive therapy is unique in a number of ways. Unlike analytic psychotherapies, cognitive therapy involves an ongoing collaboration between therapist and patient, complete with two-way feedback. Additionally, cognitive therapy posits that important subjective data are readily accessible to consciousness without the need for analytic interpretation. Unlike behavior therapy, cognitive therapy utilizes behavioral change processes not as ends unto themselves but rather as means to achieving cognitive change (Beck et al., 1979). In contrast to Ellis's (1962) Rational Emotive

Therapy, the cognitive therapist examines the unique and idiosyncratic cognitions of the patient instead of trying to "fit the patient to the irrational belief." Furthermore, the cognitive therapist uses subtle, Socratic questioning, not dramatic persuasion. The goal is to lead the patient to draw upon his or her own conclusions.

CHARACTERISTICS AND COMPONENTS OF COGNITIVE THERAPY

Cognitive therapy is an active, structured, psychoeducational treatment. Patients are taught that their emotional distress is mediated by the content and the process of their thinking styles, that they can learn to monitor and identify such cognitive patterns, and that modification of their thoughts to make them more objective and scientifically systematic (cf. Evans & Hollon, 1988) can lead to therapeutic changes in affect and behavior. From the outset of therapy, the cognitive therapist endeavors to highlight the intimate interrelations among the patient's thoughts, feelings, actions, and physiology and collaboratively engages the patient in evaluating and making changes in these areas of functioning. These activities proceed best when the cognitive therapist communicates the basic therapeutic characteristics of warmth, genuineness, and openness (cf. Truax & Mitchell, 1971) and is adept at empathically listening to and understanding the patient's unique phenomenology. These ideal characteristics of cognitive therapists should highlight the fact that, although they need to be critical thinkers, they do *not* merely engage the patient in arid intellectual debate, nor do they exhort or harangue patients into "accepting" the therapists' points of view. A friendly, trusting, mutually respectful therapeutic relationship is a necessary foundation on which to build the specific techniques of cognitive therapy.

Prior to the beginning of treatment, it is strongly recommended that patients be given a comprehensive diagnostic evaluation (Sacco & Beck, 1985). This is important for a number of reasons. First, the complaint of depressed affect may actually be secondary to another, perhaps more primary psychological disorder (e.g., obsessive-compulsive disorder or borderline personality disorder). Additionally, the patient's dysphoria may be related to an organic disorder, such as hypothyroidism, hypoglycemia, diabetes, epilepsy, or postconcussive syndrome (Hall, Gardner, Stickney, LeCany, & Popkin, 1980). Furthermore, the severity of the depression, along with the degree of suicidality, should be assessed as soon as possible. In serious cases, medication (e.g., lithium for bipolar depressives) and/or hospitalization may be indicated. Moreover, it makes good clinical sense to gather as much background information as possible about the patient prior to starting treatment. This would include information on current life situation, as well as historical information on the patient's upbringing, schooling, vocations, and significant relationships.

This latter point calls to mind a common myth about cognitive therapy—that it ignores the patient's past experiences. Quite to the contrary, a complete cognitive conceptualization of the patient's problems requires the assessment of past learning experiences. For example, it is frequently found that some of the patients' most dysfunctional beliefs about themselves have their roots in early-life (and present-time) negative feedback from the family of origin. Although the cognitive therapist attempts to deal with such beliefs as they pertain to the patient in the here and now, a conscious, rational exploration of the past is an important part of this process of cognitive reevaluation.

Socializing the Patient into the Cognitive Therapy Model

During the initial session, the therapist attempts to begin at least three important processes: (a) establishing therapeutic rapport, (b) defining the problem and setting goals of treatment, and (c) educating the patient in the cognitive therapy model. In order to set these processes into motion, the therapist establishes an important precedent by asking the patient to suggest items for an *agenda* for the session. The therapist may suggest some items, elicit others, and then ask for feedback on the overall plan for the session. A prototypical "opening statement" for the first cognitive therapy session is as follows:

> [Introductions and establishing rapport, followed by . . .] One of the things we do in cognitive therapy is to set an agenda for each session. This helps to make certain that we cover all the points that are important to you, and to make the best use of our time together. I have some ideas for agenda items for today's session, and then I'd like to hear what *you'd* like to focus on, and then maybe we can come to some agreement [checks for understanding and acknowledgment]. For starters, I'd like to check on how you're feeling today, and see if there are any pressing issues that you'd prefer to discuss right away. Then we could summarize your general life concerns that are bringing you to therapy, and perhaps establish a problem list to begin work on. In addition, I'd like to tell you a bit about cognitive therapy, so you'll have a better understanding about what to expect in this model of treatment. How do these ideas sound to you?

The agenda items suggested in the above example usually serve as appropriate starting points, except in cases where the patient is feeling particularly hopeless and/or suicidal. In such instances, it is imperative for the therapist to attend to the patient's immediate state of mind, to make every effort to offer realistic hope for relief from suffering, and to ask direct questions about suicidal ideation and/or intent. Formulating a verbal antisuicide contract, along with giving the patient the therapist's home phone number, may suffice. For some patients, hospitalization may need to be suggested and encouraged. In any event, the therapist can naturally begin to take note of the kinds of thoughts that are contributing to the patient's feelings of hopelessness, as reflected by the patient's spontaneous discourse or revealed in the patient's answers to therapeutic questions directly aimed at what is on the patient's mind.

In a typical first session where there is no suicidal crisis, more time can be spent in clarifying presenting problems and in setting general therapeutic goals. It is important that the therapist refrain from jumping in and challenging the patient's thinking before the patient even has a chance to comprehend what the therapy is about. Instead, it is wise to simply listen, reflect, be attentive, and give summary feedback and suggestions. Such summary feedback can be used to highlight for the patient the connection between his or her thoughts and feelings, thus subtly initiating the education process. If time permits, the therapist may choose, with the patient's consent, to present a more direct and comprehensive preview of cognitive therapy, in the form of a short monologue. For example, the therapist might say:

> Mr. X, I'd like to tell you a bit about what you can expect to be doing in cognitive therapy. Is that OK with you? OK. One of the fundamental principles of cognitive therapy is that a person's thoughts are very much responsible for how he feels. That's not to say that he has no "real" problems in life, or that his problem "is all in his head." Not at all. But we know from years of clinical experience and experimental research that depressed people tend unwittingly to add to their own burdens by having certain negative biases in their thinking, and that these biases are dysfunctional because they make people even more depressed, and interfere with their ability to help them solve their own problems. So, what we'll be doing here will involve trying to identify the thoughts that *you* have that may be making *you* more depressed, and then talking about ways to make your thinking more objective, even-handed, and constructive, so that you learn how to deal effectively with the kinds of life stresses that would otherwise get you down.

Note that the therapist implicitly presents cognitive theory as a diathesis-stress model (Abramson, Alloy, & Metalsky, 1988; Beck & Young, 1985; Evans & Hollon, 1988; Sacco & Beck, 1985; Weishaar & Beck, 1986), according to which maladaptive thinking patterns interact with real life events to create a depressive episode. The therapist may then proceed with the following:

> Cognitive therapy is a very active treatment. By that I mean that we work together quite intensively to help you to learn to help yourself. For

example, we'll set agendas to make the best use of our sessions, we'll work on a number of antidepression techniques, and we'll give each other ongoing feedback and suggestions. Perhaps most importantly, you'll be asked to practically apply the things you learn in these sessions to your everyday life, in the form of self-help homework assignments. We've found that patients who apply therapeutic skills between sessions recover more rapidly, and learn valuable coping skills that can be effectively used long after therapy is done. Let me emphasize that throughout this process you will have the final say on what courses of action are chosen. Your opinions and requests will be respected, and we'll try at all times to maintain a spirit of teamwork. Do you have any questions or concerns about what I've just said? Could you give me some feedback on the main points you've heard me make just now? I want to make certain that I've been clear.

Sometimes a depressed person may feel a bit overwhelmed by the prospects of an active treatment, especially if inertia and low motivation are part of the clinical picture. By asking for the patient's concerns about the course of therapy, the therapist sets the tone for a collaborative relationship and provides fertile ground for eliciting the patient's "hot cognitions." This enables the therapist once again to highlight the interrelation of thoughts and emotions.

Identifying Automatic Thoughts and Underlying Assumptions

Early in therapy, patients are taught about the phenomena that Beck (1963) called "automatic thoughts," the thoughts that mediate between environmental events and a person's emotional reactions to those events. These thoughts often go unnoticed because they are habitual and take place very quickly (hence, the term "automatic"). Because these thoughts are often not attended to, people will generally conclude that a particular external stressor directly "causes" their emotional upset, as if the negative emotion were reflexive and completely out of voluntary control. For example, Mr. X might say that a job interview "caused" him to be anxious, while not taking into account the cognitive *appraisals* of the job interview that were mediating such anxiety. He may have been covertly saying to himself: "I know I'm going to slip up somewhere in this interview and I won't get the job. I'll probably make a fool of myself in the process. Everyone will think I'm a real loser. Maybe I really am a loser." Such thinking may be commonplace for a person with low self-esteem, but he may not realize that these thoughts do not necessarily represent objective reality, and that he therefore may be subjecting himself to needless distress and may be interfering with his actual abilities to perform well on the interview. The therapist can help the patient to understand this concept by saying:

One of the most important aspects of cognitive therapy will be for you to become more aware of your thoughts when you become upset, and to learn how to be a "healthy skeptic" with regard to your own viewpoints. In other words, if you catch yourself saying self-defeating things to yourself, you need not accept these thoughts as 100 percent true. There will usually be at least one other plausible way to look at the situation, one that may be less upsetting and more constructive.

In order to assist patients in noticing such automatic thinking, therapists instruct them to use their emotional upset (e.g., sadness, hopelessness, or anger) as a *cue* to ask themselves the following question: "What am I saying to myself right now that could be causing me to feel so badly?" Patients are encouraged to jot their thoughts down on paper, thus concretizing the upsetting notion and starting the process of finding alternative, more adaptive responses.

Another important means by which to ascertain patients' automatic thoughts is to ask, whenever an affective shift takes place in the session, "What was going through your mind just now?" For those patients who have difficulty in articulating their thoughts, the therapist may use *imagery* by asking them to picture the upsetting situations in detail (Beck & Young, 1985) and then to give a running account of what they're thinking and feeling and what it all means to them. If the upsetting event is in the interpersonal sphere, the therapist can role-play the situation with the patient, so as to elicit the automatic thoughts that might actually occur in the heat of the moment (hence the term "hot cognitions").

Beck (1967) identified several common systematic errors in the way depressed patients process information, and these errors are often quite evident in their automatic thoughts. It is often helpful to describe and review these types of distortions with patients, and to instruct them to match their own automatic thoughts to the corresponding depressogenic style as it occurs. The goal is not to teach patients to denigrate themselves for their "irrational thinking," but rather to help them gain a valuable self-help skill. The systematic errors in logic that Beck (1967) discussed are:

1. All-or-none thinking. The tendency to see things in black-and-white terms; anything less than perfect is seen as utterly terrible. For example, a less than idyllic but basically solid marriage may be viewed as a total failure.

2. Overgeneralization. Drawing broad-sweeping conclusions on the basis of isolated incidents. For example, a woman who argues with her mother and then sees her cry concludes, "I always hurt everyone I care about."

3. Arbitrary inference. Jumping to conclusions, fortune-telling, mindreading, and/or mistaking emotion for fact. For instance, a woman doesn't receive a phone call from her boyfriend on a

given day, and erroneously concludes that he no longer cares for her.

4. Selective abstraction. Focusing on one negative detail of a situation out of context, thereby missing the bigger picture, which may be more hopeful. For example, a man receives a job evaluation which is 90 percent positive and 10 percent critical. He dwells on the critical 10 percent and becomes convinced that his job is in danger.

5. Magnification and minimization. Overestimating the importance of undesirable events, and downplaying the significance of positive events. As an example, a woman may feel terribly guilty as she magnifies the fact that she lost her temper with her son on one occasion, while she systematically forgets or diminishes the importance of the numerous times she has been patient, attentive, and loving.

6. Personalization. Taking responsibility for negative happenstances that are realistically out of the person's direct control. A teenager may blame herself for her father's drinking, believing that it would never happen if she were truly a good daughter.

Patients frequently find that their automatic thoughts fall into a number of the categories listed above. It is clearly a positive therapeutic step when a patient is able to say something along these lines: "Oops. There I go again, jumping to conclusions. I guess that things might not necessarily turn out as badly as I expect."

As treatment progresses, the cognitive therapist begins to help the patient to attend to the basic underlying beliefs, assumptions, or life rules that predispose him or her to depressogenic thinking. These underlying assumptions typically represent themes that tie together the various automatic thoughts that the patient is prone to have. These assumptions often take shape during the primary socialization period of a person's life (childhood and adolescence) and, like religious or cultural rules, are extremely fundamental to the way a person views the self, the world, and the future. Because they are so basic (deep cognitive structure), the patient's particular *maladaptive* assumptions are more difficult to ascertain than are the more transient automatic thoughts (surface structure). Careful observation on the part of both patient and therapist is needed to consolidate a seemingly disparate set of automatic thoughts into the themes that represent the patient's specific areas of vulnerability. For example, Ms. W had the following automatic thoughts when she began treatment with one of us (CFN):

"He [the therapist] probably thinks I'm stupid."
"I'll bet he laughs at me behind my back."

"I don't want to tell him anything personal that he'll use against me."
"I really don't want to be here. This is a mistake."

These thoughts were elicited when the therapist noticed that Ms. W was growing more and more irritable as the session progressed. (This highlights the importance of dealing with the patient's thoughts about the therapeutic relationship, not only to help avert resistance and/or premature termination but to shed light on the patient's habitual automatic thoughts and assumptions about other important relationships.) After these thoughts were gently addressed, a couple of basic themes emerged:

1. People who are more educated than I am will harshly and unfairly judge me to be inferior.
2. I desperately need approval. I'm nothing without it.

Discovery of these themes ultimately led to fruitful exploration of her expectations for exploitation in relationships and of her regrets about never having gone to college. By the end of treatment, she no longer automatically assumed that others would look down on her; she was far more assertive and confident, and had begun to take college courses.

Rationally Responding to Automatic Thoughts and Assumptions

An integral component of cognitive therapy is teaching patients to reevaluate their automatic thoughts and to generate new and more adaptive responses. One method involves instructing patients to ask themselves a series of four questions whenever they catch themselves having thoughts that are upsetting them. The first of these questions is, "What is the *evidence* that supports and/or refutes this thought?" This helps the patient to steer clear of faulty inference-making that is based primarily on hunches, intuition, "gut feelings," and other forms of illogical thinking. Of course, it is important to teach the patient the kinds of information that qualify as true objective evidence (Newman, 1989), so as to avoid the same pitfalls that occur when depressogenic assumptions are made in the first place.

A second question is, "How else could I view this situation?" This asks the patient to make a conscious effort in trying to see things in a different light. For instance, the cognitive therapist can prompt answers to this question by asking, "How could this situation turn out to be a blessing in disguise?" It is important to keep an open mind when answering this question, and it is often advisable to brainstorm possible alternatives.

The third question asks, "Realistically, what is the worst thing that could happen in this situation, and what implications would it have for my life?" This question provokes an earnest analysis of the degree of seriousness of the situation or feeling and has as its goal the task of helping patients to "de-catastrophize" their thinking.

The final question is quite pragmatic and constructive: "Even if there is reason to believe that my depressing viewpoint is warranted, what can I *do* to help remedy this situation?" This question sets the stage for constructive problem solving, which is especially important in helping patients to decrease their sense of helplessness and hopelessness and to learn to engage in rational self-help behaviors.

One particularly useful format for organizing, concretizing, and recording the self-help process described above is the Daily Thought Record (DTR) (see Table 17.1). Once patients have become familiar with the methods of identifying automatic thoughts, they are asked to use DTRs to articulate upsetting thoughts, and their concomitant situations and emotions, that occur *between sessions.* Additionally, the DTR requires that patients generate and record more objective, functional thoughts, and then notice and write down any improvement in mood that they perceive. The DTR often serves as an excellent cognitive self-help assignment and may also be used collaboratively by patient and therapist *during* the session, especially if the patient needs extra instruction in learning to use this tool or if emotional upsets occur. In any case, a review of the patient's work on the DTR is a typical agenda item for each session. (For a more complete description of use of the DTR, see Beck et al., 1979; Sacco & Beck, 1985).

Table 17.1 depicts an actual DTR completed by one of our patients (with certain details altered to protect confidentiality). Mr. A, already feeling quite depressed and thinking of suicide, suffered a severe blow when his beloved dog was killed by a car. Admirably, he was able to help himself get through this ordeal without an increased risk of suicide via a most skillful use of the DTR. (Note the dramatic reduction in the patient's report of feelings of suicidality.)

The DTR is by no means the only method by which to reevaluate dysfunctional thinking. Another method involves reverse role playing: the therapist plays "devil's advocate" (Goldfried & Davison, 1976) and argues in favor of the patient's negative automatic thoughts and assumptions; the patient has the responsibility to counter these arguments with rational responses. This process can be accentuated if the patient is asked to imagine that a "best friend's" automatic thoughts are being challenged. Frequently, depressed patients are far more understanding and even-handed when looking at their friends' problems than when looking at their own. Assuming that the patient is successful in rationally responding to the "friend's" or the "devil's advocate's" stated concerns, the patient can be asked whether those same responses could be self-applied. If the answer is "yes," the technique has been helpful. If the answer is "no," the therapist can then

TABLE 17.1. Mr. A's Daily Record of Dysfunctional Thoughts

Date	Situation	Emotion(s)	Automatic Thought(s)	Rational Response	Outcome
	Describe: 1. Actual event leading to unpleasant emotion, or 2. Stream of thoughts, daydream, or recollection, leading to unpleasant emotion.	1. Specify sad/anxious/angry, etc. 2. Rate degree of emotion, 1–100.	1. Write automatic thought(s) that preceded emotion(s). 2. Rate belief in automatic thought(s), 0–100%.	1. Write rational response to automatic thought(s). 2. Rate belief in rational response, 0–100%.	1. Re-rate belief in automatic thought(s), 0–100%. 2. Specify and rate subsequent emotions, 0–100.
	I found Bucky dead by the side of the road. He was hit in the head by a car.	unbearable pain and anguish (100) devastated (100) crushed (100) suicidal (100)	1. You were my best friend and now you're gone and you didn't even say goodbye. Why did you have to leave me. (No rating) 2. I might as well be dead too. (80)	1. Don't hurt yourself more by saying he left you. He didn't leave you. He may have been on his way home when he was hit. (No rating) In his heart, Bucky was always thinking about you. He didn't want to get hit any more than the driver wanted to hit him. But these things happen and it does little good to try and find an answer to why he died. He's at peace. At least you don't have to wonder where he is or whether he's alive or dead. (No rating) 2. I'm very, very upset that Bucky is dead. Now think about yourself and how others close to you would feel if out of the blue you were no longer alive. Probably the same way. Is that what you want to do to them? You would have accepted Bucky back under any circumstances, blind, lame . . . and others would rather see you alive with a few problems than not at all. (100)	pain (80) anguish (80) devastated (70) crushed (80) suicidal (10)

EXPLANATION: When you experience an unpleasant emotion, note the situation that seemed to stimulate the emotion. (If the emotion occurred while you were thinking, daydreaming, etc., please note this.) Then note the automatic thought associated with the emotion. Record the degree to which you believe this thought: 0% – not at all; 100% – completely. In rating degree of emotion: 1 – a trace; 100 – the most intense possible.

engage the patient in a discussion of the issues surrounding a double standard—the patient is selectively tougher on himself or herself than on anyone else. The rationality of this cognitive pattern can then be challenged in its own right.

Another technique involves the use of imagery. Weishaar and Beck (1986) presented a number of applications of imagery, including:

1. Time projection. Having the patient imagine his or her life months or years in the future, so as to gain some detachment and perspective about the current upsetting event.
2. Goal rehearsal. Covertly imagining solving a current problem, so as to increase a sense of self-efficacy.
3. Coping imagery. Imagining: changing the features of a situation to make it less threatening, dealing with a range of possible outcomes (from best to worst), and/or how someone else would cope in the same circumstances.

Behavioral experiments represent yet another way to test and challenge depressive expectations. For example, if a patient is convinced that her situation is hopeless, she may systematically avoid doing anything to help herself. She may think that "nothing will work anyway . . . I'll just fail again and be even more miserable." In this case, the therapist asks her to treat the above thought as a hypothesis to be behaviorally tested. The patient is asked to generate a proposed self-help behavior (e.g., getting up at 8 A.M. so as not to sleep too much and then feel that the day has been wasted) and then to predict the outcome if she puts it into action (e.g., "I'll feel sick, I'll stay in bed, and wind up not only wasting a day but loathing myself for being a lazy good-for-nothing"). The patient is then asked if she would go forth with the self-help behavior and see if her prediction is confirmed or disconfirmed.

If the negative prediction is disconfirmed, the patient has had an important corrective experience that dispels the hopeless assumption and demonstrates how thinking patterns alone, rather than an actual lack of capacity for change, may be hindering her recovery. If the prediction is borne out, all is not lost, because the patient can be instructed to monitor her automatic thoughts at the time the experiment is carried out, thus helping the therapist and patient to gain access to key hot cognitions that are hampering progress.

The above description does not represent an exhaustive review of potential strategies for identifying and changing dysfunctional thoughts and beliefs. Any ethical, mutually agreed-upon technique that serves to deal constructively with depressive thinking is consistent with cognitive therapy. Although a number of tried-and-true methods for cognitive restructuring have been found to be consistently helpful, the notion that cognitive therapy represents a cookbook application of a specified number of rigid techniques is simply a myth.

Behavioral Techniques

Cognitive therapy incorporates behavioral procedures in order to alter depressogenic belief systems and to facilitate problem solving (Beck et al., 1979; Evans & Hollon, 1988). Although they are employed throughout the course of therapy, they are generally concentrated in the earlier stages of treatment, especially with more severely depressed patients who may be suffering from lethargy, inertia, and a sense of helplessness and hopelessness (Beck & Young, 1985; Sacco & Beck, 1985). The immediate goal is to counteract the patient's avoidance and/or withdrawal, and to begin to engage him or her in constructive activity. The long-range goals are to decrease discouragement that is born of inactivity and therefore to positively alter the patient's negative views of the self, the world, and the future.

The most frequently utilized behavioral techniques include: (a) scheduling of activities, (b) mastery and pleasure ratings, (c) graded task assignments, (d) assertiveness practice, and (e) problem solving, to name a few. The scheduling of activities usually goes hand-in-hand with mastery and pleasure ratings. For example, in order to combat low motivation, hopelessness, and excessive rumination, the therapist and patient may generate and plan a daily schedule for the patient to follow. Furthermore, the patient may be asked to rate each activity on a 1–10 scale of pleasure ("How much did I *enjoy* this activity?"), and a separate 1–10 scale of mastery ("How much did I accomplish, and how well did I perform and cope with this activity?").

Each scale is important in its own right. The pleasure scale serves to contradict the patient's assertion that nothing can be enjoyable anymore; the mastery scale focuses the patient's attention on the ability to act constructively on the environment. The mastery scale is also useful in that it may increase the patient's sense of self-efficacy (thus lifting mood and hopefulness), even as the patient engages in some relatively unenjoyable tasks that are necessary in successful day-to-day responsible living. Again, if the patient's self-ratings are consistently low in both pleasure and mastery, the therapist can assist in identifying the various dysfunctional cognitions that are responsible for such negative feelings and impressions and are therefore important to cognitive assessment.

When the patient endeavors to achieve a given goal that seems overwhelmingly difficult (e.g., finding appropriate employment), a graded task assignment can be introduced. Here, the overall goal is subdivided into easier stages that are more concrete and less formidable to achieve (e.g., revising a résumé, scanning the classified section of the newspaper, and so on). The patient then performs the tasks one by one, focuses on the success and productivity generated by each task, and counters negative thoughts that may interfere with the appreciation of each accomplished task or with expectations for the next task. Ultimately, the patient learns that by breaking down a major goal into more manageable components, difficulties that previously seemed insurmountable can be overcome.

When the patient's depressive symptoms are exacerbated by social withdrawal and/or a lack of assertiveness in social encounters, role playing can be used in the session to practice new, adaptive behaviors in this realm. After identifying problematic situations, the therapist and patient work together to brainstorm possible verbal and behavioral responses and then put them into simulated action by role playing. The patient is encouraged to try these new, assertive responses in actual situations between sessions and to monitor the results. Cognitions that might inhibit the patient from following through on such an assignment should be assessed and dealt with in the session.

Another integral cognitive-behavioral component of cognitive therapy is problem solving. This general strategy is comprised of (a) defining the problem, (b) brainstorming the potential solutions, (c) examining the pros and cons of each proposed solution, (d) choosing and implementing the chosen course of action, and (e) evaluating the results. (For a comprehensive explication of problem solving, see D'Zurilla & Nezu, 1982). The third step (examining pros and cons) has alternative applications in cognitive therapy. For example, when a patient staunchly persists in holding on to a dysfunctional thought, belief, and/or behavior in spite of rational responses to the contrary, the patient can be asked what is gained by maintaining that position and what is lost by doing so. Conversely, the patient is asked to consider what is gained or lost by *changing* the belief and/or actions. This approach serves at least two functions: (a) to elucidate idiosyncratic or "secondary" gains that the patient may be deriving from the seemingly maladaptive stance, and (b) to highlight the patient's self-defeating thoughts and behaviors and demonstrate that there *are* viable, more adaptive alternatives that would clearly benefit the patient more in the long run.

Homework Assignments

Consistent with cognitive therapy's emphasis on teaching patients to become their own "therapists," homework assignments are included as a vital part of treatment. We have found that when patients systematically apply what they have learned in the session to their everyday lives between sessions, they make more rapid and more lasting progress. Homework assignments help patients solidify and generalize their new skills and foster a sense of therapeutic self-reliance.

Homework assignments are not given in a gratuitous manner, just to keep the patient busy. Rather, each assignment should be directly related to the content of the therapy session and should be explained so that the patient understands its rationale. For example, if a depressed patient states that she is lonely but is avoiding making contact with a particular long-distance friend because she assumes that "she won't really want to talk to me . . . I'd just be bothering her," the therapist may suggest an assignment whereby the patient is to call or write to this friend and then compare the outcome of this communication to her original negative expectations. This assignment would serve to counteract the patient's inclination to socially isolate herself, would potentially highlight the erroneous and self-defeating nature of her original expectations, and/or could provoke the uncovering of other inhibitory cognitions that need to be addressed.

In the spirit of collaboration that is one of the hallmarks of cognitive therapy, it is important that the therapist not merely "order" the patient to follow through on a given assignment, without first checking to see if the patient agrees that it could be important and useful to do. Qualms about doing homework assignments should be respected and, at the same time, looked at as automatic thoughts subject to the same rational evaluation as any other automatic thoughts that may be contributing to the patient's condition. If a patient steadfastly declines to do a particular assignment, he or she can be asked to generate an assignment. In fact, as therapy progresses it is a good idea to encourage patients to develop their own assignments, as yet another step toward self-sufficiency. If the patient refuses to do any assignments at all and/or does not seem responsive to the therapist's sincere rationales behind the homework, it is important that the therapist not assume that the patient is "resistant" or "passive-aggressive." Otherwise, the therapist runs the risk of engaging in dysfunctional, nonobjective thinking as well, for example, by *labeling* a patient and *jumping to conclusions* about his or her character. (This example brings up the fact that therapists, as human beings, are subject to their own erroneous thinking at times, and need to be willing to look at their *own* automatic thoughts and beliefs when therapy is not going smoothly and frustrations build.) When such difficulties arise, the therapist can model appropriate problem-solving behavior by working with the patient to identify the sources of the difficulties and by collaboratively attempting to overcome them.

Additionally, the therapist would do well to explain that homework assignments are a "no-lose" proposition. They cannot be failed; doing an assignment partially is better than not doing it at all, and even if the outcome of the assignment seems less than helpful, it may serve to highlight problems that still need to be worked on. In any event, valuable therapeutic information is gained, and the patient has taken a step toward self-help in the long run (if not in the short run).

SPECIAL ISSUES IN ADAPTING COGNITIVE THERAPY TO DYSTHYMIC AND BIPOLAR DISORDERS

The affective disorders, in spite of being described by a rather consistent set of phenotypic symptoms, are quite heterogeneous in terms of etiology and response to treatment (Hollon & Beck, 1978, 1979). Although cognitive therapy was originally developed as a treatment for unipolar depression, the reality is that many patients who come to therapy complaining of depressed mood may be better diagnosed as suffering from dysthymia, bipolar disorder (depressed phase), major unipolar depression superimposed on a long-standing dysthymia (the so-called "double-depression"), or an atypical depression (e.g., secondary to a borderline personality disorder). While some of the above subclasses of the affective disorders seem to beg for a pharmacological approach to treatment, we have found that cognitive therapy is still an efficacious element of the treatment plan, in much the same way that a treatment package of cognitive therapy and pharmacotherapy has been found to effect clinically significant treatment and maintenance gains in certain unipolar-depressed populations (Blackburn et al., 1981; Hollon et al., 1986; Hollon & Beck, 1978).

Although the empirical literature is sparse in this area, the following is a brief overview of issues that are pertinent to the application of cognitive therapy to dysthymic and bipolar disorder populations.

Dysthymic Disorder and "Double Depression"

Dysthymic disorder, a chronic subtype of depression, is characterized by "low-level" dysphoria, anhedonia, low self-esteem, low energy, and a fairly rigid pessimistic outlook on life (Kocsis & Frances, 1987; Yee & Miller, 1988). Dysthymia, especially the early-onset variety, seems to render individuals at increased risk for developing full-blown major depression (Yee & Miller, 1988). This resultant "major depression on top of dysthymia" condition has been observed to hinder the patient's recovery from the major depressive episode, when compared to patients who do not suffer from underlying dysthymia in the first place (Miller, Norman, & Dow, 1986). Furthermore, the continuance of dysthymia after a major depression remits has been found to increase a patient's risk for subsequent major depressive relapse (Keller, Lavori, Endicott, Coryell, & Klerman, 1983). Interestingly, the data are still very unclear as to whether dysthymia and major depression lie on a continuum of severity or constitute qualitatively different disorders (Keller et al., 1983).

Cognitive therapy is known for, among other things, being a short-term therapy. Most outcome studies involving cognitive therapy specify an average of 12 to 16 sessions before termination (Beck et al., 1985; Evans et al., 1986; Hollon et al., 1986; Kovacs et al., 1981; Rush et al., 1977), and many therapists and patients alike have come to expect that treatment will be no longer than this. However, the chronic nature of dysthymia dictates the treatment will run a longer course. Cognitive therapists must be aware of their own and their patients' expectations regarding length of treatment and be prepared to deal with thoughts and feelings of hopelessness in both parties as therapy goes beyond three or four months. In fact, assuming that the patient has been properly diagnosed at intake, the cognitive therapist would do well to exercise a psychoeducational role by explaining to the patient what is known about the disorder and what to expect in terms of course and length of treatment. A conservative estimate, leaving room for wide patient variability, would be six months to two years.

A patient who is suffering from "double-depression" may seek treatment for the major depressive episode but be relatively resigned to a usual low-level dysphoric condition. Indeed, the patient may not be aware of having a chronic mood disorder at all, not having known anything different. The patient may therefore be prone to leave therapy prematurely, once the major depression has been treated, unaware that further improvement is possible and that he or she is at risk for subsequent major depressive relapse (Keller et al., 1983; Miller et al., 1986; Yee & Miller, 1988).

At the Center for Cognitive Therapy in Philadelphia, it is standard practice that when a patient's depression remains at a high level for a prolonged period (e.g., even after 12 to 16 sessions), a medication consultation is suggested. Many of the patients who become candidates for antidepressant medication are diagnosed as having dysthymic disorder. While there are numerous studies demonstrating the efficacy of a combination of cognitive therapy and pharmacotherapy for unipolar depression (e.g., Blackburn et al., 1981, Blackburn et al., 1986; Hollon et al., 1986; Hollon & Beck, 1978), more data are needed to make this same assertion for the treatment of dysthymia. One clue that this may be so was provided by Kocsis and Frances (1987), who concluded that antidepressants are an effective treatment for dysthymia but added that cognitive factors are very important and must be addressed as part of therapy as well.

For those dysthymic patients who report having "always been a sad person," a truly successful treatment would need to focus on enhancing the patient's capacity for experiencing joy, rather than solely "taking the edge off" the dysphoria (cf. Lutz, 1985; Menzel, 1987). Often, such patients operate on the implicit assumption that it is "wrong" to feel good (especially those who have been raised with religious guilt) or have fears about "jinxing" themselves into a disaster if they let their guard down and allow themselves to be happy or hopeful. These beliefs, and others related to them, would need to be identified and challenged in order to combat the patient's habitual anhedonia. Imagery, facilitated by a relaxation induction, can be utilized to remember times when the patient felt happiness or love, or to imagine joyous life events in the future. Behaviorally, dysthymic patients can be encouraged to engage in pleasant events (Lewinsohn, 1975), to initiate social contact with others, and to more freely accept positive attention from others.

Therapists must recognize that dysthymic patients are often low in motivation and may also represent mild chronic suicide risks. Therefore, it is important to regularly monitor suicidal ideation and intention and to be prepared to deal with the patient's (and one's own) hopelessness and frustration.

Bipolar Disorder

Patients who are experiencing a manic episode rarely feel that they are in need of therapy. However, it is not uncommon for a bipolar disordered patient to seek treatment when in the throes of the depressive phase. When treating these patients, cognitive therapists may find themselves in a bind. The bipolar depressive's rapid lifting of mood, unlike that of the unipolar patient, does not necessarily portend a positive therapeutic effect. Indeed, the therapist may need to help the patient to recognize and reevaluate dysfunctional *hyperpositive* thinking, including dangerously inflated ideas about invulnerability, excessively optimistic expectations for success in various life ventures, and denial of all problems. (This point highlights the fact that cognitive therapy is *not* equivalent to "the power of positive thinking" approach. The goal of cognitive therapy is to teach *adaptive, constructive, functional* thinking, whether it be positive, conservative, or cautionary in tone.)

Lithium carbonate is a well-documented treatment of choice for bipolar disorder (Chor, Mercier, & Halper, 1988; Cochran, 1984). However, noncompliance in taking medication is a prevalent problem with this population. Cochran (1984) demonstrated the effectiveness of cognitive therapy in improving patients' compliance in taking their prescribed dosages of lithium, both during adjunctive cognitive therapy and at six-month follow-up. She noted that a thorough assessment of patients' beliefs and attitudes toward their illness and toward medication can successfully predict risk for noncompliance, and that high-risk beliefs can then become targets for cognitive therapy. Table 17.2 presents the DTR of Ms. J, one of our patients suffering from bipolar disorder. She had been given the assignment of completing a thought

TABLE 17.2. Ms. J's Daily Record of Dysfunctional Thoughts

Date	Situation	Emotion(s)	Automatic Thought(s)	Rational Response	Outcome
	Describe: 1. Actual event leading to unpleasant emotion, or 2. Stream of thoughts, daydream, or recollection, leading to unpleasant emotion.	1. Specify sad/anxious/angry, etc. 2. Rate degree of emotion, 1–100.	1. Write automatic thought(s) that preceded emotion(s). 2. Rate belief in automatic thought(s), 0–100%.	1. Write rational response to automatic thought(s). 2. Rate belief in rational response, 0–100%.	1. Re-rate belief in automatic thought(s), 0–100%. 2. Specify and rate subsequent emotions, 0–100.
	It's early Sunday morning and I realize I forgot to take my midday and nightly dosage of Lithium the day before.	annoyed (85) apathetic (50)	1. Oh well. It isn't going to kill me if I miss a few times. (100) 2. I probably don't need Lithium anyway. (90) 3. I don't want people to think I'm a freak or psychotic or something. I want to be regarded as a normal person!!!!	1. Well, should I suddenly plummet into a depression I might very well feel suicidal again. So it might actually kill me if I skip a few times. (90) 2. Most signs show that I do need Lithium. It's to my advantage to take the medication. It isn't painful and I have few side effects. And it isn't worth going off the medication and taking the risk of going through all that pain and craziness again. (90) 3. I'm not crazy. I have a treatable disorder that many successful and creative and important people have had. If someone does, by chance, regard me as abnormal, it's not worth my time to have them as friends. People who really care about me won't stop being my friend because I take Lithium. (100)	1. annoyed (20) 2. apathetic (0)

EXPLANATION: When you experience an unpleasant emotion, note the situation that seemed to stimulate the emotion. (If the emotion occurred while you were thinking, daydreaming, etc., please note this.) Then note the automatic thought associated with the emotion. Record the degree to which you believe this thought: 0% = not at all; 100% = completely. In rating degree of emotion: 1 = a trace; 100 = the most intense possible.

record each time she noticed that she missed taking her medication, so as to catch the thoughts that might be hindering her from complying with treatment. Her successful completion of this DTR, which led to the revelation that she worried about being labeled as a "psychotic" if she were to be seen taking the lithium, represented a significant breakthrough in treatment. She is currently still in cognitive therapy, takes her lithium routinely, and maintains a stable enough mood to rationally address problematic issues in her life with some success.

Cognitive therapy is also useful in treating the depressive aftereffects of a manic episode (Jacobs, 1982) and serves as a viable replacement treatment when there are significant medical contraindications to taking lithium (e.g., when the patient is pregnant; see Chor et al., 1988). Chor et al. (1988) noted several important components to a cognitive therapy for bipolar disorder, including: (a) mood monitoring, with predetermined precautions to be implemented when the patient's mood would get too high or too low, (b) anticipatory problem solving, (c) stimulus control (e.g., avoiding risky situations such as bars, drugs, and driving, when in a manic state), (d) planning more activities when mood is low and fewer activities when mood is high, and (e) challenging of hyperpositive cognitions (e.g., "assuming superiority," "I can do no wrong" statements, jumping to conclusions based on impulsive emotional desires, and inclinations toward overaggression). Again, the data are quite limited in this area, but one can readily hypothesize that a combination of cognitive therapy and lithium would create a positive synergistic therapeutic effect and would lead to greater maintenance of gains that either treatment alone or alternative treatments. This remains to be empirically tested.

SUMMARY

There is considerable evidence that cognitive therapy is an effective short-term therapy for unipolar depression. Clinical evidence suggests that cognitive therapy may also be efficacious in the treatment of dysthymic disorder and as part of a package treatment for bipolar disorder.

Cognitive therapy teaches patients to become skilled reality testers via monitoring thoughts and basic assumptions about the self, the world, and the future and then putting these cognitions to empirical tests. These tests include examining evidence for one's beliefs, setting up behavioral experiments and graded tasks, weighing the pros and cons of maintaining or changing certain cognitive and behavioral patterns, and a host of additional interventions. Through this process, learned in session and applied between sessions, patients begin to take a more constructive, hopeful view of themselves and their problems, learn to take steps to help themselves, and therefore feel happier.

The cognitive therapist's role is one of teacher and collaborative facilitator, actively helping the patient to gain new perspectives, behaviors, and skills that can help toward better functioning now and in the future, long after therapy is completed.

Cognitive theory of the affective disorders is parsimonious, has heuristic value, and is testable. The corresponding therapy is eminently teachable and has an excellent track record in outcome studies in the treatment of depression. Demonstrating the utility of cognitive therapy for other subtypes of the affective disorders (e.g., dysthymia, bipolar disorder) will be an important future direction in the ongoing study of this therapeutic approach.

REFERENCES

Abramson, L. Y., Alloy, L. B., & Metalsky, G. I. (1988). The cognitive diathesis-stress theories of depression: Toward an adequate evaluation of the theories' validities. In L. B. Alloy (Ed.), *Cognitive processes in depression* (pp. 3–30). New York: Guilford.

Adler, A. (1936). The neurotic's picture of the world. *International Journal of Individual Psychology, 2,* 3–10.

Beck, A. T. (1961). A systematic investigation of depression. *Comprehensive Psychiatry, 2,* 163–170.

Beck, A. T. (1963). Thinking and depression: 1. Idiosyncratic content and cognitive distortions. *Archives of General Psychiatry, 9,* 324–333.

Beck, A. T. (1967). *Depression: Clinical, experimental, and theoretical aspects.* New York: Harper & Row.

Beck, A. T. (1974). The development of depression: A cognitive model. In R. Friedman & M. Katz (Eds.), *Psychology of depression: Contemporary theory and research* (pp. 3–28). Washington, DC: Winston/Wiley.

Beck, A. T. (1976). *Cognitive therapy and the emotional disorders.* New York: International Universities Press.

Beck, A. T., Hollon, S. D., Young, J., Bedrosian, R. C., & Budenz, D. (1985). Treatment of depression with cognitive therapy and amitriptyline. *Archives of General Psychiatry, 42,* 142–148.

Beck, A. T., & Hurvich, M. S. (1959). Psychological correlates of depression. 1. Frequency of "masochistic" dream content in a private practice sample. *Psychosomatic Medicine, 21,* 50–55.

Beck, A. T., Rush, A. J., Shaw, B. F., & Emery, G. (1979). *Cognitive therapy of depression: A treatment manual.* New York: Guilford.

Beck, A. T., & Ward, C. H. (1961). Dreams of depressed patients: Characteristic themes in manifest content. *Archives of General Psychiatry, 5,* 462–471.

Beck, A. T., & Young, J. E. (1985). Cognitive therapy of depression. In D. Barlow (Ed.), *Clinical handbook of psychological disorders: A step-by-step treatment manual* (pp. 206–244). New York: Guilford.

Blackburn, I. M., Bishop, S., Glen, A. I. M., Whalley, L. J., & Christie, J. E. (1981). The efficacy of cognitive therapy in depression: A treatment trial using cognitive therapy and pharmacotherapy, each alone and in combination. *British Journal of Psychiatry, 139,* 181–189.

Blackburn, I. M., Eunson, K. M., & Bishop, S. (1986). A two-year naturalistic follow-up of depressed patients treated with cognitive therapy, pharmacotherapy, and a combination of both. *Journal of Affective Disorders, 10,* 67–75.

Chor, P. N., Mercier, M. A., & Halper, I. S. (1988). Use of cognitive therapy for treatment of a patient suffering from a bipolar affective disorder. *Journal of Cognitive Psychotherapy: An International Quarterly, 2,* 51–58.

Cochran, S. D. (1984). Preventing medical non-compliance in the outpatient treatment of bipolar affective disorders. *Journal of Consulting and Clinical Psychology, 52,* 873–878.

Dobson, K. S. (in press). A meta-analysis of the efficacy of cognitive therapy for depression. *Journal of Consulting and Clinical Psychology.*

D'Zurilla, T. J., & Nezu, A. (1982). Social problem-solving in adults. In P. C. Kendall (Ed.), *Advances in cognitive-behavioral research and therapy* (Vol. 1, pp. 201–274). New York: Academic Press.

Ellis, A. (1962). *Reason and emotion in psychotherapy.* New York: Lyle Stuart.

Evans, M. D., & Hollon, S. D. (1988). Patterns of personal and causal inference: Implications for the cognitive therapy of depression. In L. B. Alloy (Ed.), *Cognitive processes in depression* (pp. 344–377). New York: Guilford.

Evans, M. D., Hollon, S. D., DeRubeis, R. J., Piasecki, J., Tuason, V. B., & Garvey, M. J. (1986). *Relapse/recurrence following cognitive therapy and pharmacotherapy for depression: 4. Two-year follow-up in the CPT project.* Unpublished manuscript, University of Minnesota and St. Paul-Ramsey Medical Center, Minneapolis–St. Paul.

Gallagher, D. E., & Thompson, L. W. (1982). Treatment of major depressive disorder in older adult outpatients with brief psychotherapies. *Psychotherapy: Theory, Research and Practice, 19,* 482–490.

Goldfried, M. R., & Davison, G. C. (1976). *Clinical behavior therapy.* New York: Holt.

Hall, R. C. W., Gardner, E. R., Stickney, S. K., LeCany, A. F., & Popkin, M. K. (1980). Physical illness manifested as psychiatric disease (Analysis of a state hospital inpatient population). *Archives of General Psychiatry, 37,* 989–995.

Hamilton, E. W., & Abramson, L. Y. (1983). Cognitive patterns and major depressive disorder: A longitudinal study in a hospital setting. *Journal of Abnormal Psychology, 92,* 173–184.

Hollon, S. D., & Beck, A. T. (1978). Psychotherapy and drug therapy: Comparisons and combinations. In S. L. Garfield & A. E. Bergin (Eds.), *The handbook of psychotherapy and behavior change* (2nd ed., pp. 437–490). New York: Wiley.

Hollon, S. D., & Beck, A. T. (1979). Cognitive therapy of depression. In P. C. Kendall & S. D. Hollon (Eds.), *Cognitive-behavioral interventions: Theory, research, and procedures* (pp. 153–203). New York: Academic Press.

Hollon, S. D., DeRubeis, R. J., Evans, M. D., Tuason, V. B., Wiemer, M. J., & Garvey, M. (1986). *Cognitive therapy, pharmacotherapy, and combined cognitive therapy-pharmacotherapy in the treatment of depression: 1. Differential outcome.* Unpublished manuscript, University of Minnesota and St. Paul-Ramsey Medical Center, Minneapolis–St. Paul.

Horney, K. (1950). *Neurosis and human growth: The struggle toward self-realization.* New York: Norton.

Jacobs, L. I. (1982). Cognitive therapy of postmanic and postdepressive dysphoria in bipolar illness. *American Journal of Psychotherapy, 36,* 450–458.

Karoly, P., & Ruehlman, L. (1983). Affective meaning and depression: A semantic differential analysis. *Cognitive Therapy and Research, 7,* 41–50.

Keller, M. B., Lavori, P. W., Endicott, J., Coryell, W., & Klerman, G. L. (1983). Double depression: Two-year follow-up. *American Journal of Psychiatry, 140,* 689–694.

Kelly, G. (1955). *The psychology of personal constructs.* New York: Norton.

Kocsis, J. H., & Frances, A. J. (1987). A critical discussion of DSM-III dysthymic disorder. *American Journal of Psychiatry, 144,* 1534–1542.

Kovacs, M., Rush, A. J., Beck, A. T., & Hollon, S. D. (1981). Depressed outpatients treated with cognitive therapy or pharmacotherapy: A one-year follow-up. *Archives of General Psychiatry, 38,* 33–39.

Krantz, S., & Hammen, C. (1979). Assessment of cognitive bias in depression. *Journal of Abnormal Psychology, 88,* 611–619.

Lewinsohn, P. M. (1975). Engagement in pleasant activities and depression level. *Journal of Abnormal Psychology, 84,* 729–731.

Lewinsohn, P. M., Larson, D. W., & Muñoz, R. F. (1982). The measurement of expectancies and other cognitions in depressed individuals. *Cognitive Therapy and Research, 6,* 437–446.

Lutz, R. (1985). *Zum Konzept euthymer Behandlungsstrategien.* Unveroeffentlichter Vortrag, Philipps-Universitaet Marburg.

Menzel, S. J. (1987). *Therapieprogramm zum Aufbau von positivem Verhalten und Erleben bei Depression.* Unveroeffentlichter Diplomarbeit Westfaelische Wilhelm-Universitaet Muenster.

Miller, I. W., Norman, W. H., & Dow, M. G. (1986). Psychosocial characteristics of "double depression." *American Journal of Psychiatry, 143,* 1042–1044.

Murphy, G. E., Simons, A. D., Wetzel, R. D., & Lustman, P. J. (1984). Cognitive therapy and pharmacotherapy: Singly and together in the treatment of depression. *Archives of General Psychiatry, 41,* 33–41.

Newman, C. F. (1989). "Where's the evidence?" Helping patients to rationally respond to their automatic thoughts. *International Cognitive Therapy Newsletter, 5,* 4–8.

Rogers, T. R., & Forehand, R. (1983). The role of parent depression in interactions between mothers and their clinic-referred children. *Cognitive Therapy and Research, 7,* 315–324.

Roth, D., & Rehm, L. P. (1980). Relationships among self-monitoring processes, memory, and depression. *Cognitive Therapy and Research, 4,* 149–158.

Rush, A. J., Beck, A. T., Kovacs, M., & Hollon, S. D. (1977). Comparative efficacy of cognitive therapy versus pharmacotherapy in outpatient depressives. *Cognitive Therapy and Research, 1,* 17–37.

Sacco, W. P., & Beck, A. T. (1985). Cognitive therapy of depression. In E. E. Beckham & W. Leber (Eds.), *Depression: Treatment, assessment, and research.* New York: Dow Jones-Irwin.

Shaw, B. F. (1977). Comparison of cognitive therapy and behavior therapy in the treatment of depression. *Journal of Consulting and Clinical Psychology, 45,* 543–551.

Simons, A. D., Murphy, G. E., Levine, J. L., & Wetzel, R. D. (1986). Cognitive therapy and pharmacotherapy for depression: Sustained improvement over one year. *Archives of General Psychiatry, 43,* 43–48.

Sullivan, H. S. (1953). *The interpersonal theory of psychiatry.* New York: Norton.

Taylor, F. G., & Marshall, W. L. (1977). Experimental analysis of a cognitive-behavioral therapy for depression. *Cognitive Therapy and Research, 1,* 59–72.

Teasdale, J. D., & Fennell, M. J. V. (1982). Immediate effects on depression of cognitive therapy interventions. *Cognitive Therapy and Research, 6,* 343–352.

Truax, C. B., & Mitchell, K. M. (1971). Research on certain therapist skills in relation to process and outcome. In A. E. Bergin & S. L. Garfield (Eds.), *Handbook of psychotherapy and behavior change: An empirical analysis.* New York: Wiley.

Weishaar, M. E., & Beck, A. T. (1986). Cognitive therapy. In W. Dryden & W. Golden (Eds.), *Cognitive-behavioral approaches to psychotherapy* (pp. 61–91). London: Harper & Row.

Weissman, A., & Beck, A. T. (1978). *Development and validation of the dysfunctional attitude scale.* Paper presented at the meeting of the Association for the Advancement of Behavior Therapy, Chicago.

Yee, C. M., & Miller, G. A. (1988). Emotional information processing: Modulation of fear in normal and dysthymic subjects. *Journal of Abnormal Psychology, 97,* 54–63.

CHAPTER 18

Interactional Psychotherapy

BENJAMIN B. WOLMAN, PhD

One can distinguish three basic types of social interaction: "taking," which is *instrumental,* "taking and giving," which is *mutual,* and "giving," which is *vectorial.* People are born *instrumental* in their attitude, that is, they are "selfish"; the child in utero is a taker, and the mother's body is the giver. As the child grows, it gradually learns that peer relationships are *mutual;* one must give and take. In adult life the relationships of friendship, love, and marriage are all mutual interactions based on giving and taking. Taking care of one's children is *vectorial;* the parent gives without thought of reciprocation. Well-adjusted adults function in all three dimensions; they are *instrumental* in their breadwinning activities, *mutual* in their friendships and marriage, and *vectorial* in their parenting and in the pursuit of idealistic purposes (Wolman, 1958).

There are three types of psychosociogenic mental disorders. Some individuals, rejected in childhood, develop an extremely selfish attitude; they are *hyperinstrumental sociopaths.* Children forced to worry about their overdemanding parents, who reverse the social roles and expect their children to function as caretakers, become *hypervectorial schizotypes.* Children exposed to a seesaw of parental acceptance-rejection attitudes become *dysmutual depressives* (Wolman, 1973).

CORRECTIVE EMOTIONAL EXPERIENCE

One can treat dysmutual-depressive patients in many ways, as described in the chapters of this volume. In developing the interactional method of psychotherapy I was influenced by the ideas of Alexander and French (1946), who introduced the concept of "corrective emotional experience." Adults who come for help are mature in many areas of their lives, but in some areas they retain childlike emotions and attitudes. A certain part of their personality remains infantile—"fixated," or "regressed" to the early stages of development (Freud, 1919/1962).

In psychotherapy the process of regression is facilitated by the inevitable dependence of the patients on their therapists. This dependent patient–therapist relationship was named "transference" by Freud.

TRANSFERENCE

People seek psychotherapy when they are unhappy about themselves and/or about their life. They go to someone who they believe can help them. Seeking psychological help and guidance resembles a child's dependence on its parents, and patients tend to *transfer* their child-versus-parent emotions onto their psychotherapists (Fenichel, 1945; Langs, 1976; Mendelson, 1960; Tarachow, 1963; Wolman, 1972).

The type and intensity of transference depend on the type and intensity of the disorder. The schizo-hypervectorials tend to develop intense and lasting transference. The sociopathic-hyperinstrumentals tend to develop superficial transference or no transference at all. The depressive dysmutuals tend to develop intense transference that swings from positive to negative attitudes toward the therapist (Bemporad, 1976; Lewin, 1959; Wolman, 1984).

The initial reaction of depressed patients to the therapist is blissful euphoria. "Finally," they say, "I have found someone who understands me and cares for me." They tend to believe that the therapist is an omnipotent and benevolent person, and they ascribe to him or her all the virtues their parents never had. The usual therapeutic signs of friendliness are interpreted as evidence of great love. Most of their symptoms disappear temporarily, and they tend to love themselves, the therapist, and everyone else. However, quite soon their euphoria comes to an end, and the patients' love turns into resentment. As Wolberg (1954) put it:

> Psychotherapy is also very difficult with depressed patients because their demands for help and love are insatiable. No matter how painstaking the therapist may be in supplying their demands, they will respond with rage and aggression.
>
> *(p. 628)*

Woe to the therapists who allow themselves to be caught in the web of their patients' insatiable demands. Therapists must state their position clearly, when male or female patients ask accusingly: "You don't love me, do you?" My answer has always been: "I care for your well-being. My responsibility is to help you and not to please you."

Depression can be *exogenous* if it is caused by real misfortunes, such as a serious disease, the loss of someone beloved, financial catastrophe, and so on. When the exogenous depression is related to the patients' neglect or error, it requires a realistic appraisal of the situation and a rational search for remedies. *Endogenous* depression is not related to any true setback or defeat. Sometimes a patient says, "I have no reason to complain, but I feel miserable. Everything bothers me and I don't know why." Endogenous depression requires a more thorough investigation of the patient's personality.

Reassurance does not work, and showing compassion makes the situation worse because, if the doctor is so concerned, it must be very bad. Instead, a calm and steadfast attitude in the therapist is reassuring because it shows that there is no reason for alarm.

Depressed patients try to use the therapist's reserved attitude to make themselves more unhappy. A female patient told me, "I know that you don't love me anymore. You're right. I don't deserve to be loved. I'm a terrible person. Everybody hates me; I hate myself too."

One must adjust one's therapeutic method to the particular needs of a particular patient. Once, when a patient said, "I wish you would love me," I counteracted the need to be loved by a realistic remark: "What would you gain by my love? What would my love contribute to your life? Suppose you saw not me, but another therapist; should that therapist love you too? What for?"

One of the main tasks of psychotherapy with depressed patients is to increase their love and respect for themselves. Quite often, depressed patients practice willful regression and self-defeating behavior, hoping to get more attention and love from the therapist, instead of trying to act in a constructive manner. Their *resistance* is quite persistent. Their emotional involvement with the therapist, that is, their transference, may become a source for *resistance* and a wish to stay in therapy as long as possible.

EGO THERAPY

Interactional psychotherapy *aims at strengthening the patient's ego,* and the therapist's strategy must be adjusted to the level of mental disorder. At this point it is necessary to introduce the concept of *interindividual cathexis.* A lot of nonverbal communication goes on in psychotherapy, and the therapist's attitude is usually more important than his or her words. The therapist's friendly and reassuring attitude cathects (invests) loads of neutralized libido. It makes patients feel accepted and conveys the therapist's concern for the patients' well-being and the determination to help them.

Psychotherapy, following Alexander's definition, should be a "corrective emotional experience," and transference on too deep a level must be prevented, especially in depressive disorders (Schuyler, 1983; Wolman, 1984). Too deep a transference makes the patients overdependent on the therapist and slows down their progress toward depending on themselves.

THERAPEUTIC INTERACTION

I have called my method of treatment of mental disorders *interactional psychotherapy* because psychotherapy is *always a two-way relationship*. In a dentist's or opthamologist's office the patients are passive recipients of treatment. In psychotherapy the patients' active participation is essential, and no psychotherapist can help a patient without his or her cooperation.

Freud (1919) realized that a totally passive attitude may not be appropriate and in some instances the psychoanalyst ". . . must help the patients by interpreting to them their unconscious." In Freud's relatively stable era, direct help was an exception from the abstention rule, but today no therapist can abstain from direct guidance. Several psychoanalysts have introduced significant modifications to psychoanalytic theory and practice; among them are Jacobs (1983), Langs (1976), Selesnik (1967), Stone (1961), and Tarachow (1963). Eissler (1953) introduced the concept of "parameters," which implies giving direct guidance to the patients. Zetzel (1965) suggested a far-reaching deviation from the classic psychoanalytic detachment attitude. According to Zetzel, the psychoanalyst should ". . . respond at all times to affects which indicate the patients need to feel respected and acknowledged as a real person." In other words, the psychoanalyst should give up the "evenly hovering attention" and convey an expression of friendliness and sympathy.

Interactional psychotherapy applies some psychoanalytic concepts, but it definitely advocates *direct intervention* in patients' lives, for the job of psychotherapy is to *help people who need help*.

BODY LANGUAGE

My modifications of the psychoanalytic treatment method are related to years of clinical experience. Some instances deserve to be mentioned. For years I used the psychoanalytic couch with all patients except schizophrenics, whose anxiety state demands to be able to look at the therapist (Wolman, 1966).

The radical change came about when I taught resident-psychiatrists in a university hospital. One resident-psychiatrist was treating a female patient behind a one-way screen, while the other residents and myself watched his work. The patient was on the couch, and the young psychiatrist asked her a question, to which she responded briefly, "Okay, I agree." The psychiatrist could not see her face, but those of us behind the screen could clearly read her facial expression of dismay and anger. Obviously her face communicated her true feelings, whereas what she said was intended to appease the young doctor.

I have realized that the use of a couch deprives the therapist of nonverbal communication. In several instances of one-way screen observation and from my own experience, I have learned a great deal about body language. When I subsequently became involved in supervising private practitioners of psychology and psychiatry, I guided them to use not only their ears, but their eyes as well.

THE THREE PHASES

The therapeutic strategy must be adjusted to the personality of the patients and the level of their mental disorder. There are five levels of mental disorders: (a) neurosis, (b) character neurosis, (c) latent psychosis, (d) manifest psychosis, and (e) total collapse of personality structure. The interactional psychotherapy is applicable mainly to depressive neurosis and depressive character neurosis. On these two levels of depression, interactional therapy operates in three phases: *the analytic phase, the search for identity, and becoming: self-realization.* The three phases can overlap one another (Krauss & Krauss, 1977; Wolman, 1972, 1978, 1982, 1984).

The first task of the analytic phase is to analyze the etiology and symptomatology of depression. The analytic phase probes the mental obstacles that prevent the patients from attaining emotional maturity. It deals with the patients' past experiences and helps them to cope with their problems in a rational way. Not all patients are capable of going beyond the analytic phase but those who are move on to the second phase, where they become aware of their own potentialities, and then to the third phase—inner harmony and full realization of what they wish and can accomplish.

INTERPRETATION

Communication and direct guidance are the two main methods of the analytic phase. Communication is the indispensable tool used in all psychotherapeutic methods; there is no psychotherapy without two-way communication. The patients communicate their worries, anxieties, inner conflicts, and guilt feelings, and the psychotherapist interprets them, thus helping to solve their problems and enabling the patients to cope with both their inner and social hardships. Awareness and understanding of one's problems are the first steps leading to their solution. Moreover, depressed patients quite often respond well to the interpretation of their unconscious processes, but this response does not necessarily lead to immediate changes in their emotions and behavior. Interpretation and insight are important therapeutic tools, and their usefulness can be substantially increased by treatment of transference and resistance (Mendelson, 1960).

Interpretation of unconscious material, and especially of dreams, requires considerable caution; premature interpretation may cause more harm than help, and interpretation of emotionally loaded dreams should not start at the beginning of psychotherapy.

A realistic appraisal of oneself and one's life situation is a highly relevant element of mental health. A great many depressed patients underestimate their own resources and overestimate the hardships and dangers they face; occasionally, in an elated mood, they may also over-estimate resources and underestimate hardships as well. Therapeutic interpretation helps them to see things as they are and makes them aware of their potentialities, but their resistance can be formidable.

DIRECT GUIDANCE

As a rule, therapists should not tell patients what to do, but depressed patients often act in an immature and irrational way that could cause harm beyond repair to their careers and personal relationships. Thus, quite often, the following five behavioral rules must be repeatedly explained to them.

1. The first and foremost method of fighting depression is *testing reality and counteracting guilt feelings and anxiety.* Have you really done all the wrong things you blame yourself for? Are your fears justi-fied? Are you really helpless? What can you do to cope with whatever adversities you are facing?

2. Passivity fosters depression and increases the foreboding feeling of disaster. *Active life reduces depression, and constructive efforts en-hance the person's feeling of power and self-esteem.* Active pursuit of goals presents a challenge: victory will bring joy, but even failure need not affect self-esteem; it is easy to be proud in victory, but even in disappointment a person can be proud of his or her courage and tenac-ity. Thus, never give up; go on fighting against all odds.

3. Depressed people are often self-defeating as if hoping to win approval and love by their own misery; many are often accident-prone. One can fight depression by rejecting infantile dependence on others and by *building self-reliance and self-respect.* What's good in trying to have others love you? Even the Bible says, "Love thy neighbor as

thyself"—that is, *love for oneself comes first.* You cannot please every-body, but you must please yourself.

4. Depressed people tend to withdraw from social contacts and perpetuate their depressive moods. Life is with people; loneliness increases depression, *social interaction reduces it.* Depressed individuals must force themselves to be with people.

5. Choose *"S-D" for self-discipline, not self-defeat.* Infants are unable to control their impulses; they cry in pain, scream in anger, and fall asleep when tired. Mature adults exercise *rational control* over their behavior.

THE LEVELS OF DETERIORATION

The five rules of direct guidance with patients on neurotic levels should be adjusted to the more severe levels of depression. On the character neurotic level one must pay attention to the evasive defense mechanism of character neurotics who tend to hide their depression behind a smoke screen of humor and self-satisfaction. They often deny that anything bothers them and that they are depressed. A female patient tried to convince me (and herself) that "everybody has some problems" and "everyone should keep smiling." It took a while before she admitted, crying, that she was spending sleepless nights in a state of acute anxiety and worry about her future. She needed a great deal of reassurance and emotional support before she could admit this. She was afraid that the therapist, like everyone else she knew, would be critical of her. "I had to pretend to be strong," she explained, "to impress people and to win their approval. I was afraid to admit my weaknesses." For a while she resisted therapeutic interpretation, but ultimately her neurotic character defenses were removed, and we could follow the above described five rules of direct guidance.

The latent depressive psychotics require a more cautious approach, as a therapist's errors can throw a patient into a iatrogenic psychosis. Latent psychotics can barely hold onto their defenses and are exceedingly sensitive; however, as long as their ego keeps functioning and retains contact with reality, it is a *latent* and not a *manifest* psychosis. In many cases the interpretation of dreams could be counterproductive or even harmful. When unconscious and morbid fears and wishes break through the weak defenses, therapeutic interpretations can cause a collapse of personality structure and turn the latent depressive psychosis into a manifest depressive psychosis. Some cases of manifest depressive psychosis may need, at least temporarily, pharmacological help and hospitalization (Denber, 1977; Wolman, 1983).

SUICIDAL PATIENTS

As a rule, the more severe the depression, the greater the danger of suicide. The psychotherapist's task is to teach people to swim in the stormy waters of life, but a cautious lifeguard does not teach drowning people how to swim; the main obligation is to save the person's life. Apparently, in suicidal cases direct guidance is an absolute necessity (Shneidman, 1976; Wolman & Krauss, 1976).

Whenever patients have communicated suicidal thoughts, or whenever I have the slightest suspicion that the patients harbor suicidal thoughts, I confront them in more or less the following way:

> Our work is a two-way street. It is my moral obligation to help you, but I need your help. Please help me to help you, for I cannot help you without your help. We must have a two-way commitment; I will not let you down, and you will not let me down. Whenever you have suicidal thoughts, you must call me. Whenever possible, I will cancel another patient to see you immediately. If I cannot do that or you cannot reach me, you will not do anything—you will wait until you see me. I demand your word of honor, or I refuse to work with you.

I have never failed. In forty years of practice I have treated several suicidal patients; some of them tried to kill themselves before I saw them, but in my entire practice I have not had one suicide on my conscience. I prevent suicides by building self-respect and moral commitment. "Suicide," I tell my patients, "is a murder of someone who cannot defend himself or herself." If the patient lives at home, I take additional precautions and make sure that family members keep a close watch on the patient 24 hours a day, 7 days a week, and I give them all my phone numbers where they can reach me at any time.

SUMMARY

1. There are two parties in combating depression: the therapist and the depressed person. Psychotherapists should be aware of the fact that their job is *emotional re-education*. Physical or chemical treatment can remove the symptoms but cannot remove the causes of depression and bring a complete cure.

2. In working with depressed patients the psychotherapist must avoid the pitfalls of the patients' masochistic love–hate manipulations. A good therapist must get involved with the patients' case without ever getting involved with the patients' person. The therapist must always retain the *professional distance* separating the helper from the one who

is being helped. Depressed patients often play on their therapist's sympathy; should they succeed, the therapist's work is rendered useless.

3. The therapist should help the depressed person to see things as they really are. Exaggerated notions and distorted perceptions must be corrected; a firm grip on *reality* is an indispensable prerequisite of mental health. *Testing reality* is especially important in depressed people, who tend to underestimate themselves and overestimate the potential odds and dangers.

4. Low self-esteem and continuous self-deprecation and self-accusation must be therapeutically corrected. A fair, objective, and realistic appraisal of one's abilities and potentialities will contribute toward healthy and balanced *self-esteem* and *self-confidence,* which will successfully counteract the feelings of inadequacy and inferiority.

5. The patients' feeling of helpless anger, directed mostly against themselves and those who do not love them, must be channeled across the two channels of love and hate. People who have adequate love for themselves do not need so much love from others. Thus, "*love yourself* and you'll not need so much love from without" is an important therapeutic approach.

6. Passive and idle life perpetuates depression. Passivity deepens the feelings of weakness and facilitates the morbid Cinderella mentality, always waiting for salvation from without. *Active life and constructive efforts* improve self-esteem. Success has always been a good doctor.

7. *Social involvement* is a necessary antidote to depressive isolation. Depressed people tend to brood and imagine nonexisting dangers. Being actively involved with other people gives them the chance to face real hardship, instead of imaginary misery.

8. To live with a depressed person could overtax one's patience. *People close to a depressed person need guidance* to avoid infantilizing compassion and/or rejecting impatience. They must remain cool in the face of demands of "great love" and accusations of rejection. The family members of a depressed person may need therapy themselves (Wolman & Stricker, 1983).

9. Depressed patients *must actively participate in their own recovery* through either self-discipline or self-defeat. They must be willing to renounce their infantile, bittersweet masochism and look forward to the adult feelings of responsibility, self-esteem, and self-confidence.

REFERENCES

Alexander, F., & French, T. (1946). *Psychoanalytic Therapy.* New York: Ronald Press.

Bemporad, J. (1976). Psychotherapy of the depressive character. *Journal of the American Academy of Psychoanalysis, 4,* 347–372.

Denber, H. C. B. (1977). Depression: Pharmacologic treatment. In B. B. Wolman (Ed.), *International encyclopedia of psychiatry, psychology, psychoanalysis and neurology* (Vol. 4). New York: Aesculapius–Van Nostrand Reinhold.

Eissler, K. R. (1953). The effect of the structure of the ego on psychoanalytic technique. *Journal of the American Psychoanalytic Association, 1,* 104–143.

Fenichel, O. (1945). *Psychoanalytic theory of neurosis.* New York: Norton.

Freud, S. (1962). Turning in the ways of psychoanalytic psychotherapy. In J. Strachey (Ed. and Trans.). *The standard edition of the complete psychological works of Sigmund Freud* (Vol. 17). London: Hogarth Press. (Original work published 1919.)

Jacobs, T. (1983). Psychoanalytic technique: Changing views. In B. B. Wolman (Ed.), *International encyclopedia of psychiatry, psychology, psychoanalysis and neurology—Progress* (Vol. 1). New York: Aesculapius—Van Nostrand Reinhold.

Krauss, H. H., & Krauss, B. J. (1977). Nosology: Wolman's system. In B. B. Wolman (Ed.), *International encyclopedia of psychiatry, psychology, psychoanalysis and neurology* (Vol. 8). New York: Aesculapius—Van Nostrand Reinhold.

Langs, R. (1976). *The therapeutic interaction.* New York: Jason Aronson.

Lewin, B. D. (1959). Some psychoanalytic ideas applied to elation and depression. *American Journal of Psychiatry, 116,* 38–43.

Mendelson, M. (1960). *Psychoanalytic concept of depression.* Springfield, IL: Thomas.

Schuyler, D. (1983). Treatment of depressive disorders. In B. B. Wolman (Ed.), *Therapist's handbook* (2nd ed.). New York: Van Nostrand Reinhold.

Selesnick, S. T. (1967). The techniques of psychoanalysis developed by Franz Alexander and Thomas French. In B. B. Wolman (Ed.), *Psychoanalytic techniques: A handbook for the practicing psychoanalyst.* New York: Basic Books.

Shneidman, E. S. (Ed.). (1976). *Suicidology: Contemporary developments.* New York: Grune & Stratton.

Stone, L. (1961) *The psychoanalytic situation.* New York: International Universities Press.

Tarachow, S. (1963). *An introduction to psychotherapy.* New York: International Universities Press.

Wolberg, L. R. (1954). *The technique of psychotherapy.* New York: Grune & Stratton.

Wolman, B. B. (1958). Instrumental, mutual acceptance, and vectorial groups. *Acta Sociologica Scandinavia, 3,* 19–28.

Wolman, B. B. (1966). *Vectoriasis praecox or the group of schizophrenias.* Springfield, IL: Thomas.

Wolman, B. B. (1972). *Success and failure in psychoanalysis and psychotherapy.* New York: Macmillan.

Wolman, B. B. (1973). *Call no man normal.* New York: International Universities Press.

Wolman, B. B. (Ed.). (1978). *Clinical diagnosis of mental disorders: A handbook.* New York: Plenum.

Wolman, B. B. (Ed.). (1982). *Psychological Aspects of Obesity: A Handbook.* New York: Van Nostrand Reinhold.

Wolman, B. B. (Ed.). (1983). *Therapist's handbook* (2nd ed.). New York: Van Nostrand Reinhold.

Wolman, B. B. (1984). *Interactional psychotherapy.* New York: Van Nostrand Reinhold.

Wolman, B. B., & Krauss, H. H. (Eds.). (1976). *Between survival and suicide.* New York: Gardner Press.

Wolman, B. B., & Stricker, G. (Eds.). (1983). *Handbook of family and marital therapy.* New York: Plenum.

Zetzel, E. R. (1965). The theory of therapy. *International Journal of Psychoanalysts, 46,* 39–52.

CHAPTER 19

Interpersonal Psychotherapy for Depression

MYRNA M. WEISSMAN, PhD and GERALD L. KLERMAN, MD

This chapter will describe Interpersonal Psychotherapy (IPT) for depression, including the theoretical and empirical bases, efficacy studies, and derivative forms, and will also make recommendations for its use in clinical practice.

Interpersonal Psychotherapy (IPT) is based on the observation that major depression—regardless of symptom patterns, severity, presumed biological or genetic vulnerability, or the patients' personality traits—usually occurs in an interpersonal context, often an interpersonal loss or dispute. By clarifying, refocusing, and renegotiating the interpersonal context associated with the onset of the depression, the depressed patient's symptomatic recovery may be accelerated and the social morbidity reduced.

IPT is a brief, weekly psychotherapy that is usually conducted for 12 to 16 weeks, although it has been used for longer periods of time with less frequency as maintenance treatment for recovered depressed patients. It has been developed for ambulatory, nonbipolar, nonpsychotic patients with major depression. The focus is on improving the quality of the depressed patients' current interpersonal functioning and the problems associated with the onset of depression. It is suitable for use, following appropriate training, by experienced psychiatrists, psychologists, and social workers. Derivative forms have been developed for nonpsychiatric nurse practitioners. It can be used alone or in combination with drugs.

IPT has evolved over 20 years' experience in the treatment and research of ambulatory depressed patients. It has been tested alone, in

Portions of this chapter derive from: Weissman, M. M., & Klerman, G. L. (1990). Interpersonal Psychotherapy (IPT) and its derivatives in the treatment of depression. In D. Manning & A. Francis (Eds.), *Combining drugs and psychotherapy in depression* (Progress in Psychiatry Series). Washington, DC: American Psychiatric Press.

comparison with, and in combination with tricyclics in six clinical trials with depressed patients—three of maintenance (Frank, Kupfer, & Perel, 1989; Klerman, DiMascio, Weissman, Prusoff, & Paykel, 1974; Reynold & Imber, 1988) and three of acute treatment (Elkin et al., 1986; Sloane, Staples, & Schneider, 1985; Weissman et al., 1979). Two derivative forms of IPT (Conjoint Marital (IPT-CM); Foley, Rounsaville, Weissman, Sholomskas, & Chevron, 1990), and Interpersonal Counseling (IPC; Klerman et al., 1987), have been developed and tested in pilot studies. Six studies have included a drug comparison group (Elkin et al., 1986; Frank et al., 1989; Klerman et al., 1974; Reynold & Imber, 1988; Sloane et al., 1985; Weissman et al., 1979), and four have included a combination of IPT and drugs (Elkin et al., 1986; Klerman et al., 1974; Sloane et al., 1985; Weissman et al., 1979). Two studies (Reynold & Imber, 1988; Sloane et al., 1985) have modified the treatment to deal with special issues of elderly depressed patients.

The concept, techniques, and methods of IPT have been operationally described in a manual that has undergone a number of revisions. This manual, now in book form (Klerman, Weissman, Rounsaville, & Chevron, 1984), was developed to standardize the treatment so that clinical trails could be undertaken. A training program developed (Weissman, Rounsaville, & Chevron, 1982) for experienced psychotherapists of different disciplines provides the treatment for these clinical trials. To our knowledge, there is no ongoing training program for practitioners, although workshops are available from time to time, and the book can serve as a guide for the experienced clinician who wants to learn IPT.

It is our experience that a variety of treatments are suitable for major depression and that the depressed patients' interests are best served by the availability and scientific testing of different psychological as well as pharmacological treatments, to be used alone or in combination. Clinical testing and experience should determine which is the best treatment for a particular patient.

THEORETICAL AND EMPIRICAL BACKGROUND

The ideas of Adolph Meyer (1957), whose psychobiological approach to understanding psychiatric disorders placed great emphasis on the patient's environment, comprise the most prominent theoretical sources for IPT. Meyer viewed psychiatric disorders as an expression of the patient's attempt to adapt to the environment. An individual's response to environmental change and stress was mostly determined by prior experiences, including early experiences in the family, and by affiliation with various social groups. Among Meyer's associates, Harry Stack Sullivan (1953) stands out for his emphasis on the patient's current psychosocial and interpersonal experience as a basis for treatment.

The empirical basis for IPT includes studies associating stress and life events with the onset of depression; longitudinal studies demonstrating the social impairment of depressed women during the acute depressive phase and the following symptomatic recovery; studies by Brown, Harris, and Copeland (1977) which demonstrated the role of intimacy and social supports as protection against depression in the face of adverse life stress; and studies by Pearlin and Lieberman (1979) and Ilfield (1977) which showed the impact of chronic social and interpersonal stress, particularly marital stress, on the onset of depression. The works of Bowlby (1969) and Henderson and associates (1978) emphasized the importance of attachment bonds, or, conversely, showed that the loss of social attachments can be associated with the onset of major depression; and recent epidemiologic data showed an association between marital dispute and major depression (Weissman, 1987). The sequence of causation between depression and interpersonal dispute is not clear from any of this research.

Components of Depression

Within the framework of IPT, major depression is seen as involving three components:

1. *Symptom formation,* which includes the depressive affect and vegetative signs and symptoms, such as sleep and appetite disturbance, loss of interest and pleasure;
2. *Social functioning,* which includes social interactions with other persons, particularly in the family, derived from learning based on childhood experiences, concurrent social reinforcement, and/or current problems in personal mastery of social situations;
3. *Personality,* which includes more enduring traits and behaviors, such as the handling of anger and guilt, and overall self-esteem. These constitute the person's unique reactions and patterns of functioning and may contribute to a predisposition to depression, although this is not clear.

IPT attempts to intervene in the first two processes. Because of the brevity of the treatment, the low level of psychotherapeutic intensity, the focus on the context of the current depressive episode, and the lack of evidence that any psychotherapy changes personality, no claim is made that IPT will have an impact on the enduring aspects of personality, although personality functioning is assessed. While some longer-term psychotherapies have been designed to achieve personality change using the interpersonal approach (Arieti & Bemporad, 1979), these treatments have not been assessed in controlled trials.

THE CHARACTERISTICS OF INTERPERSONAL PSYCHOTHERAPY

Goals of IPT with Depression

A goal of IPT is to relieve acute depressive symptoms by helping the patient to become more effective in dealing with those current interpersonal problems that are associated with the onset of symptoms. Symptom relief begins with educating the patient about depression—its nature, course, and prognosis, and the various treatment alternatives. Following a complete diagnostic evaluation, the patient is told that the vague and uncomfortable symptoms are part of a known syndrome that has been well described, is understood, is relatively common, responds to a variety of treatments, and has a good prognosis. Psychopharmacological approaches may be used in conjunction with IPT to alleviate symptoms more rapidly. Table 19.1 describes the stages and tasks in the conduct of IPT.

Treating the depressed patient's problems in interpersonal relations begins with exploring which of four problem areas commonly associated with the onset of depression is related to the individual patient's depression: grief, role disputes, role transition, or interpersonal deficit. IPT then focuses on the particular interpersonal problem as it relates to the onset of depression.

TABLE 19.1.   Stages and Tasks in the Conduct of IPT

Stages	Tasks
Early	Treatment of depressive symptoms
	Review of symptoms
	Confirmation of diagnosis
	Communication of diagnosis to patient
	Evaluation of medication need
	Education of patient about depression (epidemiology, symptoms, clinical course, treatment prognosis)
	Assessment of interpersonal relations
	Inventory of current relationships
	Choice of interpersonal problem area
	Therapeutic contract
	Statement of goals, diagnosis, problem area
	Medication plan
	Agreement on time frame and focus
Middle	Treatment focusing on one or more problem areas
	Unresolved grief
	Interpersonal disputes
	Role transition
	Interpersonal deficits
Termination	Discussion of termination
	Assessment of need for alternate treatment

IPT Compared with Other Psychotherapies

The procedures and techniques in many of the different psychotherapies have much in common. Many of the therapies have as their goals helping the patient develop a sense of mastery, combating social isolation, and restoring the patient's feeling of group belonging.

The psychotherapies differ, however, as to whether the patient's problems are defined as originating in the distant or immediate past, or in the present. IPT focuses primarily on the patient's present. It differs from other psychotherapies in its limited duration and in its attention to the current depression and the related interpersonal context. Given this frame of reference, IPT includes a systematic review of the patient's current relations with significant others.

Another distinguishing feature of IPT is its time-limited nature. Even when used as maintenance treatment, there is a definite time course (Frank et al., 1989; Klerman et al., 1974; Reynold & Imber, 1988). Research has demonstrated the value of time-limited psychotherapies (usually once a week for less than nine to 12 months) for many depressed outpatients (Klerman et al., 1987). While long-term treatment may still be required for changing chronic personality disorders, particularly those with maladaptive interpersonal and cognitive patterns, and for ameliorating or replacing dysfunctional social skills, evidence for the efficacy of long-term, open-ended psychotherapy is limited. Moreover, long-term, open-ended treatment has the potential disadvantage of promoting dependency and reinforcing avoidance behavior.

In common with other brief psychotherapies, IPT focuses on one or two problem areas in the patient's current interpersonal functioning. Because the focus is agreed upon by the patient and the psychotherapist after initial evaluation sessions, the topical content of sessions is focused and not open-ended.

IPT deals with current, not past, interpersonal relationships; it focuses on the patient's immediate social context just before and since the onset of the current depressive episode. Past depressive episodes, early family relationships, and previous significant relationships and friendship patterns are, however, assessed in order to understand overall patterns in the patient's interpersonal relationships.

IPT is concerned with interpersonal, not intrapsychic phenomena. In exploring current interpersonal problems with the patient, the psychotherapist may observe the operation of intrapsychic mechanisms such as projection, denial, isolation, or repression. In IPT, however, the psychotherapist does not work on helping the patient see the current situation as a manifestation of internal conflict. Rather, the psychotherapist explores the patient's current psychiatric behavior in terms of interpersonal relations.

EFFICACY OF IPT

The efficacy of IPT has been tested in several randomized clinical trials. Table 19.2 describes the efficacy data on IPT and its derivatives—alone, in comparison with, or in combination with drugs (Weissman, Jarrett, & Rush, 1987).

TABLE 19.2. Efficacy Studies of IPT and Its Derivatives

Study No.	Treatment Condition	Diagnosis (No. of patients)	Time weeks/ (years)	Reference
Acute Treatment Studies				
1	IPT + amitriptyline/ ami/IPT/nonscheduled treatment	MDD ($N = 96$)	16	Weissman et al. (1979)
2	IPT/nortriptyline/ placebo	MDD or dysthymia, age 60+ ($N = 30$)	6	Sloane, Staples, & Schneider (1985)
3	IPT/CB/imipramine + management/placebo + management	MDD ($N = 250$)	16	Elkin, et al. (1986)
Maintenance Treatment Studies				
4	IPT/low contact + amitriptyline/placebo/ no pill	Recovered MDD ($N = 150$)	32	Klerman, Weissman, Rounsaville, & Chevron (1974)
5	IPT/IPT + placebo/ IPT + imipramine/ management + imipramine management + placebo	Recovered recurrent MDD ($N = 125$)	(3)	Frank, Kupfer, & Perel (1989)
6	Same design as #5	Recovered recurrent MDD, geriatric ($N = 120$)	(3)	Reynold & Imber (1988)
Derivative IPT				
7	Conjoint IPT-CM/ individual IPT for marital disputes	MDD + marital disputes ($N = 18$)	16	Foley, Rounsaville, Weissman, Sholomskas, & Chevron (1990)
8	Interpersonal Counseling (IPC) for distress/treatment as usual	High score GHQ ($N = 64$)	6	Klerman et al. (1987)

IPT as Maintenance Treatment

The first study of IPT began in 1967 and was on maintenance treatment (study 4 in Table 19.2). At that time, it was clear that the tricyclic antidepressants were efficacious in the treatment of acute depression. The length of treatment and the role of psychotherapy in maintenance treatment were unclear. Our study was designed to answer those questions.

One hundred and fifty acutely depressed outpatients who had responded to a tricyclic antidepressant (amitriptyline) with symptom reduction were studied. Each patient received eight months of maintenance treatment with drugs alone, psychotherapy (IPT) alone, or a combination. We found that maintenance drug treatment prevented relapse and that psychotherapy alone improved social functioning and interpersonal relations, but had no effect on symptomatic relapse. Because of the differential effects of the treatments, the combination of the drugs and psychotherapy was the most efficacious (Klerman et al., 1974) and no negative interaction between drugs and psychotherapy was found.

In the course of that project, we realized the need for greater specification of the psychotherapeutic techniques involved and for the careful training of psychotherapists for research. The psychotherapy had been described in terms of conceptual framework, goals, frequency of contacts, and criteria for therapist suitability. However, the techniques, strategies, and actual procedures had not been set out in a procedure manual, and there was no training program.

IPT as Acute Treatment

In 1973 we initiated a 16-week study of the acute treatment of 81 ambulatory depressed patients, both men and women, using IPT and amitriptyline, each alone and in combination, against a nonscheduled psychotherapy treatment (DiMascio et al., 1979) (study 1 in Table 19.2). IPT was administered weekly by experienced psychiatrists. A much more specified procedural manual for IPT was developed. By 1973, the Schedule for Affective Disorders and Schizophrenia (SADS) and Research Diagnostic Criteria (RDC) were available for making more precise diagnostic judgments, thereby assuring the selection of a more homogeneous sample of depressed patients.

Patients were assigned randomly to IPT or the control treatment at the beginning of treatment, which was limited to 16 weeks since this was an acute and not a maintenance treatment trial (Weissman, Klerman, Prusoff, Sholomskas, & Padian, 1981). Patients were assessed up to one year after treatment had ended to determine any long-term treatment effects. The assessment of outcome was made by a clinical evaluator who was independent of and blind to the treatment the patient was receiving.

In the latter part of the 1970s, we reported the results of IPT compared to tricyclic antidepressants alone and in combination for acute depressions. We demonstrated that both active treatments, IPT and the tricyclic, were more effective than the control treatment and that combined treatment was superior to either treatment (DiMascio et al., 1979; Weissman et al., 1979).

In addition, we conducted a one-year follow-up study which indicated that the therapeutic benefit of treatment was sustained for a majority of patients. Patients who had received IPT either alone or in combination with drugs were functioning better than patients who had received either drugs alone or the control treatment (Weissman et al., 1981). There remained a fraction of patients in all treatments who relapsed and for whom additional treatment was required.

Other Studies of IPT for Depression

Other researchers have now extended IPT to other aspects of depression. A long-term period of maintenance of IPT is underway at the University of Pittsburgh, conducted by Frank, Kupfer, and Perel (1989) to assess the value of drugs and psychotherapy in maintenance treatment of chronic recurrent depressions (study 5 in Table 19.2). Preliminary results recently published on the first 74 patients, studied over 18 months, showed that maintenance IPT as compared to maintenance imipramine in remitted patients with recurrent major depression (three or more episodes) significantly reduced recurrence of new episodes. Fifty percent of the patients receiving maintenance medication had experienced a recurrence by 21 weeks, while those assigned to IPT did not reach the 50 percent recurrence rate until 61 weeks. The presence of a pill or no pill did not significantly relate to patient recurrence. A similar study in a depressed geriatric patient population is also underway at the University of Pittsburgh (study 6 in Table 19.2).

Sloane (study 2 in Table 19.2) completed a pilot six-week trial of IPT as compared to nortriptyline and placebo for depressed elderly patients. He found partial evidence for the efficacy of IPT over nortriptyline for elderly patients, primarily due to the elderly not tolerating the medication. The problem of medication in the elderly, particularly the anticholinergic effect, had led to the interest in psychotherapy for this age group.

The NIMH Collaborative Study of the Treatment of Depression

Given the availability of efficacy data on two specified psychotherapies for ambulatory depressives, in the late 1970s, the NIMH, under the leadership of Drs. Parloff and Elkin, designed and initiated a multicenter, controlled, clinical trial of drugs and psychotherapy in the treatment of depression (study 3 in Table 19.2). Two hundred and fifty outpatients were randomly assigned to four treatment conditions: (a) cognitive therapy; (b) interpersonal psychotherapy; (c) imipramine; and (d) a placebo-clinical management combination. Each patient was treated for 16 weeks. Extensive efforts were made in the selection and training of psychotherapists. Outcome was assessed by a battery of scales which measured symptoms, social functioning, and cognition. The initial entry criteria were a score of at least 14 on the 17-item Hamilton Rating Scale for Depression. Of the 250 patients who entered treatment, 68 percent completed at least 15 weeks and 12 sessions of treatment. The preliminary findings from three Centers (Oklahoma City, Washington, DC, and Pittsburgh) were reported at the American Psychiatric Association Annual Meeting, May 13, 1986, in Washington, DC (Elkin et al., 1986). The full data have not yet been published. Overall, the findings showed that all active treatments were superior to placebo in the reduction of depressive symptoms over a 16-week period.

1. The overall degree of improvement was highly significant clinically. Over two-thirds of the patients were symptom-free at the end of treatment.

2. More patients in the placebo–clinical management condition dropped out or were withdrawn—twice as many as for interpersonal psychotherapy, which had the lowest attrition rate.

3. At the end of 12 weeks of treatment, the two psychotherapies and imipramine were equivalent in the reduction of depressive symptoms and in overall functioning.

4. The pharmacotherapy, imipramine, had rapid initial onset of action, but by 12 weeks, the two psychotherapies had produced equivalent results.

5. Although many of the patients who were less severely depressed at intake improved with all treatment conditions—including the placebo group—more severely depressed patients in the placebo group did poorly.

6. For the less severely depressed group, there were no differences among the treatments.

7. Forty-four percent of the sample were severely depressed at intake. The criteria of severity used was a score of 20 or more on the Hamilton Rating Scale for Depression at entrance to the study. Patients in IPT and in the imipramine groups consistently and significantly had better scores than the placebo group on the Hamilton Rating Scale. Only one of the psychotherapies, IPT, was significantly superior to placebo for the severely depressed group. For the severely depressed patient, interpersonal psychotherapy did as well as imipramine.

8. Surprisingly, one of the more important predictors of patient response for IPT was the presence of an endogenous depressive symptom picture measured by RDC following an interview with the SADS. This was also true for imipramine; however, this finding for drugs would have been expected from previous research.

DERIVATIVES OF IPT

IPT in a Conjoint Marital Context

Although the causal direction is unknown, clinical and epidemiologic studies have shown that marital disputes, separation, and divorce are strongly associated with the onset of depression (Weissman, 1987). Moreover, depressed patients in ambulatory treatment frequently present marital problems as their chief complaint (Rounsaville, Prusoff, & Weissman, 1980; Rounsaville, Weissman, Prusoff, & Herceg-Baron, 1979). Yet, when psychotherapy is prescribed, it is unclear whether the patient, the couple, or the entire family should be involved. Some evidence suggests that individual psychotherapy for depressed patients involved in marital disputes may promote premature separation or divorce (Gurman & Kniskern, 1978; Locke & Wallace, 1976). There have been no published clinical trials comparing the efficacy of individual versus conjoint psychotherapy for depressed patients with marital problems.

We found that marital disputes often remained a complaint of the depressed patient despite the patient's symptomatic improvement with drugs or psychotherapy (Rounsaville et al., 1980). Because IPT presents strategies for managing the social and interpersonal problems associated with the onset of depressive symptoms, we speculated that a conjoint version of IPT, which focused intensively on problems in the marital relationship, would be useful in alleviating those problems (study 7 in Table 19.2).

Individual IPT was adapted to the treatment of depression in the context of marital disputes by concentrating its focus on a subset of one of the four problem areas associated with depression for which IPT was developed—interpersonal marital disputes. IPT-CM (Conjoint Marital) extends individual IPT techniques for use with the identified patient and his or her spouse. The treatment incorporates aspects of currently available marital therapies, particularly those that emphasize dysfunctional communication as the focus on interventions. In IPT-CM, functioning of the couple is assessed in five general areas: communication, intimacy, boundary management, leadership, and attainment of socially appropriate goals. Dysfunctional behavior in these areas is noted, and treatment is focused on bringing about improvement in a small number of target problem areas. A treatment manual and a training program like those used in IPT were developed for IPT-CM.

Only patients who identified marital disputes as the major problem associated with the onset or exacerbation of a major depression were admitted into a pilot study. Patients were randomly assigned to IPT or IPT-CM, and received 16 weekly therapy sessions. In IPT-CM the spouse was required to participate in all psychotherapy sessions, while in IPT the spouse did not meet with the therapist. Patients and spouses in both treatment conditions were asked to refrain from taking psychotropic medication during the study without first discussing it with their therapists; therapists were discouraged from prescribing any psychotropic medication.

Three therapists (a psychiatrist, a psychologist, and a social worker) administered individual IPT to depressed married subjects. Three therapists (social workers) administered conjoint marital IPT. All therapists had extensive prior experience in the treatment of depressed patients. At the end of treatment, patients in both groups expressed satisfaction with the treatment, felt that they had improved, and attributed improvement to their therapy (Table 19.3). Patients in both groups exhibited a significant reduction in symptoms of depression and social impairment from intake to termination of therapy. There was no significant difference between treatment groups in the degree of improvement in depressive symptoms and social functioning by endpoint (Foley et al., 1990).

The Locke–Wallace Marital Adjustment Test Scores at session 16 were significantly higher (indicative of better marital adjustment) for patients receiving IPT-CM than for patients receiving IPT (Locke &

TABLE 19.3. Symptom and Social Functioning at End of Treatment in Depressed Patients with Marital Disputes Receiving IPT vs. IPT-CM

	Treatment Condition	
Outcome of Termination	IPT ($N = 9$)	IPT-CM ($N = 9$)
Depressive symptoms (Hamilton Rating Scale)	12.4	13.0
Overall social functioning	2.8	3.0
Marital adjustment* (Locke–Wallace)	4.7	5.8**
Affectional expression* (Spanier Dyadic)	6.5	8.6[†]

*Higher score = better marital adjustment
**$p < .05$
[†]$p < .10$

Wallace, 1976). Scores of the Spanier Dyadic Adjustment Scale (Spanier, 1976) also indicated greater improvement in marital functioning for patients receiving IPT-CM, as compared to IPT, and reported significantly higher levels of improvement in affectional expression (i.e., demonstrations of affection and sexual relations in the marriage).

The results must be interpreted with caution because of the pilot nature of the study—the small size of the pilot sample, the lack of a no-treatment control group, and the absence of a pharmacotherapy or combined pharmacotherapy–psychotherapy comparison group. If the study were repeated, we would recommend that medication be freely allowed or used as a comparison condition and that there be more effort to reduce the symptoms of depression before proceeding to undertake the marital issues.

Interpersonal Counseling (IPC) for Stress/Distress

Previous investigations have documented high frequencies of anxiety, depression, and functional bodily complaints in patients in primary care settings (Brodaty & Andrews, 1983; Goldberg, 1972; Hoeper, Nycz, Cleary, Regier, & Goldberg 1979). Although some of these patients have diagnosable psychiatric disorders, a large percentage have symptoms that do not meet established criteria for psychiatric disorders. A mental health research program, part of a large health maintenance organization (HMO) in the greater Boston area, found that "problems of living" and symptoms of anxiety and depression were among the main reasons for individual primary care visits. These clinical problems contribute heavily to high utilization of ambulatory services.

We developed a brief psychosocial intervention, Interpersonal Counseling (IPC), to deal with patients' symptoms of distress. IPC is a brief, focused, psychosocial intervention for administration by nurse practitioners working in a primary care setting (Weissman & Klerman, 1988). It was modified from interpersonal psychotherapy (IPT) over a six-month period, through an interactive and iterative process in which the research team met on a weekly basis with the nurse practitioners to review previous clinical experience, discuss case examples, observe video tapes, and listen to tape recordings.

IPC comprises a maximum of six half-hour counseling sessions in the primary care office, focused on the patient's current functioning. Particular attention is given to recent changes in the person's life events; sources of stress in the family, home, and workplace; friendship patterns; and ongoing difficulties in interpersonal relations. IPC assumes that such events provide the interpersonal context in which bodily and emotional symptoms related to anxiety, depression, and distress occur. The treatment manual describes session-by-session instructions as to the purpose and methods for the IPC, including "scripts" to ensure comparability of procedures among the nurse counselors.

Subjects with scores of 6 or higher were selected for assignment to an experimental group that was offered interpersonal counseling (IPC), or to a comparison group that was followed naturalistically (study 8 in Table 2). Subjects selected for IPC treatment were contacted by telephone and invited to make an appointment promptly with one of the study's nurse practitioners. During this telephone contact, reference was made to items of concern raised by the patient's response to the General Health Questionnaire (GHQ), and the patient was offered an appointment to address these and other health issues of concern. Sixty-four patients were compared with a subgroup of 64 untreated subjects with similar elevations in GHQ scores during June 1984, matched to treated subjects on gender.

IPC proved feasible in the primary care environment (Klerman et al., 1987). It was easily learned by experienced nurse practitioners during a short training program of from eight to 12 hours. The brevity of the sessions and short duration of the treatment rendered IPC compatible with usual professional practices in a primary care unit. No significantly negative effects of treatment were observed, and with weekly supervision, nurses were able to counsel several patients whose levels of psychiatric distress would normally have resulted in direct referral to specialty mental health care. In comparison with a group of untreated subjects with initial elevations in GHQ scores, those patients receiving the IPC intervention showed a significantly greater reduction in symptoms and improvement in social functioning over an average interval of three months. Many IPC treated patients reported significant relief of symptoms after only one or two sessions. Many of the patients had substantial depressive symptoms when they entered into the study.

This pilot study provided preliminary evidence that early detection and outreach to distressed adults, followed by brief treatment with IPC, can, in the short term, reduce symptoms of distress as measured by the GHQ. The main effects seem to occur in symptoms related to mood, especially in those forms of mild and moderate depression that are commonly seen in medical patients.

Although definitive evaluation of IPC awaits further study, this report of short-term symptom reduction suggests that this approach to outreach and early intervention may be an effective alternative to current practices. If so, then IPC may be a useful addition to the repertoire of psychosocial intervention skills that can be incorporated into routine primary care.

CONCLUSIONS

The Current Role of IPT in the Psychotherapy of Depression

While the positive findings of the clinical trials of IPT in the NIMH Collaborative Study and other studies described are encouraging and have received considerable attention in the popular press (Boffey, 1986), we wish to emphasize a number of limitations in the possible conclusion regarding the place of psychotherapy in the treatment of depression. All the studies, including those by our group and by the NIMH, were conducted on ambulatory depressed patients or patients experiencing distress. There are no systematic studies evaluating the efficacy of psychotherapy for hospitalized depressed patients or bipolar patients who are usually more severely disabled and often suicidal.

It is also important to recognize that these results should not be interpreted as implying *all* forms of psychotherapy are effective for depression. One significant feature of recent advances in psychotherapy research is in the development of psychotherapies specifically designed for depression—time-limited and of brief duration. Just as there are specific forms of medication, there are specific forms of psychotherapy. (See Weissman et al., 1987 for a review of other brief psychotherapies, particularly cognitive therapy for depression.) It would be an error to conclude that all forms of medication are useful for all types of depression; it would be an equal error to conclude that all forms of psychotherapy are efficacious for all forms of depression.

These investigations indicated that for outpatient ambulatory depression there is a range of effective treatments, including a number of forms of brief psychotherapy, as well as various medications, notably monoamine oxidase inhibitors and tricyclic antidepressants. These therapeutic advances have contributed to our understanding of the complex interplay of psychosocial and biological factors in the etiology and pathogenesis of depression, particularly ambulatory depression.

IPT and Drug Therapy Combined

A number of studies in the program described above compared IPT with medication and also evaluated the combination of IPT plus medication. Unlike other forms of psychotherapy, we have no ideological hesitation in prescribing medication. The decision to use medication in the treatment of depression should be based upon the patient's severity of symptoms, quality of depression, duration of disability, and response to previous treatment. It should not be based on the loyalties or training of the professional, as is too often the case in common clinical practice.

In our studies, IPT and medication, usually tricyclic antidepressants, have had independent additive effects. We have not found any negative interactions; in fact, patients treated with the combination of medication and psychotherapy have a lower dropout rate, a greater acceptance of the treatment program, and more rapid and pervasive symptom improvement. Contrary to many theoretical discussions, the prescription of medication does not interfere with the patient's capacity to participate in psychotherapy. In fact, the opposite occurs. A reduction of symptoms facilitates the patient's capacity to make use of social learning.

A variety of treatments may be suitable for depression. The depressed patient's interests are best served by the availability and scientific testing of different psychological as well as pharmacological treatments, which can be used alone or in combination. The ultimate aim of these studies is to determine which treatments are best for specific subgroups of depressed patients.

REFERENCES

Arieti, S., & Bemporad, J. (1979). *Severe–mild depression: The psychotherapeutic approach.* New York: Basic Books.

Boffey, P. M. (1986). Psychotherapy is as good as drugs in curing depression, study finds. *New York Times,* May 14, pp. A1, A17.

Bowlby, J. (1969). *Attachment and loss* (Vol 1). London: Hogarth Press.

Brodaty, H., & Andrews, G. (1983). Brief psychotherapy in family practice: A controlled perspective intervention trial. *British Journal of Psychiatry, 143,* 11–19.

Brown, G. W., Harris, T., & Copeland, J. R. (1977). Depression and loss. *British Journal of Psychiatry, 130,* 1–18.

DiMascio, A., Weissman, M. M., Prusoff, B. A., Neu, C., Zwilling, M., & Klerman, G. L. (1979). Differential symptom reduction by drugs and psychotherapy in acute depression. *Archives of General Psychiatry, 36,* 1450–1456.

Elkin, I., Shea, T., Watkins, J. T., Collins, J. F., Docherty, J. P., & Shaw, B. F. (1986). *The NIMH Treatment of Depression Collaborative Program: Outcome findings and therapist performance.* Paper presented at the annual meeting of the American Psychiatric Association, Chicago.

Foley, S. H., Rounsaville, B. J., Weissman, M. M., Sholomskas, D., & Chevron, E. S. (1990). Individual versus conjoint interpersonal psychotherapy for depressed patients with marital disputes. *International Journal of Family Psychiatry, 7,* 10.

Frank, E., Kupfer, D., & Perel, J. M. (1989). Early recurrence in unipolar depression. *Archives of General Psychiatry, 46,* 397–400.

Goldberg, D. P. (1972). *The detection of psychiatric illness by questionnaire.* Institute of Psychiatry, Maudsley Monograph No. 21. London: Oxford University Press.

Gurman, A. S., & Kniskern, D. P. (1978). Research on marital and family therapy: Progress, perspective and prospect. In S. Garfield & A. Bergin (Eds.), *Handbook of psychotherapy and behavior change* (pp. 817–902). New York: Wiley.

Henderson, S., Byrne, D. G., Duncan-Jones, P., Adcock, S., Scott, R., & Steele, G. P. (1978). Social bonds in the epidemiology of neurosis. *British Journal of Psychiatry, 132,* 463–466.

Hoeper, E. W., Nycz, G. R., Cleary, P. H., Regier, N. A., & Goldberg, I. D. (1979). Estimated prevalence of RDC mental disorder in primary medical care. *International Journal of Mental Health, 8* (2), 6–15.

Ilfield, F. W. (1977). Current social stressors and symptoms of depression. *American Journal of Psychiatry, 134,* 161–166.

Klerman, G. L., Budman, S., Berwick, D., Weissman, M. M., Damico-White, J., Demby, A., & Feldstein, M. (1987). Efficacy of a brief psychosocial intervention for symptoms of stress and distress among patients in primary care. *Medical Care, 25,* 1078–1088.

Klerman, G. L., DiMascio, A., Weissman, M. M., Prusoff, B. A., & Paykel, E. S. (1974). Treatment of depression by drugs and psychotherapy. *American Journal of Psychiatry, 131,* 186–191.

Klerman, G. L., Weissman, M. M., Rounsaville, B. J., & Chevron, E. S. (1984). *Interpersonal psychotherapy of depression.* New York: Basic Books.

Locke, H. J., & Wallace, K. M. (1976). Short-term marital adjustment and prediction tests: Their reliability and validity. *Journal of Marriage and Family Living, 38,* 15–25.

Meyer, A. (1957). *Psychobiology: A science of man.* Springfield, IL: Charles C. Thomas.

Pearlin, L. I., & Lieberman, M. A. (1979). Social sources of emotional distress. In R. Simmons (Ed.), *Research in community and mental health.* Greenwich, CT: JAI Press.

Reynold, C., & Imber, S. (1988). Unpublished manuscript, University of Pittsburgh.

Rounsaville, B. J., Prusoff, B. A., & Weissman, M. M. (1980). The course of marital disputes in depressed women: A 48-month follow-up study *Comprehensive Psychiatry, 21,* 111–118.

Rounsaville, B. J., Weissman, M. M., Prusoff, B. A., & Herceg-Baron, R. (1979). Marital disputes and treatment outcome in depressed women. *Comprehensive Psychiatry, 20,* 483–490.

Sloane, R. B., Staples, F. R., & Schneider, L. S. (1985). Interpersonal therapy versus nortriptyline for depression in the elderly. In G. D. Burrows, T. R. Norman, & L. Dennerstein (Eds.), *Clinical and pharmacological studies in psychiatric disorders. Biographical psychiatry: new prospects.* London: John Libbey.

Spanier, G. B. (1976). Measuring dyadic adjustment: New scales for assessing the quality of marriage and similar dyads. *Journal of Marriage and Family Living, 38,* 15–25.

Sullivan, H. S. (1953). *The interpersonal theory of psychiatry.* New York: Norton.

Weissman, M. M. (1987). Advances in psychiatric epidemiology: Rates and risks for major depression. *American Journal of Public Health, 77,* 445–451.

Weissman, M. M., Jarrett, R. B., & Rush, A. J. (1987). Psychotherapy and its relevance to the pharmacotherapy of major depression: A decade later (1976–1985). In H. Y. Meltzer (Ed.), *Psychopharmacology: The third generation of progress* (pp. 1059–1069). New York: Raven Press.

Weissman, M. M., & Klerman, G. L. (1988). *Manual for interpersonal counseling for stress and distress.* Unpublished manuscript, Columbia University and Cornell University.

Weissman, M. M., Klerman, G. L., Prusoff, B. A., Sholomskas, D., & Padian, N. (1981). Depressed outpatients: Results one year after treatment with drugs and/or interpersonal psychotherapy. *Archives of General Psychiatry, 38,* 52–55.

Weissman, M. M., Prusoff, B. A., DiMascio, A., Neu, C., Gohlaney, M., & Klerman, G. L. (1979). The efficacy of drugs and psychotherapy in the treatment of acute depressive episodes. *American Journal of Psychiatry, 136,* 555–558.

Weissman, M. M., Rounsaville, B. J., & Chevron, E. S. (1982). Training psychotherapists to participate in psychotherapy outcome studies: Identifying and dealing with the research requirements. *American Journal of Psychiatry, 139,* 1442–1446.

CHAPTER 20

Marital and Family Therapy for Depression

IAN H. GOTLIB, PAMELA M. WALLACE, and CATHERINE A. COLBY

INCIDENCE

Depression is the most common of all the psychiatric disorders, and is perhaps the most lethal. It has been estimated that one in five depressed persons receives psychiatric treatment, that one in 50 is hospitalized, and that one in 100 commits suicide. Each year, more than 100 million people worldwide develop clinically recognizable depression, an incidence 10 times greater than that of schizophrenia. Furthermore, the World Health Organization expects that this number will increase over the coming years (Sartorius, 1979). Epidemiological studies indicate that 18 to 26 percent of female adults and 8 to 12 percent of males will experience at least one clinically significant episode of depression at some time in their lives (Weissman & Boyd, 1983); currently, there are estimated to be between 10 million and 14 million people in the United States who are exhibiting diagnosable depression (Weissman & Boyd, 1983).

There is also a significant cost associated with depression, in terms of suicide. The National Institute of Mental Health has reported that, of the 22,000 suicides committed each year in the United States, 80 percent can be traced to a precipitating depressive episode. The mortality risk from all causes appears to be elevated in depressed individuals (Lehmann, 1971). Therefore, when one considers the various medical and diagnostic categories of which depression is an intricate part or with which it is frequently associated and the number of patients who show a

Preparation of this chapter was facilitated by Grants No. 6606-3465-51 from Health and Welfare Canada and No. 997-87-89 from the Ontario Mental Health Foundation to Ian H. Gotlib. Correspondence concerning this chapter should be addressed to Ian H. Gotlib, Department of Psychology, University of Western Ontario, London, Ontario, Canada N6A 5C2.

subclinical form of this disorder, it is apparent that the problem of depression is considerable.

No single set of factors can adequately explain the full range of phenomena associated with depression, but, over the past decade, researchers have gained a growing appreciation of the significance of the psychosocial aspects of this disorder (Brown & Harris, 1978; Cane & Gotlib, 1985; Coyne, Kahn, & Gotlib, 1987; Hooley, 1985; Kessler, Price, & Wortman, 1985). As part of this examination of interpersonal functioning, investigators have begun to assess the role of intimate relationships in the etiology, course, and treatment of depression, as well as the negative impact of depression on close relationships. In this context, the marital and family relationships of depressed persons have recently become a major focus of interest.

Paralleling this escalation of research examining interpersonal aspects of depression is a growing interest in marital and/or family-oriented approaches to the treatment of this disorder. Thus, there has been a considerable increase in both the number and the methodological sophistication of studies assessing the efficacy of therapies for depression that focus on altering depressed persons' problematic relationships with their spouses and families. In this chapter, we will examine the current state of knowledge concerning the use and effectiveness of marital/family therapy for depression. We will begin with a brief examination of the literature that has underscored the importance of focusing on interpersonal factors in depression. In this context, we will review two distinct groups of investigations: those assessing the marital relationships and interactions of depressed persons, and those examining the effects of parental depression on the adjustment and psychosocial functioning of children in the family.

Following this review we will examine the results of outcome studies conducted to assess the efficacy of marital and/or family-oriented therapies for depression. We will outline the basis of an interpersonal systems approach to the treatment of depression (Gotlib & Colby, 1987), and will conclude the chapter with a case example illustrating the application of this therapy in the treatment of a depressed woman.

THE FAMILY RELATIONSHIPS OF DEPRESSED PERSONS

The literature examining the relationships of depressed individuals with their spouses and children developed, in part, from a sizable body of studies demonstrating that depressed persons are characterized by problematic interpersonal functioning. For example, at a broad level, depressed individuals report having smaller, less integrated, and less supportive social networks than do their nondepressed counterparts

(Brim, Witcoff, & Wetzel, 1982; Lin, Dean, & Ensel, 1986). Indeed, Henderson, Byrne, and Duncan-Jones (1981) found that depressed persons also judged a higher portion of their interactions with others to be affectively unpleasant. In a study recently completed in our laboratory, Gotlib and Lee (in press-b) found depressed psychiatric outpatients to report that they engaged in fewer social activities and had fewer close relationships than did nondepressed psychiatric outpatients and nondepressed community controls. The depressed patients in this study also rated the quality of their significant relationships more negatively and reported that there were arguments in their families over a greater number of issues than was the case for the nondepressed subjects. Moreover, results from a diverse set of investigations have implicated a lack of supportive interpersonal relationships in the etiology of depression (Barnett & Gotlib, 1988; Brown & Harris, 1978; Costello, 1982). A number of investigators have demonstrated in observational studies that depressed persons are characterized by deficits in social skills (Gotlib, 1982; Libet & Lewinsohn, 1973) and that people interacting with depressed persons respond to them in a negative manner (Coyne, 1976; Gotlib & Robinson, 1982). Considered collectively, these findings underscore the importance of interpersonal aspects of depression and provide the impetus for investigations examining the marital and family relationships of depressed persons.

Depressed Persons and Their Spouses

There are clear indications in the psychiatric literature that the relationships between depressed individuals and their spouses may be problematic. For example, epidemiological investigations indicate not only that women are 1.6 to 3 times more likely to be depressed than are men (Weissman & Klerman, 1977) but that married women are at significantly greater risk for developing depression than are unmarried women (Overall, 1971). In a finer-grained analysis, Renne (1971) reported that both males and females who were unhappily married were more depressed than were those who were separated and divorced. Beach, Winters, Weintraub, and Neale (1983, July) found 84 percent of the depressed patients in their sample to show a "negative course" of marital change in the four years following discharge from hospital, and Merikangas (1984) found the divorce rate in depressed patients two years after discharge to be nine times that of the general population. It has long been accepted that living with a psychiatrically disturbed person exerts a significant toll on the individual's spouse and family (Claussen & Yarrow, 1955). Targum, Dibble, Davenport, and Gershon (1981) found that over half of the spouses of bipolar depressed patients indicated that they regretted having married; similarly, Coyne et al. (1987) found that 40 percent of the spouses of depressed persons were themselves sufficiently distressed to warrant referral for psychotherapy.

The results of other studies provide more direct evidence of the link between marital distress and depression. Both Coleman and Miller (1975) and Crowther (1985), for example, obtained significant correlations between depressive symptomatology and marital distress in samples of psychiatric patients. Paykel et al. (1969) found that the most frequent life event preceding the onset of depression was a reported increase in arguments with the spouse. Schless, Schwartz, Goetz, and Mendels (1974) demonstrated that the impact of marriage- and family-related stresses persists after depressed patients recover. Finally, as we noted earlier, a number of recent investigations have reported that the lack of an intimate relationship with a spouse or boyfriend increased women's vulnerability for depression (Brown & Harris, 1978; Costello, 1982; see Gotlib & Hooley, 1988, for a more detailed review of this literature).

These and other similar findings have provided the foundation for studies examining more explicitly the nature of the marital relationships of depressed persons. In an early investigation, Weissman and her colleagues (Rounsaville, Weissman, Prusoff, & Herceg-Baron, 1979; Weissman & Paykel, 1974) interviewed depressed female psychiatric patients over the course of their treatment. Weissman found these patients to report marital relationships characterized by friction and hostility; they also reported being more dependent and less affectionate toward their spouses than did nondepressed controls (see Freden, 1982, for similar findings from a study conducted in Sweden). Rounsaville et al. (1979) noted subsequently that the presence of marital disputes was an important determinant of treatment outcome for these depressed women. Those women who reported marital difficulties on entry to treatment showed less improvement in their depressive symptoms and social functioning and were more likely to relapse after a course of individual therapy. In fact, these marital problems were found to persist at a one-year follow-up, even though the women had recovered symptomatically. These findings led Weissman to view the marital relationship as a "barometer" of clinical status.

Subsequent research replicated and extended Weissman's results. In one of the first observational studies of depressed patients, Hinchliffe, Hooper, and Roberts (1978) examined the marital interactions of male and female depressed inpatients and their spouses while in the hospital and again after recovery. These interactions were compared with the interactions of nonpsychiatric surgical patients and their spouses and with the interactions of the depressed patients with strangers. Hinchliffe et al. found that, while they were in hospital, the conversations of couples with a depressed spouse were marked by conflict, tension, negative expressiveness, high levels of disruption, negative emotional outbursts, and a high frequency of interruptions. Moreover, on almost every dimension measured, the interactions of the depressed patients with their spouses were more negative than were their interactions with strangers, indicating that the marital couple behaves as a "system." After recovery, the marital interactions of the male depressed patients were less negative, resembling those of the surgical controls; in contrast, the depressed women and their spouses continued to show high levels of tension and negative expressiveness.

In a similar study, Hautzinger, Linden, and Hoffman (1982) examined the marital interactions of couples seeking marital therapy, half of whom had a depressed spouse. Consistent with Hinchliffe et al.'s (1978) results, Hautzinger et al. found that communication in couples with a depressed spouse was more disturbed than in couples without a depressed partner. Couples with a depressed spouse more frequently discussed emotional difficulties; their conversations also tended to be more uneven, negative, and asymmetrical than were those of the distressed but nondepressed couples. Spouses of depressed partners seldom agreed with the depressive, offered help in an ambivalent manner, and evaluated the depressed spouse negatively. In contrast, the depressed spouses spoke positively of their partners and negatively of themselves.

Several studies have found the marital interactions of depressed persons to be characterized by hostility. Kahn, Coyne, and Margolin (1985) reported that, compared to nondepressed control couples, couples with a depressed spouse were more sad and angry following marital interactions and experienced each other as more negative, hostile, mistrusting, and detached, as well as less agreeable, nurturant, and affiliative. Biglan and Hops and their colleagues (Biglan et al., 1985; Hops et al., 1987) examined the marital interactions of couples in which the wife was clinically depressed. These authors found that depressed women exhibited higher rates of depressive affect and behavior and lower rates of problem-solving behavior than did either their husbands or nondepressed control spouses.

Three studies conducted in our laboratory provided further evidence of the negative marital interactions of depressed persons. Kowalik and Gotlib (1987) had depressed and nondepressed psychiatric outpatients and nondepressed nonpsychiatric controls interact with their spouses while simultaneously coding both the intended impact of their own behavior and their perceptions of their spouses' behavior. Compared with the nondepressed controls, the depressed patients were found to code a lower percentage of their messages as positive and a higher percentage as negative, indicating that they perceived the interactions and their spouses as problematic. Ruscher and Gotlib (1988), who examined the effects of depression on the marital interactions of depressed couples from the community and nondepressed control couples, found that couples in which one partner was depressed emitted a relatively low proportion of positive verbal behaviors and a high proportion of negative verbal and nonverbal behaviors. In the third study, Gotlib and Whiffen (1989) examined marital satisfaction and interpersonal behavior in groups of depressed psychiatric inpatients, nondepressed medical patients, and nondepressed community controls. Both the depressed and the medical patients and their spouses reported significantly lower marital satisfaction and exhibited more negative behavior during the interactions than did the nondepressed control couples.

The results of recent investigations suggest that the behavior of the depressed patients' spouses may be as influential in predicting clinical course and outcome as the patients' own symptoms and behaviors. Vaughn and Leff (1976), for example, interviewed family members (typically spouses) of depressed patients around the time of the patients' hospitalizations. On the basis of the extent to which they expressed critical or hostile comments to the researcher when talking about the patient, relatives were classified as high or low in expressed emotion (EE; Hooley, 1985). Hooley (1986) demonstrated that spouses who were classified as high-EE on the basis of what they said to an interviewer *about* their depressed partners were also significantly more negative in interactions *with* their partners than were low-EE spouses. Vaughn and Leff found that depressed patients who returned from the hospital to live with high-EE spouses were more likely to relapse during a nine-month follow-up period than were patients who returned home to live with low-criticism family members (Hooley, Orley, & Teasdale, 1986). Both Vaughn and Leff and Hooley et al. found that depressed patients relapsed at even lower rates of criticism than those typically associated with relapse of schizophrenic patients.

It is clear, therefore, that the marital relationships of depressed persons are characterized by tension and hostility and that negative marital interactions can increase the likelihood of depressed patients' relapse. In an attempt to gain a broader understanding of the interpersonal functioning of depressed persons, investigators have recently begun to examine the relationships of depressed individuals with their children.

Depressed Persons and Their Children

Although the relationships of depressed women with their children have received less attention than have their marital relationships, results of a number of diverse studies suggest that this may be an important area of investigation. For example, epidemiological investigations indicate that women who are raising children and who are not employed outside the home are particularly vulnerable to depression (Brown & Harris, 1978; Gotlib, Whiffen, Mount, Milne, & Cordy, 1989). Depressed women have also been found to report difficulty being warm and consistent mothers, and they indicate that they derive little satisfaction in being mothers and feel inadequate in this role (Bromet & Cornely, 1984; Weissman, Paykel,

& Klerman, 1972). Interestingly, several studies have found currently depressed adults to report having experienced difficult early family environments and problems in their relationships with their parents (Gotlib, Mount, Cordy, & Whiffen, 1988; Parker, 1981). Given these findings, it is not surprising that accumulating evidence suggests that the children of depressed parents are at increased risk for a variety of psychological and social difficulties (Beardslee, Bemporad, Keller, & Klerman, 1983; Gotlib & Lee, in press-a).

A number of studies have examined the relationships between depressed women and their children. Compared with their nondepressed counterparts, depressed mothers have been found to report being less involved, less affectionate, and more emotionally distant with their children, and to experience more irritability and resentment (Weissman et al., 1972). Depressed mothers have also been found to report various psychological and physical problems in their children, including depressed and anxious mood, suicidal ideation, and difficulties in school (Billings & Moos, 1983; Weissman et al., 1984). Furthermore, Billing and Moos (1986) found that depressed mothers continued to report problems in their children's functioning even after remission of their own depressive symptoms.

Several investigators have moved beyond the self-reports of depressed women to examine more directly and objectively both the interactions of depressed mothers and their children and the psychosocial functioning of the children themselves. Bettes (1988), for example, found that depressed mothers took longer to respond to their infants' vocalizations than did nondepressed mothers and, further, failed to modify their own speech after their infants had vocalized. In addition, the speech of the depressed women was more monotonous, failing to provide "affective signals" that allow infants to regulate their affective state. In a study conducted in our laboratory, Whiffen and Gotlib (in press) examined the effects of postpartum depression on infant cognitive and socioemotional development. Depressed mothers in this study rated their infants as more temperamentally difficult than did nondepressed mothers. Independent observers also rated the infants of the depressed mothers as more tense, less happy, and deteriorating more quickly under the stress of testing (Cohn, Matias, Tronick, Connell, & Lyons-Ruth, 1986; Ghodsian, Zayicek, & Wolkind, 1984; Zekoski, O'Hara, & Wills, 1987).

Two studies have attempted to delineate the specific characteristics of depressive mothering. Breznitz and Sherman (1987) reported that in a nonthreatening situation, depressed mothers of two- to three-year-old children spoke less than did nondepressed mothers. When placed in a more stressful situation, however, they increased their speech rate and decreased their response latency, a speech pattern indicative of anxiety. Breznitz and Sherman proposed that the children of depressed mothers were being socialized to respond to stress with exaggerated emotionality. In a similar study, Kochanska, Kuczynski, Radke-Yarrow, and Welsh (1987) compared the interactions of depressed and control mothers in situations in which the mother initiated an attempt to control or influence the child's behavior. Kochanska et al. found that the depressed mothers were more likely than were the nondepressed mothers to terminate the attempt before resolution, and were less likely to reach a compromise solution. These investigators proposed that the premature termination of control attempts may have been due to the depressed mother's fear of confrontation, a hypothesis consistent with the results of studies demonstrating that depressed adults cope by avoiding stressful situations (Coyne, Aldwin, & Lazarus, 1981).

Studies of the older children of depressed mothers indicated that these children demonstrate poorer functioning than do children of nondepressed parents. Welner, Welner, McCrary, and Leonard (1977) reported that the children of the depressed parents had more depressed mood, death wishes, frequent fighting, somatic complaints, loss of interest in usual activities, hypochondriacal concerns, and disturbed classroom behavior. The results of a recent observational study indicated that children of depressed mothers emit more irritated affect than do children in nondepressed families (Hops et al., 1987). Lee and Gotlib (1989a, 1989b) recently examined child adjustment in families in which the mother was diagnosed as suffering from a nonpsychotic, unipolar depression. Lee and Gotlib found that children of depressed mothers demonstrated higher rates of both internalizing and externalizing problems than did children of nondepressed psychiatric and medical control mothers. Clinical interviewers identified a greater number of psychological symptoms and poorer overall adjustment in the children of depressed mothers than they did in the children of community control mothers. Moreover, these deficits appeared to persist at a 10-month follow-up, even after the mothers' depressive symptoms had dissipated (Hammen et al., 1987; Hirsch, Moos, & Reischl, 1985; Turner, Beidel, & Costello, 1987).

Several investigators have demonstrated that a remarkably high proportion of children of depressed parents meet diagnostic criteria for psychiatric disorder. Beardslee, Schultz, and Selman (1987), Klein, Clark, Dansky, and Margolis (1988), and Orvaschel, Walsh-Ellis, and Ye (1988), for example, found that between 40 and 50 percent of the adolescent children of depressed parents met criteria for a diagnosis of past or current psychiatric disturbance. Hammen et al. (1987) obtained similar results in a more extensive investigation, but also reported that group differences were attenuated when psychosocial stresses were covaried. Finally, in a study described earlier, Lee and Gotlib (1989a, 1989b) reported that two-thirds of the children of the depressed mothers in their sample were placed in the clinical range on the Child Behavior

Check List, an incidence three times greater than that observed in the nondepressed controls.

Children of depressed mothers have been found in a number of studies, using a diverse range of methodologies, to demonstrate problematic psychosocial adjustment and functioning. Moreover, these difficulties are apparent at a wide range of ages. A consistent finding in this literature is that, even when their mothers are no longer overtly symptomatic, children continue to demonstrate behavioral difficulties, indicating that there may be a substantial lag between alleviation of maternal symptomatology and improvement in child functioning. This finding parallels results of studies reviewed earlier, suggesting that marital difficulties also persist beyond the depressive episode. Thus, alleviation of maternal symptomatology should not be taken as a signal that all family members are functioning adequately. Given the pervasiveness of the problematic interpersonal functioning of depressed persons, a number of interventions for depression have been developed that focus on the marital and family relationships of the depressed patient.

MARITAL AND FAMILY THERAPY

Descriptions of the problematic marital relationships of depressed persons and of the adverse impact of parental depression on young children in the family have provided the impetus for investigations assessing the efficacy of therapies for depressed persons focused on improving the quality of their marital and/or family interactions. The concept of treating depression from a marital/family perspective is a relatively new one and, consequently, there is not a large body of outcome studies in this area. There are, however, a small number of investigations that have reported the successful treatment of depression using marital or family-oriented therapies.

In an early series of case studies, Lewinsohn and his colleagues described an approach to the treatment of depression that focuses on re-establishing an adequate schedule of positive reinforcement for the individual by increasing the quality and range of interpersonal interactions. Lewinsohn postulated that providing depressed patients and their spouses with feedback about their interpersonal behaviors in the home can lead to a decrease in the level of depression and an improvement in their social relationships. Thus, Lewinsohn and Atwood (1969) and Lewinsohn and Schaffer (1971) presented cases in which feedback about interpersonal behavior between depressed women and their husbands was used in combination with conjoint marital therapy to effect behavior change. The results demonstrated significant decreases in the women's MMPI-Depression scores and improvement in their marital communication and family interactions.

In a subsequent controlled investigation, McLean, Ogston, and Grauer (1973) examined the effects of behaviorally oriented conjoint marital therapy on the valence of the marital communications of depressed outpatients and their spouses. McLean et al. compared a nontreatment control group of depressed couples with a group of couples who received behavioral marital therapy. Twenty married depressed outpatients received either conjoint behavioral marital therapy with their spouses or "treatment as usual," which typically involved medication, group therapy, individual psychotherapy, or some combination of these treatments. Couples in the behavioral marital therapy treatment group received eight one-hour-weekly sessions with male and female cotherapists. During these sessions they received training in social learning principles, and the spouses were given feedback regarding their partners' perceptions of their verbal interactions. Using reciprocal behavioral contracts, spouses were taught how to communicate to their partners the changes they desired in their relationships and how to monitor the feedback they were giving to their spouses. Couples were given "feedback boxes" designed to signal positive and negative feedback during ongoing conversation.

Prior to beginning treatment, patients were assessed with the Depression Adjective Checklist (DACL). They were tape-recorded at home, discussing their problems with their spouses, and were asked to list five target behaviors that were attributed to the patients' depression. Both at the end of treatment and at a three-month follow-up, couples indicated any changes they noted in these five target behaviors. McLean et al. (1973) found that, overall, patients in the marital therapy group demonstrated greater improvements than did the control patients. At both review points, couples in the marital therapy group reported significantly greater reductions in their DACL scores and greater improvements in their problematic interpersonal behaviors. In contrast, couples in the comparison group exhibited only minor improvement in these areas. Finally, couples who received marital therapy demonstrated more adaptive verbal behavior, including a significant reduction in the frequency of their negative interchanges.

In a widely cited investigation of the effectiveness of marital therapy in the treatment of depression, Friedman (1975) conducted a 12-week therapy program designed to assess the separate and combined effects of amitriptyline and "marital and family-oriented psychotherapy" in depressed patients. Subjects were male and female depressed outpatients whose spouses agreed to make regular visits to the clinic. Patients were randomly assigned to one of four treatment conditions: drug therapy and marital therapy, drug therapy and minimal contact, marital therapy and placebo, and placebo and minimal contact. A total of 150 depressed patients completed the full course of treatment. In the drug treatment groups, patients received amitriptyline hydrochloride for the first 10 weeks of treatment; during the last two weeks they were drug-free, in order to assess withdrawal reactions. Patients in the marital therapy conditions had 12 hours of contact with a therapist using marital and family-oriented psychotherapy. Finally, patients in the minimal contact group received seven individual sessions with a physician, each lasting a half-hour.

Several assessment measures were utilized to evaluate outcome at the end of treatment, including a Psychiatric Rating Scale, a Global Improvement Clinical Scale, a self-report Inventory of Psychic and Somatic Complaints, a Family Role Task and Activity Scale, and a Marital Relations Inventory. Essentially, Friedman (1975) found that both drug and marital therapy were more effective than were their respective control conditions (placebo and minimal individual contact). However, there also appeared to be differential effects of these two types of treatment. Whereas drug therapy was associated with early improvement in clinical symptoms, marital therapy was associated with longer-term improvement in the patient's participation in and performance of family role-tasks, the reduction of hostility in the family, and the patient's perceptions of the quality of the marital relationship. Overall, for most of the outcome measures, the combined drug-marital therapy group demonstrated the greatest improvement. In discussing these results, Friedman stated that it is possible that "the marital therapy approach is more effective and quicker to achieve a positive effect with neurotically depressed married patients than is either individual or peer group therapy" (p. 634).

The usefulness of including the spouse in therapy was also examined in an uncontrolled retrospective study of 100 couples in which one partner was diagnosed with a primary affective disorder (PAD). Greene, Lustig, and Lee (1976) examined 40 unipolar depressed, 42 bipolar depressed, and 18 unipolar manic patients and their spouses. All PAD spouses received psychotherapy and/or somatotherapy, while the therapist gave supportive psychotherapy to the non-PAD spouse. The major emphasis of Greene et al.'s approach was to utilize the non-PAD partner as an "assistant therapist," with the goal of stabilizing the marriage. Greene et al. reported that approximately 10 percent of the couples receiving this treatment achieved stabilization for at least 15 years. Nevertheless, the authors cautioned that "our current practice in premarital counseling is usually to advise against marriage when there is a history of a primary affective disorder. . . . Marriage to an individual with a PAD involves serious risks: the deep emotional consequences of suicide attempts or suicide, the strong hereditary component, and the intermittent incompatibility of the marriage are emotionally disturbing not only to the spouses but also to the children" (p. 829).

Davenport, Ebert, Adland, and Goodwin (1977) also reported on the effectiveness of couples therapy in the treatment of bipolar affective disorder. Sixty-five married bipolar patients who had been previously hospitalized for an acute manic episode were followed for two to 10 years subsequent to their discharge. The patients and their spouses were arbitrarily assigned to one of three groups at the time of discharge: a couples psychotherapy group with lithium maintenance ($N = 12$), a lithium maintenance group with no regular psychotherapy ($N = 11$), and home community aftercare ($N = 42$). Each couples group consisted of three to five couples who met for approximately 90 minutes per week with male and female cotherapists. The focus of therapy, conducted with cotherapists, was on couple interactions and the acquisition of more adaptive behaviors. Davenport et al. found the overall outcome to be quite poor for those couples who did not receive the couples therapy. Patients in the lithium/no psychotherapy and home aftercare groups demonstrated high rates of rehospitalization and marital failure; in fact, three of these patients committed suicide. In contrast to this pattern of functioning, none of the 12 patients in the couples group required rehospitalization or experienced marital failure. Although there were a number of demographic differences among these groups that must be taken into account, Davenport et al. concluded that bipolar patients and their spouses can benefit from participation in a homogeneous conjoint marital therapy group.

Two preliminary reports on the effectiveness of marital therapy for the treatment of depression, both with small samples, warrant mention. Waring et al. (1988) described an ongoing investigation in which they used essentially the same four treatment groups as did Friedman (1975). They reported results from 12 couples who had completed the 10 weeks of therapy sessions. The subjects were all dysthymic women whose husbands agreed to participate in treatment. Patients received either doxepin or a placebo drug crossed with either minimal contact or cognitive marital therapy, selected for its focus on the intimacy between couples and the use of self-disclosure to improve intimacy. Waring et al. found that all patients showed an improvement in depressive symptomatology and an increase in reported intimacy. In addition, there was a trend for these effects to be most pronounced for patients in the cognitive marital therapy condition. Waring et al. suggested that the simple presence of dysthymic women's spouses in therapy may itself be beneficial.

In the second preliminary study, Beach and O'Leary (1986) described the clinical outcome for eight couples in which the wife met diagnostic criteria for unipolar depression. Couples were randomly assigned to one of three groups: conjoint behavioral marital therapy, cognitive therapy for the depressed spouse only or a wait-list control group. Whereas the marital therapy treatment focused on improving communication and problem-solving, cognitive therapy focused on examining the manner in which the patients structured their worlds and how this in turn influenced their affect and behavior. Couples in the wait-list control group were told that they could request therapeutic consultation, although none did during the 14 weeks of treatment. Beach and O'Leary assessed depressive symptoms and marital discord at every second week throughout treatment, by having subjects complete the Beck Depression Inventory and the Dyadic Adjustment Scale. Couples also completed these measures one week after the last session and at a three-month follow-up. The results of this study indicated that both active treatment conditions were more (and equally) effective than was the wait-list condition in reducing depressive symptoms. In addition, however, couples in the behavioral marital therapy condition reported significantly more rapid and larger increases in marital functioning than did couples in either the cognitive therapy or the wait-list control groups, and similar data were obtained for their husbands. Beach and O'Leary found this pattern of results to persist at the three-month follow-up assessment. Because this study is based on only eight couples, it is inappropriate to draw firm conclusions about the differential effectiveness of these intervention approaches. Nevertheless, it is noteworthy that whereas wives receiving behavioral marital therapy and individual cognitive therapy showed clinically significant reductions in depressive symptomatology, only those wives receiving the conjoint marital therapy also showed a marked reduction in marital dissatisfaction.

O'Leary and Beach (1988) reported the results of an expanded version of their study. Married women who received a diagnosis of dysthymia or major depressive disorder were randomly assigned to conjoint marital therapy, cognitive therapy for the depressed spouse only, or a wait-list control group. Both the behavioral marital therapy and the individual cognitive therapy involved 15 or 16 weekly sessions. As was the case in the earlier study, at the end of the treatment patients in both therapy groups demonstrated a significant reduction in depressive symptomatology, whereas the wait-list control group did not. In addition, patients who received marital therapy demonstrated higher marital satisfaction scores at the end of treatment than did patients in either of the other groups, who did not differ significantly from each other in this regard. At a one-year follow-up, although patients in the marital therapy and the cognitive groups did not differ on depressive symptoms, patients who had received marital therapy continued to report greater marital satisfaction than did patients in the other two groups. O'Leary and Beach suggested that the fact that the marital therapy subjects demonstrated as much change in depression as the cognitive behavior therapy subjects reflects the impact that marital satisfaction can have on depression.

They further suggested that when significant marital discord is found in conjunction with clinically significant depression, marital therapy may be the most effective and appropriate treatment.

Two recently developed interpersonal approaches to the treatment of depression have yielded promising results. Klerman, Weissman, Rounsaville, and Chevron (1984) described their Interpersonal Psychotherapy (IPT) for depression, which is based on the assumption, corroborated by the findings of the empirical investigations reviewed earlier in this chapter, that depression can result from difficulties in the interpersonal relationships between depressed persons and their significant others. IPT, therefore, attempts to improve interpersonal functioning and to alleviate depressive symptoms by focusing on how the patient is coping with current interpersonal stressors. DiMascio et al. (1979) and Weissman et al. (1979) demonstrated that IPT is as effective as pharmacotherapy in reducing depressive symptomatology and is more effective than pharmacotherapy in improving interpersonal functioning. At a one-year follow-up, patients who had received IPT alone or in combination with pharmacotherapy demonstrated significantly better social functioning than did patients who had received only pharmacotherapy (Weissman, Klerman, Prusoff, Sholomskas, & Padian, 1981). Foley, Rounsaville, Weissman, Sholomskas, and Chevron (1987, May) reported preliminary results of an important study designed to compare the effects of IPT conducted with and without the depressed person's spouse. While both treatment conditions led to a reduction in depressive symptomatology, patients who received IPT with their spouses showed greater improvement on measures of marital functioning.

The second interpersonal approach to therapy for depression is Inpatient Family Intervention (IFI; Clarkin et al., 1986), developed for the treatment of depressed inpatients. In IFI, depressed patients and relevant family members meet regularly during the patient's hospitalization, with a family therapist and the patient's primary therapist acting as cotherapists. IFI is a brief, problem-focused therapy aimed at helping patients and their families accept and understand the current illness and identifying possible precipitating stressors, both within and outside of the family. IFI also attempts to identify family interaction patterns that may produce stress for the patient, and helps the family to plan strategies to minimize potential stressors.

In the first report of the efficacy of IFI, Glick et al. (1985) randomly assigned 54 schizophrenic and 47 depressed inpatients to either standard hospital treatment, which included individual, group, and milieu activities, and somatic therapy, or to standard treatment plus IFI. The IFI patients participated in at least six one-hour family sessions. The goals of these sessions included the identification of precipitating and/or future stressors, identification of stressful family interactions and strategies for dealing with these interactions, and acceptance of the need for continuing treatment. Glick et al. reported that, at discharge as well as at the six-month follow-up, there were no significant treatment differences for the depressed patients. The schizophrenic patients with good prehospital functioning, however, demonstrated a more favorable response to IFI, exhibiting better global outcomes at discharge.

In a second report, on a somewhat larger sample, Haas et al. (1988) provided greater detail concerning group differences in treatment outcome at discharge. Although IFI was found to be generally more effective than standard hospital treatment, female patients, particularly depressed female patients, appeared to benefit more from this form of treatment than did male patients. This pattern of results was also maintained at six-month and 18-month follow-ups, at which time female schizophrenic and depressed inpatients and their families demonstrated greater improvement with IFI than did their male counterparts (Clarkin, Haas, & Glick, 1988; Spencer et al., 1988). In general, therefore, IFI seems most effective in the treatment of female inpatients.

Interpersonal Systems Treatment of Depression

Gotlib and Colby (1987) presented an interpersonal systems approach to the conceptualization of depression and outlined explicit strategies and procedures to be used in assessing and treating depressed patients and their spouses. The conceptualization of depression proposed by Gotlib and Colby, and subsequently expanded upon by Gotlib (in press), maintains that depression has both cognitive and interpersonal aspects and that an effective approach to the treatment of this disorder must therefore consider both these areas of functioning. Essentially, Gotlib and Colby suggested that, because of aversive early experiences, some individuals develop cognitive and/or personality characteristics that predispose them to become depressed in the face of certain types of circumstances or life events, such as marital turmoil or the behavior of a high-EE spouse. If these individuals then begin to exhibit depressive symptoms, two factors may interact to maintain or exacerbate the depression. First, as the literature we reviewed earlier in this chapter clearly indicated, depressed persons are less skillful and, perhaps because of the aversiveness of their symptomatic depressive behavior, they engender less social support from others in their environment than do nondepressed persons. Second, depressed individuals have been found to be characterized by a "readiness" to perceive and attend to negative aspects of their environment (Gotlib, 1983; Gotlib, McLachlan, & Katz, 1988), and to be more sensitive to negative stimuli than are nondepressed individuals (Lewinsohn, Lobitz, & Wilson, 1973). Thus, depressed persons will readily perceive the lack of support and the negative behavior in others around them and may respond by becoming more depressed and more symptomatic. Significant others, in turn, become even more negative and rejecting, and a vicious cycle continues (see Gotlib, in press, for a more detailed discussion of this conceptualization).

It is clear from this formulation that clinicians must attend to both the individual and his or her significant others if they are to deal comprehensively with the depression. In terms of dealing with the individual, it is important that therapists assess both the nature of aversive early experiences that may increase the individual's vulnerability to depression and the cognitive or information-processing style of the depressed person. With respect to the interpersonal system of the depressed person, therapists must focus on the marital or family dynamics and must attempt to understand the depression within the context of the family system. Therapists must examine what the family is doing that may be maintaining or exacerbating the depression and must also explore what the family can do differently. Finally, therapists must integrate the diverse information obtained through this assessment in developing an appropriate intervention designed to alter the dysfunctional patterns of cognitive and interpersonal behavior.

In terms of assessment, Gotlib and Colby (1987) suggested that three specific aspects of depressed patients' functioning be examined in a comprehensive assessment: the symptomatology manifested by the patients, their current cognitive functioning, and the nature and quality of their current interpersonal behavior. A number of psychometrically sound measures are available to assess these aspects of the patients' functioning. To assess depressive symptomatology, we recommend the clinician-completed Schedule for Affective Disorders and Schizophrenia (SADS; Endicott & Spitzer, 1978) and the self-report Beck Depression Inventory (BDI; Beck, Ward, Mendelson, Mock, & Erbaugh, 1961). The cognitive functioning of depressed patients can be assessed with the Dysfunctional Attitude Scale (Weissman & Beck, 1978, April) and the Attributional Style Questionnaire (Peterson et al., 1982). A number of measure are available to assess various aspects of the depressed patient's interpersonal functioning, including the self-report Social Support Questionnaire (Sarason, Levine, Basham, & Sarason, 1983), Family Environment Scale (Moos & Moos, 1981), and Dyadic Adjustment Scale (Spanier, 1976); the clinician-rated Social Adjustment Scale (Weissman & Paykel, 1974); and the spouse-completed Spouse Observation Checklist (Weiss, Hops, & Patterson, 1973). The clinician should observe the interactions of patients and their spouses and families, both to gain a more complete understanding of the nature and quality of the depressed patients' interactions and to identify potential targets for intervention.

In terms of treatment, it is important that the principles and strategies utilized by the therapist to alleviate the patients' depression focus on both cognitive and interpersonal functioning. Briefly, with respect to cognitive functioning, the therapist must recognize that depressed individuals demonstrate increased attention and sensitivity to negative aspects of their environment. A major goal in working individually with depressed patients is to attenuate this accessibility to negative stimuli. This goal is typically accomplished through education and through making the patients aware of how they are processing information and how this manner of processing affects their perceptions of their interactions with others. It is also important to help depressed individuals become more accurate in monitoring their own and other people's behaviors. Keeping daily records and increasing the number of pleasurable experiences in which they engage are useful procedures in meeting this objective.

Treatment strategies and procedures aimed at improving the depressed patients' interpersonal functioning are more complex. Because depression was conceptualized by Gotlib and Colby (1987) as involving not only the depressed persons but people with whom they have an intimate relationship (most typically, their spouses and families), attempts to alleviate the depression often involved concomitant changes in the interpersonal system. It is to the therapist's benefit, therefore, to have a working knowledge of principles of General Systems Theory (von Bertalanffy, 1968). Gotlib and Colby described a number of intervention strategies and procedures, derived from systems theory, in outlining an interpersonal systems approach to the treatment of depression. The primary goal of this therapy is to stimulate new patterns of communication and behavioral sequences that interrupt the depression-maintaining interactions that brought the depressed person into therapy. In general, therefore, interpersonal systems therapy focuses on the present rather than on historical events, with the therapist adopting an active, problem-solving approach to treatment. The therapist typically broadens the focus of treatment from the depressed patient in order to involve as much of the system (i.e., the marital dyad or the family) as possible in therapy.

Gotlib and Colby (1987) specified circumstances under which the spouses or relatives of depressed individuals should be involved in therapy and described the effective use of a number of techniques and procedures that the systems-oriented therapist can utilize to initiate change in depressed patients and their families. They described such therapeutic procedures as joining, enactment, reframing, restructuring, and altering family boundaries. Although additional empirical work is required to refine these techniques and to further validate the efficacy of this intervention, the results of preliminary work utilizing this interpersonal systems approach to the treatment of depression are promising. In the following section we present the case of a depressed woman who was assessed and treated from an interpersonal systems perspective.

CASE EXAMPLE

Brenda T., a 38-year-old mother of three, was the youngest daughter of a well-known public figure. Brenda described her early years at home as replete with episodes of "despair and rejection." She portrayed her father as a cold, demanding, and self-absorbed authority figure. Her mother was painted with gentler strokes—artistic, emotional, and devoted to her husband and children. Brenda's relationships with her siblings were characterized by fluctuating periods of intense closeness and profound separation. Her views of her current family closely matched these early childhood perceptions. Brenda felt that from a very early age there was enormous pressure in her family to achieve outstanding accomplishments, a pressure she thought emanated primarily from her father. Her two older siblings had measured up to the family standards and had both been quite successful in achieving high-profile careers. In contrast, Brenda viewed herself as the "family failure." Although she had made early attempts to match the success level of her family, she was repeatedly faced with obstacles she could not overcome. Brenda ultimately abandoned her own career efforts and turned instead to the task of raising a family. She married a somewhat older man who was well on his way to acquiring the same type of public image as her father had.

At the time Brenda was referred for counseling by her family physician, she was very depressed. Although she was somewhat vague in her initial descriptions of her concerns, she was specific in detailing the intense degree to which she felt she was suffering. After several interviews it was clear to both the therapist and Brenda that she felt little satisfaction in the major areas of her life. Specifically, Brenda described her current marital satisfaction as "rock bottom"; she was only slightly more satisfied with her parenting skills. Brenda's career satisfaction was minimal; her relationship with her family of origin was minimal as well. She noted that her outside interests and hobbies were in need of improvement and that her friendships, such as they were, were impoverished. In sum, Brenda presented as a bright, talented woman who, despite her "assets," was a troubled and needy person. Compounding her difficulties was Brenda's strong tendency to blame others (husband, father, children) for her failures and consequent despair.

In the initial assessment phase of therapy, both interview and self-report measures were administered to determine Brenda's psychological profile. She was interviewed with the SADS, and the Hamilton Rating Scale for Depression, and she completed the BDI. The results of these measures were consistent with a diagnosis of depression. Brenda's repeated statements about her marital dissatisfaction, coupled with her clear belief that her father and her husband were the primary sources of her unhappiness, suggested the utility of involving her husband in therapy. Although initially reluctant, Brenda and her husband, John, finally agreed to this approach. They completed the Dyadic Adjustment Scale, indicating their perceptions of their marital adjustment, and the Family Environment Scale was administered to assess the interpersonal relationships among family members and the social-environmental characteristics of the family.

During the assessment phase of therapy, the therapist was careful to elicit both Brenda's and John's perceptions about the problems facing their family. The therapist was also actively involved in observing the quality and pattern of interaction between the couple. The integration of interview, self-report, and observational data provided the therapist with the necessary information to formulate at least preliminary hypotheses concerning the dynamics of this couple's relationship and the role played by Brenda's depressive symptomatology. Case formulation is a challenging task, as it must include an integration of all available information and should be presented to the couple in a meaningful and coherent manner. The second important function of the assessment phase of therapy is to determine specific treatment goals and a consequent treatment plan aimed at achieving these goals.

Based on an interpersonal systems approach, the therapist hypothesized the following case formulation: Brenda, faced with a long history of failure, was able to shed some of her resulting esteem problems by blaming her father and/or her husband, and their lack of support and encouragement, for her perceived low level of achievement. In her marriage, this resulted in frequent, scathing outbursts at John for his selfish concern for his own needs and career interests at the expense of Brenda's needs. John's reaction to these often unpredictable attacks was to completely withdraw from Brenda, focusing his energies on his career and public interests, where he received much appreciation and positive reinforcement. During these periods John was totally absorbed in his life away from home and treated Brenda in a cold, critical, and often indifferent manner. Of course, the more John devoted his attention to people and activities outside the family, the more rejected and isolated Brenda felt. Brenda interpreted John's lack of interest in her as evidence of her unworthiness, which further fostered her low self-esteem, feelings of depression, and depressive behaviors. In a recurring pattern in the relationship, this depression or state of despondency led to hostility toward John and was followed by his withdrawal and lack of interest. This circular pattern had existed for so long that Brenda's depression was reaching extreme depths and the marriage was hanging by a thread. Both saw the other as selfish, demanding, and uncaring. John and Brenda agreed that two important treatment goals were to find more constructive ways to communicate their needs and feelings to each other and to help Brenda find appropriate avenues to pursue her own talents. Toward this end, therapy involved both marital and individual counseling.

Throughout the therapy sessions, the therapist actively joined with one spouse and then with the other. The therapeutic activity of joining served the function of offering support and understanding to the "joinee" as well as serving as a role model to the other spouse. Through this process the couple was able to begin the lengthy task of nurturing and understanding each other. Even with a slight indication of improved communication, the therapist was able to reframe the original problem description from selfish, uncaring spouses to one of a fear on both their parts that they would not be able to meet each other's needs. Framed in this way, both spouses were able to make more of an effort to give to each other in ways they had not previously been able to do. Given the long history of pathology in their relationship, however, this was a fragile improvement. In order to clarify the negative pattern of their interaction as well as to solidify the improvements, the therapist repeatedly had the couple involved in enactments, in which they were required to "act out" in complete detail both the negative and positive situations that had transpired between therapy sessions. An ongoing challenge throughout the sessions was the therapist's task of dealing with the couple's resistance to change and to acceptance of new ways of dealing with problems; both spouses were quick to blame, retaliate, and feel cheated.

In the individual sessions with Brenda, the therapist explained how depressed persons process and attend to negative information from their environment and how they can have an adverse impact on significant others around them through their depressive behavior. Brenda was taught to monitor her own behavior, to keep a daily record of the occurrence of positive and negative events, and to increase her involvement in pleasant activities. In the marital sessions the therapist actively sought to highlight the strengths of each spouse. John and Brenda had been so accustomed to being viciously attacked by the other spouse that they eagerly absorbed this type of response. Over time the therapist turned more and more to the couple to generate their own solutions. As a result of greater mutual support and understanding, Brenda was able to refocus some of her energies into career planning. In a pragmatic way, she developed both a short-term and long-term set of objectives. John was instrumental in bringing the short-term goals to fruition; his increased parenting responsibilities allowed Brenda to take the first step toward her career objectives.

Therapy came to a close over a period of two months, with longer intervals between sessions. Progress was evaluated by a comparison of the initial therapy goals with the couple's current functioning. To substantiate their impressions, the couple completed the original interview and self-report measures. Although progress had actually been only moderate, both spouses and therapist concluded that any further change would be a slow process. Follow-up sessions were set for two six-month intervals. At the first follow-up, it was clear that the couple had continued to maintain their original therapeutic gains, although only marginal progress had been made beyond that point. Brenda was showing no signs of depression and was happily progressing in her career. It was agreed at this session that, with the career issue more stable, the couple could afford to devote more time to their marriage. In two additional sessions, specific goals were established toward this end. By the second follow-up session, Brenda and John were devoting more time to their marriage, and both expressed satisfaction with their current functioning as a couple. No further follow-ups were scheduled, and the couple was invited to contact the therapist if they felt the need to do so.

SUMMARY

We have attempted in this chapter to provide an understanding of the theoretical and empirical foundations of marital and family-focused therapies for depression and an overview of research examining the efficacy of marital and family therapy in the treatment of this disorder. We described the basis of an interpersonal system therapy for depression and presented a brief case study that was conceptualized and treated from this framework.

It should be clear from our review that marital/family therapy or family involvement in therapy represents a promising direction in the treatment of depression. Although individual therapy has been demonstrated to be effective in reducing the level of depressive symptomatology, it has been found to be less effectual in ameliorating difficulties in marital and family functioning. In contrast, marital therapy has been demonstrated to achieve both symptom relief and a reduction in marital discord. Although few studies report data addressing the long-term effectiveness of marital therapy, given the role played by marital and family discord in relapse of depression, it is possible that marital/family therapy would prove to be more effective than individual therapy in the prevention of further depressive episodes. This hypothesis, of course, awaits additional research.

There are a number of issues that, because of space limitations, we could not address here. The differential importance of marital discord and depression in contributing to the outcome of therapy and the importance of the causal nature of the relation between depression and marital/family distress in affecting outcome are but two issues that clearly warrant further investigation. Similarly, we reviewed research examining the efficacy of marital and family therapy in alleviating depression. The use of marital/family therapy in the *prevention* of depression is an area of study that deserves serious consideration (Haas, Clarkin, & Glick, 1985). We believe that the application of interpersonally focused therapies to the treatment of depression is an exciting development in the study of this disorder. It is our hope that this chapter will serve to stimulate further research in this field.

REFERENCES

Barnett, P. A., & Gotlib, I. H. (1988). Dysfunctional attitudes and psychosocial stress: The differential prediction of future psychological symptomatology. *Motivation and Emotion, 12,* 251–270.

Beach, S. R. H., & O'Leary, D. K. (1986). The treatment of depression occurring in the context of marital discord. *Behaviour Therapy, 17,* 43–50.

Beach, S. R. H., Winters, K. C., Weintraub, S., & Neale, J. M. (1983, July). *The link between marital distress and depression: A prospective design.* Paper presented at the World Congress of Behavior Therapy, Washington.

Beardslee, W. R., Bemporad, J., Keller, M. B., & Klerman, G. L. (1983). Children of parents with major affective disorder: A review. *American Journal of Psychiatry, 140,* 825–832.

Beardslee, W. R., Schultz, L. H., & Selman, R. L. (1987). Level of social-cognitive development, adaptive functioning, and DSM-III diagnoses in adolescent offspring of parents with affective disorders: Implications for the development of the capacity for mutuality. *Developmental Psychology, 23,* 807–815.

Beck, A. T., Ward, C. H., Mendelson, M., Mock, J., & Erbaugh, J. (1961). An inventory for measuring depression. *Archives of General Psychiatry, 4,* 561–571.

Bettes, B. A. (1988). Maternal depression and motherese: Temporal and intonational features. *Child Development, 59,* 1089–1096.

Biglan, A., Hops, H., Sherman, L., Friedman, L. S., Arthur, J., & Osteen, V. (1985). Problem-solving interactions of depressed women and their husbands. *Behavior Therapy, 16,* 431–451.

Billings, A. G., & Moos, R. H. (1983). Comparisons of children of depressed and nondepressed parents: A social-environmental perspective. *Journal of Abnormal Child Psychology, 11,* 463–486.

Billings, A. G., & Moos, R. H. (1986). Children of parents with unipolar depression: A controlled one-year follow-up. *Journal of Abnormal Child Psychology, 14,* 149–166.

Breznitz, Z., & Sherman, T. (1987). Speech patterning of natural discourse of well and depressed mothers and their young children. *Child Development, 58,* 395–400.

Brim, J. A., Witcoff, C., & Wetzel, R. D. (1982). Social network characteristics of hospitalized depressed patients. *Psychological Reports, 50,* 423–433.

Bromet, E. J., & Cornely, P. J. (1984). Correlates of depression in mothers of young children. *Journal of the American Academy of Child Psychiatry, 23,* 335–342.

Brown, G. W., & Harris, T. (1978). *Social origins of depression.* New York: Free Press.

Cane, D. C., & Gotlib, I. H. (1985). Implicit theories of psychopathology: Implications for interpersonal conceptualizations of depression. *Social Cognition, 3,* 341–368.

Clarkin, J. F., Haas, G. L., & Glick, I. (Eds.). (1988). *Affective disorders and the family: Assessment and treatment.* New York: Guilford.

Clarkin, J. F., Spencer, H. H., Lestelle, V., Peyser, J., DeMane, N., Haas, G. L., & Glick, I. D. (1986). *IFI for affective disorder: A manual of inpatient family intervention.* Unpublished manuscript, Cornell University Medical College.

Claussen, J., & Yarrow, M. (1955). Introduction: Mental illness and the family. *Journal of Social Issues, 11,* 3–5.

Cohn, J. F., Matias, R., Tronick, E. Z., Connell, D., & Lyons-Ruth, K. (1986). Face to face interactions of depressed mothers and their infants. In E. Tronick and T. Field (Eds.), *Maternal depression and infant disturbance: New directions in child development.* San Francisco: Jossey-Bass.

Coleman, R. E., & Miller, A. G. (1975). The relationship between depression and marital maladjustment in a clinic population: A multi-trial, multi-method study. *Journal of Consulting and Clinical Psychology, 43,* 647.

Costello, C. G. (1982). Social factors associated with depression: A retrospective community study. *Psychological Medicine, 12,* 329–339.

Coyne, J. C. (1976). Depression and the response of others. *Journal of Abnormal Psychology, 85,* 186-193.

Coyne, J. C., Aldwin, C., & Lazarus, R. S. (1981). Depression and coping in stressful episodes. *Journal of Abnormal Psychology, 90,* 439–447.

Coyne, J. C., Kahn, J., & Gotlib, I. H. (1987). Depression. In T. Jacob (Ed.), *Family interaction and psychopathology* (pp. 509–533). New York: Plenum.

Coyne, J. C., Kessler, R. C., Tal, M., Turnbull, J., Wortman, C. B., & Greden, J. F. (1987). Living with a depressed person. *Journal of Consulting and Clinical Psychology, 55,* 347–352.

Crowther, J. H. (1985). The relationship between depression and marital maladjustment: A descriptive study. *Journal of Nervous and Mental Disease, 173,* 227–231.

Davenport, Y. B., Ebert, M. H., Adland, M. L., & Goodwin, F. K. (1977). Couples group therapy as an adjunct to lithium maintenance of the manic patient. *American Journal of Orthopsychiatry, 47,* 495–502.

DiMascio, A., Weissman, M. M., Prusoff, B. A., Neu, C., Zwilling, M., & Klerman, G. L. (1979). Differential symptom reduction by drugs and psychotherapy in acute depression. *Archives of General Psychiatry, 36,* 1450–1456.

Endicott, J., & Spitzer, R. L. (1978). A diagnostic interview: The Schedule for Affective Disorders and Schizophrenia. *Archives of General Psychiatry, 35,* 837–844.

Foley, S. H., Rounsaville, B. J., Weissman, M. M., Sholomskas, D., & Chevron, E. (1987, May). *Individual vs. conjoint interpersonal psychotherapy for depressed patients with marital disputes.* Paper presented at the annual meeting of the American Psychiatric Association, Chicago.

Freden, L. (1982). *Psychosocial aspects of depression.* Chichester, England: Wiley.

Friedman, A. S. (1975). Interaction of drug therapy with marital therapy in depressive patients. *Archives of General Psychiatry, 32,* 619–637.

Ghodsian, M., Zayicek, E., & Wolkind, S. (1984). A longitudinal study of maternal depression and child behavior problems. *Journal of Child Psychology and Psychiatry, 25,* 91–109.

Glick, I. D., Clarkin, J. F., Spencer, J. H., Haas, G. L., Lewis, A. B., Peyser, J., DeMane, N., Good-Ellis, M., Harris, E., & Lestelle, V. (1985). A controlled evaluation of inpatient family intervention: I. Preliminary results of the six-month follow-up. *Archives of General Psychiatry, 42,* 882–886.

Gotlib, I. H. (1982). Self-reinforcement and depression in interpersonal interaction: The role of performance level. *Journal of Abnormal Psychology, 91,* 3–13.

Gotlib, I. H. (1983). Perception and recall of interpersonal feedback: Negative bias in depression. *Cognitive Therapy and Research, 7,* 399–412.

Gotlib, I. H. (in press). An interpersonal systems approach to the conceptualization and treatment of depression. In R. E. Ingram (Ed.), *Contemporary approaches to the study of depression.* New York: Plenum.

Gotlib, I. H., & Colby, C. A. (1987). *Treatment of depression: An interpersonal systems approach.* New York: Pergamon.

Gotlib, I. H., & Hooley, J. M. (1988). Depression and marital distress: Current status and future directions. In S. Duck (Ed.), *Handbook of personal relationships* (pp. 543–570). Chichester, England: Wiley.

Gotlib, I. H., & Lee, C. M. (in press-a). Children of depressed mothers. In N. S. Endler & C. D. McCann (Eds.), *New directions in depression research, theory and practice.* New York: Academic Press.

Gotlib, I. H., & Lee, C. M. (in press-b). The social functioning of depressed patients: A longitudinal assessment. *Journal of Social and Clinical Psychology.*

Gotlib, I. H., McLachlan, A. L., & Katz, A. N. (1988). Biases in visual attention in depressed and nondepressed individuals. *Cognition and Emotion, 2,* 185–200.

Gotlib, I. H., Mount, J. H., Cordy, N. I., & Whiffen, V. E. (1988). Depressed mood and perceptions of early parenting: A longitudinal investigation. *British Journal of Psychiatry, 152,* 24–27.

Gotlib, I. H., & Robinson, L. A. (1982). Responses to depressed individuals: Discrepancies between self-report and observer-rated behaviour. *Journal of Abnormal Psychology, 91,* 231–240.

Gotlib, I. H., & Whiffen, V. E. (1989). Depression and marital functioning: An examination of specificity and gender differences. *Journal of Abnormal Psychology, 98,* 23–30.

Gotlib, I. H., Whiffen, V. E., Mount, J. H., Milne, K., & Cordy, N. I. (1989). Prevalence rates and demographic characteristics associated with depression in pregnancy and the postpartum. *Journal of Consulting and Clinical Psychology, 57,* 269–274.

Greene, B. L., Lustig, N., & Lee, R. R. (1976). Marital therapy when one spouse has a primary affective disorder. *American Journal of Psychiatry, 133,* 827–830.

Haas, G. L., Clarkin, J. F., & Glick, I. D. (1985). Marital and family treatment of depression. In E. E. Beckham & W. R. Leber (Eds.), *Handbook of depression: Treatment, assessment, and research* (pp. 151–183). Homewood, IL: Dorsey Press.

Haas, G. L., Glick, I. D., Clarkin, J. F., Spencer, J. H., Lewis, A. B., Peyser, J., DeMane, N., Good-Ellis, M., Harris, E., & Lestelle, V. (1988). Inpatient family intervention: A randomized clinical trial. II. Results at hospital discharge. *Archives of General Psychiatry, 45,* 217–224.

Hammen, C., Adrian, C., Gordon, D., Burge, D., Jaenecke, C., & Hiroto, D. (1987). Children of depressed mothers: Maternal strain and symptom predictors of dysfunction. *Journal of Abnormal Psychology, 96,* 190–198.

Hautzinger, M., Linden, M., & Hoffman, N. (1982). Distressed couples with and without a depressed partner: An analysis of their verbal interaction. *Journal of Behaviour Therapy and Experimental Psychiatry, 13,* 307–314.

Henderson, A. S., Byrne, D. G., & Duncan-Jones, P. (1981). *Neurosis and the social environment.* Sydney, Australia: Academic Press.

Hinchliffe, M., Hooper, D., & Roberts, F. J. (1978). *The melancholy marriage.* New York: Wiley.

Hirsch, B. J., Moos, R. H., & Reischl, T. M. (1985). Psychosocial adjustment of adolescent children of a depressed, arthritic, or normal parent. *Journal of Abnormal Psychology, 94,* 154–164.

Hooley, J. M. (1985). Expressed emotion: A review of the critical literature. *Clinical Psychology Review, 5,* 119–139.

Hooley, J. M. (1986). Expressed emotion and depression: Interactions between patients and high- versus low-expressed-emotion spouses. *Journal of Abnormal Psychology, 95,* 237–246.

Hooley, J. M., Orley, J., & Teasdale, J. D. (1986). Levels of expressed emotion and relapse in depressed patients. *British Journal of Psychiatry, 148,* 642–647.

Hops, H., Biglan, A., Sherman, L., Arthur, J., Friedman, L., & Osteen, V. (1987). Home observations of family interactions of depressed women. *Journal of Consulting and Clinical Psychology, 55,* 341–346.

Kahn, J., Coyne, J. C., & Margolin, G. (1985). Depression and marital disagreement: The social construction of despair. *Journal of Social and Personal Relationships, 2,* 447–461.

Kessler, R. C., Price, R. H., & Wortman, C. B. (1985). Social factors in psychopathology: Stress, social support, and coping processes. *Annual Review of Psychology, 36,* 531–572.

Klein, D. N., Clark, D. C., Dansky, L., & Margolis, E. T. (1988). Dysthymia in the offspring of parents with primary unipolar affective disorder. *Journal of Abnormal Psychology, 97,* 265–274.

Klerman, G. L., Weissman, M. M., Rounsaville, B. J., & Chevron, E. (1984). *Interpersonal psychotherapy of depression.* New York: Basic Books.

Kochanska, G., Kuczynski, L., Radke-Yarrow, M., & Welsh, J. D. (1987). Resolutions of conflict episodes between well and affectively ill mothers and their young children. *Journal of Abnormal Child Psychology, 15,* 441–456.

Kowalik, D. L., & Gotlib, I. H. (1987). Depression and marital interaction: Concordance between intent and perception of communication. *Journal of Abnormal Psychology, 96,* 127–134.

Lee, C. M., & Gotlib, I. H. (1989a). Clinical status and emotional adjustment of children of depressed mothers. *American Journal of Psychiatry, 146,* 478–483.

Lee, C. M., & Gotlib, I. H. (1989b). Maternal depression and child adjustment: A longitudinal analysis. *Journal of Abnormal Psychology, 98,* 78–85.

Lehmann, H. E. (1971). Epidemiology of depressive disorders. In R. R. Fieve (Ed.), *Depression in the 70's: Modern theory and research.* Princeton, NJ: Excerpta Medica.

Lewinsohn, P. M., & Atwood, G. E. (1969). Depression: A clinical research approach. *Psychotherapy: Theory, research, and practice, 6,* 166–171.

Lewinsohn, P. M., Lobitz, W. C., & Wilson, S. (1973). "Sensitivity" of depressed individuals to aversive stimuli. *Journal of Abnormal Psychology, 81,* 259–263.

Lewinsohn, P. M., & Schaffer, M. (1971). The use of home observations as an integral part of the treatment of depression: Preliminary report of case studies. *Journal of Consulting and Clinical Psychology, 37,* 87–94.

Libet, J., & Lewinsohn, P. M. (1973). The concept of social skill with special reference to the behavior of depressed persons. *Journal of Consulting and Clinical Psychology, 40,* 304–312.

Lin, N., Dean, A., & Ensel, W. M. (Eds.). (1986). *Social support, life events, and depression.* Montreal: Academic Press.

McLean, P. D., Ogston, L., & Grauer, L. (1973). Behavioral approach to the treatment of depression. *Journal of Behaviour Therapy and Experimental Psychiatry, 4,* 323–330.

Merikangas, K. R. (1984). Divorce and assortative mating among depressed patients. *American Journal of Psychiatry, 141,* 74–76.

Moos, R., & Moos, B. (1981), *Family Environment Scale manual.* Palo Alto, CA: Consulting Psychologists Press.

O'Leary, K. D., & Beach, S. R. H. (1988). *Marital therapy: A viable treatment for depression and marital discord.* Unpublished manuscript, State University of New York, Stony Brook.

Orvaschel, H., Walsh-Ellis, G., & Ye, W. (1988). Psychopathology in children of parents with recurrent depression. *Journal of Abnormal Child Psychology, 16,* 17–28.

Overall, J. (1971). Associations between marital history and the nature of manifest psychopathology. *Journal of Abnormal Psychology, 78,* 213–221.

Parker, G. (1981). Parental reports of depressives: An investigation of several explanations. *Journal of Affective Disorders, 3,* 131–140.

Paykel, E. S., Myers, J. K., Dienelt, M. N., Klerman, G. L., Lindenthal, J. J., & Pepper, M. P. (1969). Life events and depression: A controlled study. *Archives of General Psychiatry, 21,* 753–760.

Peterson, C., Semmel, A., VonBaeyer, C., Abramson, L. Y., Metalsky, G. I., & Seligman, M. E. P. (1982). The Attributional Style Questionnaire. *Cognitive Therapy and Research, 6,* 287–300.

Renne, K. S. (1971). Health and marital experience in an urban population. *Journal of Marriage and the Family, 33,* 338–350.

Rounsaville, B. J., Weissman, M. M., Prusoff, B. G., & Herceg-Baron, R. L. (1979). Marital disputes and treatment outcome in depressed women. *Comprehensive Psychiatry, 20,* 483–489.

Ruscher, S. M., & Gotlib, I. H. (1988). Marital interaction patterns of couples with and without a depressed partner. *Behavior Therapy, 19,* 455–470.

Sarason, I. G., Levine, H. M., Basham, R. B., & Sarason, B. R. (1983). Assessing social support: The social support questionnaire. *Journal of Personality and Social Psychology, 44,* 127–139.

Sartorius, N. (1979). Research on affective psychoses within the framework of the WHO programme. In M. Schon & E. Stromgren (Eds.), *Origin, prevention and treatment of affective disorders.* London: Academic Press.

Schless, A. P., Schwartz, L., Goetz, C., & Mendels, J. (1974). How depressives view the significance of life events. *British Journal of Psychiatry, 125,* 406–410.

Spanier, G. B. (1976). Measuring dyadic adjustment: New scales for assessing the quality of marriage and similar dyads. *Journal of Marriage and the Family, 38,* 15–28.

Spencer, J. H., Glick, I. D., Haas, G. L., Clarkin, J. F., Lewis, A. B., Peyser, J., DeMane, N., Good-Ellis, M., Harris, E., & Lestelle, V. (1988). A randomized clinical trial of Inpatient Family Intervention, III: Effects at

6-month and 18-month follow-ups. *American Journal of Psychiatry, 145,* 1115–1121.

Targum, S. D., Dibble, E. D., Davenport, Y. B., & Gershon, E. S. (1981). Family attitudes questionnaire: Patients and spouses view bipolar illness. *Archives of General Psychiatry, 38,* 562–568.

Turner, S. M., Beidel, D. C., & Costello, A. (1987). Psychopathology in the offspring of anxiety disorder patients. *Journal of Consulting and Clinical Psychology, 55,* 229–235.

Vaughn, C. E., & Leff, J. P. (1976). The influence of family and social factors on the course of psychiatric illness: A comparison of schizophrenic and depressed neurotic patients. *British Journal of Psychiatry, 129,* 125–137.

von Bertalanffy, L. (1968). *General systems theory.* New York: Braziller.

Waring, E. M., Chamberlaine, C. H., McCrank, E. W., Stalker, C. A., Carver, C., Fry, R., & Barnes, S. (1988). Dysthymia: A randomized study of cognitive marital therapy and antidepressants. *Canadian Journal of Psychiatry, 33,* 96–99.

Weiss, R. L., Hops, H., & Patterson, G. R. (1973). A framework for conceptualizing marital conflict, technology for altering it, and some data for evaluating it. In L. A. Hamerlynck, L. C. Handy, & E. J. Mash (Eds.), *Behavior change: Methodology, concepts, and practice.* Champaign, IL: Research Press.

Weissman, A. N., & Beck, A. T. (1978, April). *Development and validation of the Dysfunctional Attitudes Scale: A preliminary investigation.* Paper presented at the annual meeting of the American Educational Research Association, Toronto.

Weissman, M. M. (1979). The psychological treatment of depression. *Archives of General Psychiatry, 36,* 1261–1269.

Weissman, M. M., & Boyd, J. H. (1983). The epidemiology of affective disorders: Rates and risk factors. In L. Grinspoon (Ed.), *Psychiatry update* (Vol. II). Washington, DC: American Psychiatric Press.

Weissman, M. M., & Klerman, G. L. (1977). Sex differences in the epidemiology of depression. *Archives of General Psychiatry, 34,* 98–111.

Weissman, M. M., Klerman, G. L., Prusoff, B. A., Sholomskas, D., & Padian, N. (1981). Depressed outpatients: Results one year after treatment with drugs and/or interpersonal psychotherapy. *Archives of General Psychiatry, 38,* 51–55.

Weissman, M. M., & Paykel, E. S. (1974). *The depressed woman: A study of social relationships.* Chicago: University of Chicago Press.

Weissman, M. M., Paykel, E. S., & Klerman, G. L. (1972). The depressed woman as a mother. *Social Psychiatry, 7,* 98–108.

Weissman, M. M., Prusoff, B. A., DiMascio, A., Neu, C., Goklaney, M., & Klerman, G. L. (1979). The efficacy of drugs and psychotherapy in the treatment of acute depressive episodes. *American Journal of Psychiatry, 136,* 555–558.

Weissman, M. M., Prusoff, B. A., Gammon, G. D., Merikangas, K. R., Leckman, J. F., & Kidd, K. K. (1984). Psychopathology in the children (ages 6–18) of depressed and normal parents. *Journal of the American Academy of Child Psychiatry, 23,* 78–84.

Welner, Z., Welner, A., McCrary, M. D., & Leonard, M. A. (1977). Psychopathology in children of inpatients with depression: A controlled study. *Journal of Nervous and Mental Disease, 164,* 408–413.

Whiffen, V. E., & Gotlib, I. H. (in press). Stress and coping in maritally satisfied and dissatisfied couples. *Journal of Social and Personal Relationships.*

Zekoski, E. M., O'Hara, M. W., & Wills, K. E. (1987). The effects of maternal mood on mother-infant interaction. *Journal of Abnormal Child Psychology, 15,* 361–378.

Author Index

Subject Index

(continued from front)

Hyperactivity: Current Issues, Research, and Theory (Second Edition) *by Dorothea M. Ross and Sheila A. Ross*

Review of Human Development *edited by Tiffany M. Field, Aletha Huston, Herbert C. Quay, Lillian Troll, and Gordon E. Finley*

Agoraphobia: Multiple Perspectives on Theory and Treatment *edited by Dianne L. Chambless and Alan J. Goldstein*

The Rorschach: A Comprehensive System. Volume III: Assessment of Children and Adolescents *by John E. Exner, Jr. and Irving B. Weiner*

Handbook of Play Therapy *edited by Charles E. Schaefer and Kevin J. O'Connor*

Adolescent Sexuality in a Changing American Society: Social and Psychological Perspectives for the Human Service Professions (Second Edition) *by Catherine S. Chilman*

Failures in Behavior Therapy *edited by Edna B. Foa and Paul M.G. Emmelkamp*

The Psychological Assessment of Children (Second Edition) *by James O. Palmer*

Imagery: Current Theory, Research, and Application *edited by Aneés A. Sheikh*

Handbook of Clinical Child Psychology *edited by C. Eugene Walker and Michael C. Roberts*

The Measurement of Psychotherapy Outcome *edited by Michael J. Lambert, Edwin R. Christensen, and Steven S. DeJulio*

Clinical Methods in Psychology (Second Edition) *edited by Irving B. Weiner*

Excuses: Masquerades in Search of Grace *by C.R. Snyder, Raymond L. Higgins and Rita J. Stucky*

Diagnostic Understanding and Treatment Planning: The Elusive Connection *edited by Fred Shectman and William B. Smith*

Bender Gestalt Screening for Brain Dysfunction *by Patricia Lacks*

Adult Psychopathology and Diagnosis *edited by Samuel M. Turner and Michel Hersen*

Personality and the Behavioral Disorders (Second Edition) *edited by Norman S. Endler and J. McVicker Hunt*

Ecological Approaches to Clinical and Community Psychology *edited by William A. O'Connor and Bernard Lubin*

Rational-Emotive Therapy with Children and Adolescents: Theory, Treatment Strategies, Preventative Methods *by Michael E. Bernard and Marie R. Joyce*

The Unconscious Reconsidered *edited by Kenneth S. Bowers and Donald Meichenbaum*

Prevention of Problems in Childhood: Psychological Research and Application *edited by Michael C. Roberts and Lizette Peterson*

Resolving Resistances in Psychotherapy *by Herbert S. Strean*

Handbook of Social Skills Training and Research *edited by Luciano L'Abate and Michael A. Milan*

Institutional Settings in Children's Lives *by Leanne G. Rivlin and Maxine Wolfe*

Treating the Alcoholic: A Developmental Model of Recovery *by Stephanie Brown*

Resolving Marital Conflicts: A Psychodynamic Perspective *by Herbert S. Strean*

Paradoxical Strategies in Psychotherapy: A Comprehensive Overview and Guidebook *by Leon F. Seltzer*

Pharmacological and Behavioral Treatment: An Integrative Approach *edited by Michel Hersen*

The Rorschach: A Comprehensive System, Volume I: Basic Foundations (Second Edition) *by John E. Exner, Jr.*

The Induction of Hypnosis *by William E. Edmonston, Jr.*

Handbook of Clinical Neuropsychology, Volume 2 *edited by Susan B. Filskov and Thomas J. Boll*

Psychological Perspectives on Childhood Exceptionality: A Handbook *edited by Robert T. Brown and Cecil R. Reynolds*

Game Play: Therapeutic Use of Childhood Games *edited by Charles E. Schaefer and Steven E. Reid*

The Father's Role: Applied Perspectives *edited by Michael E. Lamb*